DREAMS OF A SUMMER NIGHT

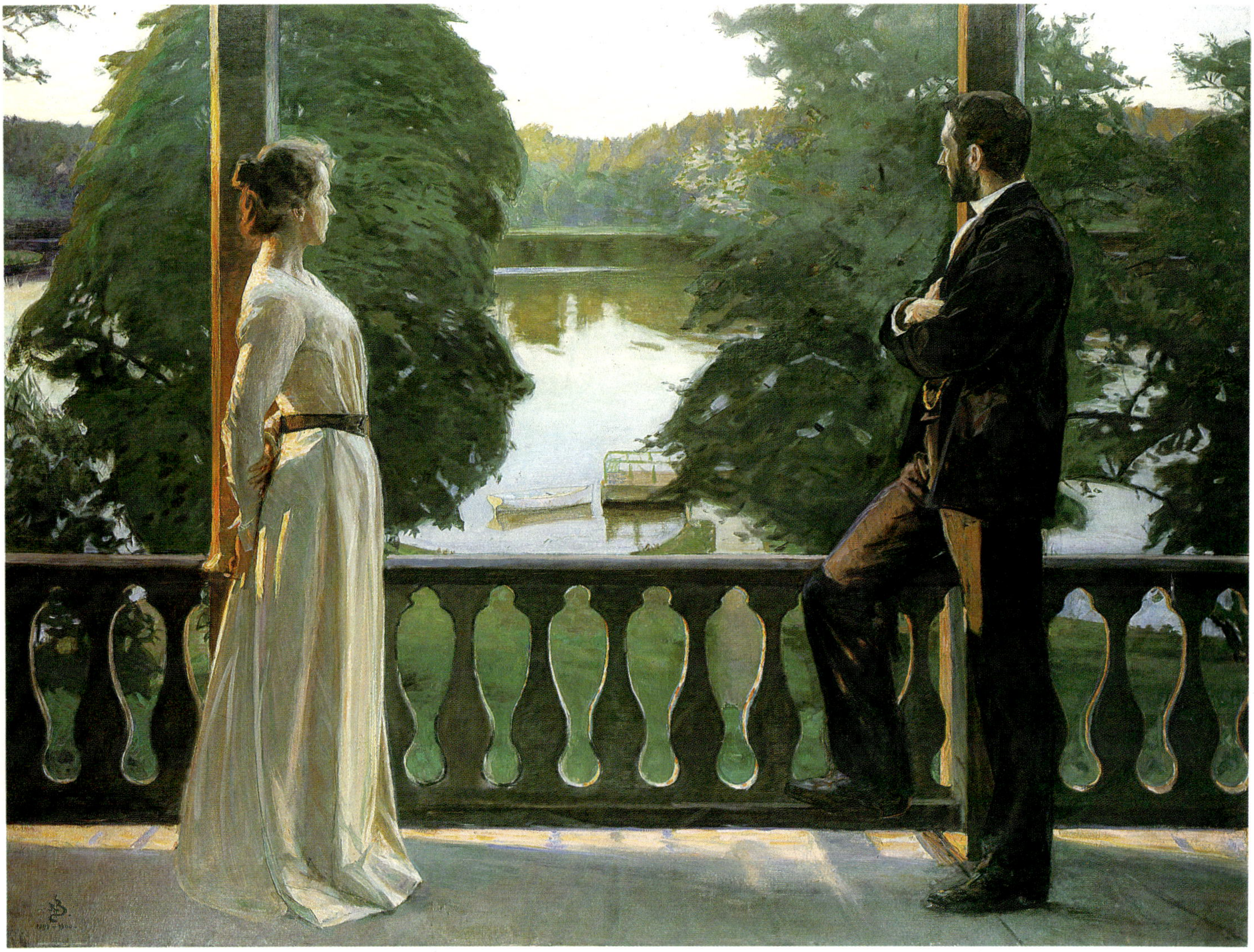

DREAMS OF A SUMMER NIGHT

Scandinavian Painting at the Turn of the Century

Hayward Gallery, London

10 July to 5 October 1986

Organized by the Nordic Council of Ministers
and the Arts Council of Great Britain

ARTS COUNCIL OF GREAT BRITAIN

ISBN 0-7287-0497-8

Catalogue edited and produced for the Arts Council of Great Britain by Leena Ahtola-Moorhouse, Carl Tomas Edam and Birgitta Schreiber

Catalogue design Osmo Pasanen

Catalogue printed by Bohusläningens Boktryckeri AB, Uddevalla, Sweden

Translations by Martha Gaber-Abrahamsen, Margaret Plesner, Patrick Hort

English text edited by Diana Phelan

Cover: Harald Sohlberg, *Summer Night* (detail) (No. 88)

Frontispiece: Richard Bergh, *Nordic Summer Evening* (No. 6)

PATRONS: H.M. Queen Elizabeth II

H.M. Queen Margrethe II of Denmark

H.E. Mauno Koivisto, President of the Republic of Finland

H.E. Vigdís Finnbogadóttir, President of the Republic of Iceland

H.M. King Olav V of Norway

H.M. King Carl XVI Gustaf of Sweden

HONORARY COMMITTEE

Scandinavia:	Hans Peter Clausen, Minister of Culture, Denmark
	Gustav Björkstrand, Minister of Culture and Science, Finland
	Sverrir Hermannsson, Minister of Culture and Education, Iceland
	Hallvard Bakke, Minister of Culture and Science, Norway
	Bengt Göransson, Minister for Cultural Affairs, Sweden
Great Britain:	The Rt. Hon. Richard Luce, MP, Minister for the Arts
	Sir William Rees-Mogg, Chairman, Arts Council of Great Britain
	Sir Roy Strong, Chairman, Advisory Panel on Art, Arts Council of Great Britain
	Mr Ronald Grierson, Chairman, South Bank Board

EXHIBITION COMMITTEE

Scandinavia:

Hanne Westergaard, Senior Curator, Statens Museum for Kunst, Copenhagen

Salme Sarajas-Korte, former Director of Exhibitions, Suomen taideakatemia, Helsinki

Leena Ahtola-Moorhouse, Curator, Suomen taideakatemia, Helsinki

Selma Jónsdóttir, Director, Listasafn Íslands, Reykjavík

Knut Berg, Director, Nasjonalgalleriet, Oslo

Tone Skedsmo, Curator, Nasjonalgalleriet, Oslo

Pontus Grate, Deputy Director, Nationalmuseum, Stockholm

Carl Tomas Edam, Special Projects Director, Nordic Council of Ministers, Copenhagen

Birgitta Schreiber, Administrative Assistant, Nordic Council of Ministers, Copenhagen

Great Britain:

Mr David Thompson, Chairman, Exhibitions Committee, Arts Council of Great Britain

Dr John House, Courtauld Institute of Art

Miss Joanna Drew, Director of Art, Arts Council of Great Britain

Mr Andrew Dempsey, Assistant Director for London exhibitions, Arts Council of Great Britain

The exhibition and catalogue have been generously supported by Volvo

Table of contents

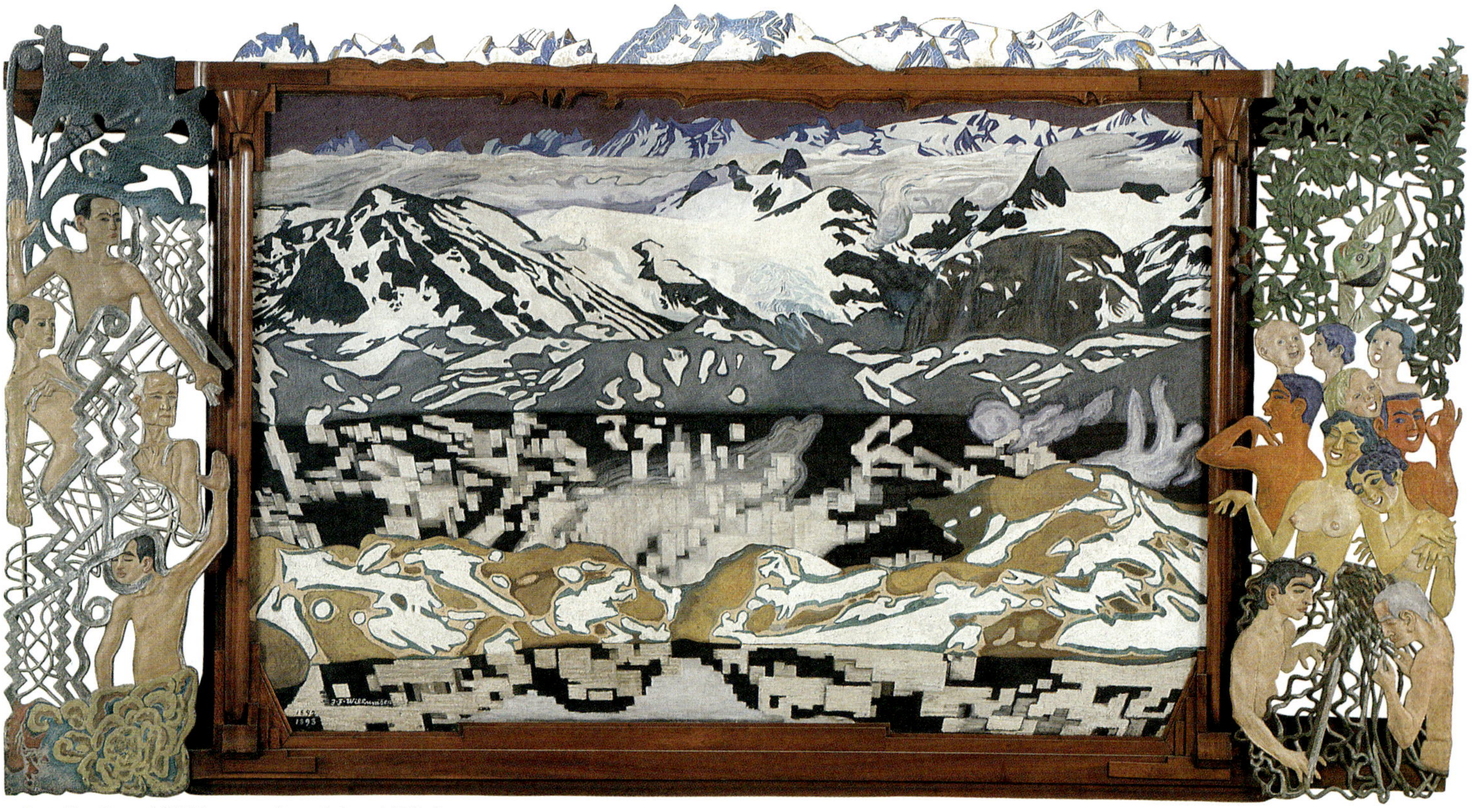

Jens Ferdinand Willumsen, Jotunheim, 1892–3.
Oil painted zinc and enamelled copper. 105 × 277 cm. J. F. Willumsens Museum, Frederikssund, Denmark.
(This work could not be exhibited because of its fragile condition.)

'The clouds drifted away and I found myself at the edge of an abyss, looking over a mountainous landscape in the far North, grim and harsh, covered by eternal snow and ice, a world uninhabitable for human beings.

The symbolic figures in the relief were formed under the influence of this grim atmosphere.

The figures on the left of the relief represent those who steadfastly seek through learning and reason the link between the infinitely great and the infinitely small. The infinitely great is symbolized by a stellar nebula, the infinitely small by microbes. The figure below is inspired; the figure above is convinced of the true outcome of his researches.

The right side of the relief is in contrast to the left and represents the purposeless; below are two men, one of whom is weaving a net which the other is as quickly unravelling; in the centre a group of those who are indifferent; above a figure representing chimeric dreams' (artist's commentary, 1895).

Preface and Acknowledgements

'WHAT MAGIC IN THESE WHITE NIGHTS!'

Our title is not entirely fanciful. The long northern summer night is the subject of many of these pictures; and a preoccupation of Nordic literature too – the quotation comes from Hamsun's novel of 1892 with the very nineties title of *Mysteries*.

The immediate appeal of these paintings makes it odd that this is the first full survey of turn of the century Scandinavian art to be held in this country. We do not seem to have looked much further than the admittedly towering figure of Munch. And yet visitors to the Nordic countries have frequently returned with enthusiasm for artists such as Vilhelm Hammershøi, Akseli Gallen-Kallela and Carl Larsson. This exhibition is long overdue. These artists and many others should be better known here.

The reason for this neglect is perhaps partly a result of our fixation on Paris as the centre of the art world in the late nineteenth and early twentieth centuries. But there is also the fact that the works of these painters were bought early by both the museums and private collectors of the Nordic countries. Very few indeed have entered collections in this country.

It would be appropriate therefore to begin by thanking, on behalf of the Arts Council and our co-organizers the Nordic Council of Ministers, the lenders in each of the five countries. We are especially indebted to the national collections: the Statens Museum for Kunst in Copenhagen; the Suomen taideakatemia in Helsinki; the Nasjonalgalleriet in Oslo; the Listasafn Íslands in Reykjavik and the Nationalmuseum in Stockholm. The full participation of these national museums as well as many other collections has meant that our exhibition includes the very finest painting of the nineties.

The selection of the exhibition has been made by a group of scholars representing each of the Nordic countries. The individual members of this group are listed on page 7. They have also been responsible for preparing the entries in the catalogue, with contributions from other specialists. The work involved has been considerable and we are indebted to each member of the Scandinavian Exhibition Committee and the scholars they have consulted, especially Professor Matti Klinge of Helsinki University, Assistant Professor Gunnar Broberg of Uppsala University and the art historian Jørn Otto Hansen.

We also wish to express our gratitude to Tuula Arkio, Deputy Director, and Leena Peltola, former Deputy Director of the Ateneumin taidemuseo, Helsinki, and Karla Kristjánsdóttir, Head of Department of the Listasafn Íslands, who have provided further assistance.

Making the practical arrangements for an international exhibition involving five countries with showings in three other countries – the exhibition moves on from London to Düsseldorf and Paris – has been particularly complicated. This has been undertaken for the Nordic Council of Ministers by Carl Tomas Edam, Special Projects Director. We are grateful to him and to his Administrative Assistant, Birgitta Schreiber, and to Kerstin Dahlman, Görel Wapner Kjeldsen, Margaretha Persson and Bente Wagnkilde.

Although the choice of artists and works has been made by our Scandinavian colleagues, we have benefited from the advice of Dr John House of the Courtauld Institute of Art. Taking our cue from him, we have been able to suggest balance, or even imbalance, bearing our public in mind. Dr House has also contributed an 'outside view' to this catalogue. Further advice has come from the two other museums where the exhibition is to be shown, the Kunstmuseum in Düsseldorf and the Musée du Petit Palais in Paris. In this connection we are grateful to Dr Hans Albert Peters and Dr Rolf Andree in Düsseldorf, and to Mlle Thérèse Burollet in Paris.

Virtually all the works in the exhibition are reproduced in colour in this catalogue. That this has been possible is due to the generous support of the exhibition and its publication from a most appropriate source, the Swedish-based international company Volvo. We are indebted to Volvo and would like to take this opportunity of thanking their Chief Executive Officer and Chairman of the Board of AB Volvo, Dr Pehr G. Gyllenhammar.

The embassies of the five Nordic countries in London have been involved in preparations for the exhibition from the outset and we are particularly grateful to their cultural and press representatives for help with all the liaison such a multinational venture entails. Our thanks in particular to Mr Jørgen Anker Nielsen, Minister-Counsellor of the Royal Danish Embassy; Mr Lasse Lehtinen, Counsellor for Press and Cultural Affairs of the Embassy of Finland; Mr Sveinn Björnsson, Minister-Counsellor of the Icelandic Embassy; Mr Jan Flatla, Counsellor for Press and Cultural Affairs of the Royal Norwegian Embassy; Mrs Kerstin Asp-Johnson, Cultural Attaché of the Swedish Embassy.

Finally we should like to thank the Scandinavian editor of the catalogue, Leena Ahtola-Moorhouse, who has been a member of the selection committee in respect of the Finnish contribution but has also acted as co-ordinating editor in the Nordic countries. She has been assisted by our English editor Diana Phelan. Both have had a difficult task and, as is usual with exhibitions, far too little time to do it in. The result however is a book which will long be a standard work on its subject.

Joanna Drew

Director of Art, Arts Council

Andrew Dempsey

Assistant Director for London exhibitions, Arts Council

LENDERS TO THE EXHIBITION

Aarhus	Aarhus Kunstmuseum
Bergen	Rasmus Meyers Samlinger
	Hilmar Rekstens Almennyttige Fond
Copenhagen	Davids Samling
	Den Hirschsprungske Samling
	Det kongelige Bibliotek
	Ordrupgaardsamlingen
	Statens Museum for Kunst
Gothenburg	Göteborgs konstmuseum
Helsinki	Ateneumin taidemuseo/Konstmuseet i Ateneum
(Helsingfors)	Helsingin kaupungin taidemuseo/
	Helsingfors stads konstmuseum
	Professor Kai Otto Donner
	Mrs Maija-Liisa Masalin
Mora	Zornmuseet
Mänttä	Gösta Serlachiuksen taidesäätiön kokoelmat
Oslo	Nasjonalgalleriet
	Oslo Kommunes Kunstsamlinger, Munch-museet
Oulu	Mrs Inger Korkeakivi
(Uleåborg)	
Randers	Randers Kunstmuseum
Reykjavík	Listasafn Íslands
	Mr Sverrir Thórdarson
Seltjarnarnes	Mr Hilmar Gardarsson
Skagen	Skagens Museum
Stavanger	Stavanger Faste Galleri
Stockholm	Nationalmuseum
	Nordiska Museet
	Prins Eugens Waldemarsudde
	Thielska galleriet
	f.d. Stenmanska samlingen
Trøndheim	Trondelag Kunstgalleri
Turku	Turun taidemuseo/
(Åbo)	Åbo konstmuseum
Vaasa	Pohjanmaan museo/
(Vasa)	Österbottens museum
Vejen	Vejen Museum
	and
	Private Collections

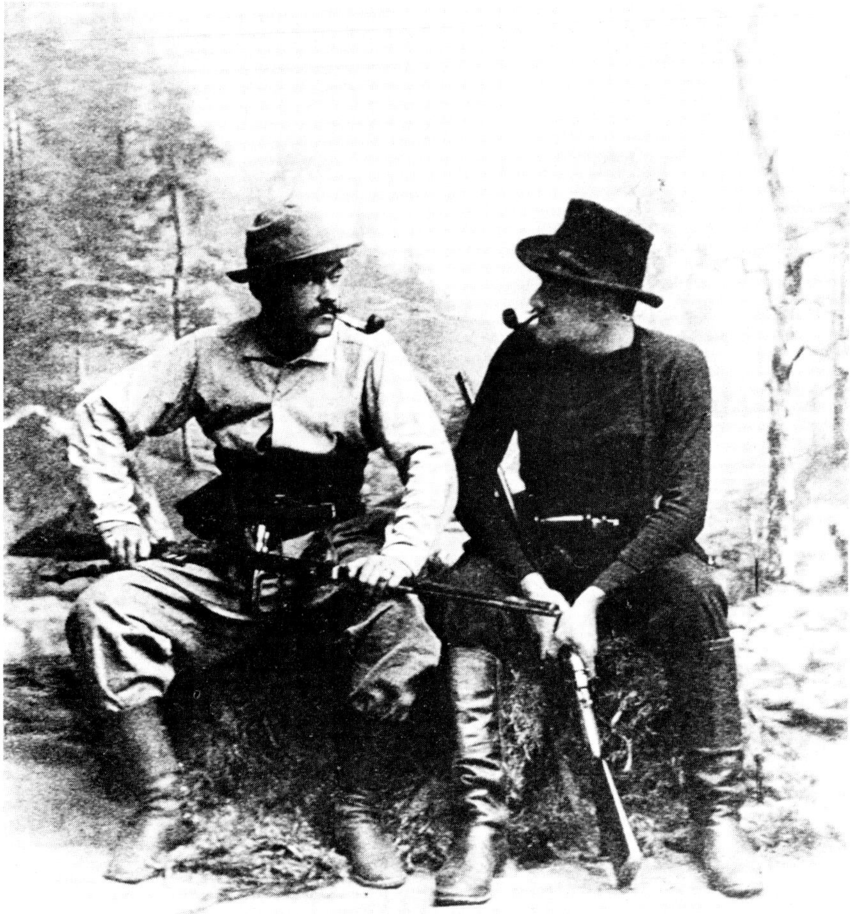

Akseli Gallen-Kallela (on right) and Louis Sparre in Helsinki in 1890 (photo Daniel Nyblin). Gallen-Kallela museo, Espoo

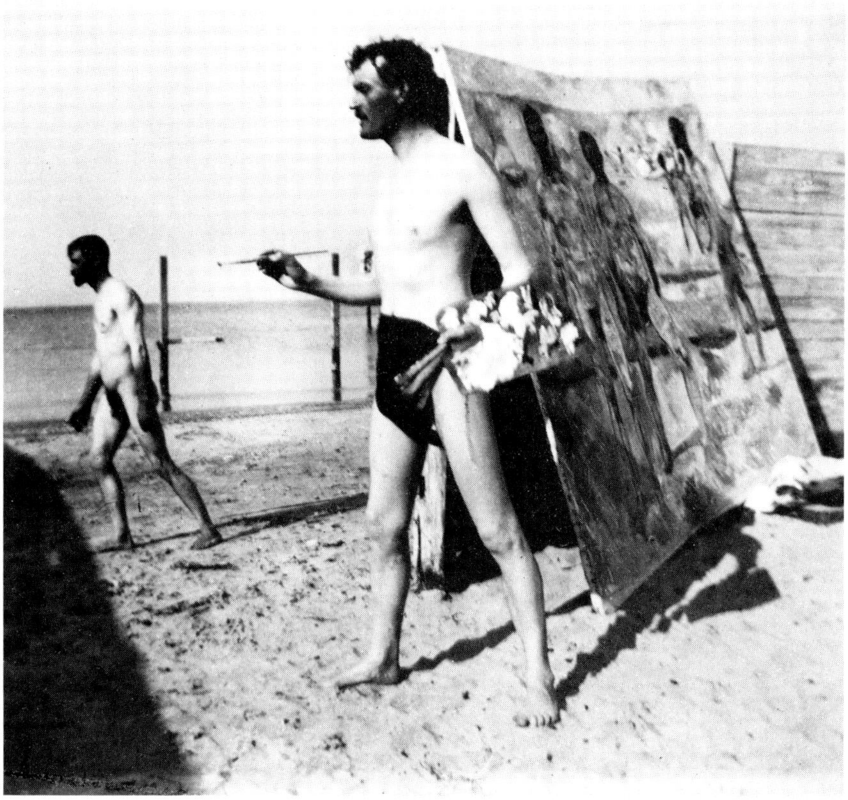

Edvard Munch on the Beach in Warnemünde in 1907 (photo Edvard Munch). Oslo Kommunes Kunstsamlinger, Munchmuseet, Oslo

Foreword

In the late nineteenth century, artists broke with old traditions and sought new ways to express themselves and a new era. This newly found artistic freedom paved the way for movements in the arts which still have a strong influence. In Denmark, Finland, Iceland, Norway and Sweden, as in many other countries, many new artists were recognized, not only in pictorial art but also in the applied arts, literature and music.

This exhibition – DREAMS OF A SUMMER NIGHT – gives the British public a unique opportunity to discover some of the major Scandinavian painters at the turn of the century. With few exceptions, the works by these artists are unknown outside Scandinavia.

The exhibition 'Northern Light: Realism and Symbolism in Scandinavian Painting, 1880–1910', shown in the United States in 1982–83, however, presented some of the works in this exhibition to an international audience for the first time.

It is my hope that through this exhibition and the accompanying catalogue, these works of art by major Scandinavian artists will reach a wider audience and be appreciated for their contribution to the understanding of ourselves and the world at large. It is my hope that you will discover the special quality of these works from a period of important social changes and outstanding artistic achievements. Together they represent an inherent part of the cultural heritage of the Nordic countries.

We at Volvo are pleased to support this exhibition to be presented in London, Düsseldorf and Paris. It gives Volvo a renewed opportunity to further cultural exchange and thereby international understanding through the world of art.

Pehr G. Gyllenhammar
Chief Executive Officer
Chairman of the Board
AB Volvo

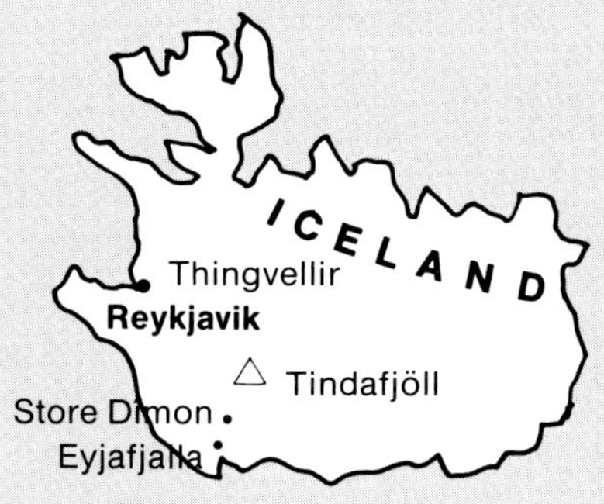

NORTHERN EUROPE 1900

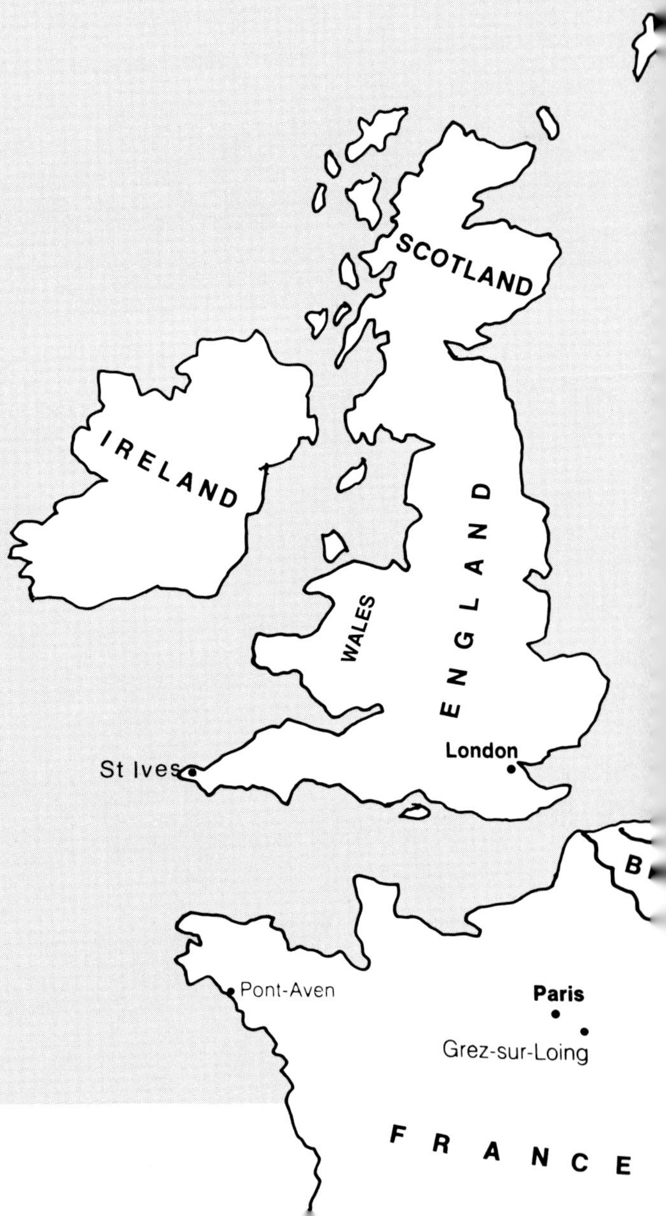

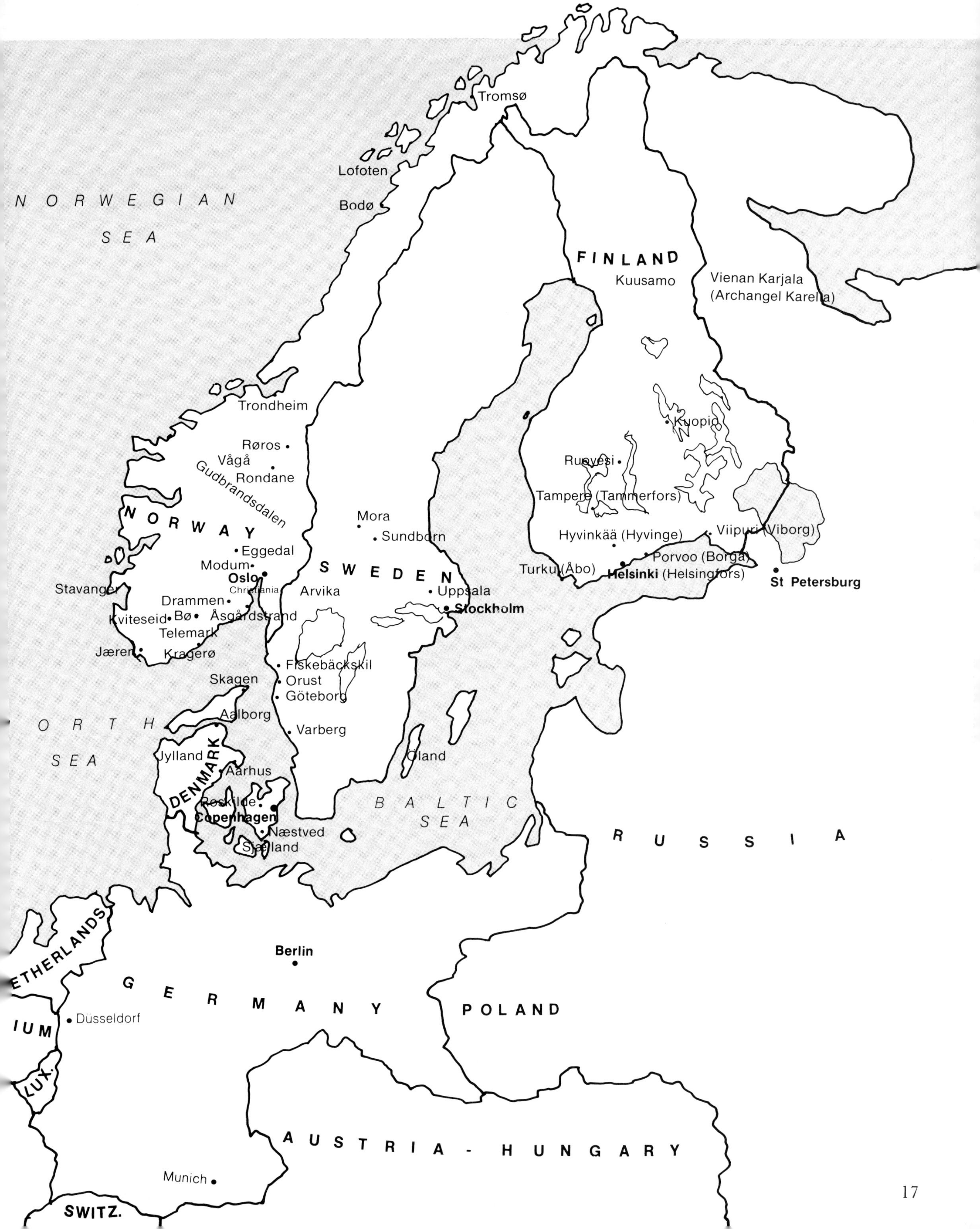

Tromsø
Lofoten
Bodø
NORWEGIAN
SEA
FINLAND
Kuusamo
Vienan Karjala
(Archangel Karelia)
Trondheim
Kuopio
Røros
Vågå
Rondane
Gudbrandsdalen
Ruovesi
Tampere (Tammerfors)
NORWAY
Mora
Sundborn
Viipuri (Viborg)
Hyvinkää (Hyvinge)
Eggedal
Modum
Oslo
Christiania
Porvoo (Borgå)
Turku (Åbo)
Helsinki (Helsingfors)
St Petersburg
SWEDEN
Stavanger
Arvika
Uppsala
Stockholm
Drammen
Kviteseid
Bø
Åsgårdstrand
Telemark
Jæren
Kragerø
Fiskebäckskil
Orust
Göteborg
Skagen
Aalborg
NORTH
SEA
Varberg
Jylland
Öland
DENMARK
Aarhus
Roskilde
Copenhagen
Næstved
Sjælland
BALTIC
SEA
RUSSIA
NETHERLANDS
Berlin
GERMANY
POLAND
Düsseldorf
BELGIUM
LUX.
AUSTRIA - HUNGARY
Munich
SWITZ.

An Outside View

JOHN HOUSE

Exhibition-goers in London will be largely unfamiliar with the painters included in *Dreams of a Summer Night*, apart from one – Edvard Munch. Munch has been presented in single-artist shows, notably the one at the Hayward Gallery, and also as the solitary Scandinavian artist in the Royal Academy's *Post-Impressionism*; but he has always been marooned from his contemporaries and the original contexts of his art. The present exhibition seeks to fill this gap, not just as a foil for Munch, but in order to reveal a particularly vital phase in Scandinavian art.

In the English-speaking world, conventional accounts of late nineteenth-century painting have focused primarily on developments in Paris, and have isolated one key moment of change: Gauguin's rejection of Naturalism and Impressionism in 1886–8, in favour of imagined subjects, painted in an emphatically flat, anti-illusionist style. This emphasis on the flatness of the painting, in turn, has been taken up in this century as the prime characteristic of modern – or rather, modernist – painting.

Scandinavian painting of the late nineteenth century does not fit tidily into this pattern. It does, indeed, reveal a marked change in the same years, but this was not a rejection of nature in favour of imagination; rather, artists moved away from an ostensibly dispassionate, exterior view of their subjects, and sought instead to infuse nature with richer levels of meaning. It is this development which the present exhibition seeks to explore. It involved changes in the pictorial language and vocabulary of the painters – in the scenes they chose to paint and the ways they treated them; but the relationship between the artists and their natural subjects remained crucial – indeed intensified, as they explored the margins between perceived nature and inner feeling.

Naturalist painting in the 1880s was dominated, in Scandinavia as in many other countries, by the example of French painters such as Jules Bastien-Lepage; the influence of the Impressionists was of far less importance. This naturalist vision emphasized the painters' detachment from their subjects. Figures – generally peasant

Fig. 1. Erik Werenskiold, Peasant Burial, 1885, Nasjonalgalleriet, Oslo

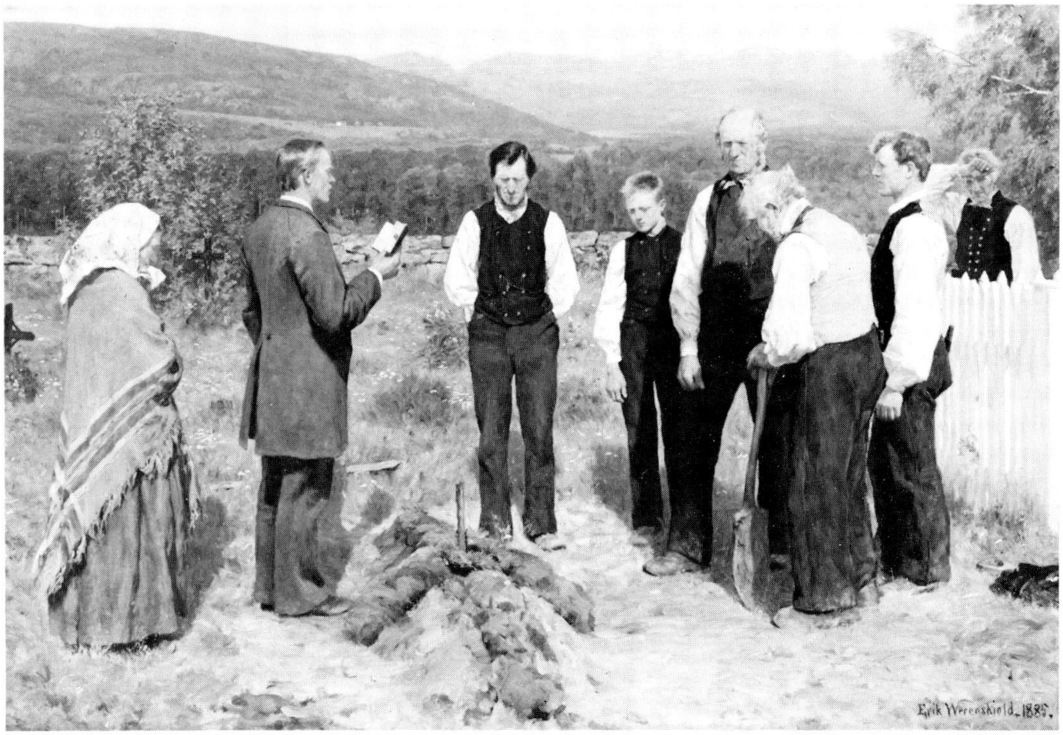

figures – play a central role; they are laid out for the scrutiny of the spectator, but in no way acknowledge our presence. As viewers of the painting, we occupy a quite different world, and cannot visualize ourselves in any way participating in the scene depicted. Erik Werenskiold's *Peasant Burial* (Fig. 1) is a prime example of this: the figures are spread across the canvas before us, but their activity is entirely self-contained, and we take no part in their mourning. Carl Larsson wittily played on this process of distancing in *The Open-Air Painter* (Fig. 2); we, outside the picture, watch the painter, shown at the left, painting the snow scene – or rather, watch the onlookers at far left watching the painter as he paints. Our access to the picture is mediated by these successive stages, or stepping-stones, between us and the scene itself. The painting was first exhibited at the Paris Salon in 1886 with the title *In Sweden*, which further emphasized the distance between the viewers, in a French summer, and this archetypal image of the northern winter.

In the later 1880s and early 1890s, this detachment became unviable for many of the younger painters in all these Scandinavian countries. The reasons for such a change were complex and multifarious, but of central importance was the increasing emphasis on each country's national characteristics and culture, and a growing feeling that the detachment of the typical naturalist viewpoint was quite inappropriate as an expression of man's relationship to his surroundings in the northern countries.

Travellers from England and France in the later nineteenth century constantly reiterated their surprise in Scandinavia at the close conjunction between raw nature and urban culture – at the outcrops of rock which thrust through the soil even in the centre of Stockholm and Christiania (Oslo), and at the proximity of the cities to areas of uncultivated wilderness. Likewise, the Scandinavian peoples were described as living far closer to nature than their southern counterparts, both because of the harshness of the long northern winter and because, during the summer, the Scandinavians enjoyed to the full the long hours of daylight, and the twilight of the midsummer

Fig. 2. Carl Larsson, The Open-Air Painter (In Sweden), 1886, Nationalmuseum, Stockholm

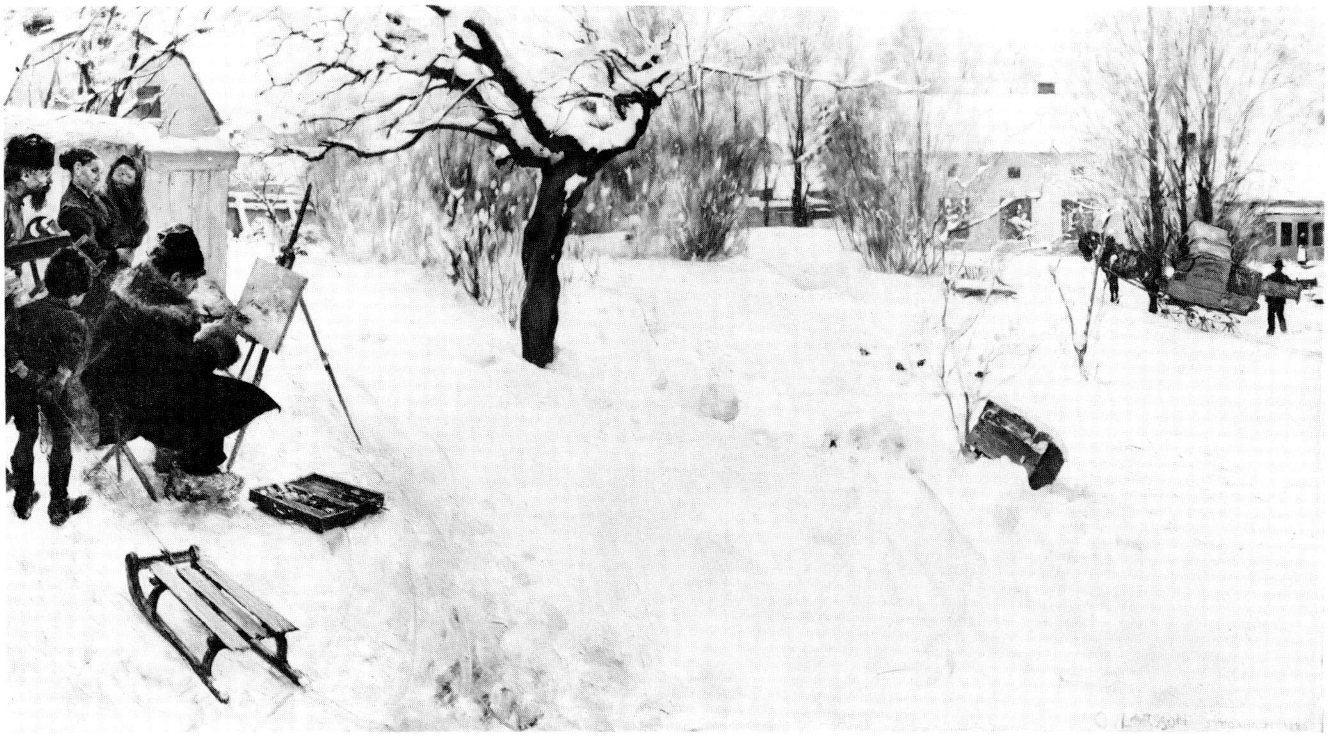

nights. Moreover, a far larger proportion of the population lived in the country than in France and England, and industry, comparatively late in arriving, was concentrated primarily on harnessing natural resources, and was thus scattered, not concentrated in any great industrial metropolis.

The rocky coastlines of Brittany or Cornwall – archetypal images of harsh nature in France and England in the 1880s – were far away from the cultural centres where the paintings of these places found their audiences, whereas in the North the distance, both physical and cultural, was much less. Indeed, several of the Scandinavian painters, Anders Zorn, for instance, and Laurits Andersen Ring, specialized in depicting the regions from which they themselves came.

Many southern viewers described the Scandinavians' paintings as the work of peasants; thus the French critic Gustave Geffroy wrote of Juho Rissanen's works exhibited at the Paris Exposition Universelle in 1900 (including No. 77): 'M. Rissanen is a peasant living among peasants; with a harsh, determined art, which seeks to pin life down, he has painted physiognomies which are astonishing in their naive thought, their child-like malice, or their simple kindness.' But such images of the artist are myths, and cannot be taken at face value; Rissanen had studied in St Petersburg, and his pictorial image of the Finnish peasant was a synthesis of the lessons of Dürer's drawing and Ilya Repin's paintings of Russian history; he was not a primitive, but a conscious primitivist. Likewise, the other painters of the deep country had all spent extended periods studying painting in the city and, almost without exception, had also studied abroad. Thus the vision which they evolved was distilled from a variety of artistic stimuli, as they sought to give pictorial form to their ideas of their essential national landscape; and during their travels overseas, they too, like the foreign visitors to their countries, would have contributed to the developing popular image of the northern countries.

It is this which gives particular point to their rejection of the Bastien-Lepage naturalist tradition in the later 1880s and early 1890s. Reacting against the detachment of the naturalist viewpoint, they sought to immerse themselves in their subjects, inviting the viewer to share this involvement: in place of ethnography, they sought empathy. This they achieved by a number of paths.

First, there was a change in the subjects they chose. Rather than concentrating on peasant life and labour – on a social landscape from which the painter, by virtue of being a painter, was inevitably excluded – they focused more on nature's effects, on the changing seasons and particularly on the 'blue hour', the long twilight of the summer night. And second, they presented these effects in such a way that the viewer gained a more immediate access to them; their chosen viewpoints place no obstacles between the scenes and their viewers, but rather draw the viewer in, to appreciate the subject to the full. Figures now play a far less important role; no longer do we view the scene from outside, as the scenario for the action of the figures that dominate it, but instead we can engage directly with the effect depicted.

Akseli Gallen-Kallela's *Waterfall at Mäntykoski* (No. 21) illustrates this change in a particularly acute form. Originally it included the figure of a water nymph playing nature's harp, and a human listener, thus leaving the spectator quite outside a rather literal-minded allegory of the spirit of the waterfall; but Gallen-Kallela erased the figures and replaced them with the five golden harp strings which run right down the surface of the picture, seeking to evoke the resonance of the waterfall directly in the viewer. The transition can be seen, too, in the change between Werenskiold's *Peasant Burial* (Fig. 1), with its self-contained figure group, and his *Autumn* (No. 103), in which we are poised above a secluded uplands farm, and seemingly enfolded by foliage and hillside; the later picture's title directs our attention towards the overall effect, not the individual contents of the scene.

Werenskiold's *Autumn* is still in a sense a social landscape, though one to which the viewer is given ready access; however, many artists moved further away from the social concerns of the 1880s, by focusing instead on nature unadulterated by man. This appears first in the *Summer Night* paintings by Kitty Kielland and Eilif Peterssen of 1886 (Nos. 47 and 67), where the viewer is placed right by the edge of a secluded Norwegian lake, contemplating in solitude the play of light on water. By the early 1890s this quest for the solitary, untainted view of nature led painters to pilgrimages deep into the wilds; Gallen-Kallela in Finland, Bruno Liljefors in Sweden, and the Dane Jens Ferdinand Willumsen, travelling in the mountains of Norway, created images of the extreme limits of human access. Gallen-Kallela's *Great Black Woodpecker* (No. 20) presented the wilderness as viewed from the furthest point he could reach, with the woodpecker's red hood standing for 'the cry of life of the individual in the silence of the wilderness', while Willumsen's *Jotunheim* of 1892–3 (illustrated page 10) showed 'a mountainous landscape in the far North, grim and harsh, covered by eternal snow and ice, a world uninhabitable for human beings', viewed from 'the edge of an abyss', with the added allegorical figures on its frame symbolizing, on the left, those who seek true knowledge, and, on the right, those without a purpose to their lives.

Viewpoints such as these presented painters with particular problems, for they could not be accommodated within the conventional structures of landscape painting. Different conventions were needed in order to capture the distinctive types of scenery of the northern countries. Indeed, painters of the Danish 'Golden Age', notably Christen Købke and his successors Johan Thomas Lundbye (see No. 73) and Peter Christian Skovgaard, had already sought ways of giving pictorial form to the horizontal panoramas of Denmark's lowlands. As Richard Bergh put it, the North was 'the land without *motifs*'; 'where is the architectonic or painterly unity that makes the landscape of the South, with its clear and serene lines, so seductive to artists? Not here.' Neither the viewpoints of Gallen-Kallela and Pekka Halonen (No. 27), perched on the edge of the wilderness, nor Denmark's open panoramas, depicted by Ring, Viggo Johansen and Vilhelm Hammershøi (Nos. 74, 40, 35), could be formulated according to the conventions of the picturesque, which placed the landscape at the disposal and in the control of the viewer, whose viewpoint is the focus for measured recessions from foreground into distance. In their search for means to express these subjects, northern landscapists in the late nineteenth century looked to Japanese prints, with their emphasis on pattern and their taut linear structures, created from even the most unexpected angles of vision. But more significant was their determination to reject the imported artifices of the picturesque: the structures they found for their visions of their own national landscapes gained their distinctive value by virtue of their difference; they seemed natural because of the absence of such artificial conventions.

In contrast to the picturesque, which belonged to a vision of the Roman Campagna or the English landscape garden, the sublime glorified nature's most powerful forms and forces; both Norway and Sweden had had a significant group of painters who had used the rhetoric of the sublime to depict its national scenery – notably Johan Christian Dahl and Marcus Larson. The sublime, again, places the landscape at the disposal of the viewer; it elevates the spectator above the natural material, by adopting a raised viewpoint which allows the eye to survey and control the whole scene – and, indeed, incorporates into the picture a more comprehensive view than can be seen from any single natural viewpoint. In a sense, the sublime was the ideal art of the grand tourist, assimilating nature's most dramatic manifestations into the education of the cultured eye. Willumsen's encounter with Jotunheim, and Harald Sohlberg's with the mountains of Rondane (No. 89) were quests of a quite different order – private encounters with the forces that lay outside man's grasp. Hence they adopted viewpoints which emphasized man's vulnerability, poised above a plunging drop, with the unattainable mountains high up and beyond them; public admiration has been replaced by private awe.

For the northern landscapist, there was nothing incompatible between deep involvement with the idea of nature and the personal emotion of the artist. The antithesis between nature and the imagination, propounded by French Symbolism in the later 1880s, is singularly inapplicable to Scandinavian painting (as indeed it is to another northern landscapist who worked in France, Vincent van Gogh). Richard Bergh discussed this issue in particularly relevant terms in an essay in 1896: 'the landscape, that tract in which we live, affects our lives, not just in the superficial sense of enforcing on us certain fixed living conditions, but also by the purely suggestive influence it has on our soul. That drama which daily is in front of our eyes puts its mark on our inner being... Every landscape is a state of mind.' Crucial to Bergh's argument are the particular characteristics of life in the North – the immediacy of man's confrontation with the extremes of nature: the harsh winter, the liberation of spring culminating in midsummer. These natural phenomena come to evoke the key elements in human experience: growth and death, joy and sorrow.

Bergh's monumental painting, *Nordic Summer Evening* (No. 6), enshrines these ideas in pictorial form. This picture has recently been the subject of vigorous debate between American and Scandinavian historians, the Americans tending to see it as involving a level of suggestive meaning, symbolism even, concerning the awakening of sexuality, while the Scandinavians prefer to view it in essentially naturalistic terms. Viewed in terms of Bergh's own writings, these two positions need not be incompatible: the image of nature may evoke human experience without recourse to allegory. In the painting, the two figures are presented with a monumental symmetry, both of them looking out towards the lake; no clear-cut narrative reading is possible. But their poses are contrasting: the man looks out in a matter-of-fact way, one foot on the balustrade, with his arms folded, while the sun lights up the terrace around him; the woman arches herself backwards into the sunlight, shown in slashes of colour across her back and hands. The man, turned towards the light, sees the sun; the woman feels it. This contrast enshrines the traditional identification of woman with nature and instinct, and man with culture and reasoning. But these signs, presented as effects of nature, cannot be read allegorically as symbols for a further level of meaning; their resonance lies precisely in the fusion of nature with the suggestion of inner experience – of observation with evocation.

This enriched vision of nature – a form of nature mysticism – runs throughout Scandinavian painting at this period. Nature and the countryside are seen as the expression of the life-force and as the repository of essential values, in contrast to the shallowness and artificiality of urban civilization. At times, the meanings of the pictures are enriched by comparatively explicit symbols, such as the dandelions in Ejnar Nielsen's *The Blind Girl* (No. 65) and Ring's *Girl Blowing Dandelion Seeds* (No 72), or the myrtle tree in Ring's *At the Garden Steps; The Artist's Wife* (No. 70). But generally the mood is evoked by the suggestive juxtaposition of the elements in the scene, particularly by the interrelationships between figures and their natural surroundings, as in Bergh's *Nordic Summer Evening*; this leaves the viewer of the pictures free to explore their resonance. For the present-day viewer in Britain, many of the associations which the pictures would have evoked in their original audience are lost, because of the very different roles that ideas of nature now play in our culture, in which 'nature mysticism' has little place.

It is in this historical context, in relation to Scandinavian ideas about the resonance of nature, that Munch's 'psychic naturalism' should be discussed. Certainly, his preoccupation with the most destructive areas of human experience – sickness and death, of course, and sexuality and jealousy – set him apart from his contemporaries, and gained him the outspoken condemnation of Bjørnstjerne Bjørn-

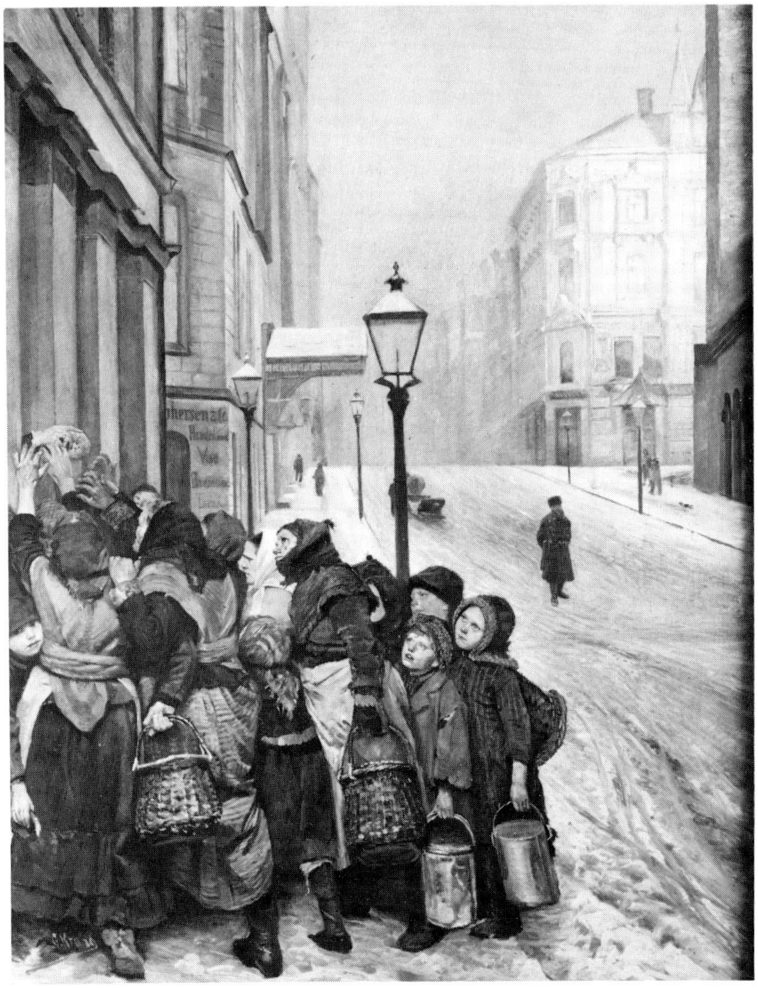

Fig. 3.
Christian Krohg, Struggle for Existence, 1899, Nasjonalgalleriet, Oslo

son, leading figure in the propagation of Norwegian cultural values, and strong supporter of artists such as Werenskiold; yet Werenskiold continued to support Munch's art, however unsympathetic he may have been to its moods. Munch's images of seashore and woods as scenarios for explorations of human experience (e.g. Nos. 56, 57, 59–61) invite comparison with his contemporaries' treatments of similar scenes. Indeed Prince Eugen (cf. Nos. 15–17) wrote of one of his landscapes of the early 1890s in a way particularly comparable to Munch: 'I will paint a canvas with only great disharmony, so that it will cut into every other person who sees it. It will have the effect of a scream.'

Among Munch's other main themes, his treatment of city streets also has a close context in Norwegian art, in the modern urban subjects of the 1880s by Christian Krohg, Munch's mentor and friend in the artistic circles of the Christiania Bohemian life at the time. But whereas Krohg's paintings, such as *Struggle for Existence* (Fig. 3), are primarily concerned with issues of social injustice, Munch, in paintings like *Evening on Karl Johan Street* (Fig. 4), transformed the rhetoric of Krohg's picture – the plunging diagonal, the crowd on the pavement set against the solitary figure on the road – from an image of social division (Krohg's isolated figure is a policeman) to one of personal isolation. In this sense, Munch's image of man's relations to his surroundings, in city and country, can be compared most closely to the early novels of the Norwegian writer Knut Hamsun, *Hunger*, of 1890, set in Christiania, and *Mysteries*, of 1892, set in a small coastal town.

Another of Munch's favoured themes, of figures in an enclosed interior, recurs frequently in the Scandinavian art of the period. Just as the human experience of outdoor nature is depicted as essentially private, rather than social, in the art of the end of the nineteenth century, so the interior scenes are presented in ways which

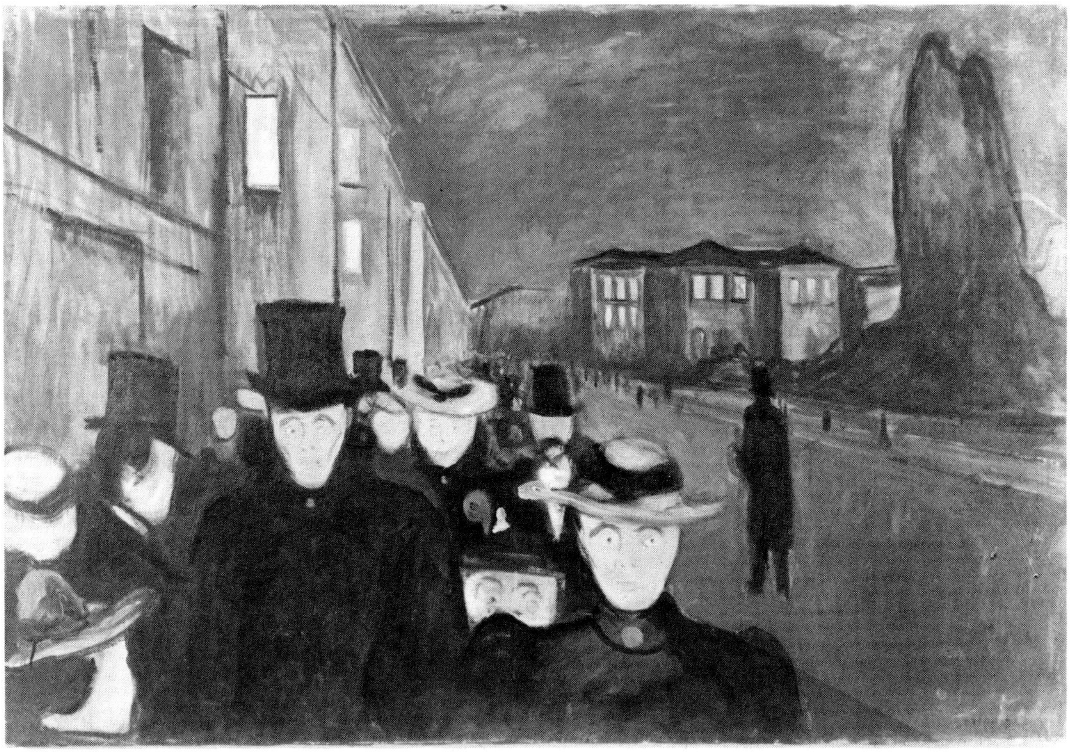

Fig. 4. Edvard Munch, Evening on Karl Johan Street, 1893, Rasmus Meyers Samlinger, Bergen

heighten the sense of the inner experience of the protagonists. Even in group situations, emphasis is thrown on the experience of the individual – on the single woman watching for the arrival of the baptismal party in Harriet Backer's *Christening in Tanum Church* (No. 4), or the woman in August Eiebakke's *Laying the Table* (No. 11), performing her task under the scrutiny of the figures beyond. But more often the focus is on a single figure, whose expressions, gestures and surroundings evoke moods and suggestions. In Magnus Enckell's *Awakening* (No. 14), almost a male equivalent to Munch's celebrated *Puberty*, the title hints at ideas of youth and growth, while in Nielsen's *And in his Eyes I Saw Death* (No. 66), the man looking blankly out into space suggests the other end of the cycle of life. In Hammershøi's interiors (Nos. 30, 32, 34, 36), the tautly structured pictorial organization complements the stillness of the figures, lit by candlelight or by daylight filtered through doors and windows. Hammershøi deliberately avoids signposting further levels of meaning through his titles or by using expressive gestures, allowing the placing of his figures to evoke the privacy of an inner world, whereas Halfdan Egedius, in *The Dreamer* (No. 7), invites us more immediately into the reverie of his friend Stadskleiv, as he gazes down into the splash of sunlight on the floor of the humble rural interior.

A prime element in the emergence of nationalistic feelings in Norway, Sweden and Finland in the mid- and later nineteenth century was the preservation – or revival – of their traditional folk cultures. The first open-air museum, Skansen in Stockholm, was created in 1891 for the preservation and display of traditional Swedish country buildings and artefacts, and the similar museums in Oslo and Helsinki followed soon afterwards. By 1883, Anders Zorn was collecting folk art and local costume in his native town of Mora, in the heart of Dalarna, the Swedish province with the richest surviving traditional culture; in later years he and his wife founded a local folk art museum and craftworkshops, and encouraged the reintroduction of folk customs which had become obsolete, such as the setting up of the maypole at midsummer (see No. 111). Here, we cross the borderline from the maintenance of a living tradition to the self-conscious revival of customs from the past in the pursuit of notions of national identity; Zorn's celebration of Swedish culture, and of a particularly Swedish notion of female beauty, presented as natural and belonging to the national soil (cf. *Red Sand*,

No. 112), can be closely compared with the contemporary emergence of *volkisch* ideology in Germany, in which the revival of national festivals also played an important part.

Larsson's watercolours of home life in Sweden (No. 52), so popular and influential through their publication in book form, also reflect this renewed interest in Swedish folk art and decoration. The ideas of arts and crafts movements, from England in particular, played their part in Larsson's enterprise, but, in the texts which accompanied the illustrations, he emphasized that the roots of the domestic aesthetic he was propagating lay firmly in Swedish national traditions:

> Our farmers and their wives... let nothing leave their hands without giving it an artistic or personal touch. All these cheery peasant patterns that you find everywhere are to me in most cases more significant works of art than most oil paintings. And the scrupulously fabricated cottage with its façade, its floor, its veranda and its leaded-glass windows! And their garb! Just picture what the Swedish people looked like in days of old, bursting with colour and health, as they stood radiantly outside church in the Sunday sunshine... It is the Swedish peasant painters from the end of the last century whose footsteps I follow, and I admit it freely. Think for example of the ancient painting you come upon here in Dalarna or in Norrland. Such deep, solemn feeling, coupled with such bold, healthy humour. And what a national feeling for style!

In such comments, Larsson moves effortlessly from questions of taste and style to an association between robust good health and Swedish nationhood.

Folk costumes and customs had provided subjects for painters in all the Scandinavian countries since the mid-nineteenth century. In the 1880s such themes had been treated with the detached, ethnographic viewpoint of French naturalism, for instance by the Finnish painter Albert Edelfelt in *Women of Ruokolahti on the Church Hill* (Fig. 5); here the four richly dressed figures are recorded with dispassionate detail; the painter's viewpoint is physically near them, but wholly separate from them. Zorn's *Midsummer Dance*, painted a decade later, likewise shows folk costumes, but the viewer's relationship to the image is quite different: rather than study the figures as specimens, in the clear light of day, we can now seemingly become a part of the celebrations, absorbed into the warm glow of the low night sun, and implicitly ourselves among the dancing couples; we are invited to share the intensity of this key festival in Swedish national culture.

Interest in folk culture in Finland dated back to the publication of the *Kalevala* (1835; final version 1849), the great poem which was manufactured as a Finnish national epic by Elias Lönnrot, following the model of the Homeric epic and based on Finnish folk sources. Edelfelt's *Women of Ruokolahti* reflected this interest, but Gallen-Kallela and his friend Louis Sparre gave new impetus to the movement from 1890, by their journeys into the Finnish interior in search for authentic settings and décor for their paintings and illustrations of *Kalevala* themes; Gallen-Kallela's *Great Black Woodpecker* (No. 20) derived from one of these expeditions. His first paintings of *Kalevala* subjects treated the stories in a comparatively naturalistic way, as for instance in his *Aino Triptych* (Fig. 6), where his studies of folk art are felt particularly in the remarkable carved decorative frame. By the mid-1890s, though, he had come to feel that these subjects reflected the traces of a great pre-Christian mythology, and should be treated in a quite different manner – hieratic and stylized; *Lemminkäinen's Mother* (No. 25) was his grandest realization of this new vision of the *Kalevala*.

Gallen-Kallela's *Kalevala* subjects (Nos. 23–5), with their flatly painted surfaces and decorative linear patterning, can be closely related to the stylistic modes of French synthetist painting (to artists such as Maurice Denis), and to aspects of

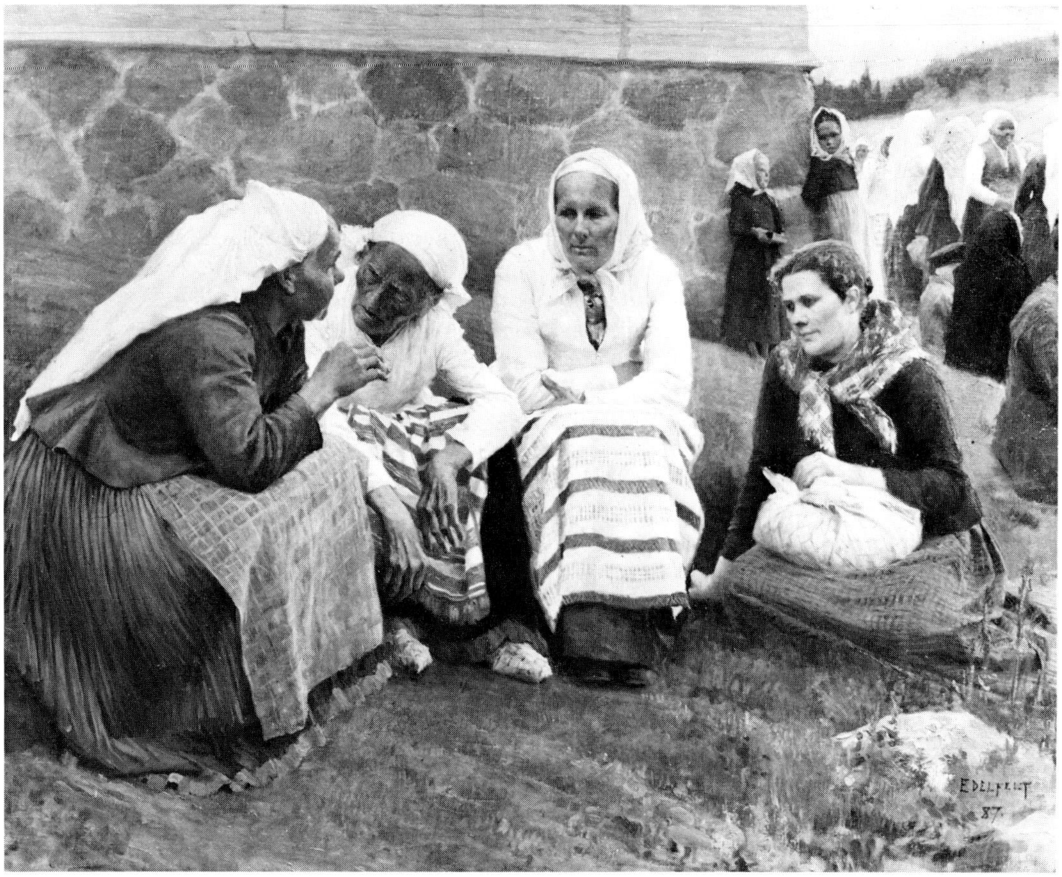

Fig. 5. Albert Edelfelt, Women of Ruokolahti on the Church Hill, 1887, Ateneumin taidemuseo, Helsinki

Fig. 6. Akseli Gallen-Kallela, Aino Triptych, 1891, Ateneumin taidemuseo, Helsinki

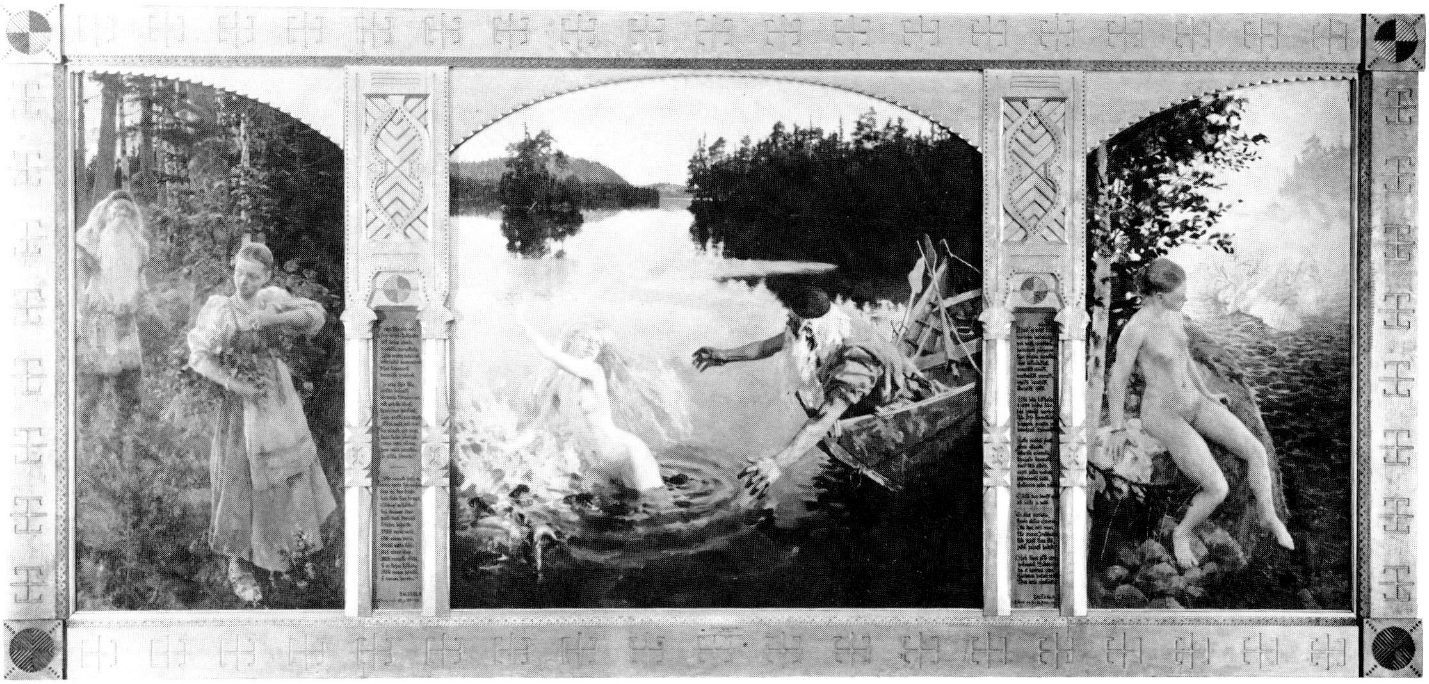

international Art Nouveau design. However, alongside these *Kalevala* canvases, Gallen-Kallela continued to paint pictures in a more naturalistic manner; this shows that he adopted this style because he felt it particularly appropriate to this sort of theme. The extreme simplification of *The Defence of the Sampo* and *Joukahainen's Revenge* (Nos. 23, 24) results from their origin as designs for tapestry.

Gallen-Kallela's use of styles as a direct complement to his subjects sets him apart from his French contemporaries, for whom the idea of style was central to their whole pictorial personality; this notion of a 'signature style', serving to differentiate and validate the work of a particular creative artist, has become crucial to the cult of artistic individuality and personality in the twentieth century, but it is very misleading to treat Scandinavian painting of the late nineteenth century in the light of these concerns. Likewise, those of Gallen-Kallela's contemporaries who adopted flatter, more linear styles also chose them for their appropriateness to particular themes and particular projects, rather than viewing them as an overriding stylistic imperative. Gerhard Munthe's themes from Norwegian legend (No. 63), conceived as designs for decorative projects, are handled in a self-consciously primitivizing style, based on Norwegian folk art traditions, yet he continued to paint atmospheric softly-brushed landscapes in oils. Larsson's technique in his *A Home* watercolours (No. 52) would have facilitated the reproduction of the images in his books; in his mural paintings, in the Stockholm Nationalmuseum and elsewhere, he adopted a rather different handling and a more mellow, nuanced colouring. Gustav Fjaestad's patterned treatment of snow scenes (No. 19) related closely to his activities as a decorative designer, particularly in tapestry (another arts and crafts type venture), while the hieratic treatment of Carl Wilhelmson (No. 106) gives his images of the peasantry of the Swedish west coast a heroic, iconic character, which transcends the detailed naturalism of peasant paintings of the 1880s such as Edelfelt's (Fig. 5).

Shared by the painters in the present exhibition was their rejection of this detailed naturalism, in favour of types of handling which, they felt, better expressed the moods they sought to convey. However, these concerns led to no one dominant stylistic solution. As we see from the contrast between Munch's rippling, cursive rhythms and scratchy drawing and Ejnar Nielsen's spare monumentality, comparable themes of sickness and death are handled very differently; likewise Sohlberg's crisp drawing in his image of a terrace on a summer night (No. 88), is a far cry from the free, often incisive brushwork of Bergh's terrace picture, *Nordic Summer Evening* (No. 6). The question of style, as such, was not their central concern, as it was to their contemporaries in the French avant-garde; rather, the manners of painting they chose were used like a flexible tool, in the service of expressive, evocative treatment of their subjects.

The position of Scandinavian artists differed from their French contemporaries in other respects, too. In France by the mid-1880s the antagonism and polarization between academic and avant-garde art was well established, and institutionalized in exhibiting societies like the Société des Indépendants; alternative exhibiting societies were set up in the Scandinavian capitals, but the resistance of the artistic establishment proved quite weak. Almost all the painters in the present exhibition were immediately recognized by their contemporaries, at home and abroad, as being among the most significant painters of their generation; moreover, paintings by most of them were quickly bought by their respective national collections. The Norwegian Nasjonalgalleriet bought its first Munch in 1891, and in 1895, on the recommendation of Werenskiold, bought Munch's newly painted and controversial self-portrait; it also bought Sohlberg's first significant painting, *Night Glow* (No. 86), in 1894. The Senate of Finland commissioned Gallen-Kallela's *Aino Triptych* (Fig. 6) in 1890, a commission which encouraged Gallen-Kallela to make his extended trip in Finnish and Russian Karelia, and bought *Lemminkäinen's Mother* (No. 25) in 1898. The Statens Museum for

Kunst in Copenhagen began to buy from Ring in 1891 and from Hammershøi in 1896, and the Stockholm Nationalmuseum bought its first Larsson in 1883, its first Liljefors and Zorn in 1886, and purchased Zorn's *Self-Portrait* (No. 110) in 1897, soon after it was painted.

Moreover, in the Nordic countries there were wealthy private collectors who bought extensively from the young and experimental artists: Heinrich Hirschsprung and later Wilhelm Hansen in Denmark; Herman Frithiof Antell and Gustav Adolf Serlachius in Finland; Pontus Fürstenberg and later Ernest Thiel and Prince Eugen in Sweden; and Olaf Schou and Rasmus Meyer in Norway. All of these collections survive intact, either as separate institutions or as donations to museums, and works from all of them are included in the present exhibition.

Thus in the late nineteenth century the notion of an avant-garde, alienated from and somehow 'ahead' of its contemporaries, had no real significance in Scandinavian art circles. Even Munch was considered an integral, if controversial, part of the art scene in his own country; it is only in our century that his work has been prised apart from that of his contemporaries, and that he alone of Scandinavian artists has been accorded a place in the international pantheon of fame which has subsequently been created from the artists of the late nineteenth century. We can witness the beginning of this process in two pioneering and monumental German histories of modern art. In Richard Muther's *The History of Modern Painting* (English edition 1895–6), virtually all of the artists in the present exhibition who had by then come before the public eye are included, with perceptive discussion of their recent work, with the exception of Munch, despite the celebrity and scandal which had surrounded Munch's recent exhibitions in Muther's home country. The picture is quite different in *Modern Art* (English edition 1908) by Julius Meier-Graefe, who had known Munch in Berlin. Meier-Graefe's account was one of the pioneering books in the establishment of the ideas about modern art traditions, as a succession of revolutionary styles, which have until recently dominated writing about late nineteenth-century art; of all the artists in the present exhibition, only Munch received extended treatment from Meier-Graefe, who classified him along with 'Gauguin and his Circle', and concluded that he alone of Scandinavian artists had succeeded in fusing 'the old Norse spirit' with a powerful expression of Nature.

The preoccupations of the earlier twentieth century have largely erased the Scandinavian painters of the later nineteenth century from international view; and the criteria by which late nineteenth-century painting has traditionally been discussed are particularly inapplicable to it. Scandinavian painting cannot be treated in terms of polarities between academic and avant-garde; between nature and imagination; between naturalism and symbolism; between free brushwork and drawing. Indeed the total inadequacy of these categories in this context should make us look again at many rooted assumptions about French art. The Scandinavian painters of the period show us exploratory art which was largely accepted by their contemporaries; they sought to infuse their visions of nature with suggestiveness and personal feeling, so that their paintings at one and the same time expressed notions of a national spirit and the artist's personal sensibility.

NOTES

The most important sources in English on late nineteenth-century Scandinavian art are two recent exhibition catalogues from North America: *Northern Light* (The Brooklyn Museum, 1982–3), and in particular the contributions by Kirk Varnedoe ('Nationalism, Internationalism, and the Progress of Scandinavian Art') and Tone Skedsmo ('Patronage and Patrimony'); and Roald Nasgaard, *The Mystic North* (Art Gallery of Ontario, Toronto, 1984), to whose discussion of landscape painting I am particularly indebted. I am also most grateful to all the Scandinavian collaborators in the present project, who have, with warmth and generosity, shown me so much and told me so much; without them, this outsider would have had few footholds in the 'northern wilderness'.

Nordic Art at the Turn of the Century

KNUT BERG

After the upheavals and bitter clashes of the 1880s, Scandinavian art in the 1890s entered into smoother waters. In all the Nordic countries, the 1880s marked a turning point in the development of art, with the breakthrough of Realism and Naturalism. The point of departure was the close contact with French art formed in this period. Paris became the unchallenged Mecca of art; almost the whole generation of young Scandinavian artists gathered there and the friendships made then laid the foundation for close relationships between the artists of the Nordic countries. The 1880s were above all an age of *plein-air* painting. Never has the sun shone so brightly in Nordic art as in this period. It was an extrovert, vital art that endeavoured to depict both man and nature as realistically as possible. Scandinavian artists followed in the path of the French Naturalists: Jules Bastien-Lepage was their idol. They also had some contact with the Impressionists, though without having any deep understanding of their art.

The leading artists of the period and those who brought the new trends from France home to their respective countries were P. S. Krøyer and Theodor Philipsen in Denmark; Christian Krohg, Erik Werenskiold, and Frits Thaulow in Norway; Ernst Josephson, Carl Larsson and Karl Nordström in Sweden. In Finland, the leaders were above all Albert Edelfelt, probably the Nordic artist who enjoyed the greatest success on the international scene, and the young Akseli Gallen-Kallela.

The 1880s were a time of transition not only on the artistic level; the period also marked an important turning point for the artists' standing in society. It was a radical and self-assured troop of young artists, with great belief in themselves, who returned to their home countries after studies in Paris. At home they promptly met with opposition from a conservative bourgeoisie and the established art institutions. The artists demanded greater influence in defining their work circumstances, and they formed their own organizations to protect their interests. Even though different solutions were found to suit the different countries, the problems themselves were largely the same. It was during this period that the artistic milieu assumed a form that has largely characterized the Nordic art world to this very day.

With the 1890s, however, the situation changed. The sun set over the Nordic landscape; the summer night and the blue hours of dusk took over, evoking a special atmosphere of magical mysticism. Harsh depictions of reality disappeared; the artist became a romantic and a dreamer seeking to fathom the depths of the soul. The strong feeling of community which marked the 1880s vanished: the individuality of each artist was brought out more clearly. French art was no longer the supreme source of inspiration. England, Germany, and Italy with the great masters of the Early Renaissance, assumed a stronger role. But above all, artists became national exponents: art was to interpret the character of each country and its people.

This new artistic mood probably emerged first in Norway. In the summer of 1886, a group of Norway's leading Naturalists, some of them coming direct from Paris, gathered at Fleskum, a farm outside Oslo, in a kind of artists' collective. The group included Kitty Kielland, Harriet Backer, Eilif Peterssen, and Erik Werenskiold. Instead of painting in the bright noon sun, as one might have expected, Kitty Kielland and Eilif Peterssen chose the quiet evening hours by a lake nearby. A pale moon is reflected in dark, shiny water, and blue tones pervade their pictures. We encounter a new feeling of peace and tranquillity which evokes an elegiac, musical atmosphere. Behind the change in style, we can probably see the influence of Puvis de Chavannes, who from this time on came to exert an increasing influence on the development of Scandinavian art.

Harriet Backer, Norway's leading woman painter, specialized in interiors. She worked slowly and methodically, and with a rare consistency followed her own line of development, never becoming what one would call a typical painter of the 1890s. Harriet Backer was above all the great colourist in Norwegian art. More than any other painter of the period, she cultivated the subtlety and sonority of colour. She used

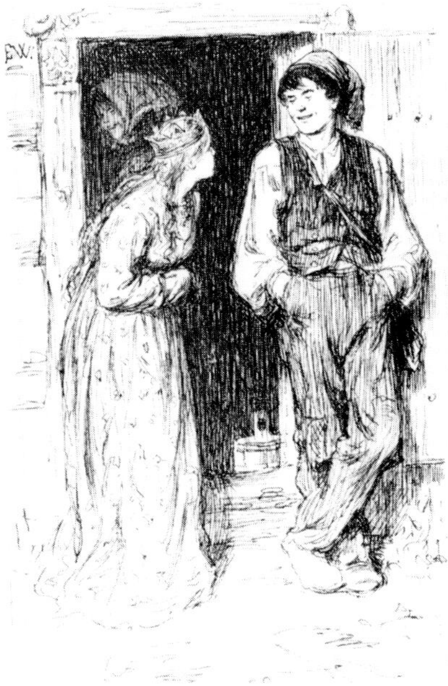

Fig. 7. Erik Werenskiold, Askeladden and the Princess (Illustration for P. Ch. Asbjørnsen and J. Moe, Norske Folke- og Huldre-Eventyr i Udvalg, Copenhagen, 1879), Nasjonalgalleriet, Oslo

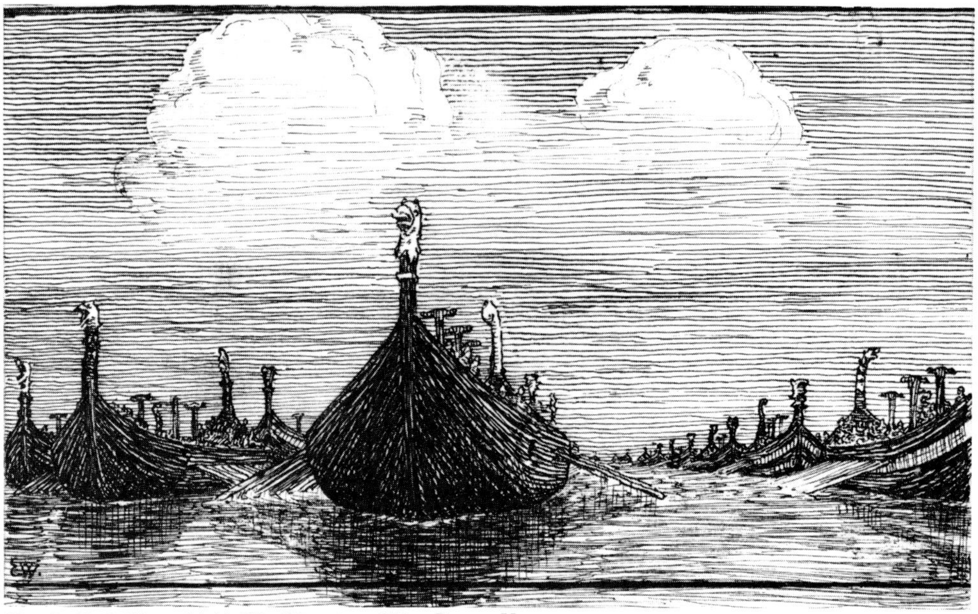

Fig. 8. Erik Werenskiold, The Victorious Ships Return Home after the Battle at Svolder (Illustration for S. Sturlason, Olav Trygvesons Saga), Nasjonalgalleriet, Oslo

colour to depict the light falling into a room; light structures and defines the space, giving life to every inch of the surface.

Erik Werenskiold remained a Naturalist at Fleskum; he did not change his style until the beginning of the 1890s. Together with Christian Krohg and Frits Thaulow, he led the struggle for artists' rights in the '80s; in the 1890s he became the unchallenged leader of the Norwegian art world. He attracted not only the artists of his own generation, but also most of the young phalanx, which for decades to come was to play a dominating role in Norwegian art. Through his illustrations to Norwegian fairy-tales in the 1880s and to Snorre's *Sagas of the Norse Kings* in the 1890s, he created a national ideal which is as alive today as it was then. The union with Sweden was approaching an end, and in Norway there was a conscious search for national roots, a harkening back to the past glory of the Middle Ages, to rural culture, and to a sense of communion with nature. Where there were no national traditions, Werenskiold considered it his task to create them.

Harald Sohlberg and Halfdan Egedius were among the young artists who belonged to the circle around Werenskiold. Sohlberg, a rather lonely figure, had a profound and highly original feeling for landscape. Combining a meticulous sense of detail with a feeling for the monumentality of his motifs, he imbued his landscape with an eerie symbolism. In many ways his pantheistic attitude towards nature suggests a return to the ideals of early Romanticism of the beginning of the century.

Egedius is the wonder child of Norwegian art. Already at the age of 16 he was a mature artist and his last paintings were created before he was 20. He devoted the rest of his short life – he died at the age of 22 – to illustrating the Sagas of Snorre. Together with Sohlberg he may be considered the leader of the Neo-Romantic movement prevailing among the young Norwegian artists of the 1890s, painting moody landscapes, with a marked tendency towards mysticism and symbolism.

One member of the young generation of artists did not join Werenskiold's circle: Edvard Munch. At a time when nearly all other Scandinavian artists were returning home, Munch went abroad. From 1889 to 1909 he lived mostly in Germany and France; only returning to Norway in the summer. This is why in many respects he remained somewhat apart from the general trends in Norwegian art; he was part of an international art world. His pictures were, however, exhibited regularly in Norway, and he was not without a certain influence. But no other artist so recklessly revealed his innermost feelings and fantasies. Munch was a controversial figure and his

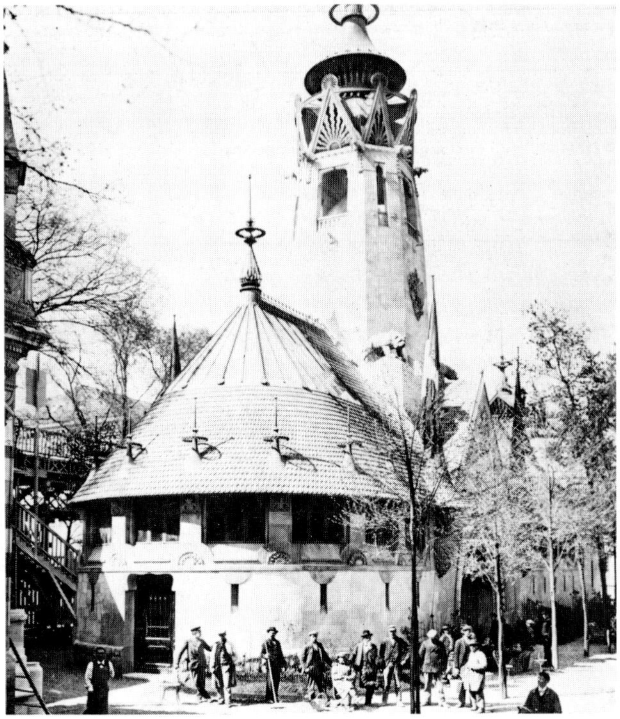

Fig. 9.
Herman Gesellius, Armas Lindgren, Eliel Saarinen, The Finnish Pavilion at the Paris World Fair in 1900. Photo: The Museum of Finnish Architecture, Helsinki

pictures often met with opposition, but to claim that he was misunderstood and not appreciated in his homeland, as has often been maintained, is an overstatement. There was never any doubt among artists and others interested in art that Munch was the greatest talent of his generation. Munch himself may have felt persecuted, but that is another matter entirely.

Developments in Finnish art in the last decades of the nineteenth century can in many respects be compared to those in Norwegian art, and the issues were largely the same: a conscious yearning to establish a national identity, a problem that was even more pertinent in Finland than it was in Norway.

The Russians, having followed a very liberal policy in the Grand Duchy of Finland which made it possible for that country to develop a fairly large degree of self-government, began to tighten their grip towards the end of the century and carry out a more thorough political integration of Finland into Russia. But the Finns not only had a Russian problem: they also needed to free themselves from the Swedish influences which had up to then dominated Finnish cultural life. One must see developments in Finnish art in the 1890s against this background.

By the 1880s, Finnish art had emerged from its relative isolation and, with Edelfelt in the lead, began to make itself felt in the international arena. It became a goal, not only in art, but also in politics, to emphasize an independent Finnish artistic and cultural profile. This development culminated with the Finnish pavilion – separate from the Russian pavilion and on a par with the displays of other countries – at the Paris Exhibition of 1900. For the Finns, it confirmed their acceptance as a nation among nations.

Towards the end of the 1880s, the Finnish Naturalists devoted their art more and more to subjects with overtly nationalistic overtones. In addition to the work of Edelfelt, one can follow this development in the works of Järnefelt, Halonen, and above all Gallen-Kallela. It culminated at the beginning of the 1890s with 'Karelianism'. The point of departure for this movement was the national epic, the *Kalevala*, which more than anything else was thought to express the Finnish national soul, free from all Swedish influences. In Karelia, the desolate and sparsely populated parts of eastern Finland on the Russian border (now Russian territory), it was believed that the spirit of the *Kalevala* tradition was still alive, and it became fashionable among artists to go out into the wilds to depict the untouched wilderness and the hard and frugal life of those who lived there.

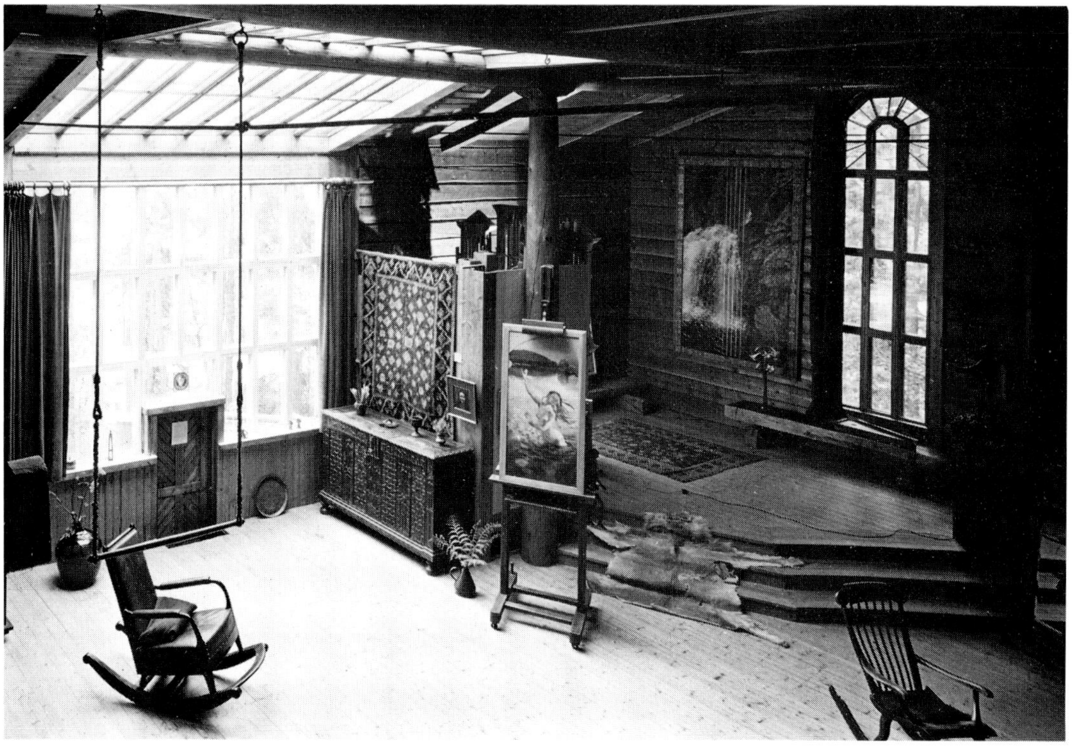

Fig. 10. Akseli Gallen-Kallela, The Interior of the Wilderness Studio 'Kalela', 1894–5, Ruovesi, Finland (Photo Simo Rista)

The central figure in this national movement was Akseli Gallen-Kallela, probably the most original talent in Nordic art of this period apart from Edvard Munch. In order to achieve the atmosphere he sought, he developed a more simplified formal language at the beginning of the 1890s, and the decorative element in his pictures was emphasized more strongly, undoubtedly inspired by his interest in Finnish folk art. But a feeling of insufficiency in his naturalistic style led to a crisis. After an extended period abroad and contact with the Symbolist and Synthetist trends in French and German art, he devised the style which characterizes his large *Kalevala* compositions from the last half of the decade. In these stylized works with their powerful contours, clear surfaces, and highly decorative overall effect, he succeeded in fully expressing the mysticism and heroic tone of the *Kalevala*. He created a style which in many respects was decisive for the development of Finnish art around the turn of the century.

Symbolism took deeper root in Finnish art than it did in the art of the other Nordic countries; in Finland, it had above all a national purpose. We meet the same trend in the work of Pekka Halonen during this period and especially in that of Hugo Simberg, who had been a student of Gallen-Kallela and whose unique world of fantasy is most evident in his small watercolours.

But not all Finnish artists were affected by the national pathos of Karelianism. At the opposite extreme stood Magnus Enckell, who at the beginning of the decade had been caught up by Parisian mysticism, with its theosophical and spiritualist overtones. He sought an almost classical purity, and in his series of pictures of nude boys, characterized by a firm line and almost ascetic restraint in the use of colour, he expresses the isolation of the individual who, sunk deep in meditation, reflects the inner mysteries of the soul.

Enckell's reaction against Karelianism was not purely artistic; it was also rooted in the Swedo-Finnish intellectual milieu which rejected Finnish nationalism, and sought contact with more cosmopolitan ideas. It was Enckell and his circle who first introduced Symbolism and the new styles of the 1890s into Finnish art. Their influence undoubtedly contributed to Gallen-Kallela's crisis and his artistic rebirth

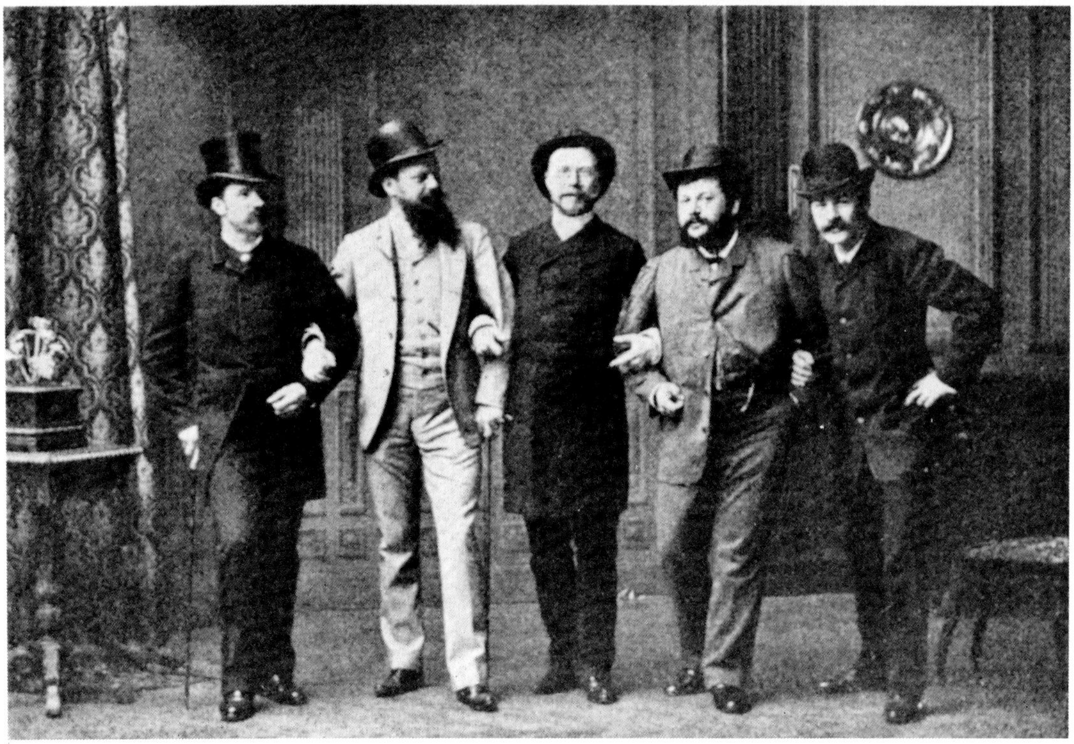

Fig. 11. The Leaders of the Opponents in Sweden in 1885. From left: Per Hasselberg, August Hagborg, Carl Larsson, Ernst Josephson and Richard Bergh (photo Sixten Strömbom, Konstnärsförbundets historia, Stockholm, 1945, p. 140)

around the middle of the decade.

Ellen Thesleff was another member of Enckell's circle. She too had come under the influence of Parisian 'soul' painting. In her small, delicate landscapes with their blurred forms, we meet a fragile mystical play of light which expresses a gentle lyricism. They are in striking contrast to the powerful, monumental landscapes we otherwise find in Finnish art.

Helene Schjerfbeck matured early as an artist, and already at the beginning of the 1880s, one finds symbolist elements in her art. Even when she works in a realistic style, her pictures have an innate spiritual quality. During most of the 1890s she taught at the Helsinki art school, a task that consumed most of her energy. However, a new period of artistic creativity followed in the early 1900s. Influenced by Whistler, she emphasized abstract values. Her pictures show a Japanese-inspired elegance, not based on the decorative effect of line, but on a suggestive colour harmony that evokes a spiritual atmosphere.

The Swedish Naturalists of the 1880s generally remained in Paris longer than their colleagues from the other Nordic countries. It was not until the last half of the decade that they set a course for home. Once there, they promptly came into conflict with 'the establishment' in the Swedish art world, especially the Academy, and they were dubbed the 'opponents'. It was this group which in 1886 created the Artists' Union, an organization that was to play a leading role in the Swedish art world far into the next century. Among the leaders of the group were Karl Nordström, Carl Larsson, Richard Bergh, Bruno Liljefors, and Anders Zorn, all artists who had a major influence on developments in the 1890s as well.

Carl Larsson, Bruno Liljefors, and Anders Zorn are considered to be the three major figures in Swedish art during the 1890s, all three of them highly different. Zorn was the 'king', the internationally fêted society painter with his portraits and sensual nudes. But at the same time, he remained tied to the rural life in Mora in the Dalarna district, where he had grown up in modest circumstances. It was here that he generally found his subject matter and the models for his buxom nudes. In 1896, he settled down in Mora and built up his open-air museum. In spite of his brilliant

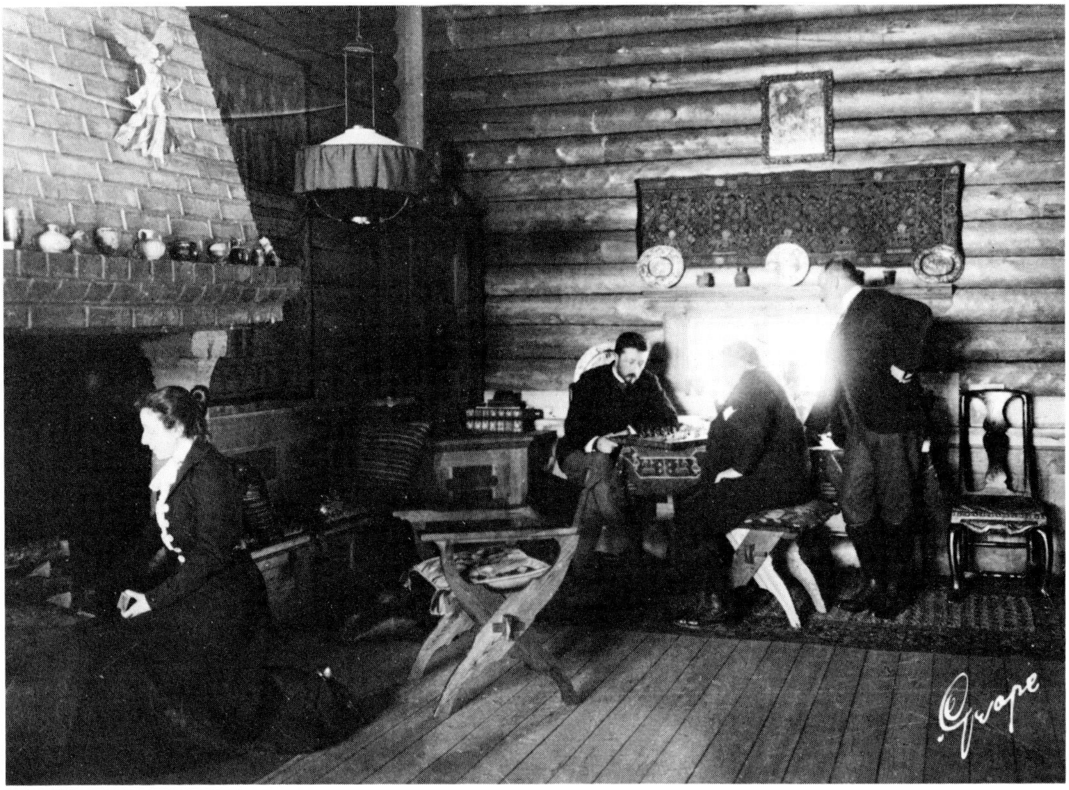

Fig. 12. The Interior of the Mora House. Prince Eugen and Anders Zorn playing chess, Emma Zorn in foreground (photo Nationalmuseum, Stockholm)

international career, Zorn can therefore also serve as a prototype for the painter of regional life in Swedish art of the 1890s. There was a general trend at the time for artists to turn away from the cities towards more rustic, rural milieux, a trend we meet in all the Nordic countries, but nowhere more markedly than in Sweden, where artists often settled permanently in their native regions, not just for short periods.

Carl Larsson's series of watercolours, 'A Home', probably one of the most-loved achievements in Swedish art, can also in a sense be called regional paintings. With their light, warm interiors furnished with characteristic simplicity, these pictures from Larsson's home in Sundborn had a great influence on interior design, not only in Sweden but also in the rest of Scandinavia.

Bruno Liljefors, with his pictures of animals, holds a unique position in Nordic art. No other painter delved so deeply into the life of animals, especially birds, and their role in nature. In his pictures from the 1890s, he often imbued these depictions with a particular mysticism.

Richard Bergh had a greater direct influence on the development of Sweden's art and art world than the 'big three'. He was an excellent organizer and in many respects the brain behind the Artists' Union. He was also one of the period's most influential writers on art. From 1893 to 1896 he lived in the little town of Varberg on the west coast, south of Gothenburg, and together with his friends from Paris in the 1880s, Karl Nordström and Nils Kreuger, he founded the 'Varberg School'. It was here that the new romantic style of Swedish landscape painting developed, characterized by the atmosphere and poetry of the Nordic summer nights. On the wall of Bergh's work-room in Varberg hung Paul Gauguin's landscape from Brittany from 1889 (now in the Nationalmuseum, Stockholm) which he had bought in Copenhagen in 1892 – perhaps an indication of the source of inspiration for Bergh's own landscapes.

Closely allied with Richard Bergh was Prince Eugen. Although his social position prevented him from taking part in the day's debates on art, he came to play a very prominent role in the Swedish art world. He also had close contacts with artists in the other countries. In his art, Prince Eugen continued the trends of the Varberg School, and he can probably be considered the leading representative in Swedish art of national romantic landscape painting, to which he gave a monumental and simplified form and highly dramatic emotional expression. Among the other painters who worked with this same kind of poetic landscape painting were Gustav Fjæstad, and to a certain extent Carl Wilhelmson, even though his genre paintings exhibit a more powerful realistic touch.

Another member of the same generation of lyrical painters in the 1890s was Eugène Jansson, who, diverging from the usual landscapes, chose the city as his subject. He was above all a painter of *l'heure bleue*, and in his townscapes we can see a move towards abstraction, with a floating, wave-like play of lines. Houses are often presented as heavy, formless masses, giving his pictures a powerful, emotionally charged effect.

Two of the Swedish artists in the exhibition, Ernst Josephson and August Strindberg, resist precise classification. Josephson, perhaps the most gifted of the Swedish painters of the 1880s, became mentally ill in 1888. His art during his illness expressed an imaginary world of a personal and literary character. In his drawings we find a deformed but expressive and refined mastery of line of often moving and charming beauty. His paintings display powerful and intense colour effects related to the freer means of expression of our own day.

August Strindberg played a role as an art critic and debater, but his paintings were probably considered eccentric experiments by his contemporaries, and it was not until recent years that he has been taken seriously in Swedish art history. His paintings can in many ways be compared to today's 'action painting'. For him, it was the artistic act of creation that was important; the subject matter played a minor role. The picture grew out of the powers which lay in the material itself.

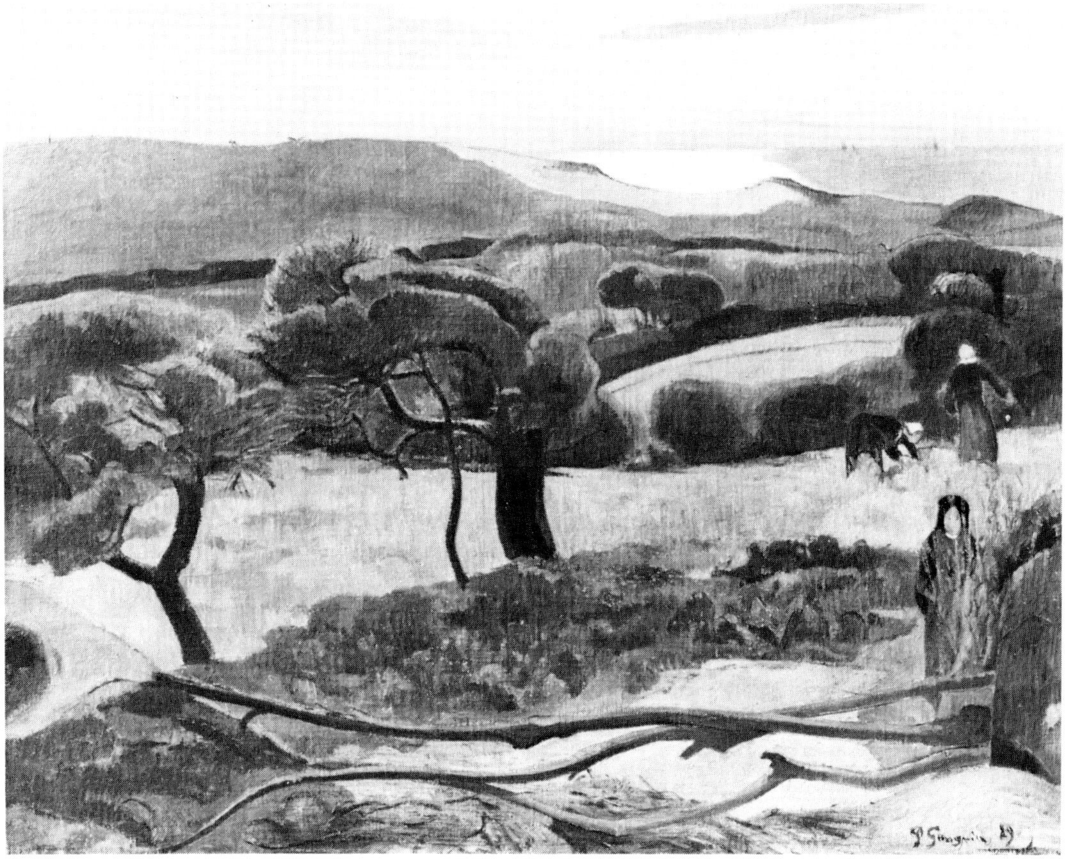

Fig. 13.
Paul Gauguin, Landscape from Brittany, 1889, Nationalmuseum, Stockholm

Denmark, in contrast to the other Nordic countries, had a strong national tradition of art which culminated in the 'Golden Age' in the first half of the century. It created an ideal whose influence was felt in many ways in Danish art even in the last half of the century as well. As was the case in the other Nordic countries, the 1880s in Denmark marked the advent of a new generation of painters and renewed contacts with international currents. There were the same conflicts between this young generation and the established institutions, which led to the foundation of independent art schools, and in 1891 to the creation of the Free Exhibition. Of the independent art schools, Krøyer's and Kristian Zahrtmann's were the most famous, and it was there that nearly all the young Danish artists received their basic training. Zahrtmann's school should also be singled out for its importance for Norwegian art. Almost all of the young Norwegian artists of the 1890s studied at the school, and it contributed in no small degree to the close contacts between Norwegian and Danish art during this period.

The Free Exhibition, an institution that still exists, became an important meeting-place for artists from all the Scandinavian countries. It also served as a major gateway for new international trends. Denmark came to play an important role as a mediator of new ideas to Scandinavia. In 1888 there was a large exhibition of French art in which the Impressionists were well represented, and in 1892 the exhibition of

Fig. 14. P. S. Krøyer, The Artists' Lunch, 1883, Skagens Museum, Denmark

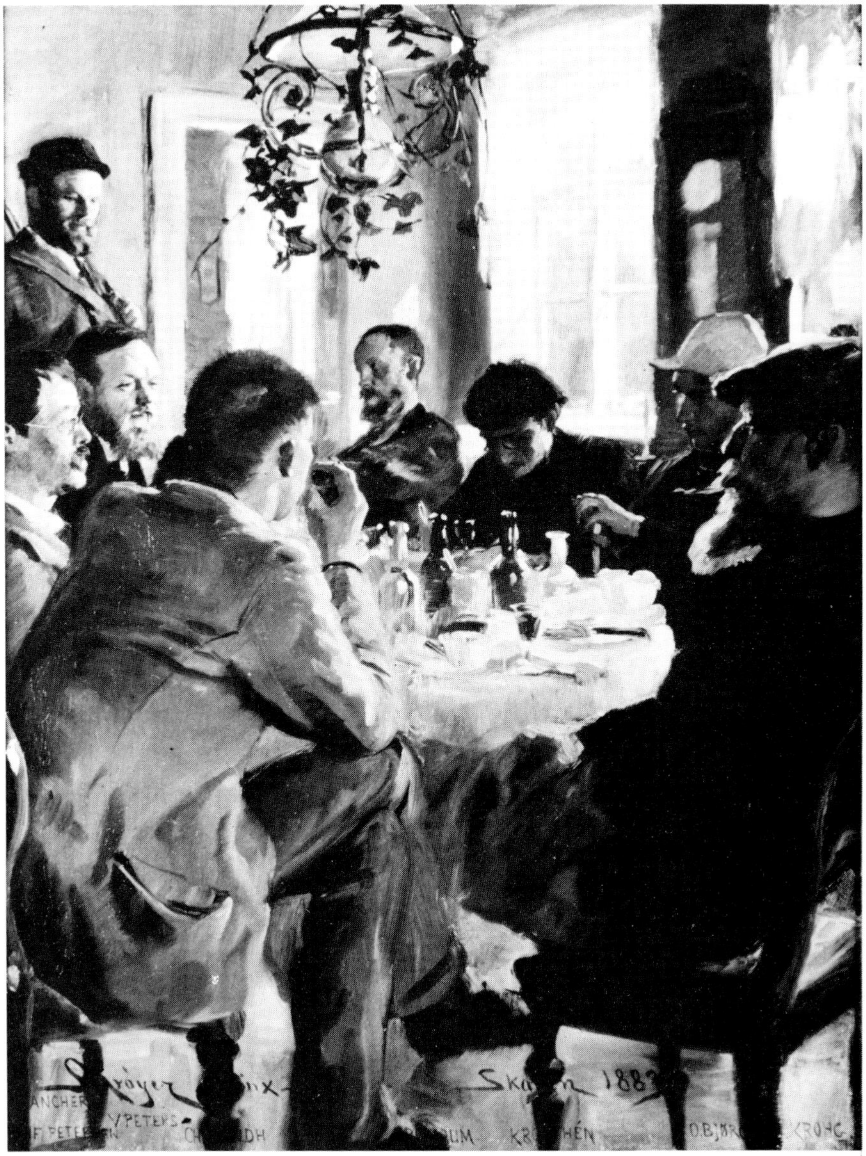

works by Paul Gauguin and Van Gogh. The collection that Gauguin's Danish wife Mette brought home with her to Denmark is also significant.

Perhaps the most important group in Danish art of this period were the Skagen painters. From the end of the 1870s Skagen, or the Skaw, a little fishing village on the northern tip of Jutland, became a meeting-place for artists not only from Denmark but also from Norway and Sweden. Here they created a Nordic artists' colony which in the 1880s played a major role in the development of Naturalism and *plein-air* painting in Scandinavia.

The Danish painters in the group remained faithful to Skagen through the 1890s too. The most prominent of them were P. S. Krøyer, Michael and Anna Ancher, and Viggo Johansen. The central figure was P. S. Krøyer, a painter who in many ways assumed the same position in Danish art as Zorn did in Swedish art. A virtuoso with a brush, he mastered a wide artistic repertoire. He was internationally orientated, travelled continuously, keeping abreast of developments in other countries. In the 1880s, he was the leading Naturalist, and in the 1890s, became the foremost Danish painter of the light northern summer nights. The delicate and finely tuned colour harmonies with blue, white and yellow predominating, give his pictures from the Skagen shore a characteristic, almost self-illuminated effect.

In sharp contrast to Krøyer as an artist and as a person was L. A. Ring. He grew up in very modest circumstances and kept close ties with the Danish countryside and the simple people who lived there. Throughout his career, he remained a committed Naturalist, painstakingly rendering his motifs with great fidelity to detail. With his tight, tersely composed landscapes, marked by an intimate objectivity, but not without feeling, he is perhaps the painter in his generation who best expressed the special features and atmosphere of Denmark's countryside.

Vilhelm Hammershøi, in turn, was a man of completely different fibre, a painter of loneliness and silence. His pictures are marked by quiet contemplation without external action, but filled with an inner tension with an undertone of mysticism and hidden drama.

His range of subjects was limited, and he never ventured far to find them. Whether in homely interiors, pictures of buildings, portraits, or landscapes, we find the same sharply sculptured forms and terse monumentality, and light is always the main theme. His palette is subdued, mostly refined nuances of grey, from the deepest black to the lightest white.

Fig. 15. Cover of Tårnet (October 1893–March 1894) and Taarnet (April–September 1894)

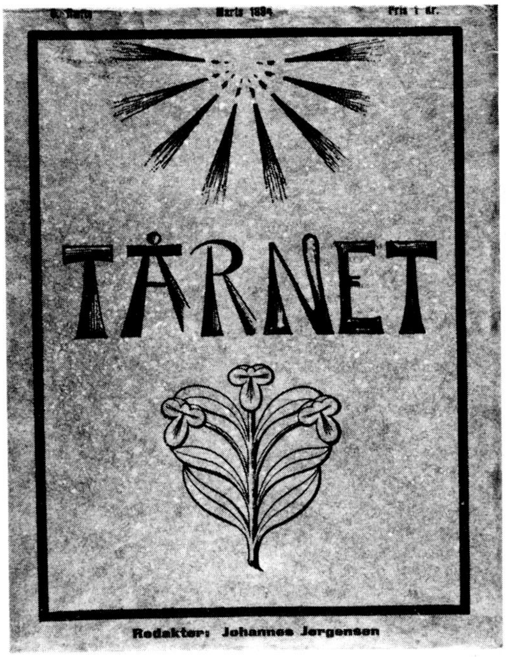

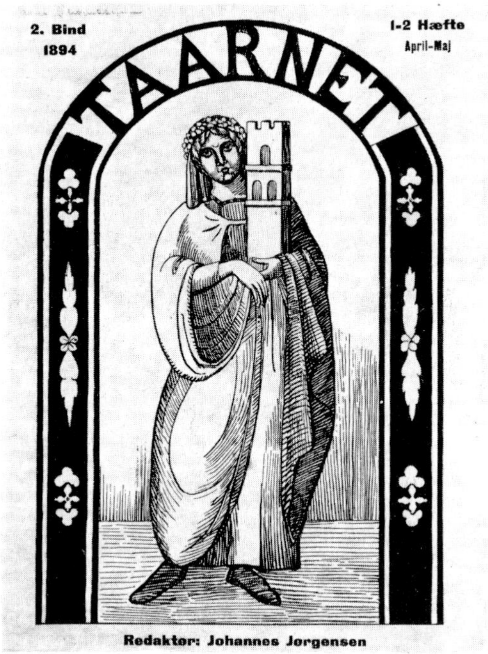

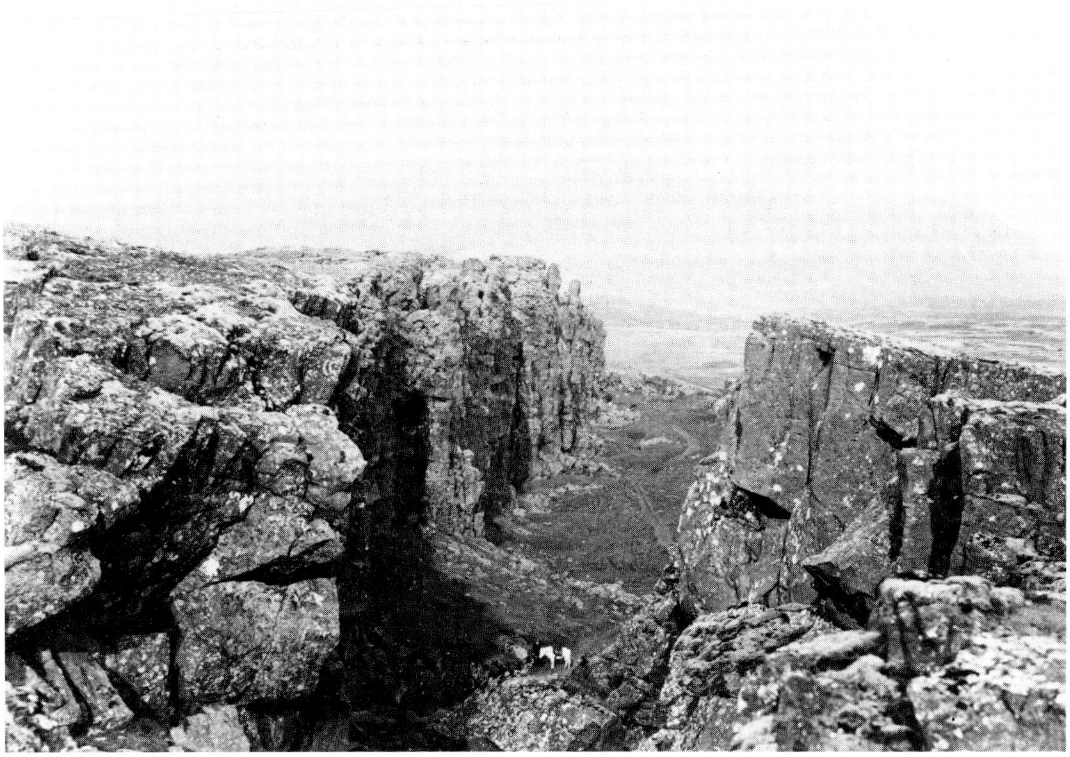

Fig. 16. Landscape at Thingvellir in Iceland (photo S. Eymundson). National Museum of Iceland

Both Ring and Hammershøi, though each in his own way is so clearly 'Danish' and brings to mind the masters of the 'Golden Age', fall to a certain extent outside the main trend in the development of Danish art in the 1890s. The dominating figure was J. F. Willumsen, a dynamic and multifaceted talent who, as well as being a painter, was also a sculptor, architect, craftsman and an influential art theoretician. He was a pioneer in introducing Symbolism and Synthetism not only to Danish art, but also to Nordic art. During his stay in France in the late 1880s and early 1890s, he had come into close contact with the leading avant-garde circles in French art, especially with Gauguin. His art at the beginning of the decade was completely under the sway of Synthetism. At around the turn of the century, however, he developed a powerful expressive style in which he attempted to illustrate his conception of nature as the moving force in life.

French Symbolism propagated by the journal 'Taarnet' and painters like Johan Rohde and Willumsen exerted a profound influence during the 1890s on the young generation of Danish painters, such as Ludvig Find, Harald Slott-Møller and Ejnar Nielsen. The most original of the three was probably Ejnar Nielsen. His pictures of the individual's struggle against old age, illness, and death also make a social comment, which was rare at the time. They keep to a very subdued palette and, in spite of their content, express a sincere and compassionate view of the world.

Iceland, which was in union with Denmark, had in 1874 received its own constitution. It had only 70,000 inhabitants, but there was a strong sense of a national identity and an awareness of cultural traditions, especially apparent in its literature. With increased independence and an improving economy, came a growing interest in art, but the sparse population and an unsophisticated urban milieu placed severe limitations upon its development. Modern Iceland's first painter, Thórarinn Thorláksson, received his training in Copenhagen during the 1890s, and was influenced by the mood prevailing in Danish art at the time. He depicted the magnificent and unique Icelandic countryside in a silent, earnest way. Today Thorláksson is considered the founder of national Icelandic art.

Aspects of Scandinavian Symbolism

SALME SARAJAS-KORTE

The romanticism of the end of the nineteenth century gave birth to a period in art in Scandinavia which was expressive and original. To some degree it was even uniform in all the Nordic countries. This period is commonly referred to simply as 'the '90s' or 'the turn of the century', but often with more preciseness, using two highly different terms, as *National Romanticism* and *Symbolism*. The art of these years proves, however, that it was possible to reconcile these two terms and at the same time find the essence of the Scandinavian art of the day. A love of nature took on a metaphysical dimension in pantheism. Patriotism in this far-off corner of the world did not necessarily conflict with the escapism of Symbolism in other parts of Europe. The synthetist style gradually superseded realistic form.

Mystical Romanticism had a strong appeal for the Nordic artistic temperament. As early as the end of the 1880s, when incipient Romanticism in the pictorial arts was just seeking its Symbolist form, Nordic painters were quick to find the mystical and romantically oriented features of prevailing Realism.

Before there was a real knowledge in Scandinavia of Symbolism as an artistic movement, attention was paid to the 'new mysticism' in European intellectual life. This was to become an inseparable part of Symbolism.

International Realism and Positivism, with their social ideology, had hardly had time to take root in Nordic art before signs were being sought of their decay. Old-fashioned romantics and enthusiastic representatives of the new generation often joined forces in this effort. One of the best examples of this is probably the popularization of Zola's ideas as interpreted by Scandinavia's leading champion of Realism, Denmark's Georg Brandes.

Brandes' articles revealed the increasing reaction to the supremacy of the Positivist ideologies of the 1880s. He argued that with Zola, as with all other poets, it is the imagination which creates works of art. The poet was not quite so detached as he pretended. His temperament transformed reality. Zola was, in fact, a Symbolist.[1] Brandes' views helped prepare the way for the poets of the 1890s.

Brandes repeated his ideas on Zola in a lecture in Helsinki in 1887. The leading Swedo-Finnish cultural periodical, *Finsk Tidskrift*, summarized the lecture more or less as follows: Zola was not a Realist at all. He was a Romantic! Zola's *temperament* was in fact the same as the romantics' *imagination*. The summary ended with the victorious claim that Brandes had led his listeners right up to the Romantic era which, at least in Helsinki, was being prophesied in some literary circles.[2] The literary works of the Norwegian Henrik Ibsen, considered a Naturalist, were an excellent parallel, the article noted.

About the same time, the Scandinavian artists' colony in Paris was pursuing the 'scientific mysticism' of the day. In 1888, Albert Edelfelt wrote home about 'the new mysticism whose representatives even included important artists'.[3] Artists attended Dr Charcot's demonstrations of hypnotism at La Salpêtrière hospital, and held seances.[4] 1888 was also the year when Gallen-Kallela's paintings began to show symbols which pointed to mysticism, when Richard Bergh finished his painting *Hypnotic Seance*, and when Ernst Josephson's occultism triggered his latent mental illness. Josephson's art during his illness was, in fact, based on his personal problems, but its deep mysticism and links with Emanuel Swedenborg, so worshipped by the Symbolists,[5] were like an urgent cry in Scandinavia's mystical atmosphere at the end of the century. Life and death, religion and art formed an impenetrable weave.

When Symbolism in the pictorial arts began to take shape in the footsteps of French Symbolist poetry, Nordic artists quickly adopted the new trend. Referring to Gauguin's art, Gustave Albert Aurier and Joséphin (Sâr) Péladan proclaimed that the artist was a *visionary* who had the gift of seeing behind *exoteric* phenomena their lasting, real, internal, *esoteric* being intuitively experiencing them, *synthetically*, in ancient times.[6]

'Ils sentent tout de suite, tout à la fois, *synthétiquement*', wrote Charles Baudelaire in *Curiosités esthétiques*.

A metaphysical understanding of the great synthesis of being was sought both in the content of the works of art and also in a simplification of form, in an effort to achieve a harmony of colour and form which corresponded to the universal harmony.

With amazing unanimity, Nordic artists turned away from the evolutionary optimism and from the bright light of the Impressionists. The new trend paved the way for an individualistic, often gloomy philosophy of life, which was connected with a mystic pantheism so characteristic of the inhabitants of the north.

The Scandinavian artists' adoption of this new metaphysical Romanticism was even more natural since Symbolism in France was seen as a non-French, northern trend. It was considered to have a haziness which stood in sharp contrast to the spiritual lucidity of the Latin world. Even *La Plume*, the periodical which promoted Symbolism, wrote of the barbarism of the 'northern dissenters, Ibsenists, Tolstoyans, and Bjørnsonists.'[8] Camille Mauclair went straight to the heart of the matter in *Mercure de France*: it had been shown that the French had banned nationalism. 'All their spiritual fathers, Tolstoy, Ibsen, Carlyle, and Fichte, all music from Bach to Wagner, from Schumann to Borodin, were foreign, and Rossetti, and Swinburne, and finally Nietzsche and everyone...'[9]

Mauclair's view shows that the nationalism which emerged in the various countries of Europe at the end of the last century formed a barrier in France to the acceptance of Symbolism. Nationalism in Scandinavia had quite the opposite effect: even though Symbolism came to Scandinavia from Paris, it was considered to be something that had fertile soil in the Nordic countries. It attracted artists back to Scandinavia to create their own national art which, however, was believed to be abreast with the newest developments in international art. These artists' self-confidence was further increased by theosophy's idea that in the universal spiritual development of mankind it was now the turn of the Nordic countries to take the lead: 'Das Licht kommt jetzt vom Norden!'.[10]

Gradually, a negative attitude to Paris emerged, towards its over-civilization and decadence. The interest in the Nordic wildernesses that had been aroused during the period of Realism took on a new dimension. The primitive life which Gauguin sought in Tahiti was found in this northern wilderness and mountain regions. Scandinavia's own national legends were seen to have the same holy wisdom as the great world religions. The North's 'own roots', the ancient world of the heroes, were found in poetic folklore.

New artistic models, a new concept of the relationship between art and life, coloured all turn-of-the-century Scandinavian art. The artist's attitude towards his work changed. Even the art of so independent an artist as Vilhelm Hammershøi, for example, so devoid of Symbolist references, would not have been possible without the existence of Puvis de Chavannes, Carrière, and Whistler, without the models of Giotto and Fra Angelico. And the works of Helene Schjerfbeck and Ellen Thesleff, simple as they were at that period, came under the same influences.

One of the earliest Scandinavian links with French Synthetist-Symbolist art was J. F. Willumsen's contact with Gauguin and the Pont-Aven group in 1888–91. In 1891, Willumsen is known to have attended Gauguin's famous farewell party as he left for the South Seas for the first time.[11] His *Jotunheim* of 1892–3 (illustrated page 10), a subject from the fells of Norway, is an excellent example of a northern variation of Gauguin's art. The rugged mysticism of nature in the north was merged with Gauguin's philosophy of art. Perhaps in no other painting did it take on such a clear – and baroque – expression. However, Willumsen's art retained more of Gauguin's Synthetist style than his art philosophy from this period. In one of his letters, Gauguin himself warned against an excessive formalistic interpretation of his art. The artistic expression should be as simple as Handel's music.[12]

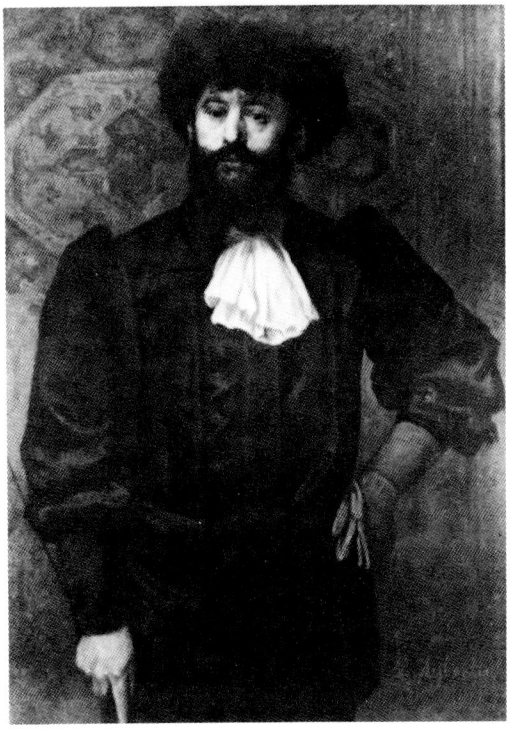

Fig. 17. Marcelin Desboutin, The Portrait of Sâr Merodack Péladan, The Salon of the Rose + Croix 1893

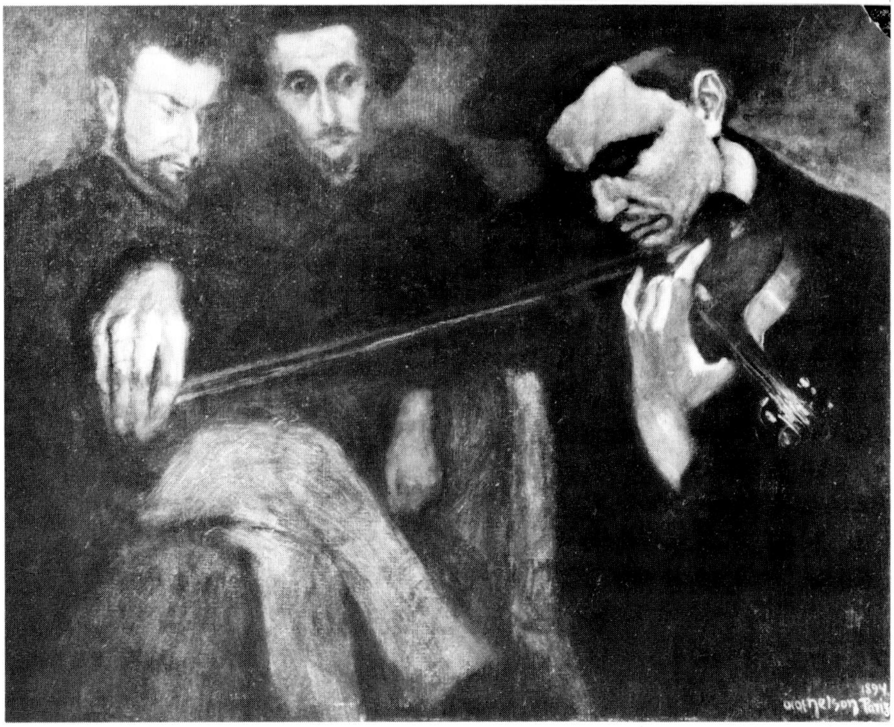

Fig. 18. Olof Sager-Nelson, The Violinist, 1894, Göteborgs konstmuseum, Gothenburg

The young Scandinavian group of artists which gathered in Paris in the early 1890s understood the deep literary and mystical tradition of Symbolism; the spiritual leaders of the group were the Swedes Ivan Aguéli and Olof Sager-Nelson, and the Finn Magnus Enckell. They joined the literary and artistic circle of Soleil d'Or and were strongly influenced by the Catholic mysticism of Joséphin Péladan. Enckell and Aguéli, in particular, were both very well read and had delved into the mystical and occult traditions of past ages, Aguéli even put aside his work as a painter during his hectic years in Paris. What was important was to take a stand on Catholic and theosophical mysticism. It became the basis for all art: music, poetry, and painting. 'Only here did I learn to understand what art is and how deep my roots are in it,' wrote Magnus Enckell, whose androgynous boy figures depicted the profound seriousness underlying the group's concept of life.[14]

The same religious and philosophical basis was found in the Danish periodical *Taarnet*, founded by Johannes Jørgensen in 1893. The idea for the periodical was formulated 'on a moonlit night... in the name of Baudelaire, Poe, and Verlaine'.[15] A belief in the transcendental, in the beyond, was the foundation for life and art, the salvation from a feeling of emptiness and harsh reality. Life itself was ugly, so why not turn to the night: the young loved its mystical darkness. In the manifesto written for the second issue of *Taarnet*, Jørgensen repeated Baudelaire's words, which can be considered to contain the basic idea of all Symbolist art. 'Dans certains états de l'âme presque surnaturels, la profondeur de la vie se révèle toute entière, si ordinaire qu'il soit, qu'on a sous les yeux. *Il en devient le symbole.*' Perhaps more clearly, Scandinavian artists remembered Henri-Frédéric Amiel's simpler idea, quoted by Jørgensen in the same connection: 'Un paysage quelconque est un état de l'âme.'[16] Amiel's spiritual landscape was the open road to nature's mysticism, which was one of the most characteristic features of Scandinavian art in the 1890s.

Only part of the Nordic Symbolist movement believed as Baudelaire did, that even the simplest view was able to reveal the profundity of life. Generally their subject-matter was composed of many elements, and embraced everything from the simplicity of Enckell's early works to melancholy nature views, profound allegories, and finally Edvard Munch's eruptive mysticism of love, fear, and death.

The formative ideas derived not only from the literary tradition, but also from the mysticism of Péladan, whose programme concentrated on classical forms and a profundity of subject-matter. Before long Péladan's eccentric behaviour drove many serious artists from his circle, but his message was carried far. Only a few Scandinavian artists have later admitted Péladan's influence. One of these few was Magnus Enckell. Although Péladan's influence is inestimably great it was exerted indirectly through his disciples, rather than directly. He himself was made a laughing-stock. 'He fell for frilled collars as Kierkegaard did for his green umbrella. He brought Germanic civilization to his own country and opened doors, that had been closed up to that time, to all of Europe,' August Strindberg wrote in 1904.[17]

Strindberg's own painting, which is quite different from typical Symbolist art, is one example of the extent of Péladan's influence. When Strindberg described the esoteric features of his art, one can clearly hear echoes of the mysticism proclaimed by Péladan. 'I have found a new art form... Each work has, I could say, a dual basis: there is the exoteric side, which everyone – though only with difficulty – can see, and the esoteric, for the artist himself and the chosen.'[8]

Strindberg also spoke of the Germanic origins of the Symbolist movement. Wagner had been a 'revelation' to Péladan, and Baudelaire had shown him the way. It followed therefore that after Paris, Berlin became the most important ideological centre for Nordic artists in the 1890s. By the middle of the decade, at slightly different times, such artists as Strindberg, Edvard Munch, J. F. Willumsen, Gustav Vigeland, and Gallen-Kallela had all spent some time there. Berlin had its own small group of artists, too, the radical Ferkel group, who were eager for the renewal of art. Its main ideology came, however, from the Pole, Stanislaw Przybyszewski, and that most important Scandinavian writer, Adolf Paul.

Undoubtedly of major significance for the history of Nordic Symbolism was the brief period (only two months), that Munch and Gallen-Kallela spent in Berlin in 1895. But their joint exhibition there seems to have left bitter memories for both. The Ferkel group discussed and philosophized. The basis of their philosophy was very similar to that of Parisian Symbolism. The main difference was that instead of the androgynous man, free from sexuality, as in French Symbolism, in Berlin the struggle between the two sexes was seen as the condition for all intellectual and artistic creativity. Man had the creative power; woman, the madonna or vampire, was the sphinx, who hid within herself the riddle of life and death.[19]

Even though Edvard Munch and Gallen-Kallela were mentioned together in the German press 'like a team of horses', the heralds of the new art,[28] they represented two very different trends in Scandinavian Symbolism of the 1890s. Both, it is true, carried the message from the North and from Paris. Gallen-Kallela was, however, a product of the Parisian Realism of the 1880s, and finally adopted the radicalism of the Norwegian Hans Jæger and the Nietzscheism mediated by August Strindberg.

Edvard Munch was in Paris from 1889 to 1892, the great years of Symbolism. Indeed, Ernest Raynaud, the authority on French Symbolism, called 1891 *la date heureuse du symbolisme*.[21] Solitary and isolated though Munch was, he was almost certainly familiar with the fundamental ideas of Symbolism. His links with Baudelaire, Mallarmé, Verlaine, and Maeterlinck seem to be well documented, and he adopted the new spiritualism of Paris quite spontaneously.

As early as 1889, he painted *Inger on the Beach*, and in 1890 his self-portrait *Night in St Cloud*, works which, with their inward sensitivity and deep melancholy, can be considered turning points in the Scandinavian art of the end of the century.

During these same years, Gallen-Kallela was in Finland on his trip of discovery to Karelia, where he sought the factual basis for the *Kalevala* epic. When he came to

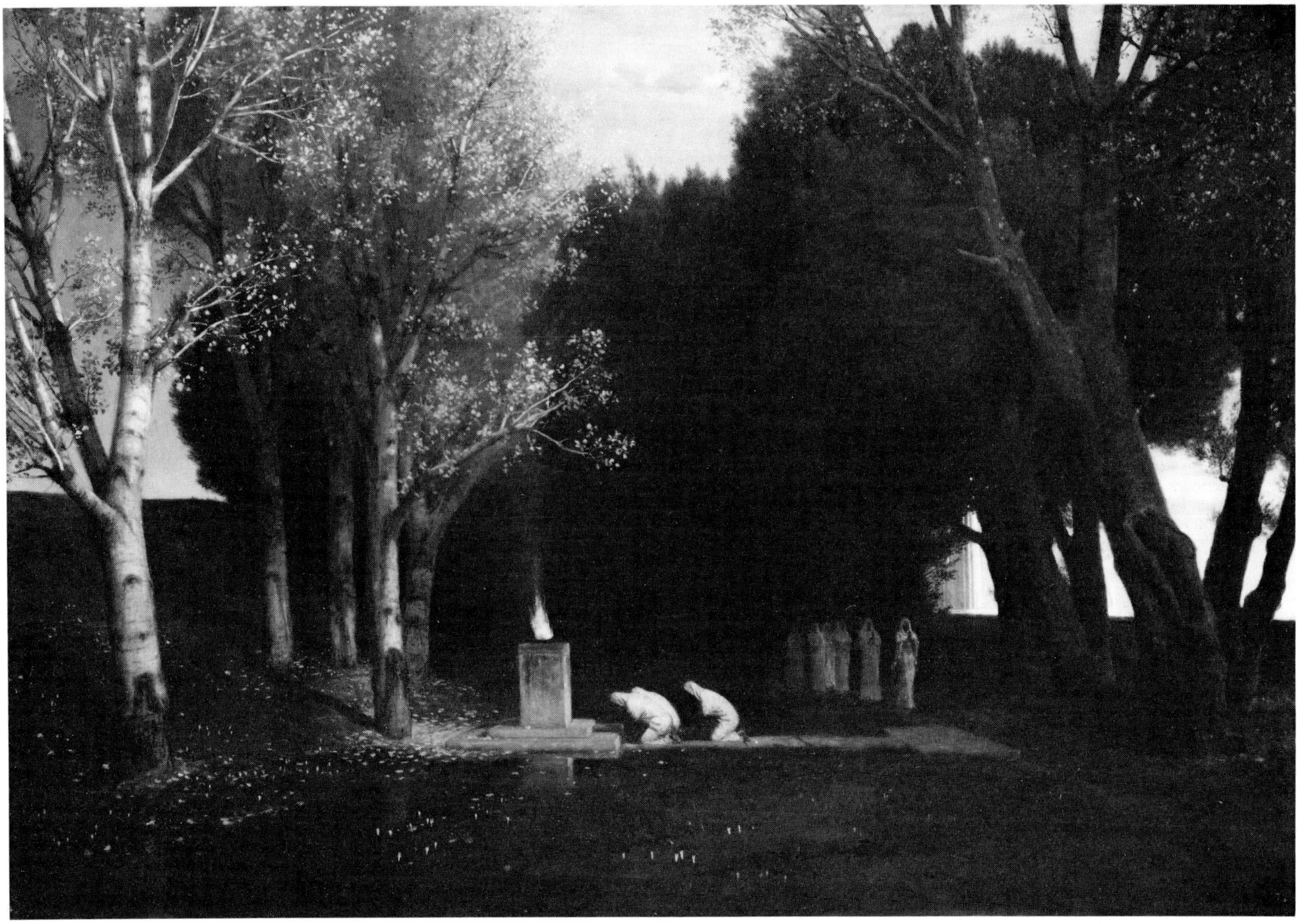

Fig. 19. Arnold Böcklin, The Sacred Wood, 1882, Offentliche Kunstsammlung, Basle

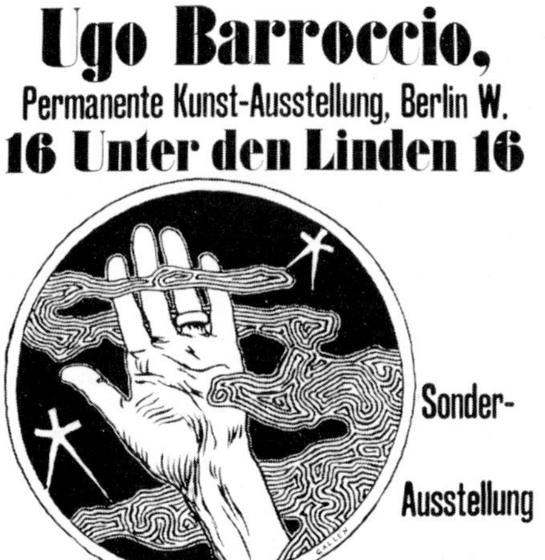

Fig. 20. The Poster of Edvard Munch's and Akseli Gallen-Kallela's Exhibition in Berlin in 1895, Gallen-Kallela museo, Espoo

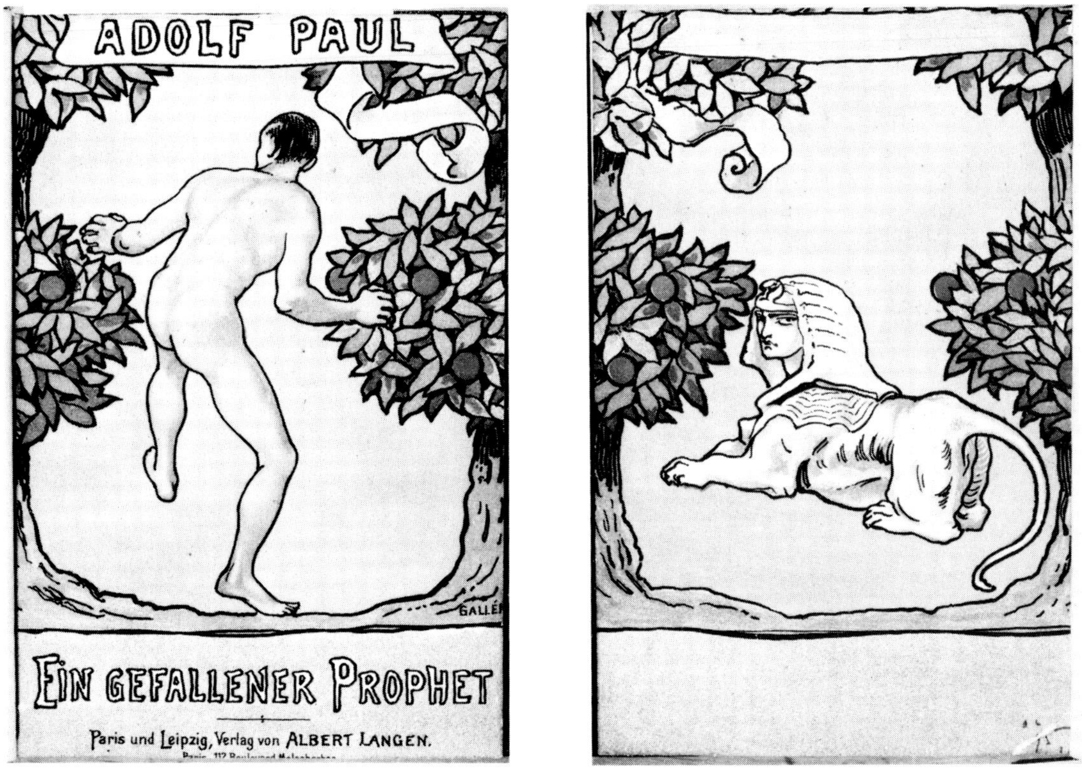

Fig. 21. The Cover by Akseli Gallen-Kallela for Adolf Paul's Collection of Short Stories 'Ein gefallener Prophet', 1894

Paris in 1892 with his first large-scale *Kalevala* painting, the *Aino Triptych* (Fig. 6), his sudden contact with Symbolist art resulted in an outburst of furious disappointment. 'Everything here is approaching an end; the signs of life which are seen here are only death throes.' The criticism was aimed at the Rose + Croix and Champ-de-Mars salons.[22]

At home in 1892–3, Gallen-Kallela underwent a serious crisis. He had to find a way between the nationalism of the 1890s and Symbolism. This course was through the medium of a pantheistic mysticism of nature.

For a brief time in 1894, Adolf Paul, who arrived in Finland from Berlin, was able to tear Gallen-Kallela away from this nationalism. The main work of art from this period, *Symposium* (No. 22), a joint idea of Adolf Paul and Gallen-Kallela, was stylistically a transitional piece. The mystery of life is revealed to night revellers, and presented in many symbols. A second work, *Conceptio artis*, was created in the same way in 1894: the artist meets a sphinx, the secret of life and death is the essence of art.

The Scandinavian artists' attitude towards Germany was ambivalent: on the one hand, they accepted German influences, while on the other, they proudly brought Germany a 'new art'. Arnold Böcklin's enormous popularity in Scandinavia at the time may seem surprising today. Even Edvard Munch wrote to his Danish friend Johan Rohde, 'No matter what complete rubbish art here in Germany is in general . . . it does have one advantage: it has produced individual artists who are so much above the others and are so lonely; for example Böcklin, who I believe is above all the others, Max Klinger, Thoma, Wagner, Nietzsche . . .'[23] The respect which Böcklin enjoyed can perhaps be compared to that almost universally accorded Puvis de Chavannes at the same time.

The Scandinavian contribution was important, in turn, for the birth of Berlin's Modernism, the ideology of the Ferkel group, and the content of the new magazine *Pan*. There were both positive and negative reactions to this Nordic influence.

'Something which strikes one here is the magnificent ring which Scandinavian names have. It is the highest possible recommendation to be a Scandinavian. They know Ibsen, Strindberg, Arne Garborg, Holger Drachmann just as well as we do.

They speak about the Nordic artists with a respect that warms the soul', wrote Edelfelt at the end of February 1895.[24]

This was confirmed at the Munch and Gallén-Kallela exhibition by the *National-Zeitung*. 'Quite recently, there was an art critic who enthusiastically greeted the young Nordic artists as the representatives of a new young culture. Finns, Danes, Norwegians, and Swedes are bringing us a new renaissance!'[25]

Adverse critical comments were also made on both sides. 'With all due respect to the abilities of these masters', the *National-Zeitung* writer continued, he wanted to know whether these artists really did come to their easels straight from the wilderness (Urwälder) of the north, or whether in fact they had not been trained according to established traditions dating back to Greek and Roman times. Edelfelt, in turn, wrote of the art in Munich: 'Certain important artists among the uninspired and artificial... If only they would take the spirit of the old masters instead of their stuffy yellowish-brown varnish.'[26]

Around 1895, Scandinavia began to react against the Symbolism of the first years of the decade. The Swedo-Finnish poet K. A. Tavaststjerna believed that 'even the word Symbolism brought with it a spiritual mist in which one gropes and gropes and experiences everything unclearly, fantastically, magnified, or awry.'[27] In Sweden, Ludvig Looström wrote in his art review in 1896 that what had been considered the art of the future a few years earlier had already lost its importance.[28]

If Symbolism as a true art movement had lost its popularity, it did not disappear without a trace. Most of the Symbolist works of individual artists such as Finland's Hugo Simberg, Norway's Halfdan Egedius, and Denmark's Ejnar Nielsen were created at the end of the 1890s. Edvard Munch continued his magnificent *Frieze of life*,

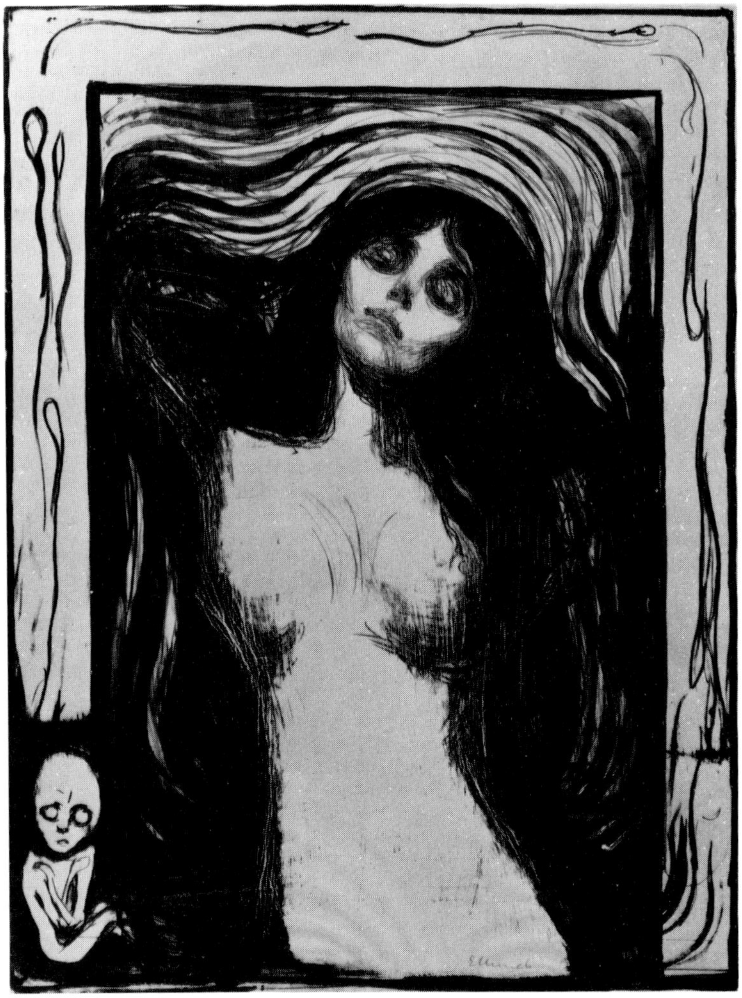

Fig. 22.
Edvard Munch, Madonna, 1895, Munch-museet, Oslo

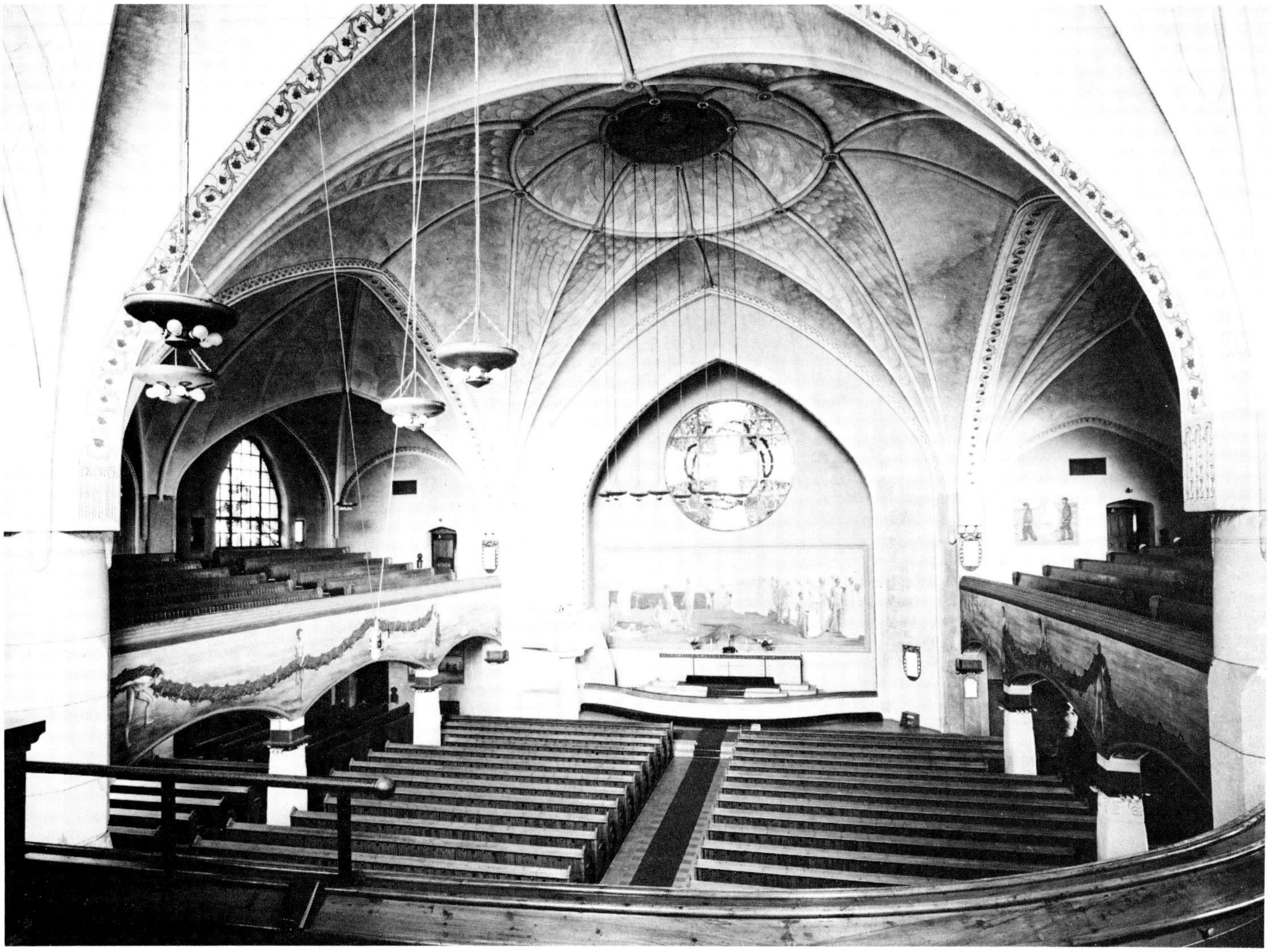

Fig. 23. Interior of St John's Cathedral, 1901–7, Tampere. Architect: Lars Sonck; altarpiece: Magnus Enckell; frescos and stained glass: Hugo Simberg, 1906–7 (photo E. M. Staf)

in which love, pain, and death form an impressive synthesis, and Gallen-Kallela finally created his series of monumental *Kalevala* paintings. He no longer sought a factual foundation for the *Kalevala* in the life of the villages of the wilderness. The *Kalevala* had become for the artist the Holy Book of the Finns.

Iceland's mighty Eddas did not influence the art of the 1890s in the same way although the Sagas found many able illustrators, for example Kittelsen and Werenskiold.

Gallen-Kallela's return to *Kalevala* subjects after his trip to Berlin and his adaptation of the new Synthetist style to Finnish folklore explain why the National Romantic style found more followers in Finland than in the other Nordic countries at the end of the century.

By the beginning of the twentieth century, one can say that the general picture of Scandinavian art had changed completely from what it had been ten years before. Instead of *plein air* and analysis, there was a synthesis of form and simple monumentality. The original basic values of Symbolism had included an admiration of the monumental art of primitive art periods.

Even after the victorious years of Symbolism, two features remained in Scandinavian art which seem to correspond to the Nordic artists' idea of pure art: a respect for Italy in the early Renaissance, and powerful clear forms. On the other hand, there was still a pantheistic mysticism of nature which was like a Nordic variation of Symbolism.

It also explains the abundance of landscape paintings in this art movement, which was generally so preoccupied with man and his metaphysical existence.

Something truly Nordic is Gallen-Kallela's credo written in 1893. Even though one can detect the ideas of Baudelaire and Oscar Wilde, the background is definitely Nordic. 'In the world, in life, and in nature, there is nothing but beautiful tales, and when the door opens, enter and accept it with all your soul. Art is an immense, eternal forest, where the trees stand as sparsely or as densely as you wish. The moon, sun, and all kinds of glittering stars move about at your will, and when you come to the shore of a lake in the wilderness it is fathomless if you so want, and lush waterlilies and wonderful red-speckled waterbirds swim on the black water. And if you want, the day will dawn on the other side of the lake behind the craggy mountain, and the yellow sun's rays shine through the delicate spiderwebs which hang between the eternal firs. The birds can begin their concert and beyond the mountain the spirit of the mountain accompanies them on the organ.'

The influence of Symbolism can be seen in Bruno Liljefors's misty views of nature, in the dense atmosphere of Prince Eugen's forest scenes, in Edvard Munch's moonlight, and in Harald Sohlberg's star-studded night on the fells. Through nature, the Nordic artist came into contact with the metaphysical world.

NOTES

1. 'Virkeligheden og Temperament hos Emile Zola.' *Tilskueren*, September 1887 (København) pp. 657–78.
2. B. Estlander, 'Dr Georg Brandes föredrag.' *Finsk Tidskrift*, 1887 (Helsingfors) p. 389. See also Z. Topelius' letter to Carl Snoilsky 15.5.1887, *Carl Snoilsky och hans vänner. Ur skaldens brevväxling* I–II, (Stockholm, 1917–18).
3. Albert Edelfelt's letter to B. O. Schauman 21.3.1888, Ateneumin Taidemuseo. See also Sarajas-Korte (Bibl. ref:15) p.17.
4. Albert Edelfelt, *Liv och arbete* (Helsingfors, 1926) p. 145. Erik Blomberg, *Ernst Josephson, Hans liv.* (Stockholm 1951) p. 652. Axel Munthe, *The Story of San Michele,* (1929). Staffan Tjerneld, *Den mystiske dr Munthe,* (Stockholm 1973) p. 73 ff.
5. Erik Blomberg 1951, Chapters 'På Brehat' och 'Sjukdomstiden'. Sarajas-Korte (Bibl.ref:15) pp. 29–33.
6. Sarajas-Korte (Bibl.ref:15) pp. 40–6.
7. *Curiosités esthétiques* . Charles Baudelaire, *Oeuvres complètes* (Paris, 1954) p. 769.
8. Huyghes Rebell, 'Menus propos sur les nouvelles Utopies'. *La Plume*, 15.3.1894.
9. *Mercure de France*, Sept. 1893.
10. Sarajas-Korte (Bibl.ref:15) p. 53 and Chapter 'Berlin 1895'.
11. Merete Bodelsen, *Willumsen i 90nes Paris* (København, 1957) English Summary, pp.63–71.
12 .J. F. Willumsen, *Mine Erindringer fortalt till Ernst Mentze* (København, 1953) pp. 72–3.
13. Sarajas-Korte (Bibl.ref:15), pp. 88–114.
14. Sarajas-Korte (Bibl.ref:15) p. 70.
15. 'Symbolisme'. *Taarnet*, (December 1893 København) pp. 51–6.
16. *Taarnet*. (December 1893 København) cit. Charles Baudelaire, *Journaux intimes*. Baudelaire (see note no. 7) p. 1194.
17. *Nittio-talet* (Stockholm, 1904) p. 114.
18. Lars-Göran Oredsson, 'Albert von Stockenström – såningsman i sekelslutets örtgård.' *Paletten* 1984 / 2 (Göteborg).
19. Sarajas-Korte (Bibl.ref:15) Chapter 'Zum Schwarzen Ferkel. Androgynen, än en gång'.
20. Sarajas-Korte (Bibl.ref:15), p. 312.
21. Sarajas-Korte (Bibl.ref:15) p. 50. Ernest Raynaud, *La Mélée Symboliste* I–III, (1918–1922).
22. Sarajas-Korte (Bibl.ref:15) pp 234–5.
23. Cit. Gösta Svenaeus, *Idé och innehåll i Edvard Munchs konst* (Oslo, 1953) p. 42.
24. Sarajas-Korte (Bibl.ref:15) p. 293. Cit. Albert Edelfelt, *Middagshöjd* (Helsingfors, 1928) p. 177. In another letter 9.3.1893 Edelfelt wrote: 'Zuerst die Franzosen, so die Skandinaven, aber jetzt werden wir auch kommen . . .' Ibid. p. 108.
25. G. V.,'Neue Bilder', *National-Zeitung*, 26.3.1895. Cit. Sarajas-Korte (Bibl.ref:15), p. 293.
26. Edelfelt (see note no. 24) pp. 106–113.
27. 'Symbolism i realism', *Hufvudstadsbladet*, 20.11.1895 (Helsingfors).
28. S. Alfons, B. Lindwall & R. Josephson, *Svensk konstkrönika under 100 år* (Stockholm, 1944), 1896.

The North, Nature, and Poverty: Some Background on the Nordic Identity

MATTI KLINGE

No other point of the compass in Europe has such a stark and clear profile as the north: a uniform area with a uniform culture, in relation to the rest of the continent. One country, Norway, takes its name expressly from its point on the compass. How important the very concept 'north' is for the 'northmen' is illustrated by the national anthems of Finland, Sweden, and Norway, where 'the North', and not the country in question, is presented as the object of love.

This clear profile of the Nordic countries as a cultural and political unit is a direct result of their geographical location. Throughout the ages they have been surrounded by other large units which have to a large extent decided their fate. The Atlantic Ocean is less important in this respect than the large states to the east and south: Russia and Germany.

The eastern border with Russia seems more sharply defined than the southern border. Contacts with the Russian empire from the Viking era to today's commercial contacts have always been lively and important, have often taken the form of wars, often that of trade. But the decisive difference when it comes to history and identification lies in religion. In the prolonged historical process which divided the Roman Empire into east and west, the Nordic countries came to belong to the west, while Russia became part of and heir to Byzantium. The Russians use the Greek-Cyrillic alphabet, while the Nordic countries use the Latin one. The Vikings did, it is true, learn Greek letters in Constantinople, and the oldest written document we have in Finnish is written in Cyrillic characters. Large parts of present-day northernmost Finland, Sweden, and Norway were within Novgorod's sphere of influence in the Middle Ages, and Lapland was not divided between the Swedish(-Finnish) and Danish(-Norwegian) kingdoms until the eighteenth and nineteenth centuries. Many Lapp villages paid taxes to two, at times three kingdoms. The northern border with Russia expanded towards the east during the long period of Russian weakness from the thirteenth century to the time of Peter the Great. Peter turned the direction of expansion in his favour at Poltava in 1709 and at Hanko in 1714.

As a result of changes in the borders and in international politics, the concept 'Norden' – the Nordic countries – is politically ambiguous even to this day, though what is generally understood by the term are the independent and intimately linked countries of Denmark, Finland, Iceland, Norway, and Sweden. Historically, Estonia and Latvia, although not part of the Nordic entity today, should at least be included in an analysis of it. All or parts of the two Baltic countries belonged to the Danish or Swedish kingdoms for centuries, and strove during their periods of independence to come closer to the Nordic countries, especially to Finland and Sweden. As far as religion and culture go, they are overwhelmingly bound to the western tradition, even though they were politically part of Russia from the beginning of the eighteenth century, with a break during their periods of independence between the two World Wars.

Geologically and agriculturally, through large farms and feudalism, the Baltic countries are similar to Denmark and to the southernmost part of Sweden, Scania. But linguistically, Estonia and to some extent Latvia are aligned with Finland, as members of the Balto-Finnic family of languages, a language group which structurally shows similarities to eastern languages and to Hungarian, but has a vocabulary strongly influenced by Germanic languages and Nordic-Lutheran semantics.

We come now to what is probably one of the most characteristic elements of the Nordic identity from a historical point of view: Lutheranism. At the Baltic Sea, it creates a clear border with the Lithuanian-Polish Catholic bloc. On the other hand, even today it theologically unites the Nordic countries with northern Germany, birthplace and stronghold of Lutheranism. Only in the Nordic countries has the

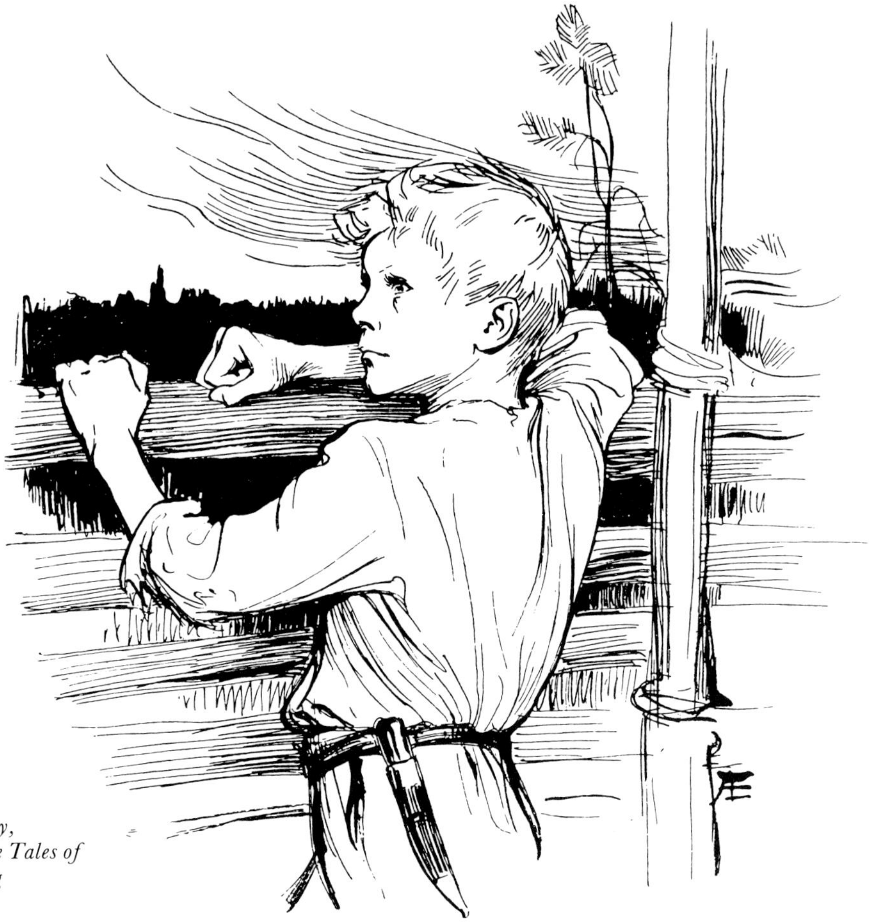

Fig. 24.
Albert Edelfelt, The Soldier Boy, 1898–1900. Illustration for The Tales of Ensign Stål by J. L. Runeberg

Lutheran state church survived in the form it took during the Reformation. In these countries it seems natural for the head of state (in Sweden, this now means the government) to appoint bishops, but from a Calvinist and Catholic point of view, this practice seems strange. Only the Anglican church can be compared to the Nordic Lutheran churches in this respect.

Lutheranism can be seen as a move towards simplicity. As a conservative movement, it turned against refinement and luxury, and emphasized primitiveness and simplicity. In this way it came to set the norms for the populist movements of the future.

In addition, Lutheranism became an important factor in the development of centrally governed states in the north during the sixteenth century. Sweden and Denmark (or Sweden-Finland and Denmark-Norway-Iceland) moved towards absolutism, in contrast to trends in Poland and even Germany for quite some time to come. Absolutism lasted in Denmark until the Napoleonic era and even longer; in Sweden, its dominance was not as continuous, but it was sufficient to allow the country to develop a sense of nationhood.

In the Baltic and North Sea areas, the German and Dutch commercial presence was always important, especially during the period of the Hanseatic League. In the Middle Ages, the Nordic countries were in a way a periphery of Germany, and German cultural and economic power started to influence politics, as royal names from the fourteenth and fifteenth centuries show: Albrekt of Mecklenburg, Erik of Pomerania, Christopher of Bavaria. But this trend was interrupted by the move towards centrally governed 'national' states in the sixteenth century. Culturally, however, the German influence was accentuated through the collapse of the Catholic church. One of the consequences of this collapse was the 'Germanizing' of the Swedish and Danish languages through sixteenth-century Bible translations and church handbooks. A large number of German-Latin concepts and structures were introduced in the same way into Finnish and Estonian. The Nordic university system, which had its beginning in the fifteenth century, was greatly expanded in the first half of the seventeenth century following German (and Dutch) patterns and scientific traditions.

But Germany's cultural influence in the sixteenth and seventeenth centuries was much greater than its political and military influence, and thus the two Nordic kingdoms were able to secure their existence in this period. During the eighteenth century, however, two modern, powerful states emerged on the borders of the Nordic countries which in their dealings with Poland had already shown what they had in store for weak neighbours. These kingdoms were the new Russia and the new Prussia. For the next two hundred years the Nordic kingdoms tested their might against these powers.

The most profound upheaval for the Nordic countries undoubtedly occurred during the Napoleonic Era when decisive political boundaries were drawn and decisive ideological positions taken. The Nordic countries as we now know them are the result of this period of turmoil. The old Danish and Swedish kingdoms were torn apart. Norway was separated from Denmark, Finland from Sweden. Old ties and traditions were lost. The new states found it difficult to build up an identity, and the old states – Denmark and Sweden – felt mutilated and threatened with annihilation like Poland in the previous century. Furthermore, the age's general ideological developments made deep wounds in the old religious and monarchistic identities.

As the number of Nordic countries rose from two to four (Norway, it is true, in union, this time with Sweden, and Finland as a Grand Duchy of Russia, but retaining its old law, religion, language, etc.), relations between the countries changed. In the wake of the tribulations brought about by international politics, the centuries-old antagonism between Swedes (Finns) and Danes (Norwegians) began to subside. A 'Nordism' or 'Scandinavianism' began to emerge. One of the uniting factors was the new belief in 'natural man', who was to be preferred to his civilized counterpart.

Rousseau and French 'provincialism' formulated and disseminated this ideology of the natural, which meant a negation of luxury, refinement, subtlety in art and science. The emphasis was no longer on industry and the cities, but on the moral superiority of rural life. Those who lived a simple and modest life were considered to be closer to the divine and the eternal than those whose minds were filled with thoughts of luxury, intrigue, and sophistry.

Nature in its unspoiled, wild form also acquired its human complement during the latter half of the eighteenth century. In the Nordic countries, Ossian and pre-Christian European mythology, together with Greece and Homer, came to represent the primitive, uncorrupted, anti-industrial and anti-Latin trend. Like Rousseauism, they were against the cities, and against luxury, science, and profit.

This interest in the primitive received support from the romantic theories propounded by Chateaubriand and Bernardin de Saint-Pierre. They turned the love of the wilderness or unspoiled nature into a fashionable movement. The Nordic countries, after a short-lived love affair with Lapland, turned to the less exotic but more convincing wildernesses of the forests and lake districts. But it was not enough to have the theme 'love of the wilderness'; it was necessary to place a moralistic interpretation on nature's beauty in relationship to man.

Neo-humanism's concept of Homeric Greece was contained in the ideal of 'noble simplicity and quiet grandeur'. The aesthetic-moral world view was thought by Winckelmann to be found in Greek art as seen in the light of the new archaeological discoveries. But it was not confined to the past. 'New Greeks' in Europe were to be sought in areas not yet spoiled by civilization.

According to Montesquieu and others experience seemed to show that barren and cold climates would produce a people who were intelligent, hardy, and freedom-

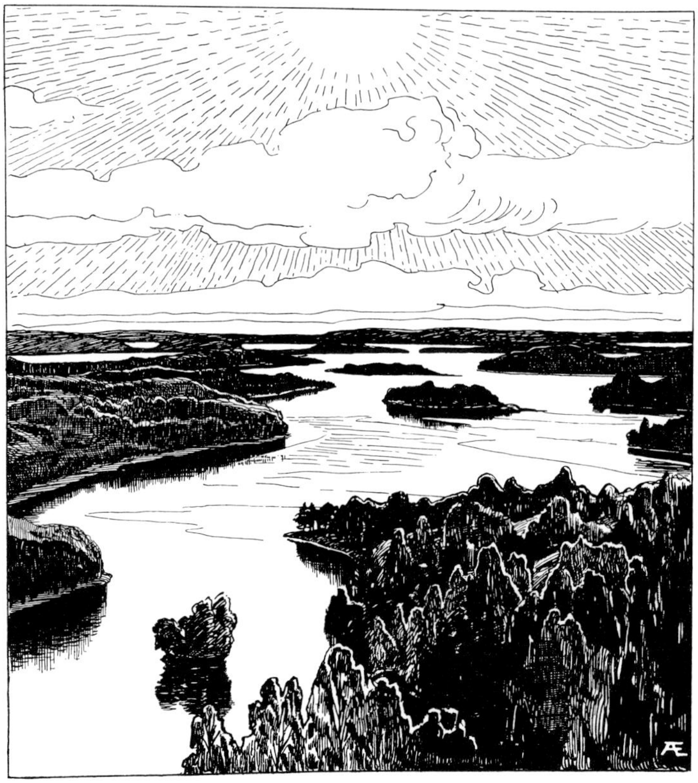

Fig. 25.
Albert Edelfelt, The Lake Panorama, 1898–1900. Illustration for The Tales of Ensign Stål by J. L. Runeberg

loving. In what could be called a pre-Darwinistic spirit, it was believed that only those who were physically and morally superior could survive in these conditions. The all too easy life in the lowlands unfortunately enabled the weak and unhealthy to flourish.

Soon these ideas found their way to the north, and people began to compare the moral characteristics of the various regions. The first landscape art which took its motives from the wilderness emerged, but it was concerned with topography, rather than with the mood of the landscape.

All these theories proved to be of the greatest importance in the difficult situation which arose in the Nordic countries during the Napoleonic Wars. And military and moral defeats, beginning with the British naval offensive against Copenhagen in 1807 and the Russian–French alliance the same year in Tilsit which decided Finland's separation from Sweden and united it with Russia in 1808–9, were followed by economic problems.

After Copenhagen's bombardment, the Danish clergyman Grundtvig began to formulate his idea of the Nordic countries as the new Greece. The inhabitants of the north and the Greeks were 'natural' people with their own mythology and folklore, as opposed to the 'artificial' people, who did not create things themselves, but borrowed their culture from others. Grundtvig's ideology made it necessary to exclude all that was Latin and Catholic. The direction was away from Rome, as during Luther's time, but now with new positive overtones.

This Nordic fusion of folk poetry and neo-humanistic ideals was populist in nature and led to a rejection of the conspicuous consumption and elegant life-style of the aristocracy and well-to-do bourgeoisie. But it was not a revolution in the French tradition. Instead of seeking freedom and equality through force, it hoped to achieve its ends through moral education.

Sweden's greatest poets in the first half of the nineteenth century, Tegnér and Geijer, were among the leaders of this development. Tegnér's *Fritiofs Saga* showed how greatness lay in conquering oneself, not in overthrowing the establishment. Geijer glorified the Nordic peasant's simple pride and freedom, and explicitly compared Greece and the Nordic countries. This ideology was carried to its extreme by J. L. Runeberg, Finland's national poet, who was also much admired and read in Sweden and Norway.

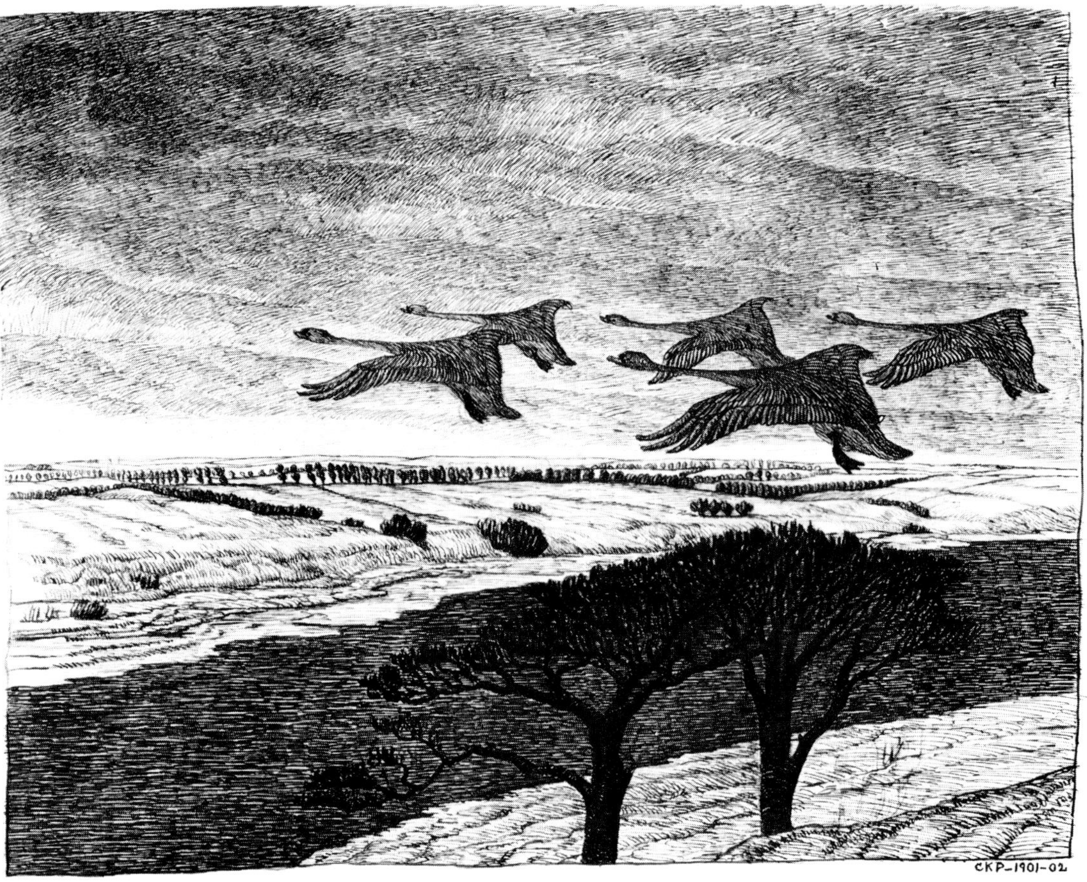

Fig. 26. Christian Kongstad Petersen, Landscape with Five Flying Swans, 1901–2, Den kongelige Kobberstiksamling, Statens Museum for Kunst, Copenhagen

Runeberg created an idealized picture of the Nordic man and his surroundings: the people of the North are like new Greeks, especially the poor and industrious people of the inland areas, who live in magnificent natural surroundings. Poverty is seen as the ideal. The poor inland dweller is closer to God than the inhabitant of the lowlands or the townsman because he lives a tranquil inner life and does not strive feverishly for worldly success. In *Our Land* (Finland's national anthem, and expressive of feelings in Sweden and Norway too), Runeberg speaks of nature, man's love of it, and the world that nature mediates. The poem concludes with the assurance of a bright and hopeful future, which comes from love as a process of maturation, and is based on a submission to fate. This view of life takes on a special meaning when contrasted with the revolutionary tendencies at the time it was written, 1846–8. For the people in the Nordic countries, nature was enough: more was not possible, nor even desirable.

The idealization of poverty became an important, almost central feature of the Nordic identity. It was given added vitality by the religious tradition and by the often harsh geographic and climatic conditions which prevailed in the north. But there was real poverty, especially in the nineteenth century, when the increase in population was not matched by an equally large increase in production. During the great famines of the 1860s, hundreds of thousands of people died of hunger and epidemics. Emigration to America was on a massive scale. From Finland, emigrants also went to the metropolis of St Petersburg. Difficult years came later, too, with the two World Wars, especially in Finland, the Nordic country which suffered most. Today the Nordic countries are among the richest in the world, but the tradition of poverty persists, often giving rise to feelings of guilt.

Alongside the tradition of poverty, however, there is also one of wealth and optimism, of industry and liberalism, which finds expression in literature and in art, for example in the works of Ibsen and Edelfelt. The *art nouveau* period of the turn of the century again sought out the wilderness. The silent land of the forests, untouched by man, became a source of inspiration, as the painting, literature and music of the time bear witness.

Much of the ideology of simplicity, poverty, and local democracy has lived on in the Nordic agrarian parties and, in some ways, in the social democratic parties. The tradition of liberalism has been relatively weak or has only emphasized religious sectarianism (resistance to the state church in Sweden). From a French or German point of view, the Nordic tradition also seems to be unscientific. German thoroughness and French logic have no obvious place in the Nordic mentality.

There is none the less an old and firm link in the Nordic tradition to the urban and intellectual world which in various ways has exerted an influence since the Middle Ages. On an ideological level, however, the traditions of populism and simplicity, and the idealization of nature have dominated. They stem perhaps from the Nordic countries' sense of being on the periphery of the world, set apart as it were from the rest of Europe.

Fig. 27. Christian Kongstad Petersen, Peasant Carrying the Ugly Duckling, 1901, Den kongelige Kobberstiksamling, Statens Museum for Kunst, Copenhagen

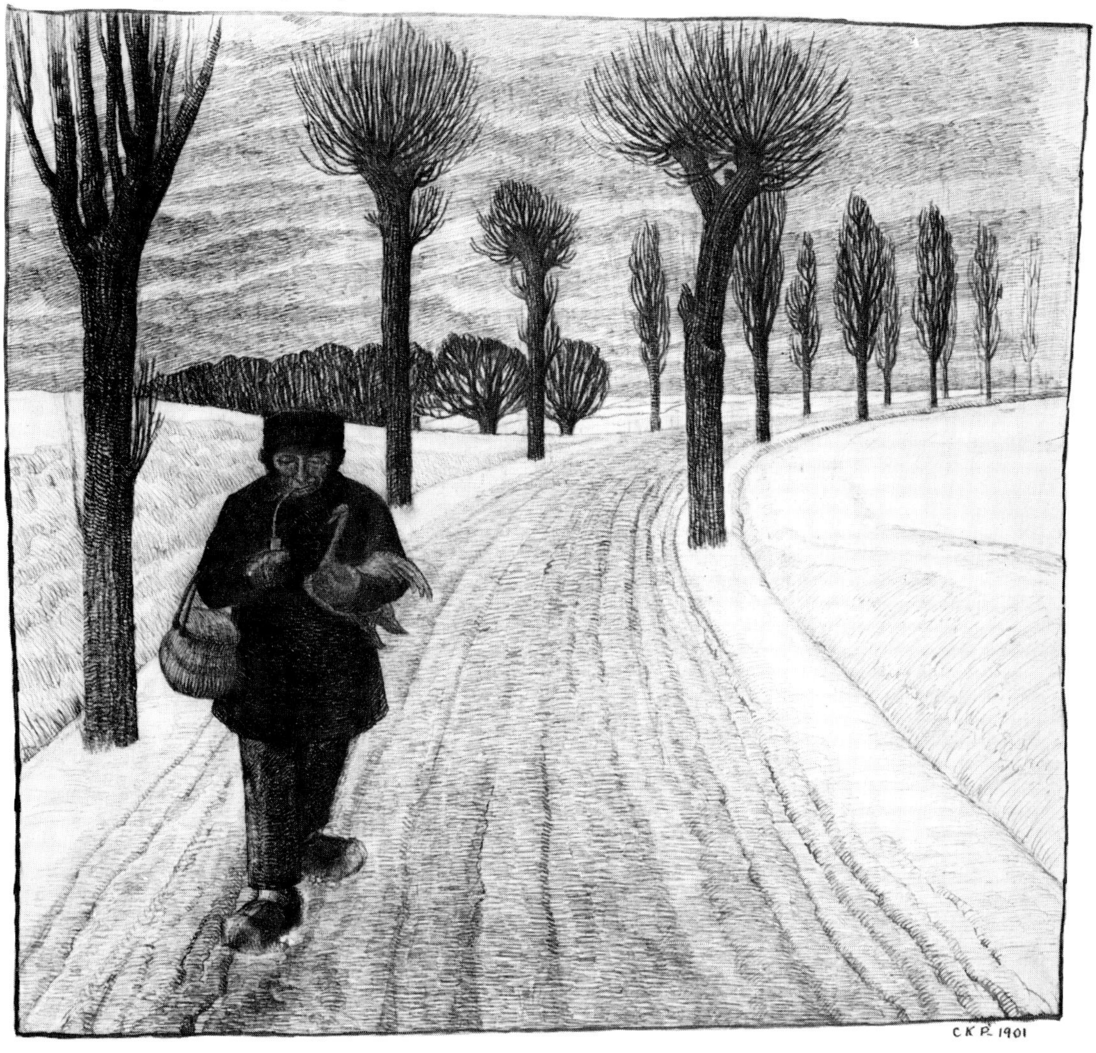

Scandinavia at the Turn of the Century

GUNNAR BROBERG

The Central European at the turn of the century probably thought of Scandinavia as an area bound by snow and ice and great forests, as a periphery of Europe proper. From the Middle Ages, frozen northerners had travelled south to warm themselves at the fires of Classical culture. Travellers in the opposite direction were less common. The philosopher Descartes reported home that in Stockholm ideas froze into ice, and shortly afterwards died of pneumonia there. And at the beginning of the nineteenth century, the poet Tegnér wrote, 'If only barbarism were even patriotic.' Scandinavian barbarism has been a concept from the Viking Age which is often felt to be all too justified.

But the term barbaric can hardly be applied to the years around the turn of the century. At this time culture was actually being borrowed from Scandinavia – from Ibsen, Strindberg, Grieg, Sibelius, Nielsen, Stenhammar, and numerous artists. Furthermore, economically and politically Scandinavia was undergoing a period of rapid development, which brought the rest of Europe closer. And this took place at a time when Scandinavia as a whole was experiencing major internal conflicts.

Population

Scandinavia is not, however, a clear entity geographically. The area is as large as France and the Iberian Peninsula together and embraces many different types of landscape and climate. The Baltic Sea can be considered a northern counterpart to the Mediterranean, that is as a body of water which divides but perhaps even more unites. The old kingdom of Sweden–Finland held together not in spite of, but because of, this broad expanse of water. Its cities lay across from one another on the Gulf of Bothnia like brother and sister. The Skagerrak was a *mare nostrum* for Denmark–Nor-

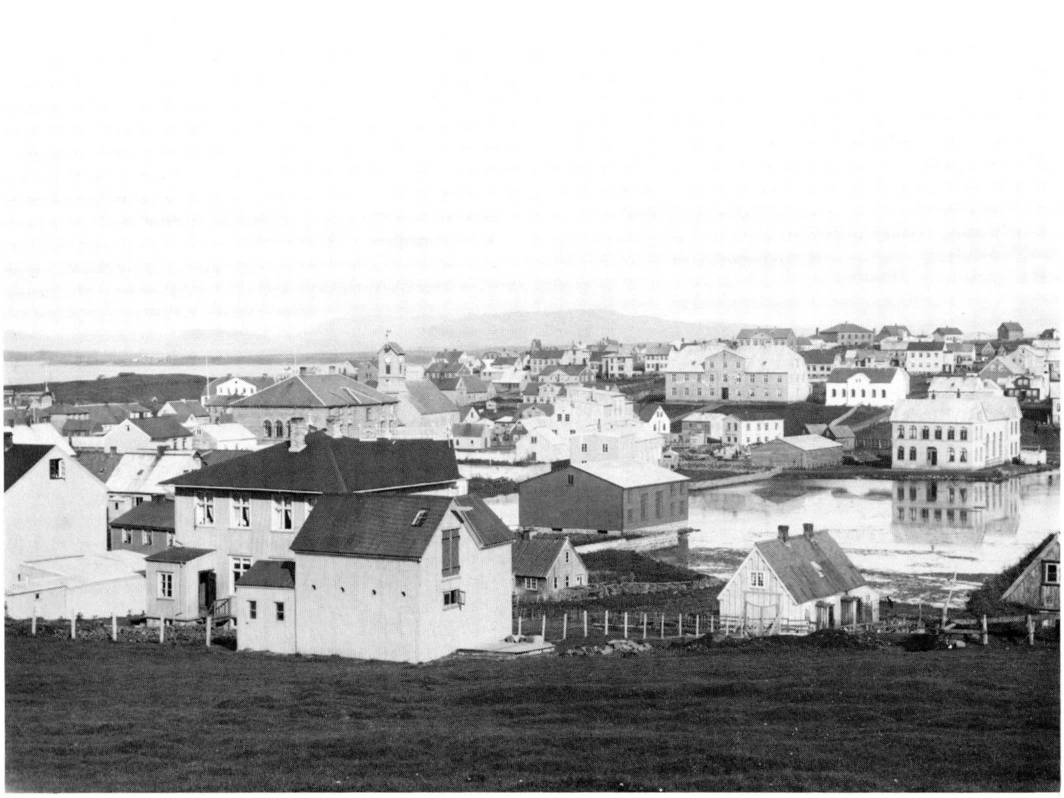

Fig. 28.
The Centre of Reykjavik about the turn of the century, National Museum of Iceland. Photo S. Eymundson

way in the same way. Norway also turns away from the rest of Scandinavia through its settlements along the Atlantic coast. The closest northern neighbour is Iceland, the hermit in the west. All this was to be changed by new means of communications, but an expression of a kind of maritime unity was still found at the turn of the century in the cultural links across the waters which bound Gothenburg, Skagen, and Christiania (Oslo).

And we must not forget the fundamental role which the inland ice played in creating Scandinavia's distinctive features, its varied landscape and wildlife. When the ice withdrew, it left innumerable lakes and an irregular archipelago. The Scandinavian model is to a large extent a result of this dispersion of natural resources, so that neither large factories nor major social problems have emerged. The road from rural culture to industrialism should have been travelled relatively painlessly, but there were of course many other factors which contributed to the changing face of the North.

Scandinavia's population at the turn of the century was around 14 million – compared with some 35 million in Britain and 40 million in France. Growth was strong, especially in the capital cities, which in the decades around the turn of the century took on much of their present-day official character and grew into almost European metropolises. Copenhagen had almost half a million inhabitants, Stockholm some 400,000, Christiania (Oslo) nearly 250,000, and Helsinki 130,000. Reykjavik, Iceland's cultural centre, had 12,000 inhabitants.

The population was also relatively homogeneous. The old ethnic minority in Finland, Sweden, and Norway were the Lapps (Sami), who though small in numbers aroused great interest. The emancipation of the Jews, so important for European turn-

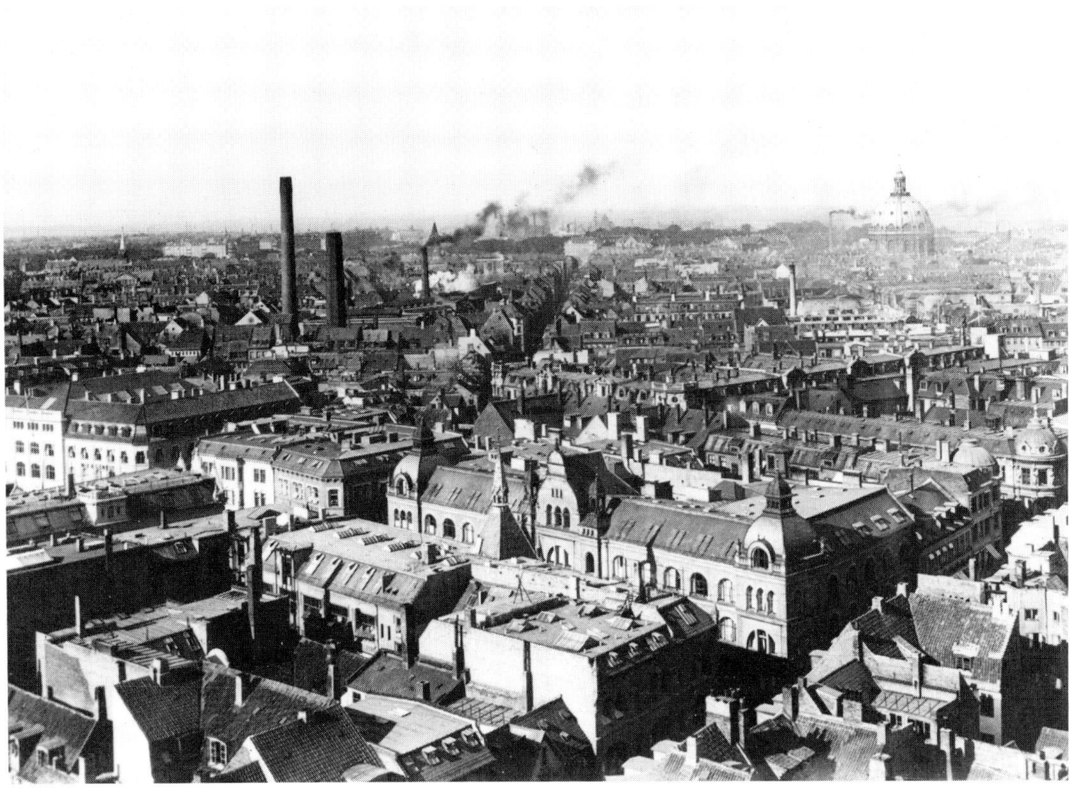

Fig. 29.
View from St Nicholas Square in Copenhagen, 1907, Københavns Bymuseum, Copenhagen

of-the-century culture, had an important impact on Sweden and Denmark: Jewish researchers, for example, created Swedish comparative literary history. But paradoxically, there was a strong nationalistic element in their research. One of the few internationalists was Georg Brandes in Denmark, the great cultural ideologist of the '80s.

Scandinavia had no major colonial experiences; only Denmark at this time had any possessions. The main current population problem, emigration primarily to North America, was one that writers and artists declined to comment on, possibly because it was so commonplace. Here we see the social limitations of turn-of-the-century art, aimed as it was at the purchasing power of the upper class. But Chicago was on its way to becoming the world's second-largest Swedish city; a Norwegian quarter was being established on New York's Manhattan; Winnipeg, in Canada, became partly an Icelandic town; and St Petersburg in Russia had a considerable Finnish population. In Norway and Sweden, especially, emigration was increasing markedly. According to many, it drained away the nation's best blood. But today most people believe it was the result of the growth in population in the poorer parts of the Northern countries. It is clear that Scandinavia was geographically 'stretched out' in a way which brought an end to some of its old isolation.

But language and religion were the main binding ties. It is impossible to sum up what the Lutheran church in general has meant for Scandinavian culture; it certainly contributed to the high level of literacy, but also to the antipathy to metaphysics and philosophy, because these were seen as the concern of the clergy and the theologians. On the other hand, the state churches' firm grip on education encouraged a strong sense of duty and nationalism. This held true for the turn of the century and certainly holds true today, no matter how secular Scandinavia has become.

In around 1900, technology made its great breakthrough in Scandinavia, as elsewhere. Electricity spread light over the Nordic darkness; railways wound their way through the endless forests and over the high Norwegian mountains; telegraph cables linked up the countries. Scandinavia was on its way to overcoming its geographical and climatological limitations – but the weather and wind were still the best-loved topics of conversation and people still fled to the silence of nature in the North.

Unity and divisions

Competition and divisions prevailed within and among the countries. Two nations were moving towards independence. Norway liberated itself from Sweden in 1905 and Finland from Russia in 1917. There were, after all, older historical links and they proved stronger. Norwegians and Icelanders made their way to Denmark; for them Copenhagen was the cultural centre of the North. The Finns ensured that contacts were maintained with Sweden and Stockholm. The struggle for freedom helped Norwegian and Finnish culture, and Swedish and Danish culture were carried along with the current.

Finland's place in the Scandinavian cultural sphere could be questioned. But in spite of its position as a Grand Duchy under Russia, Finland did have a fairly large degree of self-government, with its own laws and own church. The Finns were still judged according to Swedish laws no matter what happened politically. The question of language has many ramifications. In the middle of the century, the Finnish philosopher Johan Vilhelm Snellman, the ideologist of the 'Fennomen', had asked in the title of an article, 'Can a people's education be degraded by making their language the language of education?' The implied answer was that a powerful language for the people would form a barrier against Russification. The gradual promotion of the

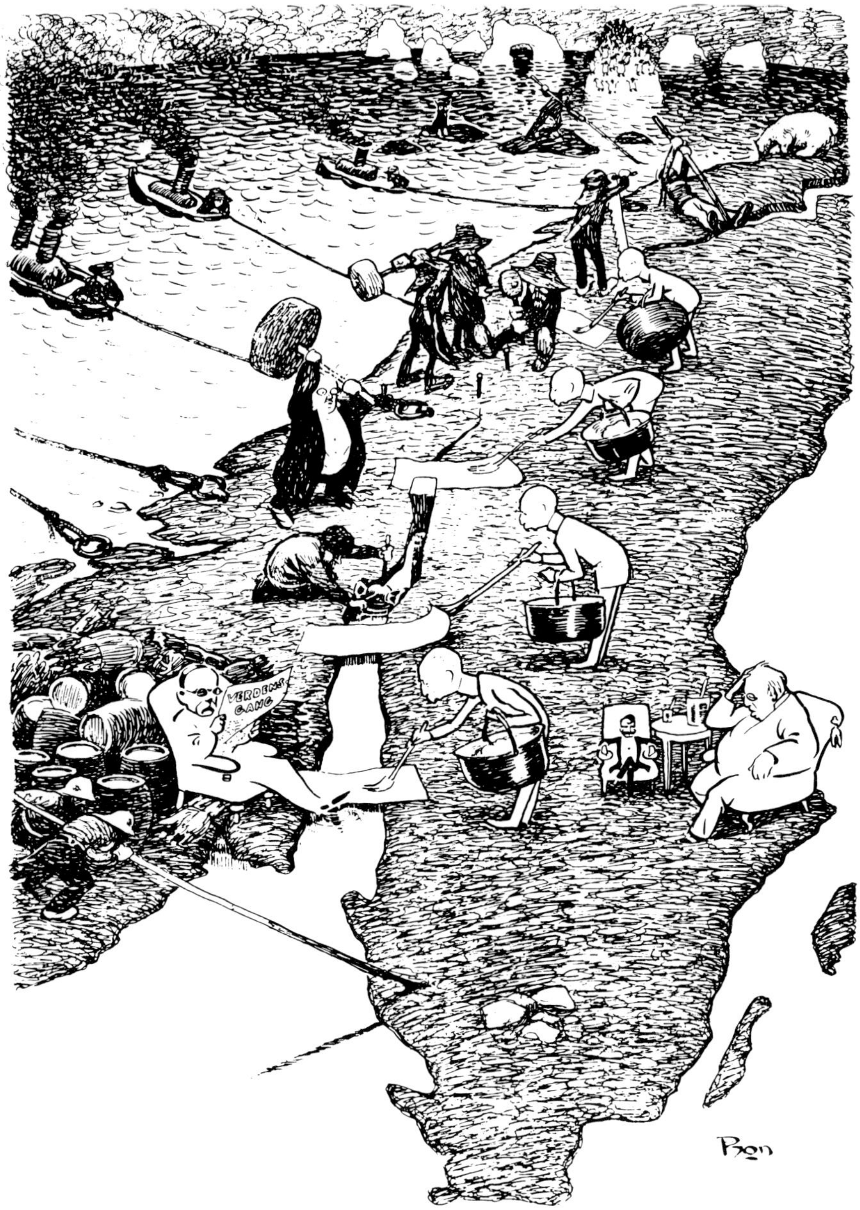

Fig. 30.
'Norway out of the Union'. Cartoon in the Swedish satirical magazine Puck, 1905

Finnish language had in the long run to influence the position of Swedish, but it was just as culturally strong and was an essential condition for Scandinavian unity. Finnish mythology, presented in the *Kalevala* epic, and with its world devoid of Norse Vikings, became increasingly important for the national identity of the Finns. In contrast, but still in harmony with the quickening of the national consciousness, was *The Tales of Ensign Stål*, Runeberg's poem in Swedish on the Finno-Russian War of 1808–9.

A comparable struggle for a national language is the rivalry which emerged in Norway in the 1880s between 'bokmaal', the language of the old Danish administration, and 'ny-norsk' (New Norwegian) or 'landsmaal', which was constructed from local dialects. The Norwegians, like the Finns, also had a large degree of self-government during their period of union with Sweden. And shortly after the turn of the century a plebiscite gave unequivocal evidence of the will of the people: 368,000 voted for a dissolution of the union while only 184 voted against. It was hardly defensible to save the union by force of arms, and anyway the Swedes had renounced their martial ideals. And so the union, created in 1814 by Karl XIV Johan, was dissolved in 1905.

The Norwegians chose a Danish prince as their ruler – Norway was to be a

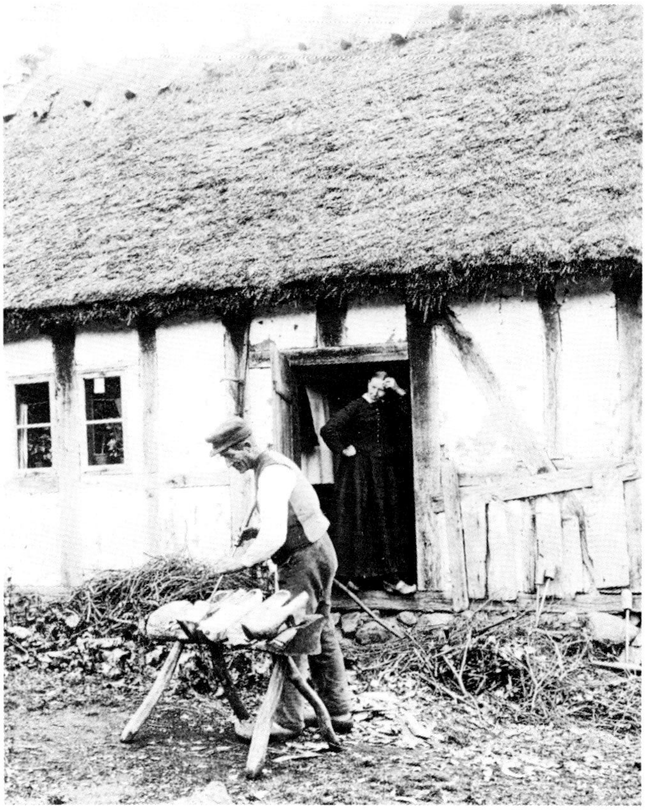

Fig. 31.
A Shoemaker from Blekinge, Sweden. Photo Alfred B. Nilsson (Rolf Söderberg, Pär Rittvel, Den svenska fotografiens historia 1840–1940, Stockholm, 1983)

kingdom just like its Scandinavian neighbours. Denmark's role as Scandinavia's heart had clearly diminished considerably since the heyday of the 'Scandinavianism' movement in the middle of the nineteenth century, when the idea of a union of the Nordic countries had flourished, nourished by hopes for an old-fashioned Viking Scandinavia. But when in 1863 Prussia attacked the southern Danish provinces of Schleswig and Holstein, Sweden refused to intervene. The dream of brotherhood vanished. Denmark and Sweden licked their wounds and gradually regained their strength from within.

Nationalism

Instead of Scandinavianism, nationalism grew. Scandinavia is, as one can see, an excellent example of how the rearrangement of the map brought about by the Napoleonic Wars created new tensions. Norwegian nationalism was conditioned by its relationship to Sweden, Finland's by its relationship to Russia and by the Swedish legacy, and Sweden's by its failure to play the role of big brother. The Icelandic nationalist movement, rooted in peasant culture, grew out of opposition to Danish rule. Denmark's own cultural development was strongly influenced by the 'folk high schools', the form of adult education created by N. F. S. Grundtvig. For 'Grundtvig, the historian must first and foremost find the essence, the 'spirit of the people'. A school should not be a musty institute of learning; it should be a 'school of life', embracing the nation's heathen antecedents as well as Christianity.

The turn of the century was full of nationalistic frenzy, but also of painful soul-searching. In Sweden, a study of the great wave of emigration inspired the researcher Gustav Sundbärg to write a collection of aphorisms, *Svenska folklynne* (1911), on the national mentality of the Swedes. His criticisms were often severe: the Swede lacks the instinct for self-preservation, he wrote, and is deficient in pride and patriotism – in contrast to the Norwegian and the Dane. On the other hand, he does have a marked inclination for science and a feeling for nature, positive characteristics which have combined to produce an impressive list of scientists. The emigrants were homesick not for the land of their fathers, but for the farms of their fathers. Sundbärg here points out a schism typical of the time between nationalism and provincialism.

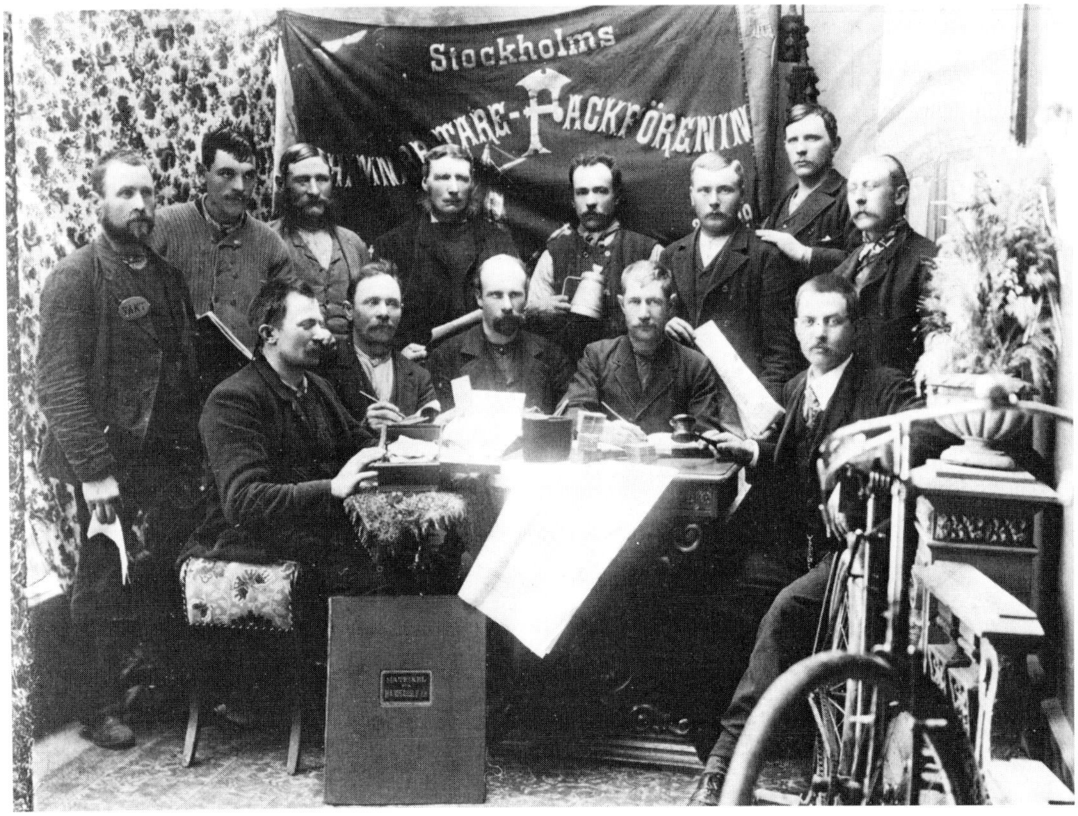

Fig. 32.
The Strikers' Committee in the first Harbour Strike in Sweden, 1896. Photo Mimmi Gustafsson (Rolf Söderberg, Pär Rittvel, Den svenska fotografiens historia 1840–1940, Stockholm, 1983)

Much of this can be seen as a reaction against the internationalism of the radicalism of the '80s and as the result of the change from economic protectionism to cultural protectionism. In Sweden, the economic debate had been carried on under the slogan 'Sweden for the Swedes', to which the pseudonymous Falstaff Fakir (Axel Wallengren) replied, 'The North Pole for the Poles!' In Georg Brandes' little essay *What is the Danish Folk Character?* (tr. 1901), the Danes are said to possess 'sluggishness, softness, phlegm, and rawness' and to stand wide open to religion's false message. The turn-of-the-century reader must have considered Brandes as a spokesman for the worst kind of Jewish cosmopolitanism and radicalism.

The relationship between socialism and nationalism is interesting, partly because it has often seemed contradictory, and partly because so many of the Scandinavian artists had radical sympathies as well as nationalist ones. Among writers and artists one can perhaps differentiate between 'political nationalists' and 'cultural nationalists'. An interest in nature and provincialism is emphasized by the latter, and many artists during their years in artists' groups abroad tried to revive the old ideals of Scandinavianism. The traditional 'historical romanticists' are found among the political nationalists.

A feeling for nature was omnipresent. In the nationalistic world of symbols at the turn of the century it is rare to find people depicted purely as people. Instead, people appear in symbiosis with nature, beautiful but poor. Verner von Heidenstam spoke of fields not people when he confessed his homesickness during his years abroad, 'I long for the fields; I long for the stones where I played as a child.' The general influence of Darwinism can be mentioned as one of many reasons for the interest in nature, but there was also the lure of the immutability of nature in an era characterized by rapid changes. Nature is also the theme of Edelfelt's illustrations for Runeberg's *Our Land*: lakes and forests as far as the eye can see. The Finnish forest was soon to gain its own composer in Sibelius.

Natural science and the belief in progress

The forest was also seen as a natural resource by the progressive industrial countries. Natural scientists and technologists covered the same terrain as artists and writers

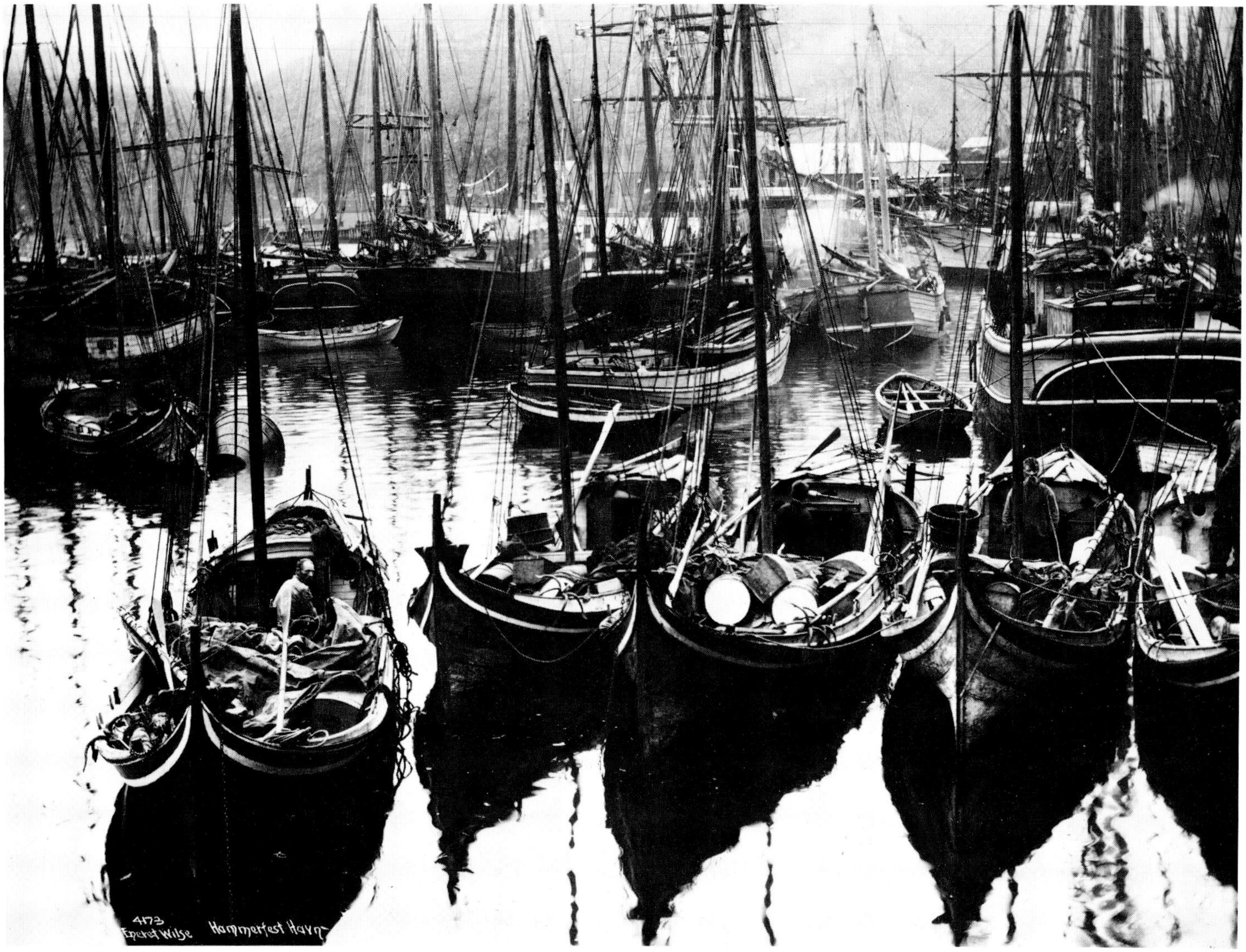

Fig. 33. Hammerfest Harbour (photo Wilse), Wilse-arkivet, Norsk Folkemuseum, Oslo

and with the same success. The turn of the century meant an upswing in Scandinavia for the natural sciences, as can be seen by the growing number of research positions and publications in this field. In Sweden, for example, there was a tripling of professorships between 1870 and 1900. Research, and not just teaching, became a matter of course in the university teachers' work, and the concept of research gained further respect with the awarding of the first Nobel Prizes in 1901 by the Swedish Academy and the Swedish Academy of Sciences in Stockholm, and the Storting (parliament) in Oslo. One legacy of the Swedish–Norwegian union is this division of labour in awarding the prizes. The fact that the Swedish Academy gave the prize in literature in 1903 to Bjørnstjerne Bjørnson can be seen as a mere good-will gesture to Norway, but also as a recognition of Scandinavian literature.

Natural scientists dedicated themselves to charting their countries' resources of timber and arable land. Numbers, tables, inventories meant certain, indisputable knowledge. Mineral resources were mapped out in Sweden, and in Lapland, while in Norway, the directorate of fisheries studied the sea's resources. In this way, geographical conditions created scientific traditions. Just before the turn of the century, Thorvaldur Thóroddsen laid the foundations for the study of Icelandic geology through his vulcanological research. Two other important figures in world science were the ecologist Eugen Warming and the geneticist Wilhelm Johannsen. Both were concerned with agriculture, Denmark's principal industry.

History and art were also surveyed. The artists' depiction of the Scandinavian landscape in all kinds of light has an inventory-like aspect. An artist like Bruno Liljefors, for example, even approached scientific exactitude in his ecological painting. The parallels between art and science should not be carried too far, but natural science generally set the tone and guided activities. It, if anything, showed progress. Its status was thus a measure of national status. It also provided work. Natural science, like art and literature, served the cause of nationalism.

The Sagas and myths also helped foster the spirit of nationalism. In Iceland, the Eddas were read as living history, and the Norwegian folk tales of Asbjørnsen and Moe were widely read. In Stockholm, the Skansen open-air museum, created in the 1890s, gave a glimpse of life in old Sweden. Here in peace and quiet it was possible to dream of the past or study the objects on exhibit, while modern life rushed by down in the city.

A new enlightenment

People were living through 'a new enlightenment', characterized by a criticism of Christianity and a changed moral code. Georg Brandes, one of the fiercest critics of the bourgeoisie, was irritated by the insularity of Danish 'hominess'. A major debate on sexual mores had been in progress at least since the 1880s when the novel by Hans Jæger, *From Christiania's Bohemia*, created a scandal with its reports on prostitution in Norway. Bjørnson, Ibsen, and Strindberg steered the debate into ever stormier waters. The critics spoke of a materialism that disintegrated morals, but perhaps a term like 'la belle époque' more aptly characterizes the increasingly continental life in Scandinavia. The question of women's status was widely debated and further upset the guardians of tradition. In his philosophical writings, the Dane Harald Höffding gently guided Scandinavian students towards a belief in the potential of the future. Life's finest principle, he taught, is the greatest possible happiness of living beings. This 'welfare principle', with its roots in utilitarianism, was to have great influence in later years.

Naturally this nationalistic optimism does not give the whole picture of the situation. A belief in progress is linked mainly to the '80s, but darker moods continually clouded the picture. A high price was paid for progress. Criminal psychology seemed to show that not everyone could keep up with developments. In his sensational theory of dreams, Freud claimed that man could not alienate himself from the animal in him, something that was anticipated in Ibsen's *The Lady from the Sea* (1888) and in Strindberg's *A Dream Play* (1901).

Nietzsche rejected Western culture as degenerate, and Durkheim found that it suffered from anomie, a lack of ethical values. And in Scandinavia, too, at least among the cultural avant-garde, the 1890s were characterized by a withdrawal into the self, by a longing for the remote past, and by mysticism. In the midst of their triumphal march, the scientists themselves admitted that it would never be possible to reveal the 'truth'. Science, like art, worked with fictions, which were called 'causality' and 'atoms'. The state of the world also gave cause for concern. When Ellen Key spoke of the new year in her famous *The Century of the Child* (1900) she compared it to a newborn child who does not dare land on our earth because the weapons there have left no room. Later, in an article on the future of Scandinavianism (1906), Key was to speak out on behalf of a united nations of Scandinavia as a peace zone, but this has not come about, at least not yet. Some maintained that a lack of values and social disorder could only be changed through a joint national effort. Others were to greet 1914 with enthusiasm.

The pendulum swung back and forth, but the turn of the century in Scandinavia was a period of enlightenment. If one wants to single out a particular feature from such a rich and contradictory epoch, then the ambition of education for the masses, the dream of a great national educational effort, is a suitable one. It was to lead to the flowering of culture and science and it was led by artists and scientists. The art critic Carl Laurin pleaded for art in the schools. Just as the enlightenment of eighteenth-century Europe was manifested by the great French encyclopedia, so the new enlightenment in Scandinavia was summed up by the large national encyclopedias published in these years. The very titles are revealing. The Swedish encyclopedia, which is still an incomparable reference work, is, for example, called a *Nordic Family* book. Popular scientific periodicals had titles like *Ljus* (Light) and *Frem* (Forward). Professors and students joined together in university organizations to campaign for national education in the press and on lecture tours.

Popular and political movements spread the message further. The old society was on its way out and the old world view crumbling. Education and science were needed to build up a new framework. The transition to a new society was not without its problems, but it succeeded. And art and literature gave the framework depth. If not before, then at least at the turn of the century, Scandinavian barbarism showed that it had humane features.

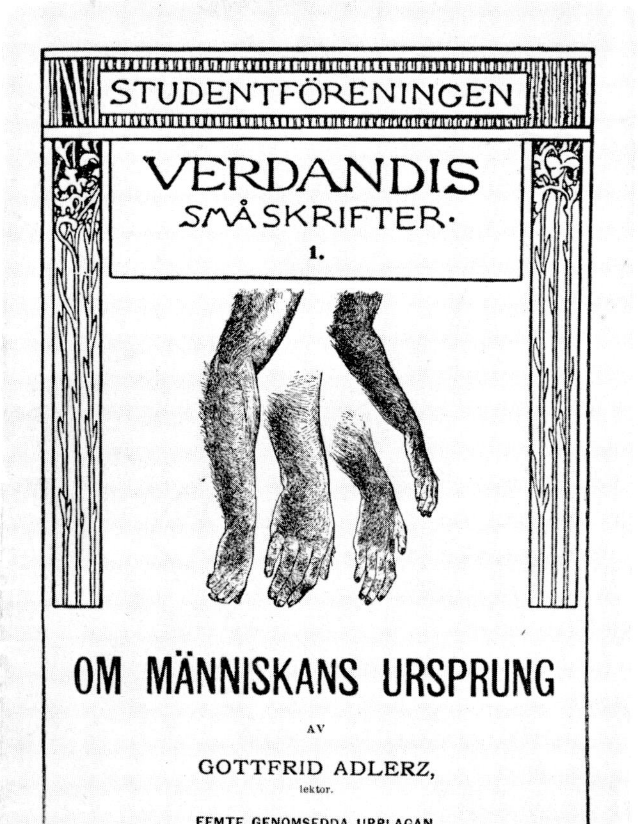

Fig. 34.
The Cover by Carl Larsson for Gottfrid Adlerz' 'The Descent of Man', 1888 (first edition)

Catalogue

Artists are listed alphabetically and works by the same artist are listed in chronological order.
The title of each work is given in English as well as in the original language.
The medium is oil on canvas unless specially indicated.
Dimensions are given in centimetres, height precedes width.
The following is a list of the artists by nationality:

DENMARK

Anna *Ancher*
Ludvig *Find*
Vilhelm *Hammershøi*
Viggo *Johansen*
Peder Severin *Krøyer*
Ejnar *Nielsen*
Laurits Andersen *Ring*
Harald *Slott-Møller*
Jens Ferdinand *Willumsen*

FINLAND

Magnus *Enckell*
Akseli *Gallen-Kallela*
Pekka *Halonen*
Eero *Järnefelt*
Juho *Rissanen*
Helene *Schjerfbeck*
Hugo *Simberg*
Ellen *Thesleff*

ICELAND

Thórarinn B. *Thorláksson*

NORWAY

Harriet *Backer*
Halfdan *Egedius*
August *Eiebakke*
Kitty *Kielland*
Theodor *Kittelsen*
Edvard *Munch*
Gerhard *Munthe*
Eilif *Peterssen*
Harald *Sohlberg*
Erik *Werenskiold*

SWEDEN

Richard *Bergh*
Prince *Eugen*
Gustaf *Fjaestad*
Eugène *Jansson*
Ernst *Josephson*
Carl *Larsson*
Bruno *Liljefors*
August *Strindberg*
Carl *Wilhelmson*
Anders *Zorn*

The following persons have contributed towards the catalogue

Leena Ahtola-Moorhouse	L. A-M.
Knut Berg	K. B.
Pontus Grate	P. G.
Torsten Gunnarsson	T. G.
Sidsel Helliesen	S. H.
Selma Jónsdóttir	S. J.
Marit Ingeborg Lange	M. I. L.
Magne Malmanger	M. M.
Salme Sarajas-Korte	S. S-K.
Tone Skedsmo	T. S.
Göran Söderström	G. S.
Hanne Westergaard	H. W.

ANNA ANCHER, née BRØNDUM

1859–1935, Denmark

Anna Ancher attended Vilhelm Kyhn's drawing school in Copenhagen from 1875 to 1878. In 1879 she began to exhibit her work, and in 1880 she married the painter Michael Ancher. In the 1880s, the Norwegian painter Christian Krohg became important for her colouristic development, and when she worked with Puvis de Chavannes in Paris, in 1888–9, the Impressionists undoubtedly influenced her. Otherwise, she developed independently from the beginning of the 1890s. The scope of her painting technique was extraordinary. She alternated between painting with thick brushstrokes and airy, modulated nuances.

She received encouragement which was rare for a married woman painter of her time. Her husband understood and respected her art. It was always possible to lighten her household duties by bringing in food from her parents' hotel kitchen, and the family's economy did not rest on her. She was free to express herself, and the other Skagen painters followed her with interest, as did the critics and others interested in art.

Anna Ancher was the only native of Skagen among the 'Skagen artists' of her generation. The unique light over the characteristic landscape did not interest her, however, nor the hard life in the rough climate. Perhaps the former was too familiar to her, while the latter bored her. Her subject-matter was the intimate life within the small cottages, the people with whom she felt so at home and could chat so gaily. She depicted them honestly and without sentimentality, without hiding their small defects or comical sides, but with a little veiled tenderness which took the sting off realism. And always with exquisite, colouristic subtlety.

1

A Funeral, 1891

(En begravelse)

103.5 × 124.5
Signed lower left: Anna Ancher 1891
Statens Museum for Kunst, Copenhagen
Inv. no. 1433 (purchased in 1891)

At Skagen, the dangerous life on the sea took its toll of men, often in their best years, without warning; the possibility was always present in most families. When Anna Ancher painted a funeral, it was a depiction of the everyday life of the people of Skagen, told straightforwardly and without heroism. Here the next of kin are gathered together while the clergyman says a prayer at the bier before the departed leaves his home for the last time. The gravity is tempered by light from the window which makes the dark group of figures stand out in bluish silhouette against the warm rose wall. The colouristic harmony is further enriched by the green wreaths.

A Funeral was shown at the Charlottenborg Palace exhibition in 1891 and in Paris in 1900.

H.W.

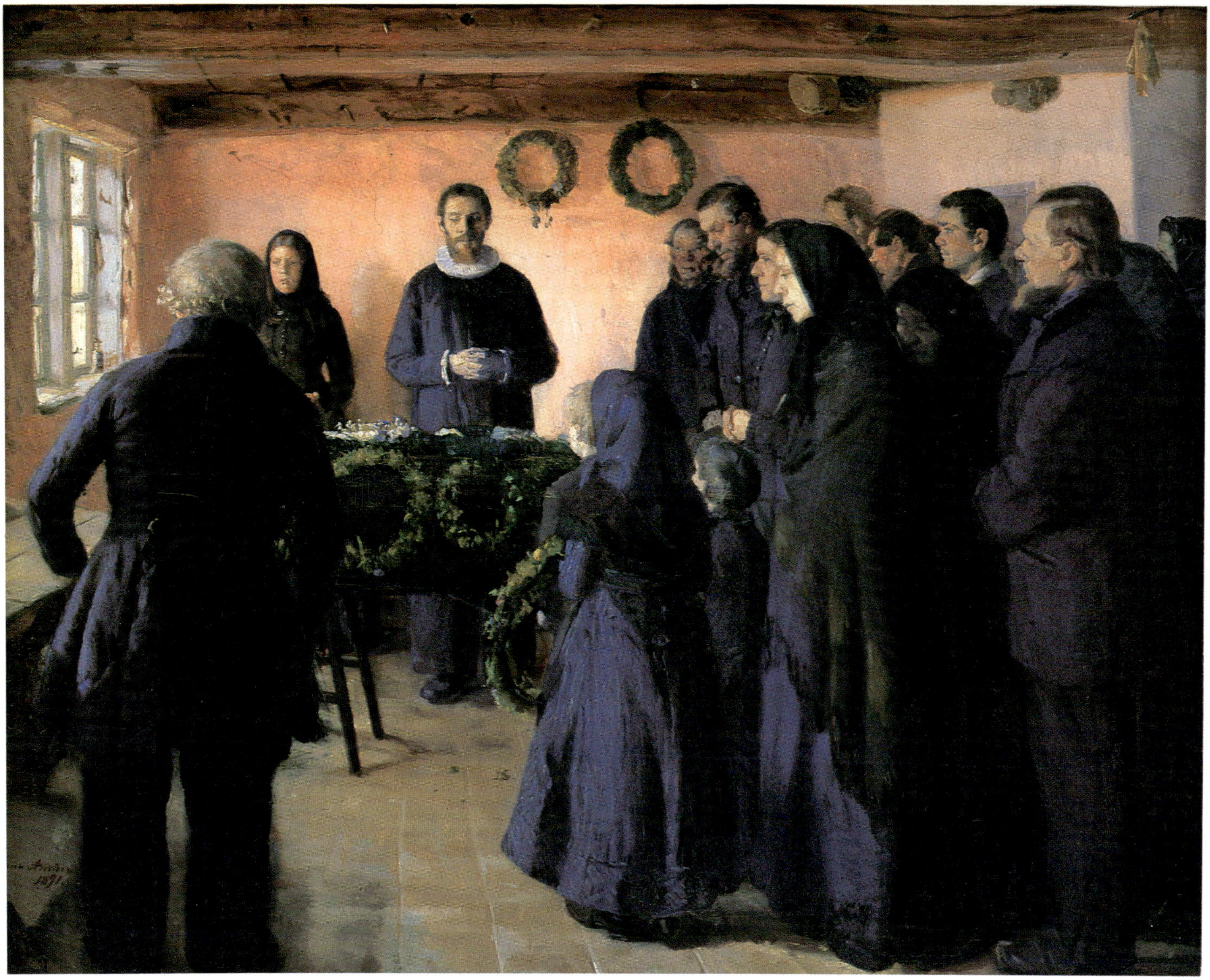

1. Anna Ancher

HARRIET BACKER

1845–1933, Norway

From 1861 to 1874, Harriet Backer received instruction in drawing and painting at art schools in Christiania. Between 1866 and 1872, she also made a number of trips abroad together with her sister, Agathe Backer Grøndahl, who later became a well-known pianist and composer. From 1874 to 1878, she studied in Munich, mainly under Eilif Peterssen, where she painted still-lifes, portraits, and her first interiors. From 1878 until 1888, she lived in Paris, but frequently spent time in Norway. She studied with L. Bonnat from 1878 to 1880.

Harriet Backer made her debut at the Salon in 1880 with *Solitude*, a Renaissance interior painted in Munich in 1878, but with a figure added in Paris in 1880. The painting won an honourable mention. From 1881 to 1888, she lived in Paris with Kitty L. Kielland, with whom she also travelled to Brittany in 1881, to Jæren in 1884, Risør in 1885, and Fleskum in 1886. She received a silver medal at the World Fair in Paris in 1889 for her *Chez moi* (1887, Nasjonalgalleriet). She returned to Norway in 1888 and there ran a popular art school from 1889 to 1912. In the 1880s, she painted a number of realistic interiors, some from bourgeois homes, some from the countryside. In the 1890s, Backer expanded her subject-matter, and church interiors became especially important. Throughout her entire career, she painted portraits and landscapes, with more still-lifes toward the end of her life. Her interiors, in particular, in which the central concern is daylight's play in a closed room, have always been considered among the finest Norwegian art has to offer.

2

By Lamplight, 1890

(Ved lampelys)

54.7 × 66.5
Signed lower left: Harriet Backer/Sandviken 90
Rasmus Meyers Samlinger, Bergen
Inv. no. 20 (purchased in 1914)

After returning from Paris in 1888 Harriet Backer spent most of the next two years in Sandviken outside Christiania. During this period she painted some of her best-known pictures, among them three shown at this exhibition.

In the early 1880s, her art had undergone important changes. Under the influence of French realism she turned from historical scenes to the depiction of contemporary interiors. She was deeply impressed by open-air landscape painting and tried in her own work to realize what she called 'the *plein-air* in the interior'. Indeed, the main theme of her pictures of those years is the play of light breaking into the room from outside: light itself is the subject. Around 1890, however, a new development took place. Harriet Backer was caught up in the general reaction against descriptive realism. But it is of particular interest to note that she was able to meet the new demands of the day without any obvious change in subject-matter, and without giving up working methods which did, after all, take visible reality as a point of departure.

By Lamplight brilliantly exemplifies the new attitude. It is the first of several interior scenes seen by artificial light. The suggestive shadows lurking in dark corners give rein to the imagination. We can no longer talk of the painting's atmosphere in a purely physical sense. Although light is studied as closely as in any of her earlier works, it has now taken on quite a new character. Radiating from the lamp it has lost its descriptive objectivity, as it is reflected in the mirror on the wall and, at the same

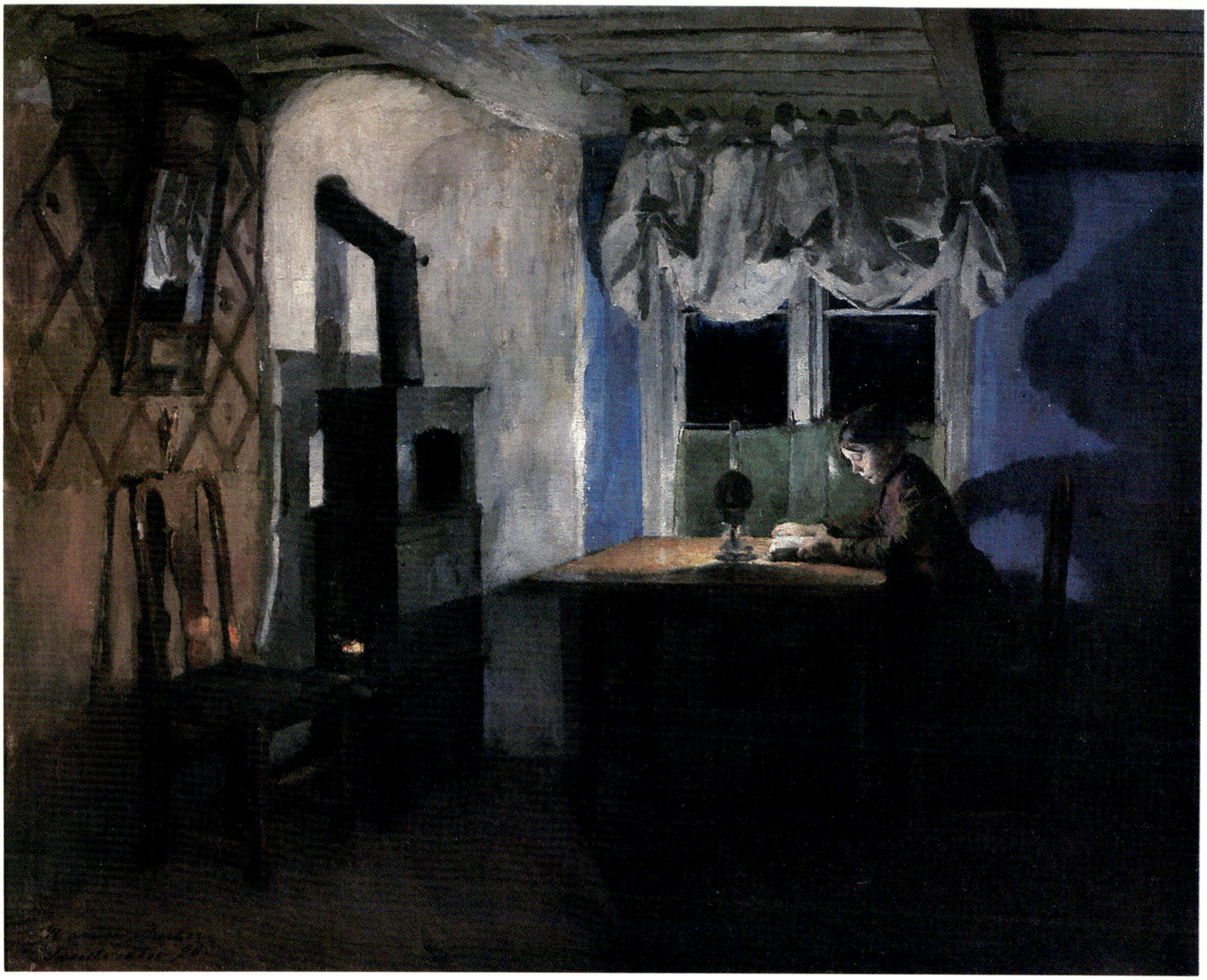

2. *Harriet Backer*

time, mysteriously broken by long shadows cast across the room. The fire in the stove sheds its flickering glow contrasting with the peacefulness of the scene. The psychological significance of the representation is brought out by the pose of the figure. The girl sits quietly at the table; but we feel her concentrating intensely on what she is reading. Perception has given way to meditation and inner recollection.

By Lamplight, or *Winter Evening*, as it was originally titled, was painted in the winter of 1889–90. It was first shown at the Autumn Exhibition in 1890. As was often the case with Harriet Backer's pictures, it did not receive much attention from the public at large, but met with great respect in more specialized circles. Admittedly, the leading art critic Andreas Aubert did not give it much space in his long review of the Autumn Exhibition in the daily *Dagbladet*. But he did make an interesting comparison by linking it to Edvard Munch's interior *Night in St Cloud*. 'If anyone has difficulty understanding it (Munch's picture)', he wrote, 'he should see it in the evening. After Harriet Backer's sensitive interior *Winter Evening*, this is the picture which gains most by electric light' (*Dagbladet*, 5 November 1890). Both pictures were described as sensitively executed, and we must assume that the comparison was made because both show a lone figure by a window in a dark room. Munch's picture is usually viewed today as an example of his neurasthenic and decadent art. Harriet Backer's painting, on the other hand, is seen as a simple depiction of a milieu, whose essential contribution is the harmonious solution of formal and colouristic problems. It is interesting to note that works which later art historians have judged to be of such unequal importance were treated on an equal footing by one of the day's leading art critics.

M.I.L.

3

Inngangskoner, 1892

90.5 × 112.5
Signed lower left: Harriet Backer
In the lower right corner: Indgangskoner./Sakristiet i Tannum/kirke. Ufærdig
Rasmus Meyers Samling, Bergen
Inv. no. 22 (purchased in 1914)

This picture was painted at Tanum church in 1892, but was set aside as unfinished. It was first shown in public at Harriet Backer's major retrospective exhibition at the Art Association in Christiania in 1914. Here, together with *By Lamplight*, it was purchased by the great art collector Rasmus Meyer of Bergen. The picture was left at the sketch stage: in places we can see the perspective drawing underneath. The colours are applied thinly, almost like watercolours. The broad strokes, the fresh, airy colours, give a much more immediate impression than we are used to seeing in her carefully calculated art.

The subject of the painting is unusual and shows a Norwegian church tradition which died out in the 1920s. After childbearing, a woman was not allowed to enter a church before being blessed and cleansed by the priest. In Harriet Backer's time, this tradition was still alive, and we see two women kneeling at the altar in the sacristy of Tanum church waiting to be cleansed so that they might once again have access to the church's holy sacraments. We do not know whether Harriet Backer found this Old Testament view of women exotic or repulsive. But as she was at this time involved with feminism in general and women's suffrage in particular, she must have found this archaic custom interesting and symptomatic of the church's conservative attitude towards women.

Her close friend Kitty L. Kielland had already been involved in heated debates with some of the country's leading theologians concerning the question of women. But neither Harriet Backer nor Kitty L. Kielland was politically committed in her art. There is no reason to interpret Harriet Backer's many depictions of lone women in quiet rooms as an expression of political feminism, even though such attempts have been made. But if her art was not political, it could certainly be cunning. It must have amused her that the man she used as the model for the minister in the picture of Tanum church was in reality a blacksmith.

M.I.L.

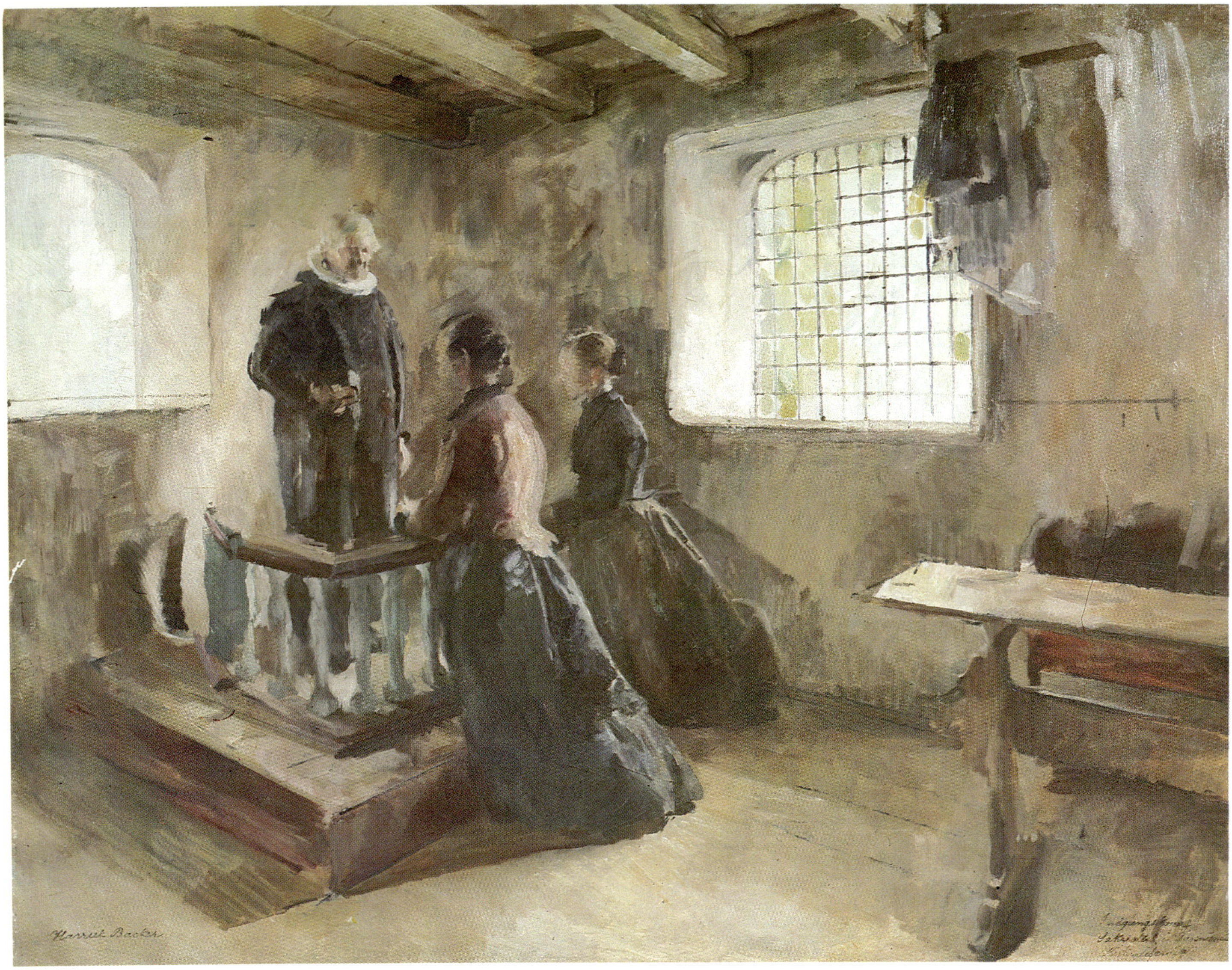

3. *Harriet Backer*

4

Christening in Tanum Church, 1892

(Barnedåp i Tanum kirke)

109 × 142
Signed lower right: Harriet Backer/Tannum, 1892
Nasjonalgalleriet, Oslo
Inv. no. 2465 (purchased in 1959)

Church interiors represented a new subject to which Harriet Backer turned in 1890. Her sudden predilection for such themes may be understood as an attempt to combine an interest in historical interiors typical of her early work with the Realist demand to stick to contemporary subject-matter. The tyranny of time is suspended by the ageless rites performed in an old and venerable church. The light streaming into these interiors takes on a double significance: physically present it also becomes a symbol of divine presence. A preoccupation with spiritual matters was an important element in the cultural life of the 1890s; it led to a religious reorientation even on the part of some of the most inveterate materialists. In Norway, Arne Garborg, a well-known author (see No. 68) and a friend of Harriet Backer's, was a leading exponent of this spiritual reorientation. In an article on spiritualism from 1893, Garborg succinctly sums up the situation: 'The sun of Realism is setting. Up rises the moon of Romanticism, with its pale and ghostly light.' (*Samtiden* 1893.)

The subject of the present painting is the medieval church at Tanum in Bærum outside Christiania. Apparently Harriet Backer discovered it in the spring of 1890; Tanum is not far from Sandviken, where she lived at the time. In a letter to Garborg she wrote enthusiastically: 'I discovered the Sunday before last that the interior of Tanum church is one of the most beautiful I have seen. The wall from the time of Olaf the Holy, otherwise furnishings from the last century. And it is uninhabited in every respect. I close the door from within and use it as my studio...' (Kielland 1958, p. 158). From 1891 to 1893 she painted no less than eight pictures of this subject.

Christening in Tanum Church is the most interesting of them, and is often considered her masterpiece. The composition is highly original: we stand inside the church, turning our back to the altar, looking out. The perspective effect is striking as our eye is drawn from the open foreground in the dark room towards the background where we find the picture's focus of interest: a woman entering the church with a child to be christened. This movement is further emphasized by the figure in the foreground turning towards the woman as she enters. In contrast to the cool and quiet interior, is the doorway itself, almost an independent little open-air painting, where the summer's glittering light and green lushness are captured with vivid, impressionistic strokes. Pulsating life outside is seen against the timeless, serene church. Harriet Backer uses this contrast in most of her pictures, but never so emphatically as here.

M.I.L.

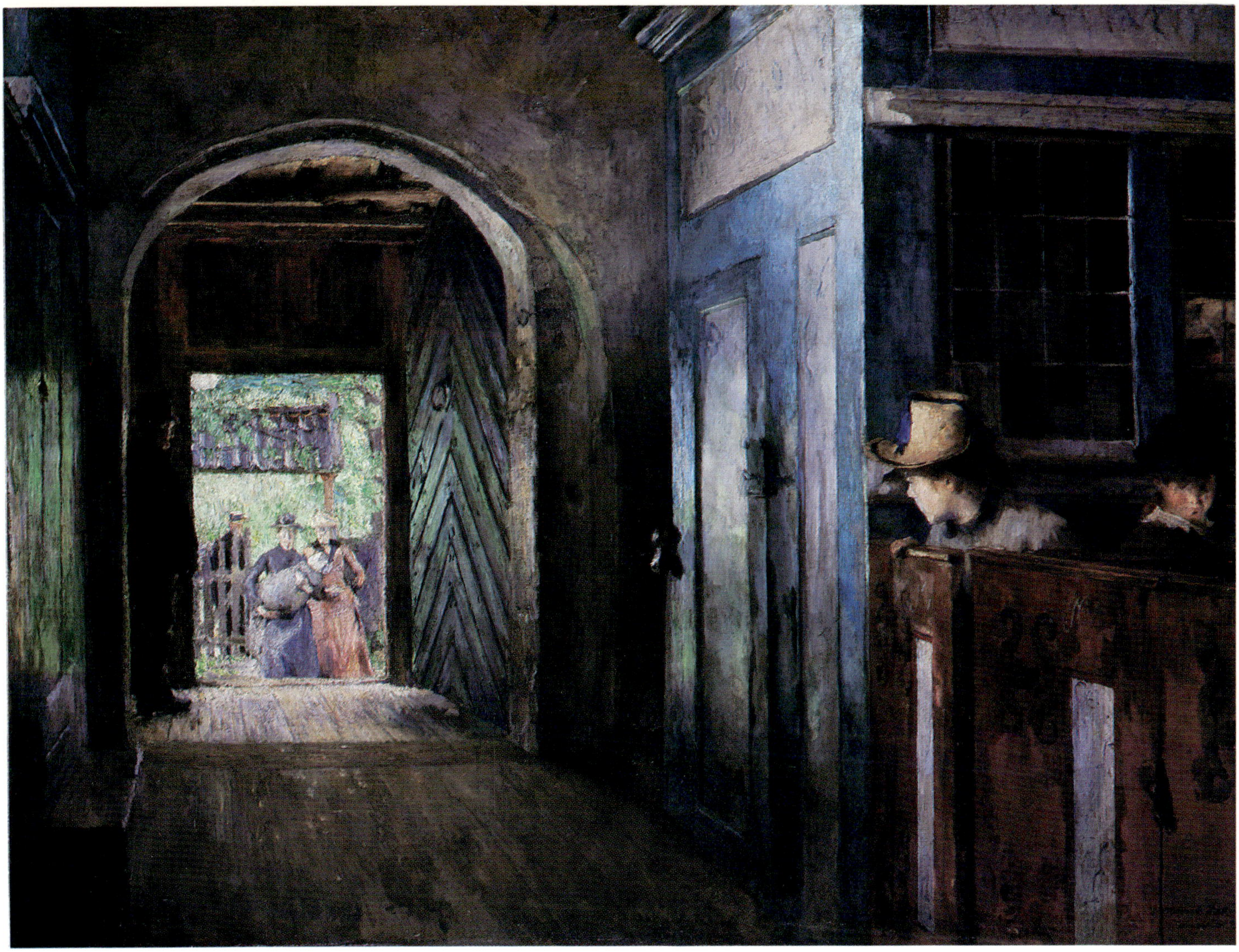

4. Harriet Backer

RICHARD BERGH

1858–1919, Sweden

Richard Bergh grew up in Stockholm in a well-to-do and artistic milieu. In 1858 his father, Edvard Bergh, one of the most distinguished Swedish landscapists of the day, was the first person to hold the new professorship of landscape painting at the Royal Academy of Fine Arts. His son first studied at the art school run by Edvard Perséus, then at the Academy from 1878 to 1881. He then divided his time between Sweden and France: Paris, Grez-sur-Loing, and the coasts of Normandy and Brittany. After making his debut at the Salon of 1883, where he won a third-class medal, he acted as main commissioner of Sweden's participation in the Paris World Fair of 1889, where he himself received a medal of honour.

He spent the rest of his life in Sweden, apart from a few visits abroad. Between 1893 and 1896, together with Karl Nordström and Nils Kreuger, he constituted the 'Varberg School' on the west coast of Sweden. All three of them were receptive to the message of continental Symbolism, and particularly to the painting of Gauguin, and their role was decisive for the development of Swedish National Romanticism.

Richard Bergh left his mark on the cultural life of Sweden of his day not only as a painter, but also as an essayist, polemicist and administrator. He was one of those who, in 1885, provoked the artists' revolt against the conservatism of the Academy and the National Museum and founded the Artists' Union the following year; he remained one of its guiding spirits for the rest of his life. He was also actively engaged in the current debates on social and political issues. Towards the end of his life, in 1915, he was appointed director of the Nationalmuseum, which he transformed into a more democratic, modern and dynamic institution.

His most important articles on the art of the past and present were collected in the volume *Om konst och annat* (On art and other things, 1919), followed by the posthumous volume *Efterlämnade skrifter om konst och annat* (Posthumous articles on art and other things, 1921).

5

Portrait of the Painter Eva Bonnier, 1889

(Porträtt av målarinnan Eva Bonnier)

123 × 120
Signed lower right: R. B. -89
Nationalmuseum, Stockholm
Inv. no. 1507

From 1882, Richard Bergh's portraits brought him his first successes in the Paris Salon and in Scandinavian exhibitions. A subtle psychologist, he presented his wife, or his friends, in their familiar milieu, creating an atmosphere of warm and subdued intimacy around them. As in the works of Bastien-Lepage, whom he admired, he sought an equilibrium between a naturalistic presentation and an expression of the inner life of his models. In the portrait of Eva Bonnier, painted in Paris in 1889, this equilibrium is broken. The surroundings are subordinate, the accent is on the kind of emotional intensity which was to characterize the art of the following decade. Bergh replaced the refinement of execution and use of colours which he had sought earlier with a broken, nervous touch and a chord of more sombre notes: black, yellow and cold green.

The dramatic, even tragic, atmosphere of this picture has given rise to comparisons with contemporary portraits of women in the dramas of Ibsen. But while Eva

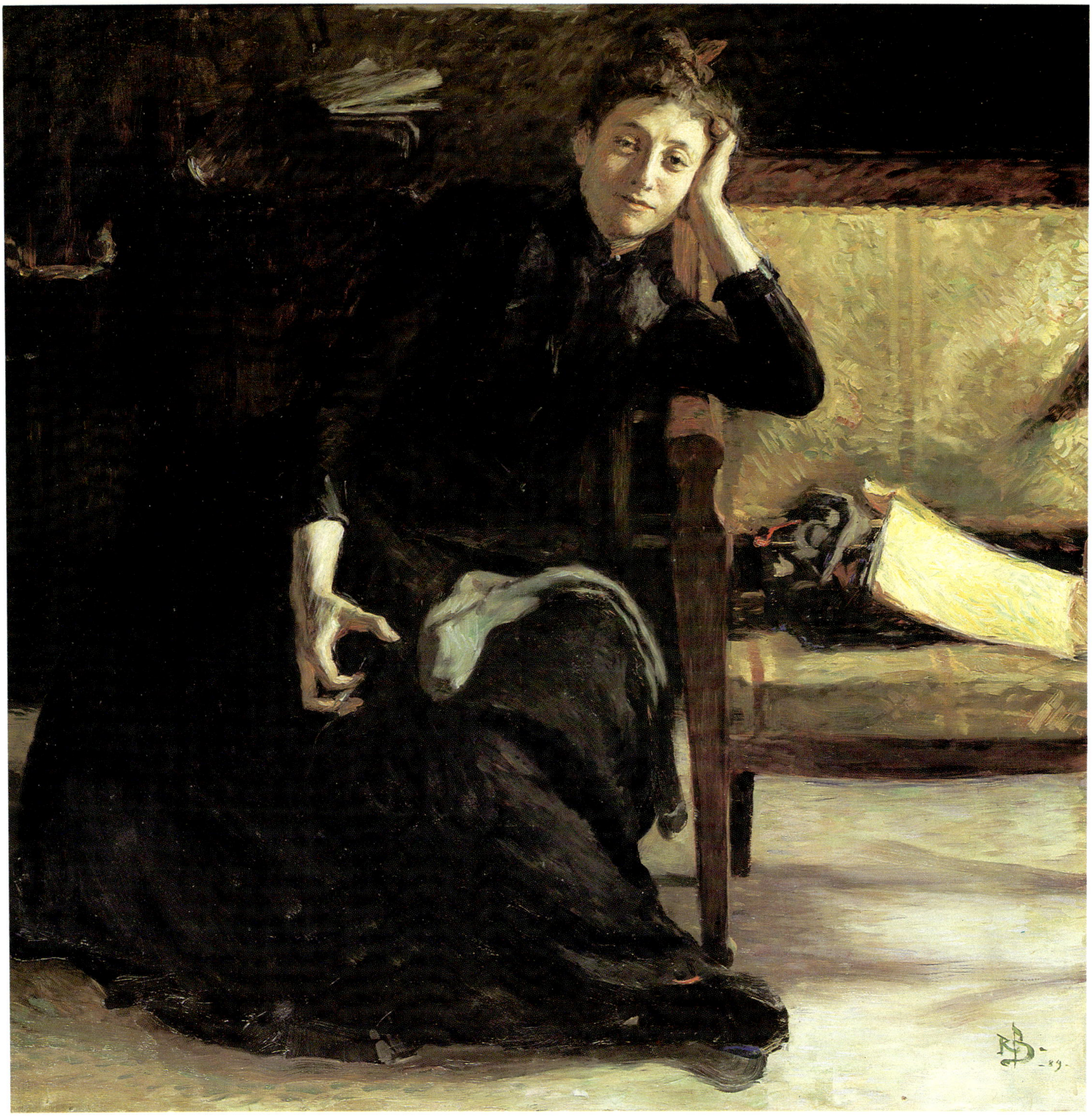

5. Richard Bergh

Bonnier's personality was strong and independent, she by no means appears to have been as highly strung, and even neurotic, as Bergh depicts her. He pushed his interpretation in a decidedly subjective direction, perhaps influenced by his personal tragedy: 1889 was the year in which he saw his young wife pine away and die of cancer.

This portrait was shown at the Paris Exposition Internationale of 1900.

P.G.

6

Nordic Summer Evening, 1899–1900

(Nordisk sommarkväll)

170 × 223.5
Signed lower left in monogram: RB./1899–1900
Göteborgs Konstmuseum, Gothenburg
Inv. no. F 7 (Fürstenberg donation, 1902)

In the articles which he published at the turn of the century, Richard Bergh developed his views on what national art ought to be: it 'should interpret *our* unique features and our heartbeat, and, as a result, use the colours and forms which are, after all, our country's and our people's.' He was convinced that a dedicated study of nature in one's own country was a natural point of departure for art. Hippolyte Taine had taught him that we are, after all, always influenced by the milieu in which we grow up. When an artist paints foreign landscapes, he lacks 'the mysterious and touching interweavings of memories, of vague feelings and imagination' which he spins into the representations of his own country.

Even if landscape painting should express this symbiosis between the artist and his homeland, Richard Bergh certainly did not see this national feeling as narrowly chauvinistic. On the contrary, he was an ardent devotee of the period's ideas on world citizenship and he hoped and believed that his countrymen – and especially artists in their painting – 'would be *Swedish* world citizens'.

This ideology is reflected in *Nordic Summer Evening*, Richard Bergh's foremost contribution to Swedish National Romanticism. In endeavouring to capture this genuinely Nordic atmosphere, he drew on many impulses from abroad. The picture's monumental Synthetist style is based not only on the painting of Puvis de Chavannes and Gauguin, but also on the Italian landscape and Renaissance paintings which he saw during his stay in Florence in 1897–8. The woman on the left displays a certain kinship with the figures of Giotto and Botticelli, for example. The way in which the railing and posts of the veranda in the foreground, together with the figures, divide the composition into three vertical parts and two horizontal sections, remind one of church triptychs, with their predellas. These figures also bring to mind the two saints flanking the Madonna in a *Sacra Conversazione.* Only in Bergh's painting, it is the *landscape* which has become the object of their devotion.

This Nordic landscape is also linked with the landscapes of the early nineteenth-century Romantics. The veranda serves a function analogous to that of the windows which open out to the outdoors in the Romantics' paintings, and the young couple play the same role, that of mediators, as the figures often found in the foreground of their landscapes. But one should note that Bergh's mediators do not passively become part of the magic of the summer evening: they do so consciously, by an act of will. For they are large and dominating, and their forms are solid and tense. We onlookers are in this way invited to reflect as they do on our experience of nature – and our Swedishness! This impression is reinforced by the fact that the couple's gaze does not lead us into an infinite distance, as in Caspar David Friedrich's mountain scenes. The panorama in *Nordic Summer Evening* is clear, close by, tangible, tightly swathed around its own core. The painting seems to tell us that our beautiful Nordic world is *here and now* for us to possess.

Still another feature which points to the painting's double origins – Swedish and foreign – is the fact that the two figures who served as models, the singer Karin Pyk and the painter Prince Eugen, had both belonged to Richard Bergh's circle of friends during his stay in Florence two years earlier. While there, he had made an oil sketch of Karin Pyk in this position. *Nordic Summer Evening* became an inspired summation of the many discussions Bergh and his friends had about Swedishness versus internationalism.

P.G.

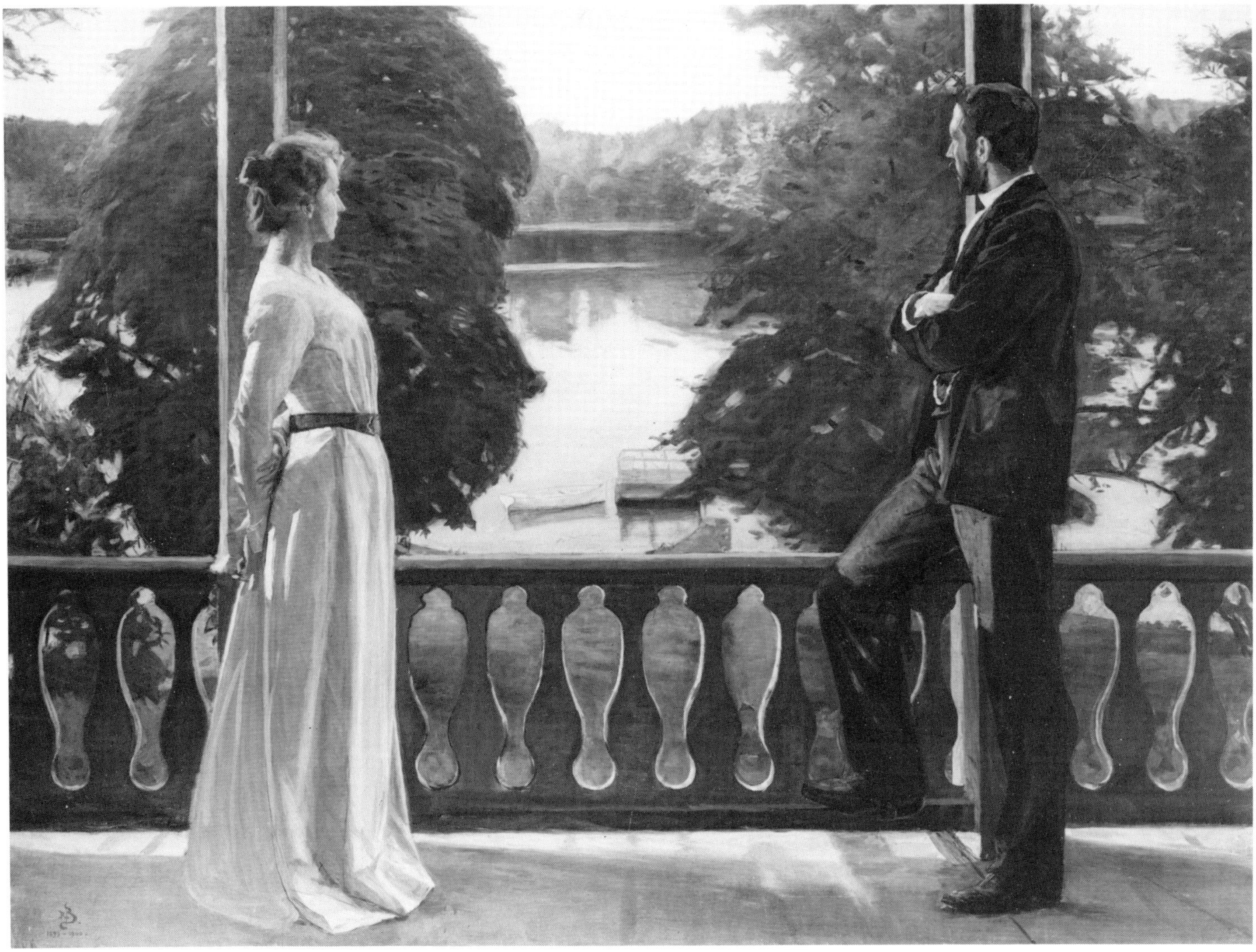

6. Richard Bergh
Reproduced in colour as frontispiece

HALFDAN EGEDIUS

1877–1899, Norway

At the early age of nine, Egedius received his first training at Berglien's art school. Later, he began to receive instruction at the Arts & Crafts School in Christiania. A three-month period of study with Kristian Zahrtmann in Copenhagen at the beginning of 1896 was of little importance. In 1894, Egedius attended Harriet Backer's art school for a time. In the summer of 1890, he took his first study trip to the Norwegian countryside together with Thorvald Erichsen. In 1892, he went for the first time to Telemark, a district whose landscape and old rural culture were to leave such profound traces in his art. Here he met the artist Torleiv Stadskleiv, who although twelve years older than Egedius became his close friend. Stadskleiv was from Bø, in Telemark, and became the most important link between the city boy Egedius and the local peasant culture with which he became so fascinated. The very next year, Egedius returned to Bø, and that summer he painted his first important work, *Saturday Evening*, also called *Night Suitors* (Nasjonalgalleriet, Oslo). The picture belongs within the tradition of 'mood painting', a trend inaugurated by such artists as Kitty L. Kielland (see Nos. 46, 47) and Erik Werenskiold (Nos. 103–5). (Werenskiold was the first to seek out the motives used by Egedius in Eastern Telemark and his influence is obvious in Egedius' earliest works.) Another interesting picture from the same summer, the portrait of a farmer's wife on one of the area's big farms, is impressive in its interpretation of the subject but was never completed (Nationalmuseum, Stockholm).

In 1894, Egedius visited Ernst Josephson's exhibition at the Art Association in Christiania and became especially interested in *Water Sprite*. The same year, he showed his *Saturday Evening* at the official exhibition in Christiania, where Sohlberg made his debut at the same time with *Night Glow* (No. 86). The two debutants received great attention and were especially honoured at the ensuing artists' party. Egedius spent the summer of 1894 in Vågå in Gudbrandsdalen, where several other artists had gathered. However, Gudbrandsdalen was never to captivate Egedius in the same way as Telemark did. He returned there in 1897, but his other excursions were to Bø, where he later periodically spent time in the winter as well. In the summer of 1895, when he was 18, he painted three of his most important works: *The Dreamer* (No. 7), *Girls Dancing* (No. 8), and the portrait of *Mari Clasen* (No. 9). He was interested in Munch's one-man show, which he saw in Christiania in the autumn. As early as 1895, he had begun preparations for his most famous work, *Play and Dance* (Nasjonalgalleriet), which was done the next year.

Even though this picture cannot be considered finished, the artist signed it, which indicates that he was satisfied with the result. Other important works from the same period are *Storm Approaching* (No. 10) and *Summer* (Nasjonalgalleriet). Egedius was a precocious artist who, although he died at the age of only 21, left a series of important and original paintings. This achievement is even more striking when we consider that he had no chance to paint at all during the last two years of his life, because all his time went on illustrating the big new edition of Snorre's *Sagas of the Norse Kings*.

7

The Dreamer, 1895

(Drømmeren)

100 × 81
Signed lower right: H. Egedius 1895.
Nasjonalgalleriet, Oslo
Inv. no. 505 (purchased in 1899)

The picture was painted in Bø in Telemark in the summer of 1895. The interior is from 'Bøstua', where Egedius rented rooms while he was in Telemark, either alone or

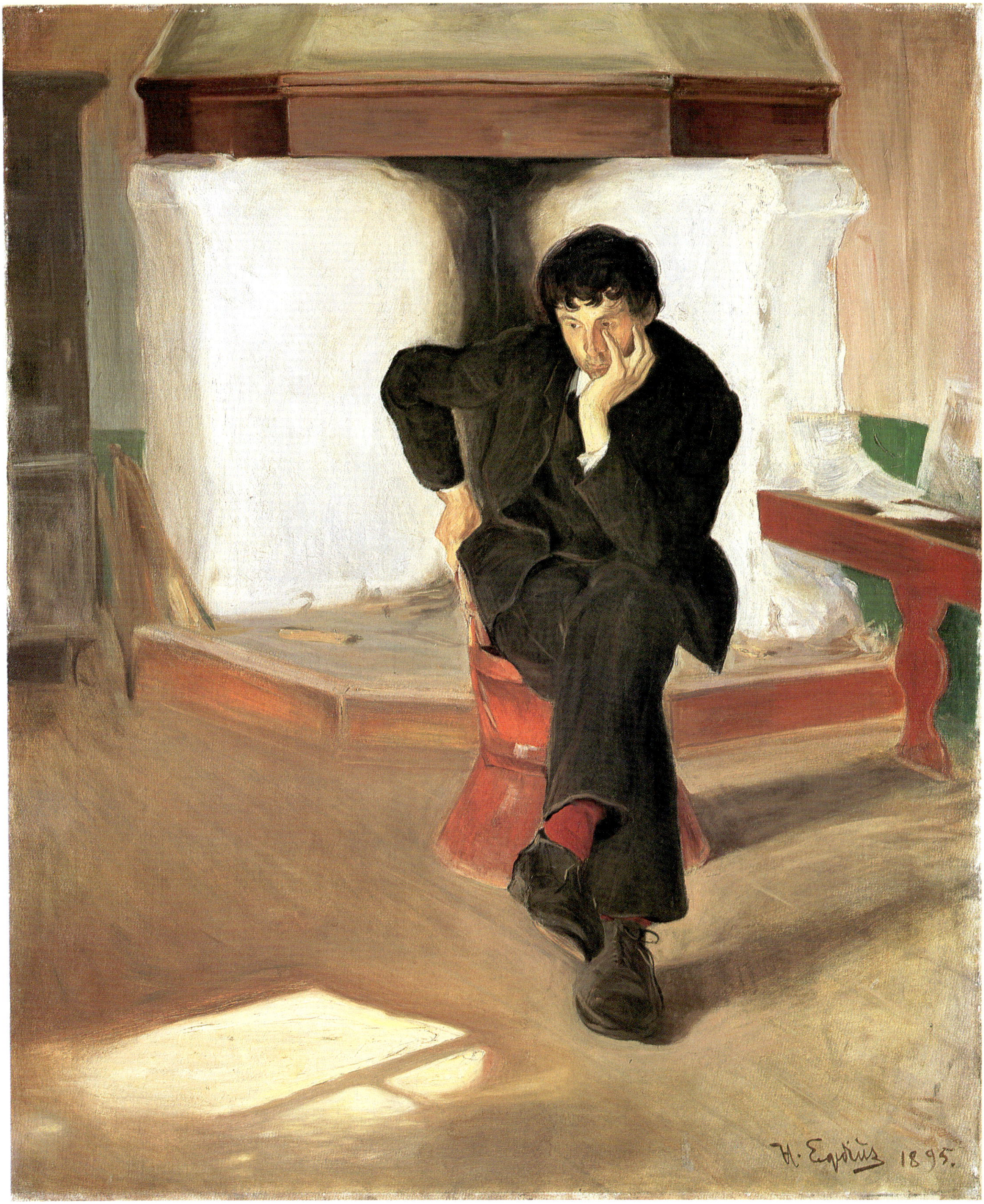

7. Halfdan Egedius

with other painters. The model is his close friend Torleiv Stadskleiv (1865–1946), a painter who was born in Bø and lived there most of his life. It is thus possible to see the painting as a depiction of the unique Telemark milieu. Egedius himself, however, considered it first and foremost a portrait of his friend and thought that he had been successful in characterizing the sitter. No doubt Stadskleiv was something of a dreamer: he indulged in strange fancies and underwent supernatural experiences. But of course the work must also be seen against a more general background. *The Dreamer* is a typical artist's portrait in the spirit of Symbolism. Since Egedius had few chances to acquaint himself with foreign painting, it is natural to seek direct influences for this picture within Norwegian art. In fact, it has interesting features in common with Edvard Munch's famous *Night at St Cloud* (1890, Nasjonalgalleriet). Both works show a man closed in, as it were, in an interior, absorbed in his own imaginary world. The light from outside breaks in through the window, whose form is reflected with insistent clarity on the floor. Thus we are made aware of exterior reality; none the less the artist's attention is directed inwards, to his own thoughts and dreams, which have a higher value than the prosaic everyday world. Despite their thematic similarity, however, the two works are composed in highly different ways. As regards the figure's pose, Egedius seems to have been influenced by Eilif Peterssen's portrait of the leading author and journalist Arne Garborg (No. 68), painted the year before. Egedius was able to mould the different influences into an original composition of great effectiveness.

By so clearly placing the artist in a traditional Norwegian rustic milieu, Egedius was also able to express his belief in the national origins of art.

M.M.

8

Girls Dancing, 1895

(Dansende jenter)

69.5 × 99.5
Signed lower left: H Egedius 95
Nasjonalgalleriet, Oslo
Inv. no. 529 (donation in 1899)

Painting in Norway in the 1890s is frequently termed 'Neo-Romantic' and Egedius' statements indicate that he had a highly romantic attitude towards his Norwegian motives. In his landscape paintings, he first and foremost sought to capture a mood; indeed he often referred to his pictures simply as 'moods'. Correspondingly, in his depictions of popular life, he tried to reach down to the irrational forces that come to the fore in fairy-tales and legends – above all in what he considered the most authentic kind of folk dancing. The popular dances in the district of Gudbrandsdalen he found rather tame: 'They could never be as wild as those of Telemark. Their fiddling was but a dim reflection of what one finds in Telemark.' His own depictions of the subject were all based on what he had seen in Telemark and they were mostly painted there. The theme of dance is central to Egedius' art. The first rough idea for such a composition goes back to 1893; some drawings of girls dancing seem to have been made then. But it was not until the summer of 1895 that he began serious work on the subject. From that year we know of studies and composition drawings which lead up to *Girls Dancing* and eventually to his most famous work, *Play and Dance* (1896, Nasjonalgalleriet).

The picture has often been called *Dance in the Barn*, a misleading title since the scene is clearly the living-room of a farm. Two women are dancing, and we can

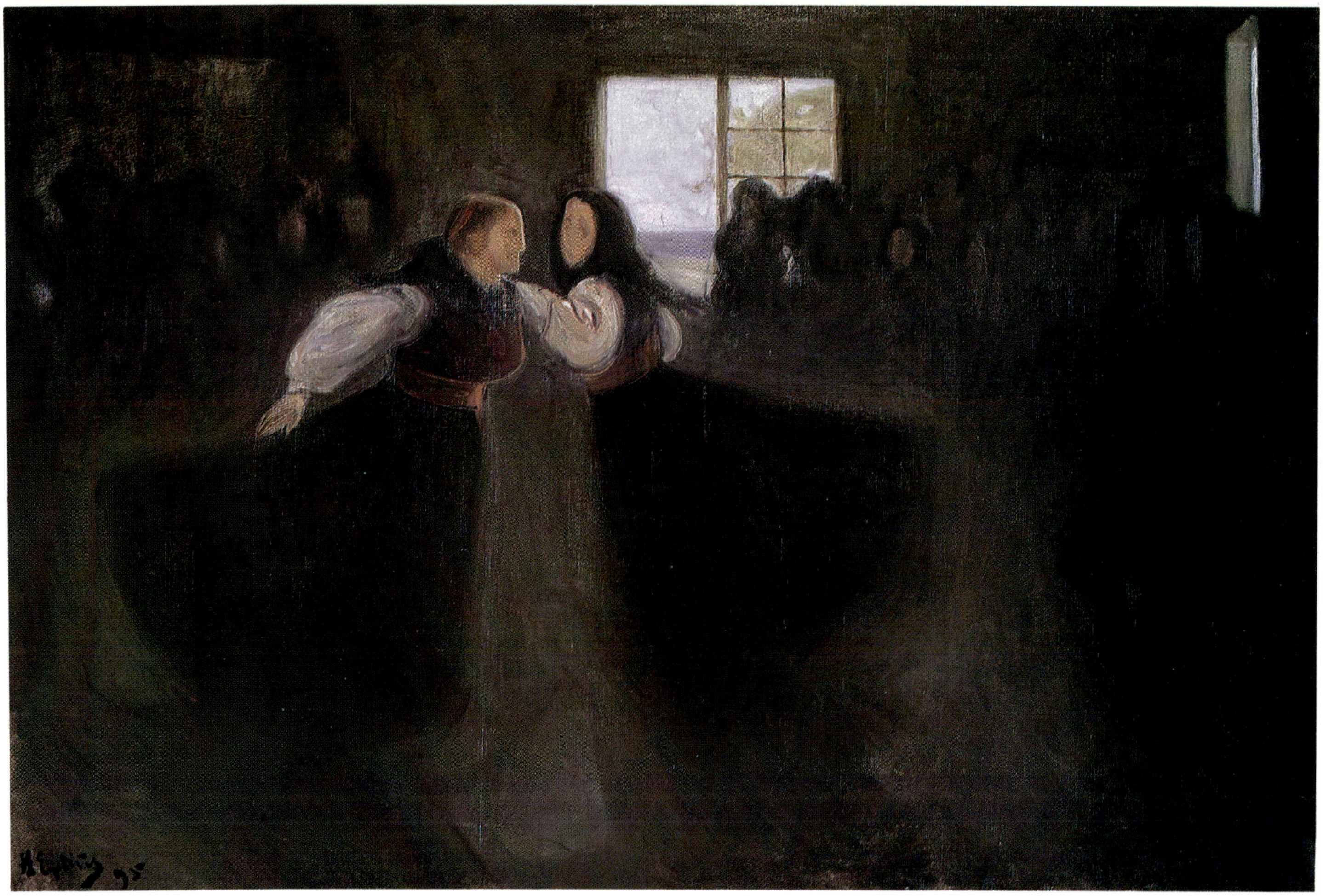

8. Halfdan Egedius

recognize one of them as Mari Clasen (No. 9). Alone on the floor they are caught up in the hectic yet monotonous rhythm of the fiddler's music. All the others have moved back and follow the movements of the dancers in breathless silence. It is difficult to say whether they are witnessing a spontaneous act or a performance. Such performances, in which the best dancers could show off their abilities, were not uncommon in Telemark, but usually three dancers participated on such occasions. No matter how one interprets the scene, the ecstatic and erotic message dominates. The room is in semi-darkness; the figures are sensed more than seen in the vanishing light of the Nordic summer night. Details disappear and the faces, in their ecstatic mood, take on a mask-like look, not unlike that found in Edvard Munch's erotic depictions from the same time. Egedius is very different from Munch in his emphasis on the local milieu and national character, which he considered the basis for any genuine art. On the other hand, in his simplified, synthetist representation, and in the picture's erotic undertones, he is indebted to his older countryman, whose works he had seen on several occasions, notably at Munch's one-man shows in Christiania in 1892 and 1895.

M.M.

9

Mari Clasen, 1895

125 × 94.5
Signed lower right: H Egedius/95
Nasjonalgalleriet, Oslo
Inv. no. 3257

The picture has personal overtones. According to Stadskleiv, there was more than ordinary friendship between Mari Clasen and Egedius. On the other hand, this painting is the most direct and immediate expression of the artist's experience of the local milieu and folk culture of Telemark. The monumental composition and the three-quarter length emphasize the heroic stance of the buxom peasant girl as she poses proudly in the region's lovely and characteristic folk costume. For Egedius, she must have stood as a symbol of the people of Telemark. Three years later, he was asked to illustrate the major work *Norway in the 19th Century* with depictions of 'Telemark types'. The most important of the three works he carried out in this connection is a large drawing of Mari Clasen – this time sitting in full-length, but otherwise with the same tautness and statuesque dignity. The pose of the figure goes back to Renaissance traditions, which were developed in the seventeenth century, especially by such artists as Van Dyck and Frans Hals. Even though Egedius had no opportunity to study such works in the original, we must naturally assume that he knew some of them through reproductions. Considering possible Norwegian models, it seems relevant to mention a youthful work by Christian Krohg. It differs, however, in being a brilliant society portrait, and the figure has not the energetic posture of the hand on the hip. This conspicuous feature had previously been reserved almost solely for portraits of men, but Egedius' choice is hardly accidental: we get the impression of willpower and almost aggressive self-awareness. This impression is emphasized by the broad, unusually free brushstrokes and the impertinently summary treatment of individual parts. The use of light articulates the characterization of the figure and emphasizes the folk costume's lush richness of colour. Within the artist's oeuvre, this portrait is a culmination of his technical skill and power of concentration.

M.M.

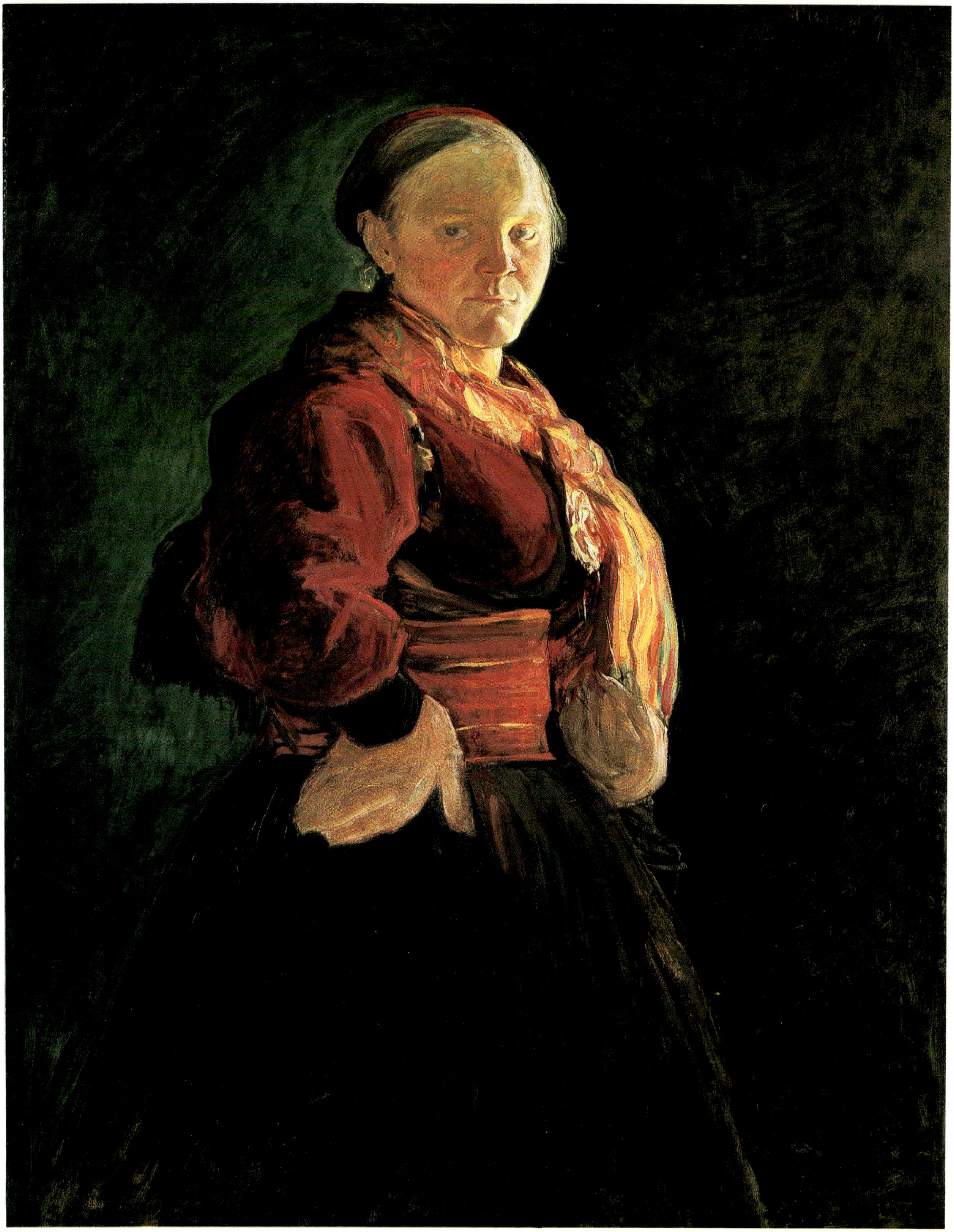

9. Halfdan Egedius

10

Storm Approaching, 1896

(Opptrekkende uvær)

63 × 79
Not signed
Nasjonalgalleriet, Oslo
Inv. no. 506 (purchased in 1899)

It has been customary to emphasize that Egedius sought above all to capture the mood in each motive, and this view is supported by his own pronouncements. 'Mood', as the Norwegian Neo-Romantics understood the word, referred to the subjective individual experience in contrast to objective interpretation. This attitude towards the artistic task is reflected in Egedius' method of work. At times he would spend months on a picture, while at others, he carried out important sections in a single sitting. *Storm Approaching* was, like all his most important pictures, done in Bø. He had made a sketch for a picture with this motive in 1895. Walther Halvorsen relates that the following year he 'continued on the sketch he had begun, but one day, when he was working on it, he threw it down and ran home for a new canvas. As it is now, it was painted at one time and not continued later'. This method of work recalls Léon Pelouse's advice '*l'ébauche sur l'ébauche*', which Egedius' teacher Harriet Backer adopted and handed down to her pupils. In this case, the method was used to give a uniform and condensed expression of the experience of an oncoming storm. The colours take on a sickly intensity and the landscape's restless forms are reflected in the panic which has suddenly possessed every living thing.

M.M.

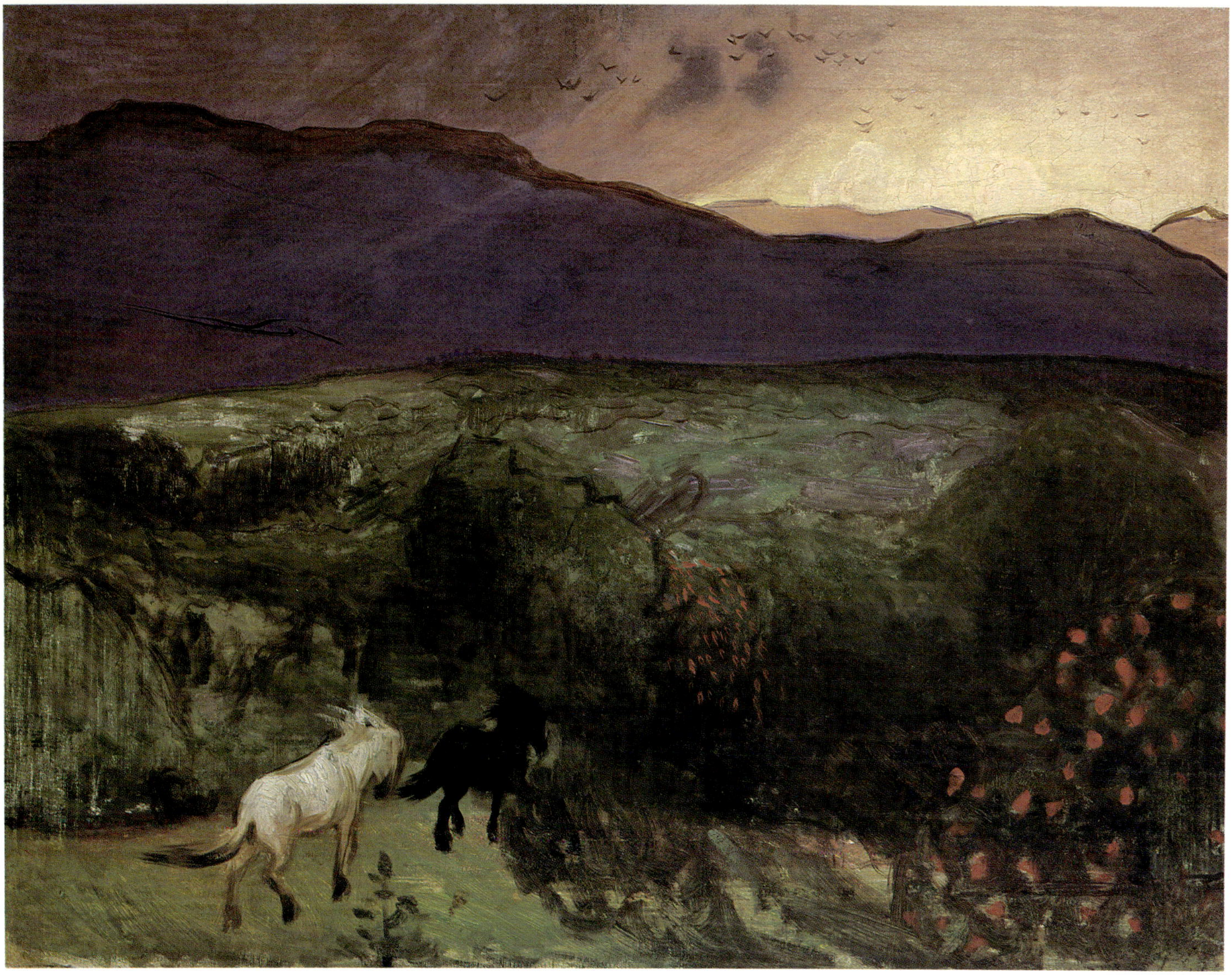

10. Halfdan Egedius

AUGUST EIEBAKKE

1867–1938, Norway

August Eiebakke was born on his parents' farm in Askim in 1867. At the age of 15 he came to Christiania (Oslo) and, an aspiring sculptor, enrolled in Christiania's Royal School of Drawing in 1883. There he developed his technical skills under the sculptor Julius Middelthun. He also studied with Mathias Skeibrok and Harald Petersen, remaining a pupil of the School until 1889.

He soon devoted himself to painting and made rather realistic paintings of folk life and landscapes. He was a great admirer of the art of Erik Werenskiold. From 1886 to 1888 Eiebakke studied under the leading Norwegian Naturalists Christian Krohg, Hans Heyerdahl, and Eilif Peterssen. He made his debut at the Christiania Autumn Exhibition in 1887, exhibiting regularly until 1933 and winning critical acclaim in 1891 with *Laying the Table*.

In January 1892 Eiebakke entered Kristian Zahrtmann's school in Copenhagen. He travelled to France in 1893 and the following year went to Italy with some Danish artists, returning there again in the winter of 1895–6. During his time in Italy he painted in a style close to the stylized New Romantic idiom of his Danish colleagues. He also started painting religious subjects in the manner of Joakim Skovgaard.

Eiebakke joined Halfdan Egedius and Erik Werenskiold in illustrating Fridtjof Nansen's Arctic Circle chronicles, *The Norwegian North Polar Expedition*, published in Norway in 1897, and later published in Germany, England, and France. He studied briefly with Kristian Zahrtmann the following year, returning to his early Naturalist style.

After the turn of the century, his works was characterized by a freer use of colours and he devoted himself to portrait painting. He made several journeys to Italy, Denmark, Holland and Germany. In 1910 he began teaching at Christiania's Royal School of Drawing, where he served as director from 1912 until 1937, when illness forced him to retire.

Eiebakke never had a one-man exhibition, but a commemorative exhibition was arranged at Oslo Kunstforening in 1939. He participated in several major showings, such as the World Fair in Paris in 1900, and the Norwegian Exhibition in Brighton in 1913.

11

Laying the Table, 1891

(Anretning)

93.5×120
Signed lower left: August Eiebakke 1891.
Nasjonalgalleriet, Oslo
Inv. no. 390 (purchased in 1891)

Laying the Table was painted when Eiebakke was recovering from an illness at his parents' farm in Askim in the spring of 1891. While working on the picture the artist wrote to the critic Andreas Aubert,

> What really troubles me these days is a picture, an interior with four figures. Oh, if I only could succeed in doing what I carry in my mind. I want to depict neither poverty with wasted faces and herring and potatoes, nor snobbish people in vulgar interiors, but a scene where well-being and satisfaction are shown as I have seen them in good periods on a simple farm like that at home, where the summer breeze filled every single corner. Yes, I have great plans in my mind—if

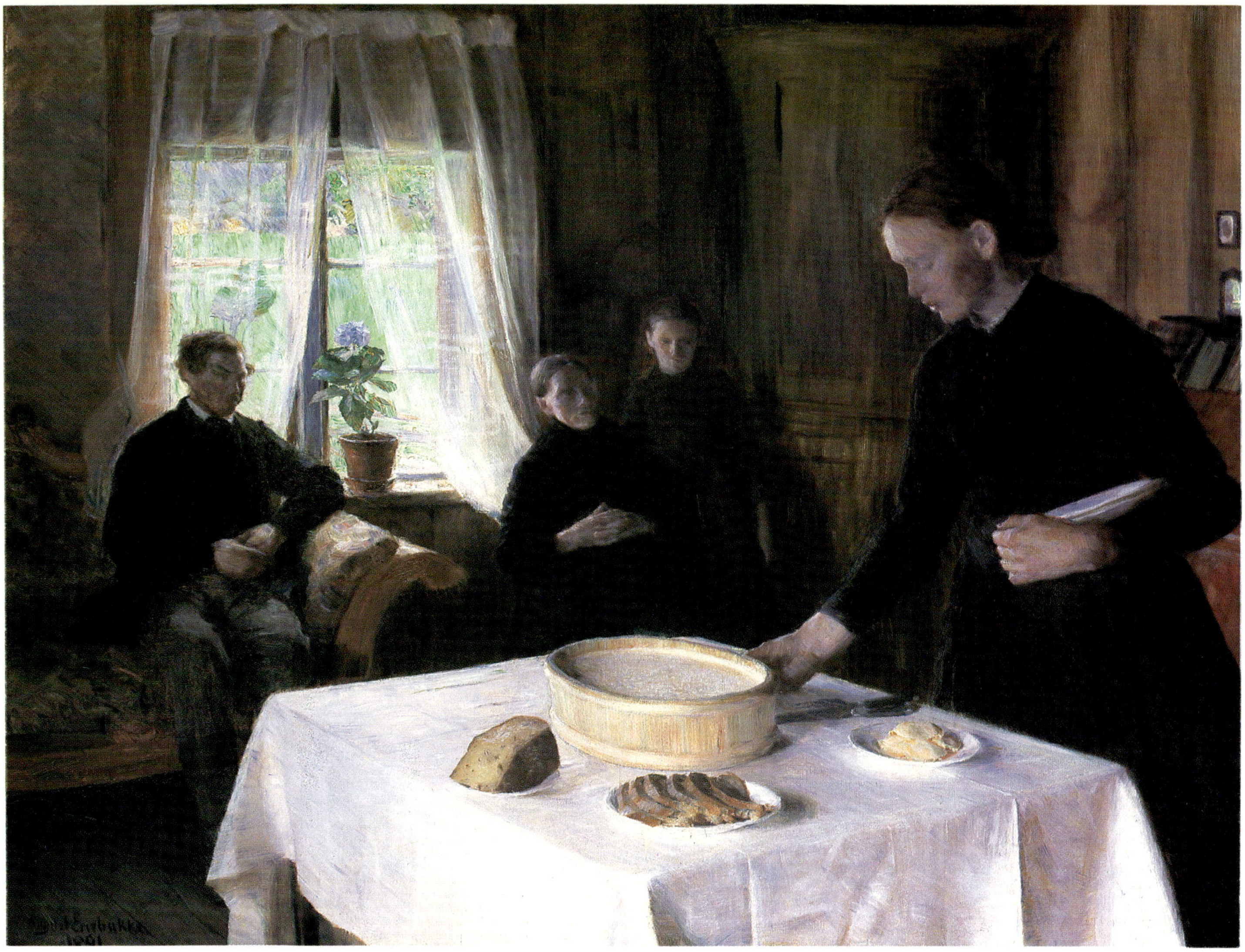

11. August Eiebakke

> only they could become a reality! But I *shall* do something here during this summer, so I can get it into the Autumn Exhibition. I feel that until then I shall have no peace in my mind . . . (Letter from Eiebakke to Aubert, 17 May 1891, University Library, Oslo).

On 2 August he wrote to Aubert again,

> My painting with the 4 figures is not yet advancing, as the models have been busy with haymaking. But I certainly hope to finish it in the course of the autumn. The matter can wait, as it is an interior. I am also working on another painting with figures—a woman making a wreath. The posture of her head, the expression in her face, the gestures of the hands are the most difficult problems to solve, but also the most interesting . . . (Letter from Eiebakke to Aubert, 2 August 1891, University Library, Oslo).

The picture tells a simple story from the artist's childhood home. His family posed in their Sunday best as models. The painting, which at one time was also called *Guests at Home*, records the strict social conventions of a Sunday or holiday visit on a Norwegian farm. The guests wait for the table to be set with cheese, butter, heavy sour cream and bread. Convention requires that they refuse several times before being served. Eiebakke captures the tension of the hostess and her guests in their introspective poses.

The painting was awarded a gold medallion at the World Fair in Paris in 1900. Critics at both the Norwegian and the French exhibition viewed the painting as a masterfully rendered tranquil interior. They particularly noted the serene backlighting and rich coloration and marvelled at the luminosity of the linen tablecloth.

The still-life objects in the painting, the cheese and the bread, the sour cream and its bowl, the cloth and the curtains, are painted with great attention to detail, but there is a special light in the grave faces in the twilight of the living-room which gives a solemn distance to the whole scene. The bluish glimmering colouring creates a picturesque unity and atmosphere that link the picture more to the '90s than the '80s, despite the realistic naturalism of its details.

The painting was bought by the Nasjonalgalleriet from the Autumn Exhibition in 1891.

T.S.

MAGNUS ENCKELL

1870–1925, Finland

Magnus Enckell was the guiding spirit of the young group of artists who, after receiving instruction in a somewhat Impressionistic style in their homeland, arrived in Paris in 1891. The group included Ellen Thesleff and Beda Stjernschantz. Ernest Raynaud, the authority on French Symbolism, calls 1891 *la date heureuse du symbolisme.* This was seen immediately in the work of these artists: clear colours disappeared; simplicity, in both composition and drawing, replaced rich nuances. Puvis de Chavannes's *Le pauvre pêcheur* and Manet's *Olympia* at the Luxemburg were the first stops on everyone's pilgrimage. The experiences that Paris had to offer and Enckell's position as the leading young artist were described by a Finnish fellow artist, Väinö Blomstedt, in the autumn of 1891. There was something new in the air. Assyrian and Egyptian art had become the models.

> There is a power in the conception of lines, a magnificent simplicity in the grandiosely decorative. It is so strange to see such old art, so little developed, but still so splendid. Now I am in a frenzy to paint; I feel that there is something that drives me with irresistible force. Everything is going to change. It is Puvis de Chavannes who in a way first came forth as the spokesman for this new art. He is childishly naive, but at the same time so supremely magnificent that it is wonderful; one cannot really understand what he has done. First one wants to turn away from it all with a laugh, but finally it grips one with a higher power. God knows what it is.

The writer did not understand Puvis any more than he understood Manet's *Olympia*, but continued,

> None other than Enckell admires it. This is what is called the art of the future. It is sad that Enckell has started with it; his drawings are very good, but his paintings are strange. He has done an old woman from Brittany in only two or three colours; he says that nowadays there are no colours at all in nature. This is a school which one will never be able to understand in Finland, and perhaps only in some quarters in France . . . it looks so awful; all objects and figures are simple to the extreme, Assyrian-like simple, surrounded by black contours, painted with one colour; . . . I think that the unfortunate thing about Enckell is that he wants to be original, and yet he is not independent enough; we could say, I believe, that he is lost to us in Finland because what he paints would never be understood and the way in which he paints would never be liked in Finland.

Enckell's great influence on his surroundings was partly due to the fact that he had studied the intellectual movements of his day, as well as its literature and music. He was also well aware of the spiritualist background of Symbolism, of Plato, Swedenborg, and Baudelaire, and during his time in Paris, which lasted to the spring of 1894, he became increasingly interested in the mysticism of Soleil d'Or and Sâr Péladan. His art took on a more mystical character. This trend culminated in Italy in the winter of 1894–5, when Enckell was strongly influenced by Böcklin. Harsh criticism in Finland quashed Enckell's interest in Symbolism, although right to the end his art was characterized by a sense of conflict. He arranged a large-scale retrospective exhibition in Stockholm in 1924 but died of pneumonia on his trip there.

Together with Hugo Simberg, Enckell executed the frescos for Tampere's St John's Cathedral, perhaps Finland's most harmonious example of Art Nouveau.

In around 1910, there was a general move in Finnish art towards the use of pure colours. This change was marked in Enckell's art, which was sharply divided into two: the dark period and the colourful, Post-Impressionistic later period. He was, however, one of the few whose art in both periods can be considered of equally high quality.

12

Two Boys, 1892

(Kaksi poikaa)

Watercolour on paper, 90 × 100
Signed upper right: M. Enckell/1892/sign. 1916
Gösta Serlachiuksen taidesäätiön kokoelmat, Mänttä
Inv. no. 67

The new conception of man, of spiritual man, in a timeless and placeless state, appeared in Magnus Enckell's early androgynous boy figures from 1892 to 1894. These boys were, on the one hand, an attempt to achieve almost sculpture-like, heavy volume, and, on the other, an attempt to create a mystical form of expression. Enckell painted *Two Boys* immediately after his first trip to Paris, where his style had undergone a radical change in the direction of archaic simplicity. He saw his art as part of the rejuvenation of art in Paris at the time. This idealistic form had links not only to Egyptian traditions, but also to those of the High Renaissance. The young sexually immature androgyne was an image of man freed from all that is incidental, frozen in its own mystical timeless existence. When these works were first exhibited in Helsinki in 1893, critics tried to treat them as pure model studies, but artists saw more in them. Albert Edelfelt told Enckell that he was especially happy that there was someone among the young artists who did not travel 'the customary old national road'.

The watercolour technique is, as in the works of Rissanen, a move towards a more spiritual form of expression that approaches fresco painting, something that could not be achieved with oils.

S.S-K.

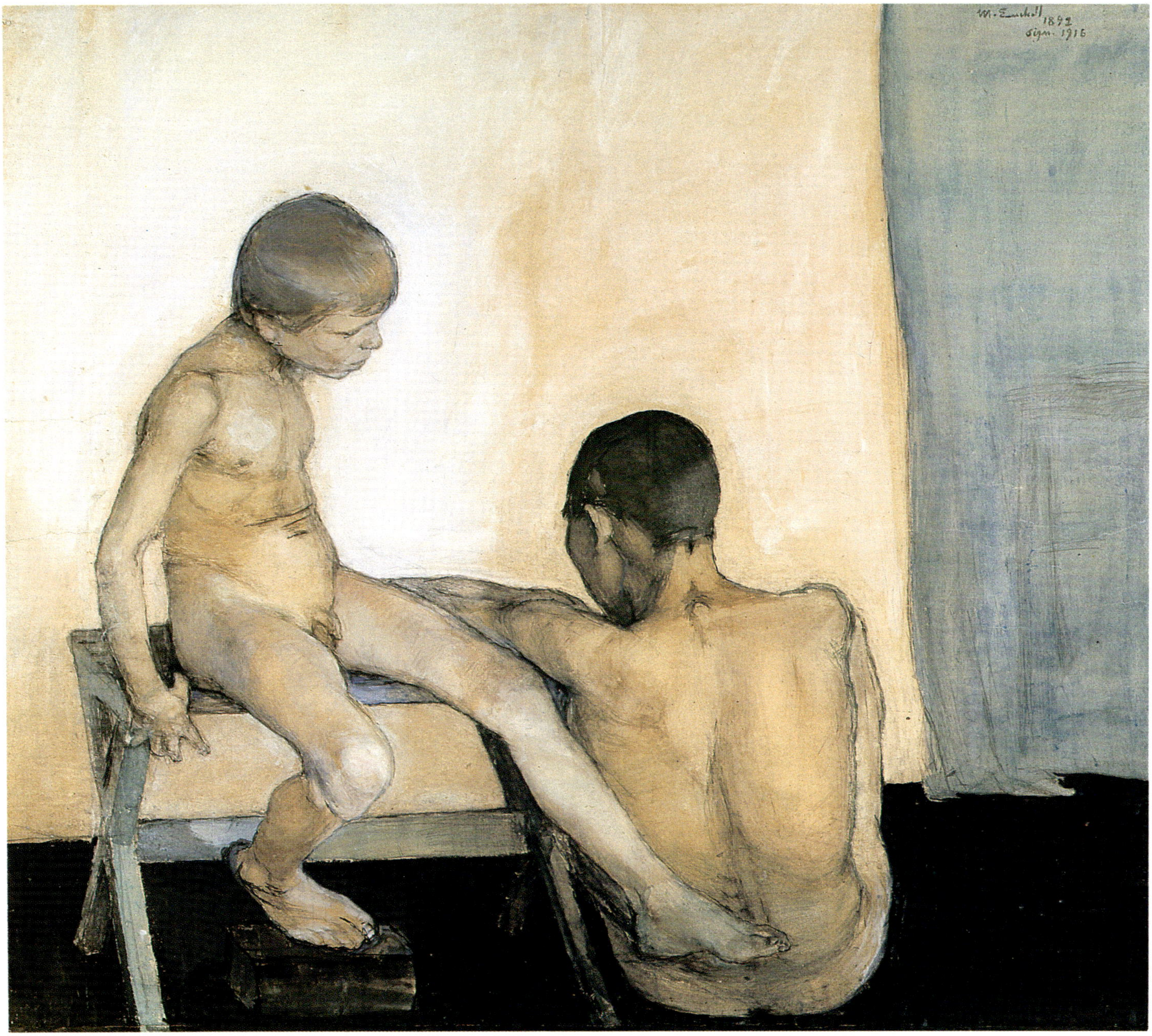

12. Magnus Enckell

13

Boy with a Skull, 1893

(Poika ja pääkallo)

Charcoal and watercolour on paper, 70 × 100
Not signed
Ateneumin taidemuseo, Helsinki
Inv. no. A I 516 (purchased in 1893)

The most clearly Symbolist of Enckell's androgynous figures, *Boy with a Skull* supports the idealistic and mystical interpretation of the whole series. The composition originally included two boys. The second, lying on his stomach, was on the left-hand side of the painting. He, too, was gazing at the skull, the symbol of life and death. The area where the second boy figure was wiped away is still visible.

Boy with a Skull is clearly linked with the ancient *vanitas* theme: man alone with the problem of eternity and the transience of life. The sparing use of colour and the stark simplicity of form, however, confused even Enckell's own Finnish artist friends. When the works were shown to the jury in 1893, Edelfelt wrote to Enckell, in Paris for the second time, 'Your three works were received with *acclamation.* Gallen-Kallela, Järnefelt, and Halonen were enchanted; they looked *very* good, fine, deep, and understood.'

Gallen-Kallela, who was just moving from Realism to Symbolism, was startled by these works. He admitted this to Enckell a decade later, in a letter which also shows the sharp differences between the two artists. 'The very first things I saw by you were a powerful stimulus to me to produce real art myself one day – I have often wanted to say this to you but couldn't: the reason must remain a mystery. You must have felt it unsaid.' And later in the same letter he added, 'You have always been a sphinx to me.'

S.S-K.

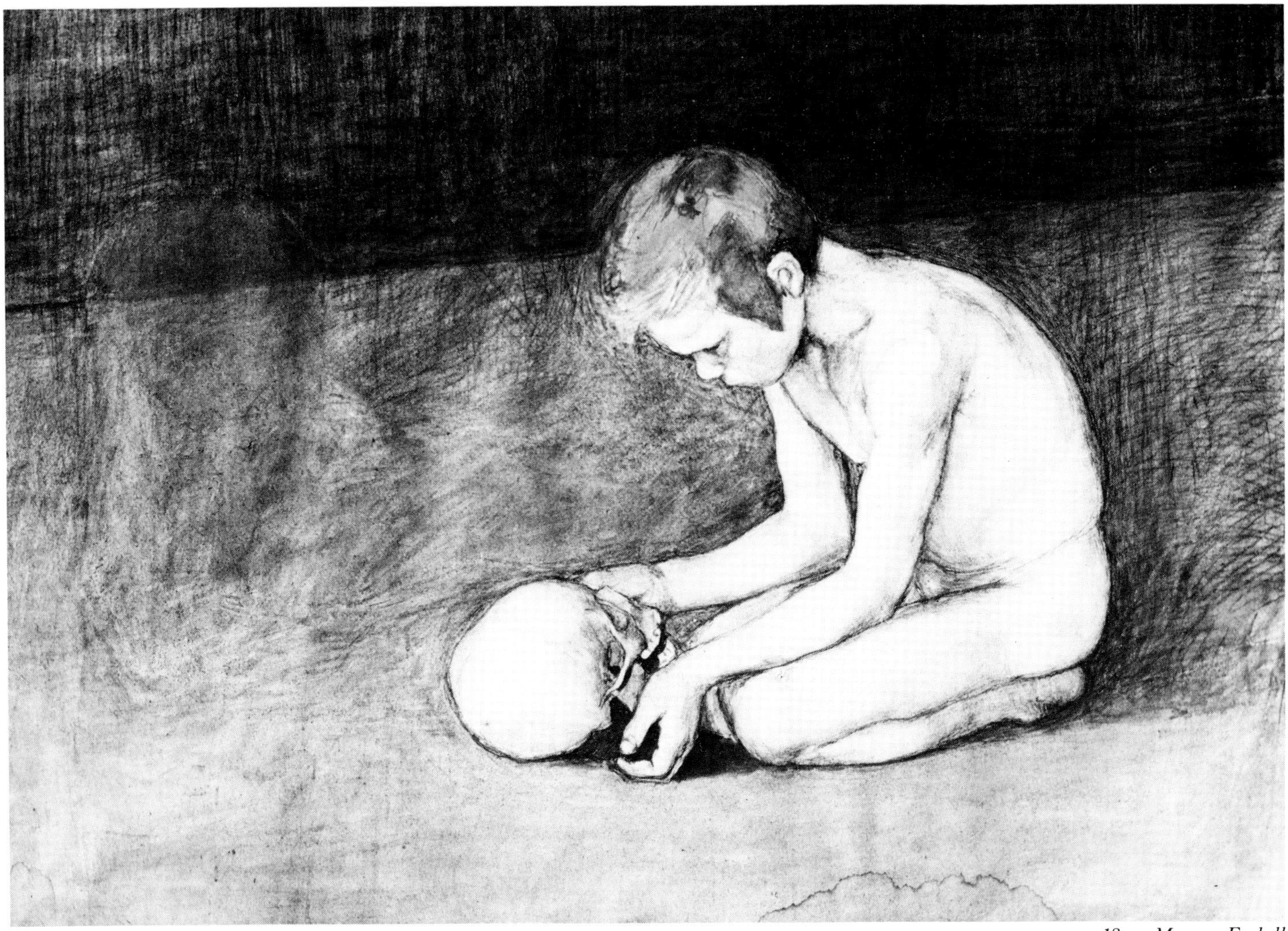

13. Magnus Enckell

14

Awakening, 1894

(Herääminen)

113 × 86
Signed lower right: M.E.
(Antell Collection) Ateneumin taidemuseo, Helsinki
Inv. no. A II 787 (purchased in 1905)

Awakening is a synthesis of Enckell's earlier boy figures. Kasimir Leino, a Finnish writer and art critic, said that the artist wanted the white background to express the fact that the youth was awakening to a brighter, more profound life. After the work had been shown at the Exhibition of Finnish Artists in 1894, Enckell's friend Bruno Aspelin noted that the public did not 'like' these works by Enckell. They did not correspond to what the 'moderns' expected of the Symbolists.

> They have too much *true* inner feeling. His picture, which represents a painful awakening from an earlier existence to a second, is so completely felt and so nobly, purely, deeply thought out. Perhaps I understand him too well to be able to value the effect properly. Enckell is perhaps too subjective! He paints too much what he himself feels and thinks for him to be understood *yet*, in this way he is ahead of his own time.

In the early years of the 1890s, Enckell was the 'artist of the future' to his fellow painters. This painting reflects the artist's own struggle, the dream of a lost paradise, the purity of childhood.It also contains the idea familiar to Swedenborgian mysticism of Adam's awakening to a bright state of consciousness. In another connection, Enckell interpreted this state as 'an instant of a brighter, crystallized life'.

With good reason, the work has been compared to Michelangelo's *Creation of Adam* and Ferdinand Hodler's *Night.* Michelangelo was one of Enckell's admired masters of the High Renaissance, and Hodler's *Night*, then called *Sommeil (Sleep)*, aroused considerable attention at the Champ-de-Mars salon in 1891, soon after Enckell came to Paris.

Awakening was exhibited at the Paris World Fair in 1900.

S.S-K.

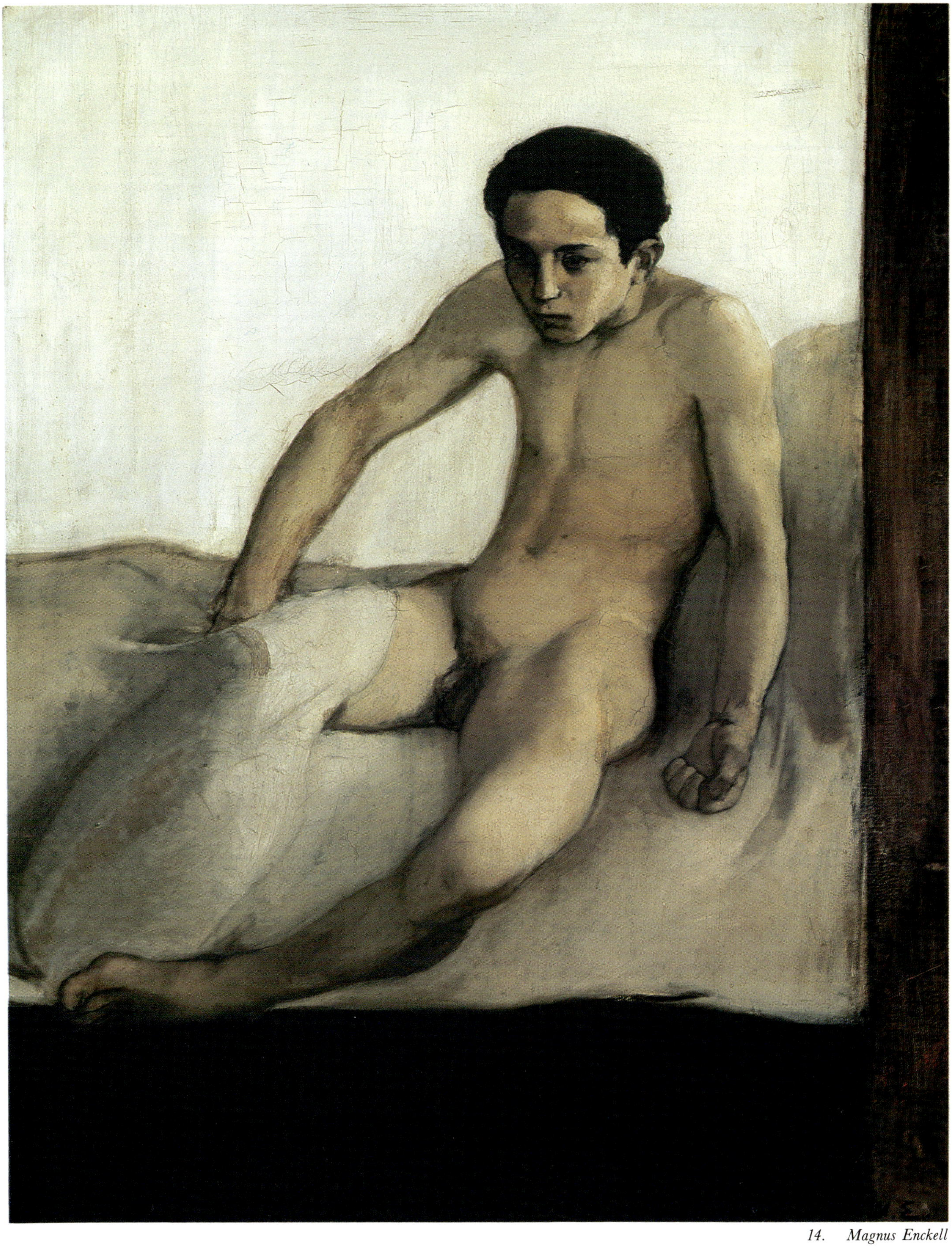

14. Magnus Enckell

PRINCE EUGEN

1865–1947, Sweden

Prince Eugen, the youngest son of the Swedish King Oscar II, showed an early interest in and aptitude for art, and started his artistic training while still in school. However, he did not arrive at the decision, at the time considered sensational, to become an artist until the age of 21. The following year, he travelled to Paris, where he became a student of Léon Bonnat. With interruptions for summer trips to Sweden, he remained in Paris until 1889, and also studied with Henri Gervex, Alfred Roll, and Puvis de Chavannes. Prince Eugen then returned to Sweden, but made a number of visits abroad, including several to Italy.

Landscape painting dominated his whole artistic production. He was one of the few to introduce landscape in a number of monumental frescos, for example at the Opera House and at the Dramatic Theatre in Stockholm, and, in a style influenced by Cubism, at Stockholm's City Hall in the 1920s.

After an initial Realist period at the end of the 1880s, Eugen became one of the leading representatives of the Swedish style of the 1890s and 1900s, with its Synthetist idiom and lyrically romantic view of the landscape.

The 'Red Prince's' liberal and unbiased view of the day's political and cultural issues also made him an important supporter of the modern art of his own period, both ideologically and financially. His support took the form of purchases, which gradually grew into one of the most comprehensive collections of Swedish turn-of-the-century art. Prince Eugen left this collection, together with his home Waldemarsudde in Stockholm, to the State as a museum.

15

The Forest, 1892

(Skogen)

150 × 100.5
Signed lower right: Eugen/1892
Göteborgs konstmuseum, Gothenburg
Inv. no. F 27 (Fürstenberg donation 1902)

1891 marked the transition from the Realism of the '80s to National Romanticism in Prince Eugen's art. The following year, he painted a winter evening landscape of a pine forest against an orange evening sky with blue shadows over the snow. It can be seen as a prelude to *The Forest*, which interprets the moody, slightly melancholy nature mysticism which was a central part of the new feeling for nature in Sweden in the '90s and so sharply emphasizes the rejection of the bright optimistic Realism of the '80s. The national art that was to be created was to emerge from the people's own feelings for their country. Prince Eugen's friend and fellow artist, Richard Bergh, a leading figure in the Artists' Union, where the art of the '90s took shape, also emphasized this. The new art, in order to be truly Nordic, must be animated by a spirit other than Realism since 'in the North, art is not a product of happiness: it is a product of longing'.

The Forest is typical of this shift in mood. It goes back to studies which Prince Eugen made in the province of Södermanland from July to October 1892. It is not, however, a portrayal of a particular forest: it is the archetype and concept of the Swedish pine forest. Through the pattern of tree trunks, our gaze is drawn inwards until we do not see the forest for the trees. As always in National Romanticism, both in literature and in the pictorial arts, the landscape is primarily the conveyor of a mood,

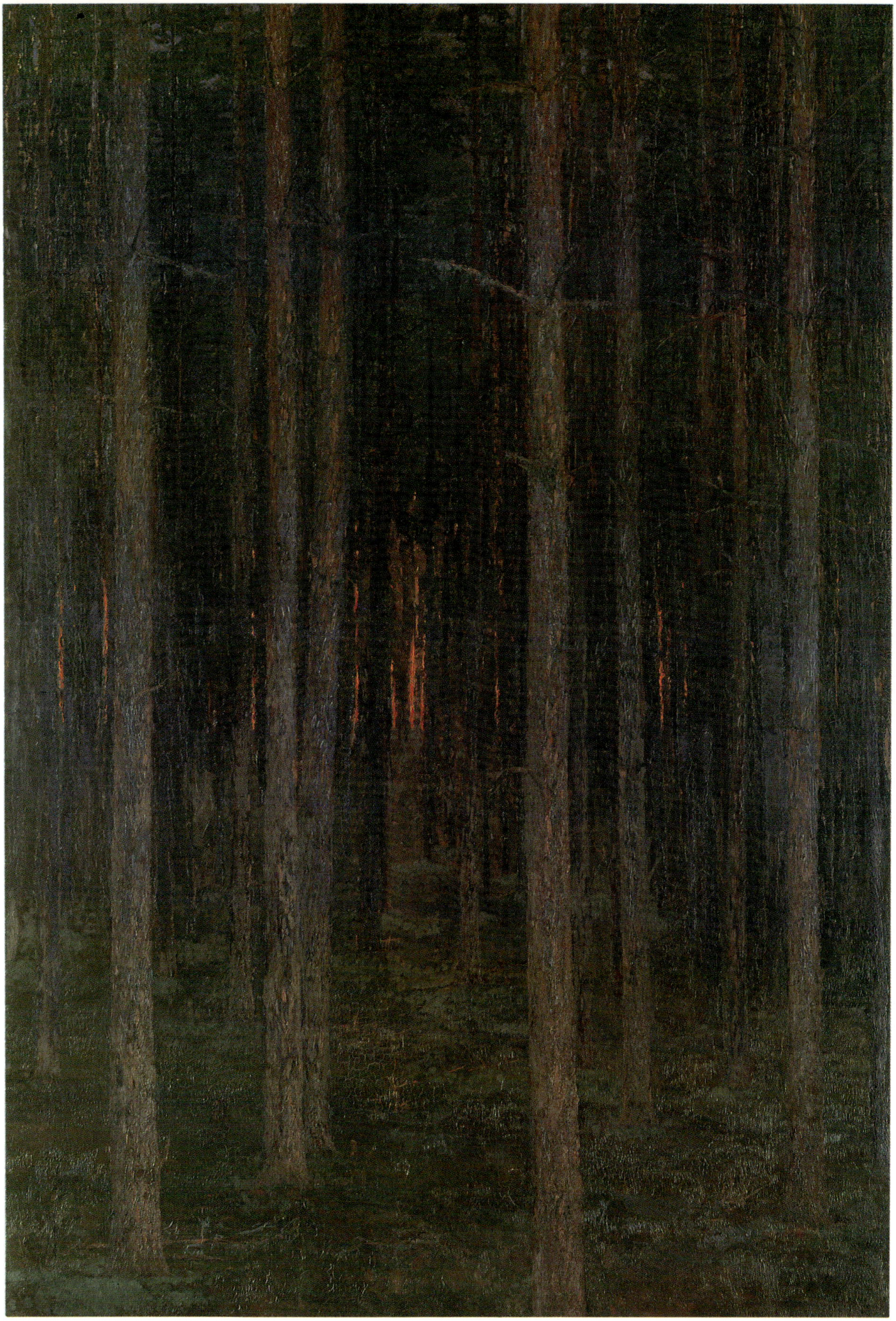

15. Prince Eugen

often with undertones of melancholy or dread, which is united with national sentiment and actually becomes part of it. In Prince Eugen's *The Forest*, we encounter his typical mood in a pictorially original and wilful composition, perhaps the most clearly Symbolist of Eugen's pictures. The motive of longing is represented by the dim light in the distance, a symbol, one could say, of another world.

The Forest was exhibited in Chicago in 1893, in Berlin in 1896 and in Stockholm in 1894 and 1897.

T.G.

16

The Cloud, 1896

(Molnet)

112 × 103
Signed lower right: Eugen 1896
Prins Eugens Waldemarsudde, Stockholm

Prince Eugen did not confine himself to 'blue pictures' in the 1890s. On the contrary, two of his best-known paintings, *The Old Castle*, 1893 and *The Cloud*, 1895 (replica in 1896) are summer pictures, painted in full daylight. They mark Eugen's breakthrough as an independently creative artist. Both are characterized by a monumental and highly simplified form, by the sky's leading role, and by a unique mood of disharmony. The pictures were painted when Eugen was around 30 years old and still felt torn between his royal duties, which King Oscar required him to perform, and his work as an artist. He himself noted in a letter that the dissonance in the much stronger palette in *The Old Castle* was intentional, and that he sought to give form to a mood of unrest and menace.

The same mood can be found to some extent in *The Cloud*, which at first glance can be interpreted as a picture of serene summer happiness. It was painted at Tyresö, south of Stockholm, which Prince Eugen visited in 1893 and where he returned for a great many years. Even though the painting has a topographical basis in the actual landscape, it has, through the consistent simplifications and monumentalization of all forms, been turned into a symbol of the landscape of central Sweden, a landscape to which Prince Eugen paid tribute throughout his entire life. Much later (1935) he commented on this stylization of the landscape: 'It is often the memory's simplified and synthetic impression of nature that inspires one to make a work of art. The artists' vaguer longing suddenly meets a response in nature... a work of art is born.' This original inspiration could, however, be transformed into something unrecognizable. Prince Eugen also related in a letter that he began *The Cloud* in front of his motive and later continued the work in his studio in the winter. When he returned the following summer, all similarities with the original motive had been obliterated.

In *The Cloud*, the sense of longing is accentuated by the path which runs over the top of the hill to an unknown destination. This motive creates a mood which recalls landscapes by Caspar David Friedrich. However, the source of inspiration should probably be sought in some of Arnold Böcklin's landscapes, which were highly thought of in Sweden at the time. Like most Swedish painters in the '90s, Prince Eugen was strongly influenced by contemporary European moods and ideas.

The Cloud was exhibited at the Paris World Fair in 1900.

T.G.

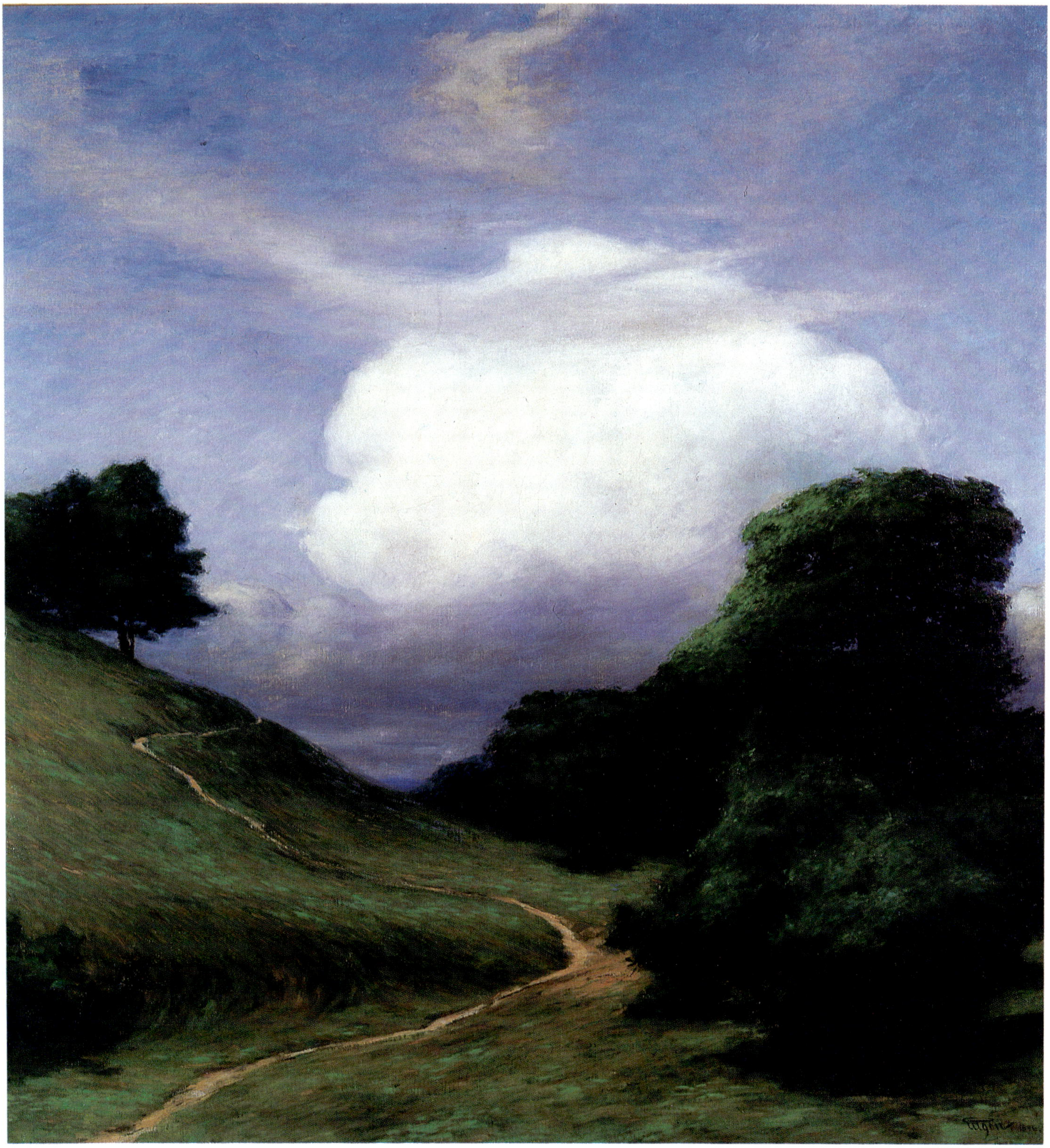

16. Prince Eugen

17

Still Water, 1901

(Det lugna vattnet)

142 × 178
Not signed
Nationalmuseum, Stockholm
Inv. no. 1609 (donation in 1903)

Still Water has its origins in a peculiarly Northern phenomenon – the long, light Nordic dusks and summer nights – which in the 1890s fostered the romanticism of the 'blue hours' in Swedish art and literature. Only in northern Sweden can one see the midnight sun, but the unique 'blue hours', which resemble neither night nor day, prevail everywhere. Two years before *Still Water* was painted, Richard Bergh wrote an article entitled *Svensk konstnärskynne* (Swedish artists' temperament) which in several respects sets out the goals of Swedish art in the 1890s. He describes how one evening, on a hill across from Florence, he was suddenly gripped by a powerful longing to return home to Sweden, to go away from the south where, in spite of everything, he would never feel at home. At that moment Bergh freed himself from the doubts about his own country's artistic potential, which he had shared with all Swedish painters who, since the early 1800s, had made their pilgrimage to Italy. He exclaimed, 'Doesn't our nature, just as well as nature in the south, reflect eternity? Do not we, too, perceive nature's great, eternal laws? Does not our gaze embrace the sky as well – and what a sky!'

It is in this spirit that Prince Eugen painted *Still Water* in 1901. He, too, sought infinity and 'nature's great, eternal laws'. Like *The Cloud* a few years earlier, *Still Water* was painted in Tyresö, south of Stockholm, Prince Eugen's summer home for many years. As in *The Cloud*, the aim is, through stylization, to emphasize the landscape, or, as Richard Bergh formulated it in another connection, 'to find the way to simplicity in matters of decorative arrangements, which alone makes loftiness possible in painting'. After his initial Realistic period in the 1880s Prince Eugen worked in this spirit throughout his artistic career. *Still Water* was, however, one of his last works to be characterized by Symbolism's view of the landscape.

T.G.

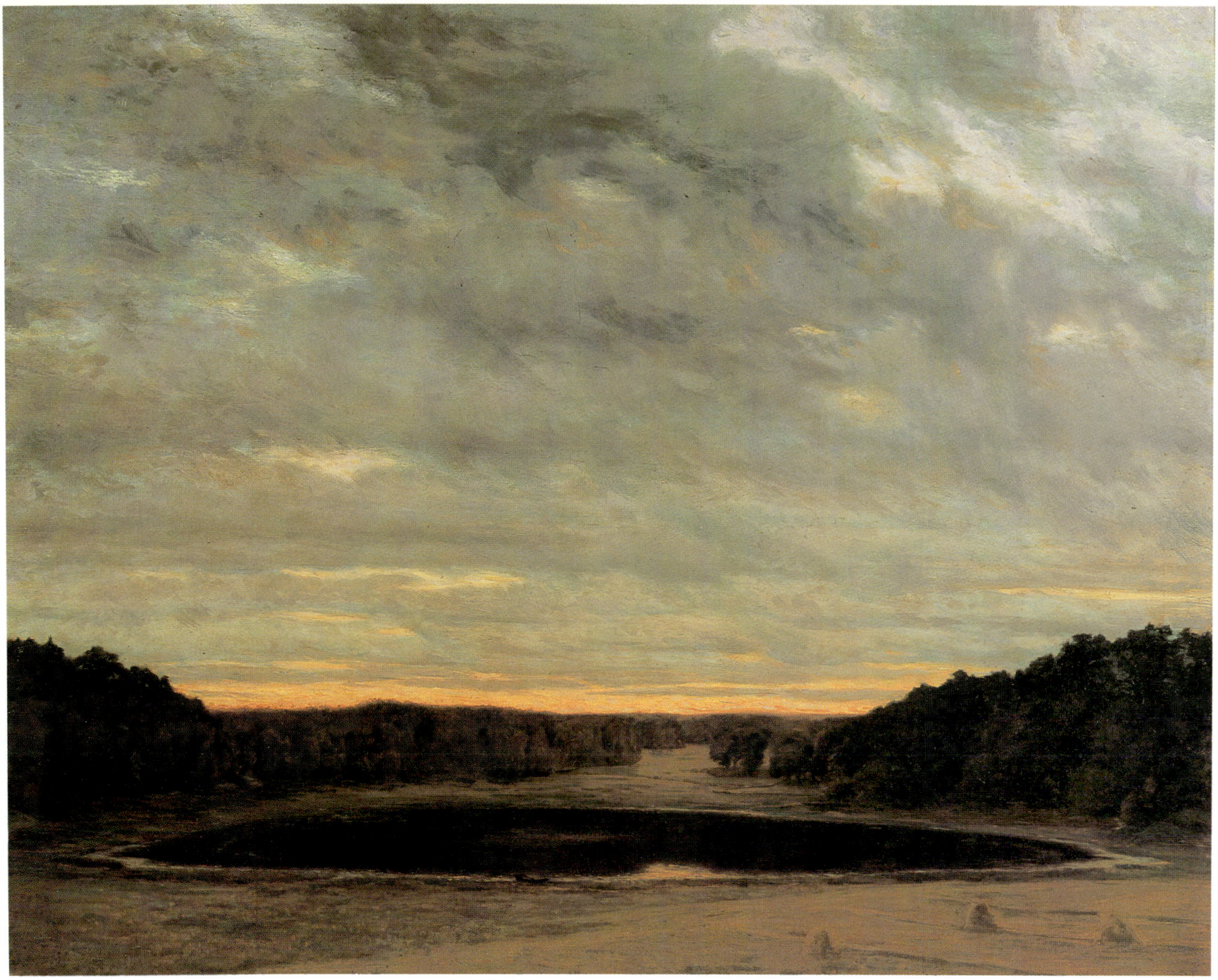

17. Prince Eugen

LUDVIG FIND

1869–1945, Denmark

In 1885 Ludvig Find was apprenticed to a housepainter. At the same time he enrolled at the Technical School in Copenhagen. In 1886, he entered the Royal Academy of Fine Arts, but he was disappointed with the teaching there and left it for the Artists' Study School. Though not a member he was invited to exhibit the present painting (No. 18) at the Free Exhibition in 1896; he became a member in 1898. In 1893 Find had had an important exhibition at the Kleis Gallery and taken part in the Study School's exhibition. He was represented at the Town Hall Exhibition in 1901.

Ludvig Find was close to the circle of the periodical *Taarnet*, and his intimate friendships with the Norwegian painters Thorvald Erichsen and Oluf Wold-Thorne date back to their days at the Study School. They all travelled to Italy on the advice of Kristian Zahrtmann and, possibly (see Slott-Møller), on that of the art historian Julius Lange. Lange's article, *The Hand on the Breast*, in which he discusses a motif in classic art and analyses the psychology of gesture, had been published in 1889 (*Tilskueren*). This essay is important as art history: it is a forerunner of Freud's theory of the unconscious and helped prepare the ground for the introverted portraits of the 1890s.

Find was in Italy for the first time in 1893–4 and again later. His interest in Quattrocento art, however, gave way after the turn of the century to a preference for French art (Bonnard).

18

Portrait of a Young Man. The Norwegian Painter Thorvald Erichsen, 1897

(Portræt af en ung man. Maleren Thorvald Erichsen)

113 × 97.5
Signed lower left: Find 97
Den Hirschsprungske Samling, Copenhagen

In the portrait of Thorvald Erichsen, Find painted his Norwegian colleague seated in the corner of a Danish Neo-Classical sofa and dressed in an old-fashioned black suit. His clenched right hand rests in the open palm of the left on his crossed knees. Light falls from high on the left and idealizes the features so that the 29-year-old artist looks younger than he does in contemporary portraits. The cut of the hair, too, seems with small alterations to have been adapted to the old-fashioned style of the suit. On the grey wall behind the birchwood sofa is a mahogany frame with brown photographs of Taddeo Gaddi's *Presentation of the Virgin*, Masaccio's *Expulsion of Adam and Eve*, and Duccio's *Washing of the Feet*.

It has been shown (*Northern Light*, Cat. no. 16) that the full-size portrait on a Neo-Classical sofa resembles C. W. Eckersberg's portrait of Madam Schmidt (1818, Den Hirschsprungske Samling, Copenhagen), and that Johan Rohde had advised Find to study Eckersberg. Find could have seen the portrait of Madam Schmidt, then privately owned, at the Eckersberg exhibition in 1895. But another Golden Age painter, J. T. Lundbye, probably influenced Find in the choice of costume and haircut, and in the sense of isolation so apparent in the portrait. An exhibition of Lundbye's work took place in 1893 and his illustrated biography appeared in 1895. If Eckersberg stands behind the composition's coolly objective Naturalism and the meticulous brushwork, then Lundbye was the Danish artist who, with his wealth of ideas and melancholy temperament, stood closest to German Romanticism and to the 'friendship portraits'. For this is what this picture must be considered. It was a manifesto not

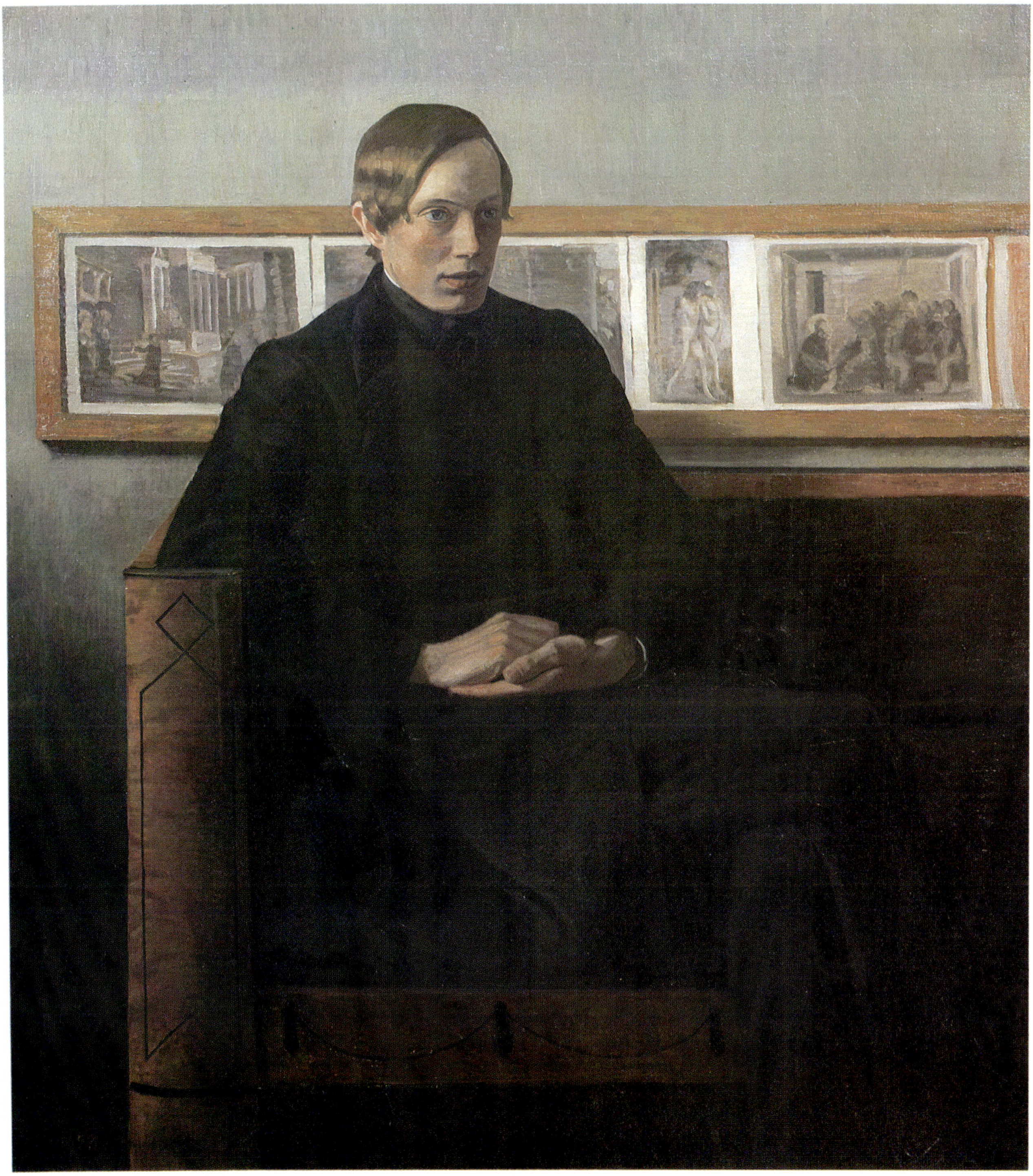

18. Ludvig Find

unusual in Danish and Norwegian art announcing a harkening back to Romanticism, including German Romanticism.

The uncomfortable and outdated Danish Neo-Classical sofa suited the ideology of the Danes. All these ideas and theories on taste are thus contained in this portrait, which is seeking a style. The psychological field of energy lies between the eyes and the hands.

H.W.

GUSTAV FJAESTAD

1868–1948, Sweden

Gustav Fjaestad was born in Stockholm and attended the Royal Academy of Fine Arts in 1891–2. He received further training under two of the leading figures in nineteenth century Swedish art, Bruno Liljefors and Carl Larsson, both of whom he helped with their monumental projects. He made his public breakthrough at the Artists' Union exhibition in 1898 with some of his snowy landscapes. The year before, he had moved from Stockholm to Lake Racken, near Arvika, in the province of Värmland, where he remained for the rest of his life. He worked there, together with his wife Maja, as a painter, craftsman, and cabinetmaker, and gathered around him a circle of artists, the 'Racken group'. Fjaestad was also a well-known athlete. He was an excellent cyclist and skater, and promoted competitive sports, which were beginning to emerge in the 1890s.

His winter landscapes quickly became popular and were often reproduced. Fjaestad had his first one-man show in Stockholm in 1908, and his paintings were highly successful in Berlin in 1914 and in London in 1927.

19

Winter Evening by a River, 1907

(Vinterafton vid en älv)

150 × 185
Signed lower right: G Fjaestad 1907/Wermland
Nationalmuseum, Stockholm
Inv. no.1703

The 1890s were the age of artists' colonies in Sweden. The radical Realists of the '80s, who had turned their backs on Sweden and left for France, Italy and Spain, began to return home at the end of the decade. They moved to different parts of Sweden and claimed them as their artistic domains. Fjaestad, although not one of the former expatriots, followed this migration to the provinces and chose forest-covered Värmland for his own.

With great consistency he cultivated landscape painting in the decorative spirit of Art Nouveau, something which can also be explained by his work as a craftsman. He united the Art Nouveau idiom with a personal form of pointillism in which he reproduced the Swedish forest landscape in its most characteristic Nordic state, winter. He covers the pictorial surface with a rhythmic pattern of dots or lines reminiscent of the technique developed by the Swedish painter Nils Kreuger in the '90s under the influence of Van Gogh's drawings.

Winter Evening by a River has a darker, more dramatic mood than many of Fjaestad's other snow-scapes. The severe limitation of the field of vision forces the viewer visually into the water, which is secret and cold, but also aesthetically appealing. Here we meet a Symbolist mood which has taken the form of Nordic sylvan mysticism, a contemplation of nature's silent and secretive life.

At the same time, Fjaestad created an elegant, decorative work. The horizonless composition is reproduced in a sharply tilted perspective and this, together with the style of drawing, emphasizes the painting's ornamental character. Its decorative quality and its cultivation of impressions from nature inevitably bring to mind Japanese coloured prints. Fjaestad himself worked with woodcuts in the first years of the twentieth century. Because of their decorative stylization he was able to work his pictures in textiles as well. An almost identical version of this motive is found in woven form at the Göteborgs konstmuseum.

T.G.

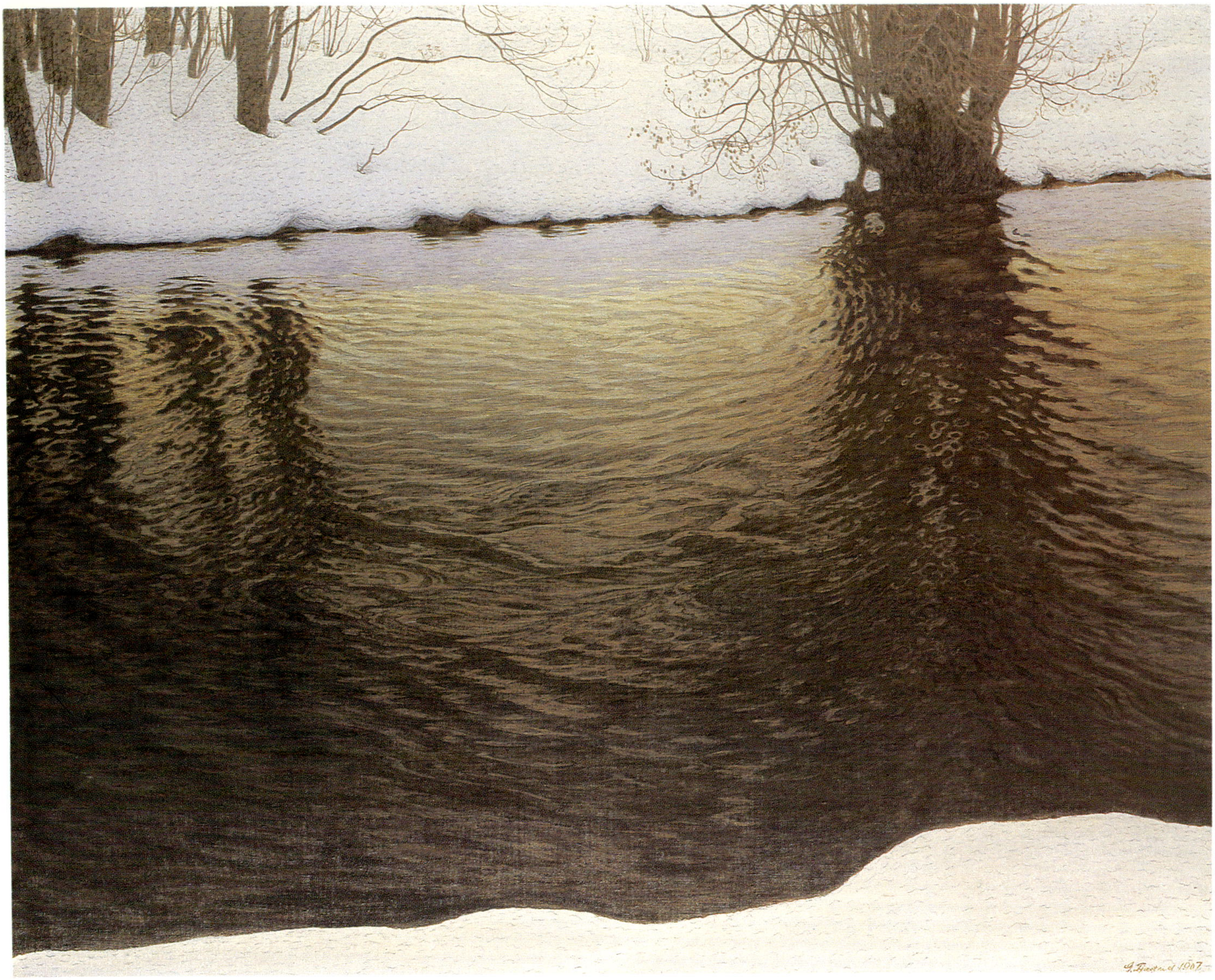

19. Gustaf Fjaestad

AKSELI GALLEN-KALLELA (Axel Gallén until 1904)

1865–1931, Finland

Akseli Gallen-Kallela began to study art in Helsinki in 1881 at the Finnish Fine Art Association and continued at Adolf von Becker's private academy. In the autumn of 1884 he went to Paris to study and attended the Académie Julian and the Académie Cormon, but was perhaps most influenced by other young Scandinavian artists.

Gallen-Kallela's art is a multifaceted reflection of the ideological and artistic developments of his time. He began as a realistic *plein-air* painter in the spirit of Bastien-Lepage, lived in the international Bohemian world of Paris, was caught up in the liberal but national ideologies of the 1880s, gradually shifted to National Romanticism, and finally assumed the role of his country's most radical Symbolist painter in the 1890s.

Gallen-Kallela became interested in Finnish mythology, the *Kalevala* epic, while he was still in Paris. He painted the first version of his large-scale painting *Aino* in 1889, at about the same time as he finished his studies there. In order to find a 'Kalevala sense of reality' for the final painting, he left for Karelia, on Finland's eastern border, in the spring of 1890. This trip started the 'Karelia' movement among Finnish artists: painters, writers, composers travelled to Karelia, where the ancient Finnish world was believed to have remained in its purest form.

After coming face to face with Symbolism and the new stylistic trends on his trip to Paris in the spring of 1892, Gallen-Kallela underwent a crisis in his art. This crisis was aggravated by the writer Adolf Paul's arrival in Finland from Berlin at the end of 1893. In 1894, Gallen-Kallela painted *Symposium*, and at the end of the year he travelled to Berlin. At this stage it became clear to him that the atmosphere of the *Kalevala* could not be captured by realistic means. The Synthetism and Symbolism of the 1890s helped him to find a new form for *Kalevala* subjects: he created highly stylized works which do justice to the heroic, epic world of the *Kalevala* and which also have a clear underlying mystical tone. The need to make his paintings into unified, decorative, monumental entities determined his style of drawing, with its powerful contours, clear surfaces and ornamental patterns.

Gallen-Kallela's influence was not confined to painting. He was a representative of Art Nouveau in Finland in the '90s in a more general way and implemented the idea of the day that different art forms are equally important. His decorative work and his designs for textiles, furniture, metal embossing, and stained glass guided future developments. His woodcuts were the first of their kind in Finnish graphics. He also initiated monumental fresco painting in Finland with his *Kalevala* frescos for the Finnish pavilion at the Paris World Fair in 1900.

The most ambitious of his frescos were the interior decorations for Sigrid Juselius's mausoleum in Pori which were, however, destroyed because of technical problems soon after they were finished. Later, in the twentieth century, Gallen-Kallela underwent still another change, towards a new use of colour in the spirit of Expressionism. He had contacts with German Expressionism and the artists of the Die Brücke group, sought new inspiration from the primitive art of East Africa, and in the 1920s made an extended visit to the United States, combining influences from Indian culture with Finnish ornamentation. This merging of sources of inspiration yielded interesting results in the mammoth plan of his last years, to illustrate the whole of the *Kalevala*.

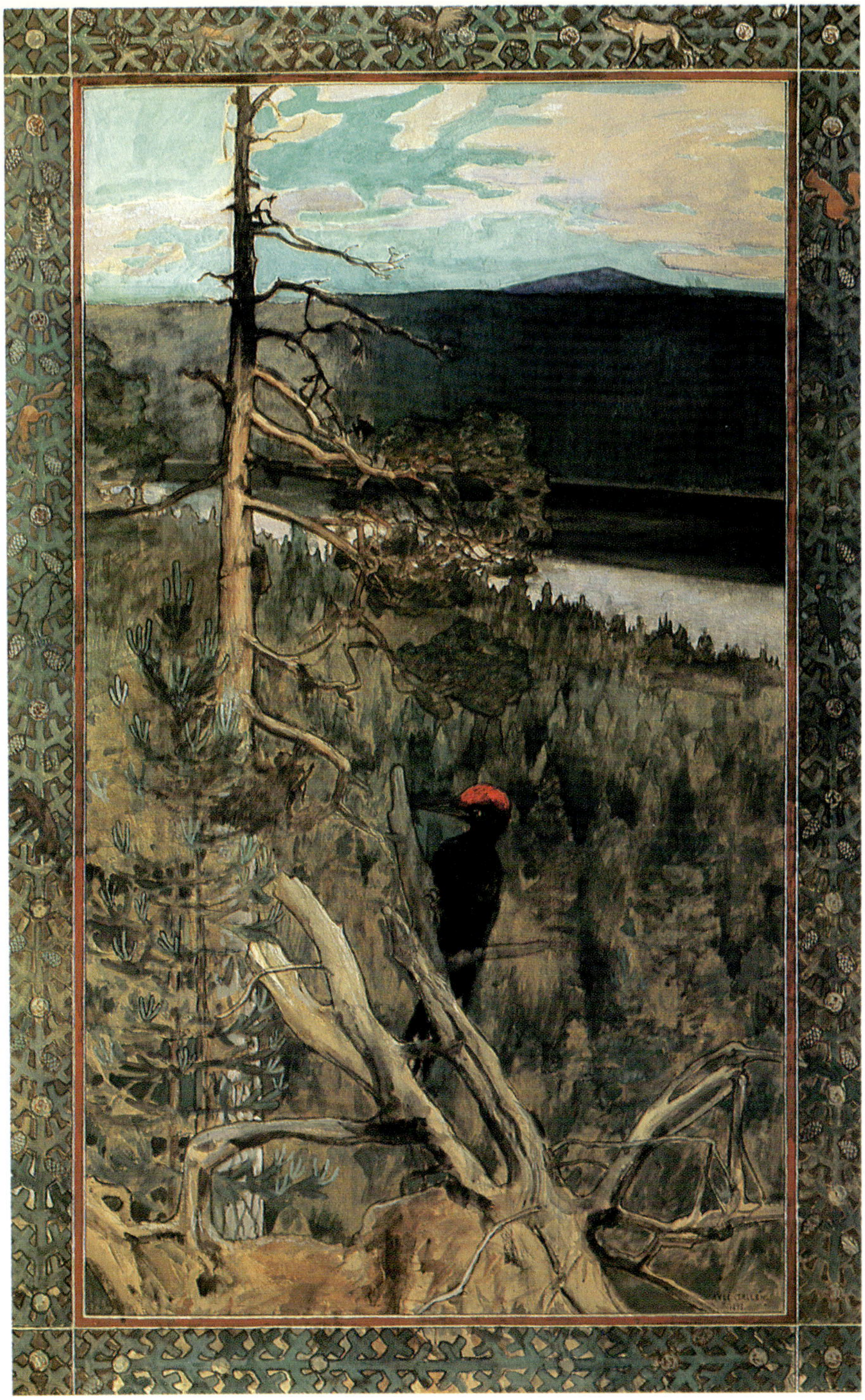

20. Akseli Gallen-Kallela

20

The Great Black Woodpecker (Wilderness), 1893

(Palokärki, Erämaa)

Gouache on carton, 144 × 89
Signed lower right: Axel Gallén/1893
Prof. Kai Otto Donner, Helsinki

After Gallen-Kallela had visited Paris in 1892, studied the new Symbolist trends in art, and received indifferent reviews at the Champ-de-Mars Salon for his *Aino*, he travelled to Kuusamo, in North Karelia, as if to seek a cure for a dangerous illness. In the profound peace of the wilderness, he found his balance again. He became part of nature as only the northern artist was able to. He experienced its pantheistic power. Gallen-Kallela himself later described the birth of the work:

> In order to see Nuorunen fell better, I went up the high boulders behind Rajala farm in Paanajärvi. I tried with binoculars to view the pink cliffs of Nuorunen. To the right I could see the crest of Vaskivaara, from whose slope gold-coloured, copper-green and dark-blue pieces of ore had been blasted out and rolled here and there in the forest. The wilderness atmosphere rules supreme here, since one does not see a trace of any settlement, and in the background there are uninhabited wilds which stretch all the way to Lapland.
>
> The great black woodpecker has always been my friend. Every time I hear its fresh, shrill voice, I get the feeling that I am so far from all human settlement that I have no contact with it – even though this might happen right in my backyard. I shot a great black woodpecker very reluctantly, because I love this bird and am glad that now it is a protected species. I shot it to use as a model, since I wanted to have it on this picture to strengthen the impression of the loneliness of the wilderness. The great black woodpecker's red crown is the individual's cry for life in the silence of the wilderness.

The Great Black Woodpecker is one of the first Finnish landscapes of the 1890s to have political and nationalistic overtones. The new stylistic features of the times are evident in the dramatic stylization of the trees and in the decorative ornamentation of the border.

S.S-K.

21

Waterfall at Mäntykoski, 1892–4

(Mäntykoski)

270 × 156
Not signed
Private Collection, Helsinki

'The waterfall's surge sang incessantly in my ears; the light night wove its dreams . . .' wrote Gallen-Kallela of the area where he painted *The Great Black Woodpecker* in the summer of 1892. 'Waterfalls have a magnetic effect', he noted to a journalist who visited his studio at the beginning of the next year. And so he chose this waterfall at Mäntykoski as his main task for the summer of 1892 and used what at the time was an immensely large canvas, almost three metres high. His aim was ambitious: to depict the powerful force of nature, the waterfall's mysterious and suggestive 'spirit', just as his Swedish fellow artist Ernst Josephson had done in his *Water Sprite*.

The point of departure was a deep involvement with the mysticism of nature. But before the painting had taken on the form it now has and in which it was seen for the first time at the Exhibition of Finnish Artists in 1894, it went through many transformations. The painting's history as seen in different drafts, and today in the painting itself thanks to modern technical means, shows the difficult road Gallen-Kallela travelled from 'nature romantic' to Symbolist artist.

Attention has been drawn to the painting's decorative, tapestry-like quality, but the depiction of the rocky landscape and the rushing water does not differ greatly from Gallen-Kallela's earlier landscape technique. The large dimensions led only to the use of broader brushes. The move closer to Symbolism was seen in a transitionary stage of the work in which there was an allegorical figure, the 'spirit' of the rapids, depicted as a nymph playing a harp, and the 'listener', a bard, sitting on the shore. The work had the romantic nature of an ancient rune. It reflected the spirit of the old incantations in which the 'power of the rapids' had its own special effect.

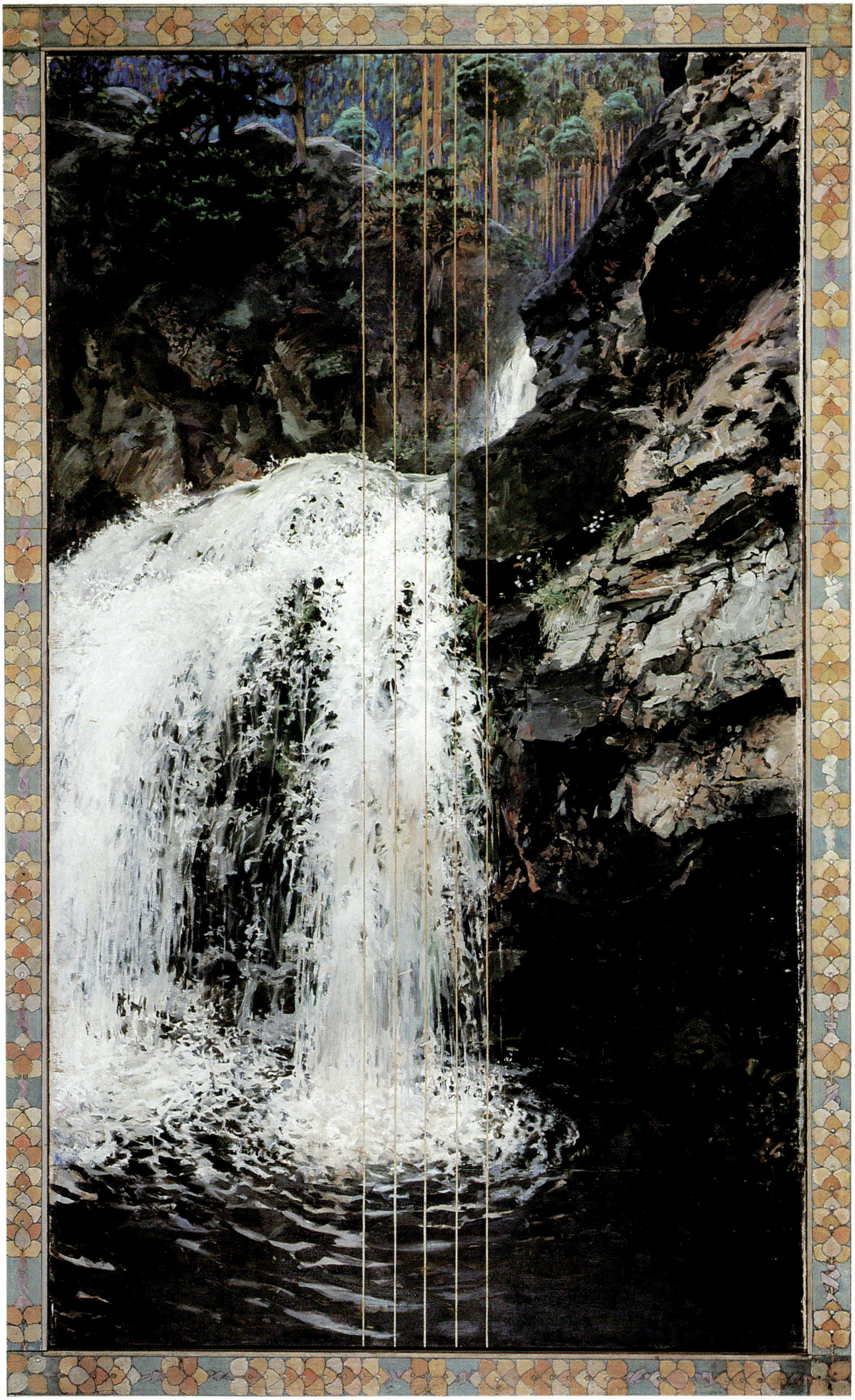

21. Akseli Gallen-Kallela

Gallen-Kallela soon realized that these allegorical figures did not suit the spirit of the times, and he removed them from the painting. Later on he turned the 'listener by the waterfall' into a marvellously evocative graphic work.

Of nature's harp, only the golden strings are left. These change the roar of the waterfall into a great symphony of nature, wonderful music which mournfully touches the strings of the human soul. It joins together past and present and lets the listener sense something for which no means of expression is found, something outside and above him.

Gallen-Kallela designed an ornamental inner frame for *Waterfall at Mäntykoski* as well as for *The Great Black Woodpecker*, which led the critics to compare the work to a tapestry. However, the 'tapestry style' which is found in Gallen-Kallela's later *Kalevala* paintings had not yet been mastered. The critic Eliel Aspelin, a personal friend of Gallen-Kallela's, saw the work as an unresolved conflict between old and new, between realistic, often carefully detailed depictions and metaphorical elements.

S.S-K.

22

Symposium (The Problem), 1894

(Symposion/Probleema)

74 × 99
Signed lower left (in monogram): AGK
Private Collection, Helsinki

This work, known today as *Symposium*, was originally titled *The Problem*, in reference to the painting's Symbolist content. Later the artist gave it a more realistic name which refers in particular to Plato's *Symposium*. After dinner, over their drinks, the artist and his friends discussed, as the ancients did, 'the deepest questions of life'. The group, all members of the Young Finland movement of the late 1880s, have gathered at their favourite meeting-place, a private dining-room at the Hotel Kämp. The leader of the symposium seated at the head of the table is the composer Robert Kajanus. The other participants are Jean Sibelius (foreground), Oskar Merikanto (head resting on the table), and Gallen-Kallela himself (upper left). The programme of the Young Finland movement was liberal, but highly Finnophile and nationalistic. They believed in the great future flowering of art, the 'Finnish Renaissance'.

'Now we must begin to create a new Renaissance in little Finland', Gallen-Kallela wrote in his diary. In around 1893, the new mystical ideology of the day had begun to unsettle the group's belief in the power of realism. When the cosmopolitan writer Adolf Paul, a friend of Strindberg and Edvard Munch, arrived from Berlin in the autumn of 1893, the situation shown in *Symposium* was ripe for change. The mood was described by Eino Leino, another member of the group.

> All old religious ideas are awakening and a time of new mysticism, new occult doctrines, invocations of the spirits and star-gazing wafts through the intellectual life of the end of the century . . . The human spirit once again feels the need to fall on its knees before the great unknown spirit of the world. The grizzled heroes of the period of enlightenment, such as Georg Brandes, warned us in vain of this new reactionary trend. It is coming indeed and will not leave anyone untouched.

Gallen-Kallela described the picture in a letter of 1894 to Robert Kajanus:

> Three men are sitting at a table covered with bottles and glasses. One of them, who appears to be leading the discussion at the head of the table, seems to be explaining some profound matter convincingly and peacefully. In order to give emphasis to his words, he raises his hand, which holds a dying cigar butt, and beats time with it to his words. Then he directs his gaze before him more intently, the eyelids which so far have been half-closed open, and he is just drawing the

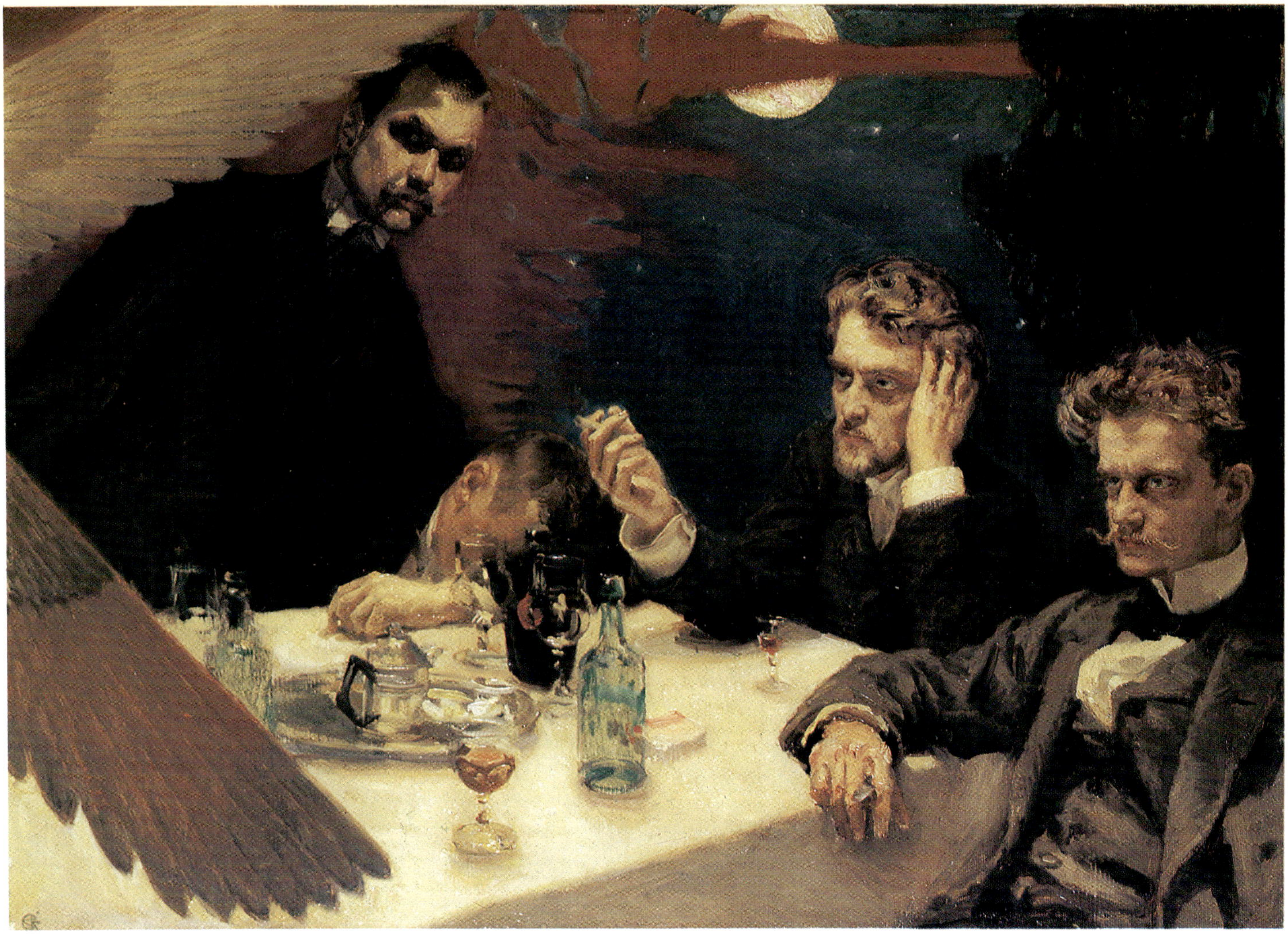

22. *Akseli Gallen-Kallela*

> others' attention to what he sees when they all shout in chorus, expressing their joy at seeing the beautiful vision . . . And what they see! I do not want to say any more . . .

Gallen-Kallela depicted the mystical vision in the flutter of the wings of the Egyptian god Osiris on the left of the picture. In the star-studded sky in the background, behind blood-red clouds, we can see the planet Jupiter, and on the right, above Sibelius' head, is a 'dark, fabulous tree on whose top the free winds of the world play their eternal songs of power'. These are the words of Kasimir Leino, a poet member of the group, giving a Nordic variation of Baudelaire's '*forêts de symboles*'.

In a draft for the painting, now in the Collection of the Gösta Serlachiuksen taidesäätiö in Mänttä, a flayed sphinx was originally placed where the wings are today, and the astral body of a human being was seen in front of Jupiter. Gallen-Kallela's fellow artist Albert Edelfelt criticized this draft, and this probably led to the changes made in the painting. Gallen-Kallela later cut out the sphinx from the draft as well.

Stylistically, *Symposium* is a transitional work in which the realistic still-life of the foreground is combined with a Synthetist-Symbolist treatment of the background.

The work caused a tremendous scandal when it was exhibited in Helsinki in 1894. This embittered Gallen-Kallela. Soon afterwards he left for Berlin at the instigation of Adolf Paul, fleeing, as Paul said, the 'patriotic naiad' of his home country.

However, *Symposium* remains his main work from the brief period during which Gallen-Kallela tried to play the role of the world citizen.

S.S-K.

23

The Defence of the Sampo, 1896

(Sammon puolustus)

Tempera on canvas, 122 × 125
Signed lower left: Axel Gallén Kallela. 1896.
Turun taidemuseo, Turku/Åbo konstmuseum, Åbo

The Defence of the Sampo was the first of Gallen-Kallela's large works, together with *Lemminkäinen's Mother*, to be exhibited in Finland after *Symposium* received such catastrophic reviews. The story of the *Kalevala* epic was familiar to the Finnish public and the work's stylistic features aroused particular interest. *The Forging of the Sampo* was like a revelation to the builders of the Finnish 'Renaissance'. Finally a form had been found, sufficiently strong, sufficiently estranged, sufficiently powerful, to give shape to the ancient shamanistic wisdom of the nation.

The picture shows the decisive battle between two tribes for a magical machine, the mysterious Sampo, which brings luck. The *Kalevala*'s hero, Wäinämöinen, together with his men, had recovered the Sampo from his arch-enemy Louhi, 'the toothless mistress of Pohjola'. The Sampo was taken back in a rowing-boat to its home, to bring wealth and happiness to the inhabitants of Kalevala. Louhi then set off in a sailing-boat to recover her lost treasure. The storm raised by Wäinämöinen destroyed the sails and the boat was torn asunder. But Louhi was transformed into a bird, taking the sides of the boat as her wings, and its oars as her tail. Gallen-Kallela's *The Defence of the Sampo* retells the story of the ensuing battle. Louhi, 'with her thousand men', has caught up with the Ossianic hero Wäinämöinen. The fierce battle is explosively dense in form and the few fighters give the impression of large groups. The furious Wäinämöinen strikes out with his sword, Lemminkäinen with his axe, Louhi with her spear. For those who do not know the story, one should perhaps reveal the outcome: the Sampo fell into the water; Wäinämöinen gathered up pieces of it, but Louhi got nothing.

Gallen-Kallela's *The Defence of the Sampo* is not entirely a product of his imagination, for the hybrid Louhi's features are fairly carefully described in the *Kalevala*. But the visual form the picture takes is naturally Gallen-Kallela's creation. There is no doubt that the hero is Wäinämöinen, not Louhi.

The Defence of the Sampo is Gallen-Kallela's first work to be carried out systematically in 'tapestry style'. A private patron had commissioned four decorative paintings for the wall panels in his dining-room and Gallen-Kallela's picture was to occupy one panel. The task admirably suited the ideals of the late 1890s about tempera and fresco paintings. The canvas was specially made out of rustic linen, and tempera, which was absorbed matt into the cloth, was chosen as the medium.

Stylization reinforced the impression that it was a decoration and not a painting in the traditional sense. The outlines were heavily emphasized; the composition was dense. The colours were decorative in an unreal manner, the colour surfaces filled by ornamental figures. It is not surprising that some critics would have liked to see the paintings as tapestries. And no wonder that the patron who commissioned the decorations for his fairly small dining-room could not use them in his home.

Finnish Art Nouveau, as a general style, was, however, emerging. Gallen-Kallela himself created a series of *Kalevala* paintings in the same spirit. The style moved towards decorative art. It lent features to architecture and to the Finnish national romantic style of the turn of the century.

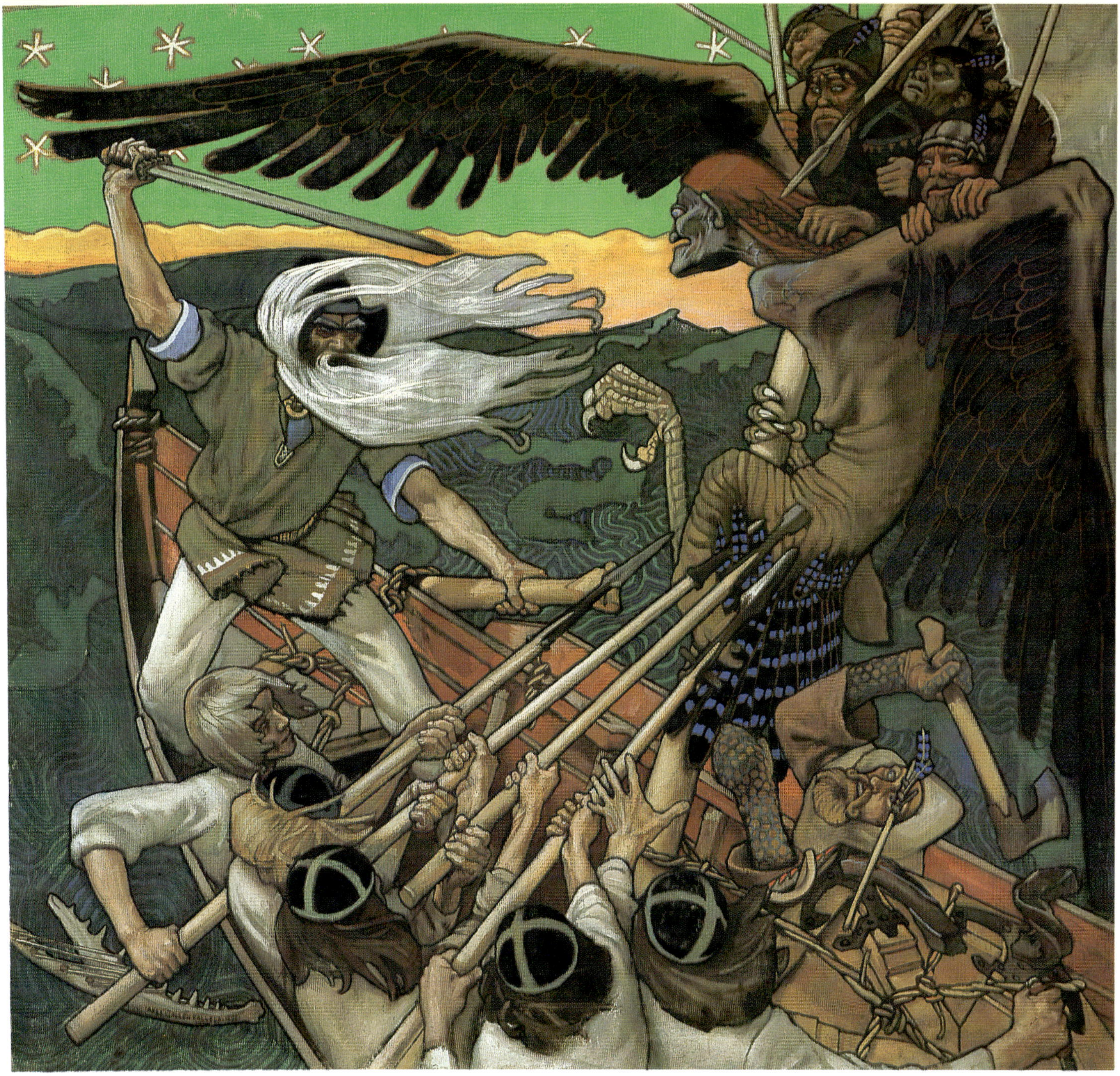

23. *Akseli Gallen-Kallela*

The Defence of the Sampo was given a surprisingly positive reception. It seemed finally to decide the question of whether a sufficiently decorative pictorial form could be found for ancient Finnish mythology. The work was shown at the Stockholm Exhibition in 1897. It was at the Munich Secessionists' exhibition the following year, and later represented the national style typical of Scandinavia at the programmatic exhibitions of turn-of-the-century art on the Continent.

The artist wanted to keep the work and its companion piece, *Joukahainen's Revenge*, in his possession. It was not until 1901 and 1904 that they were purchased by the Turun taidemuseo.

S.S-K.

24

Joukahainen's Revenge, 1897

(Joukahaisen kosto)

Tempera on canvas, 125 × 130
Signed lower left: Axel Gallen-Kallela 1897,
Turun taidemuseo, Turku, Åbo konstmuseum, Åbo
Inv. no. 81 (purchased in 1904)

Joukahainen's Revenge is a pair to *The Defence of the Sampo*. The mood and colouring are, however, completely different. *The Defence of the Sampo* depicts a battle, while *Joukahainen's Revenge* is a study of bitter hatred.

Externally, *Joukahainen's Revenge* has a more harmonious palette: yellow, grey, yellowish green and indigo. Nothing could be more pleasing than this harmony of colours. None the less, the work met with the same fate at the hands of its prospective owner as *The Defence of the Sampo*. It was never placed on the walls of the private home for which it had been commissioned.

In this case, the reason is probably the subject-matter. *Joukahainen's Revenge* depicts the repressed hatred of primitive man for the one who is the cause of his unhappiness. Joukahainen wanted to kill the great hero of the *Kalevala*, Wäinämöinen, because he had beaten him in a debate on wisdom and won the love of his sister.

The stifling hate, the threat of revenge which the unhappy mother tries to avert, the feeling of hopelessness—and the artist's knowledge that vengeance will never be carried out... all this can be found in *Joukahainen*. The style of execution is the same as in *The Defence of the Sampo*.

Interesting is the general atmosphere, the way in which internalized pain is brought out. The feeling is more reserved but, in its silent immobility, is even more intense than in *The Defence of the Sampo*. The details in the landscape emphasize the mood: the line of the horizon continues Joukahainen's gaze into infinity; the willow leaves whipped by the wind on the shore set the melancholy tone; the great boulder is like 'a bursting heart'. The landscape is the most disconsolate in the North: the dark, oppressive time of the first wet snowfall in October–November. The work's ethnographic details are correct, but they do not 'steal' from the overall mood of melancholy.

S.S-K.

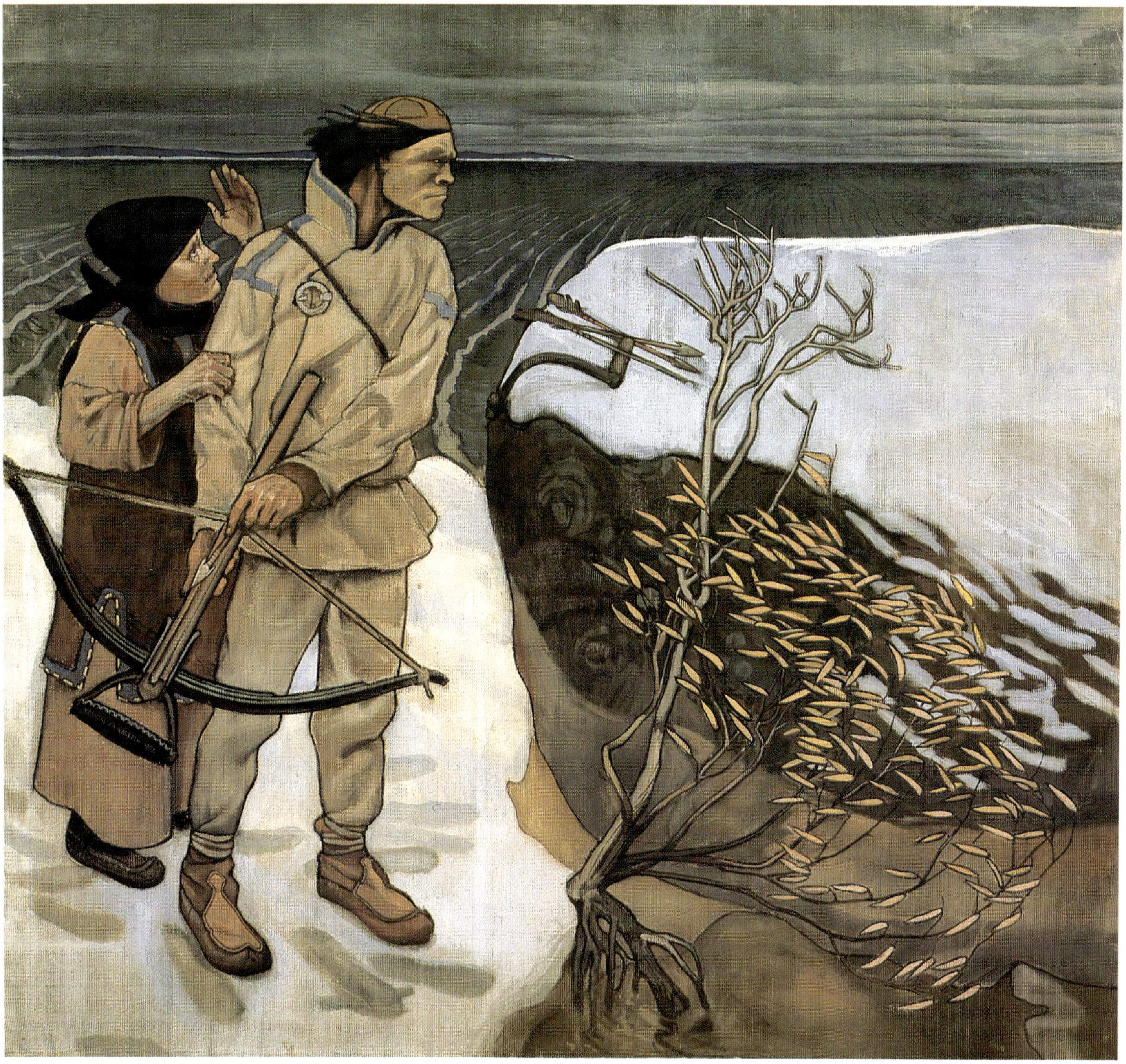

24. Akseli Gallen-Kallela

25

Lemminkäinen's Mother, 1897

(Lemminkäisen äiti)

Tempera on canvas, 85 × 118
Signed lower left on the skull: Axel Gallén-Kalela/1897.
(Antell Collection) Ateneumin taidemuseo, Helsinki
Inv. no. AA I 640 (purchased in 1898)

The most fundamental questions in *Lemminkäinen's Mother* are those of life and the ultimate aim of art. Lemminkäinen, hero and poet, wanted to master the secret of death by shooting the swan of Tuonela, the kingdom of death. Now he lies defeated beside the blood-red stones of Tuonela. The swan, the symbol of death's eternal secret, swims away majestically on the dark river. We know that Gallen-Kallela intended this symbolism because of his many comments on the painting.

> He is lying on the ground, greenly pale beside the black water, from which the swan, with a taunting lift to its neck, is swimming away. The golden shimmering rays of the sun give the mother hope, and she sends a bee to fetch balsam from the source of the rays. The deathly bitter herbs, with their pale flowers and blue-black berries, grow among the remnants of a human body.

The artist's attitude is shown perhaps even more clearly in a letter to the poet K. A. Tavaststjerna, 'Dare I tell you any more that I am still fighting in my Tuonela with my pink swan? If only I could steal even one single pink feather from its tail! I would give it to Lemminkäinen . . .'

Gallen-Kallela's portrait of his own mother, in the Nationalmuseum in Stockholm, was created at the same time as *Lemminkäinen's Mother*. Gallen-Kallela had asked his mother to sit as a model for *Lemminkäinen*. She had an inclination for theosophy and was an interesting companion for him on his mystical travels of the imagination. 'My own mother, my wise, intelligent and contemplative mother is here and I, the fruit of her womb, am teaching her everything that my senses have found out.'

In order to get his mother's face to express real pain, Gallen-Kallela told her horrifying stories as he painted.

Lemminkäinen's Mother is, as a whole, perhaps the most profound example of Gallen-Kallela's *Kalevala* mysticism, which linked the Finnish national epic with the oldest myths of mankind. The painting thus combines a universal mysticism with Finnish national aspirations, and in form as well as content is a masterly work of art.

S.S-K.

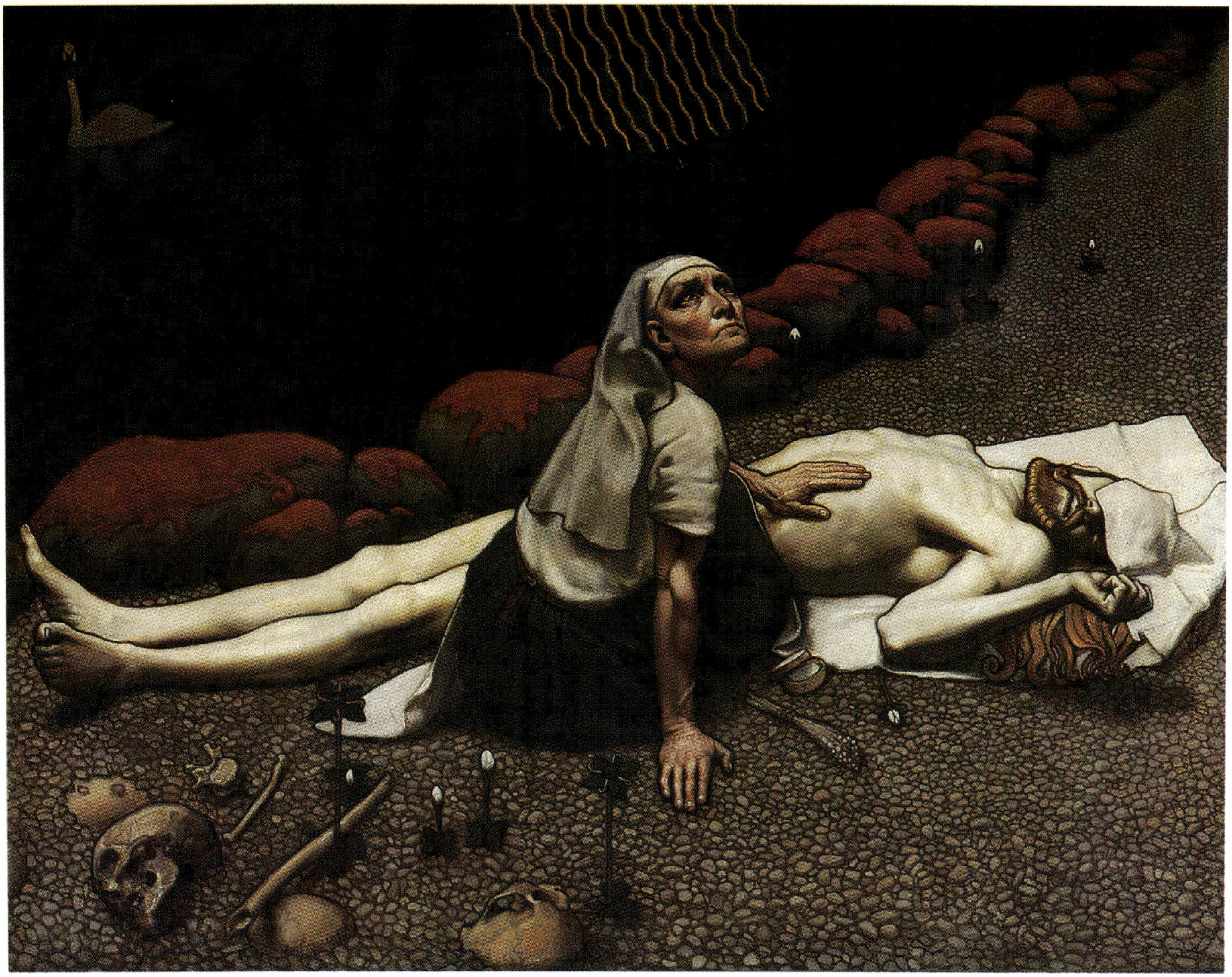

25. Akseli Gallen-Kallela

PEKKA HALONEN

1865–1933, Finland

Pekka Halonen came from a farming family and was keenly aware of his own character as an artist. Even though he was a member of the same generation as Gallen-Kallela, he did not begin his studies in Finland until 1886. He travelled to Paris for the first time in 1891, together with the younger artists Magnus Enckell and Ellen Thesleff, who soon joined the Synthetists and Symbolists in their admiration for the works of Puvis de Chavannes. From 1891 to 1892, Halonen studied at the Académie Julian but retained his realistic style and consciously stayed away from the modernistic trends of the day. However, this did not prevent him from joining Finland's national romantic movement, Karelianism, like Gallen-Kallela. He, too, made a trip in 1892 to Karelia, which was believed to be the birthplace of Finnish folklore. But his own roots lay in the soil of his own district of Central Finland.

When Halonen was in Paris for the second time in the winter of 1893, he became fascinated by theosophy, which interested almost all the Scandinavian artists studying in Paris at the time. In Finland, he had already studied the practical Christian theology of the Russian writer Leo Tolstoy, and both these religious philosophies were reflected in a spiritual crisis he experienced at this time. At the beginning of 1894, he became a pupil of Paul Gauguin for a short time. What he principally adopted from his teacher was a strong Synthetist style and an interest in the monumental power of art. This interest took him on a study trip to Italy in 1896. At the turn of the century, his art had a monumental quality, which can be seen in *Wilderness* and even more in the decorative panel paintings *Washing on the Ice* and *Lynx Hunter* executed for the Finnish pavilion at the 1900 Paris World Fair.

Gradually, however, Finland's landscape, in all its stark beauty, became increasingly important to him, and he ranks as one of the period's most important portrayers of Finnish nature. Most of his landscapes are peaceful winter or spring scenes in which he captured the essence of the Finnish countryside.

26

The Kantele Player, 1892

(Kanteleensoittaja)

53 × 51
Signed lower left: P. Halonen. 1892.
Mrs Inger Korkeakivi, Oulu

Halonen's *The Kantele Player* is an excellent example of Finland's national romanticism, also called Karelianism, at the beginning of the 1890s. The painting was done on a trip to Karelia, in a dark log cabin. Halonen made his trip in 1892, between two years of studies in Paris. His technique shows no signs of the Synthetist influence. Perhaps the best description of how he fell under the spell of folk music is given in a letter he wrote to his fiancée:

> At the moment I am painting an old man playing a kantele. I have been at his cabin for three days and you can't imagine how wonderful it is ... This is where I have spent the most pleasant times here in Ruskeala. I know that you would be enchanted to see it if you were here.
>
> The man looks very old and the kantele is just as old. The cabin is small but neat, with little windows, and straw on the floor and drying on the beams. The big room is the lightest place, the grey old man in his shirt sleeves is in the corner behind the table.

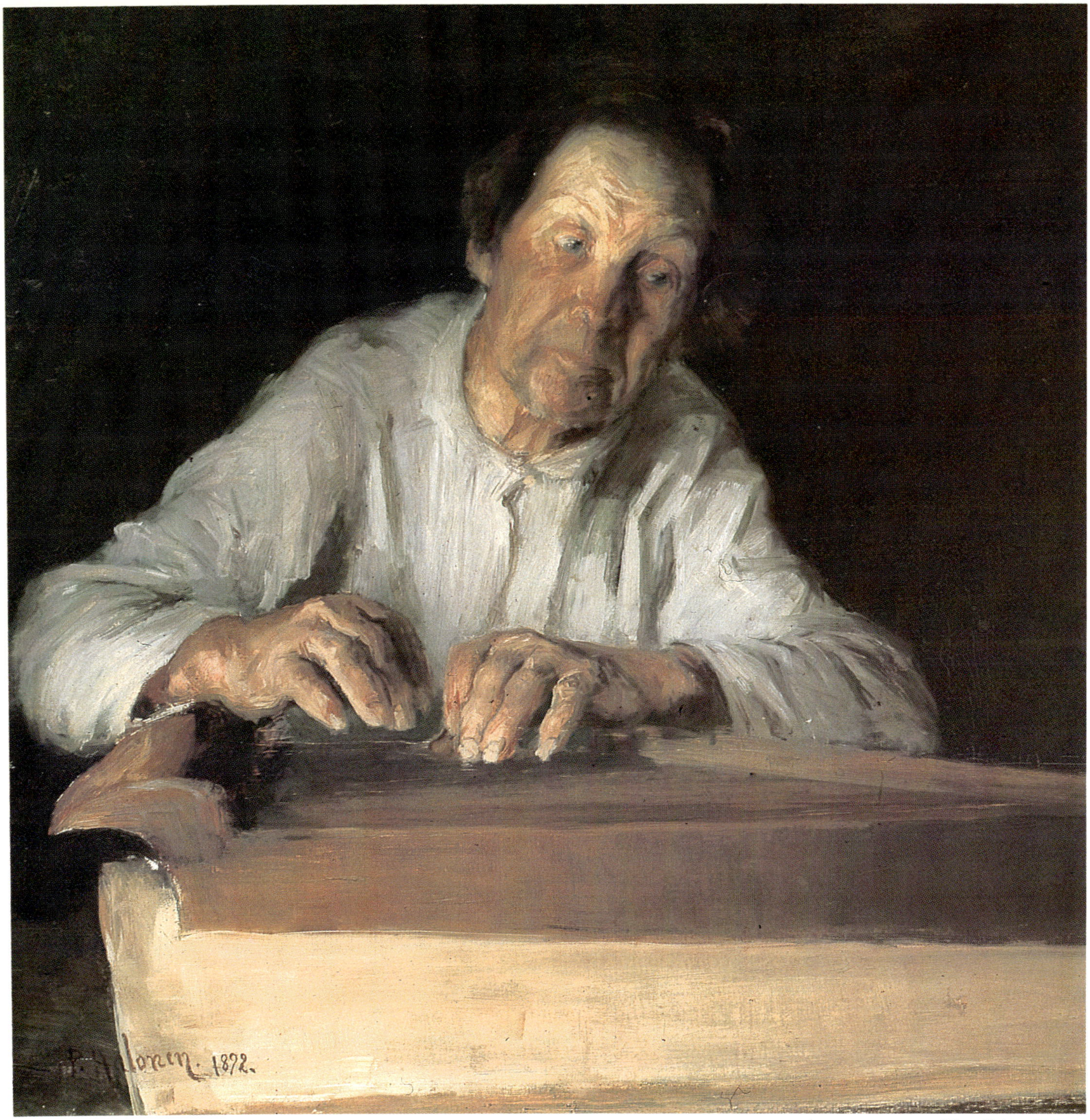

26. Pekka Halonen

When he strikes his shaky kantele with his work-worn fingers, then everything in the room is in harmony. I can't help myself: I have to take off my jacket just like the old man. And then when he gets to his favorite melody, a strange expression flits over his face and the frozen glow of his eyes seems to look back through the decades to the days of his youth and dreams, back to all kinds of adventures during his life. It is so strange to see that I have to turn my head away, because my eyes fill with tears. This is what I'm trying to do, but it is so very difficult that it's probably not possible. Especially since that expression lasts such a very short time.

S.S-K.

27

Wilderness, Karelian Landscape, 1899

(Erämaa, Karjalainen maisema)

110×55.5
Signed lower right: P. Halonen/1899
Turun taidemuseo, Turku/Åbo konstmuseum, Åbo
Inv. no. 45 (purchased in 1899)

Pekka Halonen's *Wilderness* has direct links with Gallen-Kallela's *The Great Black Woodpecker* which created the basic form for this heroic Finnish landscape type. The original name of *The Great Black Woodpecker* was also *Wilderness*. Gallen-Kallela's work should be examined against the background of his shocked reaction to French Symbolism, and as a flight from the decadence of Paris into the purity and peace of the virgin Finnish wilderness. Halonen's *Wilderness* is just as patriotic, but has a more political tone. In both paintings, the untouched Finnish landscape is presented as the symbol of Finnish primitive strength. Pekka Halonen was reacting against the political pressure exerted by Russia at the time. The despair caused by prevailing conditions and the strengthening of Finnish self-esteem which soon swept through artists' circles are reflected in a letter written by Halonen to Emil Wikström in 1899. 'We no longer exist!' he wrote, but a positive note followed: 'The Finnish people are as tough as juniper; we can't be beaten by so little... The land and the nation will live! We are God's chosen people who have a mission to mankind.' Halonen's letter has a direct reference to the collection of patriotic short stories by Juhani Aho published at the same time, *Katajainen kansani* (My Nation like Juniper). What could not be expressed directly because of censorship was said metaphorically in art, in essays, paintings, and music. For example, Sibelius' *Finlandia* was created at the same time with the same emotions in mind.

S. S-K.

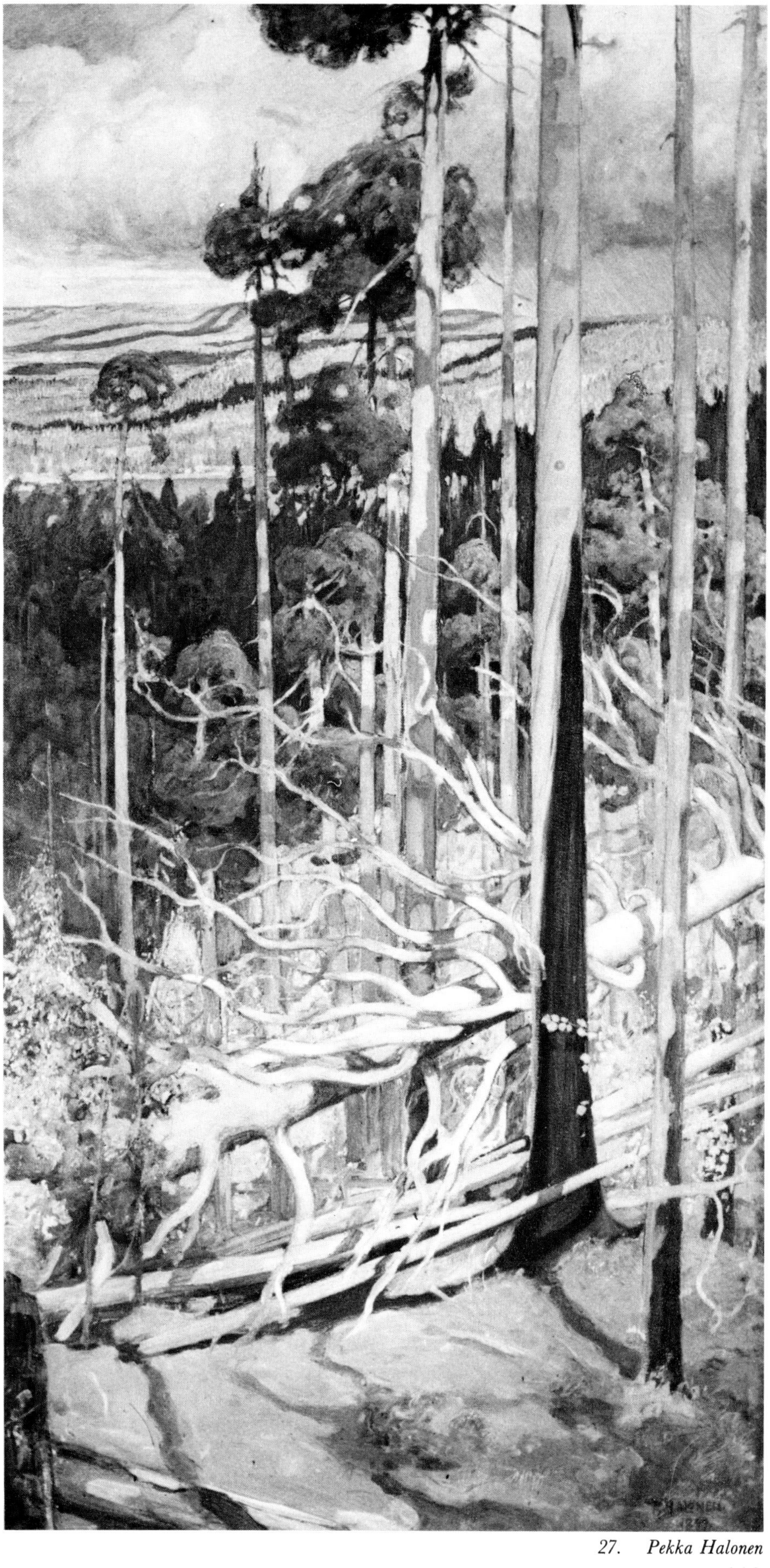

27. Pekka Halonen

28

Washing on the Ice, 1900

(Avannolla)

125×180
Not signed
(Antell Collection) Ateneumin taidemuseo, Helsinki
Inv. no. A I 781/11 (purchased in 1902)

A series of panel paintings, all the same size and portraying Finnish landscapes and ways of life, was commissioned from Finnish artists for the Finnish pavilion at the Paris World Fair. Pekka Halonen's *Washing on the Ice* and *Lynx Hunter* were two of these paintings.

The very use to which the paintings were put dictated a simplification of style which is especially clear in *Lynx Hunter*. *Washing on the Ice* gives a softer view of the landscape. The woman working at her wash stands out sharply against the soft village setting encircling the shore in the winter dusk.

In these two paintings, Halonen consciously worked to achieve a pure simplicity. They are, in fact, a kind of synthesis of all the efforts towards monumentalism in Finnish art in the 1890s. A clear source was the monumental art of Puvis de Chavannes, whom Finnish artists had admired since the beginning of the 1890s. Halonen's works recall in particular Puvis's *Winter*, painted for the Hôtel de Ville in Paris. It attracted special attention in 1892, and Halonen had the opportunity to see it in Paris. These early memories were combined with the powerful influences of early Renaissance frescos which Halonen later saw in Italy. His studies in Gauguin's studio in 1894 also helped him to develop in this direction.

Halonen said he achieved monumentalism by stylizing the colours of the landscape, the positions of the figures, and the rhythm of forms in such a way that the effect from a distance was one of peace and harmony.

When Halonen saw his paintings in place on the walls of the pavilion, he wrote to a friend in Finland,

> We must all work to create for Finland great, honest art that is our own. We will do it if only we are all interested in the cause . . . Clear evidence of it is our art here in Paris. We will soon have our own modest and honest art if only we are allowed to continue in peace. Finnish art really does seem very good here alongside the other artificial and superficial art (letter to J. J. Tikkanen, 1 April 1900).

S. S-K.

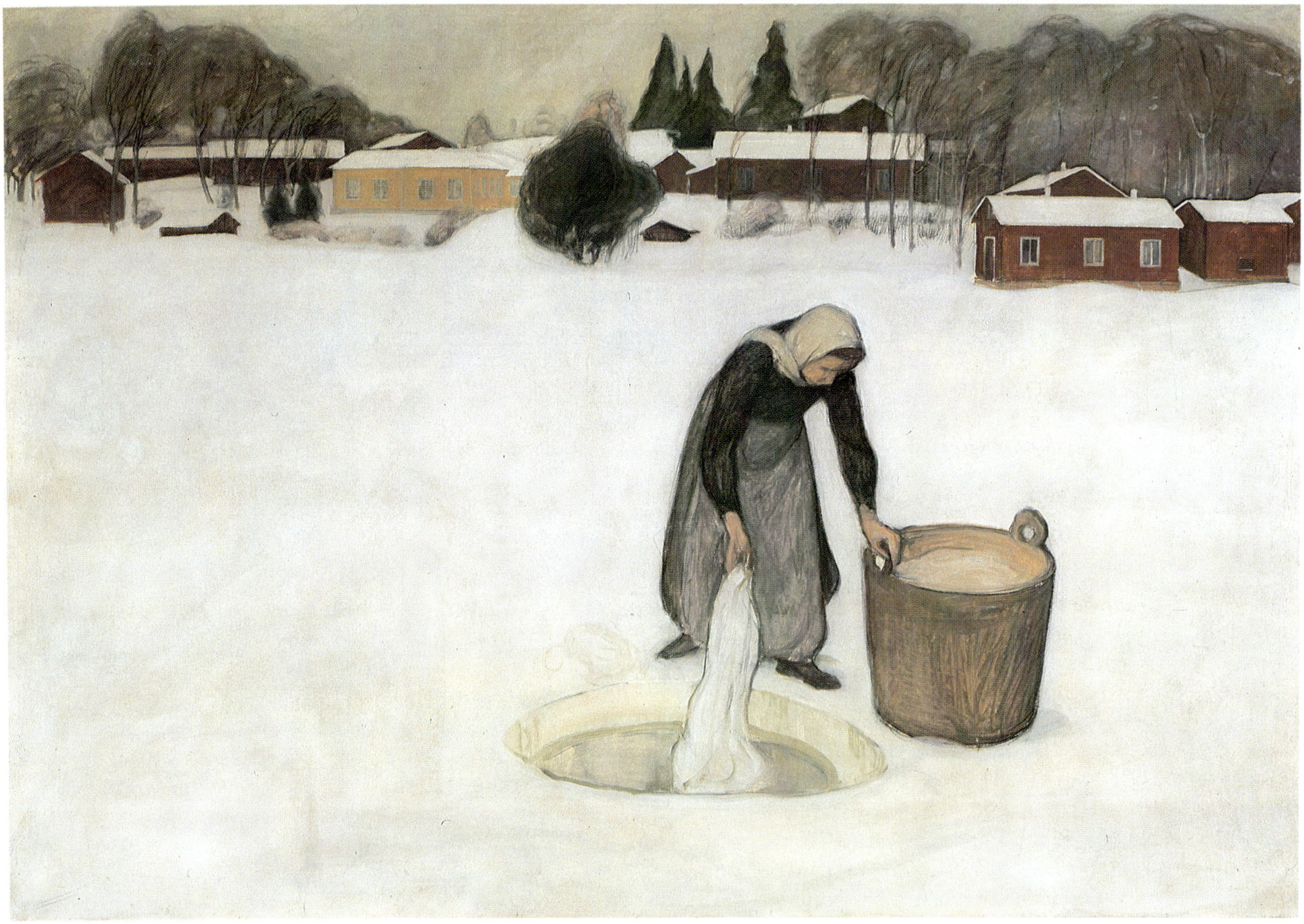

28. Pekka Halonen

VILHELM HAMMERSHØI

1864–1916, Denmark

As a child Hammershøi received private instruction in drawing before being accepted at the Royal Academy of Fine Arts, which he attended from 1879 to 1884. During the last two years, he was also a pupil at the Artists' Study School (Krøyer).

Even though his style and technique in the middle of the 1880s did not differ greatly from those of the typical painters of the decade, his psychological conception is more characteristic of the 1890s and was not always understood by his contemporaries. In fact, a portrait of his sister in 1885 (Den Hirchsprungske Samling, Copenhagen) was rejected for the Neuhausen Prize; the first step was then taken towards the creation of the Free Exhibition, of which Hammershøi was a founding member (see p. 36). His palette was already a harmonious tonality of grey from soft black, of which he was a true master, to white, accentuated by warmer colours. His interiors from the 1880s show that he had mastered the dramatic leap from intense darkness to full light; and in drawings, with a few deep black lines he could make the white paper vibrate with extraordinary illuminary power.

Hammershøi travelled to the Netherlands and Belgium in 1887. In 1889 he exhibited four pictures at the Paris World Fair and had his first opportunity to see works by Whistler. From September 1891 to March 1892 he lived in Paris, where he was frequently in the company of Willumsen. He also met Th. Durét, who later visited him in Copenhagen. From October to December 1893 he was in northern Italy. In June 1897 he went to Stockholm; in October the same year, he went by way of the Netherlands to London, where he remained until May 1898. He may have seen the major exhibition which opened there on May 16 (The Skating Rink, Knightsbridge), where, in addition to works by Monet, Manet, Bonnard, Vuillard, and German artists, there were nine oil paintings by Whistler.

From October 1902 to February 1903 he was again in Italy, and in September 1904 in London. Hammershøi's trips, especially those to London, are important for his artistic development. Part of his time in London was spent in painting street scenes around the British Museum, and part, it is said, in seeking out Whistler. In Paris the portrait of his future wife Ida Ilsted (1890) was admired by Th. Durét and Puvis de Chavannes, and Renoir was said to have been interested in some of his early portraits, among them the one of his sister which had been rejected earlier.

Like other Danish painters at the time, Hammershøi had a great deal in common with the Golden Age painters and with Eckersberg's school, both because of his training and out of personal preference. It should be noted that in the 1890s, these artists had their retrospective exhibitions, and monographs on them were published (Christen Købke: exhibition, 1884, E. Hannover's biography, 1893; Johan Thomas Lundbye: exhibition, 1893, Karl Madsen's biography, 1895; C. W. Eckersberg: exhibition, 1895, E. Hannover's biography, 1898; Constantin Hansen: exhibition, 1897, E. Hannover's biography, 1901; Wilhelm Marstrand, exhibition, 1898, Karl Madsen's biography, 1905). At the Town Hall exhibition in 1901, there was a review of Danish painting which became just as important for the acquisitions policies of Danish museums as it did for the artists' knowledge and appreciation of the art of their own country.

Hammershøi's subjects included portraits, nudes, landscapes, architecture, and interiors. The last category, with their silent, female figures, seen from the back, show the influence of Vermeer. Perhaps more interesting, however, are those interiors without figures. They, like his austere architectural paintings, are like architecture itself, Pure Art. The landscapes, too, are formally related to his architectural views because through their simplification they tell of space and structure. Even in his portraits, Hammershøi expresses an architectural feeling for structure, as in the portrait of the architect and craftsman Thorvald Bindesbøll (No. 32).

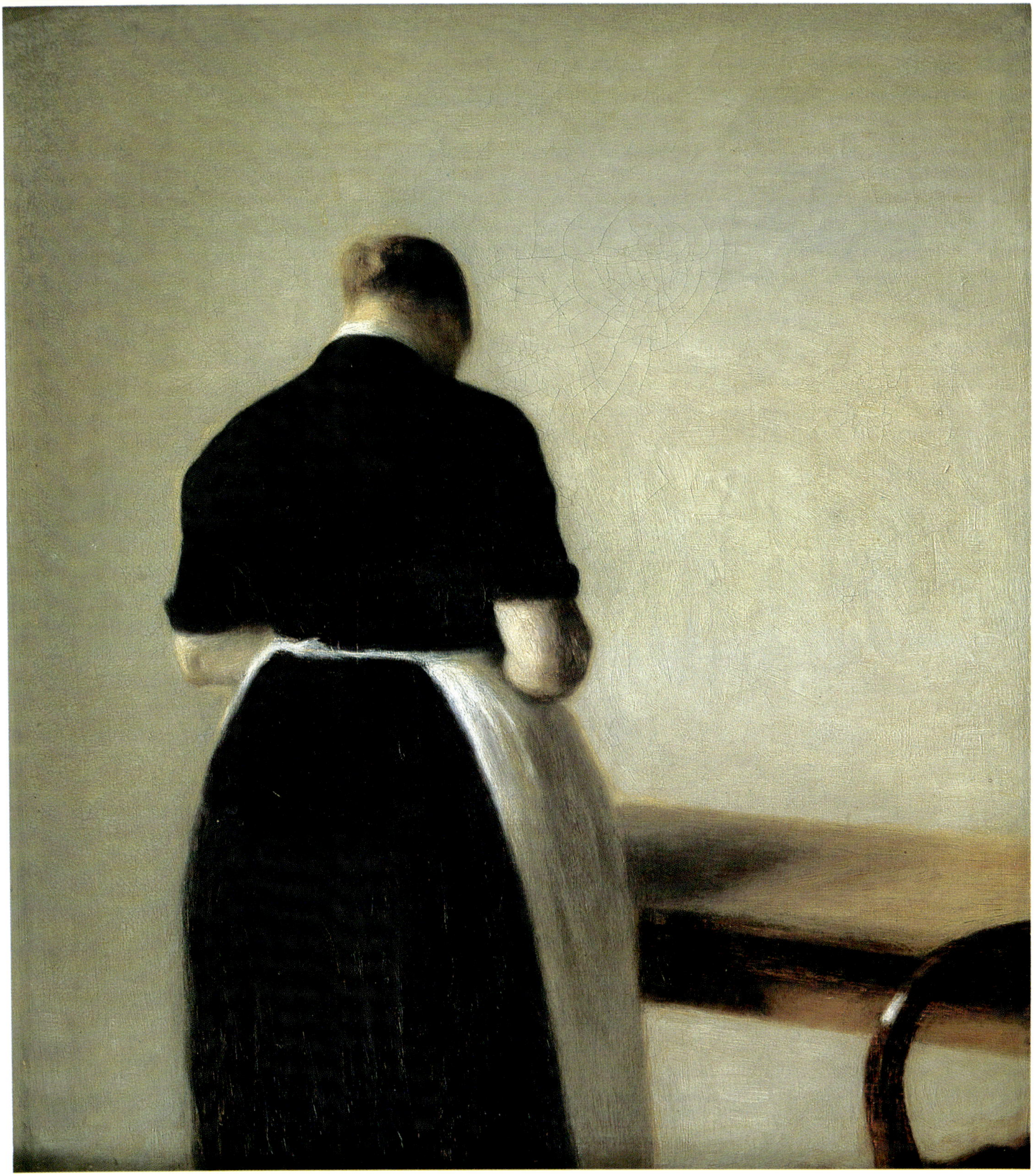

29. Vilhelm Hammershøi

In 1899, Hammershøi moved to a Renaissance house near the harbour and shipyard. Later he lived in a Neo-Classical house. It is from this period that his real interiors come, and it is his own rooms we see. Did he perhaps choose and create a setting within his home which was a point of departure for his art?

29

Study of a Woman, 1888

(Kvindefigur)

63.5 × 55.5
Not signed
Statens Museum for Kunst, Copenhagen
Inv. no. 3671 (purchased in 1924)

In 1884 Hammershøi had painted a picture of his sister and his mother by a fully set tea table. His sister stands to the left in the foreground with her back to the viewer, about to pour the kettle. To the right one sees the back of a Neo-Rococo dining-room chair. A study shows only the female figure, the back of the chair, and the table with the white cloth.

Four years later, Hammershøi resumed work on the same motive: this time with an older, stouter woman before a table without a cloth. A strong source of light from high on the left emphasizes her white apron against the black dress, the naked arms, and the white neck-band round the bowed head. In the foreground is the Neo-Rococo chair, but turned obliquely so that it gives the picture depth.

H.W.

30

A Baker's Shop, 1888

(En bagerbutik)

113.5 × 90
Not signed
Vejen Kunstmuseum, Vejen

After working tentatively on the same subject in a series of paintings, Hammershøi painted a picture of a female figure seen from behind, and with a chair beside her. In the same year he painted the final version.

In *A Baker's Shop* the chair is gone, and he has placed an area of floor and a counter between himself and the female figure, who has now been shifted to the far right of the composition. In front of her is a table, placed in an unspecified space, so that the woman stands almost pressed flat between it and the counter. Brown shelves run along the light tile-covered wall for the whole width of the picture, strongly emphasizing the horizontal movement. Light comes from an unseen source high on the left and is reflected on the shiny wall. An edge of the woman's white apron and a bit of the apron-string glow delicately against her black dress.

The white tiles give the impression of hygiene, but this is not a realistic rendering of an assistant in a baker's shop. For Hammershøi the organization of the shop itself was the inspiration for this taut composition.

A Baker's Shop was exhibited at the Paris World Fair in 1889 and in Copenhagen at the Free Exhibition in 1891 and later in his own exhibitions in Copenhagen in 1900 and 1916.

H.W.

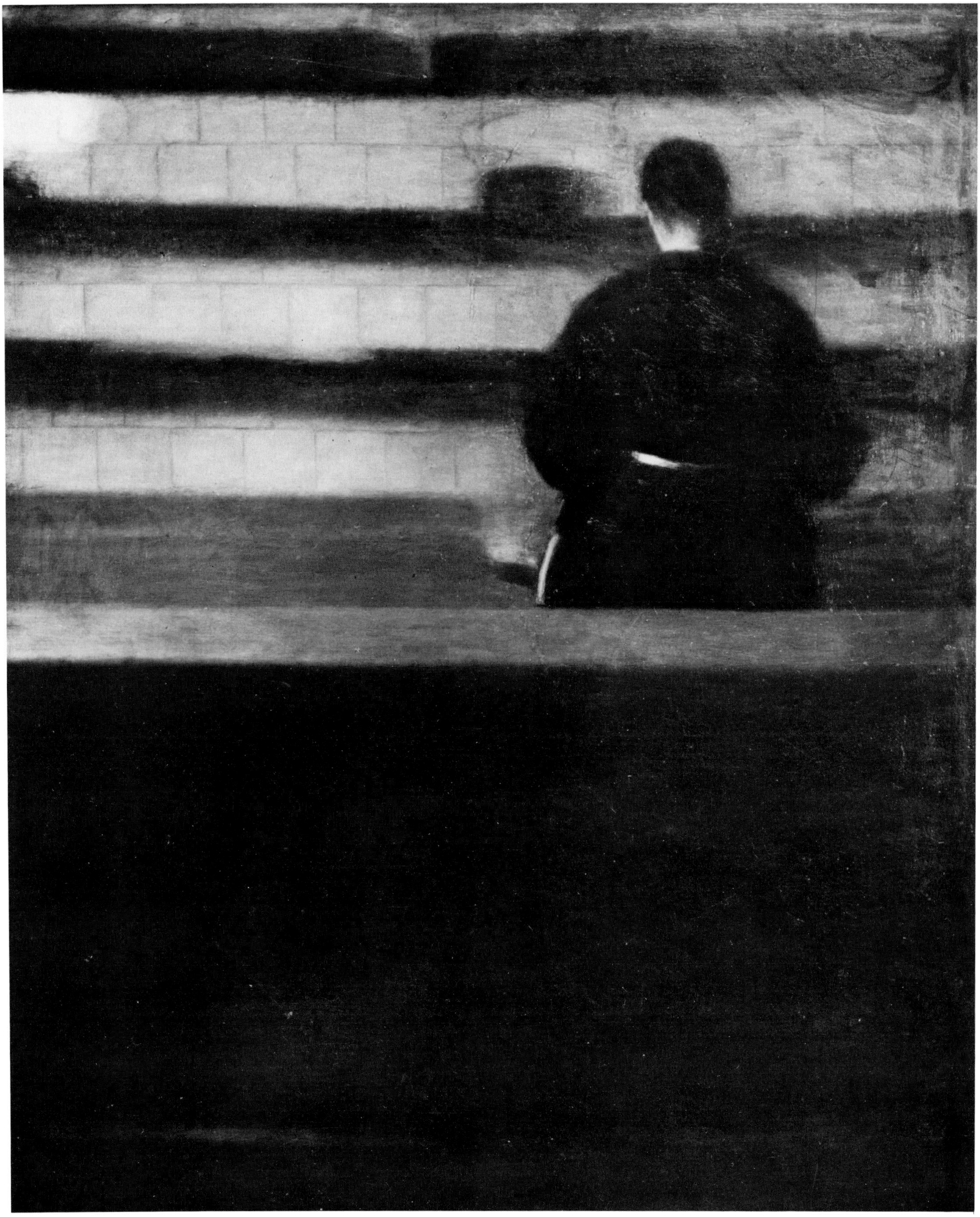

30. Vilhelm Hammershøi

31

A Farm at Refsnæs, 1900

(Bondegård. Refsnæs)

53 × 62
Signed lower right: V H.
Davids Samling, Copenhagen
Inv. no. B. 306 (purchased before 1930)

Refsnæs is a narrow peninsula, almost a spit, on the coast of north-western Zealand. It is bathed in light from the surrounding sea. Formerly the houses and farms were thatched. As is still common in northern Zealand, the houses are whitewashed, so their timber frames are not visible. The courtyards were once paved with cobblestones. In the picture we see parts of two white farm buildings. There are no figures; the sky is cloudless. Only a fine ribbon of smoke rises from the chimney.

The view is from the left, diagonally into the courtyard. The main building is not seen in its full length, and the stable hides part of the furthermost window, which receives a strong reflected light from the end of the stable. The short shadows show that the sun is almost at its zenith. It is slightly past noon in summer. The open doors confirm this. One might think that both animals and people are asleep.

Everything is simplified to the extreme: there are no details, in the yard, or on the thatched roof, door, or walls. The rhythm of the windows is determined by the timber construction, which is hinted at by lighter bands that almost imperceptibly divide the wall horizontally and vertically. Together with the carefully considered composition, they give the row of windows a rhythmic tension which is varied by the different reflections in the glass from an unseen white building.

The picture's overall tone is cool. It shows how the colour white can be made to vibrate with the greatest intensity.

H.W.

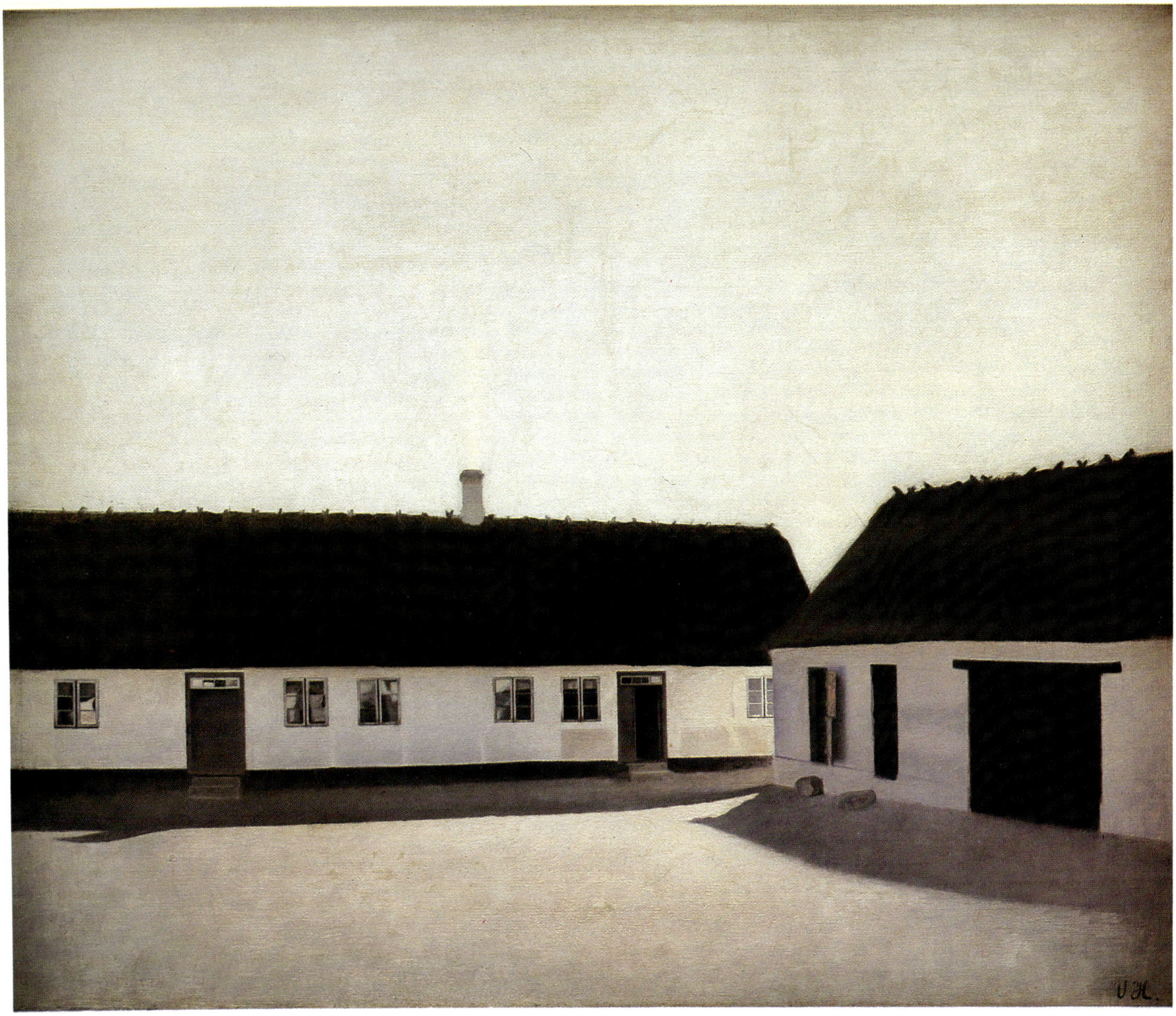

31. Vilhelm Hammershøi

32

Five Portraits, 1901

(Fem portrætter)

190 × 340
Not signed
Thielska galleriet, Stockholm
Inv. no. 117 (purchased in 1905)

In 1901 Hammershøi painted the large rather enigmatic composition *Five Portraits*. He had high hopes for it, but was deeply disappointed. No one in Denmark understood the painting, and the Statens Museum for Kunst, which he had hoped would purchase it both because of its artistic value and because of those portrayed, failed to do so. In 1905 it was sold to the Swedish collector Ernest Thiel.

In the meantime, Hammershøi had begun on a new picture with a similar subject and content, *Evening in the Living Room* (Statens Museum for Kunst, Copenhagen, inv. no. 6657), which he abandoned, however, in his despair that *Five Portraits* had left the country.

In *Five Portraits* we see five men at a table, all of them intimate friends of Hammershøi's. Farthest to the left is the architect and craftsman Thorvald Bindesbøll (1846–1908). He sits isolated from the others and also from the spectator. His position, with legs crossed and hands folded on his knees, must have been characteristic, as it is seen in other portraits of him. Next to him, behind the table, sits Karl Madsen, later director of the Statens Museum for Kunst, a critic and expert on Dutch art, especially Rembrandt. His body is turned slightly from the spectator, whom he faces. Above the white shirt front and the dark beard, his pince-nez flash towards us. We do not see his hands. In front of him on the table is a Genever glass. Genever, which is sipped like a liqueur, was a favourite drink. There is no glass in front of Bindesbøll. What might have stood there was quite a different kind of glass, for Bindesbøll preferred whiskey, at the time considered a very advanced taste in Denmark (Svend Hammershøi). Then comes J. F. Willumsen (p. 296), the man who, together with Bindesbøll, was credited with Denmark's success at the Paris World Fair the previous year. He sits with his forearms resting on the table, his hands folded around the stem of the glass. Before him stand two candles in silver candlesticks. They illuminate him, but not Karl Madsen, who receives light partly from the unseen source to the left of Bindesbøll, partly from the hidden light between him and the figure in the foreground. Willumsen, with his big bony hands in their white cuffs, his pointed beard, triangular shirt front, and his pyramid shape, formed by his elbows on the table, is the picture's main character. His heavy thoughtful gaze is Egyptian in its impenetrability. At the end of the table is the painter Carl Holsøe. He was Hammershøi's friend from his time at the Artist's Study School, and they are presumed to have influenced one another. Holsøe, too, painted interiors in Dutch eighteenth-century style. They are less refined than Hammershøi's, but were far more popular. Bald and beardless he reclines carelessly with his jacket open, hands in his pockets, and vest buttoned up to the neck. Everything emphasizes the unconventional, even though the narrow, round collar makes him look like a priest. His feet are raised and the soles of his boots project into the foreground. This rendering of his boots became the talk of the town in Copenhagen, and in a humorous periodical of the time, Holsøe's boots were the year's joke. No wonder Hammershøi was so hurt that he never completely recovered.

The table at which these men are seated is narrow like the counter in *A Baker's Shop* (No. 30), and covered with a white cloth. In the foreground sits Hammershøi's younger brother, the painter and ceramicist Svend Hammershøi, for whom Hammershøi had a deep affection and who had worked with both Bindesbøll and Willumsen. He sits modestly like a candidate for confirmation, erect on one of the uncomfortable Neo-Classical chairs one also sees in No. 18. He has a good head of hair, but no beard, and his big hands with the long, bony wrists are clasped round a pipe bowl.

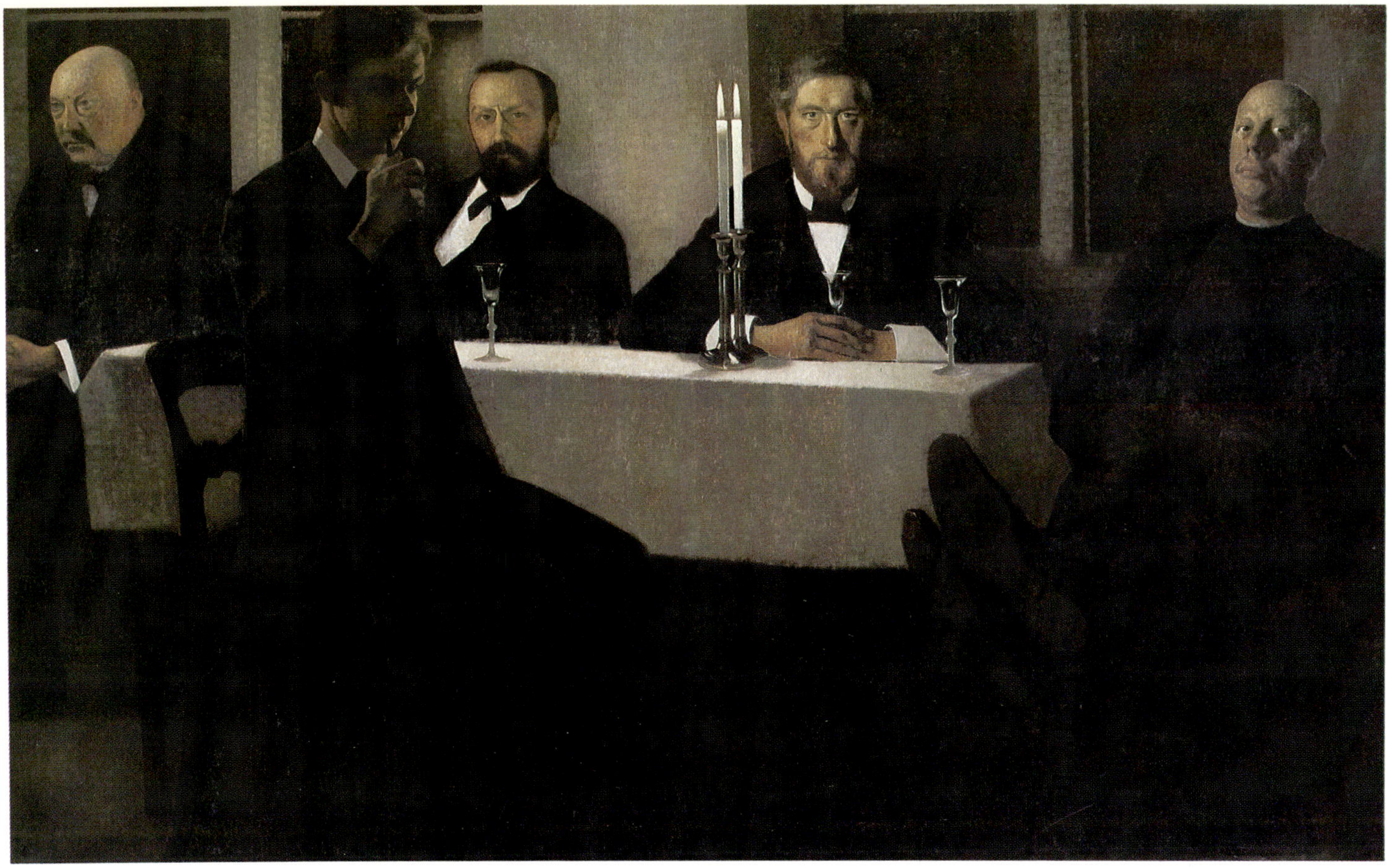

32. Vilhelm Hammershøi

The hidden source of light between him and Karl Madsen delicately outlines his young cheek.

The pictorial space is without depth, and the field of vision is so limited that we see only the lower panes of the big windows. There are no curtains and nothing is visible outside the windows. Light is reflected in the pane behind Karl Madsen.The windows completely close off the room. The world outside is irrelevant.

There is no doubt that Rembrandt's *Conspiracy of Julius Civilis* showing a group of men gathered around a narrow, self-illuminated table with hidden sources of light, was decisive for the composition. Hammershøi had had an opportunity to see it in June 1897. His painting is thus a compliment to Karl Madsen who, in 1892, had been the first to point out that the picture in Stockholm could be part of the composition intended for Amsterdam's Town Hall.

Considering how much Hammershøi had travelled in the Netherlands, it is not unreasonable to assume that he had the Dutch group portrait in mind. In Rembrandt's *Syndics of the Amsterdam Cloth Hall*, the figures, as in *Five Portraits*, have their gaze fixed on an unexpected guest, and in Frans Hals' *The Regents*, the figures portrayed are totally without mutual contact. The source of light is unseen, and the shallow pictorial space is given depth only through the person who sits in front of the table.

But the Danish Golden Age may also have been important. Hammershøi's interest in Constantin Hansen is well known. He could have become acquainted with his work at the memorial exhibition in 1897, and in the spring of 1901 he had another chance to see his work at the exhibition of Danish art at Copenhagen Town Hall.

The painting *Danish Artists in Rome*, 1837 (Inv. no 3236), was at both exhibitions. Now at Statens Museum for Kunst, but then privately owned, it shows six painters grouped around the architect M. G. Bindesbøll (1800–56), Thorvald Bindesbøll's father. He lounges on the floor, telling about a trip to Greece and Turkey, though few are listening. Small Turkish coffee cups and long-stemmed pipes provide evidence of his travels. An open balcony door gives a broad view of sunlit Rome. M. G. Bindesbøll's unceremonious position recalls Holsøe's equally informal pose in Hammershøi's picture, where it was changed from the first sketch.

Five Portraits was probably completed very late in 1901, since J. F. Willumsen did not return from his trip to America and subsequent tour in the Swiss Alps until late October. From Svend Hammershøi's description of the abandoned *Evening in the Living Room*, we know that Hammershøi painted directly from the model and not from sketches. In *Five Portraits*, the Genever glasses place the picture in some relation to the Netherlands, while the elder and the younger Bindesbøll represent the first and second generation of artists. The dark windows further emphasize the new age by proclaiming that one should not look outwards, but inwards.

If one looks on *Five Portraits* as portraiture, one sees a different side of Hammershøi. One suspects that he emphasized those traits in his friends which they wished to have: Bindesbøll, with his monumental head and compact, sculptural body; Karl Madsen, with the penetrating look behind his pince-nez; Willumsen's statuary calm; he collects his thoughts in the same way that he folds his hands; the very tall Holsøe with the very big feet, known for his open friendliness and for his pictures, which resemble Hammershøi's a little.

Hammershøi, to a greater degree than most other artists, depicted reality that went beyond realism. For example, there is the story, still told, about the empty table in *Five Portraits*: it bore no relationship to the table in Hammershøi's house, which always groaned with the weight of food.

Five Portraits has been much discussed: the table resembles a coffin and the glasses altar chalices (Wanscher); it has a mystical, ritual character. But there is no doubt that the picture is quite simply what the artist called it: five single portraits, and that one neither can nor should look deeper. The Danish art historian Julian Lange in an article in 1889, 'Erindringens kunst' (Art and memory), which was highly significant for Danish poets and painters in the 1890s, perhaps sums it up best when he says of the artist that there is 'a secret in his soul whose mystery is revealed in his work and gives it its power'.

Five Portraits was exhibited in Copenhagen, 1902, in Venice at the Biennale in 1903, in Berlin at the Secession Exhibition, 1904, and in Gothenburg in 1905.

H.W.

33

The Buildings of the East Asiatic Company in Copenhagen, 1902

(Asiatisk Compagnis bygningen)

146.5 × 140.5
Not signed
Statens Museum for Kunst, Copenhagen
Inv. no. 6657 (purchased in 1970)

Hammershøi lived in Christianshavn in Copenhagen, just across from the houses of the East Asiatic Company where he could see both the harbour and the ships. Ships had always attracted him. 'In London, he even went down the river to Greenwich, to find a good place from which to paint the ships on the Thames. But at that time of year – he had a weakness for England in the dark autumn! – there was too much fog and it was too dark to paint' (Bramsen).

Hammershøi painted the East Asiatic Company's low entrance flanked by two pavilions seen from the opposite side of the street for the first time in 1902 (A. B. no. 236). A mast and spars rise up next to the right pavilion. In 1907, he painted the motive again, but in snow and without the ship. Only the winter air lies between the buildings (A. B. no. 303). After his death, a third version was found – the one shown

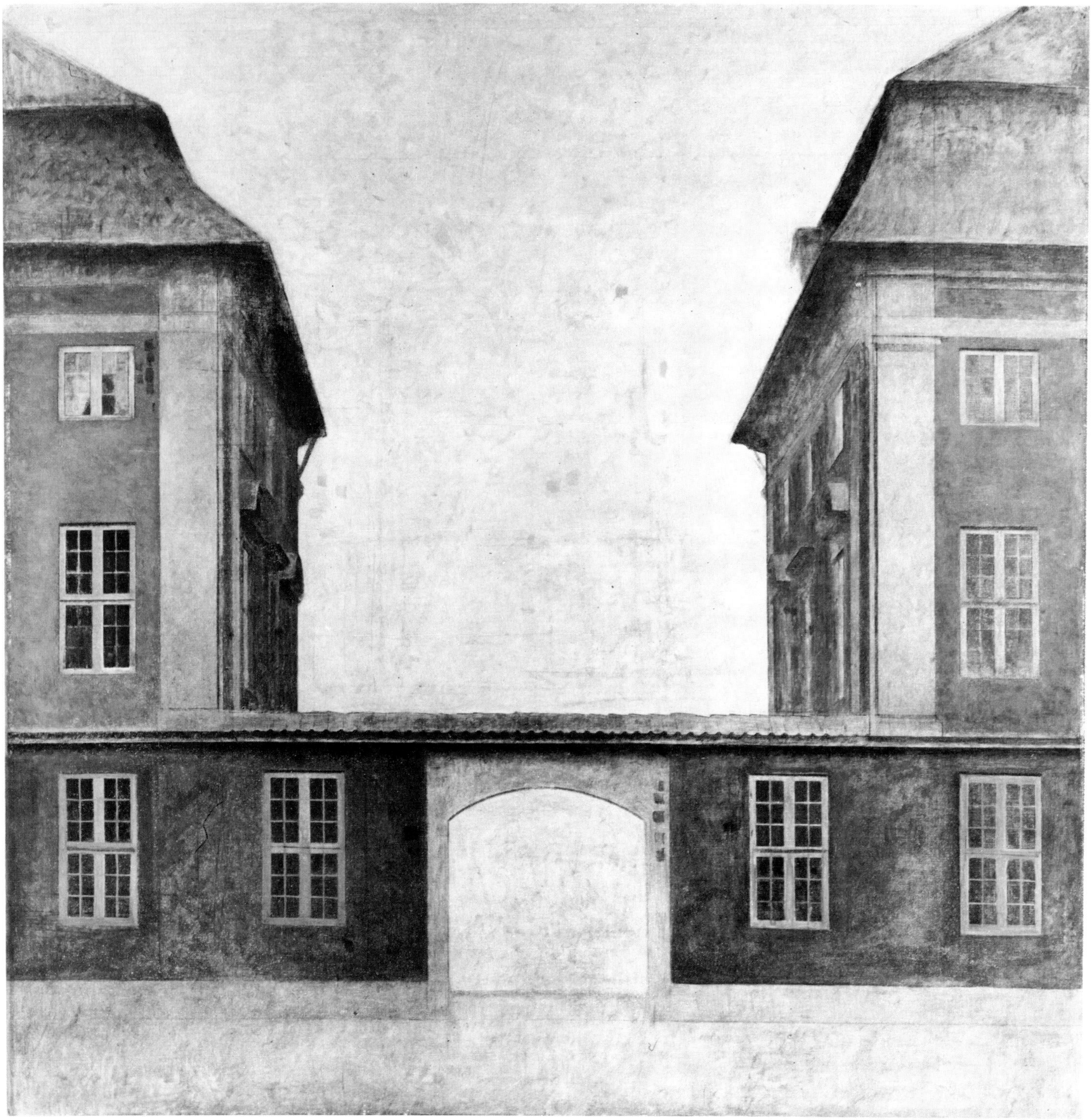

33. Vilhelm Hammershøi

here of whose existence no one had known. It was unfinished and is probably the original picture for the 1902 version, since there are slight traces of mast and spars in the painting. Hammershøi must have realized that the division of weight would be too heavy on the right-hand side and so began again with a different composition which brought the elements into balance.

In its unfinished state, the picture is mysterious, with the heavy, dark buildings, the black windows, and the gate in the middle, drawing the viewer into what? The unknown. But this magnificent architectural composition, which brings to mind

Eckersberg and the Eckersberg School, is interesting in another way as well. One sees a bit more of the gable of the right-hand building than of the left, and the vanishing point of the line of the roof is left of centre. None the less, the gate is placed precisely in the centre axis.

The composition does not conform to the laws of perspective, but this is what Hammershøi wanted. He needed the gate in the middle so as to distribute the weight and the balance of the composition. This was his main purpose. The perspective had to be adapted accordingly.

H.W.

34

The Collector of Coins, 1904

(Møntsamleren)

89 × 69.5
Not signed
Nasjonalgalleriet, Oslo
Inv. no. NG 2273 (purchased in 1953)

In the foreground on the left a young man sits by a rectangular table on which two tall candles burn in silver candlesticks. By their light 'the collector' examines a coin which he holds between the fingers of both hands. Behind him is a window with white curtains, and the candles are reflected in its panes. The palette ranges from pure white to the deepest black, and is 'texturally worked over into a dense, firm layer with a shiny, hard surface, in which the brushstrokes cannot be seen. Because of the complex left-hand side, the door on the right plays an active and dramatic role, which, in turn, makes the lonely and furtive business of this "collector of coins" become exciting and dramatic' (Vad).

H.W.

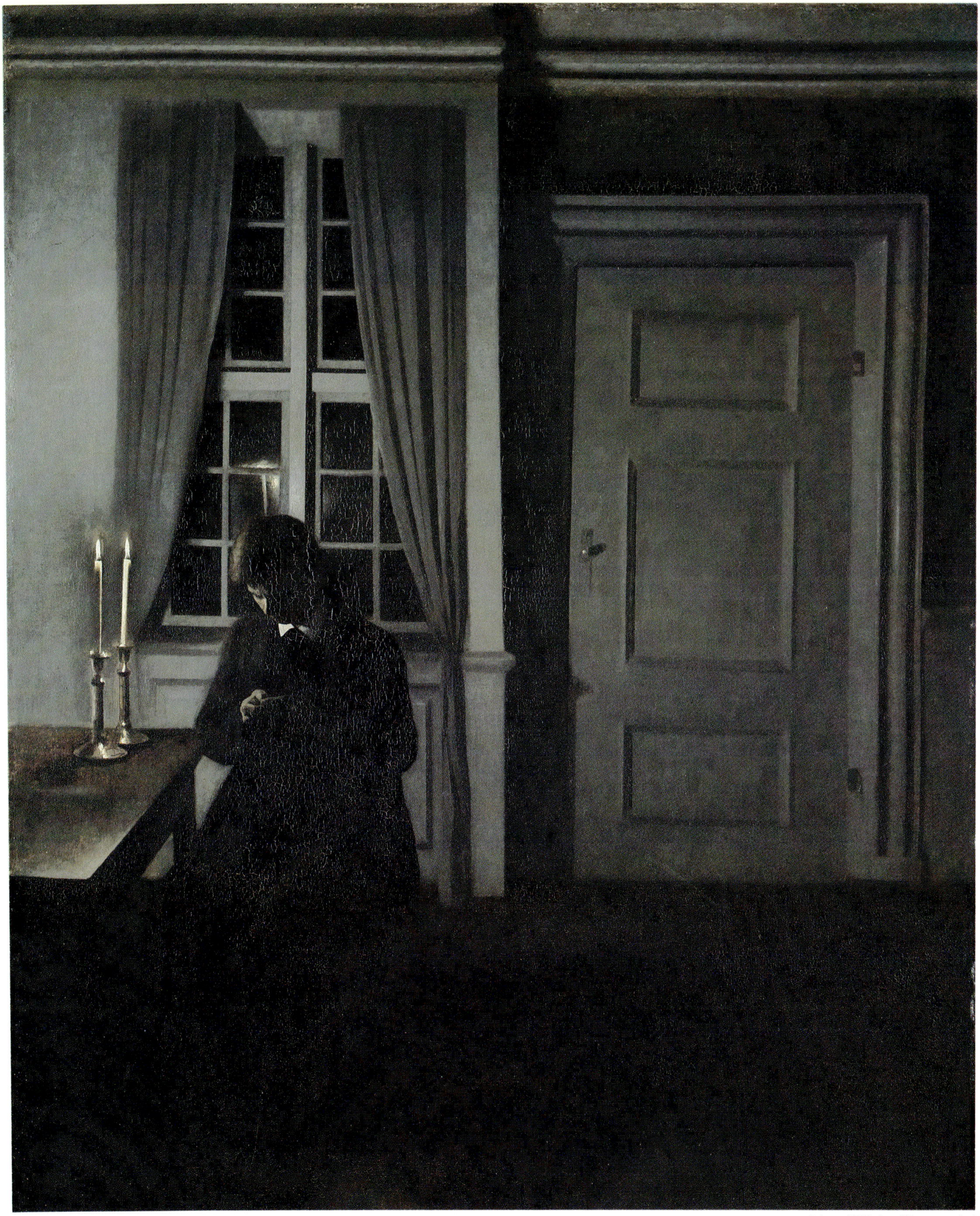

34. Vilhelm Hammershøi

35

Landscape from Lejre, 1905

(Landskab. Lejre)

41 × 68
Not signed
Nationalmuseum, Stockholm
Inv. no. NM 2248 (purchased in 1920)

In Hammershøi's landscapes, trees often play a principal part, not only because they give an architectural structure to the picture but also because they are living things. This animation of the woods and of single groups of trees can be seen in both Danish art and poetry in the years around the turn of the century.

But in 1905, Hammershøi painted a few pictures from Lejre near Roskilde. The landscape here is rolling, clearly a moraine formation. It is its gentle forms that Hammershøi sought, where the woods only emphasize the small, rounded hills, but are not closed in and secret, as in some of his other work. The horizon is low, and under the blue summer sky, where the clouds provide depth, the landscape is open and clear. There are reminders here of the Danish Golden Age; of the painter Johan Thomas Lundbye and the poet Adam Oehlenschläger, who wrote about 'Hertha's green groves' (a famous spot in Lejre is called Herthadalen). But Lundbye's pictures do not put the emphasis on the rhythm and infinite space of the landscape as Hammershøi's do and it is this which links Hammershøi's pictures with the poetry of Johannes Jørgensen and Sophus Claussen.

H.W.

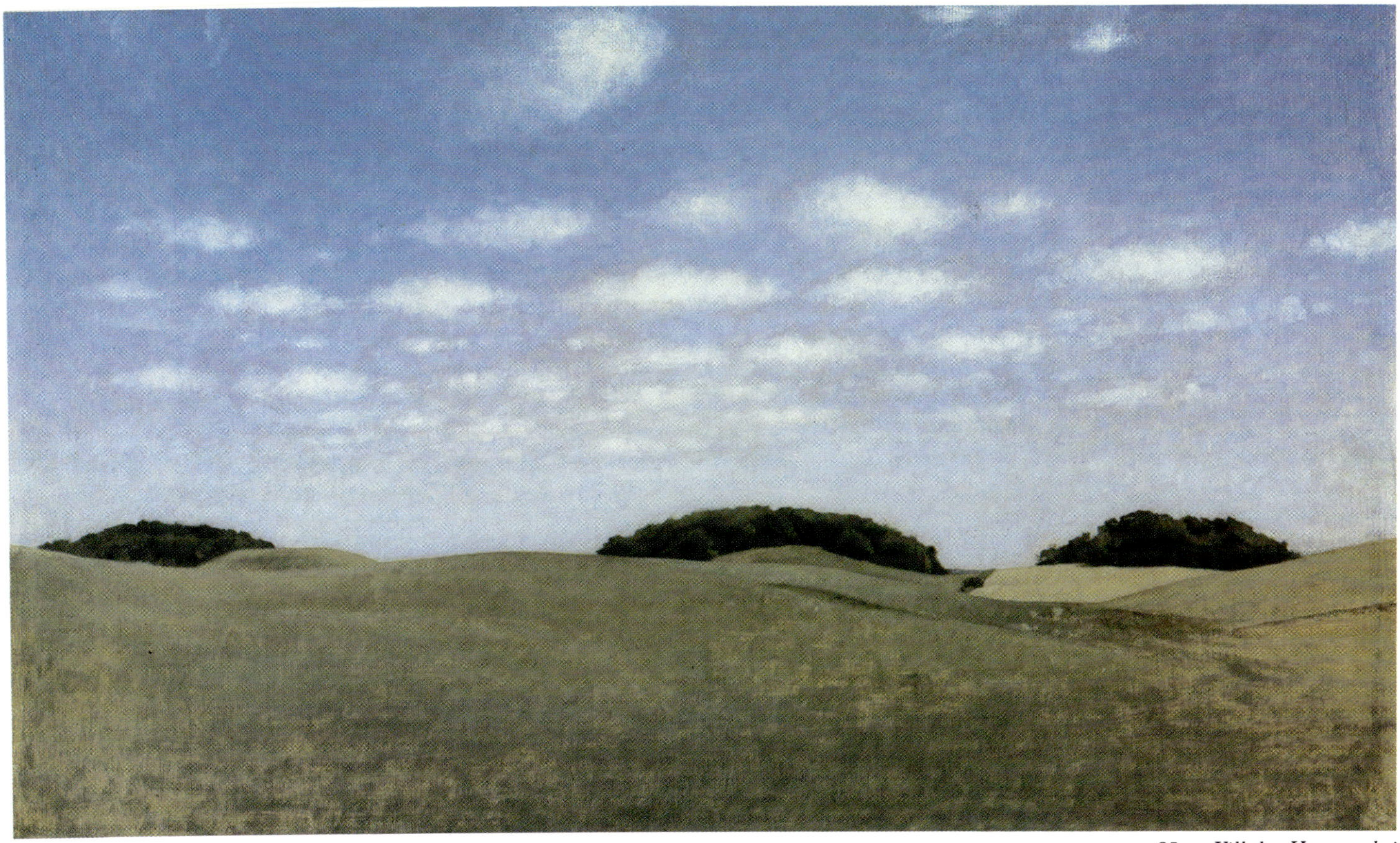

35. Vilhelm Hammershøi

36

Interior with a Seated Woman, 1908

(Interiør med siddende kvinde)

71 × 57.5
Signed lower left: V H
Aarhus Kunstmuseum, Aarhus

The first biography of Hammershøi appeared in 1905 in *Zeitschrift für bildende Kunst*, but even before this date his distinctive art had received attention abroad. In 1897, Sergei Diaghilev had arranged an exhibition of his works in St Petersburg, and in 1904 Hammershøi participated in the International Society's exhibition in London. Then things went quickly. Soon 'A Hammershøi' came to mean an interior with a solitary female figure, often seen from behind. Although Hammershøi painted many such interiors, they do not account for more than two-fifths of his total production.

These subtle daylight pictures of interiors, often with a few exquisite pieces of dark furniture, are linked to the art of the Danish Golden Age. The furniture and the open or half-open white-lacquered doors play an important part in Hammershøi's compositions. The view through several rooms with different lighting is derived from the Dutch (De Hooch), as is the woman seen from the back (ter Borch).

In *Interior with a Seated Woman* the figure is sitting to the right: before her, an open door leads into a darker room, from which yet another door permits the light to fall in from a window. Hammershøi thus worked with two main sources of light. The light in the foremost room is reflected on the dark furniture's smooth surfaces and emphasizes the white doorway against the dark floor. The placing of each piece of furniture is carefully calculated. Each surface, each cropping is part of a deliberately thought-out composition, as is always the case with Hammershøi (Vad, 1957), and it is in this, more than in anything else, that we feel his kinship with Whistler. All is contained within the picture. It is everything that the picture should be. The subject-matter itself is just an excuse.

There is, however, great intimacy in the picture. The sparse furnishings, the sparing use of colour, and the broad surfaces subtly emphasize the woman's bowed head, which, fully illuminated, rises warm, living, and with gentle defencelessness above the all-concealing black dress. The picture's soft brushwork underlines this universal human content.

H.W.

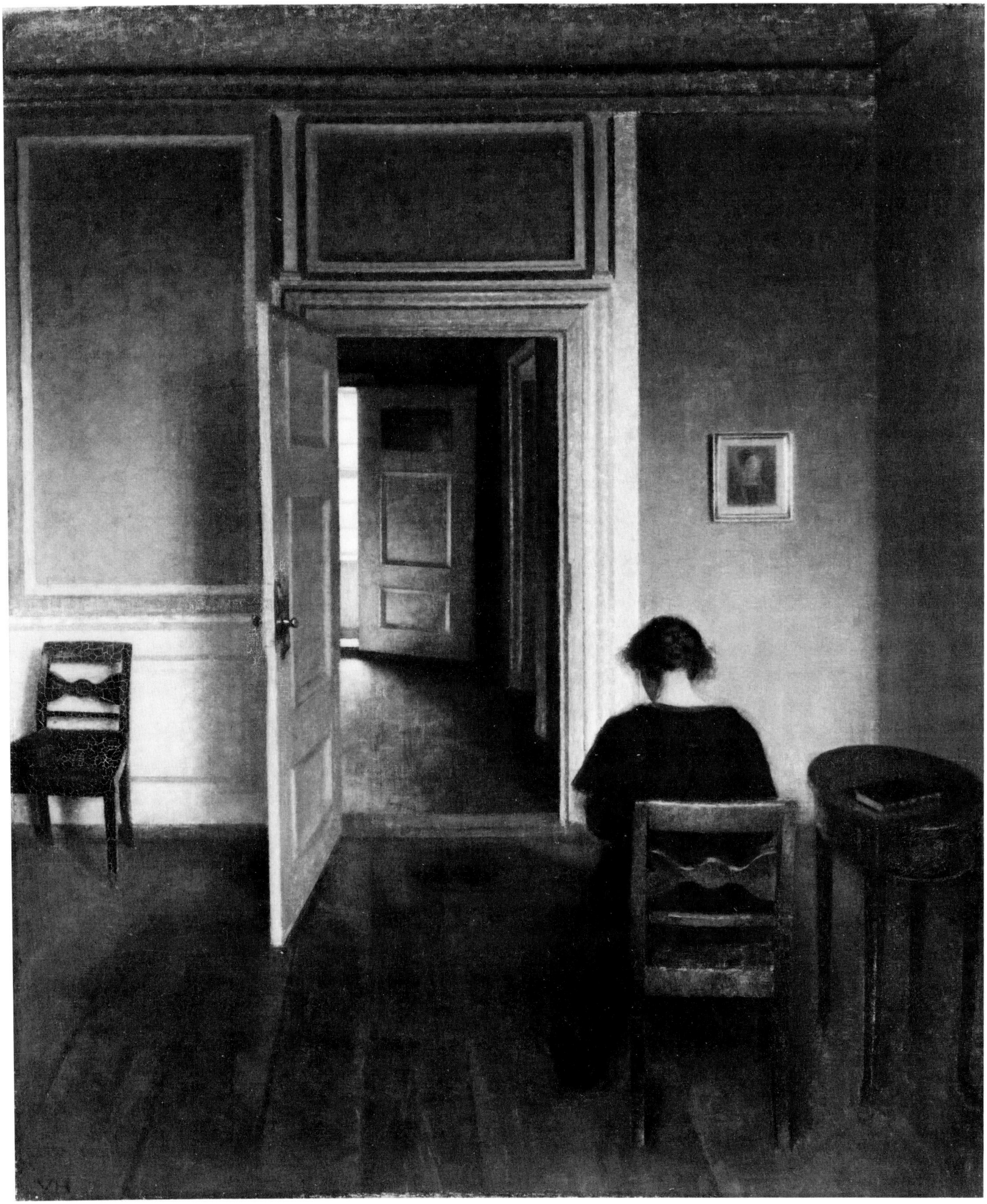

36. Vilhelm Hammershøi

EUGÈNE JANSSON

1862–1915, Sweden

Eugène Jansson came from a modest background. The son of a poor janitor, he pursued his art studies sporadically at Edvard Perséus' art school, and at the Royal Academy of Fine Arts in Stockholm, 1881–2. However, as a painter he was mainly self-taught.

Jansson's life was uneventful. He lived in Stockholm, and travelled little, but he did have contacts with the radical artists' circles which opposed the Academy. He joined the Artists' Union, which had a marked influence on National Romantic painting in Sweden in the '90s and at the turn of the century. One of his friends there was the leader of the Union, the landscapist Karl Nordström.

By nature, Eugène Jansson was a recluse, an original. Artistically, he was a pioneer as a painter of 'blue pictures' in Sweden. He tried his hand at this genre as early as 1883, and it is here that he made his lasting contribution. In 1891, he moved to the Södermalm quarter of Stockholm, from where he painted his magnificent panoramic views of the city at dusk and dawn. Jansson was a good friend of the banker and art collector Ernest Thiel, the creator of the excellent collection of turn-of-the-century art, the Thielska galleriet, in Stockholm. Like Thiel, Jansson was fascinated by Edvard Munch's art, which he had an opportunity to study at an exhibition which came to Stockholm from Berlin in 1894. Munch's work undoubtedly influenced Eugène Jansson's painting in the direction of Symbolism and Synthetism.

Eugène Jansson had a strong social conscience which at times can be seen in his painting, for example in his monumental picture of a demonstration and in depictions of dreary workers' tenements on the outskirts of town. From around 1905, his subject-matter was dominated by studies of nude male figures, bathing or doing gymnastics in the spirit of Vitalism.

Eugène Jansson's painting was not an immediate success at the time: he went too far both in his cultivation of colour and in his simplification of forms. Posterity, however, can see him as the most personal and expressive of the many 'blue painters' in Swedish art in the 1890s.

37

Riddarfjärden in Stockholm, 1898

(Riddarfjärden i Stockholm)

115 × 135
Signed lower right: Eugène Jansson/1898
Nationalmuseum, Stockholm
Inv. no. 1699 (donated in 1899)

The perspective in Eugène Jansson's large panoramas from Södermalm is remarkably topographically exact. But at the same time, he takes stylization further than any of his contemporaries and turns the subject into a kind of rhythmical, wavy ornament. The explanation for the paintings' highly visionary character probably lies in the fact that Jansson almost never made studies from nature. Instead, he studied the motive for a long time and then painted it in a single session, without first drawing it up on the canvas. In this, Eugène Jansson followed the advice of Richard Bergh. In an article on *Nordisk natur och nordisk konst* (Nordic nature and Nordic art), Bergh says that to interpret nature in painting in the Nordic countries, it is not sufficient just to open one's eyes. 'One must also close them at times, dream of what one has seen, transform it, and weigh the varied impressions the eyes have received against feeling in order to fathom the unity in this barbaric multifariousness.'

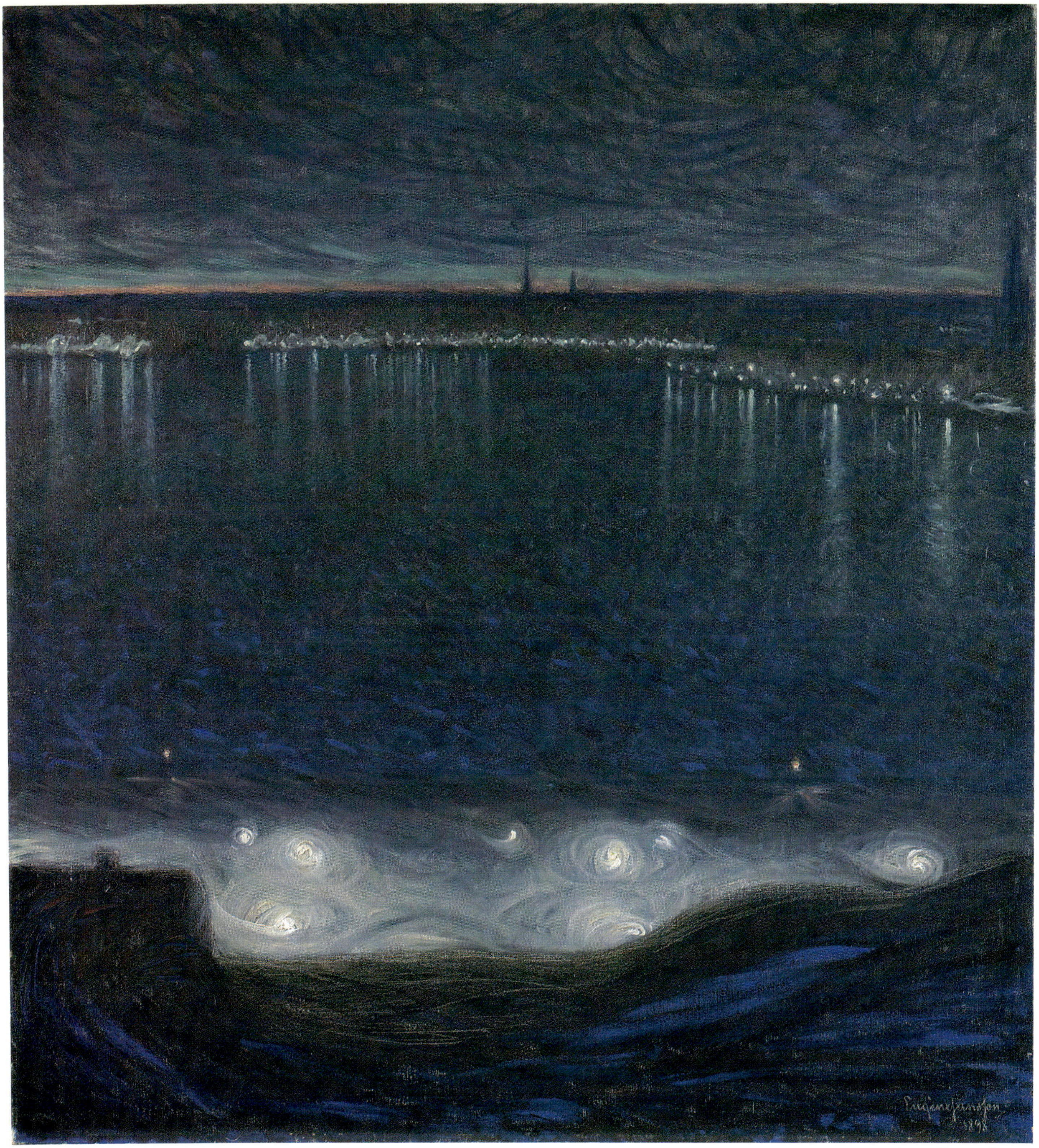

37. Eugène Jansson

Eugène Jansson's blue period lasted from 1890 to 1905, and marked the culmination of his work as an artist. His pictorial world was, as always, limited geographically – Stockholm and particularly Södermalm were his artistic domain. Through their magnificent form and suggestive mood, his paintings often take on the character of an inner landscape of dreams. At the end of his blue period, Jansson painted three thematically very similar panoramic views from his studio. *Riddarfjärden*, of 1898, is the first. Like Monet, Jansson depicted the same motive with different lighting at different times of day. As in all of Eugène Jansson's paintings, the impressive and dreamlike character are to a great extent created by the rhythmic calligraphy of his brushwork.

Riddarfjärden in Stockholm was exhibited at the Paris World Fair in 1900.

T.G.

38

The Outskirts of the City, 1899

(Stadens utkant)

152 × 136
Signed lower left: Eugène Jansson/1899
Nationalmuseum, Stockholm
Inv. no. 2134 (purchased in 1919)

In addition to the panoramic views of the city and the desolate Södermalm street scenes with their steep perspectives, Eugène Jansson also painted a number of pictures of the city's outskirts. They comprise the third element in the Symbolist urban poetry which Eugène Jansson created out of the pedestrian subjects taken from Stockholm's predominantly proletarian district. He uses chiaroscuro to express his own loneliness, but also his longing to distance himself from the banality of the everyday world through poetic visions. This metamorphosis of the subject also illustrates how the interest in the '80s in the bustling life of the city's throngs was transformed into the figureless mood pictures of the '90s.

Eugène Jansson's social conscience, which had its origin in his childhood milieu, a poor home where economic difficulties embittered everyday life, obviously guided his choice of motive in *The Outskirts of the City*. He chose to depict an otherwise forgotten part of the cityscape, finding in the workers' tenements a mood which suited his artistic temperament. The same tone of melancholy increasing to dread is also found in contemporary Swedish poetry. In *The Outskirts of the City*, however, the melancholy is redeemed by the monumentality that gives the buildings a simple dignity, something that has a precedent in the Realism of the '80s, concerned as it was with the beauty of the simple forms of everyday life. Here it is illustrated in the colouristic beauty of the play between the cultivated fields in the foreground and the simple, light masses of buildings in the background which abruptly turn their empty, windowless gables toward the surrounding countryside.

T.G.

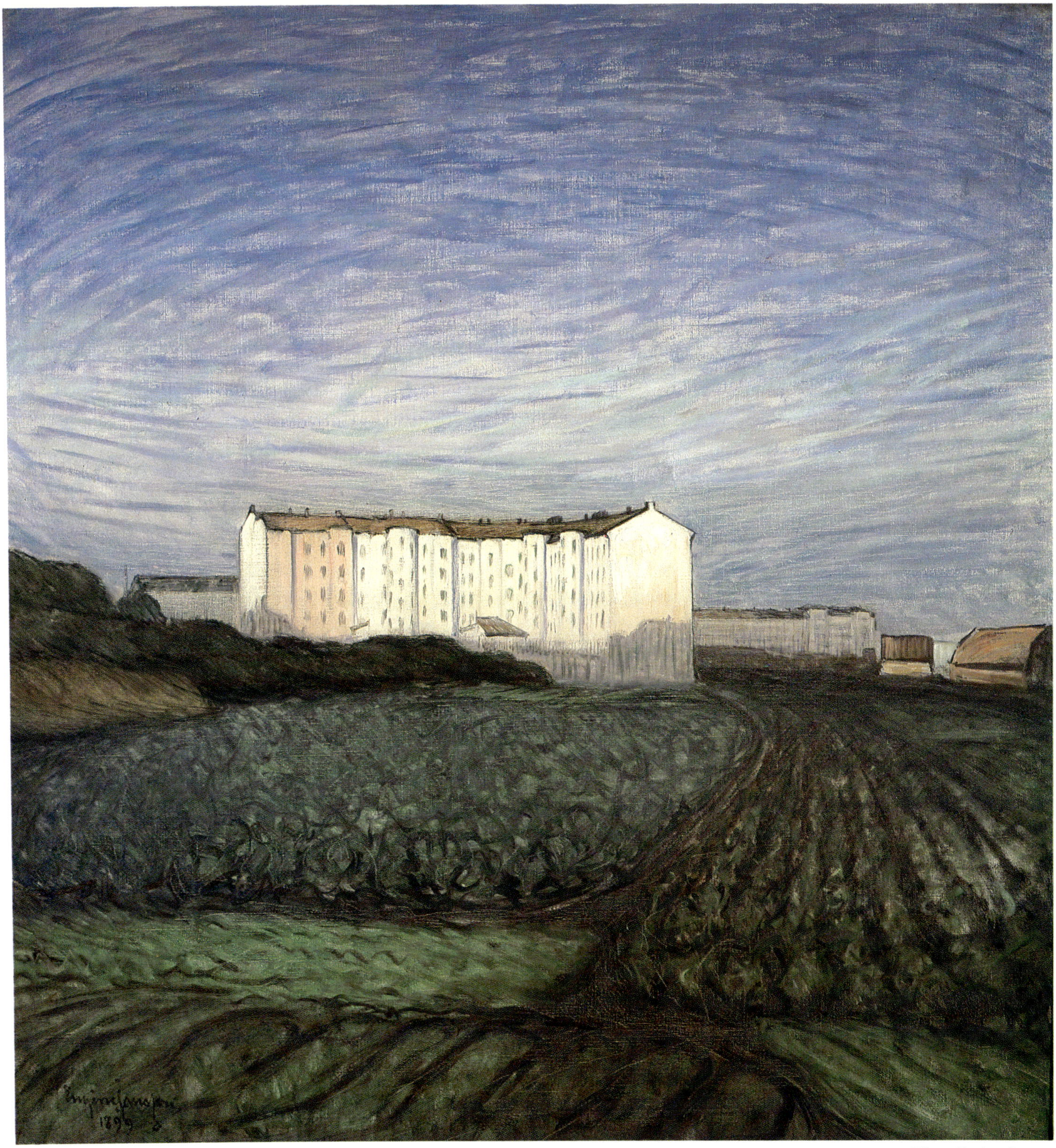

38. Eugène Jansson

39

Me. Self-Portrait, 1901

(Jag. Självporträtt)

101 × 144
Signed lower left: Eugène Jansson/1901
Thielska galleriet, Stockholm
Inv. no. 139

In this large self-portrait, Eugène Jansson has portrayed himself against the background of his favourite subject during the blue period, the view of Riddarfjärden in Stockholm in evening light. It was from this spot that his series of panoramas at dusk, night, and dawn was created. It was a view whose tense atmosphere was to be so intimately linked with his name that it was natural for him to use it as a signature in his self-portrait.

The portrait has an ascetic quality which is usually associated with Eugène Jansson's introspective nature. The deafness that struck him at the age of 14 after a serious bout of scarlet fever no doubt contributed to his introspection. A succession of illnesses also forced him to live a highly disciplined life, with the emphasis on hygiene, fresh air, gymnastics, and bathing. This was to play an important role in his paintings after the end of this blue period in 1905, when male athletes doing gymnastics and bathing in the open air became a main theme. The self-portrait, however, shows Eugène Jansson as a 'blue painter'. Here in his studio, high above the city, he watched for fifteen years, viewing dusk and dawn. The view could have inspired him to Nietzschean moods, but instead brought out the dreamy poet of light and colour.

T.G.

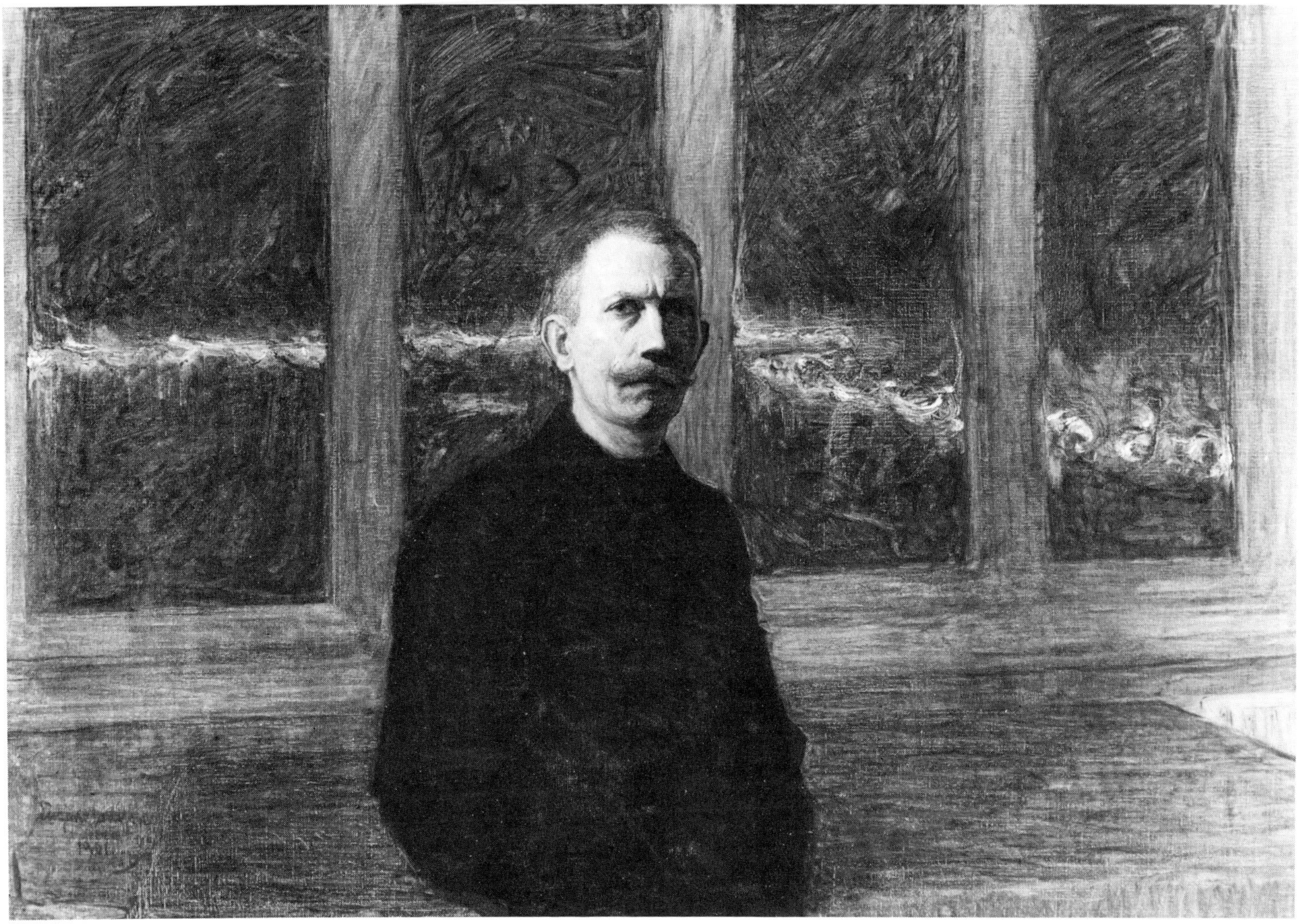

39. Eugène Jansson

VIGGO JOHANSEN

1851–1935, Denmark

Viggo Johansen was accepted at the Royal Academy of Fine Arts in 1868 and left it in 1876, without having passed the final examination. In 1880 he married a cousin of Anna Ancher's (p. 64) and found inspiration for a very important part of his work in his home. In 1882 he travelled by way of Berlin and Dresden to the World Exhibition in Vienna. He exhibited in Vienna and while there became especially interested in seventeenth-century Dutch art, which he previously had studied at the Royal Collections in Copenhagen. Viggo Johansen often had his paintings shown at international exhibitions and won recognition for his scenes from everyday life. He went to Paris for the first time in 1885 and there had the opportunity of seeing paintings by Monet. But he must certainly have heard about modern French painting before then. In the kitchen scenes and interiors, he combined Dutch intimacy with a fresh painterly concept.

Because of his studies at the Academy and through his wife's family, he became a member of the artists' colony at Skagen, but he also painted landscapes from other localities, among them the meadows near the sea on the island of Amager, just outside Copenhagen.

40

A Summer's Night, 1894

(Fra de lyse nætters tid)

79 × 121
Signed lower right: V. Johansen. 94.
Ordrupgaardsamlingen, Copenhagen
(purchased in 1902)

Viggo Johansen was the painter *par excellence* of the 1880s in his depictions of the intimacy of everyday life, and was destined to become one of those Danish painters of the 1890s whose work was characterized by strong sentiment.

This picture from the meadows on the coast of Copenhagen has for its subject flat fields, emphasized by a diagonally running ditch, low banks of earth, a waggon shed, a little group of trees, small flocks of sheep and geese, and a cow lying on the grass.

The inspiration for this highly Dutch type of landscape may have arisen in part from the locality itself, as it was colonized by Dutch vegetable-growers in the sixteenth century. Behind is a strip of water and a winking lighthouse. Above is the light summer night with a moon. The water in the calm of evening and the contrast between warm and cool light are wholly in the spirit of the 1880s. But in the 1880s, they would have been the main theme. Here it is the sky and the moon which dominate the picture, and it is from them that the landscape and animals partake of their dreamlike poetry, their *mystique*. It is the Neo-National Romanticism of the '90s in Denmark under the summer night's moon.

H.W.

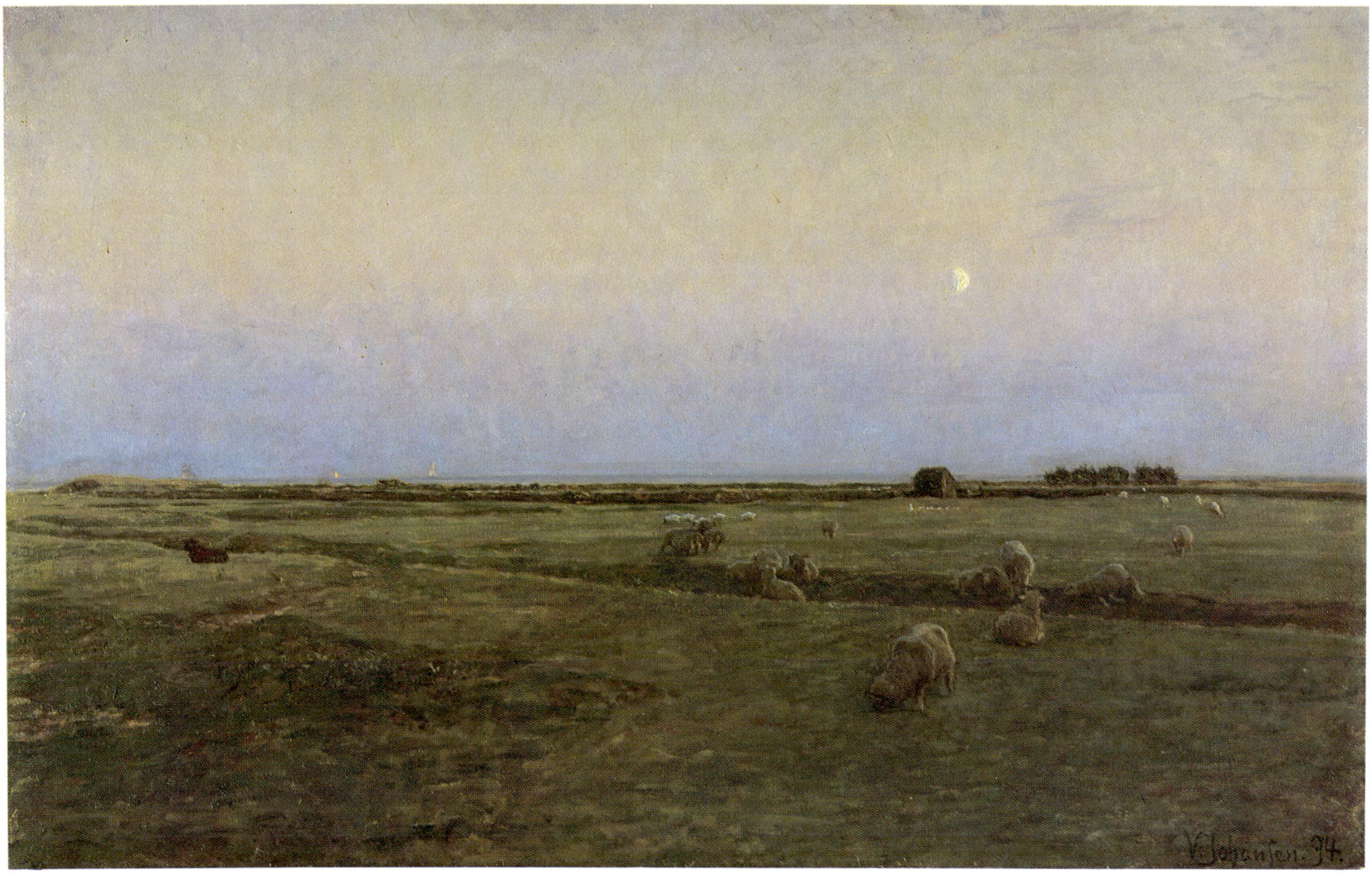

40. Viggo Johansen

ERNST JOSEPHSON

1851–1906, Sweden

During and after his years at the Academy of Fine Arts in Stockholm from 1867 to 1876, Ernst Josephson made a number of study trips to Germany, Italy, Belgium, and the Netherlands, where he copied works by Rembrandt, and to France, where he was a pupil of J.-L. Gérome in 1874. He lived in France from 1879 to 1888, first in Paris and after 1886 in the country.

He became one of the leaders of the Swedish Opponents' movement against the academy, publishing two sensational, inflammatory articles, *Om den konstnärliga uppfostran* (On Artistic Training), and in 1885 was one of the commissioners of the Opponents' first two exhibitions. In these exhibitions, sharp criticism was directed against *The Water Sprite* (Prins Eugens Waldemarsudde), the romantic scene which, together with portraits and depictions of his time, occupied Josephson for most of the 1880s.

At the age of 37 Josephson was struck by mental illness, and spent some time in hospital; he recovered sufficiently to be able to lead a fairly normal life, painting and sketching actively. In his later production, he expressed his ideas and feelings with great artistic freedom and intensity, and gave form to his personal world of fantasy. These works, which most people first considered to be the incomprehensible products of a sick mind, heralded some of the twentieth-century's expressionistic art trends and influenced a number of Swedish and foreign painters. However, it was not until after his death that Josephson's multifaceted and contradictory work as an artist became generally recognized as the most deeply personal and interesting in Swedish art of the late nineteenth century.

41

Autumn Sun, 1886

(Höstsol)

130 × 82
Signed upper left: Ernst Josephson/Tréboul 1886
Thielska galleriet, Stockholm
Inv. no. 163 (purchased in 1906)

In the 1880s, Ernst Josephson had followed the day's naturalistic and *plein-air* precepts in his portraits and genre pictures, but often endowed his colours with a powerful light and intrinsic value of a kind less common then. His fellow painter Richard Bergh wrote in 1893, 'He was the only real colourist among us, and not only because he knew how to use colour to achieve a richer and more sonorous surface than any of us, but also – and to an equally great extent – because he knew the secret of letting this harmony of colours take on a deeper meaning, a symbolic, almost musical tone.'

In 1886, Josephson left Paris and life in the big city for the country and the simple world of the peasants. In Tréboul, in Brittany, he painted *Autumn Sun*, in which the division between the descriptive narrative on the one hand, and Symbolist expression, on the other, became clear. The painting had 'caused great difficulties', he himself admitted. 'It depicts an old, decrepit woman, who is going out of a doorway, leaning on her stick, and the sun casts spots of light on the wall where the shadow falls from a dried-up tree which one cannot see, and far inside the doorway stands a little girl working. I call the picture "Autumn Sun".' Josephson had first painted it with thick colours and great detail, but he scraped off his first efforts and with light, blurred brushstrokes gave the picture an almost incorporeal look. Instead of a genre picture in the Dutch or Bastien-Lepage spirit, he created, with insight and sensitivity, an expressive symbolist picture of resigned, withered old age in profound harmony with the pale, grey-glimmering autumn light. The old peasant woman has been transformed into a 'transient vision, a figure from a saga' (E. Blomberg).

P.G.

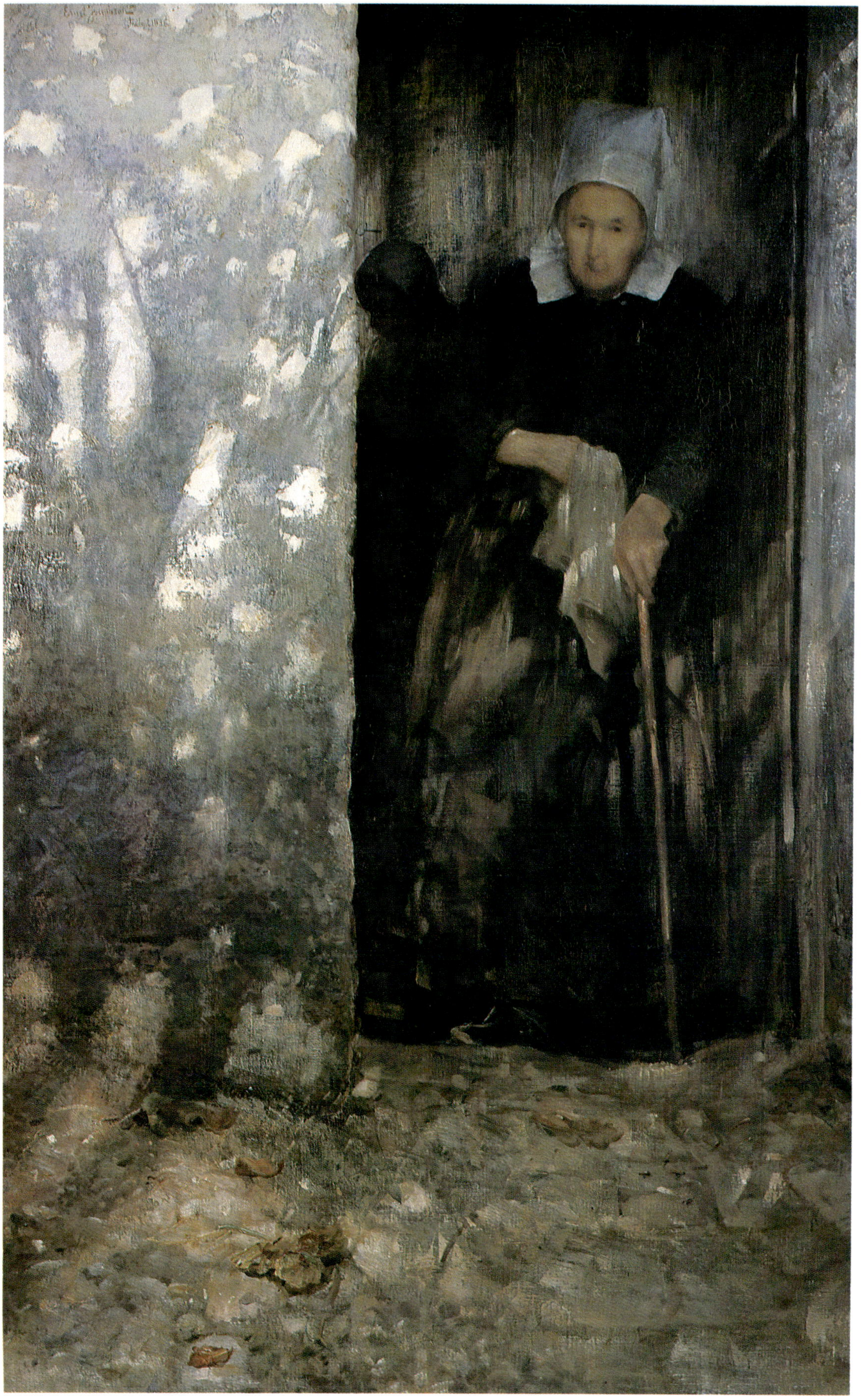

41 Ernst Josephson

42

The Holy Sacrament, c. 1890

(Det heliga sakramentet)

127 × 76
Signed lower left: Ernst Josephson
Nationalmuseum, Stockholm
Inv. no. 3602 (donated in 1915)

It was after attending spiritualist seances at Ile de Bréhat in Brittany in 1888 that Ernst Josephson first suffered from paranoia. The line between fantasy and reality was erased; delusions of grandeur alternated with feelings of terror, guilt and persecution. The paintings and drawings from the following few years were highly visionary. The artist often expressed his personal problems with religious themes. He identified himself with Christ, both the suffering Son of Man and the Savior of the World. In the central motive in his earlier works, the male figure of *The Water Sprite*, there had already been a large degree of self-identification together with a pantheistic interpretation of the Christian doctrine of atonement.

In *The Holy Sacrament*, the painter, according to analyses by E. Blomberg and I. Mesterton, may have identified himself both with Christ breaking the bread, *panis angelicus*, and with the little figure kneeling in the foreground to partake of the divine mercy and the holy communion. The figures who surround the Savior, the child to the left and the translucent female figure to the right, can be interpreted as symbols of the painter's dead mother and sister. 'The whole scene', writes Blomberg, 'gives the impression of a solemn communion, a reunification in the Swedenborgian spirit of the Son of Man, who has returned to Paradise, and his divine family.'

Emanuel Swedenborg had served as a medium for Josephson's conversations with the spirits in Bréhat; he became the one who conveyed God's message to Josephson. There are marked similarities in character and views between the great Swedish philosopher and his countryman, and the intense radiance which permeates *The Holy Sacrament* seems to derive from some of Swedenborg's dreams.

It is this powerful, intangible light which predominantly characterizes the painting. Like the life-giving sun, it emanates in yellow, orange, vermilion and green rays from the figure of Christ and drenches the rest of the painting in a blinding light. By the side stands a green-clad figure which may be either Mary Magdalene, or an angel (when first exhibited in 1893 the picture was called *The Angel's Sermon*).

It is this figure who seems to see with an inner eye the vision represented on this canvas. With its elongated body and ecstatically upturned face, it recalls figures by El Greco and representations of the apocalypse in medieval manuscripts and church porches. Josephson's art can thus be linked to an earlier visionary and expressive tradition and, in turn, heralds certain expressionistic forms of modern art.

P.G.

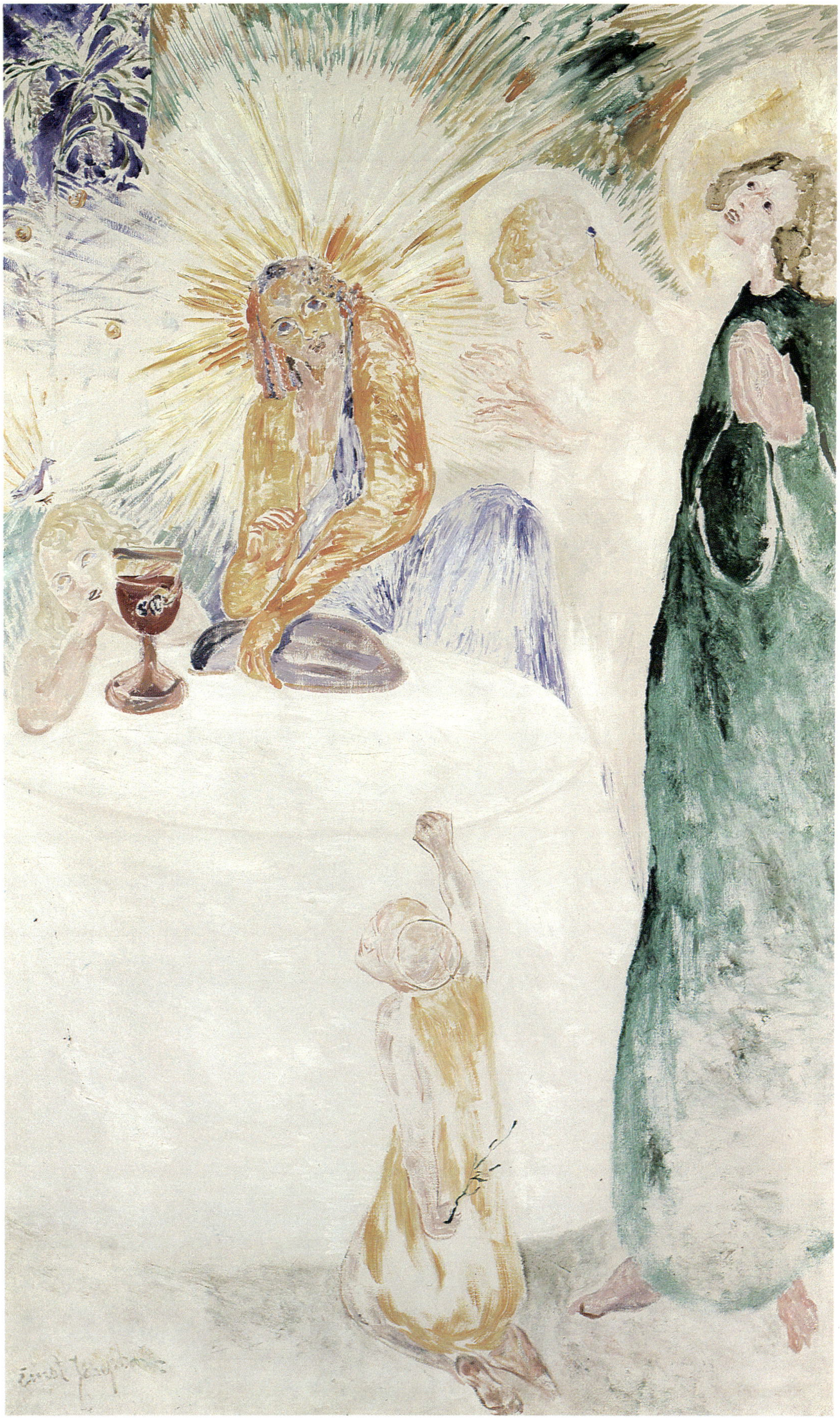

42. Ernst Josephson

43

Portrait of Ludvig Josephson, 1893

(Porträtt av Ludvig Josephson)

137 × 109
Signed upper right: Ernst Josephson/Stockholm/1893 APRIL
En midsommarn/attsdröm./SHAKSPEA/RE./W.
(Sandblom Collection) Nationalmuseum, Stockholm
Inv. no. 6352 (donation in 1970)

Ludvig Josephson was an important person in the life of his nephew Ernst, with whom he shared a passion for art, the theatre and music. He was a stage manager at the Dramatic Theatre in Stockholm and at the National Theatre in Oslo, and in 1891–2 was given the task of staging *A Midsummer Night's Dream* at the Opera in Stockholm. It is probable that Ernst Josephson attended the rehearsals and the following year chose to paint a portrait of his uncle in the course of his work. With one hand on his list, Ludvig Josephson calls the performers to rehearsal with a little bell. In the foreground, on the left, we can discern a few actors on a stage and on the right, we see written, like graffiti, the title of the play.

It is a strange and hallucinatory painting, one of the most extraordinary in Swedish art. The painter's mental illness did not impair his control of his means of expression: rather, it gave him great liberty in dealing with external reality. Thus he did not create a portrait in the ordinary sense of the word. The fantastic space of the painting is like a metaphor of the theatre's space, where all miracles and all metamorphoses are possible and where, in this case, Shakespeare's text is in the process of being transformed into a performance in flesh and blood. The stage manager in the centre looks like a magician, even like a prophet. The face is certainly that of Ludvig Josephson, with his large brown eyes, beard, and long hair, but with 'his majestic prophet's countenance he resembles Michelangelo's Moses much more than an irascible little stage manager from the provincial hole which was Stockholm' (E. Blomberg).

One gets the impression that, through Shakespeare's words, this prophet is interpreting a kind of divine message. In fact Ernst Josephson had always considered the artist – be he a painter, poet or man of the theatre – to be a creator in the image of God. In 1877 he had written to his mother, 'Do you know why the whole world bows to a great artist? Because nothing testifies to the greatness and the presence of God so much as the fact that He created a being capable of creating.'

So Uncle Ludvig could here be considered an *alter ego* of the painter.

The portrait was painted when, having recovered from the paranoid phase of his illness, Josephson felt filled with a new creative force thanks to the success of the exhibition which his friends had organized in 1893 and which marked a turning-point in the public's appreciation of his work. He painted the portrait of his uncle over an old historical composition (from 1874), which he had reversed so that the principle personage in it, an executioner in red, is clearly visible to the right, upside down. The painter also retained the Rembrandt-like chiaroscuro and the colours of the painting underneath, superimposing the portrait of Ludvig with amazing freedom and furia.

P.G.

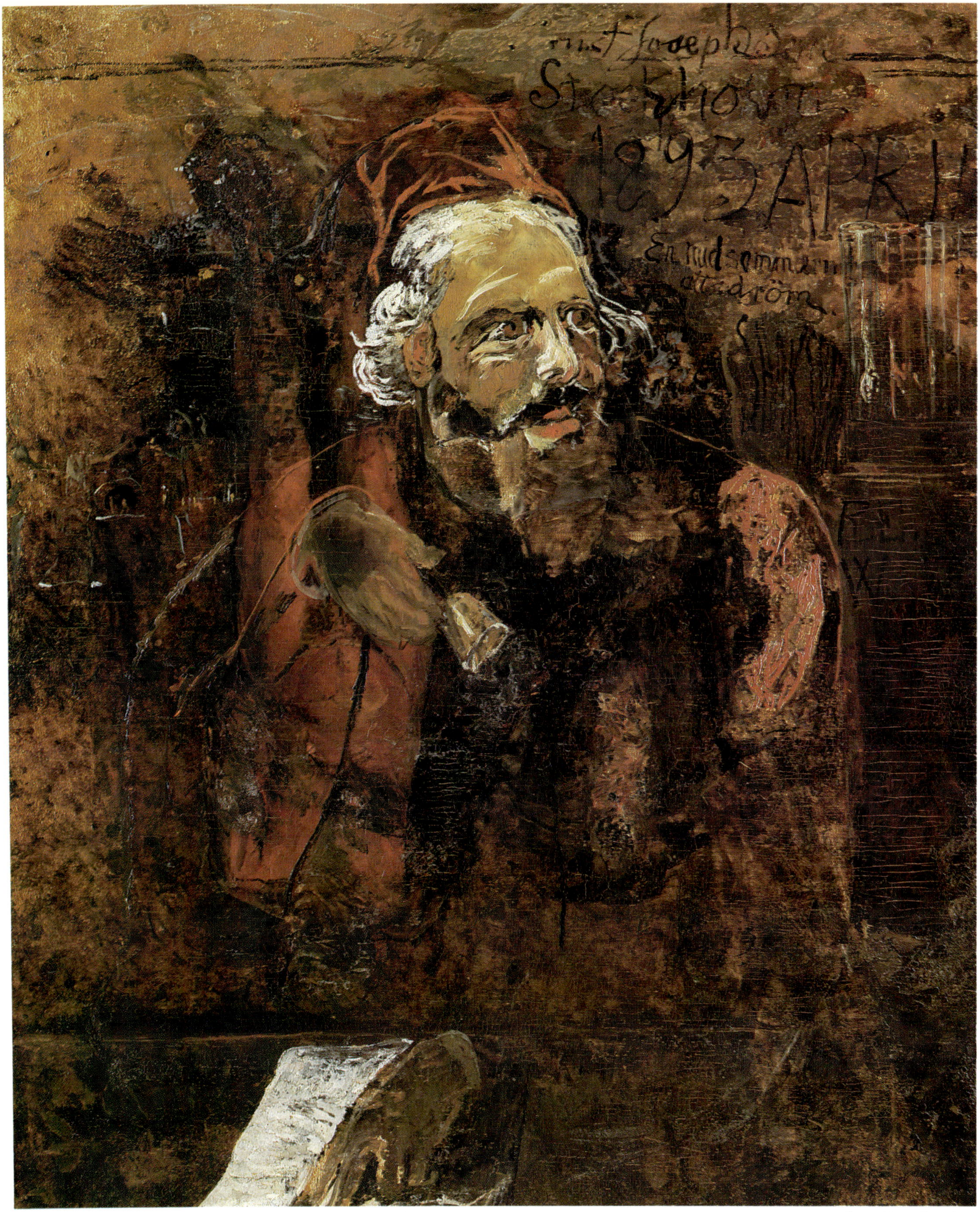

43. Ernst Josephson

44

Illustrations for E. G. Geijer's Pieces of Poetry, 1890

44a

Manhem

Pen and watercolour, 37 × 22
Signed lower right: Ernst Josephson
Formerly Stenman Collection, Stockholm

44b

Svegder

Pen and watercolour, 37 × 22
Signed lower right: Ernst Josephson
(Text lower middle: svegder)
Formerly Stenman Collection, Stockholm

44c

The Last Warrior

(Den siste kämpen)

Pen and watercolour, 37.5 × 22.5
Signed lower right: Ernst Josephson
(Text lower right above: Den Siste Kämpen)
Formerly Stenman Collection, Stockholm

44d

Charles XII

(Karl XII)

Pen and watercolour, 36.5 × 22
Signed lower right: Ernst Josephson
(Text lower right above: carl den tolfte)
Private Collection, Stockholm

44e

The Viking

(Vikingen)

Pen and watercolour, 37 × 22.5
Signed lower right: Ernst Josephson
(Text lower right above: VIKINGEN)
Nationalmuseum, Stockholm
Inv. no. H 53/1960

Historical painting in Sweden in the second half of the nineteenth century had borrowed most of its subjects from the mythology and history of the country. Ernst Josephson, when still a pupil of the Academy, was very much imbued with this spirit of nationalism. 'My ambition is to carve sagas from my homeland in noble runes', he declared in 1873.

Like most of his friends, however, he soon turned from this cult of the past. It became his programme to reflect his own age and to interpret nature with freedom and independence.

The schizophrenia that broke out in 1888 led him to people his work anew with kings and queens, with gods and legendary warriors. Political life and the ideology of the turn of the century were permeated by nationalist feelings. The glorious epochs in Sweden's history, from the age of the Vikings to Charles XII, were invoked, and its great writers read and quoted with fervour.

Josephson was particularly attracted to Erik Gustaf Geijer, poet, philosopher and historian from the Romantic era. In 1895 he illustrated Geijer's collection of poems, *Skaldestycken* (Pieces of poetry, 1811–12), with a hundred drawings. We have chosen to present here some of the most expressive of those devoted to historical themes, where Josephson recreated the rhythm and atmosphere of the poems, but with a tragic, visionary power all his own. It is clear that the poems' lofty union of heroism and longing for death struck deep chords in his soul.

Svegder, The Viking, The Last Warrior and *Charles XII* all deal with noble warriors who, after a lifetime of great feats, are accepted into another, paradisial world. One might recall Ingres' *Le Songe d'Ossian.* The legendary world evoked by the Swedish writer is the Scandinavian equivalent of these Ossian songs. But his idealized Viking

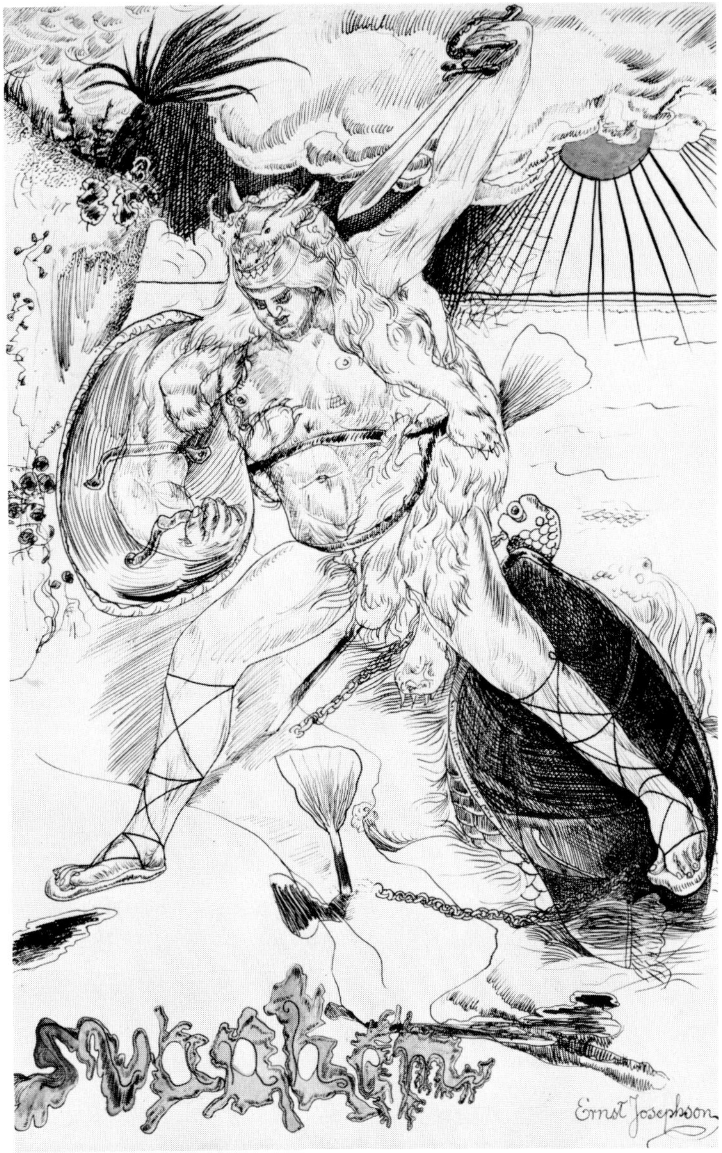

44a. Ernst Josephson

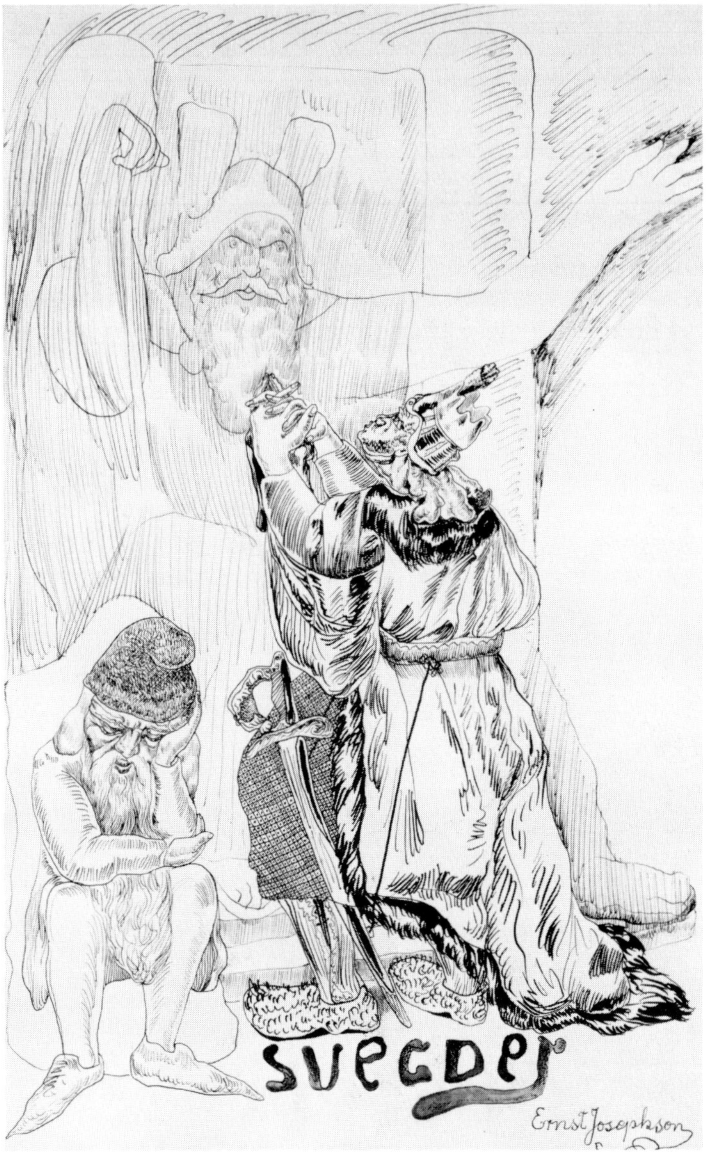

44b. Ernst Josephson

heroes, rugged and fearless, magnanimous and upright, are presented by Geijer as a condemnation of his own emasculated and mercenary age. *Charles XII*, the warrior king, appears as their descendant: on his death, he is carried away by St Michael to the 'throne of the Lamb', where he is seated beside Charlemagne and King Gustavus Adolphus. *The Last Warrior* from pagan times, rejecting Christianity and refusing to die ignominiously in his bed, is preparing to throw himself off a precipice in order to rejoin his friends in Odin's Valhalla. *Svegder*, mythical king of Svea, is enticed with secret magical powers by an old, long-bearded dwarf into the wall of a mountain, where he will behold Odin for all eternity. The heathen god which Josephson's *Svegder* is seen praying to with clasped hands could just as well be the Christian God, and he ultimately acts like an Almighty Father in whose arms a mortal longs to rest.

Even more striking is the existential symbolism of Josephson's *The Viking*. Shipwrecked on the rocks, the young Viking is on the point of being carried off by the waves: he sings to the sea where, in the tempest, he hears the 'Norns spinning their threads', because, according to Geijer's poem, 'man's fate is like the swell of the waves'. With a simple and supple line, but with extraordinary dynamics, the painter has merged the Viking and his boat and represented him in an embryonic position, ready to be received in the vast maternal bosom of the sea.

Josephson experienced 'the poems that he illustrated in a purely physical way, with all his being, and this partly explains the terrifyingly plastic power of expression which these drawings have at times' (I. Mesterton). Their delineation alternates between grand, pure lines and a detail embellished with a perseverance that is at times obsessive. This alternation is the continuation of the two work methods which had been used in parallel throughout all of Josephson's production and which undoubtedly express the fundamental dualism of his personality. He was, on the one hand, a *realist*, a temperamental, optimistic, energetic man who in the 1880s was a leader among his fellow painters and in the Opponents' movement, and, on the other, an *idealist*, a docile and anxious child, a dreamer. The insoluble conflict between these two personae was probably one of the reasons for his mental illness but, one should add, it is a dualism which is to be found at the very heart of the *fin de siècle* in Europe.

P.G.

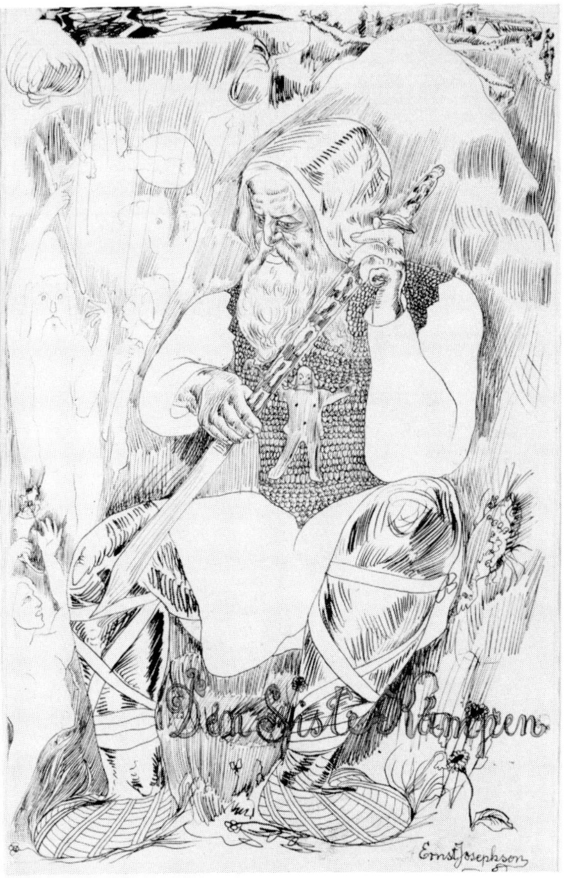

44c. Ernst Josephson

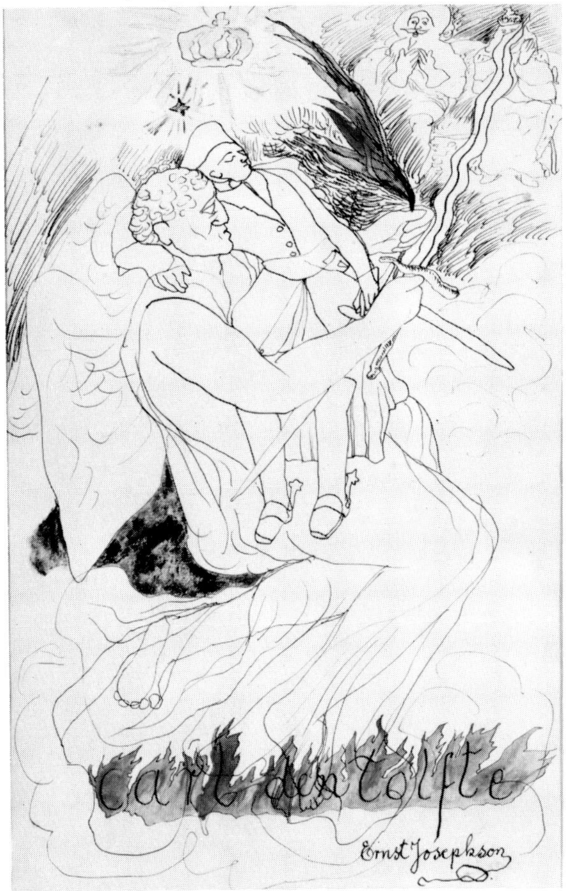

44d. Ernst Josephson

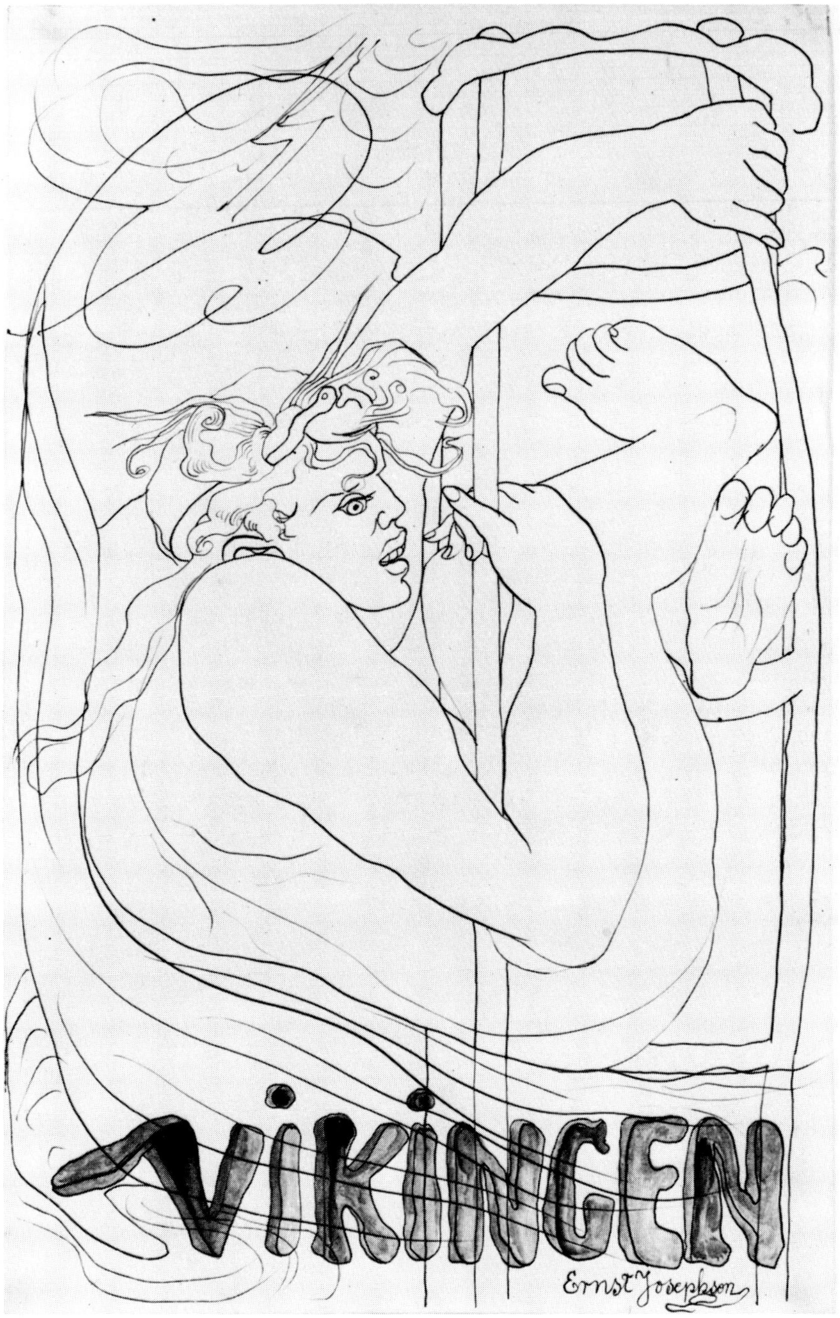

44e. Ernst Josephson

EERO JÄRNEFELT

1863–1937, Finland

'I do not care for Symbolism', wrote Eero Järnefelt in his diary in the 1890s. He also criticized 'superficial and radical trends' in Finland, the artists' need to move from one vogue to another, and the 'abuse of intelligence' which this brings with it. He wrote down these ideas in Florence in 1897, surrounded by the early art of the Renaissance. He was inspired by a new desire for humility, a desire to return to his former standpoints in art, a love of nature 'from which he had deviated for many years'.

Even though Eero Järnefelt, as we can see, could not avoid the experiments with styles and trends which the 1890s brought with them, he very soon became a true and keen observer of nature.

Eero Järnefelt came from a Swedish-speaking, but Finnophile, aristocratic family. His mother was from a Baltic–St Petersburg artistic family and brought the home a strong love of literature and art. Eero Järnefelt's older brother Arvid was a well-known writer, whose work *Herääminseni* (My Awakening) in 1894 brought Leo Tolstoy's doctrines to Finland. Tolstoy's ideas did not suit the rational Eero Järnefelt. He always remained a sceptic.

Järnefelt received his initial training from his uncle, the *plein-air* painter Mikhail Konstantinovich Klodt von Jürgensburg, a member of the Wanderers group in St Petersburg, but Järnefelt could with better reason be considered a representative of the French *plein-air* style which he studied on extensive trips to Paris. Unlike most other Finns, Järnefelt was particularly interested in the Barbizon tradition and worked at Veneux-Nadon in the spring of 1888 among Scandinavian and French painters.

Järnefelt's production was fairly evenly divided between landscapes and portraits. He continued to paint right up to his death in 1937.

45

Lake Shore with Reeds, 1905

(Kaislikkoranta, Höstlandskap)

94.5 × 75
Signed lower right: Eero Järnefelt/05.
(Antell Collection) Ateneumin taidemuseo, Helsinki
Inv. no. A II 798 (purchased in 1906)

Lake Shore with Reeds brings out the melancholy atmosphere of nature in the autumn: nature's slumber; the damp odour of decay; the pale light, the last moment before the arrival of the long period of darkness. The lone chair which has remained on the shore is waiting in vain for a human presence. Nature is becoming deserted and will soon close in.

Stylistically, Järnefelt's painting is typical of turn-of-the-century Finnish work: the age of Symbolism has not passed but gone were the dizzying wanderings among ideologies, the problems, the fairy-tales, the arabesques of Art Nouveau, all features which, in fact, had never been characteristic of Järnefelt's work. Something of the preceding decade did, however, remain, namely an effort to create a synthesis, a harmony of colours. In returning to nature artists seemed to have stopped half-way between adopting new colours which they had once rejected so defiantly and arriving at new syntheses which were no longer built upon independent, decorative, tapestry-like forms.

Järnefelt's elegiac autumn brings to mind a Chekhovian melancholy. The scene is far from Gallen-Kallela's dramatic view of barren, dying nature in for example *Joukahainen's Revenge* (No. 24). But the colours are the same in the works of both painters: ochre, brown, and lead grey – the colours of dead foliage and of icy water.

S.S-K.

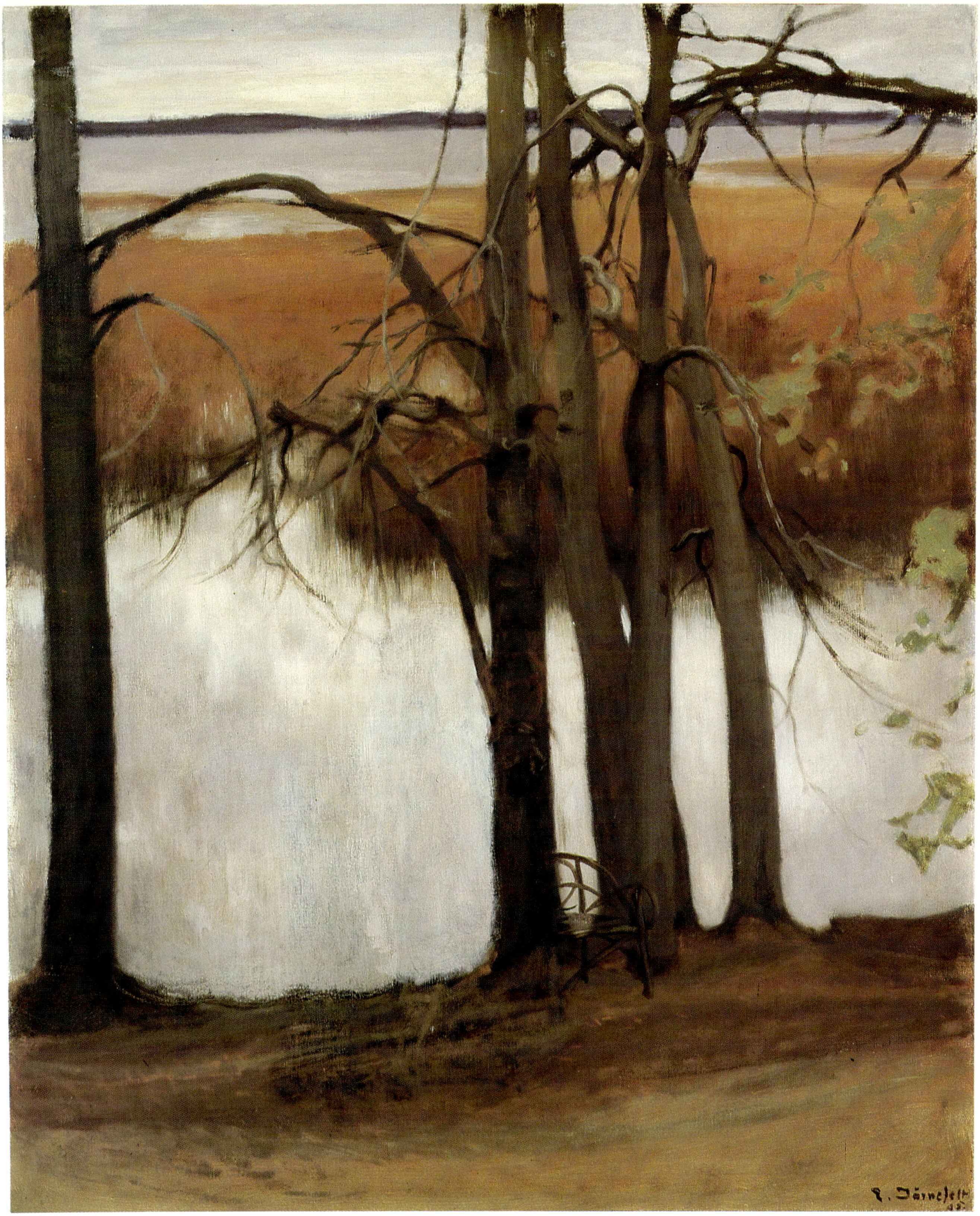

45. Eero Järnefelt

KITTY L. KIELLAND

1843–1914, Norway

Kitty Kielland was nearly thirty when she left for Karlsruhe in 1873 to begin her education as an artist under Professor Hans Gude. Earlier she had received a little instruction in drawing in her home town, where she copied works by Lars Hertervig, among others, and in 1872 she had spent a short time with Morten Müller in Christiania. In Karlsruhe, she immediately began to make open-air studies, but she also drew from plaster and live models. From 1875 to 1878, she lived in Munich, where she received instruction from Eilif Peterssen and Hermann Baisch. She then moved to Paris and studied under Léon Pelouse at the beginning of the 1880s. From 1881 to 1888 she lived with Harriet Backer in Paris and made various trips with her; to Brittany in 1881, Jæren in 1884, Risør in 1885, and Fleskum in 1886. Kitty L. Kielland made her debut at the Salon in 1879 with two landscapes from Jæren, and received a silver medal at the World Fair in Paris in 1889 for *After the Rain*, also a motive from Jæren. Her name has always been linked with Jæren. Beginning in 1876, she made a number of studies of this landscape. Another motive appeared in the middle of the '80s: moody landscapes with the still, mirror-clear water as the dominating element, as in *Summer Night* (1886, Nasjonalgalleriet), for example. She played an important role in the development of 'mood painting', but her basic philosophy remained realistic. She was one of Scandinavia's most convinced open-air painters.

46

After Sunset, 1886

(Efter solnedgang)

80 × 115.5
Signed lower left: Kitty L Kielland/Paris 1886.
Stavanger Faste Galleri, Stavanger
Inv. no. 242 (donation in 1889)

This picture, painted in Paris in the spring of 1886, is a close replica of a picture Kitty L. Kielland had painted in the summer of 1885 in Norway. She spent that summer with Harriet Backer (see Nos. 2–4) in Risør, an idyllic small town on the coast of southern Norway. The subject is from Bosvik, just outside the town. The venerable old manor, an impressive wooden house built in 1756, is still standing, and we can see that Kitty L. Kielland kept close to her model. But as the title indicates, the real subject of this picture is the mood at evening. The old house is reflected in the surface of the water in the summer evening's failing light. The mirror of water reaches across the whole length of the picture and captures the sun's last rays, which shine rose-coloured in the clouds. The composition closes around the surface of the water, and the reflecting mirror of water in the summer evening's dim light is the focus of the picture. Here the artist had discovered a subject to which she was to return again and again in the following years, a subject which stimulated a new development in Norwegian landscape painting, the so-called 'mood landscape'.

The first version of *After Sunset* was shown at the Autumn Exhibition in 1885, where the picture attracted some attention. After stating that the subject was typically Norwegian, the leading art critic Andreas Aubert wrote, 'In a French subject, it would have been difficult for her to capture the depth of feeling, the intensity of mood of the old manor with its history and its memories standing alone and silent in the summer evening's lingering, slowly fading light' (Nyt Tidsskrift, 1885, p. 526). This was considerable praise from a discriminating critic. Aubert also observed that in *After Sunset* Kitty Kielland had reached the goal her generation had set, to achieve an art that was uniquely Norwegian while still rooted in a European, professional tradition.

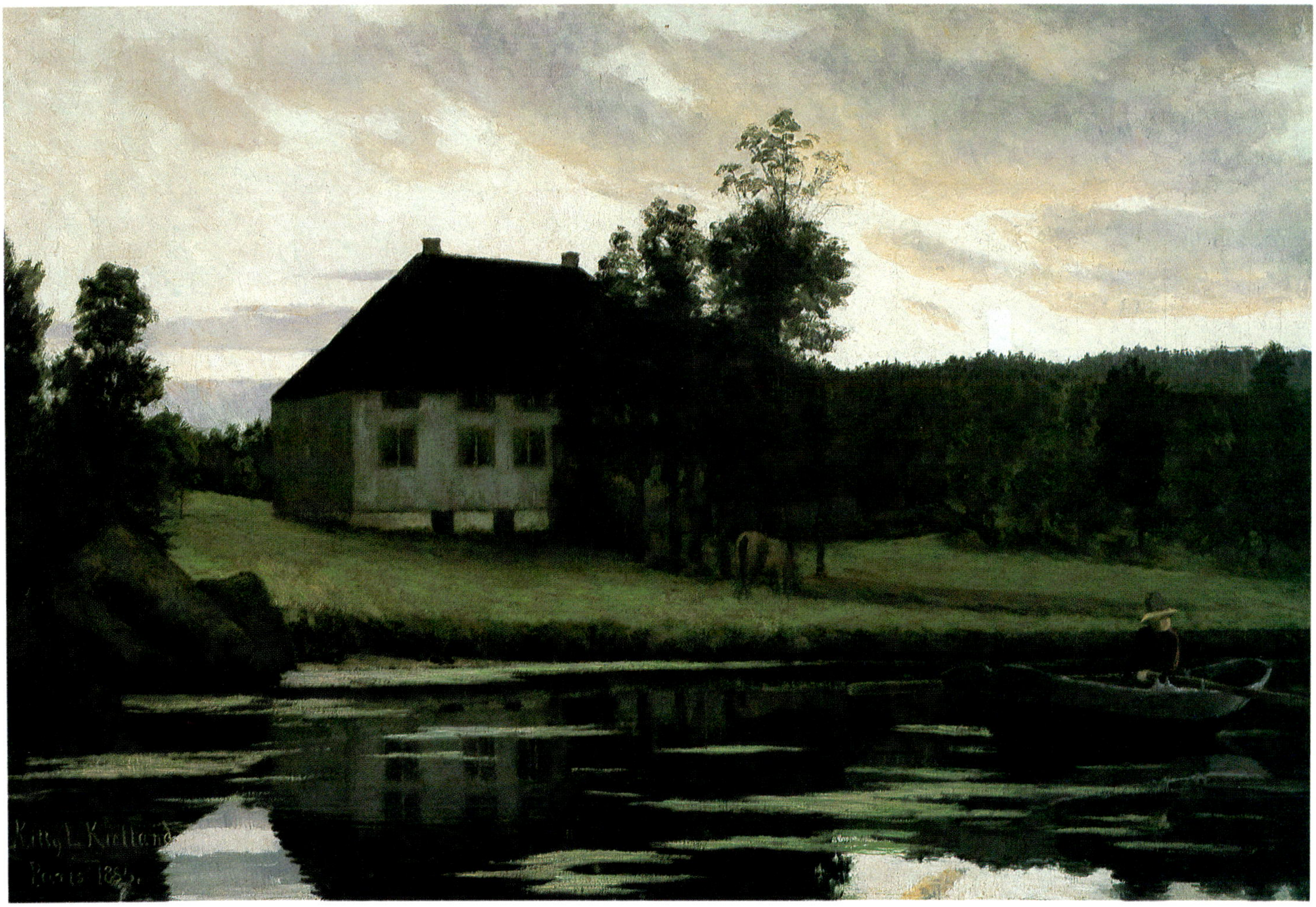

46. Kitty L. Kielland

No wonder that Kitty L. Kielland chose to paint a second version of this picture when back in Paris in the spring of 1886. *After Sunset* is the only one of her compositions which exists in several replicas. It evidently meant a great deal to her. Thus she let this picture represent her at all the important international exhibitions in the following years. As late as 1897, a version was shown at the Venice Biennale, where it was purchased by Queen Elena of Italy.

The first version was sold when first exhibited at the Autumn Exhibition. In Paris, she worked from a study taken on the spot in 1885 (Nasjonalgalleriet, Oslo) and from a photograph of the first version. The first version has rather pronounced local colour, the second one (shown here) is dominated by a harmonizing, bluish overall tone. The reasons for this development must be sought in the Paris milieu, where Puvis de Chavannes's art had again become fashionable with his famous decorations for the stairway of the museum in Lyon. The large canvas with the solemn title '*Le Bois Sacré, cher aux arts et aux Muses*' was exhibited at the Salon in 1884. It shows the Muses' sacred grove in the golden hours of evening. Even though the scene is populated by Muses inspired by Antiquity, it was Puvis's expressive landscape background which determined the character of the work. André Michel described it as follows: 'A large lake . . . which reflects a sky of gold of which only a thin band is visible above a range of mountains, of a purplish blue which closes the horizon' (A. Michel and J. Laran, *Puvis de Chavannes*, Paris, undated, p. 85). These were precisely the features which Kitty L. Kielland had noted and which inspired her own choice of a theme like *After Sunset*. So when the second version of the picture was rejected by the Salon in the spring of 1886, she was horrified. She and Harriet Backer wondered if they had gone astray as artists, and she suggested in a letter to her artist friend Erik Werenskiold that they and other painters they knew from their time in Munich get together and paint in the summer, for their mutual enjoyment and inspiration. Thus the rejection of *After Sunset* led to the famous artists' gathering at Fleskum farm outside Christiania in 1886.

Although it was rejected by the Salon, the second version of *After Sunset* was exhibited at the Gothenburg exhibition in 1886, at the Scandinavian exhibition in Copenhagen in 1888, and at the World Fair in Paris in 1889. In 1890, she donated the picture to the art association in her home town of Stavanger.

When the painting was exhibited in Copenhagen, the French critic Maurice Hamel was struck by precisely the features we have noted above. 'By saying things in the simplest way, Mlle Kielland succeeds in attaining a more penetrating impression. What translucent purity in her landscape, *After Sunset*! How the white house with its large red roof softly sinks its reflection in the water which the evening sky glazes with pale reds and greens' (*Gazette des Beaux-Arts*, 1888, II, p. 402).

M.I.L.

47

Summer Night, 1886

(Sommernatt)

100.5 × 135.5
Signed lower left: Kitty L. Kielland Fleskum 1886
Nasjonalgalleriet, Oslo
Inv. no. 357 (purchased in 1890)

In the summer of 1886, a group of artists gathered at Fleskum farm by Lake Dælivannet not far from Sandviken outside Christiania. The artists were Erik Werenskiold, Eilif Peterssen, Gerhard Munthe, Christian Skredsvig, Harriet Backer, and Kitty L. Kielland, all good friends from their study period in Munich and later in Paris. The 'Fleskum summer' of 1886 on the one hand marked the breakthrough of *plein-air* painting in Norway. But on the other, and seemingly in opposition to it, it witnessed the dawn of Romanticism. It is in landscapes that we find features which point towards the Neo-Romantic movement of the 1890s, especially in the depictions of the calm lake under the gentle, blue light of the summer night. Kitty L. Kielland's *Summer Night*, or *By the Lake*, as it was originally called, and Eilif Peterssen's *Summer Night* (No. 67) both show lake Dælivannet and are considered the masterpieces of that summer at Fleskum. This is where the close-up of nature, the quiet mirror of water, and the summer night's muted light and bluish tone came into their own. Kitty L. Kielland further developed ideas she first worked with in *After Sunset* (No. 46) and she undoubtedly influenced Eilif Peterssen in his choice of motive. These two pictures can be considered both as realistic depictions of the summer night and as Symbolist presentations of nature. The art critic Andreas Aubert had early on urged Norwegian artists to take the Nordic summer night as a motive, and let it 'become a source from which our artists could draw'. When the Fleskum painters showed their pictures at the Autumn Exhibition the same year, Aubert was able to note with satisfaction that they had followed his advice. The artists had been diligent in using the long hours of dusk for studies out in the open, something that French artists, for example, had no opportunity to do, because of 'central Europe's short dusk...' (*Morgenbladet*, 4 Nov. 1886).

Capturing the summer night as an artistic motive was wholly in keeping with the national programme of the day, to emphasize special national characteristics. But the lasting effect of the summer at Fleskum seems to have been something else: the illumination of the 'blue hour' made it sensible to simplify forms, and the picture's

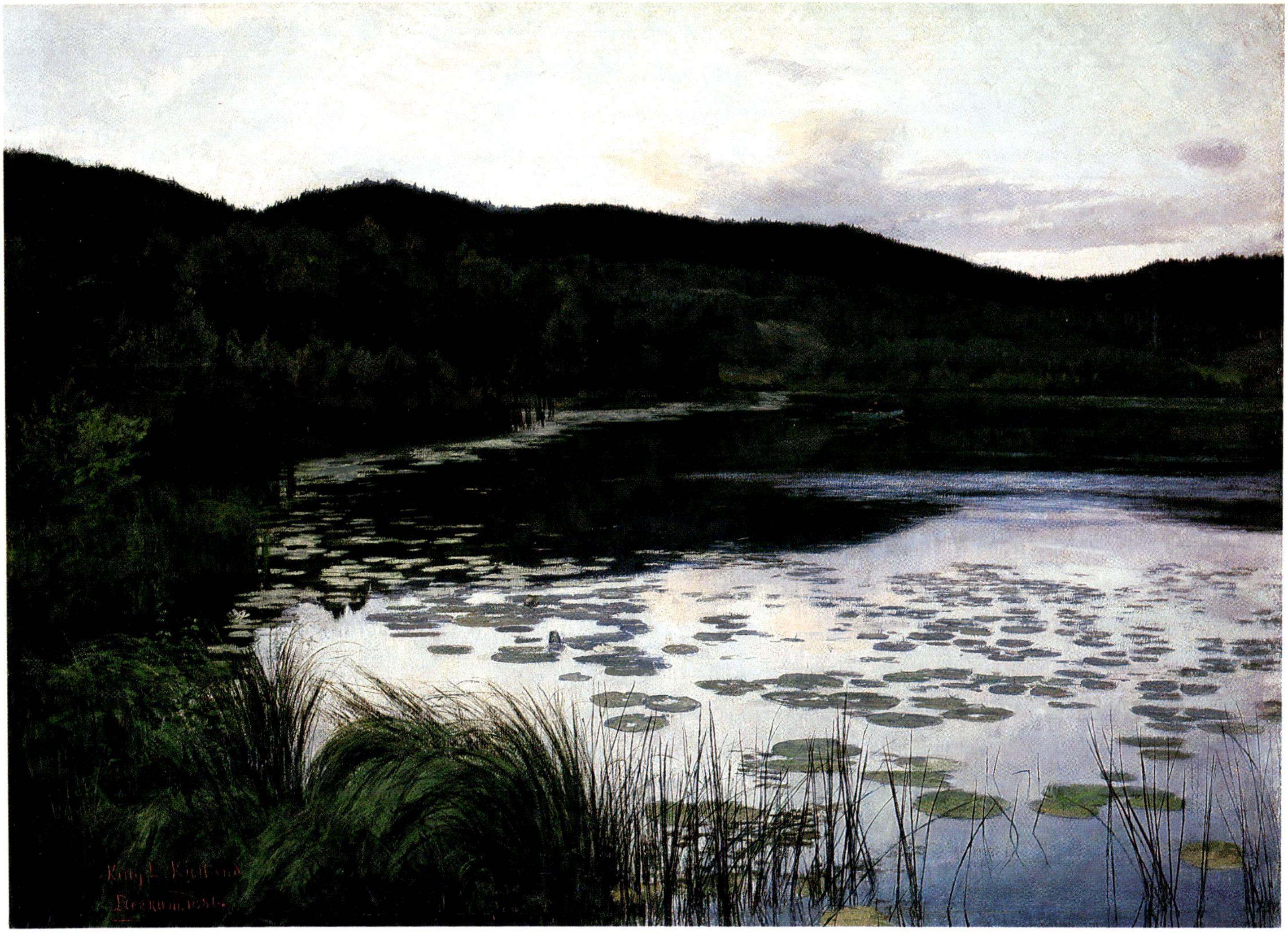

47. Kitty L. Kielland

atmospheric content could as a result be further intensified. But the synthetizing tendency also opened up the possibility of treating the motive decoratively and, as a result, prepared the way for more modern trends in Norwegian art.

Together with *After Sunset, Summer Night* was Kitty L. Kielland's most important exhibition picture in the latter part of the 1880s. It was shown at the Autumn Exhibition in 1886, at the Salon in 1887, at the Scandinavian exhibition in Copenhagen in 1888, and finally at the World Fair in 1889. In 1890, it was sold to the Nasjonalgalleriet.

At the Paris World Fair in 1889, the French critics noted landscapes in particular. André Michel drew attention to the summer night pictures in his discussion of Norwegian painting in *Journal des Debats*, 27 August 1889. He wrote, 'They speak to us above all with a vibrant tenderness of their homeland, of the brilliant, icy waters, the splendours of the harsh winters, of the sweet magic of the slow twilight and the clear summer nights . . . where the twilight of summer lingers in the skies with an exquisite sweetness, the clear nights give the painters, late-comers, a singularly alluring motive, admirably suited to capture the eye of an artist.'

M.I.L.

THEODOR KITTELSEN

1857–1914, Norway

Kittelsen grew up in difficult circumstances in Kragerø, a little coastal village south of Christiania (now Oslo). With modest local support, he received two years drawing instruction in Christiania (1874–6) and spent three years at the academy in Munich (1876–9) where he became part of the Norwegian artists' colony and formed lasting friendships with such artists as Erik Werenskiold, Eilif Peterssen, Gerhard Munthe and Christian Skredsvig. A lack of money forced him to return to Norway for two years in the autumn of 1880. He spent the winter of 1883 in Paris, but soon returned to Munich, where he remained until 1887. Kittelsen spent the rest of his life in Norway, but was rarely long in one place. Of special importance for his artistic development were the surroundings in Lofoten (where he lived from 1887 to 1888), Skåtøy at Kragerø (1889–91) and the forested valleys of Eggedal (1896–9) and Sigdal (1899–1910), where he built a house and studio for himself and his large family. In his letters and articles, he expressed increasing concern about the family's finances and the conditions under which art existed in Norway.

Kittelsen's production varied markedly in character and quality. His talent lay in exuberant, humoristic narration, and in romantic depictions of nature, which he could best express in drawings. He left his mark in Norwegian art history as an illustrator. From childhood on, caricatures and cartoons were his metier. He made a number of cartoon series intended for separate publication, as well as individual drawings, which were frequently reproduced in newspapers and periodicals. His illustrations for Asbjørnsen and Moe's *Tales for Children*, which he worked on in different periods for almost 30 years, are among the finest and best-loved drawings in Norwegian art, especially the early ones from the 1880s. In addition to these fairy-tales, which mostly depict peasant life and animals, Kittelsen's pictures of trolls and magical nature scenes are very popular. His depictions gave form to the popular fantasy of the water sprite and forest troll. Several of these pictures were originally part of a series, for which he also provided the text. Some of them were published in book form.

Kittelsen's work is more widespread and popular than most artists' because of its themes of folklore. For most Norwegians, it is part of a national cultural heritage that goes back to their childhood.

48

The Black Death, 1894–6

(Svartedauen)

12 full-page illustrations to the book Svartedauen, Christiania, 1900
Wash, pen, pencil and black chalk, c. 27.5 × 22.5
Nasjonalgalleriet, Oslo
Inv. no. 20/1983–31/1982 (purchased in 1982)

Theodor Kittelsen was first and foremost a draughtsman. His interest in anecdotes and comedy, in fairy-tales and depictions of nature are best expressed in his illustrations. At times he was commissioned to illustrate specific texts; but he also illustrated other texts on his own initiative. Sometimes, he both wrote the text and did the illustrations, and then gave full rein to his penchant for mysticism and romantic interpretations of nature. Among these works, *The Black Death* is in a special position artistically.

Of the many large and small drawings Kittelsen made for this book, all of the 12 full-page illustrations are shown in this exhibition. As the title indicates, the work deals with the great epidemic in around 1350 which, in a period of only a few years, killed two-thirds of Europe's population.

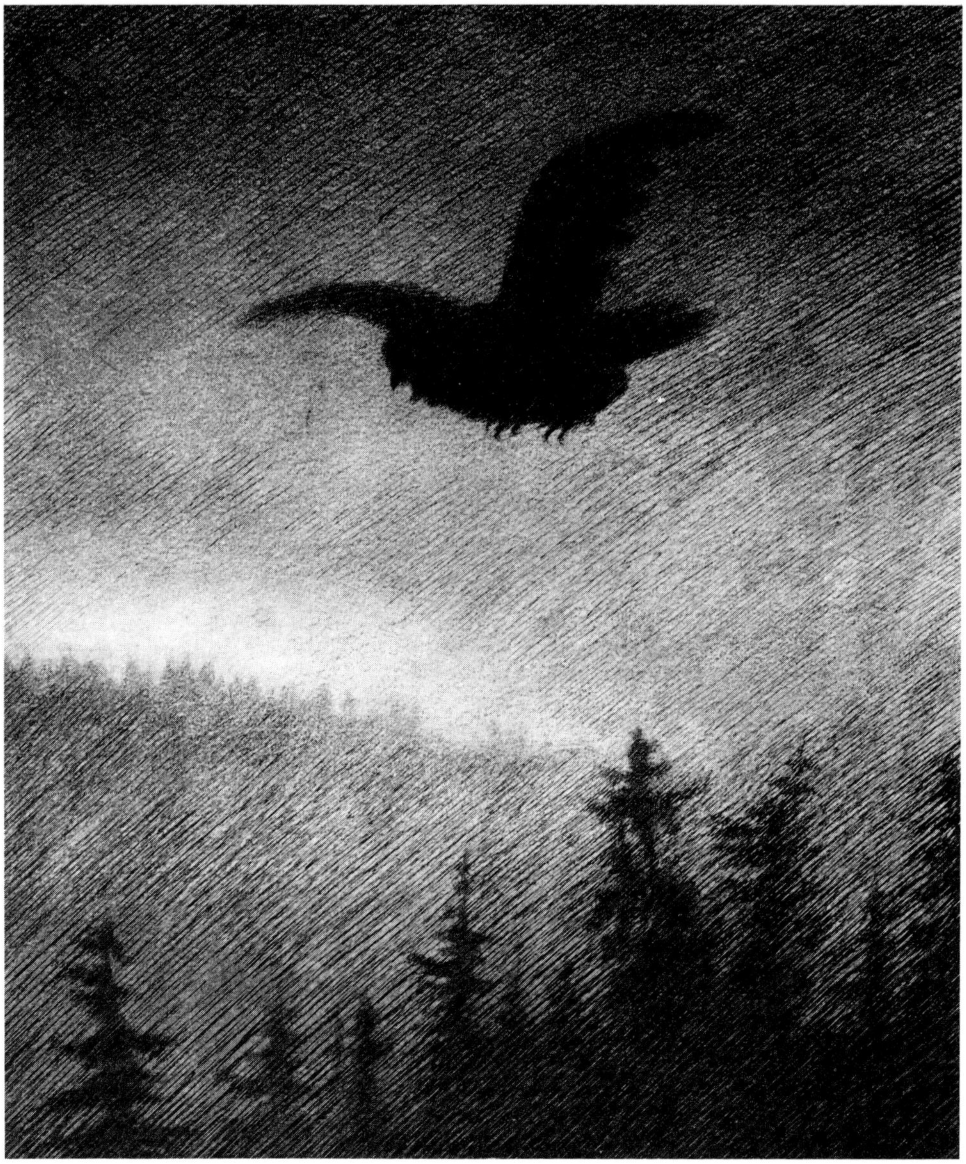

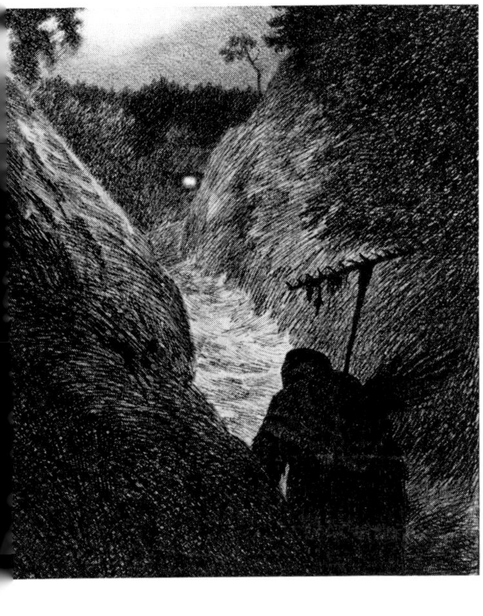

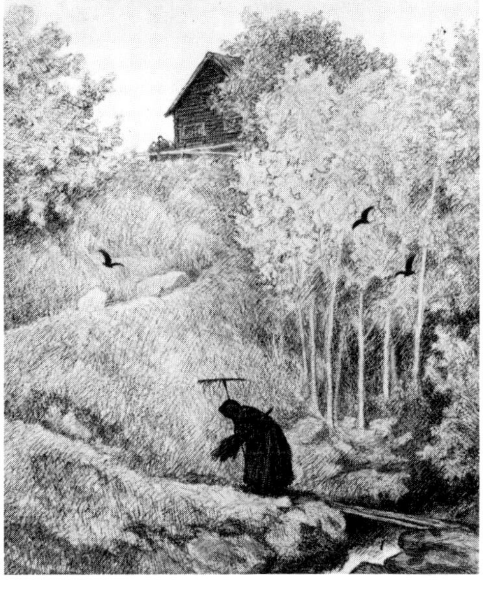

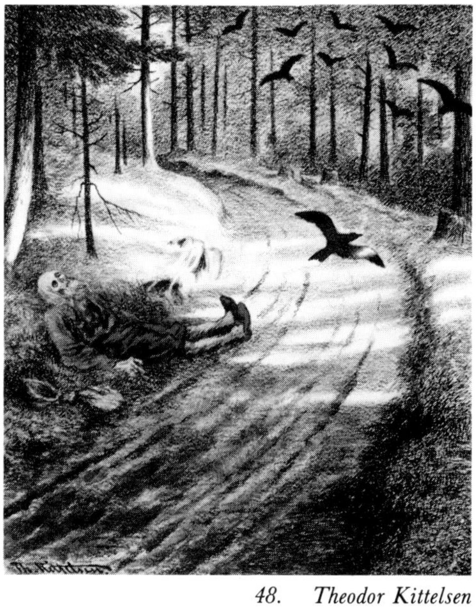

48. *Theodor Kittelsen*

In accordance with popular tradition, Kittelsen personified the plague as an old, bent woman who hobbles across the land with her rake and broom. She has a staff, shawl, and headscarf, and a horrifyingly gaping, skull-like face. Several of the illustrations show this dreaded old woman approaching or leaving a farm. She makes her inescapable progress no matter how long the journey. She sweeps people up with her wherever she goes and leaves the land devastated behind her.

Illustrations 7 and 10 are worthy of special mention as masterful examples of a pictorially concentrated expression of fear, death, and decay. In the first is *Pesta* with her foul face, sneaking from the darkness below up a narrow, creaking stairway. The figure is small, but the whole picture is concentrated on her horrible presence. There is no escape here.

In the other, it is as if we ourselves are coming up through the trapdoor to the attic room and meet the skull's vacant stare over the edge of the bed while swarms of mice flee in all directions. We can almost hear their rustling and smell the odour of closed-in putrefaction.

Kittelsen chose the barren landscape and melancholy climate of the Nordic autumn and winter as the natural surroundings for *Pesta's* fateful progress. Some of the illustrations are pure depictions of nature. In the very first, a predatory bird flies in over the tops of the spruces, gaping ferociously. The sky is dark; it is almost evening. The bird is an evil omen.

In the last illustration, the capercaillie sings on a spruce bough to a starry night sky. With wings spread and neck stretched, he calls his mate. It is spring; new life must be created in the deserted land.

All the illustrations in the book are monochrome. The large drawings were made in wash, pen and soft pencil or black chalk, a technique which made it possible to use values and texture effects in a variety of ways, and which Kittelsen exploited with impressive skill. The technique is in harmony with the pictorial composition, thus emphasizing the melancholy theme of the series.

Kittelsen worked with *The Black Death* for several years. He knew the subject from Andreas Faye's book of old Norwegian folk tales (from 1843) and several of the tales are actual retellings of Faye's work. But the subject became topical as the result of an experience he himself had on Skåtøy outside Kragerø (1889–91). An ugly old woman who came by his house every day reminded him of *Pesta*. But not until several years after he had moved from Skåtøy did he begin work on *The Black Death* in earnest. According to his letters, he did most of the illustrations in 1894. The milieu in which he found himself did not, however, give him inspiration to complete the work. What did inspire him was the deserted, decaying old *Sole* farm in Eggedal where he moved in 1896. He finished the project the same year, but several years went by before he found a publisher to print it.

In general, Kittelsen had a close and direct relationship with his sources of inspiration. In the pictures, we can recognize landscapes and buildings from Lofoten, Skåtøy and Eggedal. He had used several of the motives before, but in different ways. In spite of the different elements and the many interruptions, *The Black Death* is Kittelsen's most uniform and artistically most successful series of pictures both in idea and in execution.

S.H.

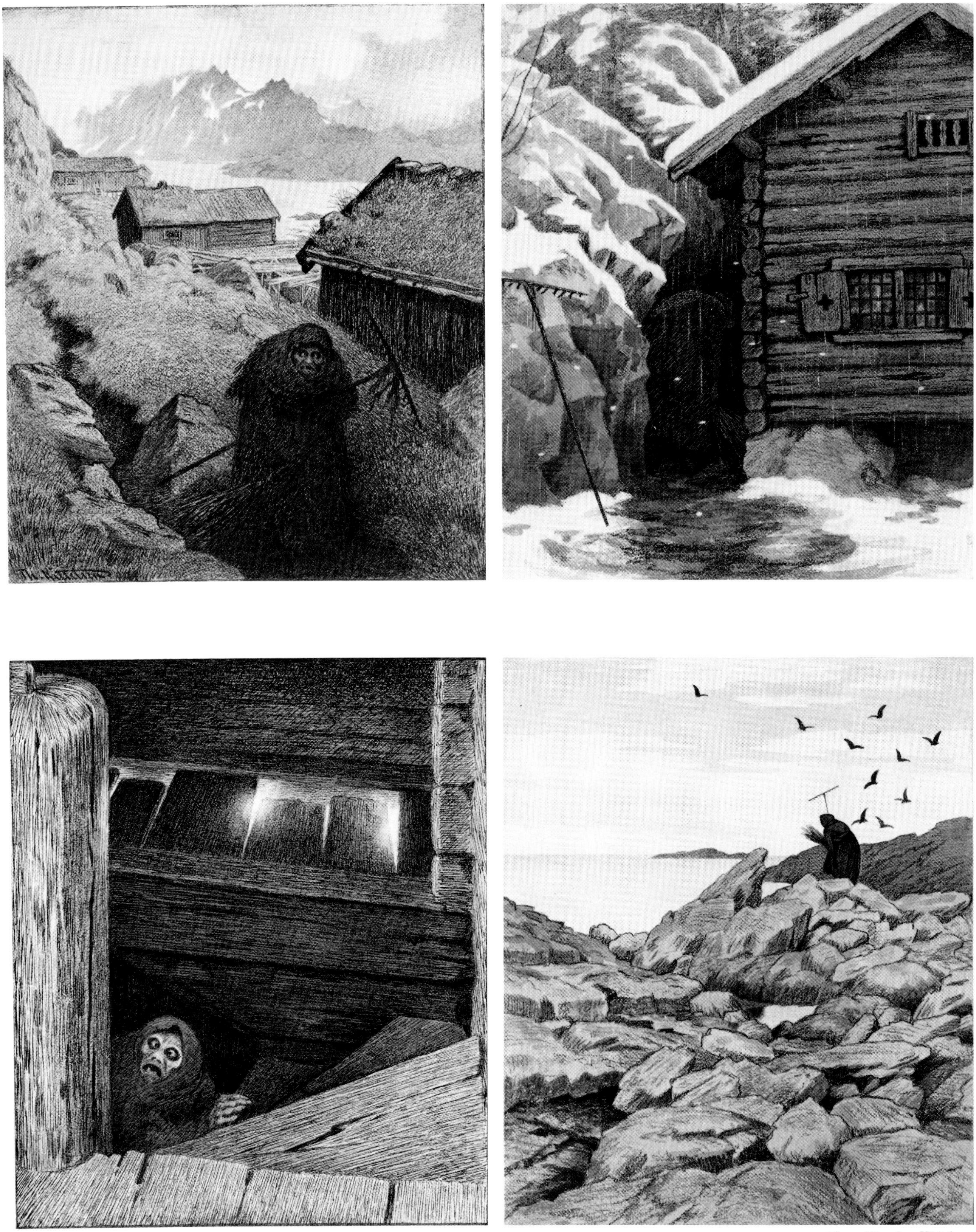

48. Theodor Kittelsen

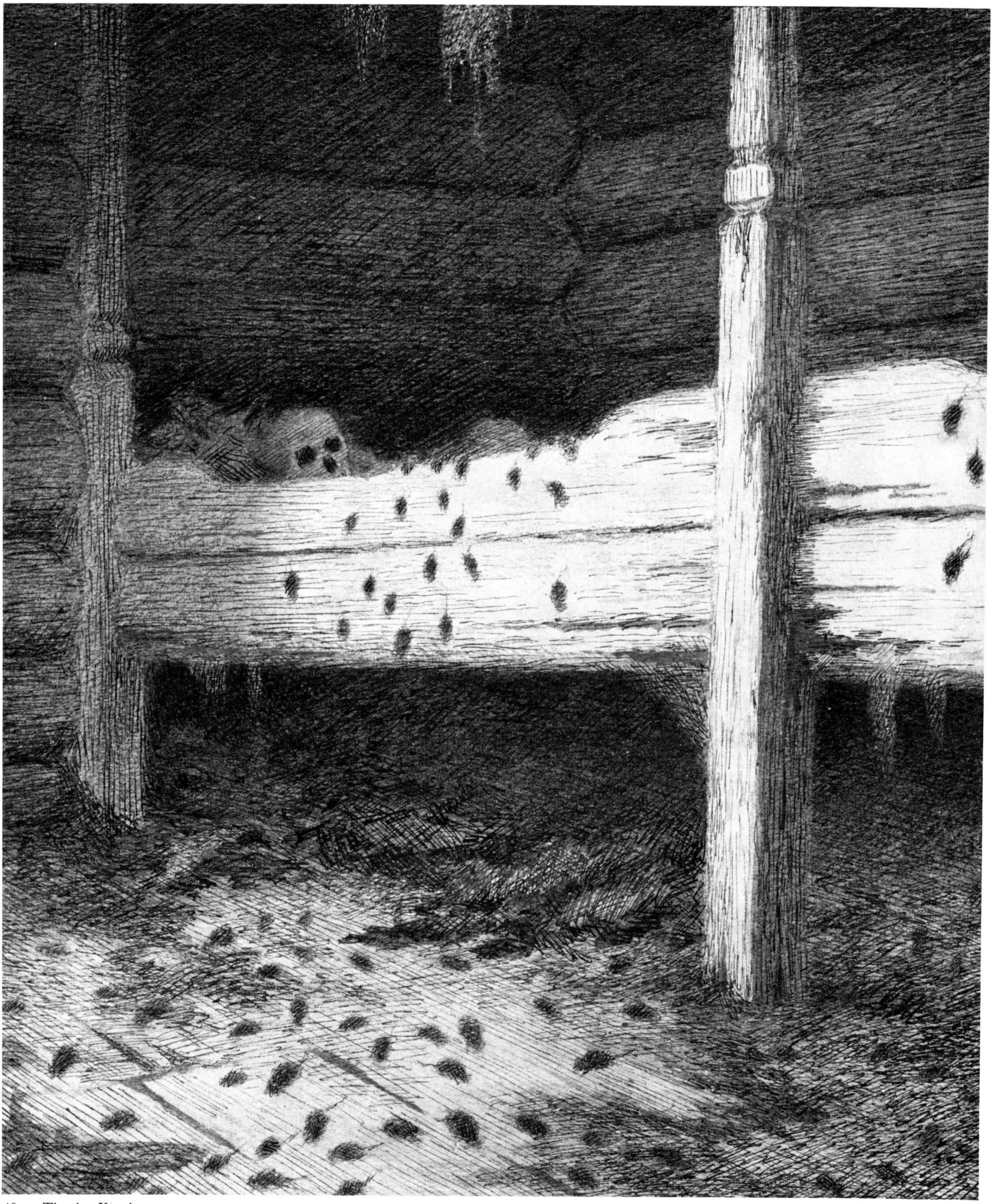

48. Theodor Kittelsen

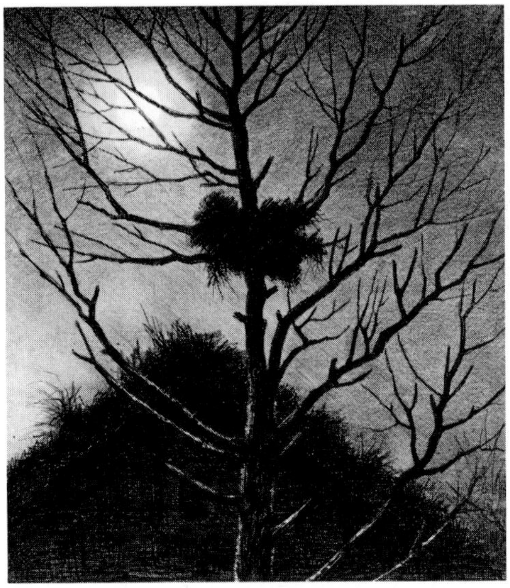

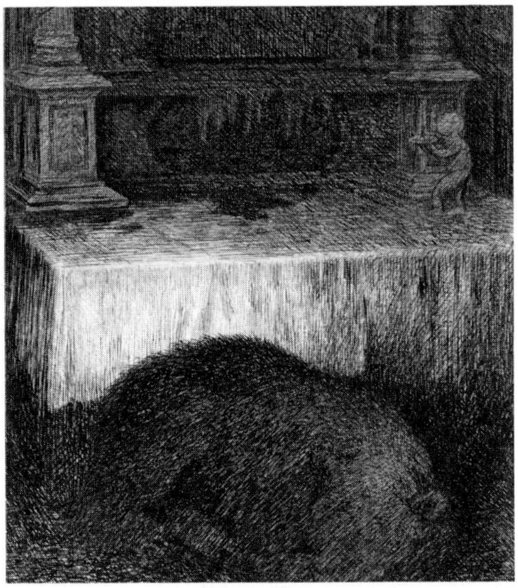

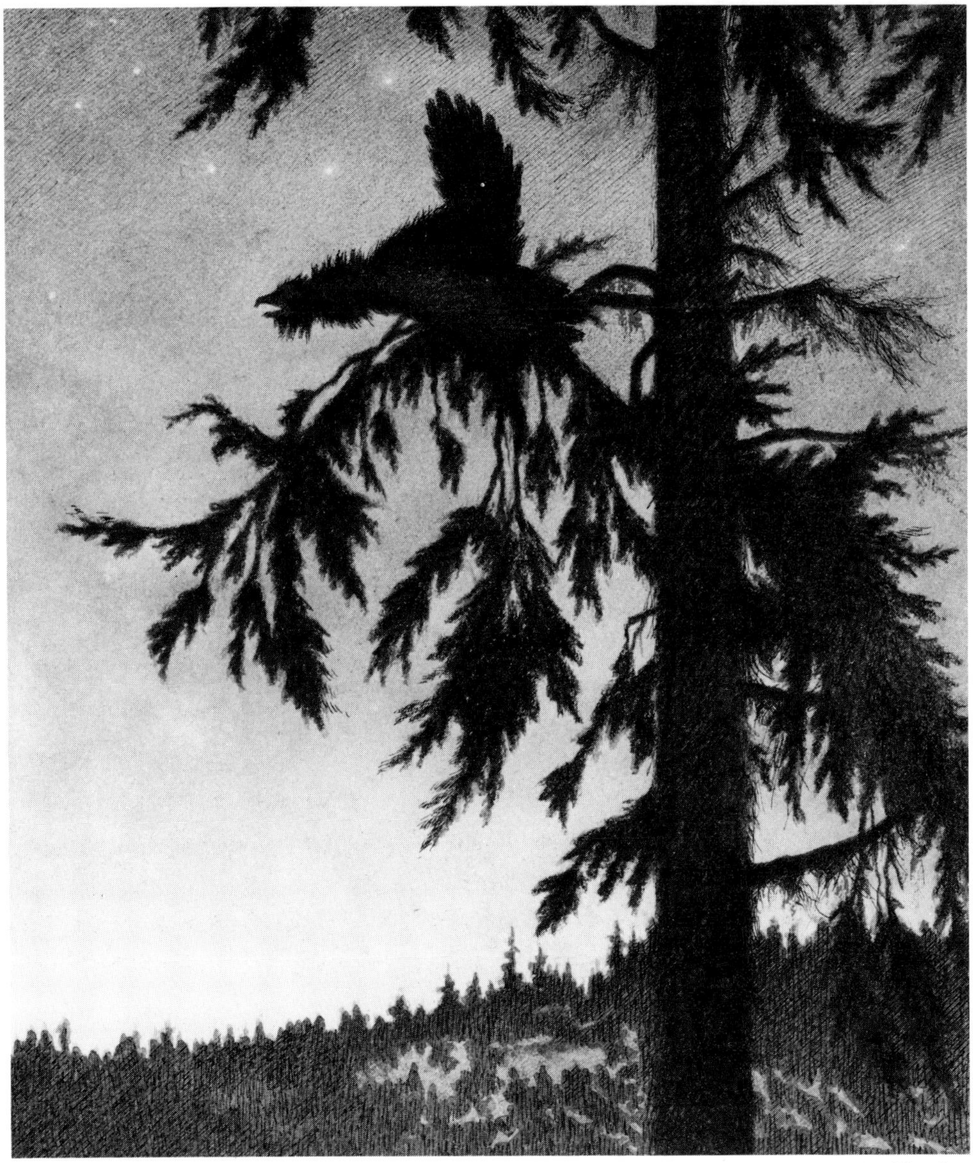

48. Theodor Kittelsen

PEDER SEVERIN KRØYER

1851–1909, Denmark

Krøyer was born in Norway but was raised in Copenhagen. His foster father was a well-known zoologist, Henrik N. Krøyer. At the early age of ten Krøyer did the illustrations for his father's book on crustacea. In 1864 he entered the Royal Academy and was taught in the tradition of the Eckersberg School. He received the small gold medal in 1873. His paintings from a fishing village in Northern Zealand are highly accomplished. But on entering Léon Bonnat's school in Paris in 1877 he was instructed to keep strictly to nature both in drawing after the nude and in tonality in painting. 'First proportions, then movement. First form, then colour. Away with the many small tones, away with the many small shapes! Look for tonality, look for simplicity and solidity. Beware of mannerisms and deftness.' (L. Tuxen: *En Malers Arbejde* (A Painter's Work), Copenhagen, 1928.)

A trip to Spain in 1878 was of importance to Krøyer. Together with the art historian Julius Lange, he went to Madrid where he copied Velázquez. In 1879 he painted in Cernay la Ville and Concarneau, and in 1880 he was in Italy with, among others, the Norwegian Eilif Peterssen. He visited the artists' colony in Skagen, on the northern tip of Denmark, for the first time in 1882, and the year after, exhibited subjects from Skagen at the Salon in Paris. In 1884 he went to London, where he saw the Summer Exhibition at the Grosvenor Gallery and Whistler's exhibition at Dowdeswell's. In Paris Krøyer also exhibited at George Petit's Gallery in the Rue de Seze.

Krøyer immediately became a leading figure in the artists' colony at Skagen. He had a light hand and was successful in everything he did. He also had a personal charm which endeared him to the artists' colony as well as to the society of Copenhagen. He painted a number of portraits of his Scandinavian colleagues – characteristic sweeping pictures. He was also a sought-after society portraitist.

Krøyer taught at the Artists' Study School from 1882 to 1904. In 1890 he turned down a professorship at the Royal Academy of Fine Arts on the grounds that he needed freedom in order to thrive.

49

Summer Evening at the South Beach, Skagen, 1893

(Sommeraften på Skagens Sønderstrand)

38.5 × 60
Signed lower left: S Krøyer, SKAGEN–Juni -93,
Til Ida og S. Schandorph. Minde om et Skagensbesøg.
Den Hirschsprungske Samling, Copenhagen
(purchased in 1901)

Krøyer came to Skagen for the first time in 1882, and was fascinated with the place, its people and the characteristically strong light. But as early as 1884, he discovered the bluish twilight poetry of the white nights. It was the beginning of the school of atmosphere and light. It is interesting to reflect that Krøyer came to Skagen directly from London, where he had had the opportunity of seeing Whistler's exhibition *Notes, Harmonies and Arrangements* at Dowdeswell's.

The artists painting in Skagen were modern people who used modern techniques. One was photography. With photography the idea for a composition could be preserved. It was a welcome aid to the memory. Because the summers were so short they had to be devoted to colour and light studies. In spite of all the *plein-air* painting, the large compositions intended for exhibition were still completed in the studio. We know that Krøyer painted one of his night pictures on the beach early in the morning

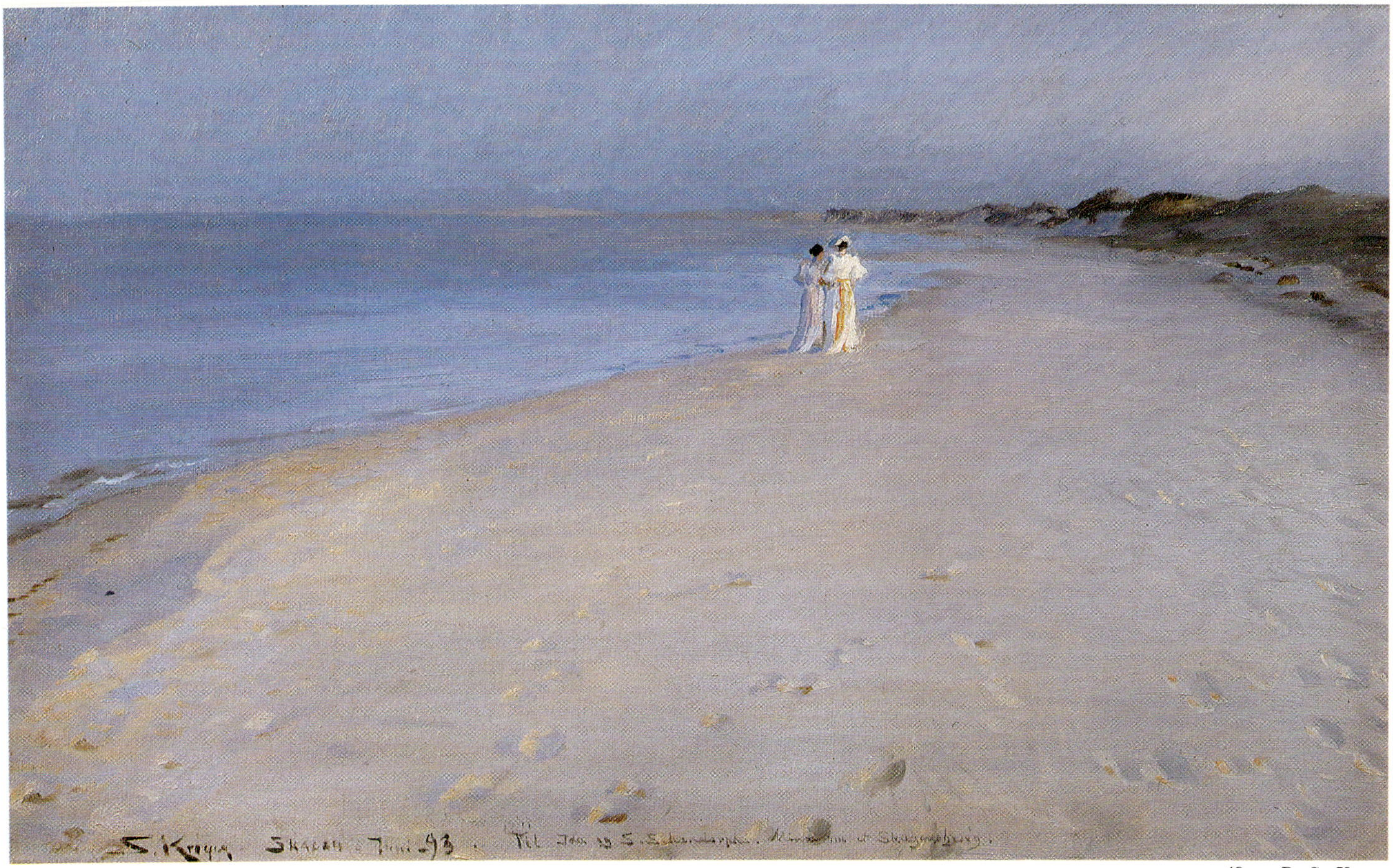

49. P. S. Krøyer

before dawn. But what does the time of day matter as long as the result is the perfect blue colour that the artist is seeking? 'Everything around me must be blue. And in the centre of the blue world, my heart will beat innocently and freely, like a wake of the boat's keel which sings, like the small drops that fall from the oars' (Karen Blixen: *Den unge Mand med Nelliken* (The Young Man with the Carnation)).

In the summer of 1893, Krøyer painted his wife, the painter Marie Krøyer (née Triepcke), promenading arm in arm with the painter Anna Ancher (p. 169) by the edge of the shore. There is a photograph for this motive too. Because of the lighting it must have been taken quite early in the evening and was utilized solely for the composition. The photograph did not need to be spontaneous, but could be carefully arranged and composed with a preconceived purpose in mind. The evening walk at sundown was not just a tradition dear to the Skagen artists. For the summer guests who gathered there in large numbers in the 1890s, it was the very essence of their stay in Skagen.

The photograph led to an impressive exhibition picture which, with its emphasis on the unending beach, the two women in the middle ground, elegantly dressed in white, and the deep blue, somewhat heavily painted evening atmosphere, corresponded to the dream of Skagen. In two small studies from June and July of the same year, it is more a question of the landscape and lighting than of the group of figures, who are drawn farther into the picture. The last sun still illuminates the dunes in places and golden spots of sun smoulder in the deep footprints in the sand in the foreground. Mrs Ancher's light dress with the cool rose sash lies in blue shadow, while

Marie Krøyer's brilliantly painted dress is the white accent which emphasizes this blue universe.

The spirit of these studies is completely different from the mood which dominated Krøyer's evening pictures from the 1880s, which capture some of the quiet moments of that decade. The intimate atmosphere of the two women's walk along the beach in confidential, muted conversation, whose words fade into the distance as they move away from the viewer, belongs to a new time and new concepts.

H.W.

50

South Beach, Skagen. A White Boat by the Edge of the Beach. A Light Summer's Night, 1895

(Skagen Sønderstrand. En hvid båd i strandkanten. Lys somerafteen)

41 × 66
Signed lower right: Sk. Skagen/-95
Skagens Museum, Skagen
(purchased in 1939)

In Skagen Krøyer was interested both in the blinding sunlight and in the gentle half-light in which several sources of light appear simultaneously, as in the picture of the white boat. Here the evening sun makes the gables and chimneys on a row of houses behind the dunes glow against the blue-violet sky, and the lighthouse in the distance has begun to send out its yellow beam. The sand on the beach in the foreground is light, while in the dune's shadows it is blue. In the still of the evening the sea is calm. A group of people in dark clothes stand by a luminous white boat in the foreground. Two women and a child are on their way home. The picture expresses the sentiments of everyday life.

H.W.

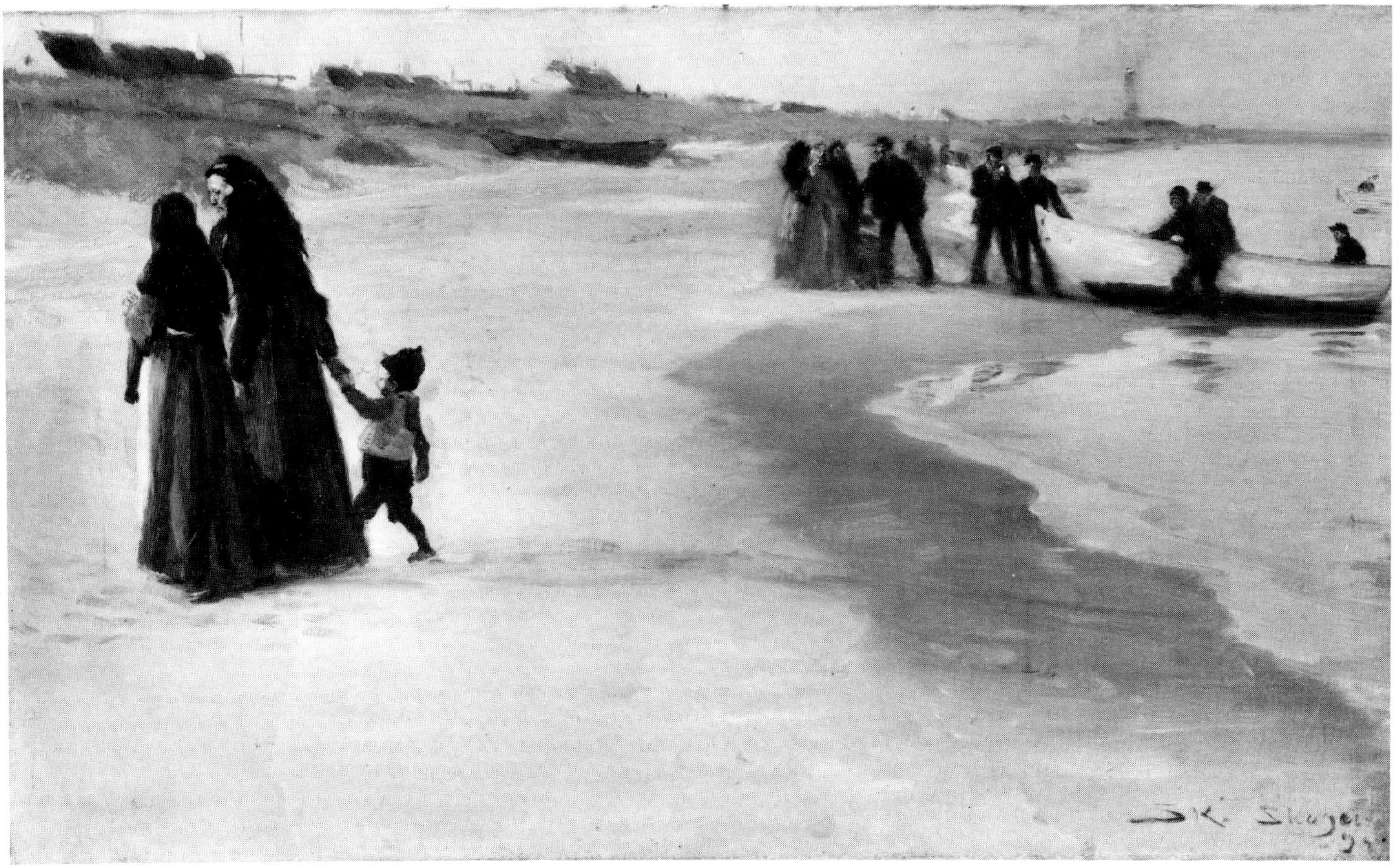

50. P. S. Krøyer

51

Boys Bathing in the Sea on a Summer Evening. Skagen, 1899

(Badende drenge ved Skagens Strand)

100.5 × 153
Signed lower right: S. Krøyer/Skagen 99
Statens Museum for Kunst, Copenhagen
Inv. no. 1658 (purchased in 1900)

The composition of the large picture of boys bathing, with which Krøyer was represented at the Paris World Fair, is taken up by the sea and the sky. Only in the lowest right-hand corner is there a little triangle of beach, where a boy is seated, drying his feet. The luminous bodies of two other boys lead from him out to two ships, whose hulls draw attention to the horizon, their masts giving the necessary vertical emphasis, which is repeated to the right by the moonlight over the water.

All this boundless, dreamy blue is part of a stringent composition. Its luminous elements capture the mood of a quiet evening, with ships on their way to port and boys bathing in the moonlight.

The painting was exhibited in Paris in 1900, and in Berlin in the Nordische Kunstausstellung, 1902.

H.W.

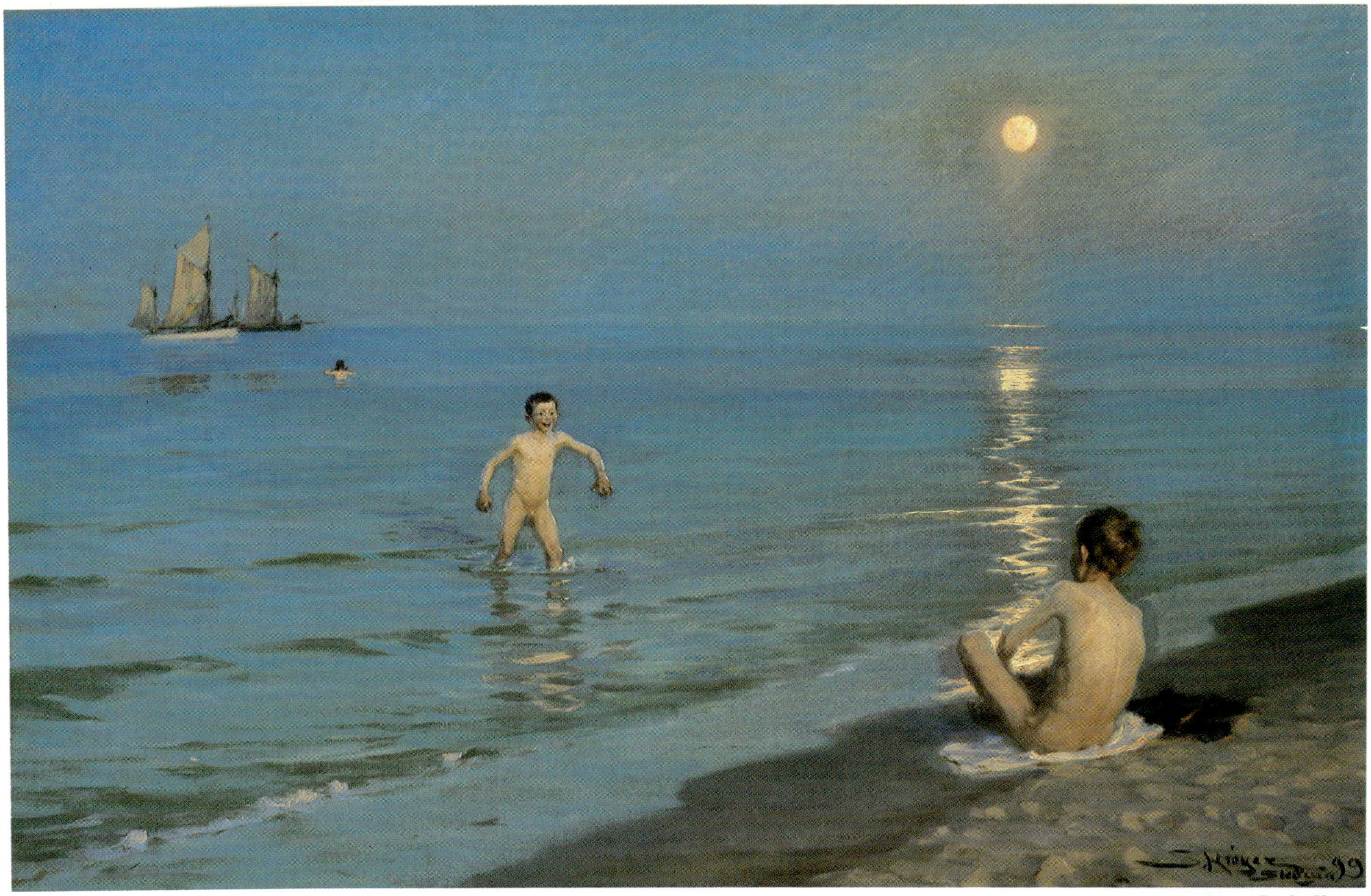

51. P. S. Krøyer

CARL LARSSON

1853–1919, Sweden

After an unhappy childhood in the working-class districts of Stockholm, Carl Larsson enrolled in the preparatory class at the Academy of Fine Arts at the age of 13. His considerable gifts as a draughtsman allowed him to finance his subsequent studies by illustrating books, magazines, and weekly newspapers. Later in his career, he illustrated books by Strindberg and Hans Christian Andersen, among others.

From 1877 onwards, Larsson paid many visits to France and from 1882 to 1884 lived in Grez-sur-Loing. Here, he abandoned historical pastiche in order to paint the modest rural life of Grez with a freshness and elegance that won him immediate success (*Médaille* at the Salon, 1883, works purchased by the French state and by the Nationalmuseum, Stockholm).

On his return to Sweden in 1885, Carl Larsson joined with other artists in opposing the Academy. Before long, he had also joined in the movement to return to nature and to the Scandinavian landscape, and lived mainly in Dalarna. Unlike many of his contemporaries, he was primarily interested in the gay and cheerful side of life. In a long sequence of watercolours which won him world-wide popularity (many of them were published in album form), he traces an idyllic image of his home in Dalarna and of his family life. At the same time, he also worked on monumental paintings, taking his inspiration from the great Italian painters of the Renaissance and the eighteenth century (frescos (1896) and *Gustavus Vasa Entering Stockholm* (1906) in the Nationalmuseum, Stockholm). His last years were darkened by the Nationalmuseum's refusal to accept his last great project, *Sacrifice at the Solstice*, in which, unusually for him, he chose to paint a dramatic subject from pagan times.

52a

A Home: Cosy Corner

(Ett hem: Lathörnet)

Watercolour on paper, 32 × 43
Signed lower middle in monogram: C.L.
Nationalmuseum, Stockholm
Inv. no. B 269 (purchased in 1900)

52b

A Home: The Kitchen

(Ett hem: Köket)

Watercolour on paper, 32 × 43
Signed lower right in monogram: C L.
Nationalmuseum, Stockholm
Inv. no. B 270 (purchased in 1900)

52c

A Home: The Studio

(Ett hem: Ateljén)

Watercolour on paper, 32 × 43
Signed lower middle in monogram: C. L.
Nationalmuseum, Stockholm
Inv. no. B 271 (purchased in 1900)

52d

A Home: Brita's Forty Winks

(Ett hem: Britas tupplur)

Watercolour on paper, 32 × 43
Signed lower middle in monogram: C.L.
(Above the door: TILL KARIN AUG. 1894)
Nationalmuseum, Stockholm
Inv. no. B 275 (purchased in 1900)

The sequence of 26 watercolours making up *A Home* immediately enjoyed an unparalleled success, and is still one of the most popular works in the whole of Swedish art. Part of the sequence was exhibited in 1897 and then again in Berlin in 1898, but it found a wider audience in 1899 when an album of colour reproductions, with vignettes and a text by the artist, was published.

The watercolours were executed from 1894 onwards at Sundborn, the small house in Dalarna which Larsson and his wife Karin had owned since 1888, and which

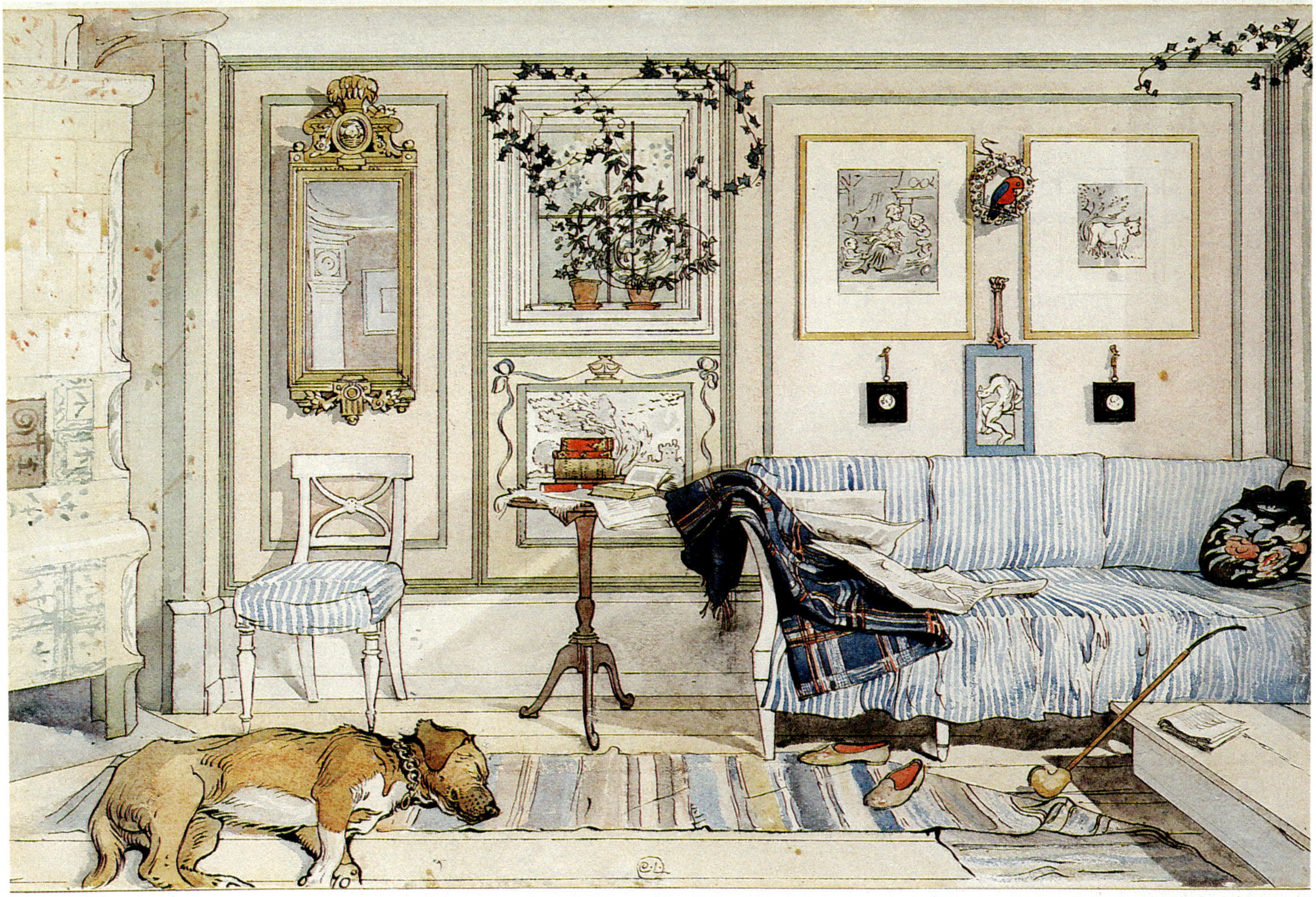

52a. Carl Larsson

they gradually enlarged, furnished and decorated together. It is now a museum open to the public.

The artist's Sundborn home has always been loved and admired, and it has often been imitated. Larsson's compatriots could not imagine anything more typically 'Swedish', but we now know that the couple owed a great deal to the new concepts of modern housing and furniture that emanated from Great Britain as a result of the work of William Morris. They came into contact with these ideas on their travels and thanks to Larsson's participation in international exhibitions, such as that of the XX in Brussels. They also subscribed to *The Studio* when it was first launched in 1893. For the Larssons, as for Voysey, Baillie Scott, Mackintosh and Briggs, the ideal house was a 'bungalow', a small country house which was simple and rustic, but above all *artistic*, flexible and comfortable, with lots of verandas and balconies, and which was furnished with high-quality handicrafts and surrounded by trees and flowers. But when Carl and Karin Larsson put their ideas into practice, they did so in a very personal – and very Swedish – manner. They also looked for inspiration to the old peasant culture of Dalarna, and to castles and country houses furnished in the Gustavus III style, which derives from Louis XV but has a more sober, 'rustic' elegance. In *Cosy Corner*, the furniture, the fireplace, the mirror and the selvage rug are all Gustavus III. The walls are panelled and decorated in an eighteenth-century style. The engravings are from the same period.

In this watercolour the artist obviously took great pleasure in the contrast between the verticals and horizontals, in the arabesques of the ivy, the mass of the sleeping dog, and the untidy couch, where he has left his newspaper, a rug and his slippers. As in all his images he takes care to stress that what he has represented is something fleeting and ephemeral: a happy moment of day-to-day life captured as it happened.

The contrast between the bright, practical bedroom we see in *Brita's Forty Winks* – it was used by both Karin Larsson and her daughters – and most contemporary bedrooms, which were still heavily decorated with mahogany, plush, and velvet, could not be greater. The whitewashed walls are decorated with stencils of superimposed motifs that recall the wallpaper of the Arts and Crafts Movement as well as that of the Gustavus III period. Larsson gives his decorative verve free rein on the doors and their surrounds.

When they lived in Grez-sur-Loing near Fontainebleau between 1882 and 1885, Karin and Carl Larsson became accustomed to a relaxed French way of life, and they tried to recreate it at their home in Dalarna. In images like *Luncheon under the Big Birch* and *Crayfishing*, the painter also remains true to the compositional style he had adopted in Grez: the vegetation invades a large part of the surface and often relegates the figures to the background.

In about 1890, however, Larsson had begun to place more emphasis on drawing and to stress the contours and decorative aspects of his surfaces. All the charming figures in *A Home* are drawn in Indian ink; the lines are at once firm and light, and sometimes break into small undulating arabesques. The artist has obvious affinities with Art Nouveau. But it is rare for him to allow line and ornamentation to take on a value of their own; he sticks closely to reality.

It should be pointed out that in the text accompanying *A Home* Carl Larsson makes it quite clear that these images were not so much intended to display how he lived at home as to provide 'a model for those who feel the need to furnish their homes agreeably'. The endless imitations of period furniture and the fussily 'artistic' mass-produced ornaments which were flooding Europe at this time threatened to wipe out entirely the old handicraft traditions. It was in order to check this trend that the Nordic Museum and the Open Air Museum in Skansen were founded in Stockholm around the turn of the century. When he published *A Home* in 1899, Larsson had similar educational aims in mind. But at the same time he obviously wanted to teach his contemporaries how to lead a happy and natural life, and he devoted infinite care and a wealth of creative imagination to making *A Home*, which is his 'map of happiness', as attractive and as exemplary as possible.

P.G.

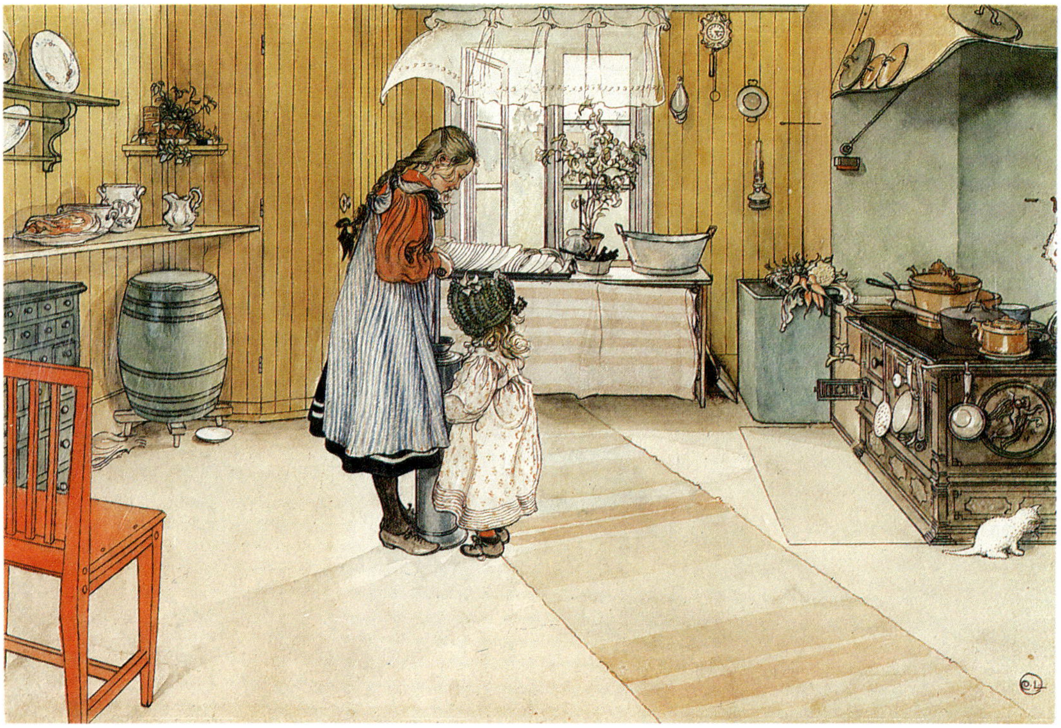

52b. Carl Larsson

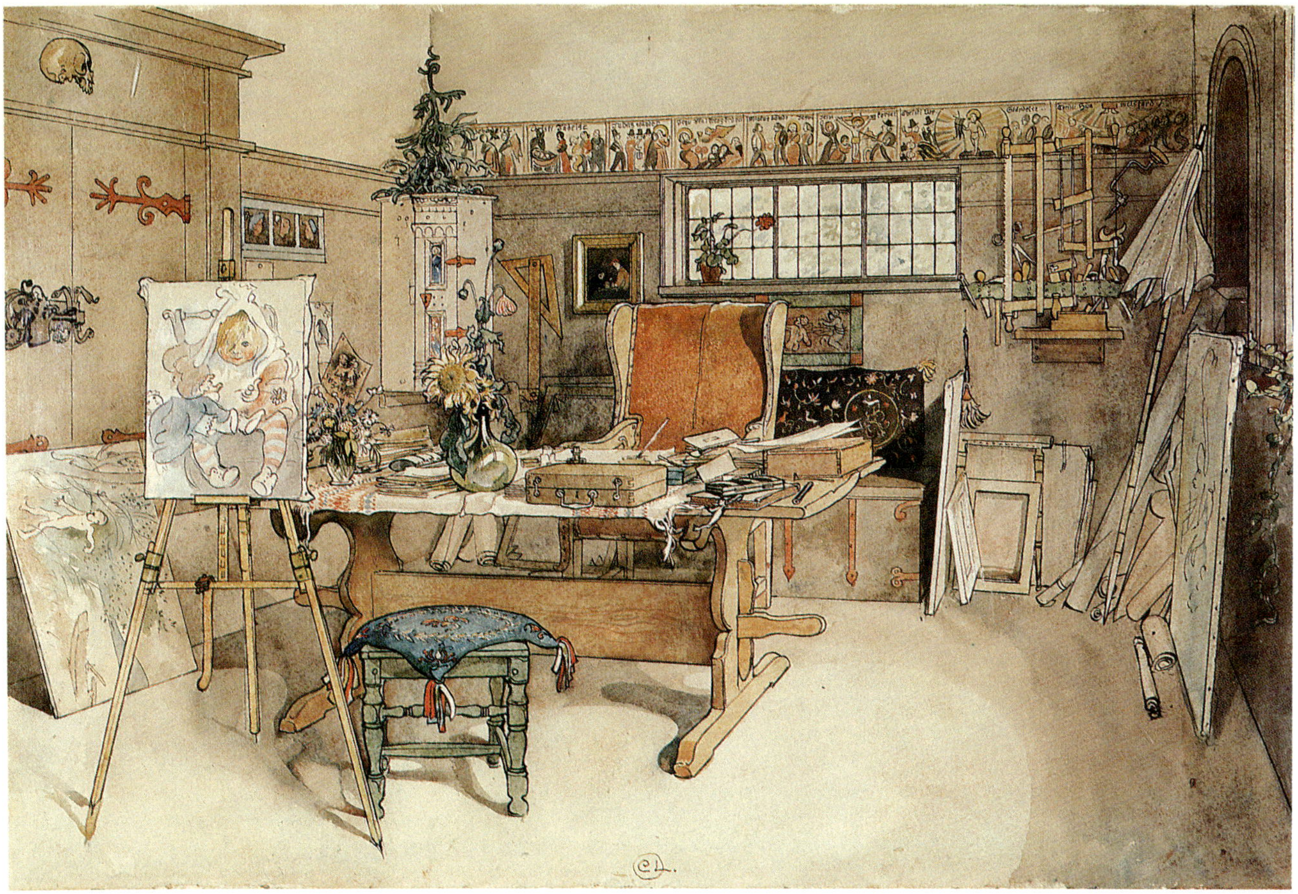

52c. Carl Larsson

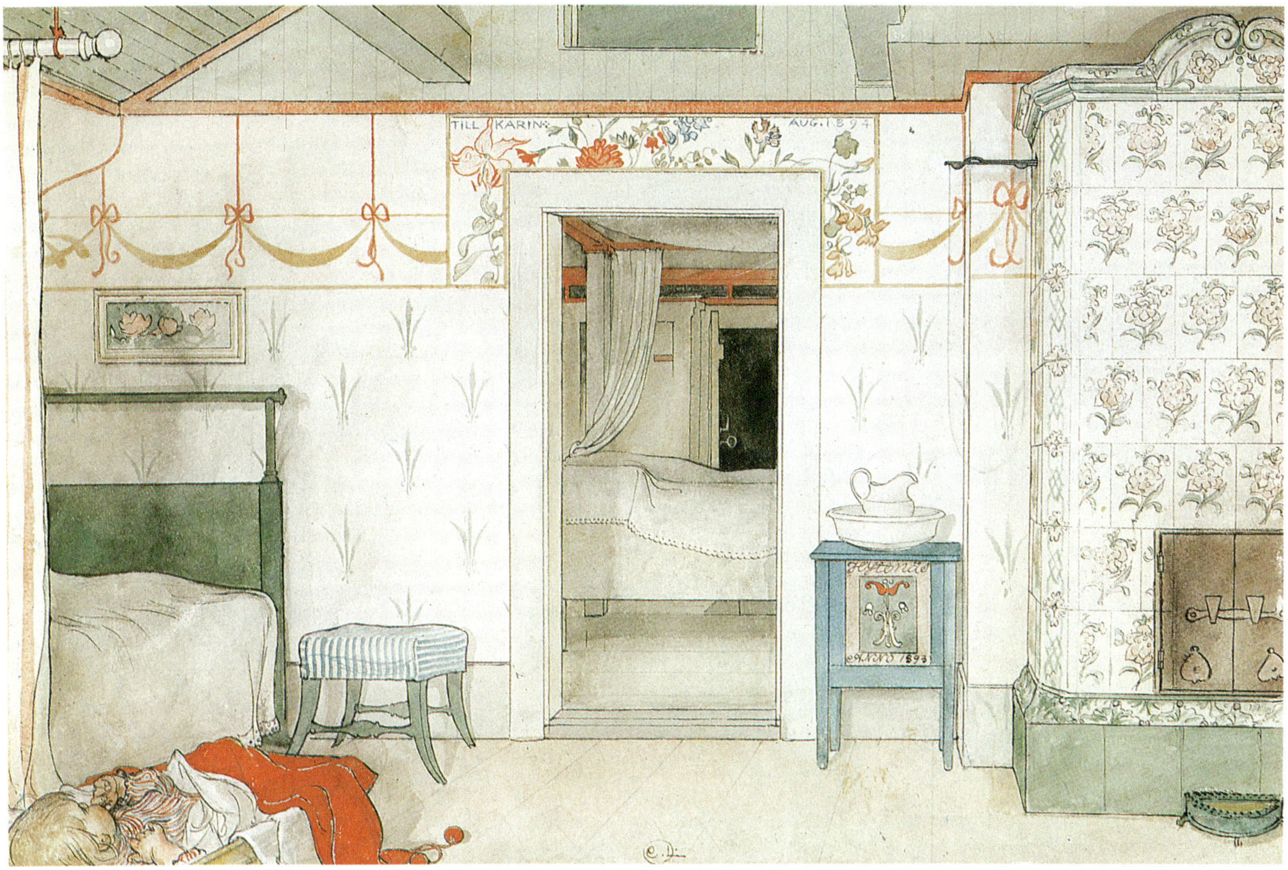

52d. Carl Larsson

52e

A Home: Between Christmas and New Year

(Ett hem: Mellan jul och nyår)

Watercolour on paper, 32 × 43
Signed lower middle in monogram: C L.
(Above the door: Guds Fred; on the door: 1891)
Nationalmuseum, Stockholm
Inv. no. B 265 (purchased in 1900)

52f

A Home: The Yard and Wash-House

(Ett hem: Gården och brygghuset)

Watercolour on paper, 32 × 43
Signed lower right in monogram: C.L.
Nationalmuseum, Stockholm
Inv. no. B 276 (purchased in 1900)

52g

A Home: Crayfishing

(Kräftfångst)

Watercolour on paper, 32 × 46
Signed lower right in monogram: C.L.
Nationalmuseum, Stockholm
Inv. no. B 278 (purchased in 1900)

52h

A Home: Luncheon under the Big Birch

(Frukost under stora björken)

Watercolour on paper, 32 × 46
Signed lower middle in monogram: C L
(On the tree trunk: CK 1894)
Nationalmuseum, Stockholm
Inv. no. 279 (purchased in 1900)

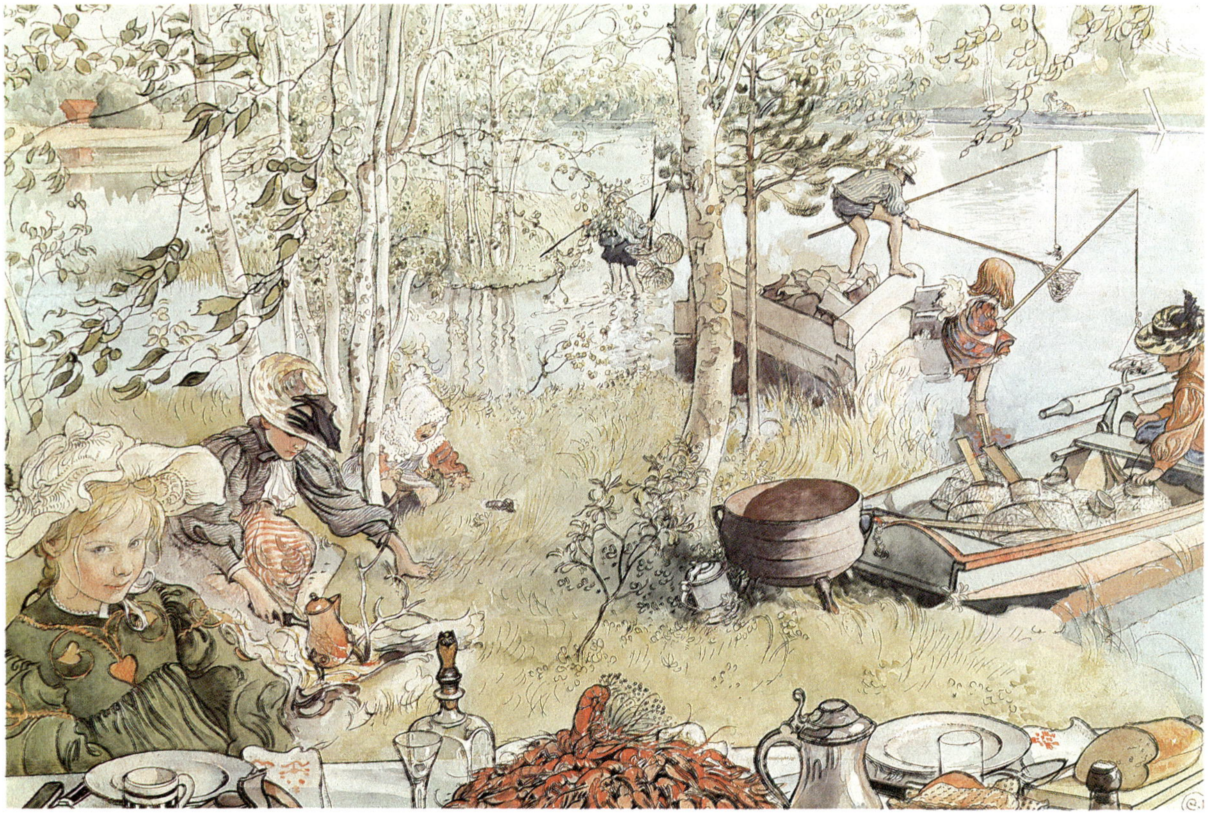

52g. Carl Larsson

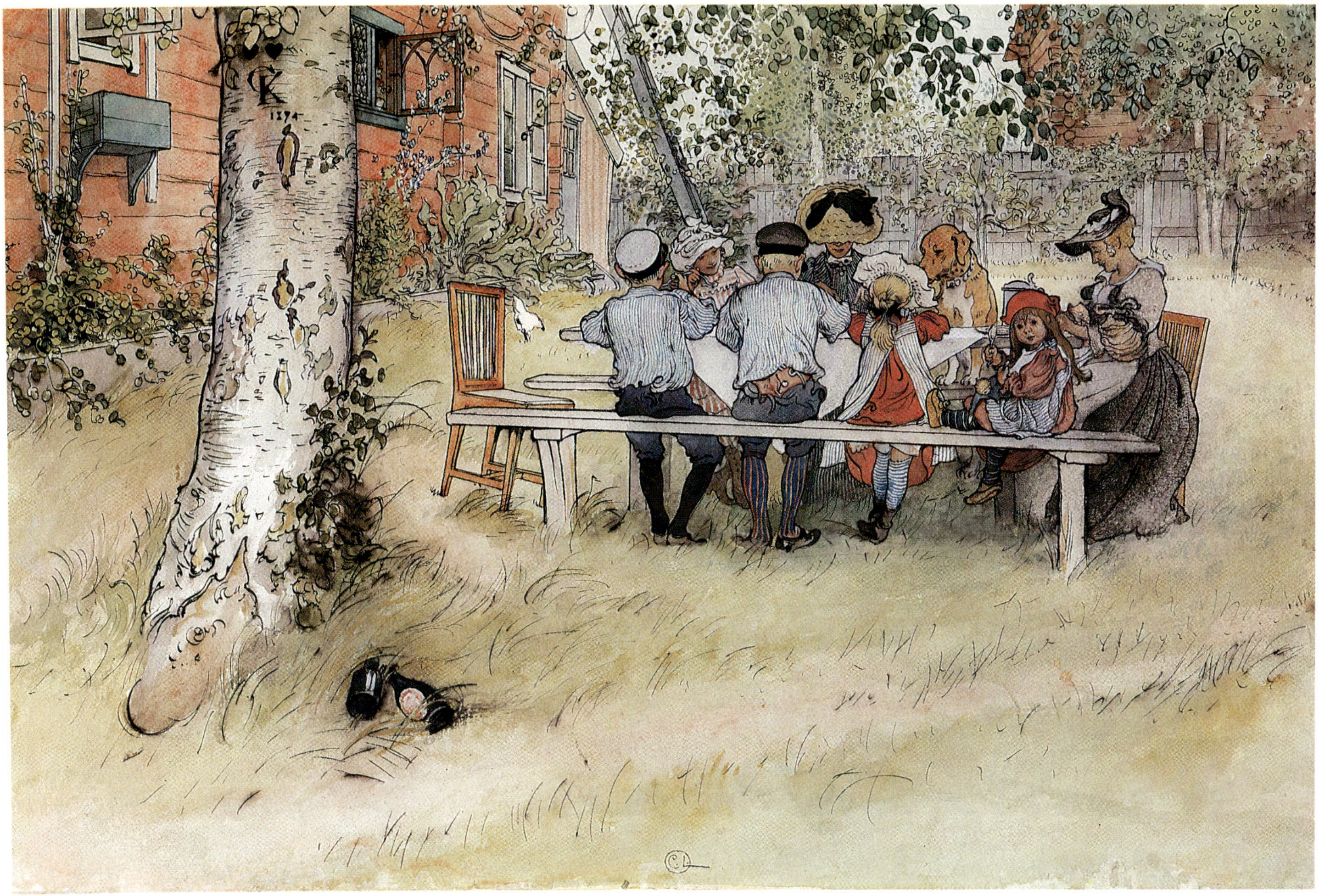

52h. Carl Larsson

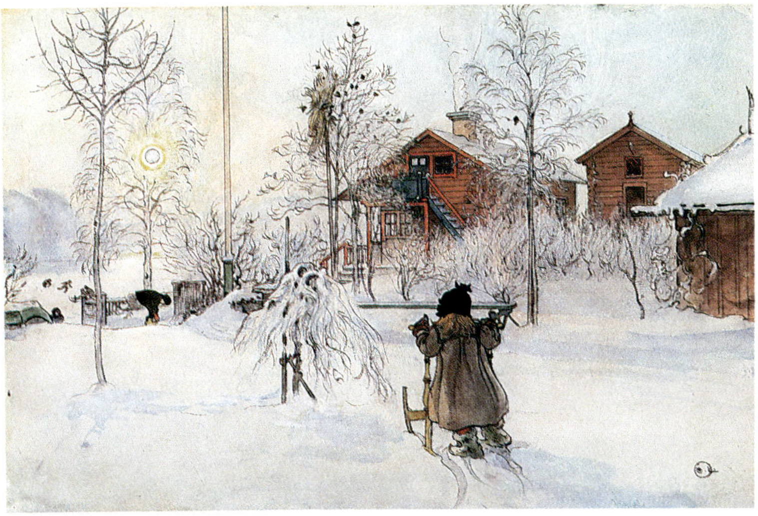

52f. Carl Larsson

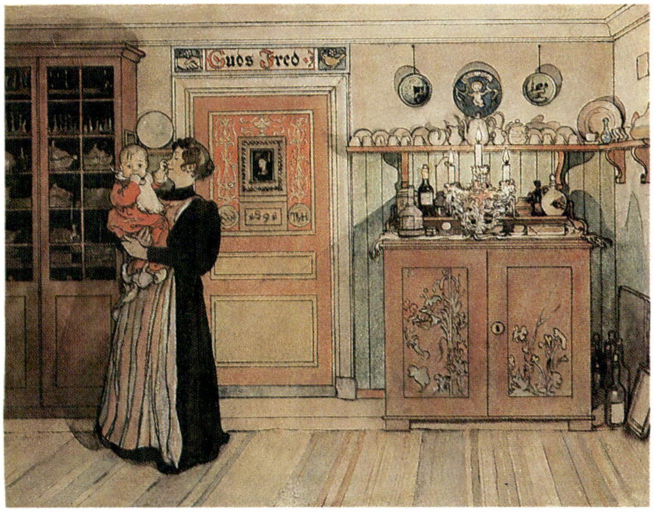

52e. Carl Larsson

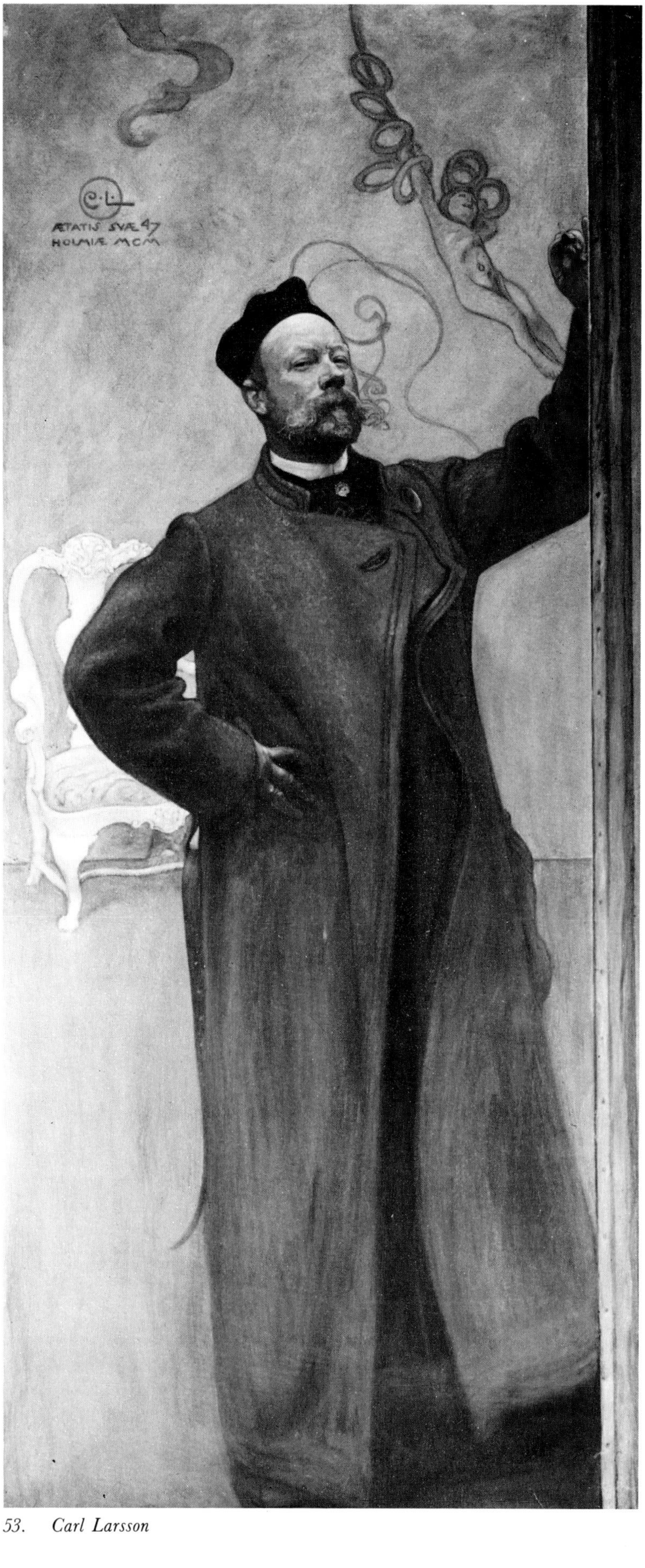

53. *Carl Larsson*

53

In Front of the Mirror. Self-Portrait, 1900

(Framför spegeln. Självporträtt)

241 × 100
Signed upper left: C.L. (in monogram) / AETATIS SVAE 47 / HOLMIAE MCM
Göteborgs konstmuseum, Gothenburg
Inv. no. F80 (Fürstenberg donation 1902)

When he executed this self-portrait in 1900, Carl Larsson was at the height of his fame. It shows him at work, a happy, self-confident man, his small, piercing eyes creased by a characteristically impish and somewhat ironic smile. He painted similar images of himself on many occasions and took an obvious narcissistic pleasure in doing so.

When Larsson's autobiography *Jag (Myself)* appeared posthumously in 1931, his readers were moved and amazed to learn that he was a complex and anxious man who suffered from nervous depression and that the mask of unclouded happiness concealed bitter memories of an unhappy childhood. It became obvious that the joy which fills his work was an ideal, a wonderful dream. Like others before him, he appears to be saying '*Et in Arcadia ego*'. His own career seemed to him to prove that everyone can attain the same happiness. Unlike most of his artist friends, he long remained true to the revolutionary optimism of the 1890s. In 1910, he wrote: 'Do not let your ego go down like some poor gravedigger into the deep, dark well of your soul. Make it climb up to the light, to the song of the birds and the scent of the flowers.'

This joyous self-portrait extols the same creed. It is a symphony in red, and the figure of the artist seems to soar up like a flame to meet the slight arabesques that ripple across the background. Larsson comes close to Art Nouveau here, and he shared two of the sources that inspired it: Japanese art and the art of the eighteenth century. The oblong format and the lay-out are reminiscent of a *kakemono*; the sinuosities of the Louis XV armchair, the artist's voluminous coat, and the background all recall the age of Rococo.

In the background we see one of the cartoons for the ceiling and lunettes which Larsson executed for the Stockholm Royal Opera House in 1897.

In Front of the Mirror was shown at the Paris World Fair in 1900, at the Artists' Association exhibition in Stockholm, and in Munich in 1901. The same year it was bought by the great patron Pontus Fürstenberg, whose important collection went to the Göteborgs konstmuseum when he died the following year.

P.G.

BRUNO LILJEFORS

1860–1939, Sweden

Born in Uppsala, which was a small town surrounded by wild countryside abounding in birds and animals, Bruno Liljefors began at an early age to spend most of his time hunting, observing and drawing wild animals. After three years at the Academy of Fine Arts in Stockholm, he studied under a German animal painter in Düsseldorf. He subsequently lived in Italy, and then in France in 1883–4 and in 1886. He made his debut at the Salon in 1884, and was greatly impressed by Courbet, Impressionism, and Japanese art. He was also impressed by the French landscape, and especially by Grez, where he found 'everything so delicate and almost flirtatious that nature at home seems boorish in comparison'.

French elegance left its mark on the paintings he executed in Sweden in subsequent years: his compositions are sophisticated and he takes infinite pains with detail. But by the end of the 1880s Liljefors began to develop the dynamic and monumental conception of nature to which he was to remain faithful until the end of his days. He also remained faithful to the landscapes and the wild life of the Uppsala region and to Stockholm and its archipelago; it was there that he established his various studios over the years.

Liljefors also produced a large number of drawings, notably the illustrations to his three books (see the Selected Bibliography in the present catalogue), which provide an insight into his vision of nature and which abound in lively poetic episodes.

His major exhibitions outside Sweden were held in Copenhagen and Paris in 1902 and in Berlin in 1910.

54

The Mating of the Capercaillies, 1888

(Tjäderlek)

145 × 200
Signed lower left: Bruno Liljefors/ 1888
Göteborgs konstmuseum, Gothenburg
Inv. no. 210 (purchased in 1888)

In Liljefors' work, many of the spiritual aspirations and pictorial experiments of the late nineteenth century – Symbolism, *plein-air* painting, Synthetism, primitivism, nationalism – take the form of images of the animal kingdom. During his long rambles through the countryside he observed animals with enthusiasm and perspicacity, intuitively experiencing the deep affinities that exist between them and their environment. His paintings display what has been termed an *ecological* awareness *avant la lettre* (Ellenius 1982), and it was this integration of Scandinavian fauna with its environment which allowed him to give new life to the genre of animal painting.

Initially, Liljefors depicted his birds, insects and carnivores, flowers and plants, by studying them at close quarters and painting them in great detail. At the same time, he was able to evoke the immensity of nature in a small landscape. In *The Mating of the Capercaillies* of 1888, however, he strikes a new chord which prefigures both his own future work and, more generally, the developments in painting that were to take place in the 1890s. Liljefors leaves behind the sunny fields, meadows and woods, and moves into the wilder forest regions of his country.

The large and heavy black game birds, to an even greater degree than his earlier foxes, hunters and little birds, stand as 'the unified expression for the ground where they have their being', to quote the artist. For this solemn mating ceremony in the silence of the spring dawn, he also resorted to a different, more homogeneous tech-

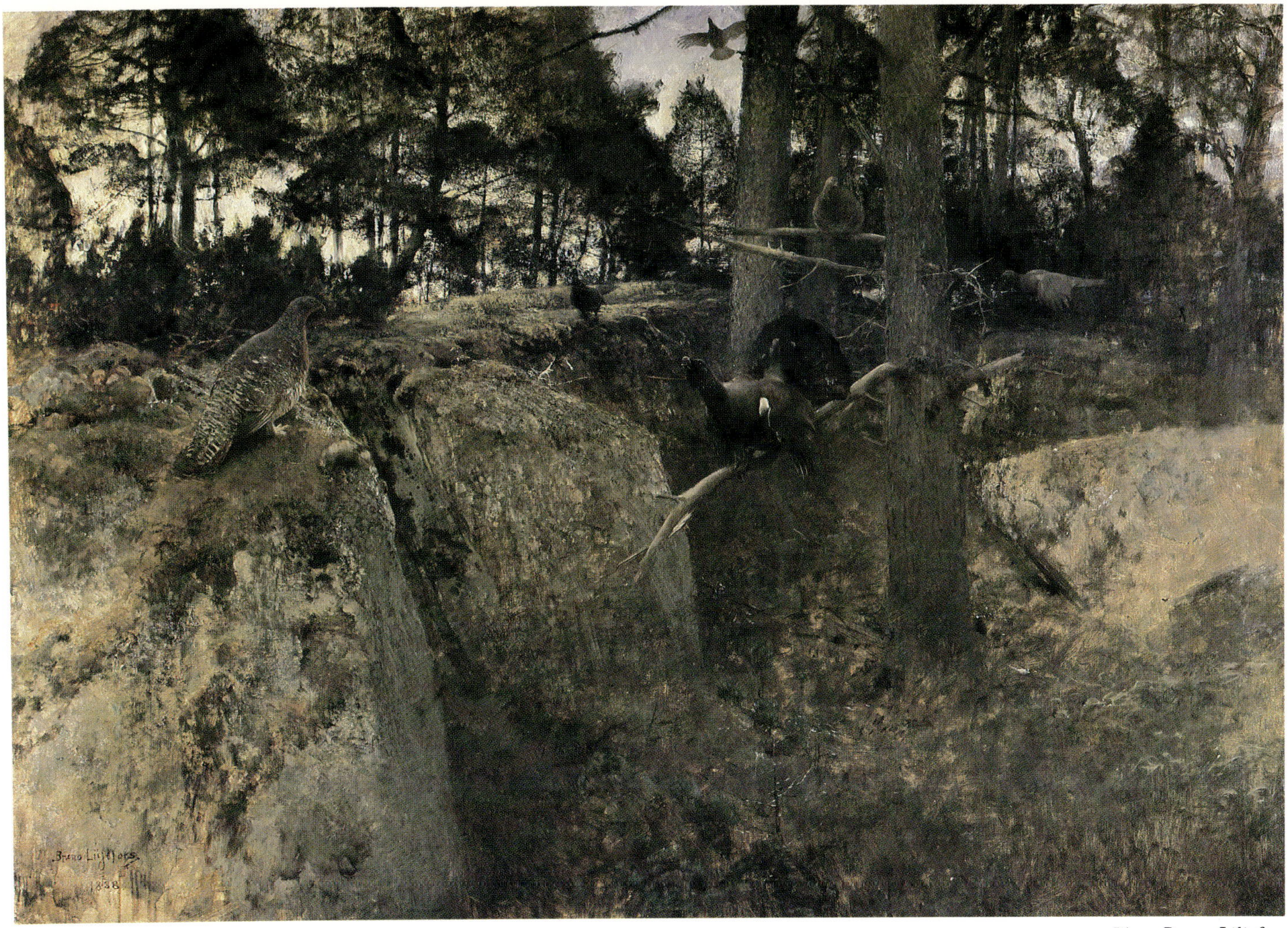

54. Bruno Liljefors

nique and palette in order to capture the quick, pulsating struggle for existence. He lets the primitive instinct which is expressed in this mating merge in intimate harmony with the primitive rock which, grey and covered with lichens, dominates most of the canvas. We are allowed to watch the performance diagonally from below and, so to speak, from the interior of the rock, 'the heart of the rock', to borrow an expression characteristic of Liljefors.

Although he is not known to have been particularly interested in the new Symbolist ideas he is spiritually allied to Symbolism's pantheistic mysticism of nature.

P.G.

55

Ducks among the Reeds, 1901

(Änder i bladvass)

131 × 137
Signed lower right: Bruno Liljefors/ 1901
Thielska galleriet, Stockholm
Inv. no. 238

By the end of the century, Liljefors had achieved a broad, dynamic vision of nature and of the fauna of Sweden. In this painting, the three ducks are fully integrated into the night scene, their dark, compact silhouettes contrasting with the frail black outline of the reeds and their shimmering reflections in the water. The painter is not trying to achieve a decorative or picturesque effect. He is attempting to show that both the birds and their environment are part of a broad indivisible totality, and that every element within it reflects every other element, as though in a mirror.

The artist's debt to Japanese art is obvious from such compositional elements as the lack of symmetry and the use of the view from above, and from the delicacy with which the reeds are drawn. But these techniques allow Liljefors to create a very special atmosphere, a *stämning*, to use the Swedish expression. Like so many of his contemporaries, he evokes the magic of the northern nights but taking care to include what he sees as one of its essential ingredients: the constant but almost imperceptible stirrings of the animal world.

The painting belonged to Ernest Thiel, the financier and collector who was at the time Liljefors' most important patron. The famous gallery he built near Stockholm in 1905 (open to the public since 1926) owns no fewer than fifty of the painter's canvases, including some of his masterpieces. Almost all of them date from between 1893 and 1907. Thiel once described how he organized an exhibition of twenty paintings by Liljefors at the Galerie Georges Petit in 1902: 'The first attempt to introduce France to Liljefors attracted a great deal of attention in artistic circles, but I did not succeed in selling a single painting – even though the exhibition was officially opened by the Swedish minister, even though the newspapers had been informed – and paid – and even though nothing had been neglected.'

When he returned to Sweden, Thiel bought most of the artist's canvases from him; the painting exhibited here was probably one of them.

P.G.

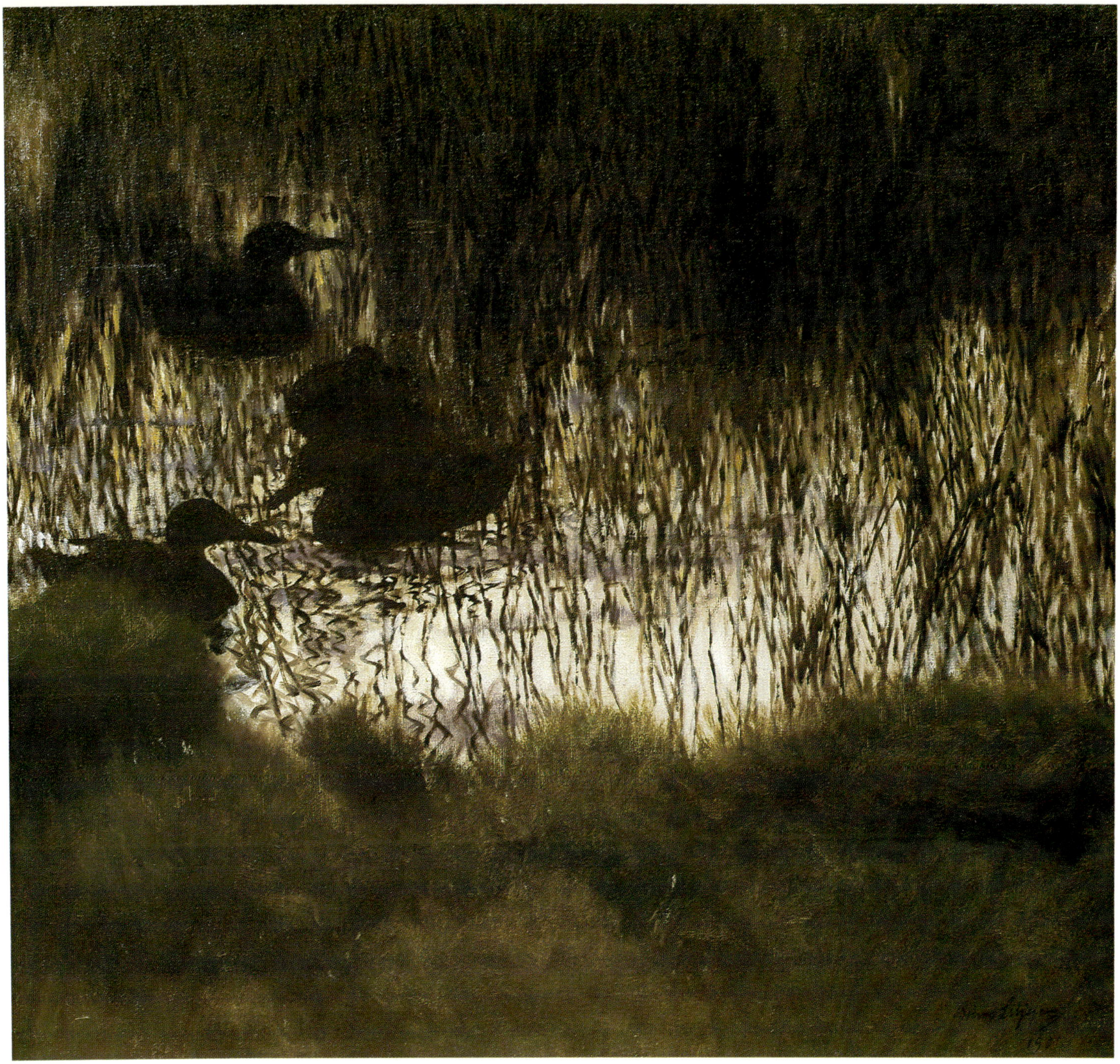

55. Bruno Liljefors

EDVARD MUNCH

1863–1944, Norway

Edvard Munch was born on Engelhaug farm into one of Norway's foremost intellectual families in the rural district of Løten at Hedmark in 1863. The following year he moved with his family to Christiania (Oslo).

Munch entered engineering school in 1879, but quickly changed course and decided to become a painter. In 1881 he enrolled at the Christiania Royal School of Drawing. The next year he moved into a studio building called 'Pultosten' together with other artists, where Christian Krohg supervised the younger ones in their work. In 1883 Munch made his debut at the Christiania Autumn Exhibition and attended Frits Thaulow's 'Open-Air Academy' at Modum. Munch's first scholarship enabled him to visit Antwerp and Paris in 1885. During the 1880s he came into contact with the Christiania bohemian set, the avant-garde of contemporary naturalistic painters in Norway, which included the writer Hans Jæger and the painters Christian Krohg and Karl G. Jensen-Hjell. Munch's first one-man exhibition was held in Christiania in the spring of 1889, and was followed by the first of his many summers in the little town of Aasgaardstrand by Christiania Fjord. In October the same year he travelled on his first State scholarship to Paris, entering Léon Bonnat's studio. In 1890 and 1891, he was again awarded State scholarships and went to Paris twice.

After a one-man exhibition in Christiania in 1892, Munch received an invitation to exhibit at the Verein Berliner Künstler. The exhibition was closed after a few days following a debate and vote in the Association. A group of artists, led by Max Liebermann, withdrew from the circle, later forming the Berlin Secession.

In the years to follow, Munch remained mainly in Berlin, although he continued to visit Paris and spend the summers in Norway. In Berlin, he fell in with such bohemian artists and writers as Richard Dehmel, August Strindberg, Holger Drachmann, Dagny Juel, and Stanislaw Przybyszewski, and the critics associated with the periodical *Pan*. In 1894 Munch produced his first etchings and lithographs and Przybyszewski published the book *Das Werk Edvard Munchs*. In 1895 Munch exhibited with the Finnish artist Axel Gallén (later Akseli Gallen-Kallela).

Munch returned temporarily to Paris in 1896, moving in the circle of artists that included Frederick Delius, William Mollard, Julius Meier-Graefe, August Strindberg, Stéphane Mallarmé, and Thadée Natansson. He printed colour lithographs and his first woodcuts at Clot's. He exhibited at the Salon des Indépendants in 1896–8 and in 1902 *The Frieze of Life* was shown at the Berlin Secession. In 1908 he suffered a nervous breakdown and was admitted to Dr Daniel Jacobson's clinic in Copenhagen. After recovering he returned to Norway in 1909 and in 1916 he purchased the Ekely property at Skøyen on the outskirts of Oslo, where he remained for the rest of his life.

T.S.

56

Inger on the Beach, 1889

(Inger på stranden)

126.4 × 161.7
Signed lower left: E.Munch 1889
Rasmus Meyers Samlinger, Bergen
Inv. no. 240

Edvard Munch painted *Inger on the Beach* during his first summer at Aasgaardstrand on Christiania Fjord. His youngest sister Inger posed on the stones as his model. In the autumn of 1889, when he himself was in Paris, the painting was shown at the Autumn Exhibition under the title *Evening* (Aften). Munch's earlier works from the

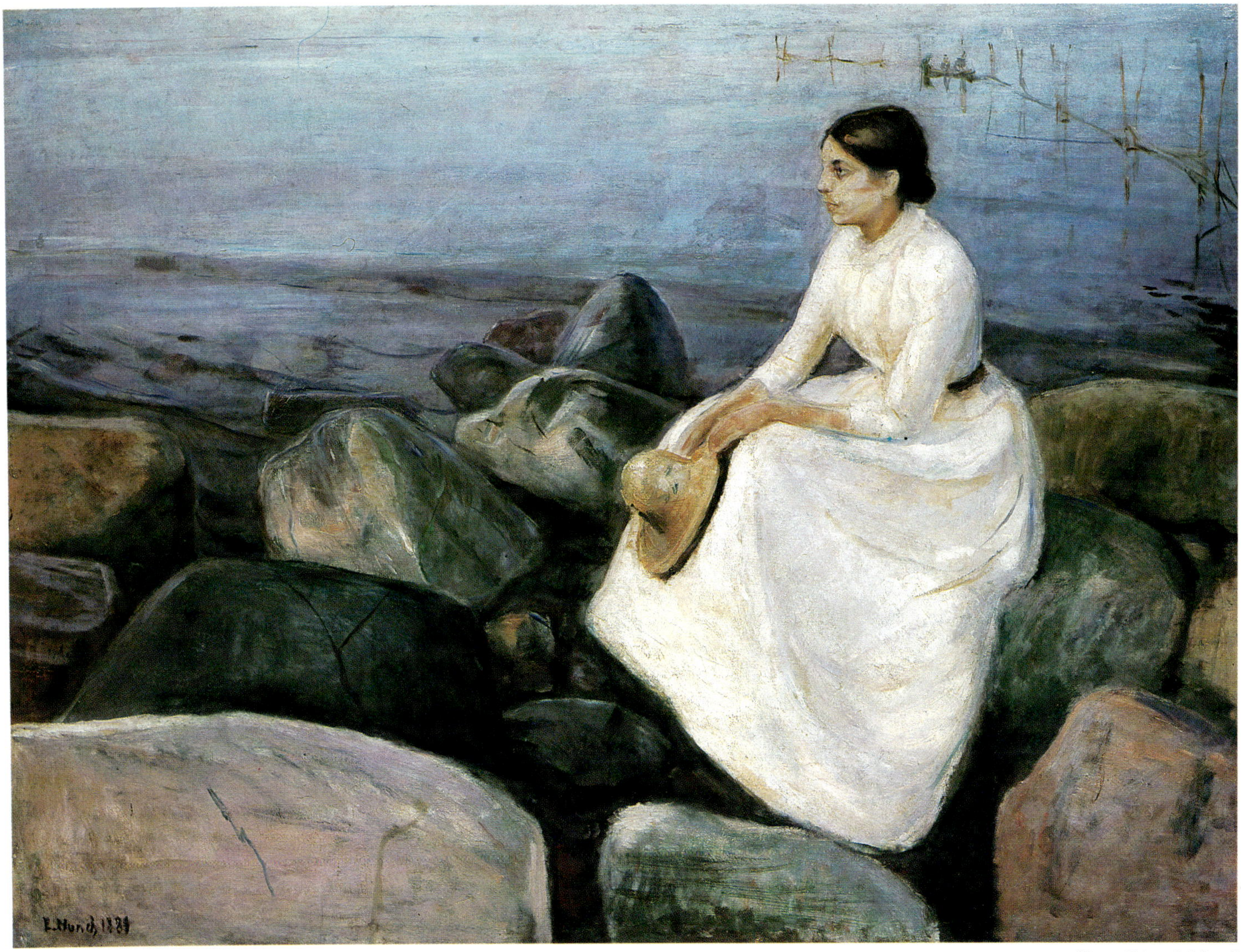

56. Edvard Munch

1880s clearly show, in both the choice of motive and its execution, influences from the art of Christian Krohg, Hans Heyerdahl and Frits Thaulow. But right after his first brief trip to Antwerp and Paris, Munch was already painting pictures which show that the naturalistic form was not enough for him. Impressions from the art he had seen in the course of his trip made it possible for him to use new artistic means, but not until his second stay in Paris in 1889 was he fully able to carry out his intentions to create subjective, highly expressionistic paintings.

As early as the last half of the 1880s, several of the leading Naturalists in Norway moved away from clear, bright Naturalism towards an emphasis on mood. This was most clearly seen in the painters who, in the summer of 1886, settled on Fleskum Farm in Bærum. This 'Fleskum colony' consisted of Christian Skredsvig, Eilif Peterssen, Erik Werenskiold, Gerhard Munthe, Kitty Kielland, and Harriet Backer. Munch was not personally close to the Fleskum painters, but the influence of these artists' interpretations of the quiet summer night's mood, and his impressions of the works of Puvis de Chavannes and Jules Bastien-Lepage which he had seen at the World Fair in Antwerp, are clearly visible in *Inger on the Beach*. Like many of Bastien-Lepage's figures in the landscape, she stares vacantly before her. The careful, slightly dry use of colour also recalls Bastien-Lepage's work.

In *Inger on the Beach*, Munch went farther than his Norwegian colleagues in a simplification of forms, and his palette has a more delicate tone. But the musical, elegiac mood and the harmony between figure and landscape have much in common with the works of several of the Fleskum painters. There are also Symbolist elements in the painting.

Munch effectively exploited nature as the factor which sets the mood and it appears as an image of the figure's state of mind. With this painting, Munch heralded much of his own development in the '90s without having been in contact with the trends in European art which were to be a prerequisite for his mature style. Aasgaardstrand's gentle coastline was also the uniting element in many of his paintings in *The Frieze of Life* in the 1890s.

Inger on the Beach was purchased by Erik Werenskiold, who sold it in 1909 to the Bergen art collector Rasmus Meyer. The painting was shown at the Munch exhibition at the Verein Berliner Künstler in Berlin in 1892, then in Düsseldorf and Cologne and at the Equitable Palast in Berlin from December 1892 to January 1893.

T.S.

57

Melancholy, 1891–2

(Melankoli)

64.5 × 96
Signed lower left: E.M.
Nasjonalgalleriet, Oslo
Inv. no. 2813 (donation in 1959)

During the course of his second stay in France, from the autumn of 1889 to 1890, Munch had an opportunity to familiarize himself with the Paris art world. The World Fair gave a good review of modern European art. The avant-garde artists of the day could be studied at the Volpini Exhibition of Impressionists and Synthetists, where Gauguin and the Pont-Aven group were very much in evidence. Van Gogh's paintings were available at Theo van Gogh's Gallery, and a number of pioneers of modern painting were represented at the Salon des Indépendants. The older Impressionists were exhibited at Georges Petit's and Durand's. Munch lived in relative isolation from the Norwegian artists' colony, but spent some time with the Danish Symbolist poet Emanuel Goldstein. In the autumn Munch moved to St Cloud outside Paris, where he received news of his father's unexpected death in December the same year. In France, he arrived at the Symbolist-Expressionistic idiom which marked his works from the 1890s. In spite of the fact that it always had a strong personal stamp, Munch's art in the '90s developed alongside the European art of his time and is unthinkable without it. His work from the early '90s clearly shows that he received important stimuli from the Neo-Impressionists, from Toulouse-Lautrec, Carrière, Gauguin, Van Gogh, Ensor, and Whistler. The day's general feel for mysticism and symbolism suited Munch in his search to create an adequate means of expression for his own experiences. The art created in the circle around Gauguin and French Symbolist poetry largely formed the background for Munch's first Symbolist-Synthetist paintings.

Melancholy marked a decisive step in Munch's development. The style which was to mark Munch's work in the '90s is formulated in this painting. His goal was to create a powerful and concentrated visual expression for a state of mind. By simplifying and stylizing line, form and colour, he sought a synthesis in order to achieve the greatest possible intensity of expression.The brushwork is broad and summary, and is consciously used as an expressive element.

Munch spent the summer of 1891 in Aasgaardstrand, where he witnessed his friend Jappe Nielsen's bouts of jealousy. *Melancholy* (also called *Jappe on the Beach* and *Jealousy*), the fruit of this summer, was considered by Christian Krohg to be the first Symbolist or Synthetist painting by a Norwegian artist when a version of it was shown at the Autumn Exhibition in 1891.

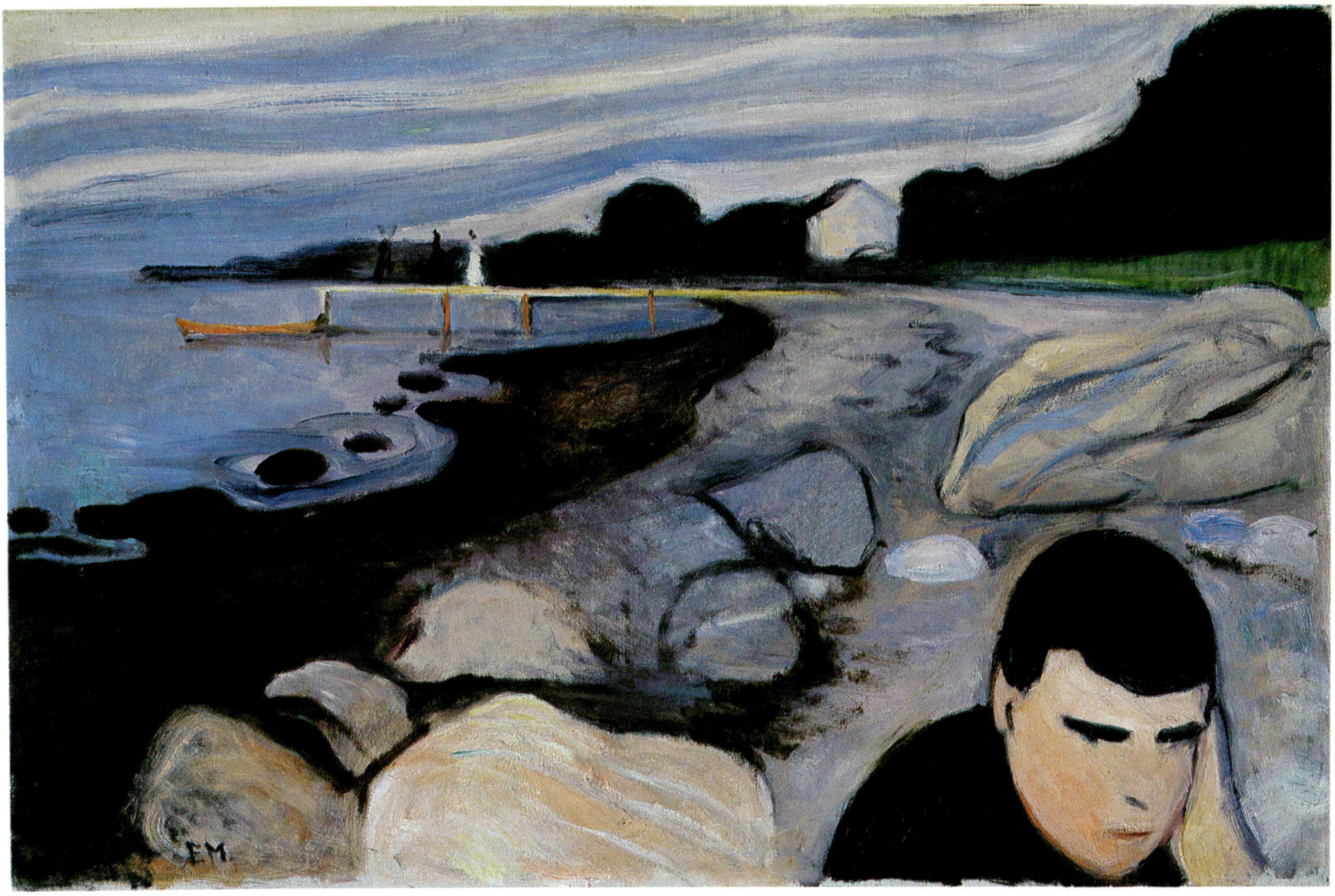

57. Edvard Munch

The picture does not show an event: it expresses a state of mind. Nature is, to a far greater degree than in *Inger on the Beach*, an expression for this state of mind. Munch achieved this through the deep, suggestive spatial effect, the wavy rhythm of the coastline, the large, simplified forms where everything is subservient to the whole, and through the blue-violet tones of the palette which are broken by the white house and the yellow boat.

Five painted versions and two woodcuts of the subject are known. The Nasjonalgalleriet's version may have formed the basis for Munch's many sketches made in the winter of 1891–2 to illustrate E. Goldstein's *Alruner* (Mandrake), or it may have resulted from this work. The painting was shown at Munch's exhibition at the Equitable Palast in Berlin, 1892–3.

T.S.

58

Portrait of Inger, 1892

(Portrett av Inger)

172 × 122.5
Signed lower left: E. Munch 1892
Nasjonalgalleriet, Oslo
Inv. no. 499 (purchased in 1899)

After the 'scandalous exhibition' at the Verein Berliner Künstler in the autumn of 1892, Munch became the major topic of discussion in Berlin's artistic circles. The uproar caused by the exhibition also led to other offers, including shows at Eduard Schulte's galleries in Düsseldorf and Cologne. In December the same year, the exhibition was already back in Berlin, where it was shown at the fashionable Equitable Palast until January 1893. Among the many works at the exhibition was the large full-length *Portrait of Inger*, painted in 1892.

In 1885, Munch had shown the first of a long line of full-length portraits at the Autumn Exhibition. It was the portrait of his friend and colleague Karl Gustav Jensen-Hjell, painted after Munch's trip to Antwerp and Paris. On this trip, Munch had studied the international portrait tradition at the Louvre and had probably also seen Manet's large full-length portraits.

In *Portrait of Inger*, Munch's ideals of the '90s in portrait presentation were already clearly formulated. He had distanced himself from the realism we find in several of his earlier portraits. The stylistic point of departure for *Portrait of Inger* is French Synthetism, which, through a stylization of form, line and colour, sought great intensity of expression. The picture is simply built; only a dividing line marks the transition between the floor on which Inger is standing and the wall behind her. The characterization is in the person herself: the room as a milieu gives no supplementary information. The figure has a closed-in form which has its balance point in the clasped hands. Munch has brought out his sister's character in the shapely face. Colour is applied in clearly pronounced planes surrounded by firm contours. The study of light which is found in several of Munch's earlier portraits is replaced by a synthetic concept of form and line, and all details which could disturb the overall impression have been removed. Munch exhibited the painting with the title *Harmony in Black and Violet*. The painting was purchased from the artist by the Nasjonalgalleriet in 1899.

T.S.

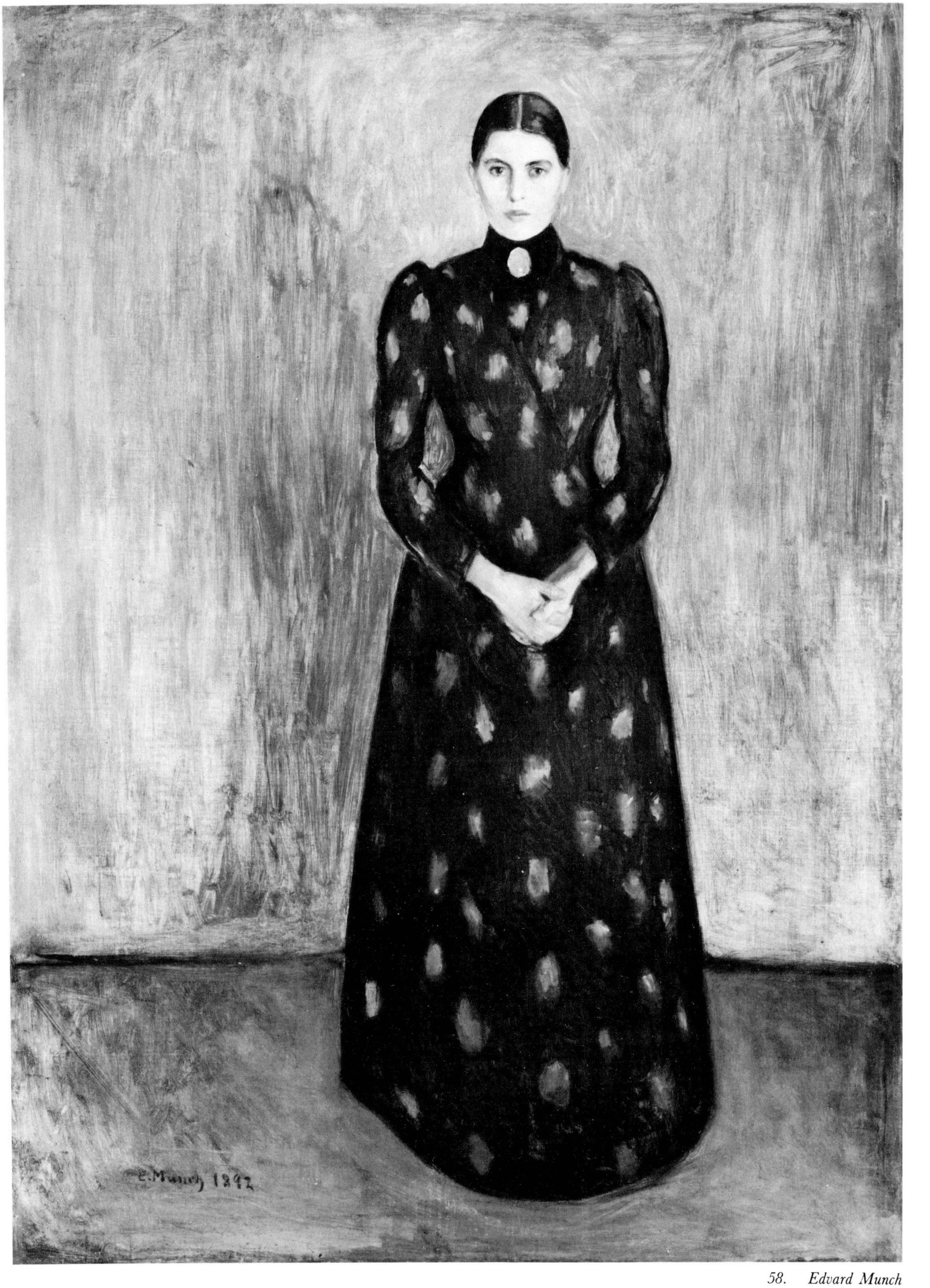

58. Edvard Munch

59

Moonlight, 1893

(Måneskinn)

140.5 × 135
Signed lower right: E. Munch
Nasjonalgalleriet, Oslo
Inv. no. 1914 (purchased in 1938)

Even though he lived abroad from 1889 to 1901, mainly in France, Munch maintained contacts with Norway through his annual summer visits. From the summers and landscape of Norway, particularly Aasgaardstrand, Munch drew inspiration for his mood-filled landscapes in which the Norwegian summer night holds a central place. In *Moonlight*, painted in Aasgaardstrand in the summer of 1893, Munch projects the mystic summer night mood onto a lone woman, who stands before a dark house in the moonlight. The woman's face lies in semi-light and has a ghostlike character. A large shadow, which does not correspond to the contours of her figure, falls on the wall of the house and gives the picture drama. The form hinted at on the left-hand lower edge has the same effect. The window frames and picket fence shine white in the summer night; so does the moon, which is reflected in the panes. Everything else lies in darkness. The shadow and the deep-green colour which follows the contours of the figure create a wave-like movement, in sharp contrast to the otherwise terse composition, dominated by horizontal and vertical lines. In *Moonlight*, Munch creates a mood and state of mind through a synthetic conception of form, line and colour. The female figure placed frontally in the lower edge of the picture played a major role in Munch's works in around the middle of the '90s.

On a brief trip to Hamburg in the autumn of 1891, Munch had seen Böcklin's work at the Kunsthalle, and was enthralled by the German's symbolic landscapes. Several of Munch's landscapes from the summer of 1893 have a deep, smouldering palette which distinguishes them from French models and, as Eggum notes, are probably due to the direct influence of Böcklin.

Moonlight was previously owned by Harald Nørregaard. It was purchased by the Nasjonalgalleriet, Oslo, at an auction at Wangs Kunsthandel in 1938.

T.S.

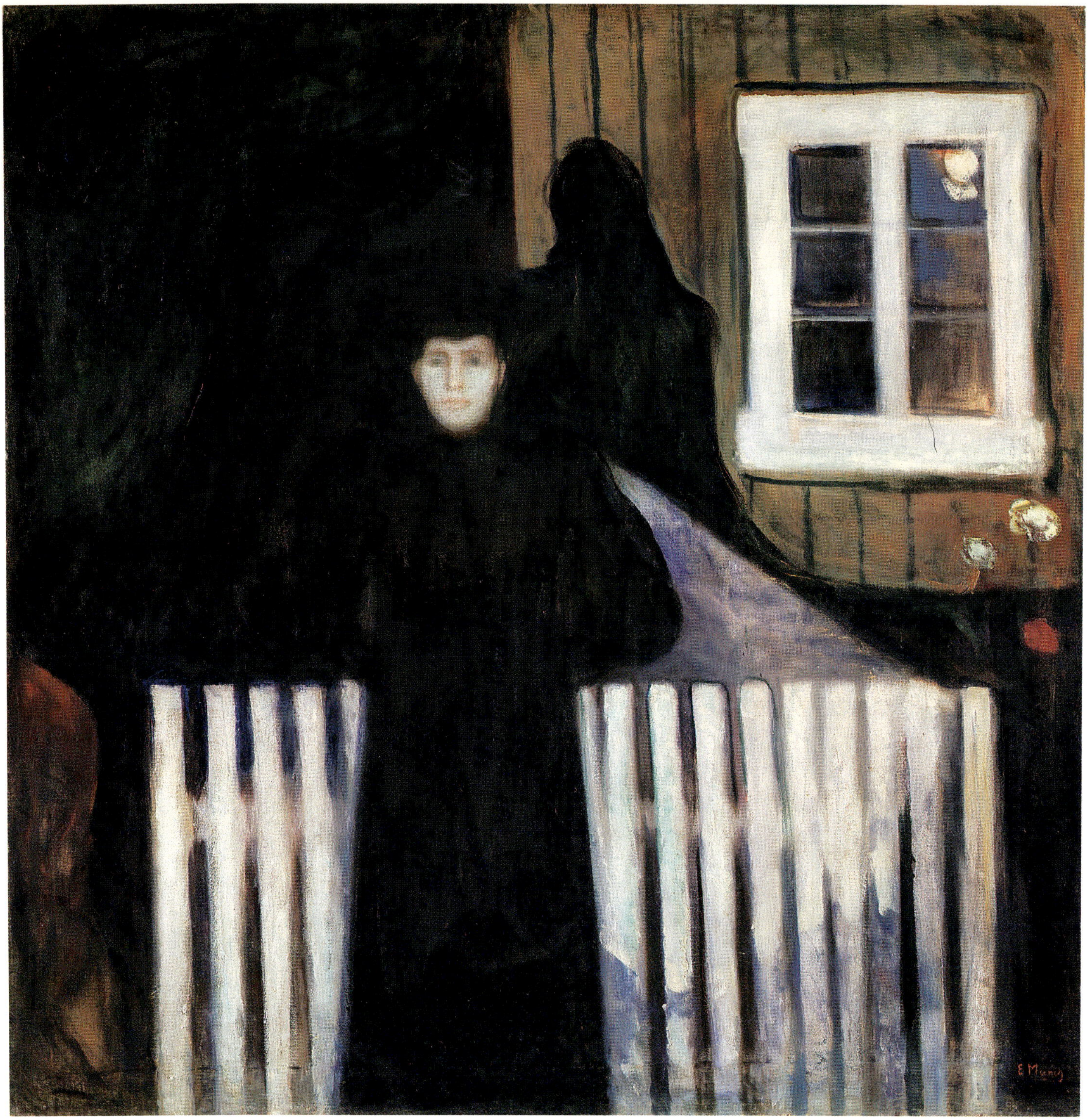

59. Edvard Munch

60

The Voice, 1893

(Stemmen)

90 × 118.5
Not signed
Oslo Kommunes Kunstsamlinger, Munch-museet, Oslo
Inv. no. M 44

In the early '90s, Munch began the series of paintings later to be called *The Frieze of Life*. One version of *The Voice* was to be the first of these paintings, and was exhibited in Christiania in 1893 in a sequence with motives dealing with love. Later, a version of *The Voice* was exhibited in the 'mature' *Frieze of Life* at the Berlin Secession in 1902.

The setting for *The Voice* is the beach at Aasgaardstrand, which provides a unifying element in the frieze. The theme recalls Munch's first romance, the moment before his first kiss. The female frontal figure plays the dominant part, as in *Moonlight*. In *The Voice*, the figure is closer to us and she seems to have great sexual power. The shaft of moonlight is used as a sign of awakening desire.

The picture expresses the tension between the couples in the background and the woman in the foreground, and, as is often the case in Munch's paintings, the main figure stands alone in contrast to the others, who are together in the boats. The woman, shown in a severe, closed form, her hands behind her back, was used in a number of other portraits by Munch around this time.

The Museum of Fine Arts in Boston has another version of *The Voice* and the motive is repeated in an etching and a woodcut. The picture was originally called *Summer Night Mood*.

T.S.

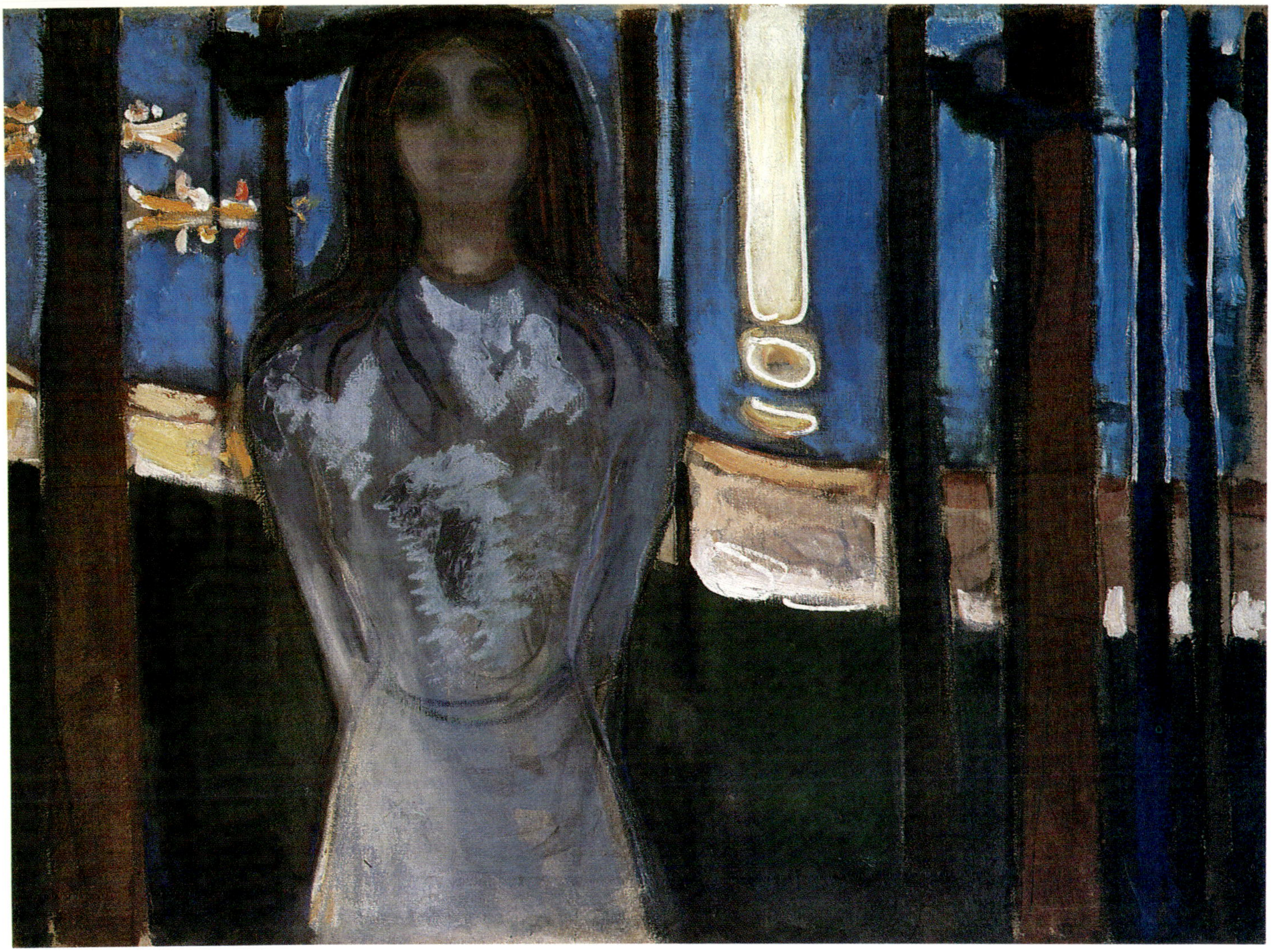

60. Edvard Munch

61

Ashes, 1894

(Aske)

Oil and tempera on canvas, 120.5 × 141
Signed upper right: E. Munch
Nasjonalgalleriet, Oslo
Inv. no. 809

When Munch exhibited *The Frieze of Life* in 1902, *Ashes* held a central place among the motives which dealt with the flowering and death of love. Munch called the painting *After the Fall*, a clear indication that the time of love in Paradise is over.

Ashes is a good example of Munch's fully developed Symbolist style of 1893–5. At the left lower edge of the picture huddles a dark-clad male figure, with ash-grey face and hand to his head. In strong contrast stands a voluptuous, red-haired, lightly clad woman with raised arms and hands in her hair. Some of her hair falls on the man's body. Her dress is open revealing a flame-red petticoat. The landscape reflects the mood. The straight trunks of the trees repeat the lines of the woman's figure while the barren stones in the foreground echo the man's huddled body. On the picture's lower edge lies an almost burned-out log, and the man is turned towards the smoke which rises from it. The message is clear. Love is dead, burned to ashes, reduced to loneliness and despair. Behind the erotic content lies a deathly fear of annihilation by woman. In the lithograph version of the picture (1896), the log in the foreground is a smoking heap of ashes. Munch himself commented: 'I felt our love lying on the ground like a heap of ashes'. The design of *Ashes* is even more simplified than, for example, that of *Melancholy* (No. 57). There is a greater fluidity of line and the palette is richer and more powerful, with more expressive contrasts. The symbolic value of colours is consciously explored.

The painting was purchased by the Nasjonalgalleriet, Oslo from Blomqvist Kunsthandel's Munch exhibition in Christiania in 1909.

T.S.

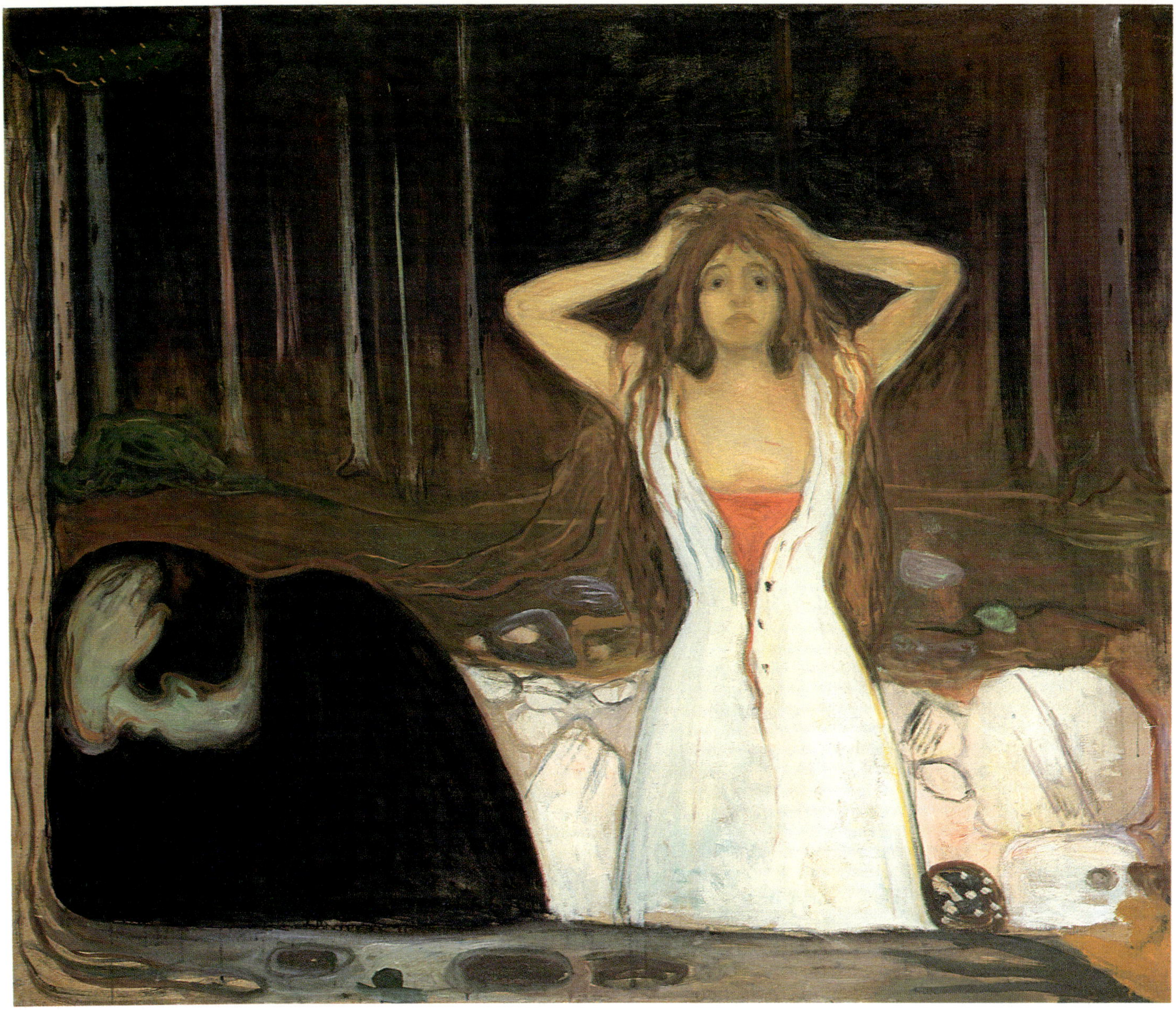

61. Edvard Munch

62

Red Creeper, 1898–1900

(Rød villvin)

119.5 × 121
Signed upper left: E. Munch
Oslo Kommunes Kunstsamlinger, Munch-museet, Oslo
Inv. no. M 503

The painting reveals a tendency towards the use of stronger colours than those which characterize Munch's work from around the turn of the century. It shows a large white house in Aasgaardstrand, Kiøsterud house, surrounded by flaming red creepers. The house with its gleaming windows stands in powerful contrast to the creepers, which seem to dance like flames.

The man in the foreground has features familiar to us from Munch's portraits of Przybyszewski. His grey-green face and staring eyes express great fear, but we are given no hint as to what he is afraid of. Fear itself and despair, expressed through the use of colour, are the subject. At the exhibition in Berlin in 1902, Munch placed *Red Creeper* among his 'fear motives'.

The painting was shown at Arno Volfframm's in Dresden in 1900 and in Christiania in 1901.

T.S.

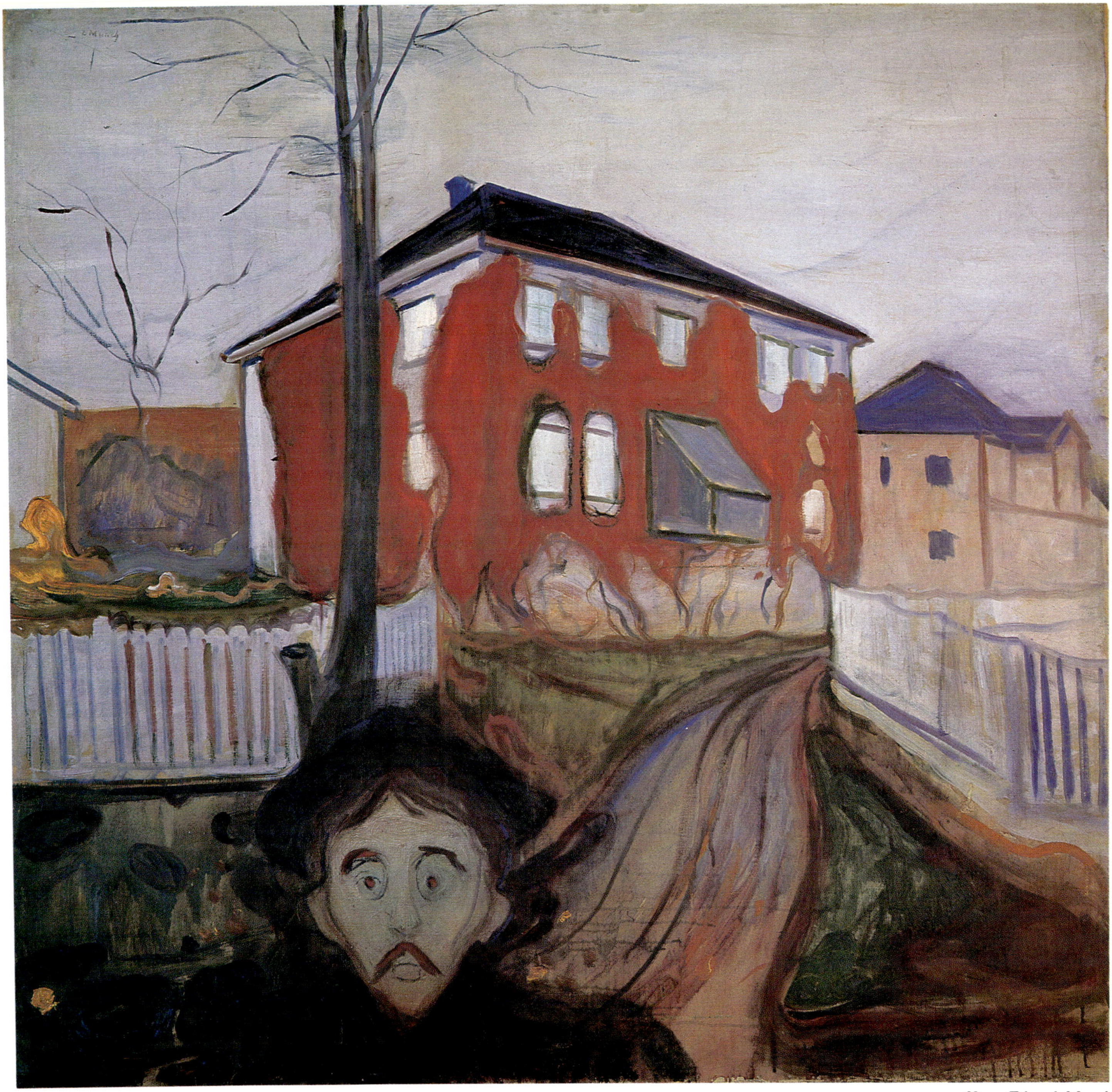

62. Edvard Munch

GERHARD MUNTHE

1849–1929, Norway

In 1874, after studies in Christiania under J. F. Eckersberg, Morten Müller and Knud Bergslien, and at the Royal School of Drawing, Munthe became one of the last young Norwegian art students to go to Düsseldorf. However, he did not join the Academy there but pursued training on his own, basing his work on a direct study of nature and of Dutch seventeenth-century landscape painting. In 1877 he went to Munich where he remained until 1882. Again, he did not attend the Academy, but continued his own course of studies.

In 1882 Munthe returned to Norway and except for short study trips abroad remained there for the rest of his life. He was thus one of the very few Norwegian artists of his generation who did not study in Paris during the 1880s – paying only brief visits to the city in 1885, and again in 1892. Through Werenskiold and his other friends from the Munich years, Munthe was, however, kept well informed about the new trends in French art, and adapted his art to the same stylistic idioms as the rest of the Norwegian Naturalist painters. In the 1880s Munthe was one of the most ardent propagators of Naturalism in Norwegian art.

During the summer of 1886 Munthe joined Werenskiold, Skredsvig, Peterssen, Kitty Kielland, and Harriet Backer at Fleskum and was influenced by the moody, emotionally charged style emerging there, though without ever becoming a fully fledged neo-romantic painter typical of the 1890s. As a painter Munthe remained, throughout his career, a faithful Naturalist.

In the 1890s, however, another side of Munthe's artistic talent emerged, namely the decorative. It was during this period that his own highly characteristic decorative style was developed, making him the great innovator of Norwegian decorative arts.

63 a

The Horse of Hades, 1892

(Helhesten)

Watercolour on paper, 79 × 112.5
Signed lower right: G. Munthe. 1892.
Nasjonalgalleriet, Oslo
Inv. no. B. 8234 (purchased in 1893)

63 b

The Suitors, 1892

(Friere (Nordlysdøtrene))

Watercolour on paper, 77 × 94
Signed lower right: G. Munthe. 1892.
Nasjonalgalleriet, Oslo
Inv. no. B. 8239 (purchased in 1893)

63 c

The Evil Stepmother, 1892–3

(Den onde stemor)

Watercolour on paper, 57.5 × 79.5
Signed lower right: G. Munthe
Nasjonalgalleriet, Oslo
Inv. no. B. 8240 (purchased in 1893)

63 d

The Wise Bird, 1892–3

(Den kloke fugl)

Watercolour on paper, 55.5 × 81
Signed lower right: G Munthe
Nasjonalgalleriet, Oslo
Inv. no. B. 8236 (purchased in 1893)

63 e

C'est ainsi, que l'amour s'allume dans le coeur, 1895

Watercolour on paper, 83.5 × 64
Signed upper right: G. Munthe -95.
Nasjonalgalleriet, Oslo
Inv. no. B. 8244 (purchased in 1895)

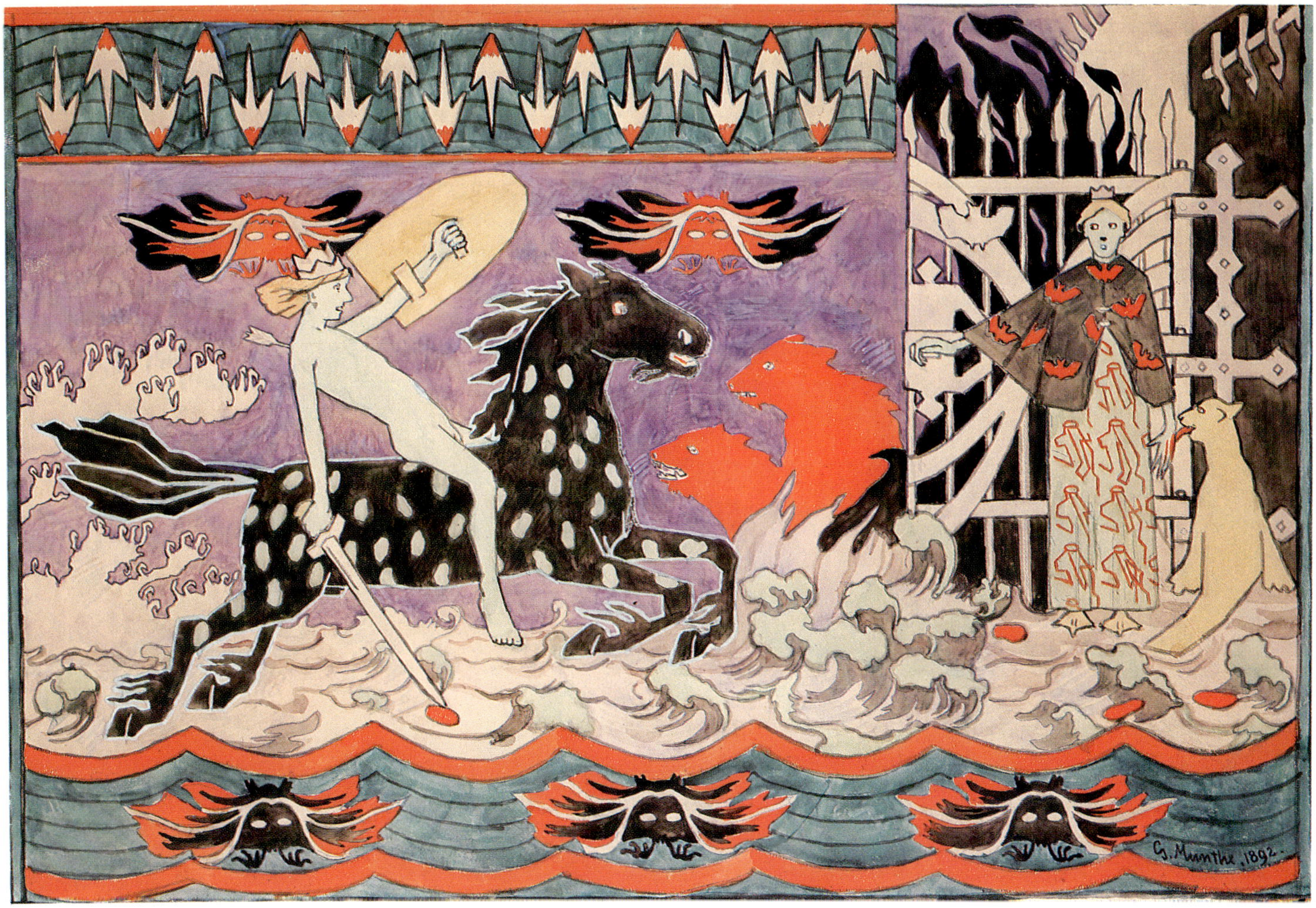

63a. Gerhard Munthe

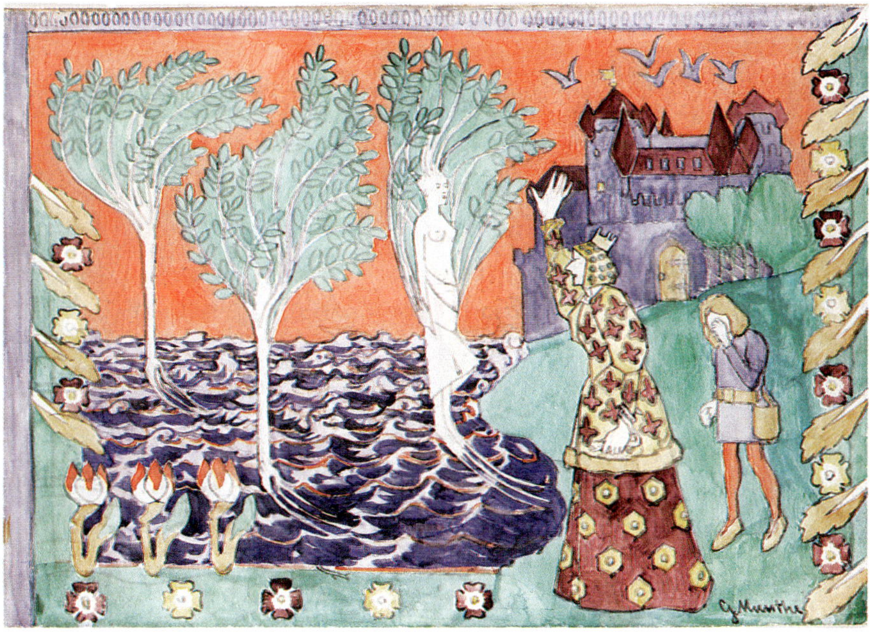

63c. Gerhard Munthe

At the so-called 'Black and White Exhibition' in Christiania in 1893 Munthe exhibited a series of 11 'decorative watercolours'. They were acclaimed by the public as well as by the critics; it was felt that they constituted a new development in Norwegian art, and eight of them were bought by the Nasjonalgalleriet. Munthe made several replicas of the series which were sent for exhibition abroad; to the Salon in Paris and the World Fair in Chicago in 1893, to Stockholm in 1894, to Venice in 1895, and elsewhere in Europe. Everywhere they evoked interest as an innovation in decorative arts. Meanwhile Munthe continued to add new motifs to the series.

The pictorial motifs appeal to the fantasy, with a tendency towards the darker, mystical, often frightening sides of life. Although clearly literary in content, the series does not, with a few exceptions, illustrate any specific text. It reflects the mystical and symbolic world of old Norwegian sagas, lores and fairy-tales, but the themes themselves were created out of his own fertile imagination. His intention was to express ideas and sentiments that could not be reached by naturalistic means, he wanted to create a new art form that in his opinion should relate to naturalism as poetry to prose. By removing perspective and using pure colour areas contained by firm contours, he created an antithesis to the illusionistic effects of Naturalism.

Munthe visited Paris in the spring of 1892 and in the autumn of the same year he must have seen J. F. Willumsen's exhibition in Christiania. It does not seem unreasonable to assume that the art of Gauguin and the French Synthetists influenced him in the formation of his decorative style. His chief source of inspiration, however, was the decorative instinct characteristic of old Norwegian art from Viking times through to the Middle Ages, surviving in the richly decorated utensils and farm houses of the Norwegian countryside. Here, he believed, was to be found the very core of the Norwegianness of Norwegian art. To create a national art was almost a moral commitment for the circle of artists to which Munthe belonged.

In working out his decorative style, Munthe assiduously studied the ornamental repertoire and decorative patterns of old Norwegian art; he was especially interested in the 'rose painting' of popular art and its colouristic effects. He thought that the fresh and lively colours he found in popular art were the result of a particular Norwegian sense of colour. In this connection one must bear in mind that his watercolours are very faded and the paper has yellowed, causing them to loose much of their original freshness. A main source of inspiration was the old Norwegian tapestries. It is, however, important to note that Munthe never actually copied any of the motifs and patterns he found in old Norwegian art, they served only as a point of departure for his own creative imagination.

When Munthe exhibited his decorative watercolours in 1893, he considered them as works of art in their own right, and he only reluctantly agreed to their use as cartoons for tapestries. He was afraid that much of their quality would be lost in the transfer. The tapestries woven after his cartoons were a great success and led to a revival in Norwegian tapestry weaving with the establishment of workshops to resurrect the old weaving techniques and colour recipes.

Munthe took a great interest in the applied arts, and he was one of the leaders, both intellectually and artistically, in the national revival movement of the decorative arts that took place at around the turn of the century. He produced designs not only for paintings and tapestries, but for works in metal, glass, furniture, and whole rooms as well. He is known especially for his book illustrations of which his participation, together with Werenskiold, Egedius and others, in the luxury edition of Snorre's *Sagas of the Norse Kings*, 1896–9, is the most famous. It has since become one of the great national monuments in Norwegian art.

K.B.

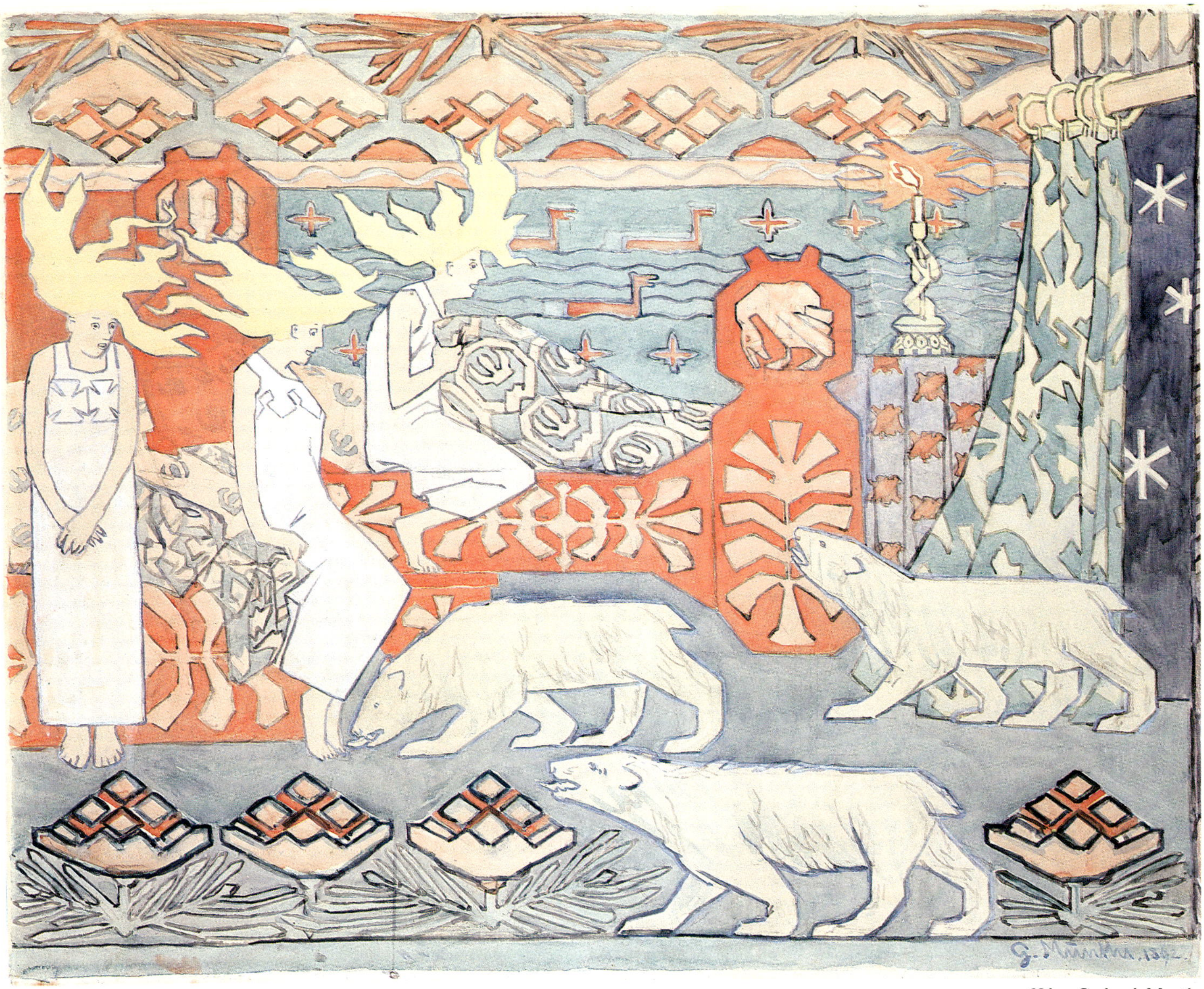

63*b*. *Gerhard Munthe*

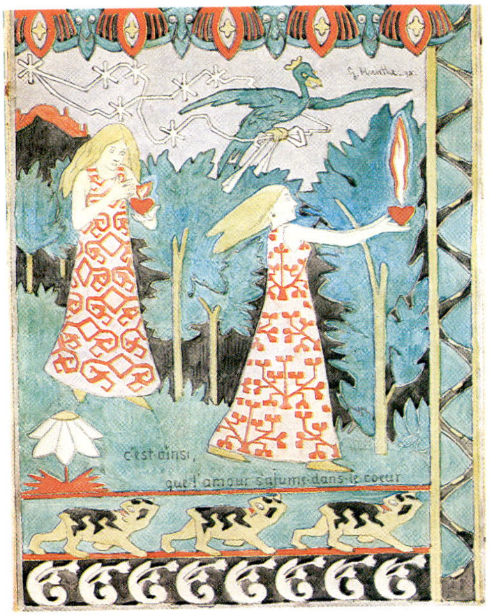

63*e*. *Gerhard Munthe*

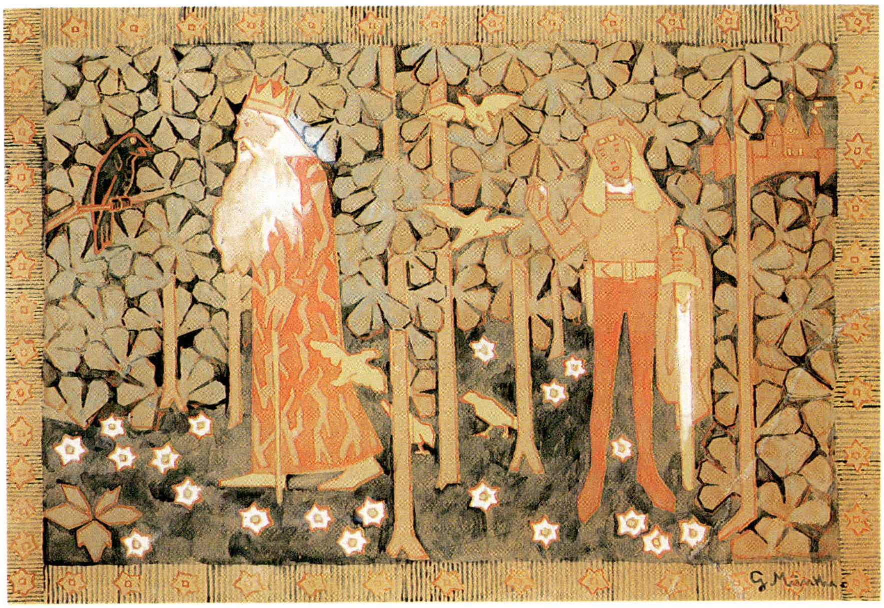

63*d*. *Gerhard Munthe*

EJNAR NIELSEN

1872–1956, Denmark

While still apprenticed to a house painter, Ejnar Nielsen was accepted at the Royal Academy of Fine Arts, Copenhagen, which he attended from 1890 to early 1893. He studied at Zahrtmann's school from 1895 to 1896. He went to Paris for the first time in 1900–1, and was in Italy the following year. He returned to both places many times.

At around the turn of the century, he did a number of book illustrations, and later received many large-scale decorative commissions.

In his youth Ejnar Nielsen admired Puvis de Chavannes, and later Andrea del Castagno. In his palette and depiction of human life, he is close to Vilhelm Hammershøi (p. 122). But he found his milieu far from Copenhagen, among the people in the village of Gjern in Jutland, where he lived from 1894 to 1900, and where he returned again and again.

64

The Sick Girl, 1896

(Den syge pige)

111 × 164
Signed lower right: SEPT = 96 – EJNAR – NIELSEN
Statens Museum for Kunst, Copenhagen
Inv. no. 1778

The picture of the sick girl was the first to make Ejnar Nielsen's name known. In the whitewashed room whose ceiling beams are just discernible, she lies parallel with the picture surface in her hard narrow iron bed before a stove, waiting for death as if she already lay in a cramped coffin. The dark cover is lifted by her pointed knees. One thin hand rests on her chest; the other hangs like a skeleton's over the edge of the bed. A dark covering underneath her brings out the delicate little emaciated head with its pale blue veins at the temples. It is painted with infinite gentleness and sensivitity. 'As with J. P. Jacobsen, the essential problem for Ejnar Nielsen is: Life seen illuminated through Death' (Zibrandtsen). In an interview (1927), the artist observed, 'Death serves life and life serves death. I do no understand why people cannot view death, with its majestic beauty, as they can life.' In the same interview he said that the sick girl was 'a totally delightful person even in her wasted state. I will never forget the child.'

'He sees a girl just before the moment of her release from suffering. She is as close as one can come to a skeleton while there is still flesh on it. The hands' tense grip is not tempered by the layer of skin. A delicate blood vessel stands out at her temple like a tree... E. N. painted the black stove like a good Naturalist, it is decorated with garlands and a baby' (Hans Helge Madsen). Attention has been drawn (Stabell) to the painting's similarities with Munch's picture of a sick girl.

The painting was shown at the Paris World Fair in 1900, where he received a bronze medal.

H.W.

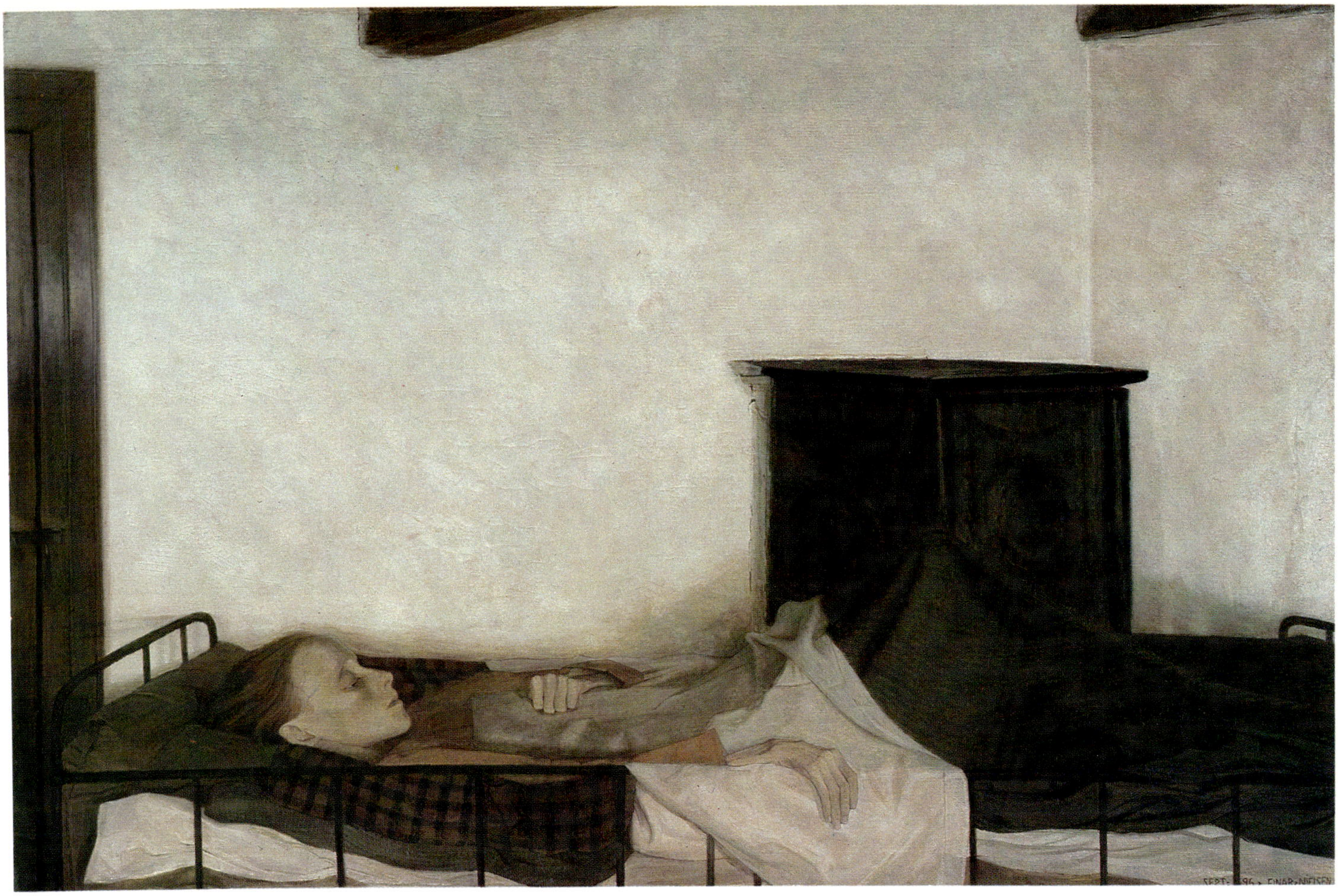

64. Ejnar Nielsen

65

The Blind Girl. Gjern, 1896 and 1898

(Den blinde. Gjern)

Oil and gold on canvas, 131.5 × 79.2
Signed lower right: EJNAR NIELSEN/GIERN = 1896 & 98
Den Hirschsprungske Samling, Copenhagen
(purchased in 1901)

The attitude of the sick child or cripple preoccupied Ejnar Nielsen. Why should those who are worn out live on? And what is life worth to one who cannot live it with all five senses? These were serious questions for the Realists of the 1880s who, in spite of their social commitment in the art they created, loved life so straightforwardly, so effortlessly. Of all the Danish artists in the 1890s, Ejnar Nielsen was the one who consistently saw life and death, poverty and illness not as descriptions of a milieu or social conditions, but as eternal questions.

From 1896 to 1905, Ejnar Nielsen was occupied with the subject of the blind girl. The model was the organist in Gjern, and the pictures all deal with the idea of seeking illumination from within.

The young woman stands slightly to the left in front of a landscape. Behind her, a golden river winds towards the background's high hills and reflects the golden sky. A row of trees with uniformly divided trunks and delicately domed tops divides the picture horizontally where the river begins. White lambs graze in the green meadows.

The Gjern hills and the winding Gjern River are real, as are the model and the trees, and were painted from photographs of Gjern which Ejnar Nielsen had made for this picture (H. H. Madsen). But they have been transformed and given meaning. The Gjern River is turned into a river of pure gold.

The dark female figure dominates the landscape. In her hands she holds dandelions.

> Through the sensitivity of her hands she is in contact with life. She holds before her a dandelion, now gone to seed. With her fingertips she delicately tries to feel the transient global shape of the flower. The double silver ring on her finger is also symbolic. These small things are worked with great delicacy into the monumental pictorial whole, where the broad features of the landscape's dreamlike unreality accentuate the blind girl's inner loneliness (Zibrandtsen).
>
> The planes and features of the face, the closed eyes, are like the forms of the hills behind. The face and the hills are part of the same zone. The hands which touch the dandelion belong to the zone with the lowlands and the sheep.
>
> The trees, which form a wreath behind her and stand along the river, are clearly rooted in nature. I consider this picture to be the most comprehensive expression of E. N.'s relationship to Gjern ... and at the same time it was painted in the midst of E. N.'s state of longing for love. *The Blind Girl* is perfect love (H. H. Madsen).

'The blind girl ... seeing though blind ... lives in love' (Karl Wåhlin, *Ord och Bild*, 1903). One is also reminded of poems by Maurice Maeterlinck, such as *Interieur, L'intruse*, and *Les aveugles*.

The dandelion *(taraxacum)* is often found in the art of the 1890s (see also No. 72). It is a plant with many properties. As far back as the Middle Ages, it was an officinal, as its juice was good for the sight, and it is also found in later pharmacopoeias. Popular belief associated it with certain oracular properties in erotic matters. The flower gone to seed symbolized both transiency and fertility. The dandelion was chosen as the symbol of the Women's Exhibition in Copenhagen of 1895, rather than the rose, on account of its excellent decorative characteristics (*Tidsskrift f. Kunst industri*, 1895).

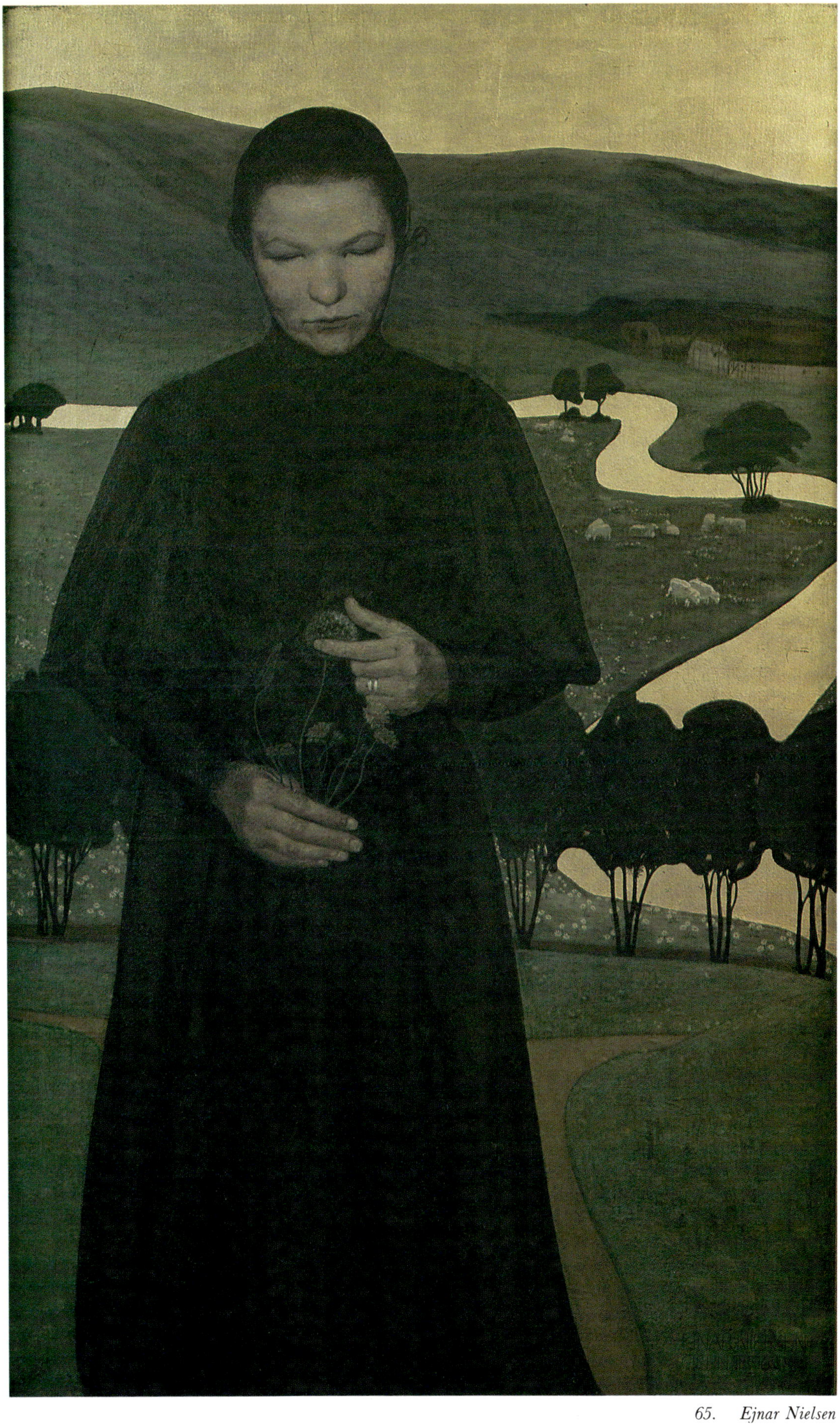

65. Ejnar Nielsen

The blind girl in Nielsen's picture holds fresh flowers with her right hand, while two fingers of the left (the one with two rings) touch a flower gone to seed.

There are similarities between this picture and Ludvig Find's portrait of Thorvald Erichsen (1897, No. 18): the figure's relationship to the background and the psychological interplay between the significance of the hands and their relationship to the eyes. These two contemporaneous pictures are perhaps the ones which most clearly reveal Danish Symbolist art, otherwise so highly individualistic.

The painting was exhibited at the Charlottenborg Palace in 1898.

H.W.

66

And in his Eyes I Saw Death, 1897

(Og i hans øjne så jeg døden)

137 × 188
Signed upper right: EJNAR NIELSEN... GIERN... 1897
and lower right: OG I HANS ØINE SAA JEG DØDEN
Statens Museum for Kunst, Copenhagen
Inv. no. 1832

This picture was composed in the same way as *The Sick Girl*: a pictorial space without depth which emphasizes the subject. On the left is a coffin; next to it is a young man sitting frontally, without movement, without life. What depth this picture has is in his eyes. Behind him is the whitewashed wall. It has been said of this picture, that 'illness is no longer the subject. Naturalism is still there, or was it imperceptibly abandoned?'

The Sick Girl had a closed-in, painful message; *And in his Eyes I Saw Death* an open, serene one. The young man is the living dead, sitting by his coffin. His gaze is not directed at you, and precisely for this reason it is universal: 'it is a confrontation with the possibility of your own death. Or with that of *your friends*!' (H. H. Madsen). The writer was referring to a portrait by Olof Wold-Torne of Alfred Hague from the same year, partly to other artists of that generation: Halfdan Egedius, Olof Sager-Nelson, and the poet Sigbjørn Obstfelder, who all died young. Death was a basic theme (H. H. Madsen and Poul Vad). As with *The Sick Girl*, comparisons have convincingly been made with works by Munch (Stabell).

Both Ejnar Nielsen and L. A. Ring found their subjects among rural people, and both treated their thoughts of death as something natural, something beautiful.

H.W.

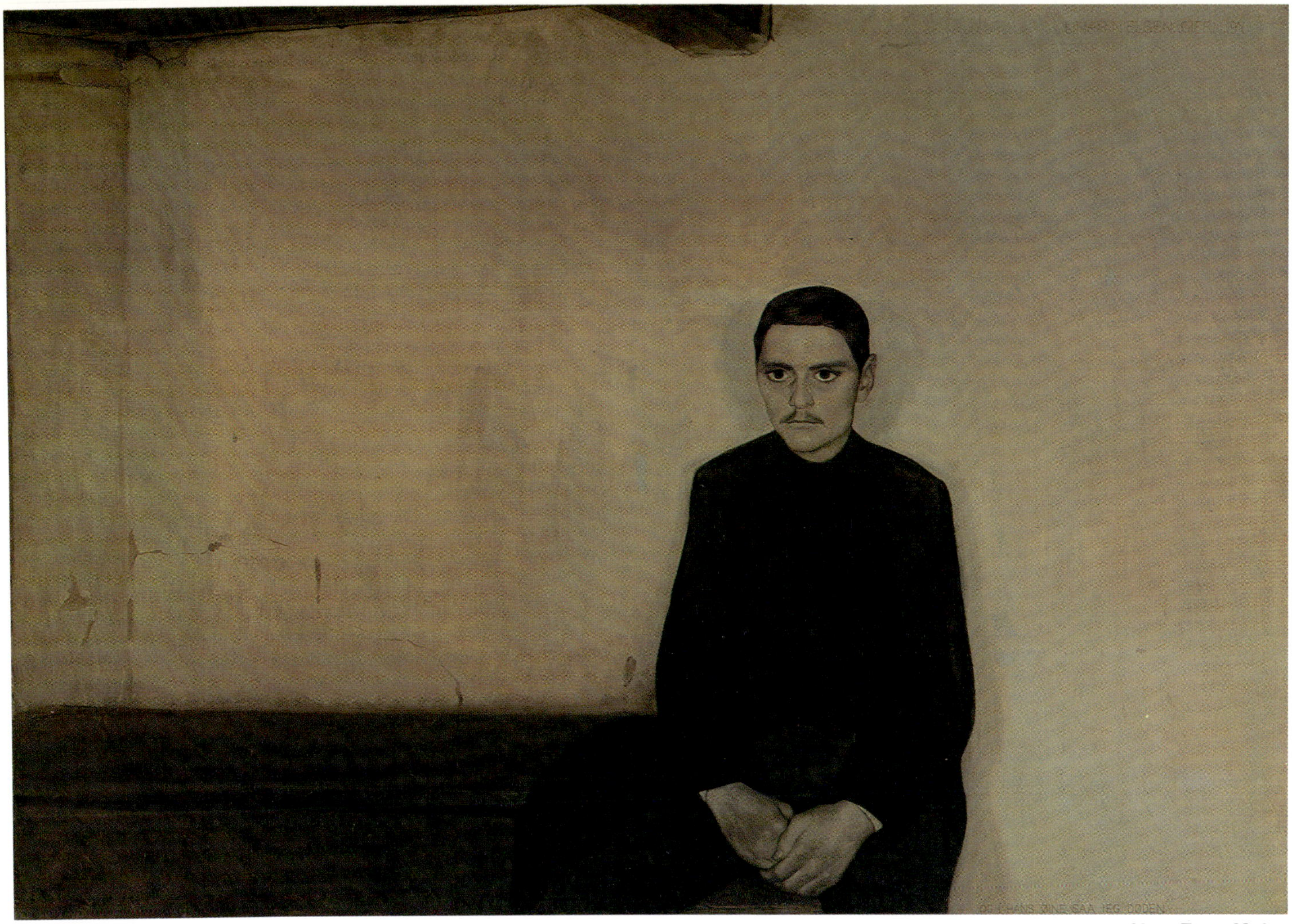

66. Ejnar Nielsen

EILIF PETERSSEN

1852–1928, Norway

Eilif Peterssen showed unusual skill in drawing even as a boy, and in 1869, at the age of 17, he began to study at J. F. Eckersberg's art school in Christiania. In 1871, after a brief period in Copenhagen, he went to Karlsruhe, and in 1873, he went on to Munich to complete his training as a painter of historical subjects.

Peterssen made his breakthrough as an artist in Munich, and since then has been considered the leading representative of the 'Munich school' in Norwegian art in the 1870s. His best-known work from this period is *Christian II Signing the Death Sentence of Torben Oxe* (Nasjonalgalleriet, Oslo) from 1874–6. The work is generally held to be the masterpiece of Norwegian historical painting, a genre which is otherwise not especially rich in Norwegian art. The painting clearly shows Peterssen's thorough study of the art of the old masters.

Peterssen left Munich in 1878, but did not follow the general Norwegian artists' migration to Paris. Instead he went to Italy where he remained, mostly in Rome, until 1883. In Italy he came into contact with the new naturalist trends in art, and the promising history painter developed into a naturalist genre painter and landscapist. His association in Italy with the Danish painter P. S. Krøyer undoubtedly furthered this development.

Right from his time in Munich and for well into the twentieth century, Peterssen held a leading place in the Norwegian art world. He became a frequent spokesman for his fellow artists, and served as board member, jury member, as well as exhibition commissioner. At various times he also worked as a teacher.

67

Summer Night, 1886

(Sommernatt)

133 × 151
Signed lower left in monogram: E P. 86.
Nasjonalgalleriet, Oslo
Inv. no. 2745 (purchased in 1968)

In the summer of 1886, a group of leading Norwegian Naturalists gathered at Christian Skredsvig's Fleskum Farm outside Christiania. In addition to Skredsvig, the group consisted of Harriet Backer, Kitty L. Kielland, Gerhard Munthe, Eilif Peterssen, and Erik Werenskiold.

It was here at Fleskum that Peterssen painted his *Summer Night.* He took as his subject Dæhlivannet, a little lake nearby. We find the same lake in two other pictures, Kitty L. Kielland's *Summer Night* (No. 47), painted the same year, and Christian Skredsvig's *The Willow Flute* (Seljefløyten) done three years later. These three pictures stand in Norwegian art history as central works in the transition from the sun-filled Naturalism of the '80s to the twilight 'mood painting' of the '90s.

The links between the summer night landscapes by Kitty L. Kielland and Eilif Peterssen are striking, and who influenced whom is an open question. However, it is clear that they must have had a joint point of departure, which probably can be found both in the classical landscapes of Puvis de Chavannes and in Whistler's atmospheric river scenes.

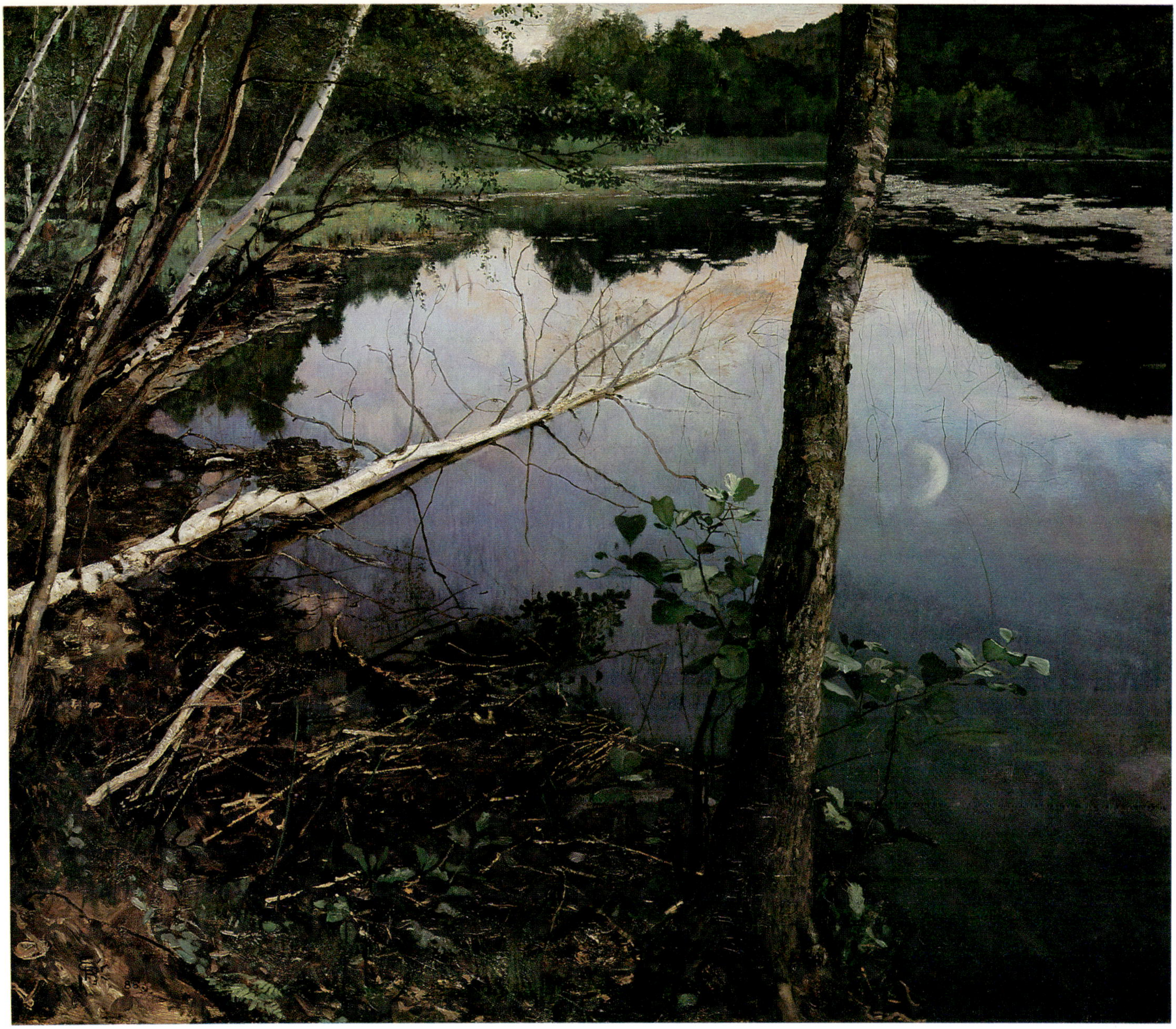

67. Eilif Peterssen

Compared with the Naturalists' open landscape compositions this picture has a new intensity. We are led into a scene of quiet contemplation, looking down into the water from a relatively high viewpoint. Only a little of the sky is visible: the rest, with the pale crescent moon, is seen as a reflection in the mirror-like water. The painting captures the 'blue hour', with its unique, musically elegiac mood.

The painting was shown at the Autumn Exhibition the same year and aroused considerable attention. There was a feeling that a new trend was in the offing. At the same exhibition, Edvard Munch showed *The Sick Girl*, a picture which also heralded a new age.

K.B.

68

Portrait of Arne Garborg, 1894

(Portrett av Arne Garborg)

133 × 106
Signed upper right: Eilif Peterssen 1894
Upper left: Arne Garborg
Nasjonalgalleriet, Oslo
Inv. no. 457 (purchased in 1895)

The portrait of the author Arne Garborg is one of the most psychologically profound in Norwegian portraiture. With seeming nonchalance, the poet sits leaning slightly forward, one arm over the back of the chair, the other hand under his chin. The complex composition creates a finely balanced rhythmic play bringing the head forward into the pictorial surface and giving the picture depth in the dark background. Realistic in presentation, with the unkempt hair and the slightly ruddy face, it is far from an 'official portrait'. The world seems to be locked out and the poet, immersed in his own thoughts, gazes before him with deep-set, dark eyes.

Here Peterssen has given an excellent interpretation of one of the most interesting personalities in Norwegian cultural life. Garborg had his roots in a modest, pietistic Norwegian rural milieu. A self-taught man in many ways, he was well read, talented and European in outlook, a reflective person who, to a greater degree than most of his contemporaries, absorbed himself in the problems of his day. He wrote most of his books in *Ny-norsk* (New Norwegian, also called Landsmaal), a merging of the different Norwegian dialects believed to represent the national linguistic tradition, in contrast to the official language, which was strongly influenced by Danish. The 'New Norwegian' movement represented a special national tradition with the emphasis on the local peasant culture. Through Garborg, the movement gained a broader horizon, and he himself did much to refine and develop the language.

K.B.

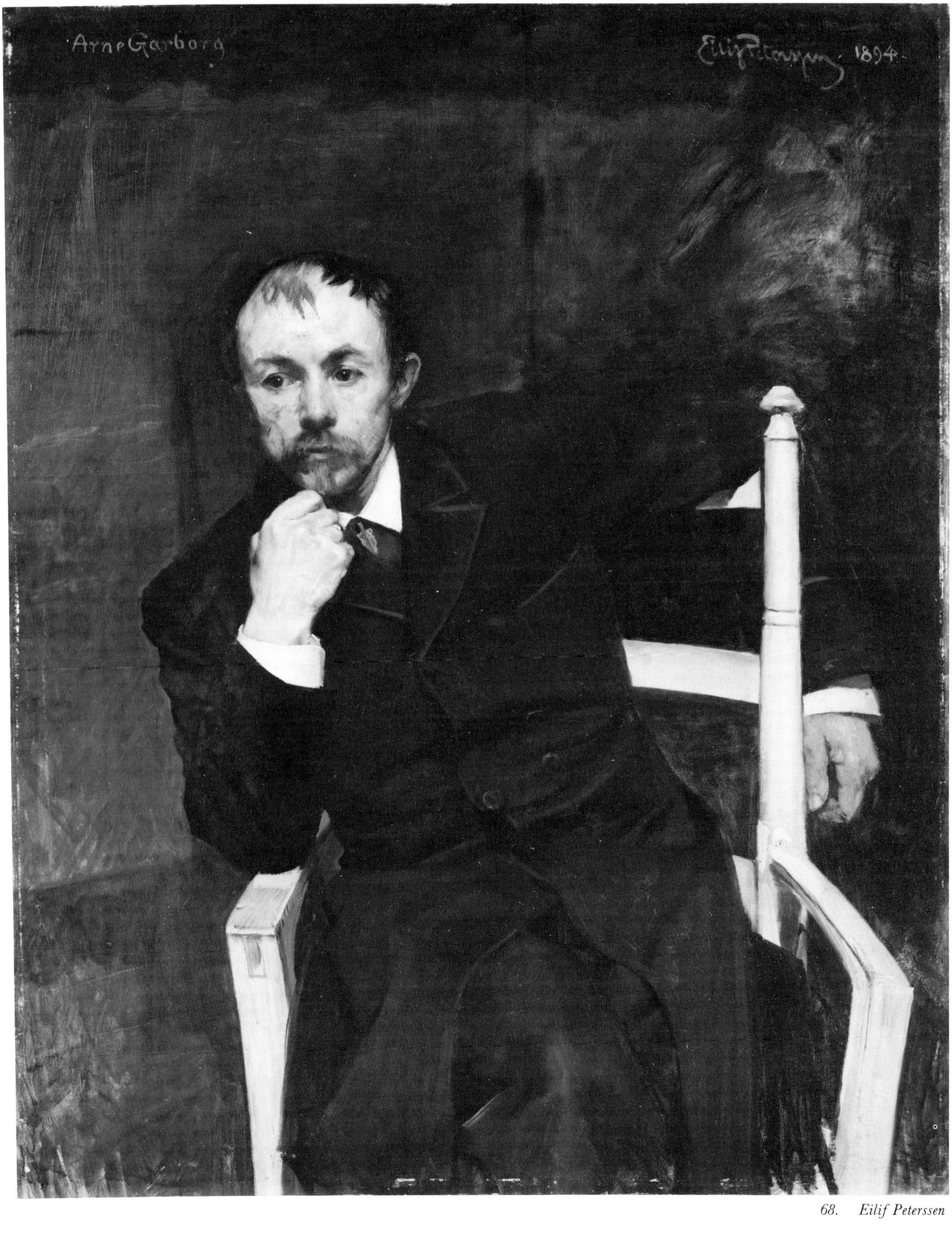

68. Eilif Peterssen

LAURITS ANDERSEN RING

1854–1933, Denmark

Ring was born in a village in the south-west of Zealand where his father was a carpenter. The rural environment and the humble people who struggled to make a living there became an important subject for him. This choice of subject-matter was related to the political ferment of the 1880s, to his own social view and his sense of justice. But the frugal world of his childhood had been deeply imprinted on his mind: the people, who all knew one another, the workshops, the year-round rhythm of work.

Ring was first apprenticed to a house painter, then studied at the Royal Academy of Fine Arts in Copenhagen from 1875 to 1877, and later for a short period at the Artists' Study School. His early years were indescribably hard. He travelled abroad for the first time in 1889, when he and the art historian Karl Madsen went to the World Fair in Paris via Hamburg. However, he had some knowledge of Scandinavian art from the major exhibitions in Copenhagen, and had studied other European art, especially French, from reproductions. J. F. Millet and Raffaelli interested him because of their subject-matter and social views. But his model was Peasant-Bruegel, who painted so clearly and described the life of everyday people. In Naples he copied *The Parable of The Blind.* He went through a period of deep depression during this trip to Italy in 1893–5, but a happy marriage after his return home resulted in a new and more optimistic expansion of Ring's subject-matter. He did, however, keep to depictions of the landscape and life in the villages where he lived, but the tone became milder.

Ring knew that he had difficulties with figure drawing. But it was precisely this awkwardness, which distorts a bit here and stunts a bit there, which makes his figures recognizable as people who have suffered from a lifetime of poverty and hard work. He was influenced too by the principles of composition he found in Japanese art, which flooded Europe during these years, whereby the moment of drama is concentrated in the foreground of the picture.

69

A Village. Jutland. Spring, 1892

(Forår i Hals)

78.5 × 103.5
Signed lower right: LA Ring 15/5 92
Statens Museum for Kunst, Copenhagen
Inv. no. 3742

Ring's life in the 1880s was characterized by financial problems and private misfortunes. He suffered from loneliness and despair and immersed himself in his work in order to avoid pointless brooding. His landscapes during this period are urgent characterizations of both the country and its colours, and of the people who inhabited it. After his trip to Paris in 1889, he often changed his place of residence, but the problems he set himself were the same as before, and he himself remained unchanged. Unrest in the art world of the day did, however, leave its mark on his pictures, which betray his own restlessness as well as his search for a form of expression.

In this spring view of Hals, a village on the coast of northern Jutland, one can see Ring's muted palette, the gentle grey-green and grey-brown tones, the dark yellow of

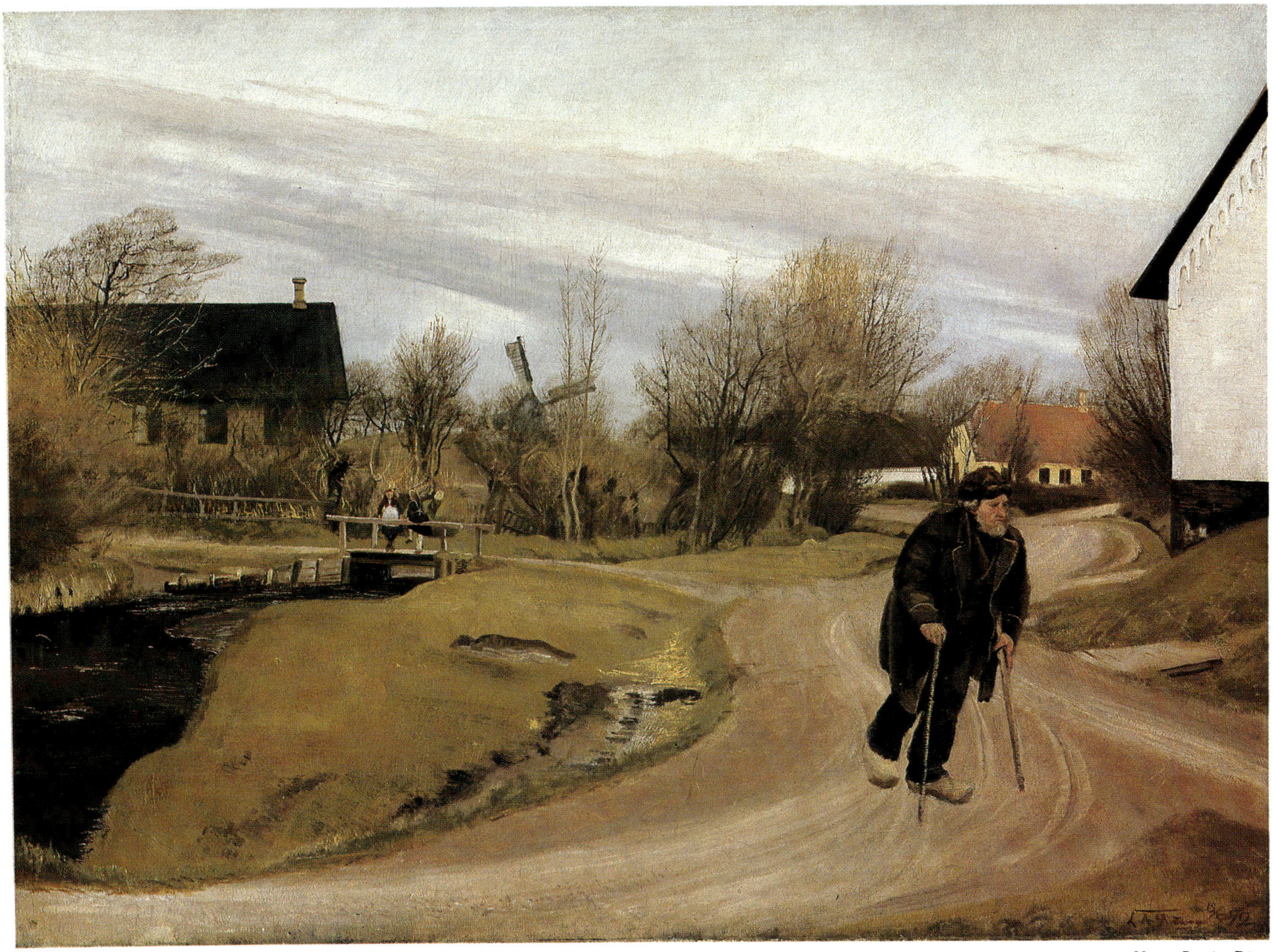

69. L. A. Ring

the house on the left. But note how boldly he lets the lighter colours into the picture at the white house on the right, and the light yellow wing of the house with the red roof in the background. One can also see how he builds up his complex composition by the use of intersecting diagonal lines, which culminate in the dark clouds' diagonal line over the grey-blue sky. Through colour and composition, he emphasizes the feeling of budding spring. But spring holds no hope for the cripple who laboriously hobbles across the road on his crutches, out of the picture, away from the two young girls who have stopped to chat on the bridge.

H.W.

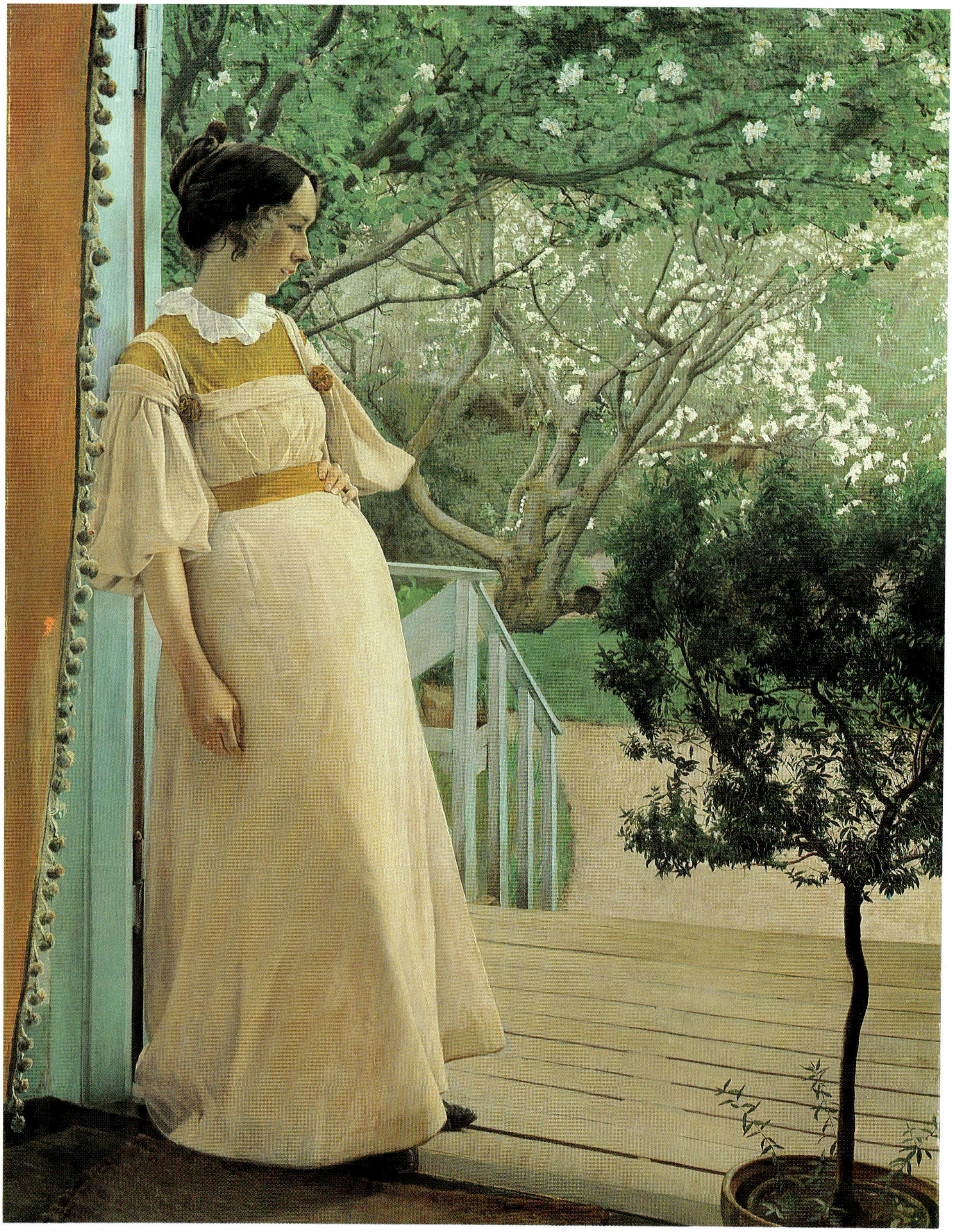

70. L. A. Ring

70

At the Garden Steps. The Artist's Wife, 1897

(I havedøren. Kunstnerens hustru)

191 × 144
Signed lower right: L.A. Ring 1897
Statens Museum for Kunst, Copenhagen
Inv. no. 3716 (purchased in 1924)

In 1896, Ring married Sigrid Kähler, the daughter of a well-known potter in Næstved whom he had known since she was a child. A number of pictures from the following years of his wife and children in the peaceful rooms of their house testify to the tranquillity which the marriage brought to his life.

The picture of the young wife in early pregnancy is one of Ring's few happy ones. One senses that he felt overwhelmed by life's goodness A few years earlier in Italy his thoughts had dwelt on death and he had expected nothing, at least nothing good, from the future.

Clad in a delicate yellow dress, which changes to light rose-ochre in the shadow, she stands leaning against the door-frame. It is the picture's stable, vertical element, tempered by a curtain whose tassels colouristically mediate the change from the golden colours of the dress and curtain to the light turquoise door-frame, which is repeated in the bannister. Opposite her stands a tall myrtle and behind lies the dense, spring-green garden, a wonder of blossoming apple trees.

It has been suggested (Nykjær) that the Romantic idea of the woman as guardian angel was taken up in Danish poetry and painting in the 1890s. Once again, she rescues man, not only in a spiritual sense, but now to a greater degree in an erotic sense, and as a result creates Paradise here on earth. In this picture, the man (the painter), though unseen, is present and sees the same as we see, Paradise. But his road must go between the woman and the tree, the twin causes of his expulsion from Paradise. The wife's role as the saviour is also supported by Dante's description of Beatrice and her flame-coloured dress. On the other hand, Realism is not excluded, and neither is the possibility of a more everyday symbolism. Which is probably just as well. Ring's roots were in the rural society and in the artisan's craft traditions, which had also been his father's (note the carefully made bannister), and it was his desire to create art which people would understand. Here is direct symbolism: youth, spring, a child expected, and faithful conjugal love expressed by the myrtle, which at Danish weddings is preferred to orange blossoms. It can be understood by the people because it has its origin among the people.

But symbolism is one thing and Symbolism something else, and the art and literature of the day were, naturally, familiar to Ring. The picture of his wife by the garden steps is perhaps the painting which most clearly expresses one of the fundamental ideas of the period: the eternal cycle. Where the garden steps end, nature begins, Pan's realm. It is life's purpose to be one with nature, for the flowers to wither before the fruit can come. It is this above all which lies behind the orchards with their white, falling petals. No matter how lovely the flowering trees, the real concerns are those of classical mysticism: Life – Death – Eternity.

There are many colouristic and thematic similarities between this picture and Maurice Denis's *L'échelle dans le feuillage*, which Johan Rohde had seen in 1892 and described in a letter to the Danish art historian Emil Hannover (Rohde, p. 134).

Perhaps Zibrandtsen (p. 71), another Danish art historian, came closest to the artist's meaning when he wrote of the young pregnant woman 'seen in pensive profile. One feels the whole of spring's echo in her mind. Ring was a great psychologist.' Zibrandtsen also called attention to the contrast between the picture's monumental size and the intimate content of the composition.

H.W.

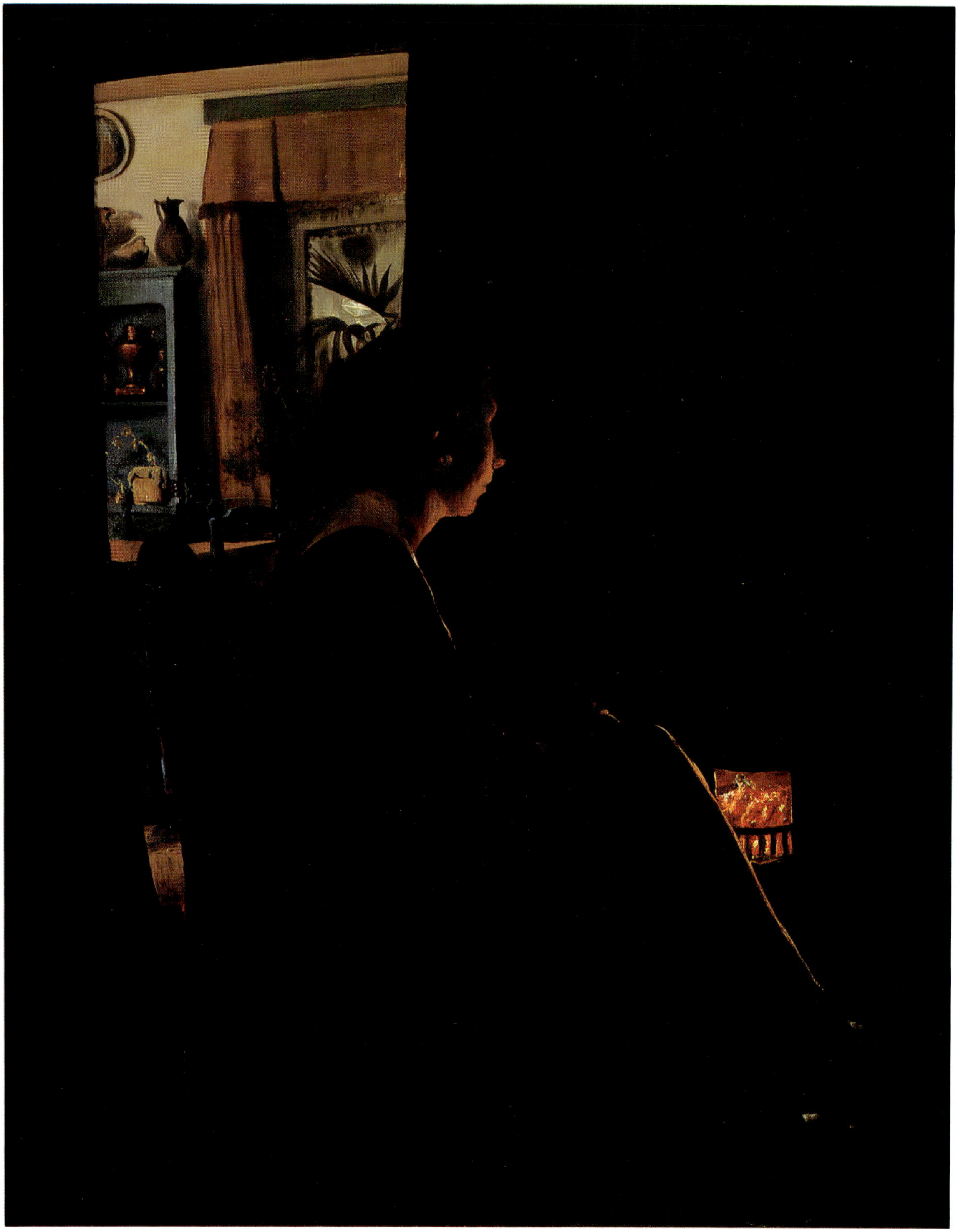

71. L. A. Ring

71

Dusk. The Artist's Wife by the Stove, 1898

(Skumring. Interiør med kunstnerens hustru)

86 × 65.6
Signed lower left: L.A. Ring 1898
Statens Museum for Kunst, Copenhagen
Inv. no. 3989 (purchased in 1936)

The year after the large spring picture of his wife at the garden steps, Ring painted two wintry evening scenes of her in the living-room of their home. Both are at the Statens Museum for Kunst in Copenhagen, and even though only one of them is shown here, they are so intimately connected that they must be considered together.

One shows his wife frontally, sitting in the golden light from a table lamp and looking up pensively from an open book. On the wall behind her hangs the sketch for a spring picture with flowering fruit trees and a picture of two young women (Den Hirschsprungske Samling, Copenhagen), for which she had served as the model the year before her marriage.

In the picture exhibited here, she sits in profile in the foreground in front of a stove, her hands idle in her lap. From the open stove door, the fire sheds its warm glow on her averted face and lays a narrow, luminous border around the edges of the dress. The light from the glowing coal is all that illuminates the room. But behind her, we see through the doorway into the dining-room, which is lit up in glaring white. And we recognize the door leading to the garden as the one from which she had looked out at the spring the year before. Now the door is closed. The light is reflected in its panes, and it is cold outside. In the living-room, the lamp sheds its gentle light, but the figure, sensitive to the cold, huddles over the oven's warmth and perhaps remembers brighter days. Or, in the hours of dusk, is she perhaps dreaming timidly of the future? Her poetic profile is turned away and silent. The picture of spring over the Neo-classical sofa is empty of people.

Sigrid and L. A. Ring expected a child in early summer 1897, but their first child was born in January 1899. It is natural to imagine that the picture of the wife by the stove is a pendant to the painting in which she stands at the garden steps, and that it is just as symbolic. The picture in which she sits in front of a sketch of flowering fruit trees may lie between these two. *The Artist's Wife by the Stove* is smaller than *At the Garden Steps*, but the composition is just as impressive. The depiction of the young wife is gentler and perhaps conveys the artist's understanding of the fragility of happiness.

H.W.

72

June. Girl Blowing Dandelion Seeds, 1899

(I Juni måned. Pige der blæser mælkebøttefrø)

87.5 × 123.5
Signed lower right: L A Ring / 1899
Nasjonalgalleriet, Oslo

Early in the first summer after Ring had moved to Frederiksværk and had paid his tribute to the landscape and to his great Danish predecessors with the picture of Lundbye's bench (No. 73), he painted a picture of a young girl in dark clothes with her hair in a braid down her back, sitting in the grass by a fence. Her almost averted profile with the high cheekbones, receding chin, and short upper lip is the type which Ring had preferred as his model since the 1880s. She resembled his wife, and the model may have been one of her sisters, perhaps Elisabeth Kähler (b. 1882). The girl's thin hand holds a dandelion and her sensitive yet primitive profile is emphasized by the lifted chin as she blows the dandelion seeds. Behind her, and diagonally into the distance, runs the fence – the nearly sawn off post in the foreground is almost brutal. The picture is closed on the right by a white building with a thatched roof. On the left there is only the pale blue sky. The grass is full of dandelions, both blooming and gone to seed.

Ring's biographer, P. Hertz, who knew him from childhood and was a close friend, sees the picture as an idyll. Kai M. Woel (1937), on the other hand, speaks of 'the almost macabre female figure. It is hardly midsummer, yet the blossoming has finished and the seeds have blown away'. The dandelion is heavily charged with symbolism (see Ejnar Nielsen, No. 65), but blowing away the dandelion seeds in one or more breaths is also a children's game, perhaps unwittingly symbolic (see Hans Christian Andersen, 'There is a difference'). The most important object in the picture is, however, the fence. Whether the girl is fenced out or fenced in and whether she is blowing the seeds before or after midsummer are less important than the picture's formal characteristics. It is at once very Japanese and very modern, as well as being extremely audacious.

H.W.

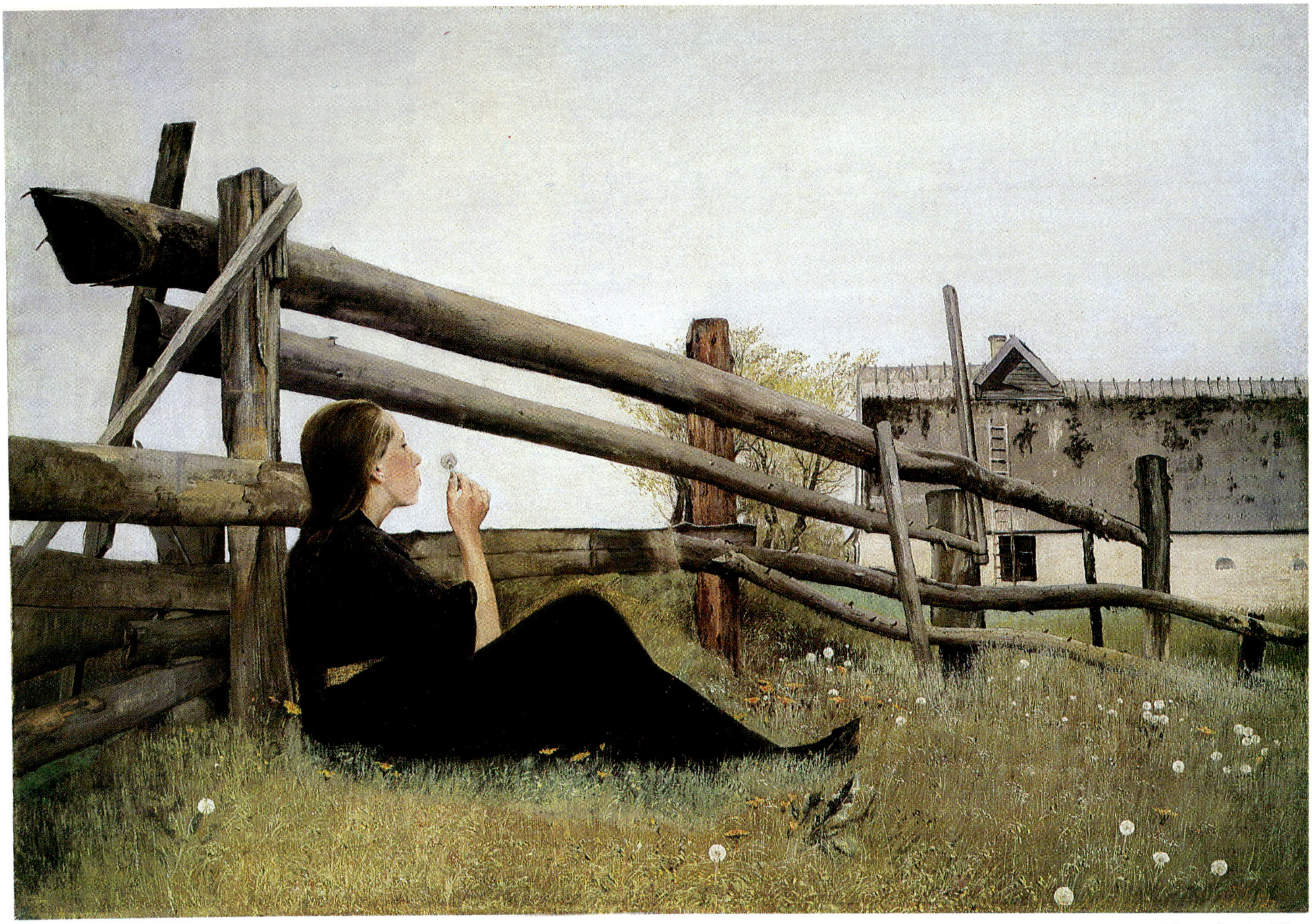

72. L. A. Ring

73

The Painter Johan Thomas Lundbye's Bench at Lake Arresø, Frederiksværk, 1899

(Lundbyes bænk ved Arresø. Frederiksværk)

43.5 × 56
Signed lower right: 99 / L A Ring
Ordrupgaardsamlingen, Copenhagen
(purchased in 1904)

On an outing in the late summer of 1898, L. A. Ring fell in love with the locality around Frederiksværk (a little village in northernmost Zealand). He moved there immediately, and lived there until 1902. This is the classical country of the 'Golden Age' painters P. C. Skovgaard and Johan Thomas Lundbye, who often found their subject-matter there. The landscape is varied, with intimate glimpses of villages and forests, and views of open countryside. The luminous blue Lake Arresø is surrounded by meadows and on the far horizon rise hills of shifting sand, crowned by large cloud formations over the sea. It was inevitable that Ring would be reminded of the Golden Age painters, whom he admired, but he did not follow them in his choice of subject.

To the left in the picture is a white-painted bench around a tree whose bare branches form a network of shadows on the foreground. The story – in fact untrue – that the bench was a favourite spot of Lundbye's was told Ring by one of his acquaintances. The bench overlooks the ploughed fields and marshes by the edge of the lake, and the hills on the other side. Ring had the rare ability to capture the viewer and bring him into the picture. He achieved this by careful cropping and by foreshortening the immediate foreground. Here we see only part of the tree whose roots touch the picture's lower edge, and we are so close that we seem to be able to touch the deeply furrowed bark. A leafless hedge shows the fall towards lower-lying land.

The whole foreground, with the strong spring light and the grotesque, contorted forms, contrasts with the neatly divided sections of fields, the warm earth tones, and the blue sky's horizontal stripes of white clouds.

Here, as elsewhere, Ring has borrowed some of the subtle pictorial effects of the East.

H.W.

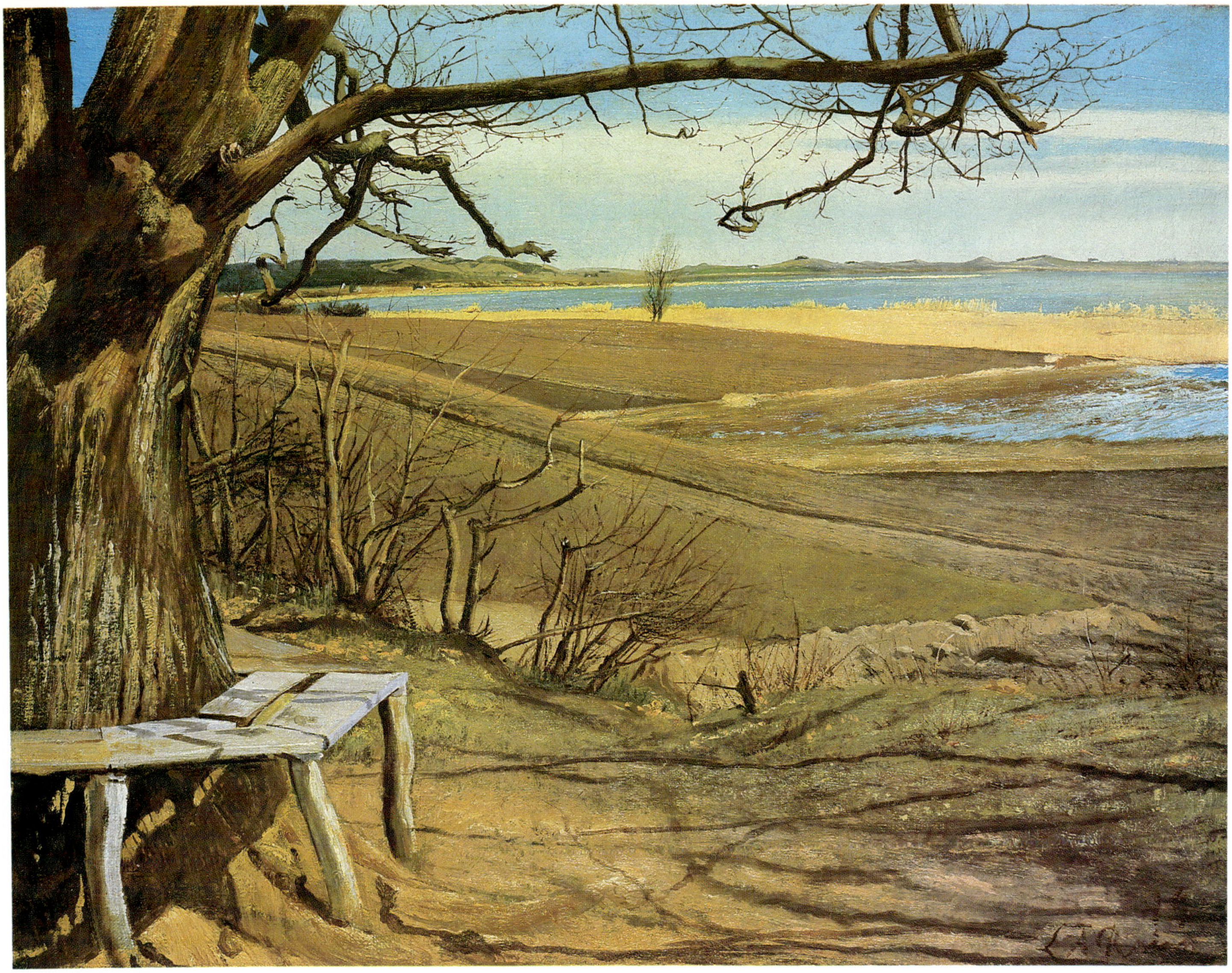

73. L. A. Ring

74

Summer's Day. Roskilde Fjord, 1900

(Sommerdag. Roskilde Fjord)

95.5 × 144.5
Signed lower right: L A Ring / 1900
Randers Kunstmuseum, Randers
(purchased in 1901)

In the summer of 1899, Ring had once again fallen prey to despair and to thoughts of death. In the autumn, he went with his wife on his second trip to Italy, and in Naples he once more copied Breugel (*The Misanthrope*, 1568). In April 1900, they returned, and Ring decided to stay at home that summer.

He found the lush green summer landscape inland too intense in colour, but the fiord and the meadows by the stream became his subject-matter. Water played a major role, not only by its presence, but particularly because it filled the picture with light, which seemed to flow out from its bed. This water was different from the fresh sea of Southern Zealand which he had previously depicted. Now he discovered the tranquil mirror-like water between the narrow river banks, where the weather rarely allowed unexpected dramatic variations.

The Danish Golden Age painters Johan Thomas Lundbye and P. C. Skovgaard had painted in the locality where Ring now lived (No. 73). They had painted Zealand's calm lakes surrounded by hills or beech forests. But there was one other Golden Age painter whom Ring greatly admired, Vilhelm Kyhn. No one else in Danish Art had been so preoccupied with the study of light on the flat beach, and the mirror-like surface of the water: all horizontal lines are accentuated by the vertical mast of a solitary boat. It is Kyhn's pictures Ring had in mind when he painted summer days by the fiord and the stream: flat landscapes where the vastness of the sky, its light, and the reflections from the water's surface are all-important.

Calm water under a peaceful sky is like a reflecting eye and in the literature of the 1890s it is often associated with the myth of Narcissus. Ring, however, is more likely to have been thinking of Danish romantic literature, such as Hans Christian Andersen's *The Little Mermaid*, with its message of flight from the world under the sea into the light, where salvation lay, and J. L. Heiberg's song about the wave which has no colour itself: 'Not heaven, only a picture of heaven do you have in your deep embrace: Your longing is never eased: it is eternal like your need.'

H.W.

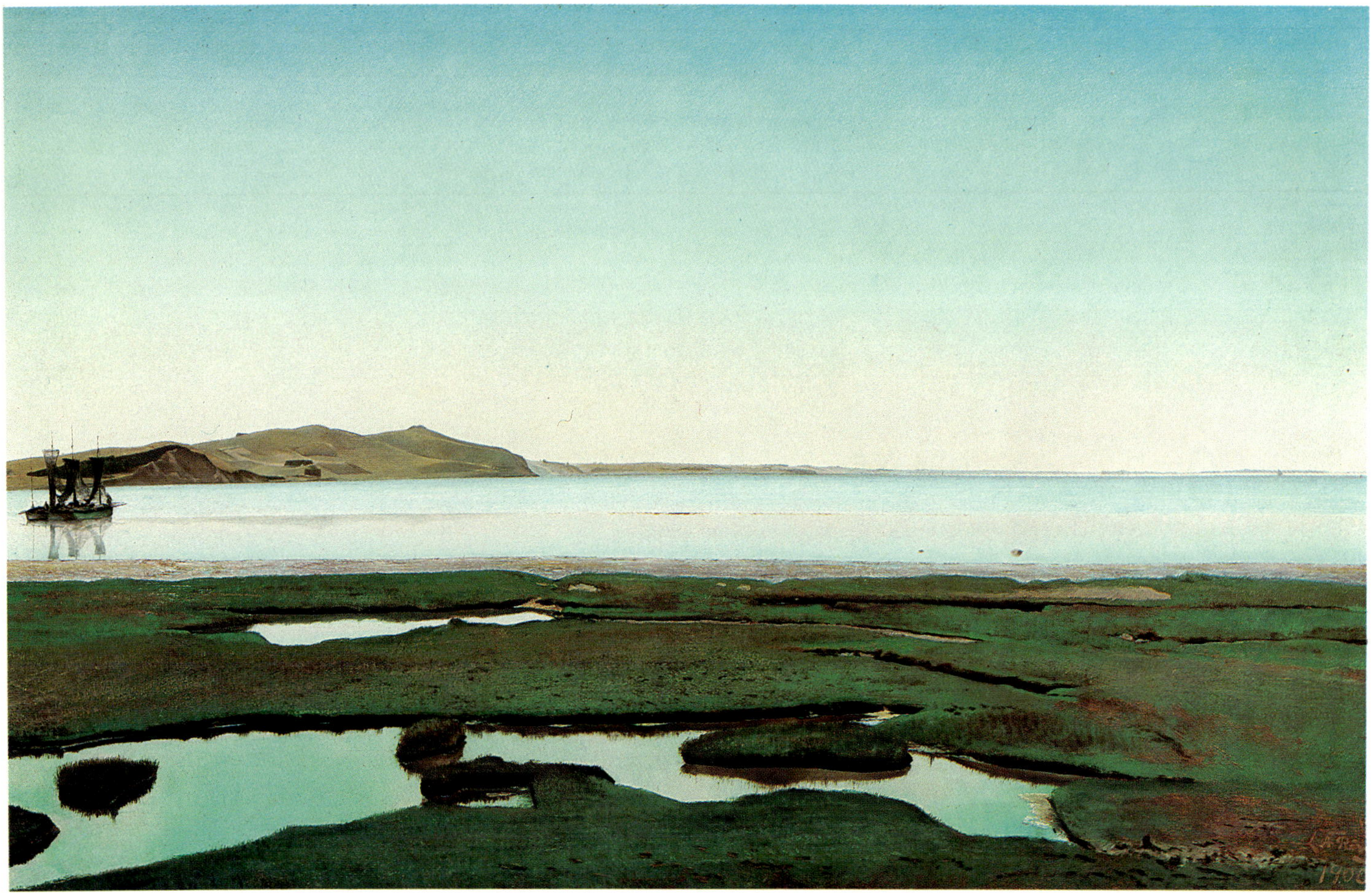

74. L. A. Ring

JUHO RISSANEN

1873–1950, Finland

Juho Rissanen's most impressive works are his early pictures, which are based on his childhood environment. As a child he had experienced pain and hardship but he avoided drama in his paintings. Instead he showed life's fateful procession. Implicit in his subjects is a social commitment and he is considered one of the most important portrayers of the Finnish people, although the number of his truly fine works is not large.

Juho Rissanen's father was an unskilled worker who died when the artist – the oldest child – was ten years old. His mother supported the family with odd jobs; four of her six children died young. Consequently Juho Rissanen's schooling was haphazard. He was apprenticed to the house painter Berg in Kuopio, and at the age of 15 was able to attend Sunday and evening classes for craftsmen.

Rissanen began his art studies in 1895 at the Helsinki Central School of Industrial Arts, where he studied full time until 1896. His studies with the artist Albert Gebhard in Rautalampi, eastern Finland, in the summer of 1896 were also important in his development. Rissanen was given special permission to study at the Finnish Fine Arts Association's art school. For six months he was Helene Schjerfbeck's private pupil. After a minor offence Rissanen was expelled from the school, but with the help of Albert Edelfelt transferred to the Association's art school in Turku, where he studied under Victor Westerholm in the spring term of 1897. He spent the summer near his birthplace in Savonkylä and Puumala studying with Albert Gebhard. Here the first works, today considered his masterpieces, were created. In the autumn he painted alone and showed his results to Edelfelt. From December 1897 to May 1898 he studied at St Petersburg's Art Academy under the guidance of Ilya Repin. According to Edelfelt's friend, the Dane Pietro Krohn, Rissanen wanted to be Ilya Repin's pupil because he had been inspired by Repin's *The Cossacks*. His interrupted but highly varied and commendable early studies ended with the 1898–9 school year, when Rissanen again went to Helsinki as Albert Gebhard's pupil.

Rissanen received international attention at the 1900 Paris World Fair. He received a bronze medal for his work. The primitive and powerful watercolour *The Blind Old Woman* (No. 77) was particularly acclaimed.

Rissanen's travels abroad began in 1900 when he went to Italy, and studied at Simi's art school in Florence. He also visited Vienna, Budapest, and the German art centres. He made another trip to Italy in 1903 to study fresco techniques. Not until 1908 did he travel to Paris and other parts of France, where he lived almost continuously from 1918 to 1939. He then moved to Florida, where he died in 1950.

Rissanen did not take an interest in oil painting until around 1908, when he prepared a series of monumental folk subjects for the Salon d'Automne in Paris. Interest there centred around Matisse and Fauvism, and Rissanen's dark works were not appreciated. Then Rissanen's artistic decline began. His private life was unsettled: his marriage to the artist Hilda Flodin lasted only a short time, from 1908 to 1914. He began to divide his interests: fresco painting, Post-Impressionist painting, and an area in which he did succeed in the 1920s, stained glass. External influences clouded his vision of his own strength and art. Rissanen's later years were also overshadowed by a neurotic fear of illnesses and war: he became restless, and subject to bouts of depression even though outwardly cheerful.

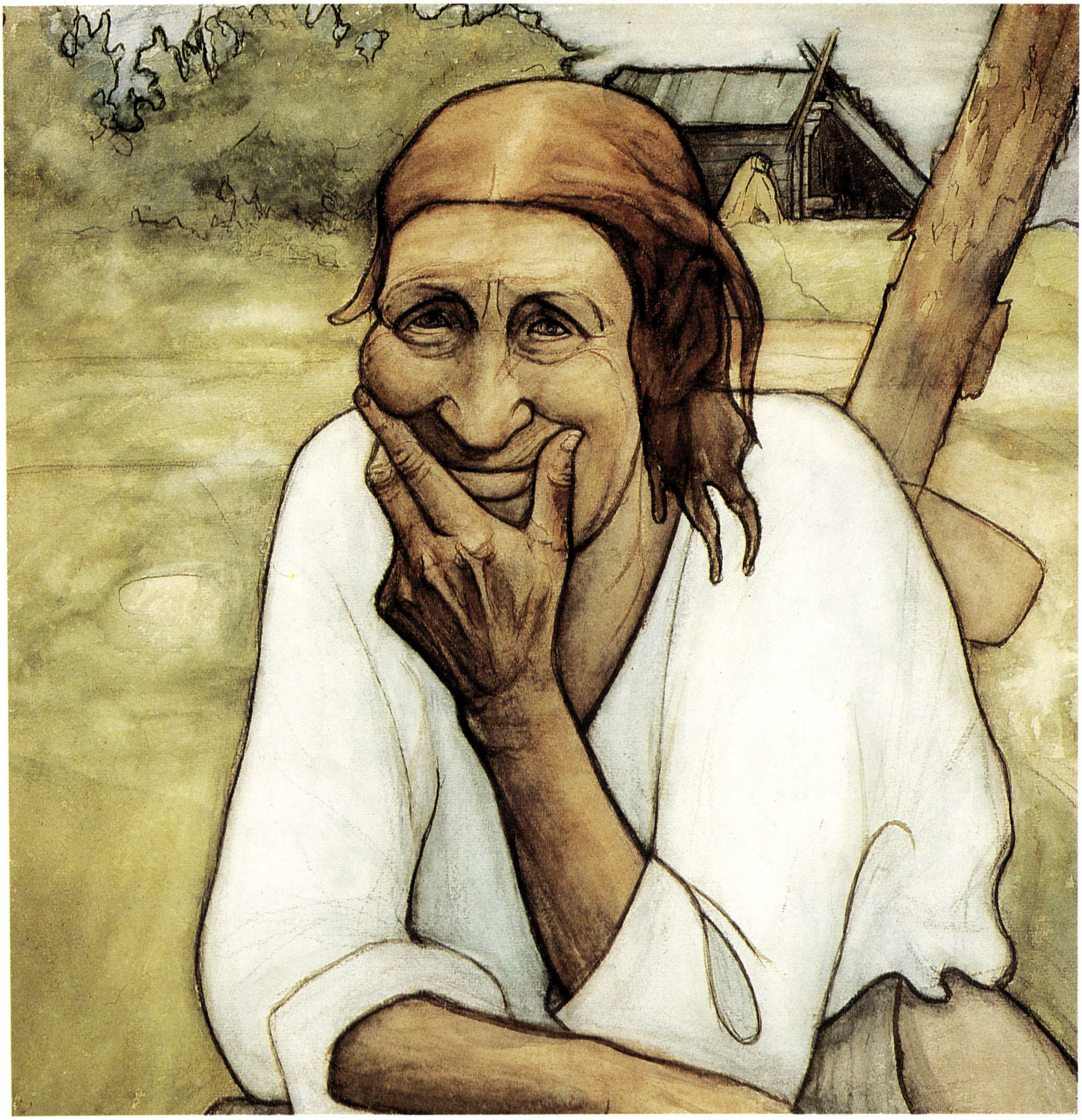

75. Juho Rissanen

75

The Old Woman, 1897

(Hauta-Heikin mummo)

Watercolour on paper, 45 × 43
Not signed
Private Collection, Kuopio

Two of Juho Rissanen's works were on show for the first time at the 1897 Finnish Autumn Exhibition: one of them was *The Old Woman.* The young artist's vision was

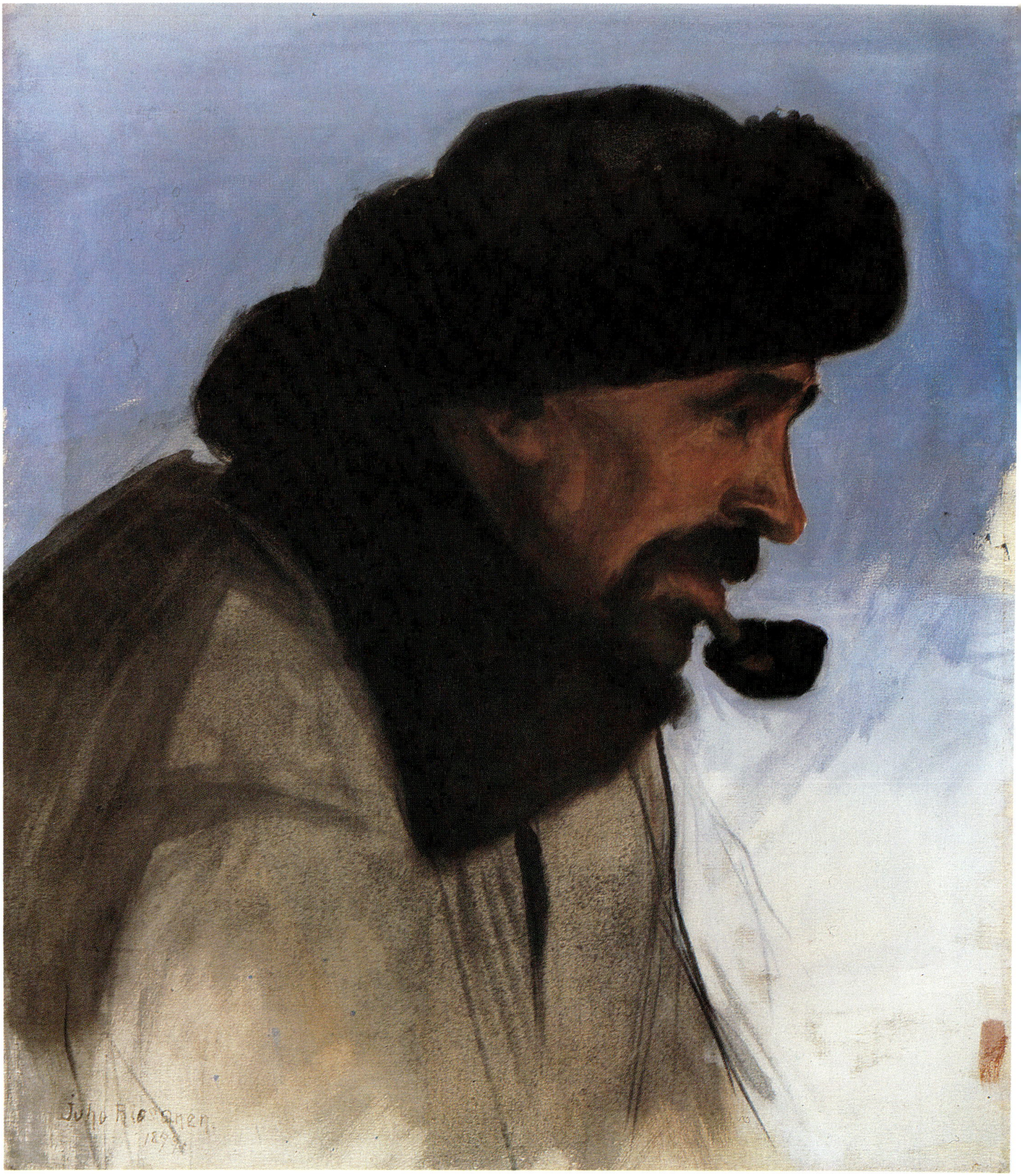

76. Juho Rissanen

firm: he had chosen his subject-matter – the people. From the beginning Juho Rissanen monumentalized and stylized; he had a natural tendency to do so and he was further influenced to emphasize decorative outlines by Albert Gebhard, who taught him in the summers of 1896 and 1897 and had been interested early on in French Synthetism.

This charcoal burner's wife from eastern Finland is shown in a white shirt, strongly outlined and with surfaces simplified in an almost Synthetist manner. The lines and composition direct one's attention to the face and eyes. In the background is a farmyard, with houses and a well. The old woman gazes out past the viewer; she seems to be concentrating on her own inner world. Her face is ambiguous: it shows sadness even though the roughened fingers pull the corners of the mouth into a smile. The portrait can be seen as Rissanen's homage to and admiration for the tough, capable peasant woman – for women like his own mother.

The Old Woman continues the realistic genre pictures of Albert Edelfelt and Akseli Gallen-Kallela. Rissanen was certainly encouraged by their examples. Stylistically it seems if Gallen-Kallela's *The Defence of the Sampo* (No. 23) and *Lemminkäinen's Mother* (No. 25), paintings shown in the winter of 1896–7, with their emphasis on contours, were particularly important to him. Rissanen's work moves us because it penetrates beneath the surface: the artist shows the peasant woman as a person capable of complex feelings and not just as a folk type.

L.A–M.

76

The Fisherman, 1899

(Kalastaja)

Watercolour on canvas, 62 × 51.5
Signed lower left: Juho Rissanen 1899
Mrs Maija-Liisa Masalin, Helsinki

Albert Edelfelt commissioned the young painter to do several panel paintings depicting the life of the people in Finland for the Finnish pavilion of the Paris World Fair. Only two were finished, however, since Rissanen's interest waned – one was *The Ice-Breaker*, the other was *Winter Fishing*. Several sketches were made for the *Winter Fishing* which can be considered completed works like this one. The fisherman's head, rendered with great character and swathed in a fur hat, is bowed against the cold blue of the sky. The peaceful expression in his eyes and the mouth sucking on the pipe reflect his stoical patience. Rissanen's outlines here are gentle and once again the silhouette is a significant stylization. Creating a winter environment was new to Rissanen, but the final result successfully captured the feeling of the cold, bright air of the Nordic winter.

L.A–M.

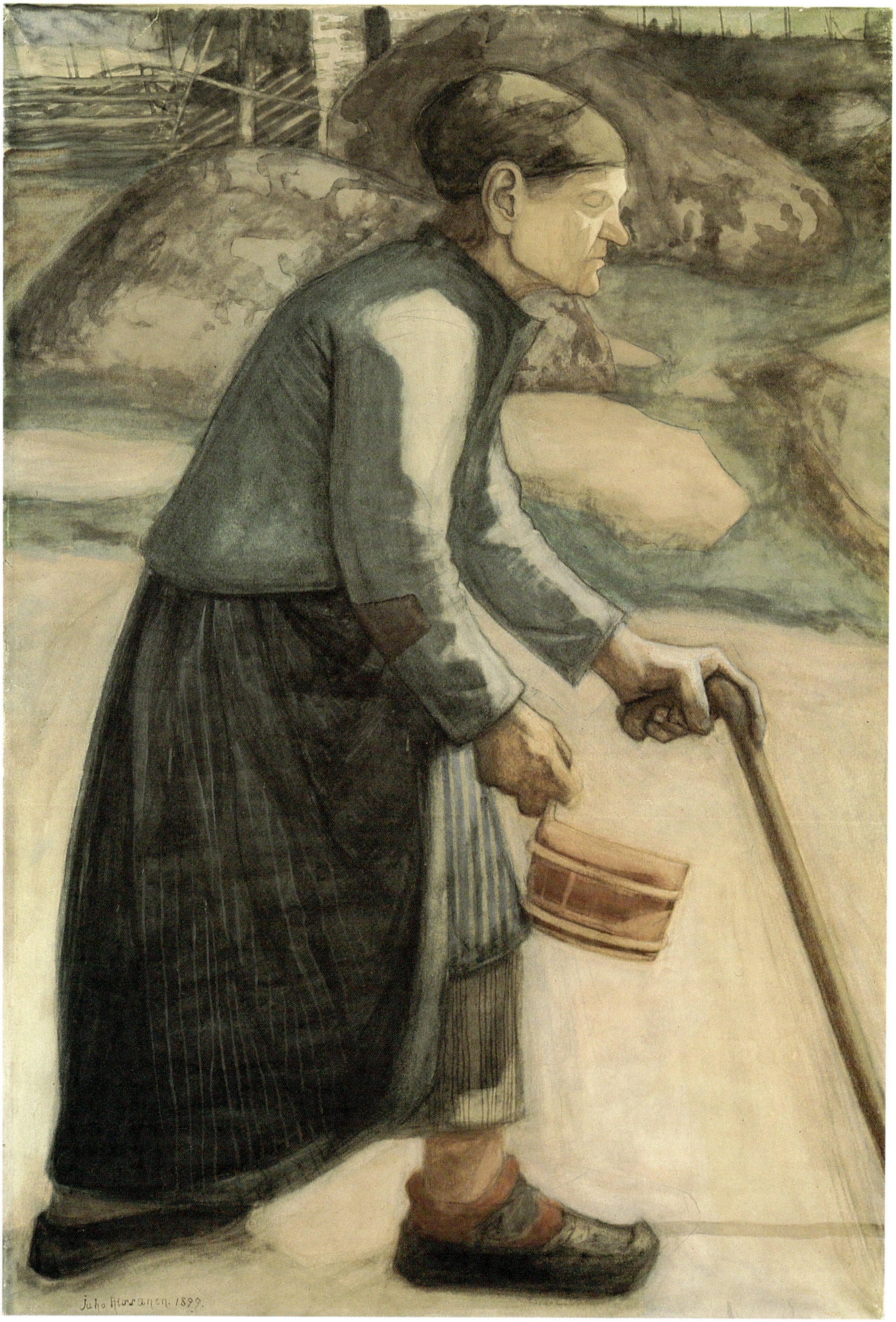

77. Juho Rissanen

77

The Blind Old Woman (Heta Kauppinen from Savonkylä), 1899

(Sokea, Heta Kauppinen Savonkylästä)

Watercolour on paper, 120.5 × 81.5
Signed lower left: Juho Rissanen. 1899
Ateneumin taidemuseo, Helsinki
Inv. no. A II 1126 (purchased in 1916)

The large watercolour *The Blind Old Woman* was one of the works at the Paris World Fair in 1900. In 1901 it was also shown in Copenhagen, at an exhibition of works by Finnish artists; in Dresden, at an international art exhibition; and in Vienna, at the Secession XII art exhibition. Rissanen had good cause to be satisfied with his reception abroad. In Finland, his primitiveness was first considered strange, but *Nya Pressen's* critic Gustaf Strengell (1 Nov. 1899) thought well of the painting, though he described it as an 'apotheosis of ugliness', the like of which had surely not been seen since the time of Gallen-Kallela's *Old Woman and Cat*. 'But all this is easily forgotten', he added, 'since its monumental grasp and warmth of feeling ennoble the painting as a whole.' The review also mentioned Rissanen's social message; according to Strengell, the artist wanted above all to arouse the viewer's sympathies for the suffering, and only secondarily did he intend his work to be artistically interesting.

The model for the portrait was the 94-year-old Heta Kauppinen from Savonkylä. As is typical of Rissanen's works, the figure fills almost the whole picture. The stony hillock and brushwood fence in the background reflect the blind woman's hard life, even though they are at the same time an inseparable part of the ordinary landscape in the region of Savo. A modern compositional device is the way in which the end of the stick groping diagonally forward is cropped. Thus Rissanen emphasized movement – here a searching movement – and the large compositional triangle formed by the figure of the blind woman and the stick.

Rissanen was called Finland's Breughel when this picture was shown, and was compared to the Belgian Eugène Laersmans (P. Krohn, 1900; Reitala, 1973). However, he was more likely to have been influenced by the Russian Wanderers group, for example by Ilya Repin's painting of a crippled boy in *Religious Procession in the Kursk Province*, and in general by the social genre pictures of Russian artists which he had seen in St Petersburg.

L.A–M.

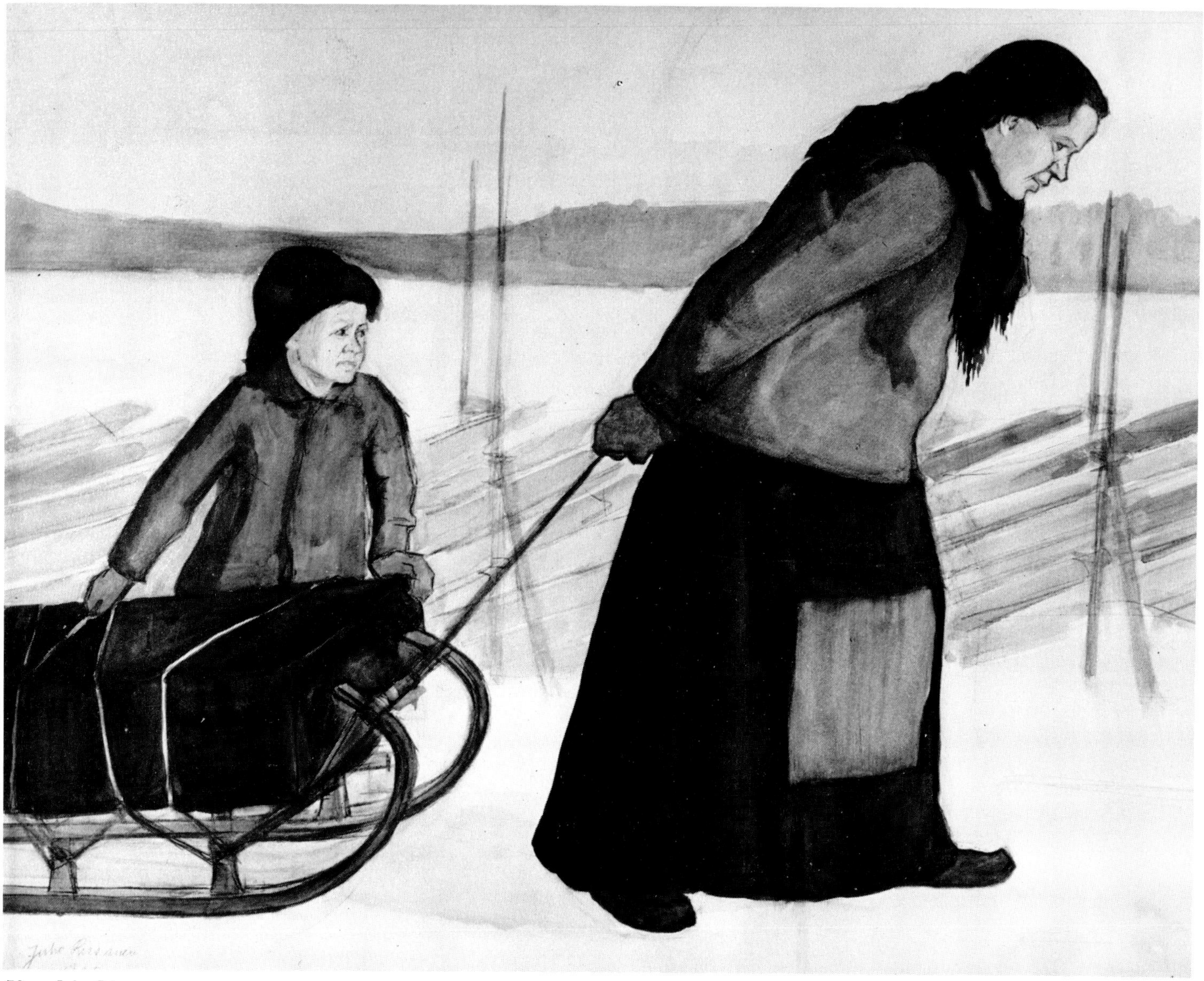

78. Juho Rissanen

78

A Memory of Childhood (Sketch), 1903

(Lapsuuden muisto, harjoitelma)

Watercolour on paper, 90 × 108
Signed lower left: Juho Rissanen / 1903.
Gösta Serlachiuksen taidesäätiön kokoelmat, Mänttä
Inv. no. 214

Juho Rissanen worked on his *A Memory of Childhood* for a long time. After his trip to Italy (1900–1), he became interested in painting it as a triptych. According to his first biographer, Onni Okkonen, the artist wanted to arouse the viewer's moral indignation at the evil caused by drink. The programme for the triptych was taken directly from his own life: his father had died on the ice on his way home from a drinking bout. Unfortunately, *A Memory of Childhood* was never completed as a triptych, but all its components have been preserved. The central part, 'bearing the body home', is in a museum in Budapest; the sketch for 'Father's death', a man lying on the ice with a bottle beside him, is at the Pohjanmaan museo in Vaasa, Finland; and this picture, intended for the right-hand side, 'pulling the coffin', is also in Finland.

While Rissanen was working on this subject, he was living in the village of Nilsiä in Savo. The region's religious revival movement made it difficult for the artist to find models, especially for this kind of 'passion play' on the theme of death. Perhaps for this reason, and also perhaps because of the artist's illness, the work was never completed as a triptych.

The picture of wife and son pulling the coffin on a sled in an expansive winter landscape has an atmosphere that can be compared to that of Hugo Simberg's *Wounded Angel* (No. 84), completed the same year. Sadness and pain are implicit in both works, and in both the landscape emphasizes the horizontal. Simberg's work, however, is more veiled and ambiguous than Rissanen's, which is taken more directly from reality. In the place of Simberg's angel we have the heavy coffin. By letting the viewer's imagination complete the dark ends of the coffin and sled the artist conveys the impression of the sled's heavy burden. Simberg's angel is a mystery even though it is shown in its entirety and subject to the laws of gravity. But both artists depicted man's fate, burdensome and wretched, based on their own experience of life.

L. A–M.

HELENE SCHJERFBECK

1862–1946, Finland

In Scandinavia, Helene Schjerfbeck is one of the best-known names in Finnish art today. During her long but difficult life, beset by illness, she moved from painting historical themes to *plein-air* painting, and then to an increasingly Synthetist style, simplified and finally expressively immaterial. A model was a necessary basis for her, but she knew that 'the painting should be a painting, and not just air or nature' (Ahtela, 1951, p. 235). Her series of self-portraits, from 1885 to 1945, is a unique pictorial record of an artist who with fierce defiance studied her own fragility.

Helene Schjerfbeck began to study art in 1873, when as a precocious student she was accepted at the Finnish Fine Arts Association's Drawing School in Helsinki. In 1877–8 she continued at Adolf Becker's private academy, where she had her first contact with French painting. From 1880 to 1886 she painted and studied mainly in France, first in the private academies of Mme Trélat and Colarossi in Paris under such teachers as Léon Bonnat, Jean–Léon Gérome, Gustave Courtois, Raphael Collin and Dagnan-Bouveret, and later in Brittany. Most significant for her development, however, were the artist colonies at Concarneau and Pont-Aven. At Pont-Aven, Bastien-Lepage noted that her works combined both sensitivity and great passion (Appelberg 1949, p. 46).

Her period of *plein-air* painting also included some years at St Ives in England, where she executed one of her major early works, *The Convalescent* (1888: exhibited at the Paris Salon of 1888 as 'Première verdure'). At the Paris World Fair in 1889 she was awarded a bronze medal. Lacking funds, she spent most of the following decade teaching in Helsinki. She also went on copying trips to St Petersburg in 1892 and to Vienna and Florence in 1894. There were also trips to the highland sanatoria of Gausdal, Norway, for reasons of health. Compared to earlier years her works were few and uneven, and this perhaps explains why she did not take part in the Paris World Fair of 1900.

In 1901, she moved with her mother to Hyvinkää, where she became isolated from Helsinki's world for a time, although she followed trends in art from newspapers and magazines. Here she developed her simplified style, the first clear example of which was *The Seamstress* of 1903–5. The painting increasingly became important on its own terms: colour pigments on a flat surface. 'I try to keep the border sharp in art and do not let it go over into reality as in old panoramas' (to Maria Wiik in 1915). During her period in Hyvinkää, Helene Schjerfbeck felt that she was caught in an eternal conflict between her household duties as a daughter and her need to paint. This conflict wore down her strength and she was often ill. She did, however, meet the art dealer Gösta Stenman, who arranged her first one-man show in 1917 and was later instrumental in making her works known in Sweden.

Schjerfbeck created an important modernistic oeuvre in her later years, and showed her fragile but passionate quality as a painter. 'It is not enough for a painter to have just an aesthetic relationship to her work; she must also have strong personal feeling. She needs warmth herself, and only then can she paint' (Ahtela, 1951, p. 179).

79

The Door, 1884

(Ovi)

40 × 32.5
Signed lower left: HS / 1884
Ateneumin taidemuseo, Helsinki
Inv. no. A IV 3680 (purchased in 1965)

Helene Schjerfbeck travelled to Paris for the first time in 1880. She was happy in that inspiring environment and, gifted as she was, did well, so that she was able to stay in

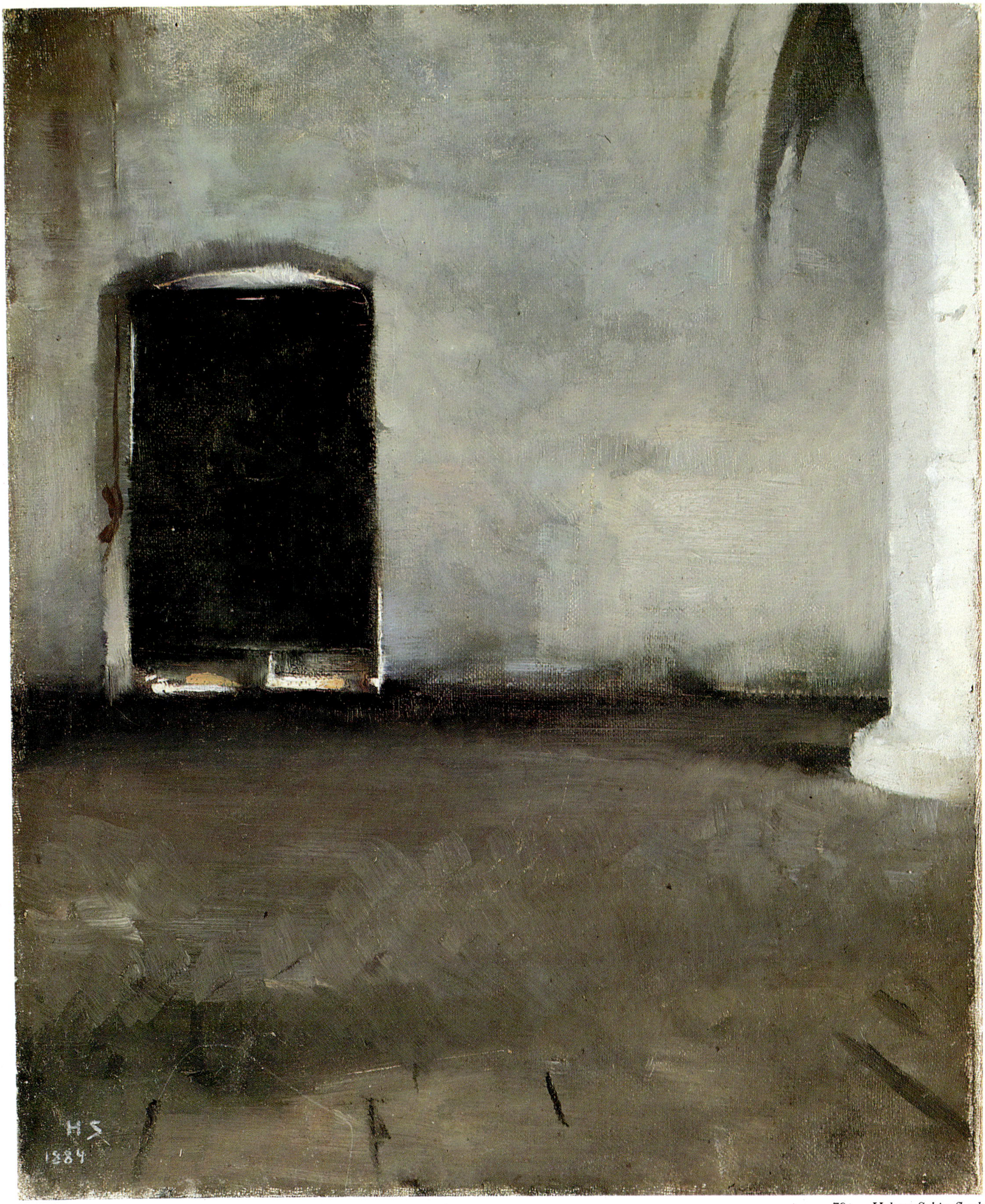

79. Helene Schjerfbeck

France almost continuously until the summer of 1884.

At this time, almost all Scandinavian artists were interested in *plein-air* painting in the spirit of Bastien-Lepage. Helene Schjerfbeck was naturally affected by this interest, but her own views on art required a more spiritual and simple direction. She mentioned in a letter to Helena Westermarck (13 Dec. 1912) that the realism of the 1880s had never suited her. We can believe this when we see *The Door*, painted when the artist was only 21, which shows either the cloister at Concarneau (Ahtela 1951, p. 302) or the interior of the chapel of Trémolo in Pont-Aven (Jacobs 1985, p.72).

The same simplicity, delicacy of grey tones and mystery created by light are found in her later works. This is not realism, but rather the creation of a spiritual feeling of time and place. The bands of light which shine around the edges of the dark door are the powerful chords which the artist also used later in her subjects. And in looking at the work, one can understand what she meant when she wrote: 'In the Middle Ages, the Soul was supposed to strengthen the body – this is where my interest begins' (letter to Helena Westermarck, 9 Oct. 1927), and 'The last stroke is always lacking from a work of art; what is complete is dead' (letter from about 1920).

L.A–M.

80

The Bakery, 1887

(Leipomo)

60 × 49
Signed lower left: H.S.
(Hedman Collection) Pohjanmaan museo, Vaasa / Österbottens museum, Vasa
(purchased in 1916)

Helene Schjerfbeck travelled to St Ives for the first time in July 1887. Her fellow artist Marianne Preindelsberger-Stokes encouraged her to come, and the financial support of the Finnish sculptor Walter Runeberg made her visit possible. The modest fishing village in Cornwall, with its mild climate, had, like Brittany, become the home of a small group of artists, and in 1887 the Swedish painter Anders Zorn and his wife also stayed there. The American painter Howard Russel Butler wrote from St Ives (1887), '... lately there has arrived a young lady from Finland – she has a wonderful talent and is a most interesting person altogether, although unfortunately lame...' (Jacobs, 1985, p. 159). The trip was intellectually important since it helped Helene Schjerfbeck to recover from the depression caused by a recently broken engagement.

The interior of the bakery, an excitingly bold composition, shows that painterly problems, above all, interested the artist. The brushstrokes are broad and free. The canvas vibrates with accents of different tones of grey, lush black, sharp blue, russet, and golden brown. The spatial composition is given added tension by the sharp perspective of the table, the diagonal position of the scales in the foreground, and the indistinct location of the background.

The balance of colours and values is built up through the row of golden brown loaves on the light table, the scales' reddish arm, and the contrast between the oven's black door and the pan of the scales. All this is counterbalanced by the blue and red splashes of colour and the cleverly glimmering grey values. The artist has captured an engaging atmosphere of time and place, as in her painting *The Door* (No. 79).

The work remained rolled up in the artist's drawer for a long time and was not shown in public until Helene Schjerfbeck had her first one-man exhibition in Helsinki in 1917, when it was already part of the Karl Hedman Collection.

L.A–M.

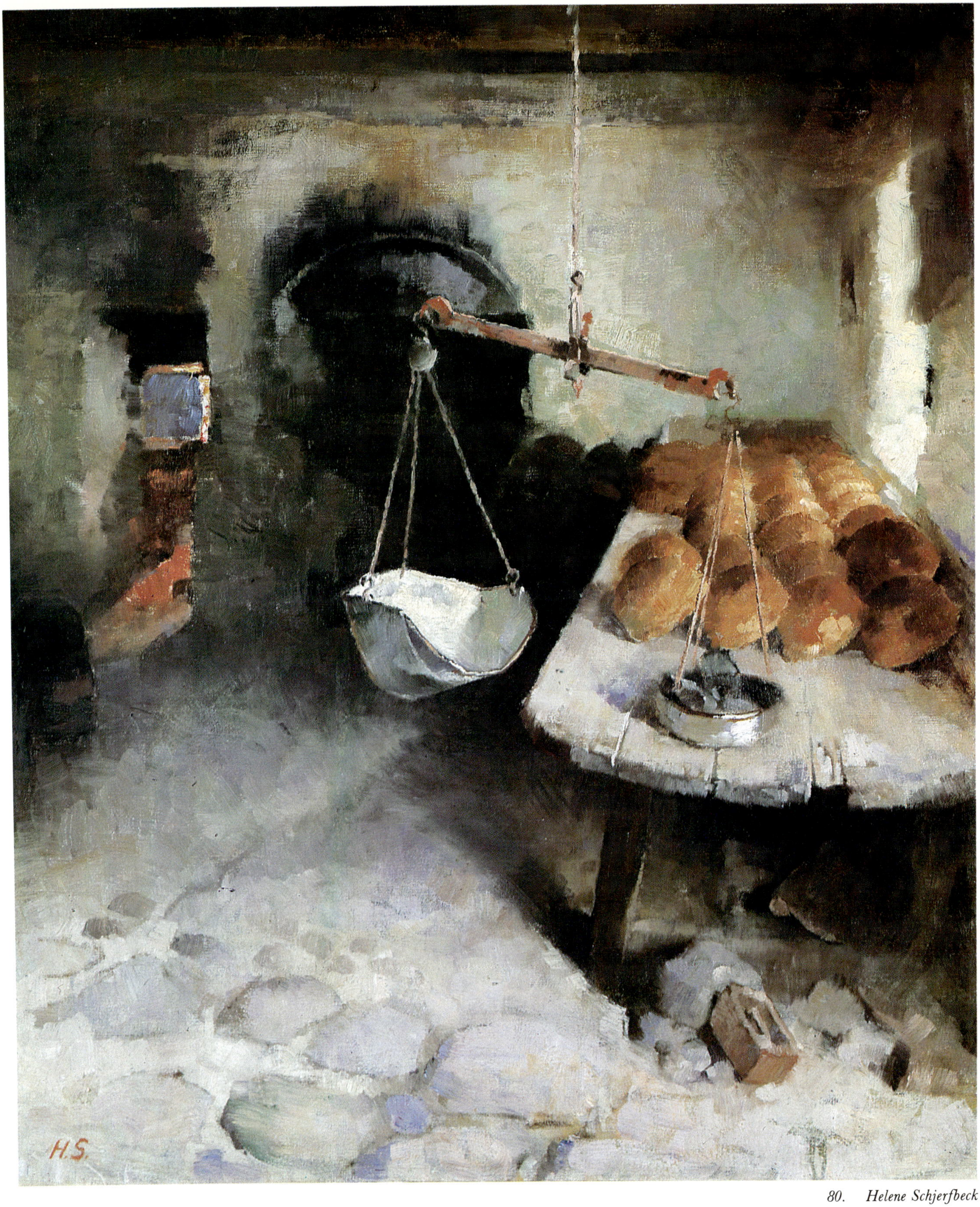

80. *Helene Schjerfbeck*

81

The Seamstress, 1903–5

(Työläisnainen, Ompelijatar)

95.5 × 84.5
Signed lower left: HS. 1903
Ateneumin taidemuseo, Helsinki
Inv. no. A IV 2994 (purchased in 1957)

The side view of the seated seamstress, whose ascetic colour scale and simple, clear composition are often compared with James McNeill Whistler's art (*Northern Light*, SMN/SSK, p. 211), is one of Schjerfbeck's most important works. It has similarities with Whistler's, but it should be noted that Schjerfbeck herself did not like Whistler; nor did she like Puvis de Chavannes, whose work has also been compared to hers (Ahtela, 1951, p. 326).

In the 1890s, Schjerfbeck sought to develop as an artist by studying the painters of the past; Holbein and Velázquez, whom she admired and copied, seem to have led her in the direction of simplicity, restraint, and lush melancholy nuances of colour. Helene Schjerfbeck said that she had learned the use of a floating black from Frans Hals, whose work she had copied at the Hermitage in 1892 (Ahtela, 1951, p. 46). These parallels link the artist with the art of her time and with the old masters, even though the final result is a product of Schjerfbeck's own spirit. The artist often used some small detail to 'electrify' the colour. In *The Seamstress* it is the green scissor band which directs the viewer's gaze diagonally downwards. The Finnish 'Shaker' rocking chair, which belonged to her mother, is an essential part of the painting, as it is in many of her other works. Helene Schjerfbeck was not afraid of outside influences. 'An artist can be cosmopolitan – and still be national. I have my roots here in the North. In this respect I am not afraid of myself. In spite of all influences, I myself create my works' (Ahtela, 1951, p. 135).

L.A–M.

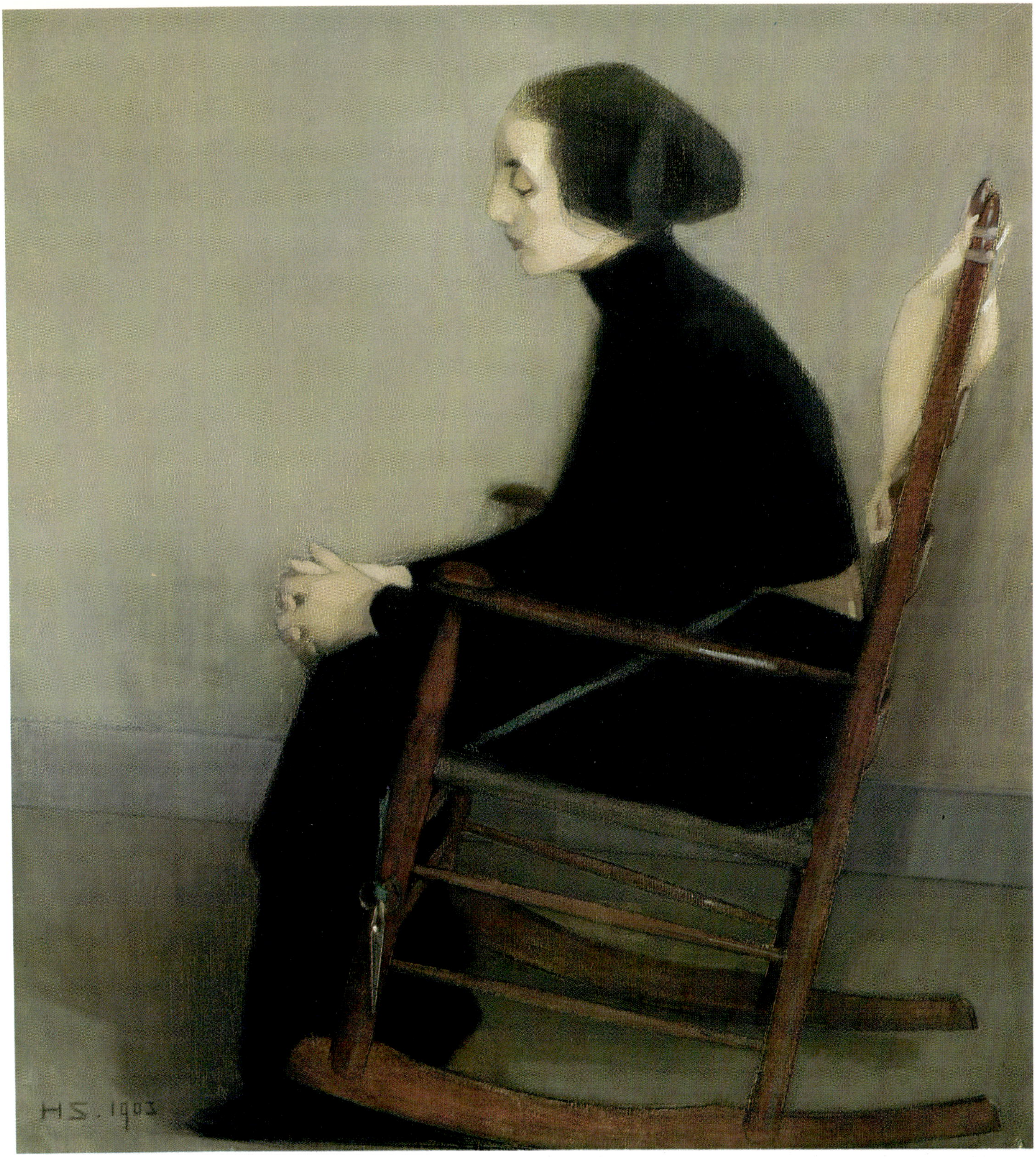

81. Helene Schjerfbeck

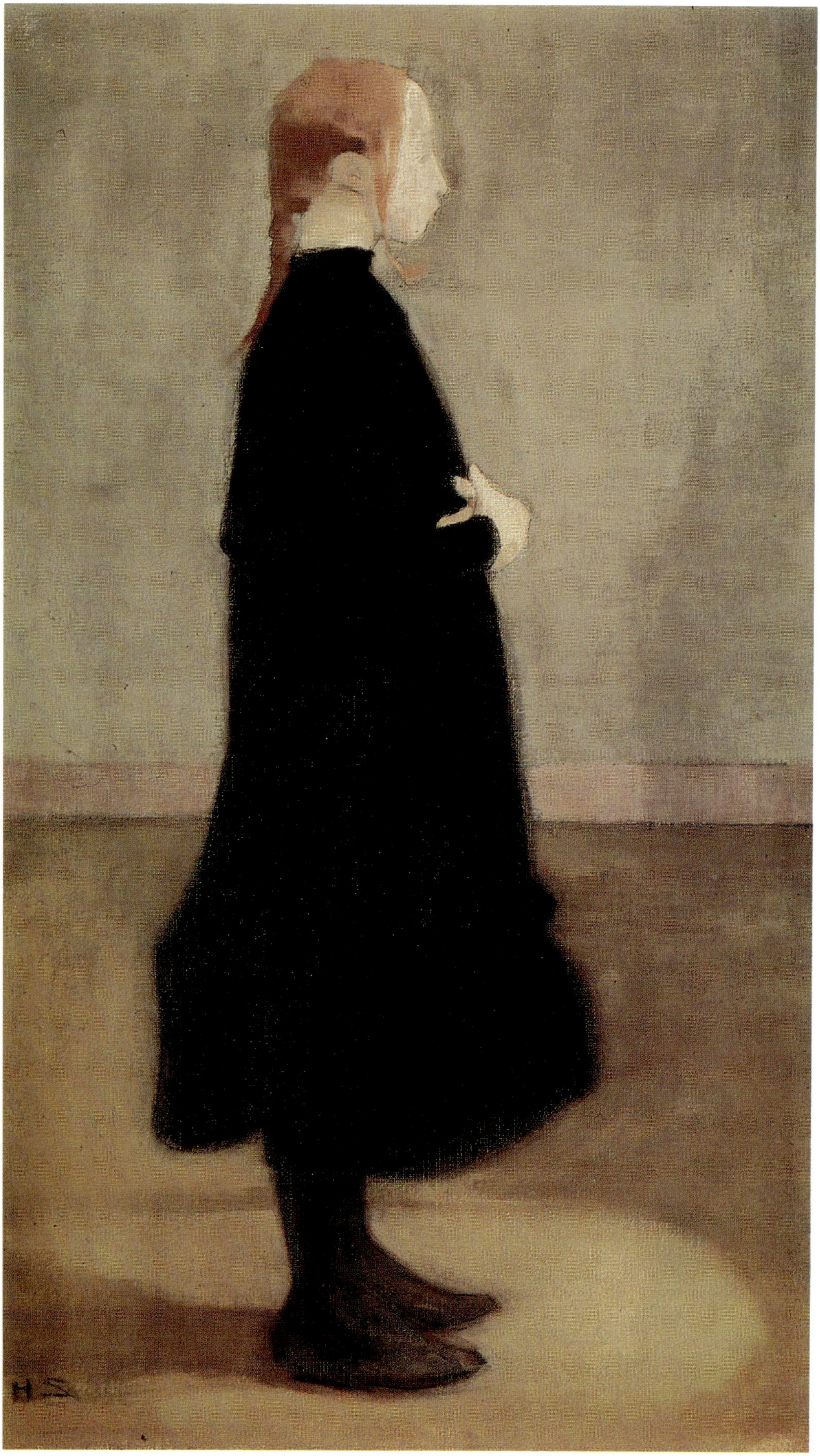

82. Helene Schjerfbeck

82

The School Girl II, 1908

(Kansakoulutyttö II)

70.5 × 40.5
Signed lower left: HS
Ateneumin taidemuseo, Helsinki
Inv. no. A II 1062 (purchased in 1915)

The School Girl is even more ascetic and sparing of detail than *The Seamstress*. The girl stands, without any accessories, against an empty background. The little figure is in profile, her hands folded on her chest, filling almost the whole length of the canvas. The work is a good example of Schjerfbeck's taut composition: an impenetrable lightly breathing black, a triangular dress, the girl's luminous delicate head with its reddish braid and side curls, the stiff boots in a pool of light. The light decorative flower-like hands are an accent typical of Helene Schjerfbeck as is the lilac border between wall and floor which divides the subtle fields of grey. The work was painted in Hyvinkää, where her models were mostly children, women and old people, and relatives.

The shy and proud artist usually withdrew from the main exhibitions at that time and only sent her paintings as lottery prize entries for the Finnish Fine Arts Association. This work was, however, an exception and was shown in the spring exhibition of the Association in 1908. She was somewhat bolder in the 1910s, when H. Ahtela, who wrote a monograph on her, and the art dealer Gösta Stenman helped the artist make her works known.

L.A–M.

HUGO SIMBERG

1873–1917, Finland

Two important influences on Hugo Simberg were his teacher Akseli Gallen-Kallela and Symbolism.

After an early artistic training in his school town of Viipuri and at the Finnish Fine Arts Association in Helsinki, Simberg studied under Gallen-Kallela in Ruovesi in the autumn of 1895. On returning home after his trip to Berlin and London Gallen-Kallela had abandoned his role as 'world citizien' to become Finland's leading national artist. Simberg did not follow his teacher in his choice of Kalevala subjects, but the primitive rural surroundings of the north helped to liberate his fantasy.

It was probably because of the influence of his teacher and the raw rural environment that his first works have a powerful mysticism in dealing with nature, but in the hybrid form of fantastic creatures typical of Simberg.

On Gallen-Kallela's advice, Simberg made his first trip abroad to London in 1895, but as the trip continued, he became more interested in visiting Paris. The separation from his Finnish environment allowed Simberg to explore more personal subjects: the problem of the individual, the struggle between life and death. Behind the joys of life lurked the devil; melancholy tenderness eased the inconsolability of death. Everything was tied to one feeling, 'which made man weep in his innermost being'.

Simberg made a weakness into a virtue. The unconscious delicate clumsiness of his technique suited a time which admired primitive art. In this respect, he was one of the purest products of the Symbolist period. When one critic commented adversely on the technical execution of his work, Simberg wrote to his brother:

> B. criticized the technical execution. He thus lost all the naive, the childishly pure, and the main thing: the devotion and love which the artist gives to his work. This love must be found in every work of art, and one can understand it when it is there. Only love makes honest and worthy works of art. If love is not present when the labour pains are felt, the child will be a miserable one. ... This shows you why I say that there is so very little art in the finest sense of the word. Since the time when all have worked to make their technique as perfect as possible, the artists' souls have withered. All care must be taken to see that the soul and body travel hand in hand through periods of development. But when will we have progressed that far!

Even though these thoughts could have been taken direct from Plato's *Symposium*, they were also the artist's own honest confession of faith.

Simberg continued to study under Gallen-Kallela in 1896 and 1897. Just before the turn of the century, he made a trip to Caucasia. More important, however, was his trip to Italy in 1898, where he studied the fresco painting of the early Renaissance. He used this knowledge when he painted the extensive fresco decorations for Tampere's St John's Cathedral in 1906–7 together with Magnus Enckell (Fig. 23) This large-scale project was also the culmination of Simberg's work. The Post-Impressionist colourism which appeared in Finnish art in around 1910 swept away the foundations of Simberg's art. Illness and the feeling that he was out of tune with his times crushed his creative power even before his early death in 1917.

Simberg's miniature art

In March 1897, after a second period of study with Gallen-Kallela in Ruovesi, Hugo Simberg explained his own view of art in a letter to his sister: 'Previously, only *well-painted oil paintings* were significant art. Now the situation is quite different. Great art can be seen on even the smallest pieces of paper, while it is often lacking in large *painted* pictures.' All this holds true for Simberg's watercolours, which combine small dimensions with fantastic subjects which come 'as if from another world'. A letter written to his twin brother Paul about a year before gives the spiritual background for Simberg's fantasy pictures.

83 a

Autumn I, 1895

(Syksy I)

Watercolour and gouache on paper, 30.1 × 14
Signed lower right: H S
Ateneumin taidemuseo, Helsinki
A II 968:1
(purchased in 1913)

83 b

Autumn II, 1895

(Syksy II)

Watercolour and gouache on paper, 12.2 × 17.9
Signed lower right on the black frame: H S.
Ateneumin taidemuseo, Helsinki
A II 968:2
(purchased in 1913)

83 c

Frost, 1895

(Halla)

Watercolour and gouache on paper, 27.1 × 18.1
Signed lower right: HS./95
Ateneumin taidemuseo, Helsinki
A II 968:3
(purchased in 1913)

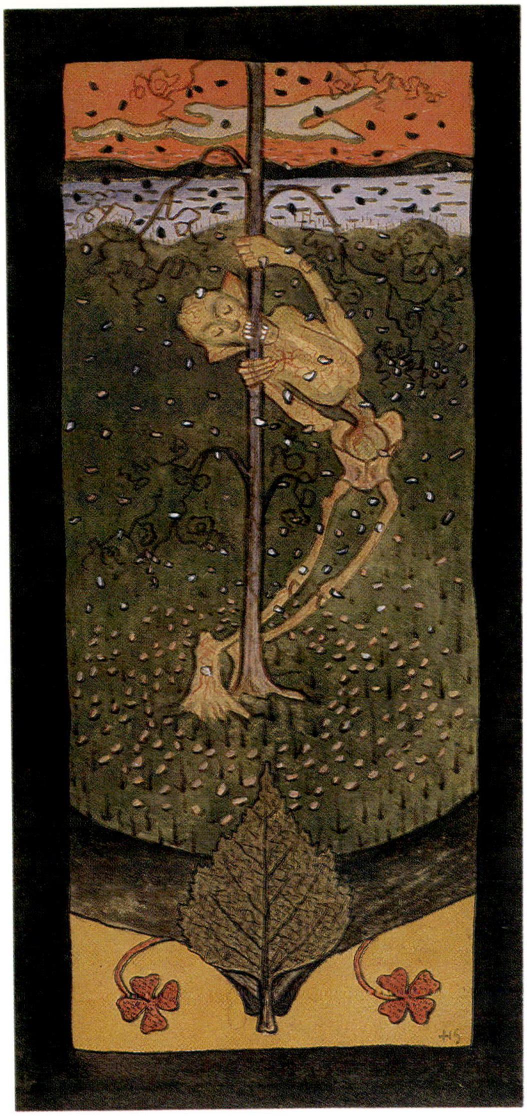

83a. Hugo Simberg

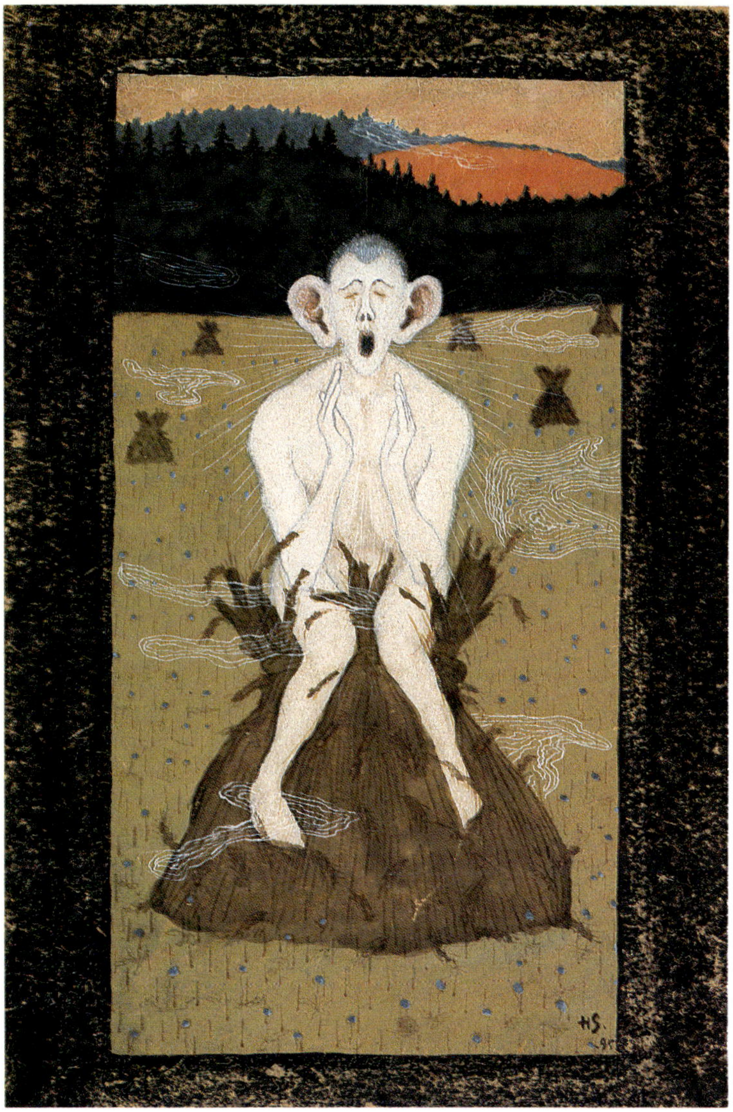

83c. Hugo Simberg

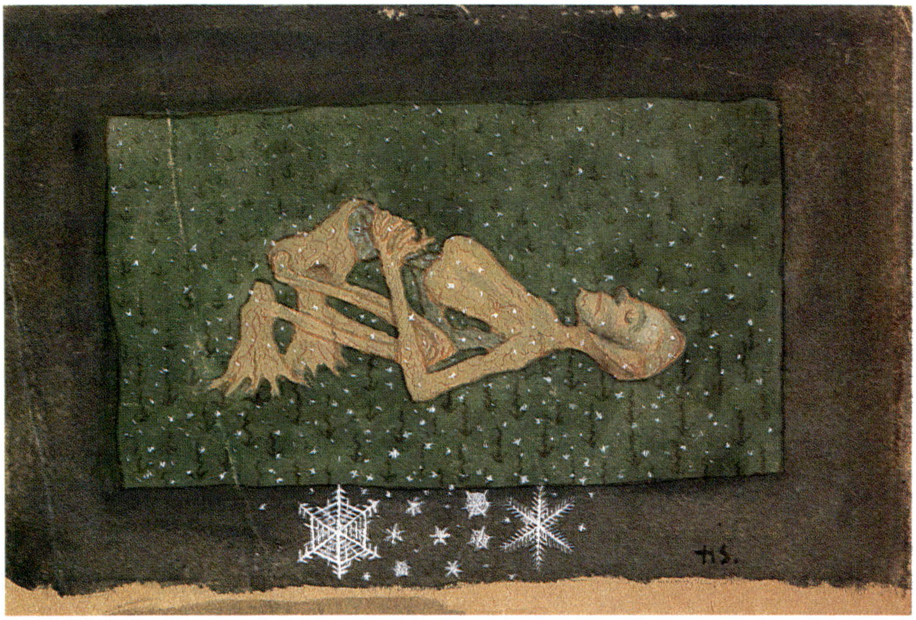

83b. Hugo Simberg

> I believe that a work of art is something which speaks to me about another world and puts me into the mood that the artist wishes to create. It should lead my thoughts to things which I don't think about every day, and I have to see these pictures and think these thoughts for a long, long time afterward.—Of course it can be achieved by Naturalism, but I believe one can achieve it much more easily through stylization. The most recent period in art, against which artists are now working, did a great deal of damage to art.

These ideas are closely linked with the theories of Symbolism. Simberg's technique in small watercolours and gouaches matured considerably during his trip to London in 1896, when he made a thorough study of Burne-Jones's small sketches and of old medieval miniatures.

The mysticism of nature

Some of Simberg's early miniatures, *Frost*, *Autumn I* and *Autumn II*, were created in the dusky days at the end of the year in Ruovesi. Their themes are clear. They are linked with everyday experiences which have, however, stimulated the artist's unique creative fantasy. Simberg describes the subject of *Frost* and his observations of nature in a letter to his brother.

> At the present time, I am painting a small picture. It shows frost which, on a still, bright autumn day at sunset, spreads above the land. It is represented by a highly stylized human figure, which has quite white skin outlined in skin-coloured contours. It is sitting on a sheaf of rye and is blowing its cold veil of mist over the harvested rye fields, where the sheaves are shown. The horizon is formed by the hills of Ruovesi. In the foreground are evergreens, blackish-green; then deciduous trees, intensive yellow, autumnly; and then finally a flowering hill. I have tried to achieve a lovely colour entity.

All three works show a unique hybrid creature. The point of departure is a human figure which grows into an increasingly horrifying symbol of destructive natural forces. Sakari Saarikivi, an authority on Hugo Simberg's art, describes them as follows:

> The palely cold Frost, sitting on top of a sheaf, blowing mist, and Autumn, growing out of the ground itself, freezing the earth's growing power, are personifications of nature's powers that are unique in European art. The latter actually rises to tragic greatness if we place it beside the small watercolour version made on the subject (Autumn II), in which Autumn's figure is convulsed on the meadow it has destroyed to await its own death as the snowflakes softly fall upon it.

Death

Hans Holbein's woodcut series *Dance of Death* interested Gallen-Kallela. As early as the spring of 1894 he asked his art historian friend J. J. Tikkanen to get him reproductions of the series, but Holbein's skeleton man does not seem to have left any direct traces in Gallen-Kallela's own art. On the other hand, his pupil Simberg's slowly moving, sometimes melancholically gentle 'Death' was created by the autumn of 1895. Simberg's 'Death' is not the cruel Reaper. His first depictions of death are set in a rustic milieu and are certainly influenced by the primitive rural man's simple, unquestioning relationship to death. The child or old person 'got away', or Death – God – 'took away the child' from the suffering and cares of life. The artist, who came from a Swedish-speaking family, gave this early work a Finnish title, 'Sallittu', which can be freely translated as 'this is our lot'. Simberg's 'Death' paintings were generally not cruel. Death does not do its destructive work among a festive crowd as Edgar Allan Poe's did. It takes the peasant, the poor old man, or – as often happened when infant mortality was high – the innocent little child.

Death and the Peasant depicts a simple man's submissive relationship to death. Death is just as natural as life itself. Simberg worked on the Death theme and on the Garden of Death in Paris, but Hans Christian Andersen depicted the Garden of Death

83 d

Death and the Peasant, 1895

(Sallittu)

Watercolour and gouache on paper, 30.1 × 20.1
Signed lower right: HS
Ateneumin taidemuseo, Helsinki
A II 968:14
(purchased in 1913)

83 e

The Garden of Death, 1896

(Kuoleman puutarha)

Watercolour and gouache on paper, 15.8 × 17.5
Signed lower right: HS./with a pencil: Paris juni/1896
Ateneumin taidemuseo, Helsinki
A II 968:16
(purchased in 1913)

83 f

Death Listens, 1897

(Kuolema kuuntelee)

Watercolour and gouache on paper, 14.6 × 16.8
Signed lower right: HS. 1897
Ateneumin taidemuseo, Helsinki
A II 968:25
(purchased in 1913)

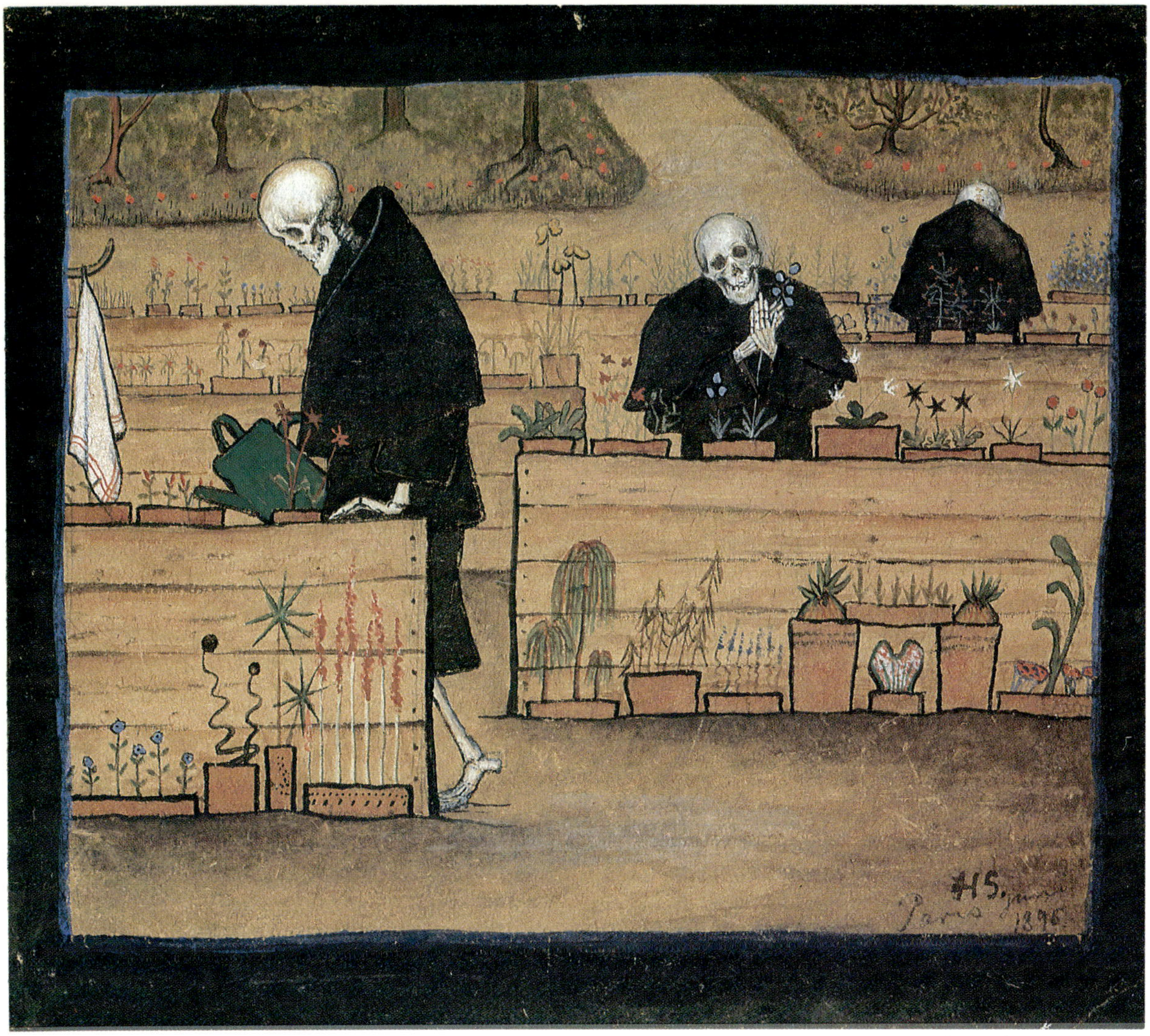

83e. Hugo Simberg

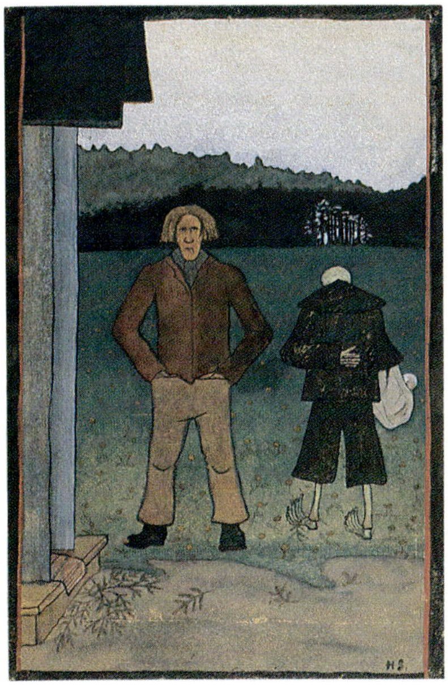

83d. Hugo Simberg

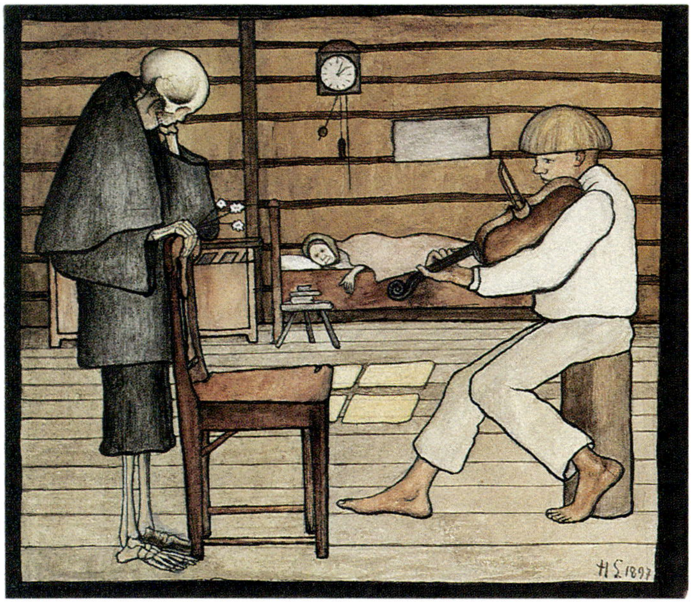

83f. Hugo Simberg

in *Historien om en Moder* in exactly the same spirit as Simberg, and these themes must in fact go back to Simberg's own childhood. He had heard Andersen's fairy-tales as a little boy, as nearly all small children in Northern countries did. Even the clothes of Death are similar in both cases: the rough horse-cloth and the hood.

In both these Gardens of Death each flower corresponds to a human soul. The Garden of Death is the waiting-room from which Death brings the souls to an 'Unknown land', to Our Lord.

The fairy-tale – a mystery of life and art

Simberg's early works include a rather clumsy piece, painted in a realistic technique, called *The Mystery*. In concept, it brings to mind Gallen-Kallela's *Symposium*, and was probably inspired by it: two men are sitting on a sofa staring at a brush dipped in red paint which has been raised by a hand appearing behind the back of the couch. Simberg's own ring is on its finger. On the lower left is the neck of a cello, also held by a human hand. The painting's artistic value is not great. It is, however, a kind of key to some of Simberg's more puzzling works, including the watercolours *Fairy-Tale* and *Fantasy*. The same disembodied hand, this time holding a shining jewel, can be seen in Simberg's watercolour *Fantasy*.

Fairy-Tale is one of Simberg's most important subjects. He made many versions of it. Its mystery is not revealed immediately, which is true also of *Frost* and *Autumn*. *Fairy-Tale* can perhaps best be explained when placed next to *Fantasy*, where a lone female figure gazes down at a hand holding a glowing jewel before her eyes. In *Fairy-Tale* a girl sitting on the back of an animal which looks like a dog is staring into the depths of a pool. Instead of a treasure, she sees a frog, with its head rising above the

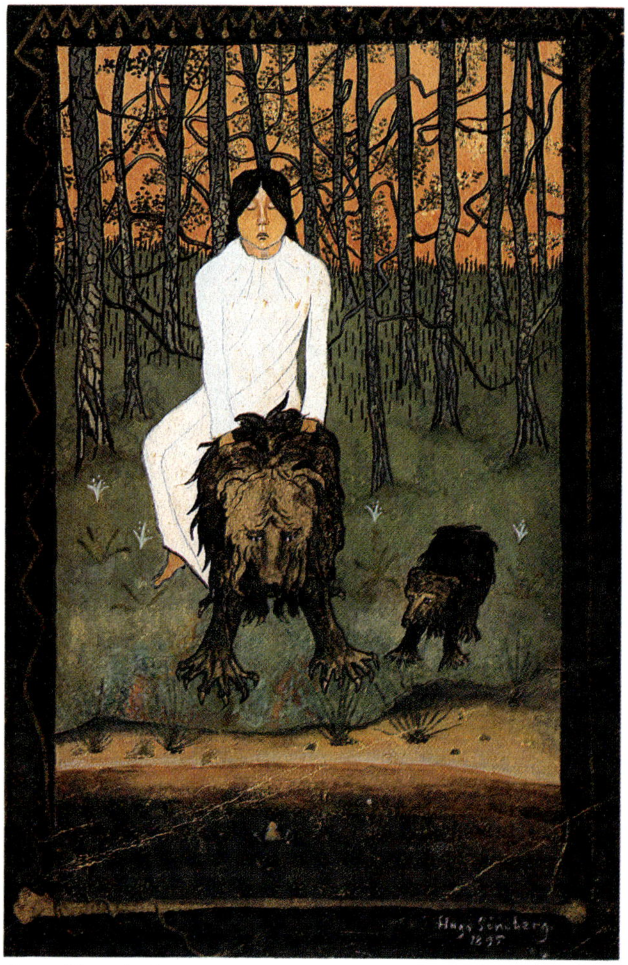

83g. Hugo Simberg

83g

Fairy-Tale I, 1895

(Satu I)

Watercolour and gouache on paper, 25.4 × 16.4
Signed lower right on the black frame: Hugo Simberg./ 1895.
Ateneumin taidemuseo, Helsinki
A II 968:4 (purchased in 1913)

83h

Fantasy, 1896

(Fantasia)

Watercolour and gouache on paper, 16 × 15
Signed upper right: HS. and above 'a monogram'.
Ateneumin taidemuseo, Helsinki
A II 968:32 (purchased in 1913)

83i

King Hobgoblin Sleeping, 1896

(Tonttukuningas nukkuu)

Watercolour and gouache on paper, 19.6 × 28
Signed lower right on the black frame: Hugo Simberg.
Ateneumin taidemuseo, Helsinki
A II 968:19 (purchased in 1913)

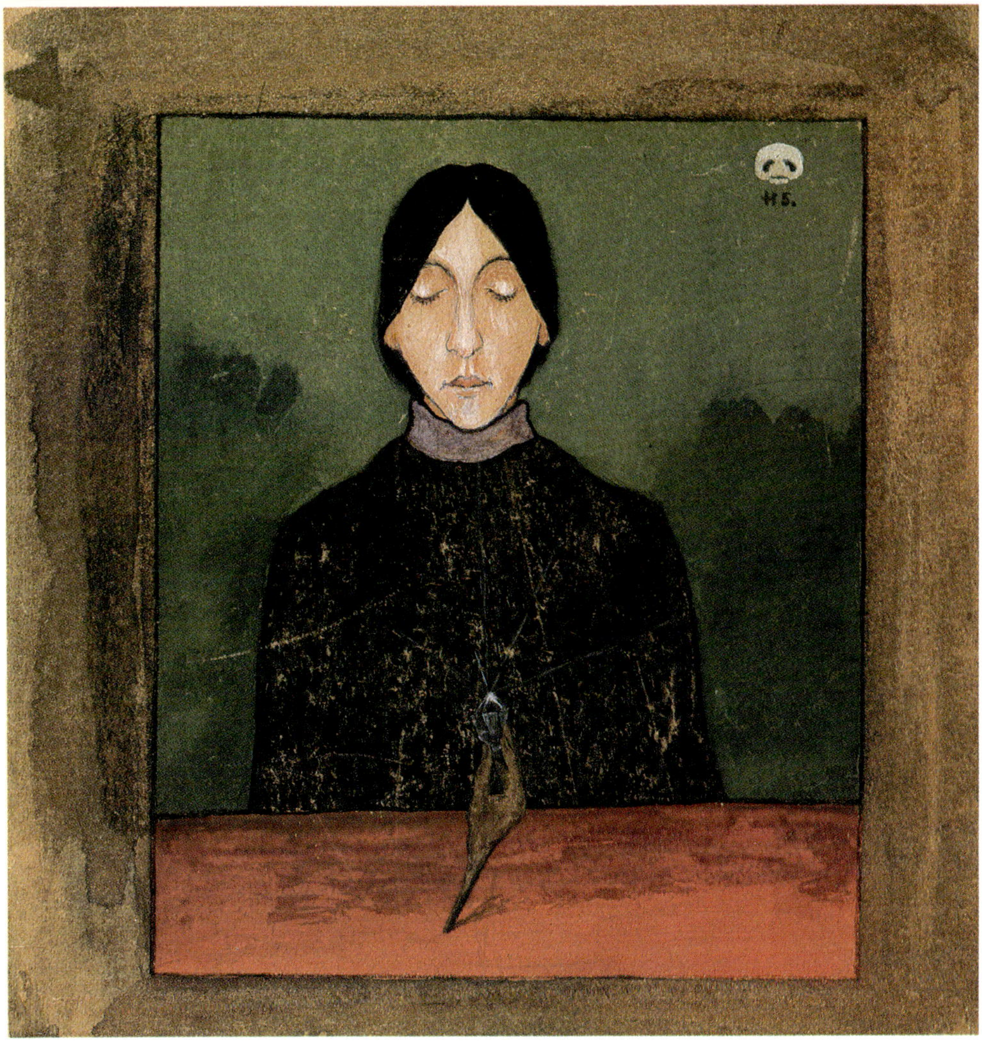

83h. Hugo Simberg

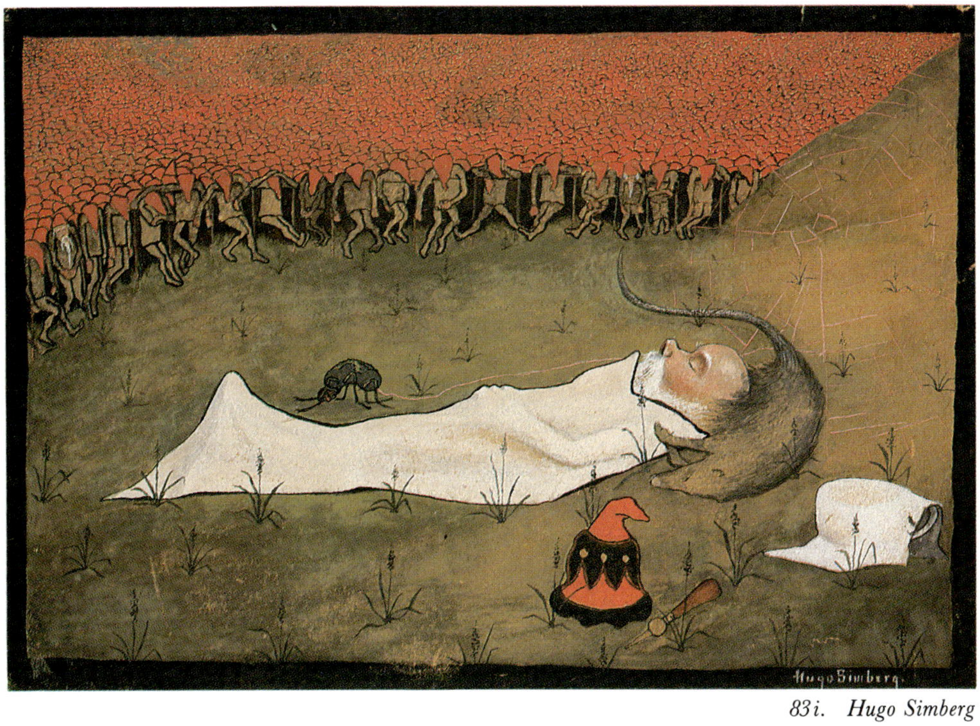

83i. Hugo Simberg

surface of the water. Again we are reminded of Hans Christian Andersen, whose fairy-tale *The Toad* (Grodan) is about an ugly toad which finally becomes a handsome prince. More important, however, is the myth that inside the ugly toad is a shining jewel. The toad seeks to escape from the depths of a well, and when it reaches the lawn, both the scientist and the poet scrutinize it. The scientist wants to operate on the toad, the poet agrees because he wants to find the jewel. This is related to Simberg's fairy-tale: '. . . isn't there something very beautiful in the folk-belief that the toad, the ugliest animal, often hides in its head the most precious jewel? Isn't it the same thing with people? What a jewel had then Aesop and Socrates!'

In another fairy-tale, *The Tinderbox*, Hans Christian Andersen tells of three dogs, each bigger than the other, which guard three treasures, each more precious than the other.

Margareta Rossholm has interpreted the *Fairy-Tale* as an erotic myth. Simberg's other works do not contradict this; however, I believe that the mystery hidden in the pool is more complicated. It is the mystery of life and death, which Gallen-Kallela was also pondering at this same time and which corresponds to the philosophy of the Ferkel group in Berlin.

Fattig fan (Poor Devil)
The contrast between the Angel and the Poor Devil, as well as that between the rose and its thorn often appears in Hugo Simberg's art. The dualism of Hugo Simberg's fantasy art is here: the dream of life's purity and its pollution, that of life's joy and its disruption, the dream of Heaven and the consciousness of Hell.

Simberg's Death was 'peculiarly laughing'. His little devil, a spoiler of life's joy, was also jesting. Death and the Little Devil, together with Father God and Angel, and the unity of life which they represented, formed the core of Simberg's philosophy of life.

Hans Christian Andersen also has his devil. In the *Snow Queen* it is 'the evil goblin, one of the most evil—Satan himself'. It gave people a mirror, which distorted everything beautiful and good and gave evil the power to grow. This is not far removed from Simberg's taunting Poor Devil.

S.S–K.

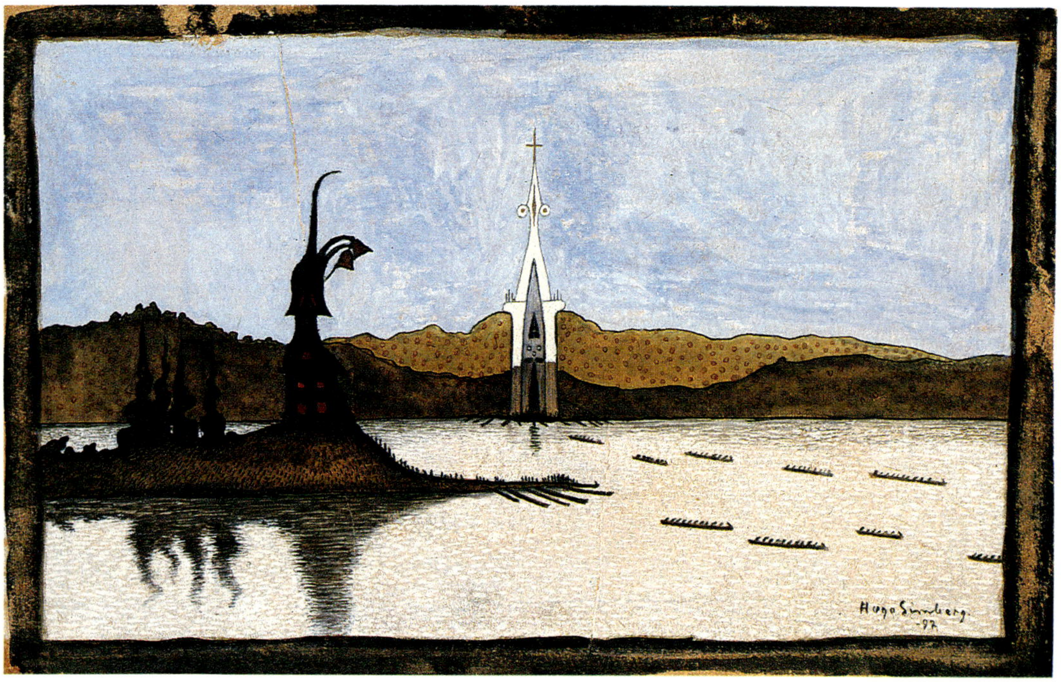

83k. Hugo Simberg

83k

The Two Churches, 1897

(Kaksi kirkkoa)

Watercolour and gouache on paper, 15.2 × 23.6
Signed lower right: Hugo Simberg./-97.
Ateneumin taidemuseo, Helsinki
A II 968:29
(purchased in 1913)

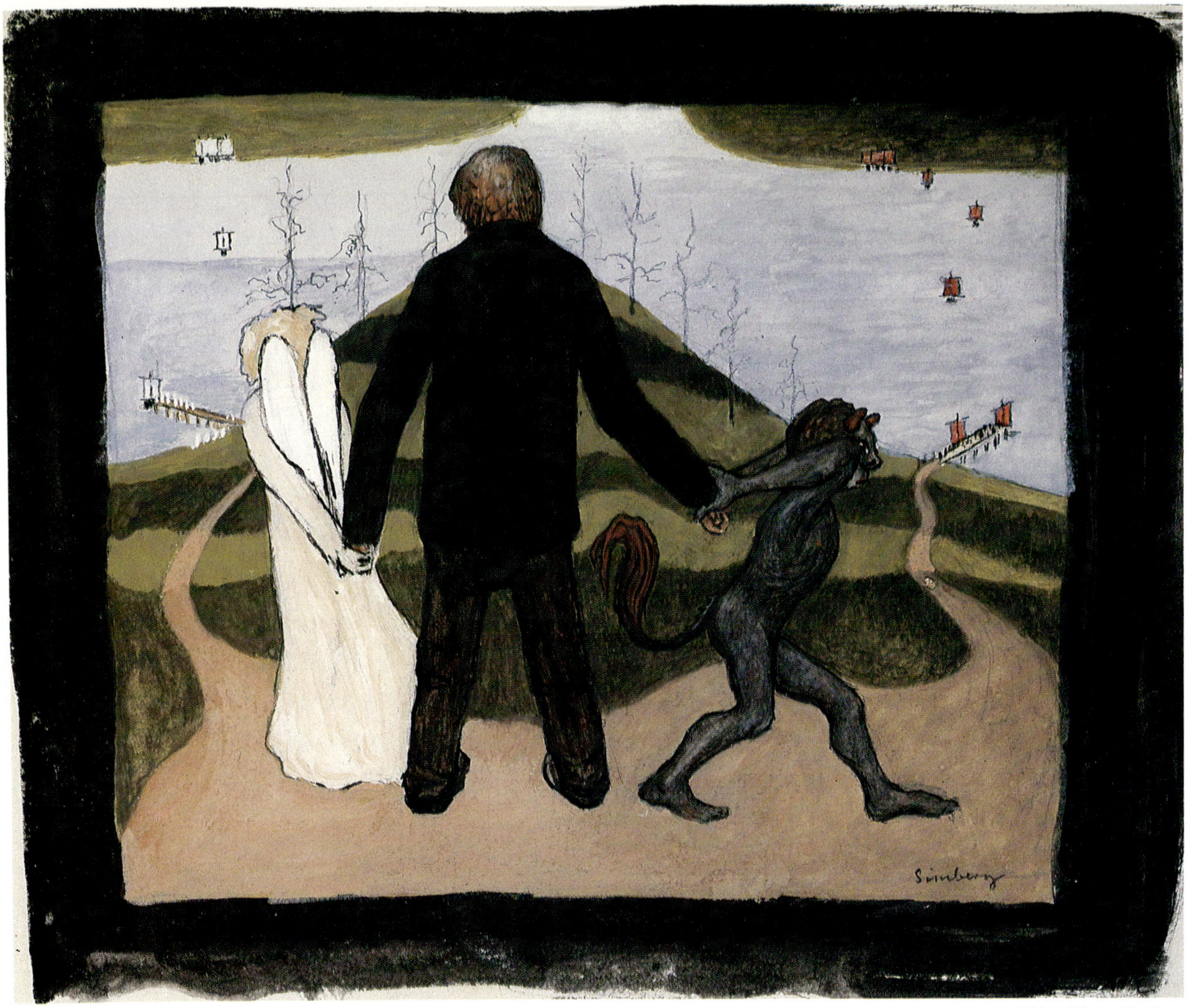

83j. Hugo Simberg

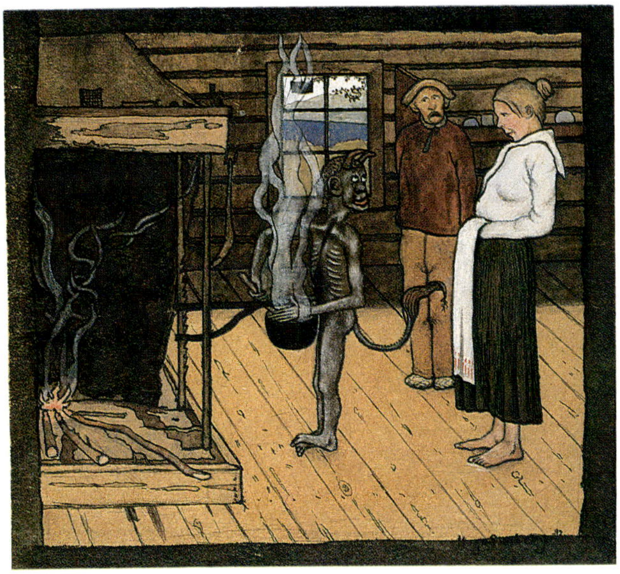

83l. Hugo Simberg

83j

At the Crossroads, 1896

(Tienhaarassa)

Watercolour and gouache on paper, 15.2 × 18
Signed lower right with a pencil: Simberg
Ateneumin taidemuseo, Helsinki
A II 968:17 (purchased in 1913)

83l

The Devil and the Pot, 1897

(Piru padan ääressä)

Watercolour and gouache on paper, 14.7 × 15.7
Signed lower right: Hugo Simberg -97
Ateneumin taidemuseo, Helsinki
A II 968:27 (purchased in 1913)

84

———, *Wounded Angel, 1903*

(———, Haavoittunut enkeli)

127 × 154
Signed lower right: Hugo Simberg / 1903
Ateneumin taidemuseo, Helsinki
A II 1703 (purchased in 1928)

The very title, just the long dash, given to the work by the artist when it was first shown at the Exhibition of Finnish Artists in 1903 shows that it was related to Simberg's own personal feelings on the enigma of life and death. His friends and those who followed his fate did not, however, need to have any detailed description of the work's content.

The theme of death in Simberg's art was already given prominence during his trip to Paris in 1895–6. A picture and appended poem have been preserved which tell that Death, The Reaper, had visited his workroom. The experience seems highly personal. 'Already?' asks the artist. 'Not yet!' replied Death, and holding out his scythe he asked the artist to draw a 'human couple on it'. From then on, love and death were inseparable for Hugo Simberg.

Wounded Angel was created after a severe crisis brought on by illness. Resignation, serenity, a feeling that life and death were inextricably connected were given form in Simberg's mind. Love and sin, life's cruelty and beauty, man's helplessness, Fate – all are contained in this one picture.

Wounded Angel is a symbol of Simberg's fate. But it also depicts one of the central themes of Symbolism, found from Plato to Swedenborg and the Symbolist poetry of France – the theme of a lost paradise, of man's original sin, of guilt, repentance, and impotence.

Simberg used the subject one more time in the frescos for St John's Cathedral in Tampere. The pictorial concept of an individual's experiences was expanded to become the symbol of redemption for the sufferings of mankind.

S.S–K.

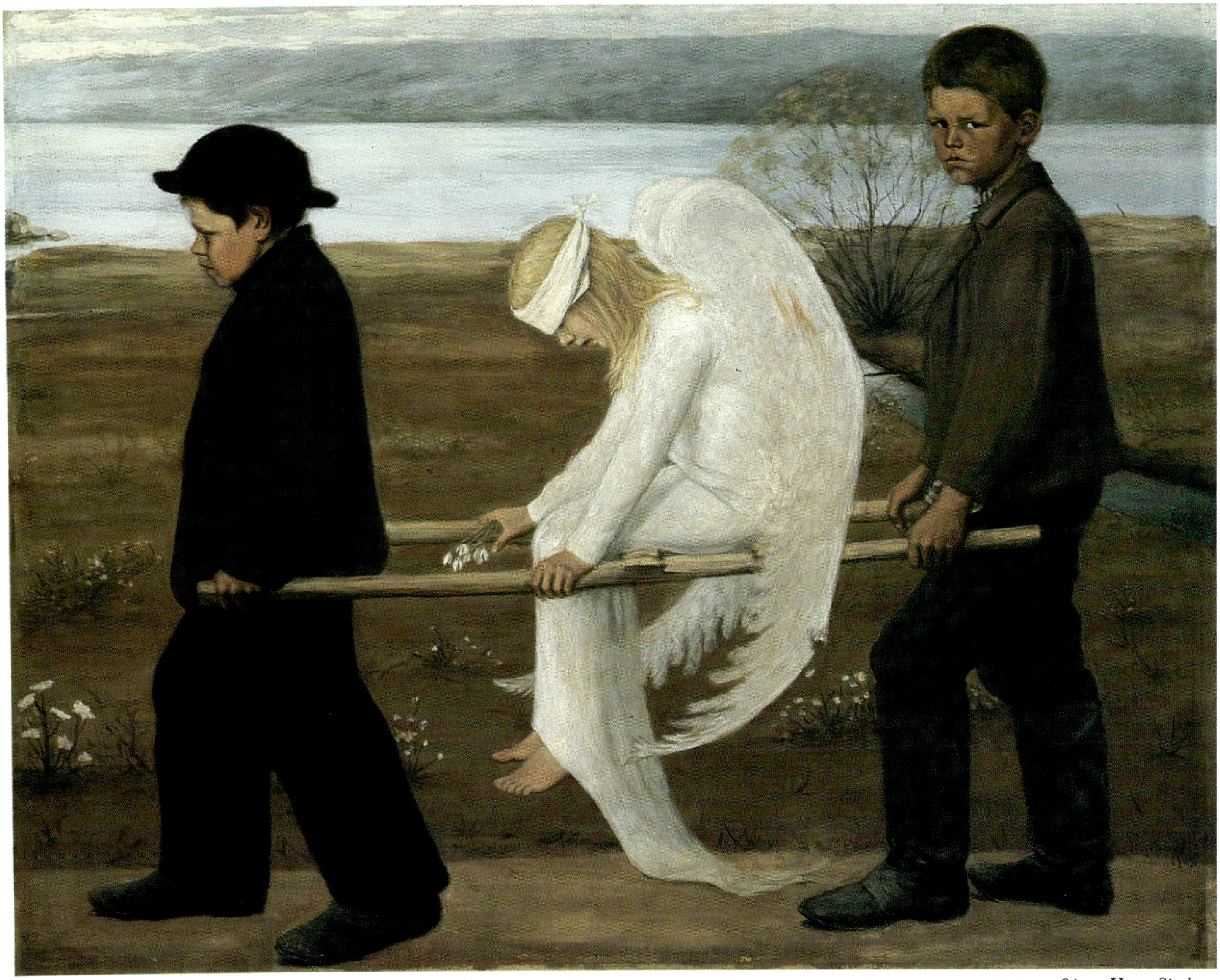

84. Hugo Simberg

HARALD SLOTT-MØLLER

1864–1937, Denmark

Harald Slott-Møller attended the Royal Academy of Fine Arts in Copenhagen from 1881 to 1883 and the Artists' Study School from 1883 to 1886. Like Johan Rohde and J. F. Willumsen (p. 296), he belonged to the generation that studied at a time when Naturalism was struggling for a foothold. They became part of this movement and Slott-Møller's early pictures reveal a Naturalism bordering on a bitter realism.

Slott-Møller won considerable recognition from the very beginning. After his marriage to the painter Agnes Rambusch in May 1888, he and his wife went to Italy for the autumn and winter of 1888–9. Both were attracted by early Italian art. A change in his painting followed: his content became more Symbolistic, and more emphasis was placed on the decorative.

His interest in Dante Gabriel Rossetti and the Pre-Raphaelites was awakened by trips to England in the 1890s. Slott-Møller also shared the interest of his age in the industrial arts and crafts, and made designs for furniture and jewellery. From 1902 to 1906, he was artistic director of the Aluminia faience factory. He held a leading position in the Arts and Crafts movement at the turn of the century and was also a member of the group which founded the Free Exhibition (see p. 36).

85

Georg Brandes at the University of Copenhagen, 1889

(Georg Brandes forelæser på Københavns Universitet)

94.5 × 82
Signed lower left: Harald Slott-Møller
Det kongelige Bibliotek, Copenhagen

Both Agnes and Harald Slott-Møller had attended Georg Brandes' lectures from their youth. A drawing (Private Collection) by her shows Brandes on the high lectern, with two lights above him and his audience below. It is dated 17 December, 1883, and inscribed 'The last lecture on Major Trends in the 19th Century'. In 1929, the writer Henri Nathansen described Brandes' lecture technique of those days. 'Georg Brandes stands there. Pale, yellow pale in the light from the gas lamp which flows over the soft yet thick and shining brown hair – even paler against the blackboard on the wall behind him. He is wearing white tie and tails. Now he lowers his head and looks over the room. The "demonic" look glides restlessly among the rows, stops to rest on a face, glides further in the breathless, tense silence ...' In the following years, Brandes reacted increasingly against Naturalism, a reaction which was crystallized in his paper on Zola (1887), where the realist writer was explained as a creator of images and myths (a Symbolist). Brandes prepared the way for what was to happen in the 1890s.

Harald Slott-Møller first painted Brandes in the spring of 1888, when he was giving his first lectures on Nietzsche. The present picture is from 1889, after Slott-Møller's return from a visit to Italy. Slott-Møller could have read the lectures which he missed because of his absence in Italy in the periodical *Tilskueren* (August 1889), in the article 'Aristokratisk Radikalism' (Aristocratic Radicalism).

Slott-Møller painted Brandes lecturing on several occasions, with small variations in the composition. The change that occurred in his art just after his trip to Italy may also have been spurred on by ideas inspired by Georg Brandes.

H.W.

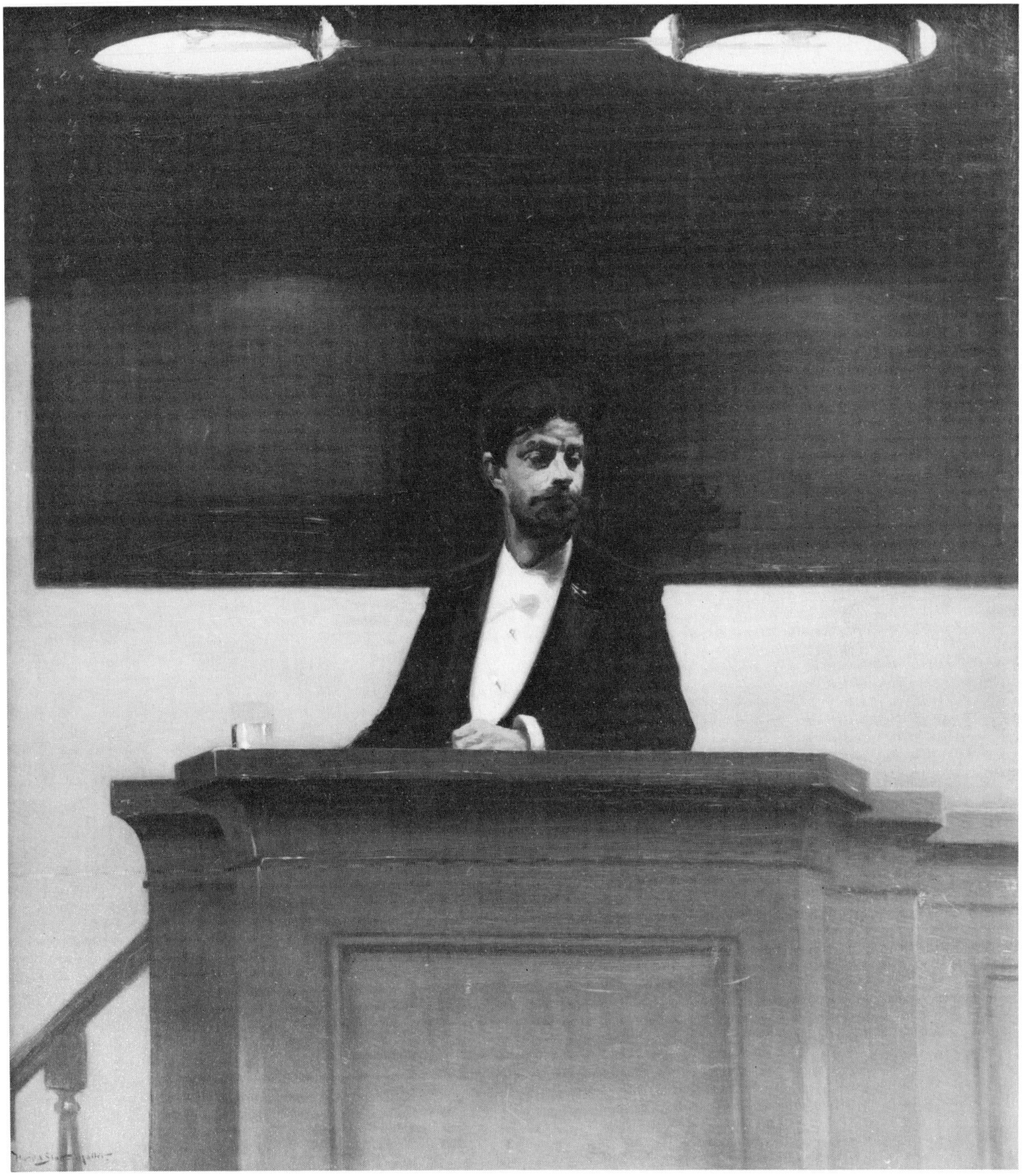

85. Harald Slott–Møller

HARALD SOHLBERG

1869–1935, Norway

Sohlberg worked mainly as a landscape painter. Of his other works only some self-portraits from the 1890s are of interest.

In his youth he was apprenticed to a decorative painter, and in 1885 or thereabouts he entered the arts and crafts school of Christiania. Four years later, his father finally allowed him to pursue his artistic inclinations. In the following years, he applied himself assiduously to his art studies, but he preferred to work on his own rather than attend formal classes. For some months in 1890 he was a private pupil of Sven Jørgensen, a rather isolated artist owing something to the Danish realist tradition. He then received some training from Eilif Peterssen and Erik Werenskiold. From late 1891 to spring 1892, he was a pupil of Kristian Zahrtmann in Copenhagen.

In the summer of 1893 Sohlberg painted his first significant picture, *Night Glow* (No. 86), which was very well received when it was shown at the official exhibition in Christiania the following year. Aided by travel grants, he went to Paris (1895–6) and then, surprisingly, to Weimar (1896–7), possibly because the Norwegian painter Frithjof Smith was a professor at the local academy. After completing his education, Sohlberg worked in Norway. He married in 1901 and went to live with his wife in the highlands of central Norway, first in the countryside near the Rondane mountain range and then (1902–5) in the small mining town of Røros. In 1906 he made another visit to Paris. On his return he moved to Kjerringvik, a village on Christiania Fjord. Four years later he settled in Christiania.

Sohlberg treated a wide range of landscape themes in his paintings, but he is best known for his views of the mountainous regions of central Norway, particularly his grandiose winter scenes from Rondane (No. 89). Roughly in the same region he found the subject-matter for his Røros townscapes (No. 90) and one or two other important works, such as *Flower Meadow in the North.*

86

Night Glow, 1893

(Natteglød)

79.5 × 62
Signed lower left: Sohlberg/ 1893
Nasjonalgalleriet, Oslo
Inv. no. 441 (purchased in 1894)

This painting represented a turning-point in Sohlberg's career. It was inspired by the view of a sunset, seen from a small island in Christiania Fjord, where he stayed during the summer in the early 1890s. In a letter written many years later, he wrote that this experience gave him the first real understanding of 'the wonderful beauty of detail'. 'Indeed', he continued, 'this subject, with its dark, detailed forms set against the brilliant sunset, impressed itself so strongly upon my mind that I had no peace till I had painted it... This awareness of details amidst the grandeur, like the overwhelmingly rich ornamentation of a church interior, also came to the fore in a couple of other works made on the same occasion.'

The work was shown at the official exhibition in Christiania in 1894. At that time it was called 'Evening Glow', but the artist himself later changed the title. The originality and importance of the painting seem to have been immediately acknowledged. It introduced a new style as well as a new contemplative attitude to nature. From then on, most of Sohlberg's landscapes were characterized by a succinct overall

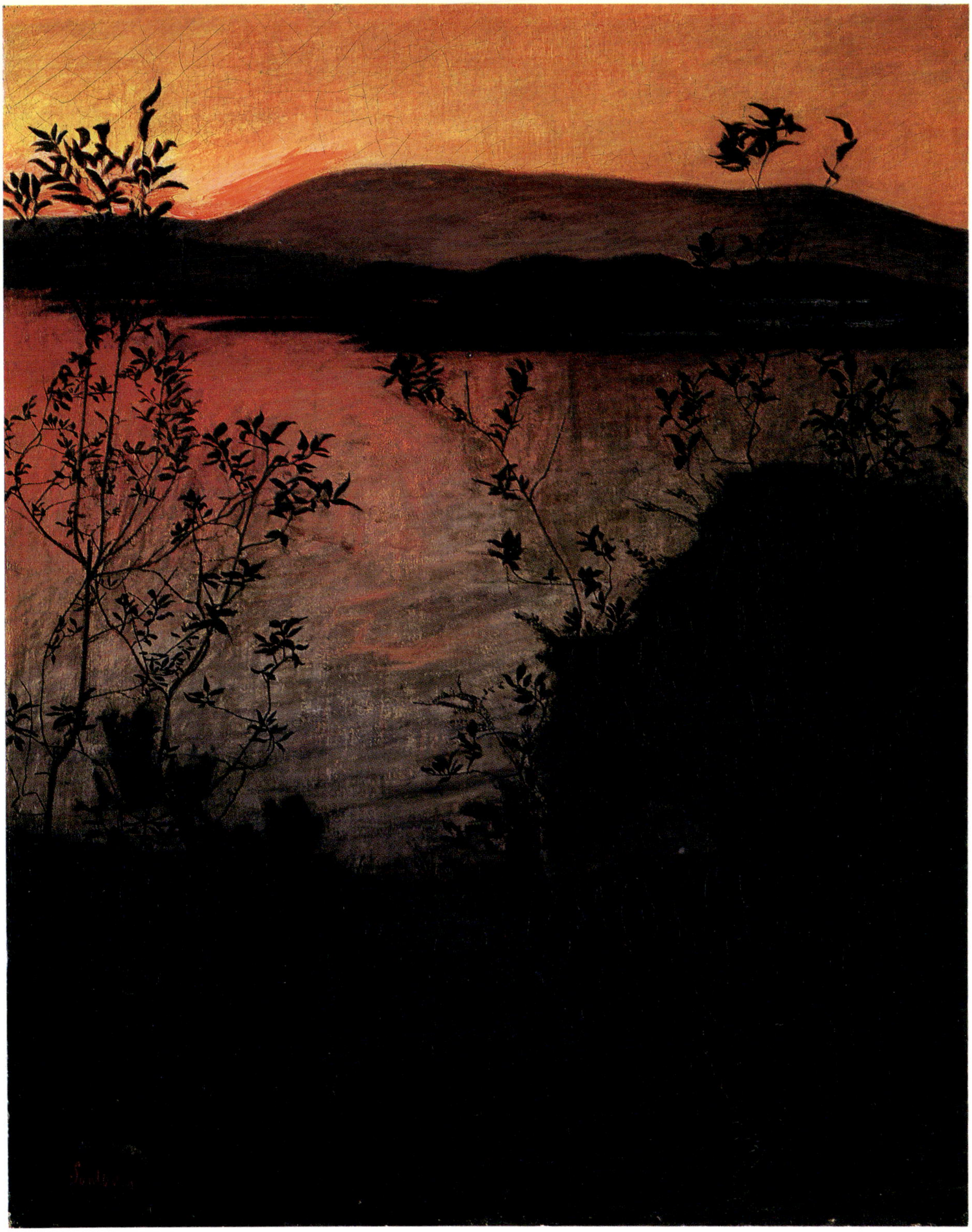

86. Harald Sohlberg

view and a rather simplified rendering of the distant parts, contrasting with meticulous attention to the details of the foreground. The tendency towards an ornamentalizing treatment of natural forms became more conspicuous in later years. The artist's reference to a church interior should perhaps not be overlooked: not infrequently a religious side to his experience of nature emerges in his paintings.

Although Sohlberg's new idiom was very personal, it did not in a more general sense break with the Scandinavian tradition. On the contrary, he continued in his own way what in Norway is generally termed 'mood painting'. This trend, which goes back to the mid-80s, aimed to achieve a subjective approach without, however, departing significantly from the realist interpretation of natural forms. Sohlberg's rather Synthetist treatment of his backgrounds as well as his increasingly ornamental arrangements were undoubtedly inspired by the second 'Free Exhibition', which he had seen in 1892 when studying in Copenhagen. Some of the artists represented at the exhibition were strongly influenced by French Synthetism, notably Johan Rohde and Willumsen. The latter's one-man show in Christiania, which opened in September the same year, included landscapes that to some extent anticipate Sohlberg's solutions. Roald Nasgaard has, I think rightly, pointed to *Spanish Chestnuts* of 1891 as especially important in this connection. This work was shown both in Copenhagen and in Christiania.

M.M.

87

Ripe Fields, 1895–7

(Modne jorder)

73 × 116
Signed lower right: Sohlberg
Private Collection

The subject represented is Rotnes farm at Nittedal, north of Christiania. The farm used to belong to friends of Sohlberg's, and he is known to have stayed there for some time during the first half of 1891.

The painting has been variously dated. Stenseng proposed 1891, allegedly on the basis of the artist's own notes. But he adds that Sohlberg brought the painting with him to Paris in 1895–6 and worked on it there. It was exhibited for the first time at the official exhibition in Christiania in 1898. Although it may be based on studies from 1891, it was surely executed later. Not only the handling but also the conception point to a date when Sohlberg's individual style was already developed. It shows the typical contrast between light and shadow, between close up and far away. We should also note the clear-cut forms and the decorative arrangement, especially in the rendering of the vegetation.

M.M.

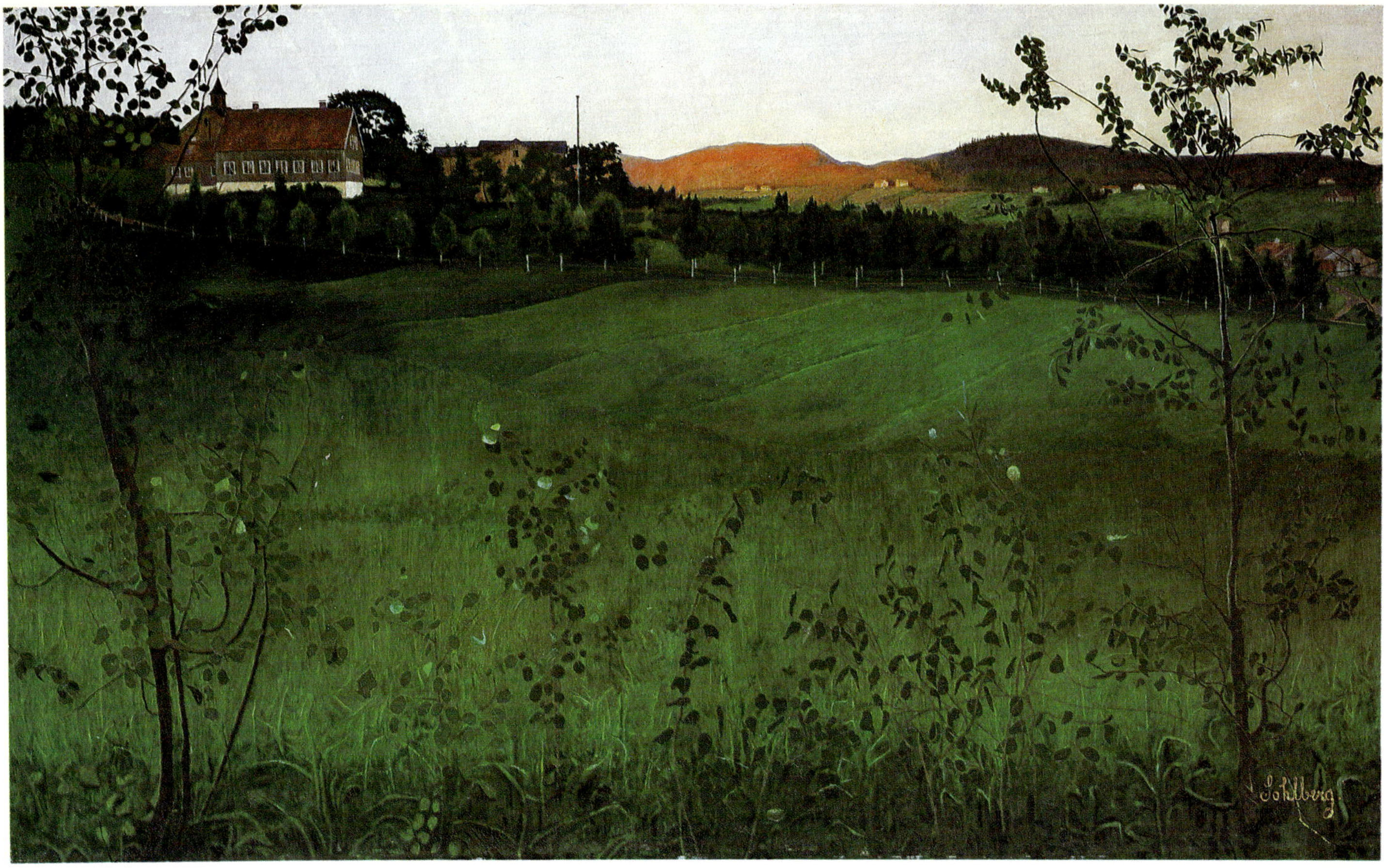

87. Harald Sohlberg

88

Summer Night, 1899

(Sommernatt)

114 x 136
Signed lower right: Sohlberg / 1899
Nasjonalgalleriet, Oslo
Inv. no. 525 (purchased in 1899)

At the time Sohlberg started on this work, he had taken a small apartment in Nordstrand, an eastern suburb of Christiania. The view is from his balcony looking westwards across Christiania Fjord. *Summer Night* is his last important painting of the 1890s, summing up his attempts and aspirations of the preceding seven years or so. Indeed, he reverted to largely the same painterly questions that had engaged him in *Night Glow* (No. 86), the work that first won him recognition. We experience much of the same tension between the immediate foreground and the infinitely distant: carefully studied details are seen against the irreducible immensity of space, represented by the magically luminous sky of the Norwegian summer night. But the stark opposites in this case are reconciled to some extent by the light of the sky reflected in the window-panes, and glowing on the flowers and the charming still-life on the balcony. The painting is thought to commemorate the artist's engagement. The table is laid for two and a lady's hat and gloves lie carelessly among the paraphernalia of youth, love, and pleasure.

This was a controversial work at the time of its appearance. In a letter from 1906, Sohlberg told the art historian and critic Jens Thiis about its reception: 'Some were angered by it, as a matter of fact they were so deeply angered that word was sent around that a public protest ought to be filed against its acquisition by the Nasjonalgalleriet. Others, again, liked it very well; some anonymous person was even moved to write a poem about it, which was sent to me.'

An oil study, differing in some parts, is in the Nasjonalgalleriet in Oslo. The artist also planned a winter version of the view (without the table); an unfinished canvas is in a private collection.

M.M.

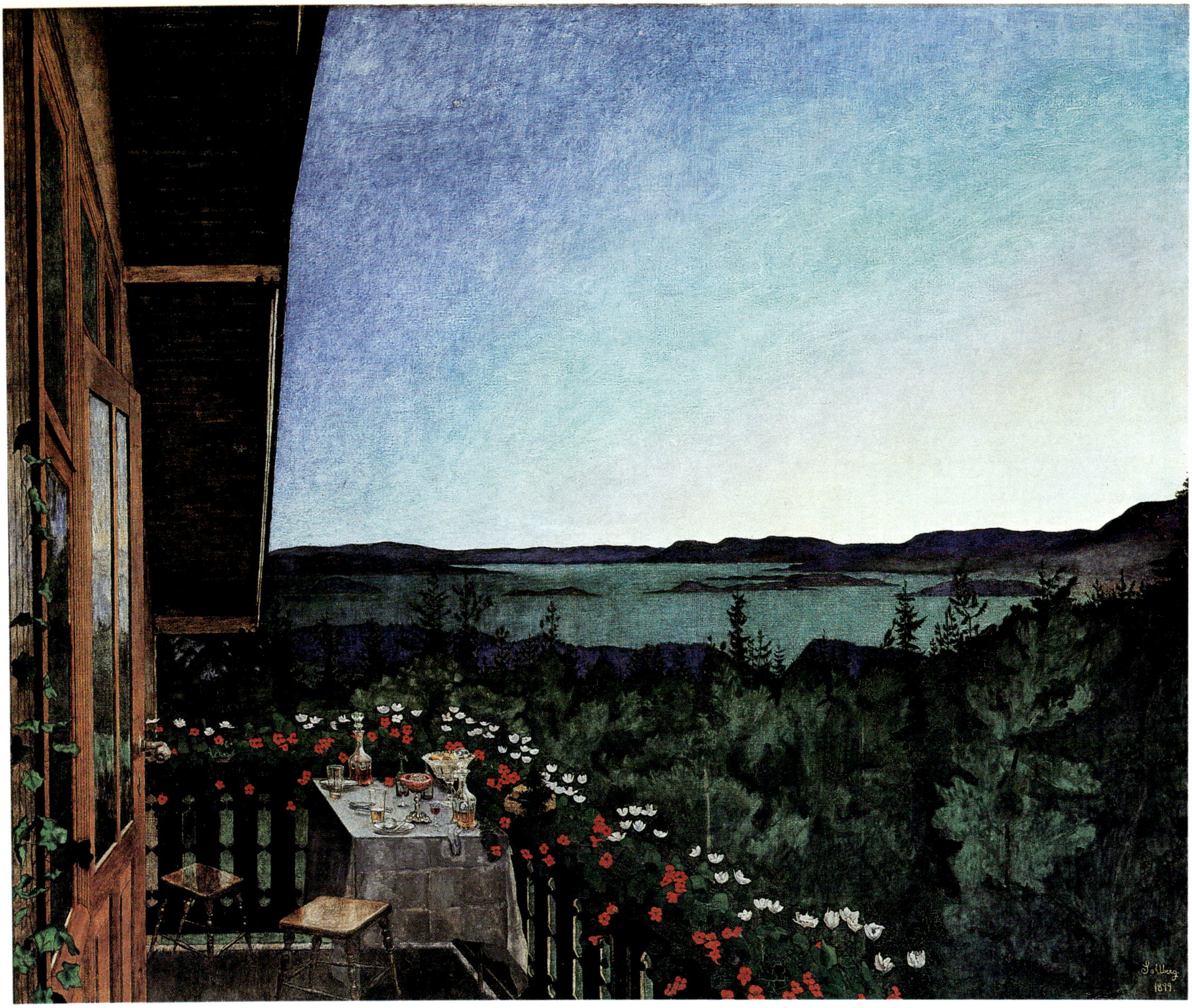

88. Harald Sohlberg

89

Winter Night in Rondane, 1901

(Vinternatt i Rondane)

68 × 91
Signed lower right: Sohlberg / 1901
Hilmar Rekstens Almennyttige Fond, Bergen

The urge towards primitivism, to an unadulterated state of nature or a primordial kind of existence, has in later years been cogently studied as an essential element of Post-Realist art (*The Mystic North* (1984); *Primitivism in 20th Century Art* (1984)). It may be interpreted in various ways, as a flight from modern decadent society, as a search for roots, or as a quasi-religious quest to confront ultimate cosmic reality. Although this last concern was never quite absent from Sohlberg's mind, it was only after the turn of the century that he came to face nature's sterner and more desolate aspects.

In late winter 1899, he joined some friends on a skiing excursion (inspired by Nansen), which led to the mountains north-west of the valley of Østerdalen. While resting not far from the mountain range of Rondane, Sohlberg was struck by its magnificent appearance under the wintry sky. He decided to give pictorial expression to his experience, and early the following year returned to the district and started work on what was to be his most ambitious composition. It eventually found its final – and to the artist definitive – form in 1914. The preparatory drawings and earlier versions (17 in all are known) that are dated, are from 1900, 1901 and 1911. Most of them are executed in watercolour or combined techniques on paper, but five are oil paintings. Among these, the work shown here is the most representative. Although slightly less formalized in conception, it comes fairly close to the final version (*Winter Night in the Mountains*, Nasjonalgalleriet, Oslo). Of this the artist wrote, in a letter to the Nasjonalgalleriet in 1914, that he thought it his most significant work because, as he said, 'more than in any other, I have succeeded in giving expression to that which is the central, the most characteristic feature of my art, i.e. the decorative, monumental and unified, in combination with the precise and detailed, in colour, form, and line, as I strongly and personally see and feel it.'

M.M.

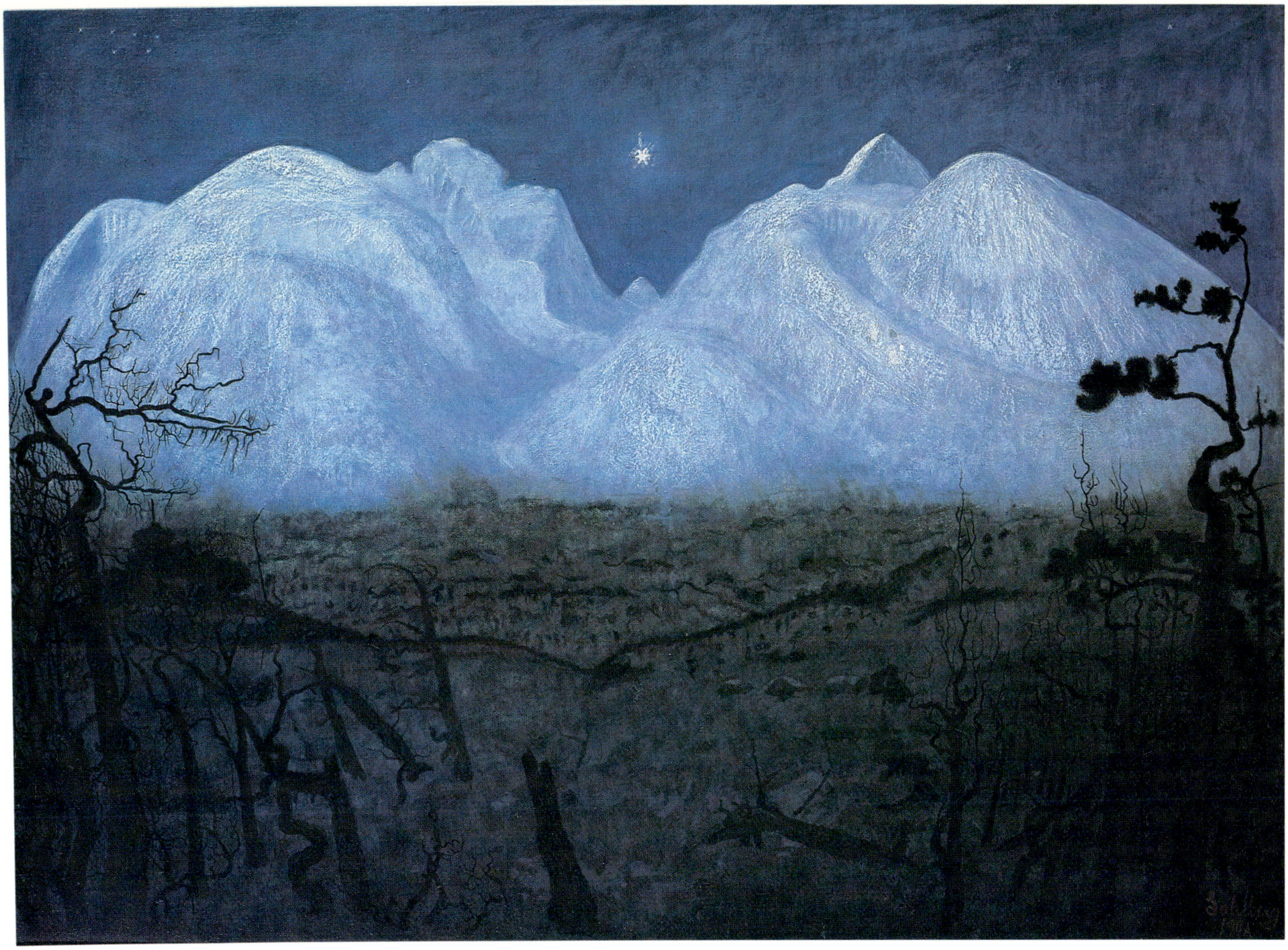

89. Harald Sohlberg

90

Night, 1904

(Natt)

113 × 134
Signed lower right: Sohlberg / Røros 1904
Trøndelag Kunstgalleri, Trondheim

The painting was excuted for the Trøndelag Kunstgalleri to replace another work lost during an exhibition abroad. Shown at the official exhibition in Christiania in 1904, it was exceptionally well received by critics and artists alike. The painter Frits Thaulow wrote in one of the leading Christiania newspapers that this work topples 'all the rules for painting that have so far been dogmas to me'. Indeed, it is quite possibly Sohlberg's most successful work.

In March 1902, the artist had moved with his wife to the small mining town of Røros, a rather bleak place high up in the mountain plains. They were to live there or near there for some three and a half years. Soon after his arrival, Sohlberg found the subject-matter for his *Night*: the (relatively) imposing late baroque church towering over the smelting works, the modest township, and the rather neglected churchyard. The churchyard lay there, he thought, 'like a frontier between the abodes of the living and the dead'. Although most of the view is depicted faithfully, the artist made some modifications. He changed the orientation of the graves by 90° so as to bring them firmly in line with the axis of the church. The freshly dug grave in the foreground is the artist's invention, and is not to be found in the preliminary oil sketch of 1903 (Nasjonalgalleriet, Oslo). As he noted, he put it in as a 'contrast to everything forgotten and decayed'.

During the first years of this century, Sohlberg showed a predilection for symmetrical arrangements not generally to be found in his work before or after that period. This hieratic kind of composition may be interpreted as an attempt to emphasize a religious experience of nature which, although never quite absent, is not always stressed to the same extent. This may therefore be the place to discuss the possible influence of German Romantic landscape painting and of C. D. Friedrich in particular. It is easy to point out similarities between the works of the two artists. Most significant, perhaps, is the tendency to stress a general tension between the intimate – or the individual – and the cosmic. It is also typical of both artists that they combine close attention to nature with a consciously built, and in that sense 'artificial', overall composition. Churchyard scenes crop up quite frequently in the *oeuvre* of Friedrich, as well as in that of some other German painters of his time. However, it is not known whether Sohlberg had actually seen any such works. (It may be worth mentioning that on his way to Weimar in 1896, he stayed in Berlin for a week to visit the galleries.)

Although Friedrich was largely a forgotten artist at the turn of the century, this was not quite the case in Norway. The Norwegian critic and art historian Andreas Aubert had been the first to rediscover the great landscape painter. As well as presenting him in several publications, he saw to it that the Nasjonalgalleriet acquired works by Friedrich – the first (*Greifswald in Moonlight*) as early as 1891. Sohlberg came to know Aubert not later than 1895–6, when they both visited Paris, and the acquaintance became sufficiently close for a correspondence to be kept up at least until 1907.

M.M.

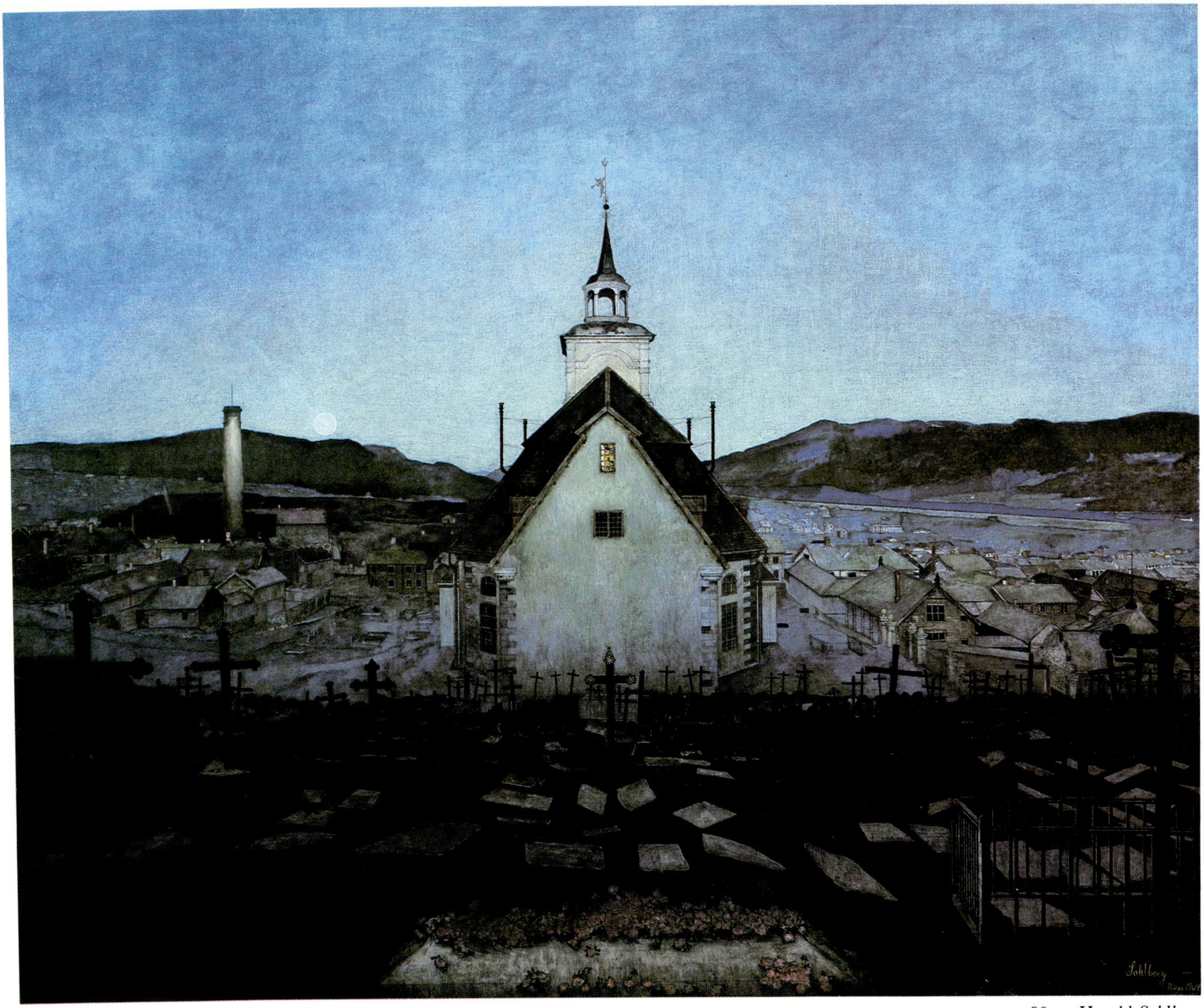

90. Harald Sohlberg

AUGUST STRINDBERG

1849–1912, Sweden

Commenting in 1899 on Strindberg's writing, his close friend the painter Richard Bergh observed that 'The aesthetic movement, which revolutionized art and literature during the 80s in the name of "Truth and Nature", was in Sweden – as in France – to no little degree a painters' movement. Even the poets were painters and foremost among them was August Strindberg. There is an eternal freshness and clarity in the pictures of nature in Sweden and of Swedish types that Strindberg painted in words. He had a painter's perception. His scenes, colourful and stark in form, were just as real in our imagination as the pictures our painterly eye conjured out of the Swedish landscape.'

A number of Swedish and foreign artists were close friends of Strindberg; besides Bergh, at various times his circle included Ernst Josephson, Carl Larsson, Karl Nordström, Christian Krohg, Edvard Munch, Paul Gauguin and Alphonse Mucha. But the 'isms' they represent are entirely absent from his painting, just as this is remarkably independent of his highly visual writing. Strindberg's artistic training consisted of painting sessions with his friend the painter Per Ekström in Stockholm in 1872. Little remains from that period, which seems to have ended in 1874. Nearly all the works are seascapes, most of them fresh but rather conventional; the last painting has a hint of Expressionism.

From 1874 to 1892 he contributed to art as a modern, perceptive critic who greatly influenced the coming generation of Swedish artists. He did not return to painting until 1892, having started on sculpture two years earlier, following the crisis in the '80s, with the blasphemy trial for *Married* and a protracted divorce from his first wife. Painting afforded a means of communication when, for one reason or another, he was incapable of writing. His activity as a painter was confined to brief, distinct periods, sometimes just a few days, principally in the years 1892–4, 1901–2, 1903 and 1905.

Membership of a group of artists was not for Strindberg but he did exhibit at the spring show of the Artists' Association (Konstnärsförbundet) in 1895. His artist friends saw to it that he was represented, together with members of the Association, at the Thielska galleriet, as well as at the famous exhibition at the Nationalmuseum in 1914, 'Breakthrough in Swedish Art'.

The foremost work on art theory by Strindberg is an essay from 1894, *Des Arts Nouveaux! ou Le hasard dans la production artistique* ('On New Art, or Chance in Artistic Production').

91 a

Stormy Sea. Broom Buoy, 1892

(Stormigt hav. Ruskprick)

Oil on cardboard, 31 × 20
Signed on back, in ink: August Strindberg / 1892
Nationalmuseum, Stockholm
Inv. no. 6175 (purchased in 1968)

91 b

Stormy Sea. Buoy without Top Mark, 1892

(Stormigt hav. Slätprick)

Oil on cardboard, 31 × 19.2
Signed on back, in ink: August Strindberg / 1892
Nationalmuseum, Stockholm
Inv. no. 6174 (purchased in 1968)

Strindberg's philosophy had disintegrated after the crisis associated with his trial for blasphemy on the publication of *Married* in 1884. A stubborn Christian since childhood, he now ceased to believe in a superior guiding force, a rational order. Bereft of ideals, illusions and faith, Strindberg preached total anarchy in politics, science and art: abandoning all scruples, one must start from scratch and compose order out of the

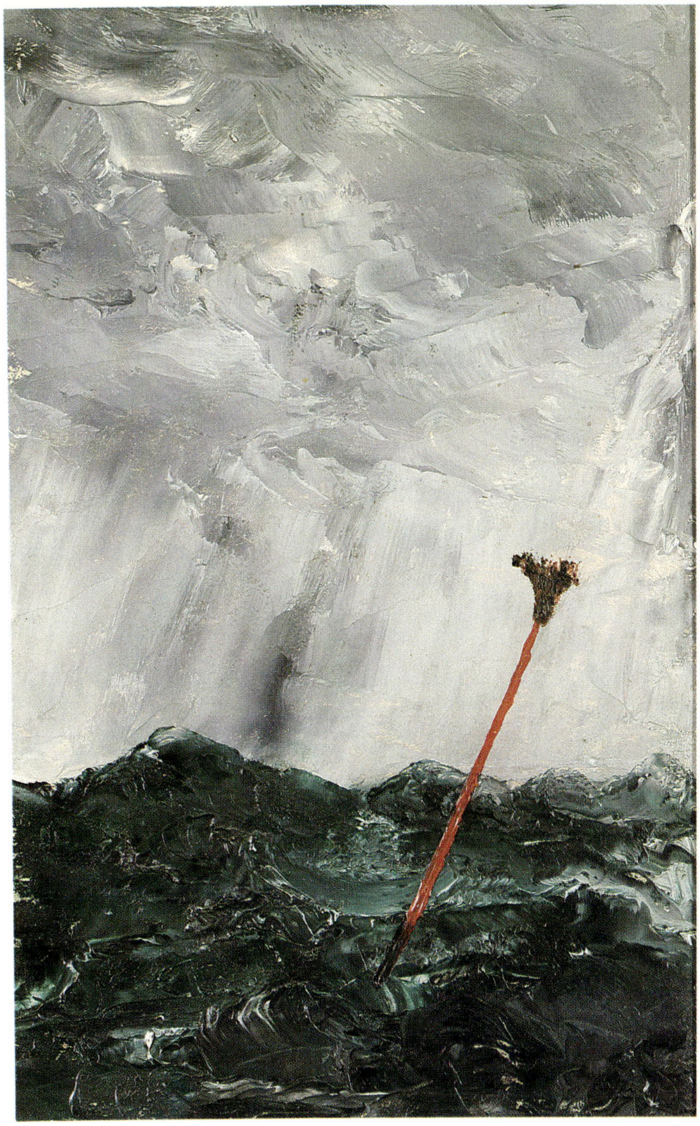

91a. *August Strindberg*

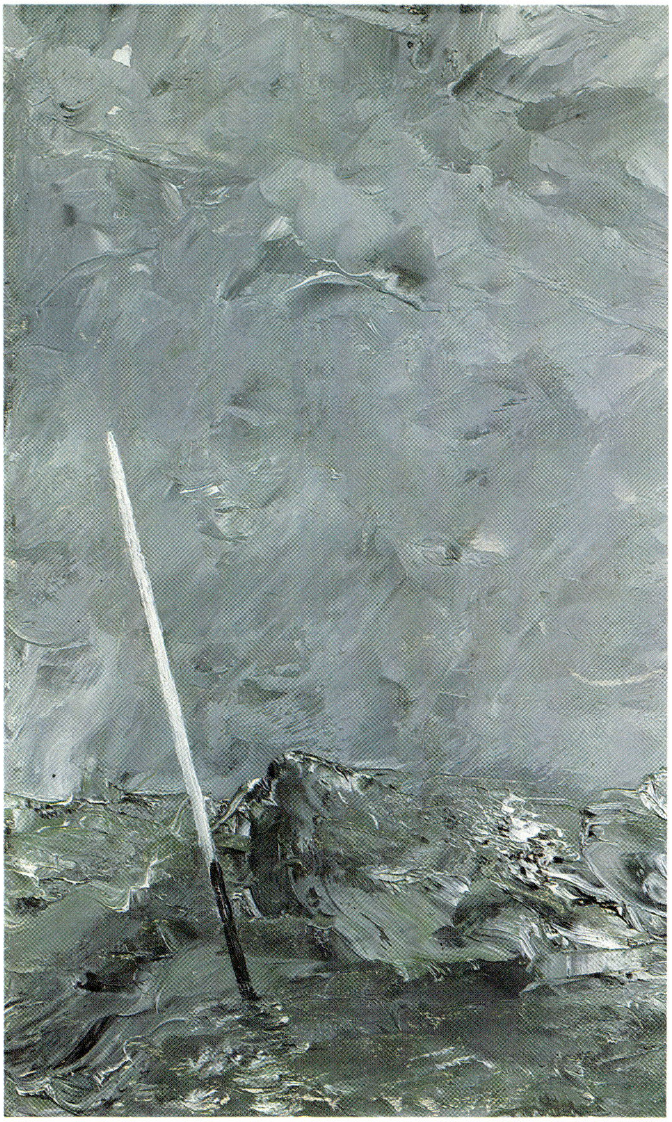

91b. *August Strindberg*

infinite chaos that is Nature. This rejection of preconceptions, established laws and lasting truths was the starting point for Strindberg's later work, not least in art.

In the early summer of 1892 Strindberg's literary work was at a dead-end; the new plays were not being staged and he was hamstrung by lawsuits arising out of the shattered marriage. He was staying in a cottage in Dalarö, a pilot station and seaside resort near Stockholm, and using materials borrowed from artist friends, with desparate courage he started to paint; miniatures at first but soon on a larger scale. There are more than thirty known paintings from this summer; all but one of them feature the sea and skerries with a varying degree of abstraction. The mood is mostly dramatic, serious, and the palette very simple, pure colours worked up with the knife. The subjects hark back to youthful encounters with nature among the Stockholm skerries but are largely fortuitous and interchangeable. Of greater importance is the structure – a faithful rendering of sky and sea ceased to be of any consequence. These two paintings are in contrasting moods, like the traditional colours of the markers. The knifework is an integral part of these storm scenes and just as important as the motif.

Commenting on himself in a letter to a friend, the writer Ola Hansson, in October 1890, Strindberg declared, 'His knowledge of his writing and its goals is nil because the inventions spring up at will in his head like grapes or mildew.' He now painted with the same spontaneity, with a modicum of realism, heralding what he wrote two years later in the manifesto on art, *Le hasard dans la production artistique: 'L'art à venir – Imiter la nature à peu près; surtout imiter la manière de créer de la nature'* (Art of the future – a close imitation of nature; above all of the manner in which nature creates).

The fact that Strindberg took the bold step of holding a one-man exhibition in Stockholm in the summer of 1892 shows that he took his painting seriously. The exhibition, which included these two pictures, was dismissed as a curiosity. Richard Bergh, for instance, was highly impressed at this time by Strindberg's literary descriptions of nature and his national aesthetics, and attempted to express them in his own paintings; as yet, however, he had no sympathy for Strindberg's paintings.

G.S.

92

Lonely Poisonous Mushroom, 1893

(Den ensamma giftsvampen)

47 × 45
Signed on back, in brown ink on paper: Målad af/ August Strindberg/ Berlin: 1893.
Private Collection, Stockholm

Strindberg continued to paint when he moved in the autumn of 1892 to Berlin, where in the tavern Zum schwarzen Ferkel he gathered a circle of Nordic and German writers and artists, among others Christian Krohg and Edvard Munch. Munch had recently created the scandal at Verein Berliner Künstler which made his name. This did not deter him or Strindberg from submitting two paintings each for the Berlin Salon in spring 1893, arranged by the conservative society. Naturally both were rejected and the paintings were showpieces instead at the parallel Salon des Refusés. Of these works, the most renowned was *The Wave*, a large picture that Strindberg later donated to Zum schwarzen Ferkel, where it hung until World War Two. It was done in a rather heavy, expressionist manner, using a palette reminiscent of contemporary work by Munch. The much smaller *Lonely Poisonous Mushroom* was painted at about the same time but is a completely independent work which Strindberg did not exhibit in Berlin. He sent it to Finland to be sold – the signature on a separate piece of paper, to be glued on the back, was dispatched later to satisfy the presumptive buyer.

The wonderfully tinted, practically abstract painting in pale blue and white with faint touches of pink, in which an ethereal atmosphere is heightened by the contrasting realism of the solitary mushroom, seems to have its immediate inspiration in the romantic seascapes of Caspar David Friedrich, which Strindberg was able to study in Berlin. The painting relates to an experience Strindberg had described in the novel *By the Open Sea* (1890), 'Now when there was nothing to catch the eye in either land or sea, just the blue vault above him, he felt free, isolated like a cosmic speck, floating in the air, subject to nothing but the law of gravity.'

The painting remained in a private collection in Finland until it was bought by the financier Ivar Kreuger. After his bankruptcy it was sold in Stockholm in 1932. With the aid of reproductions, in recent years it has come to be one of Strindberg's best-known paintings.

G.S.

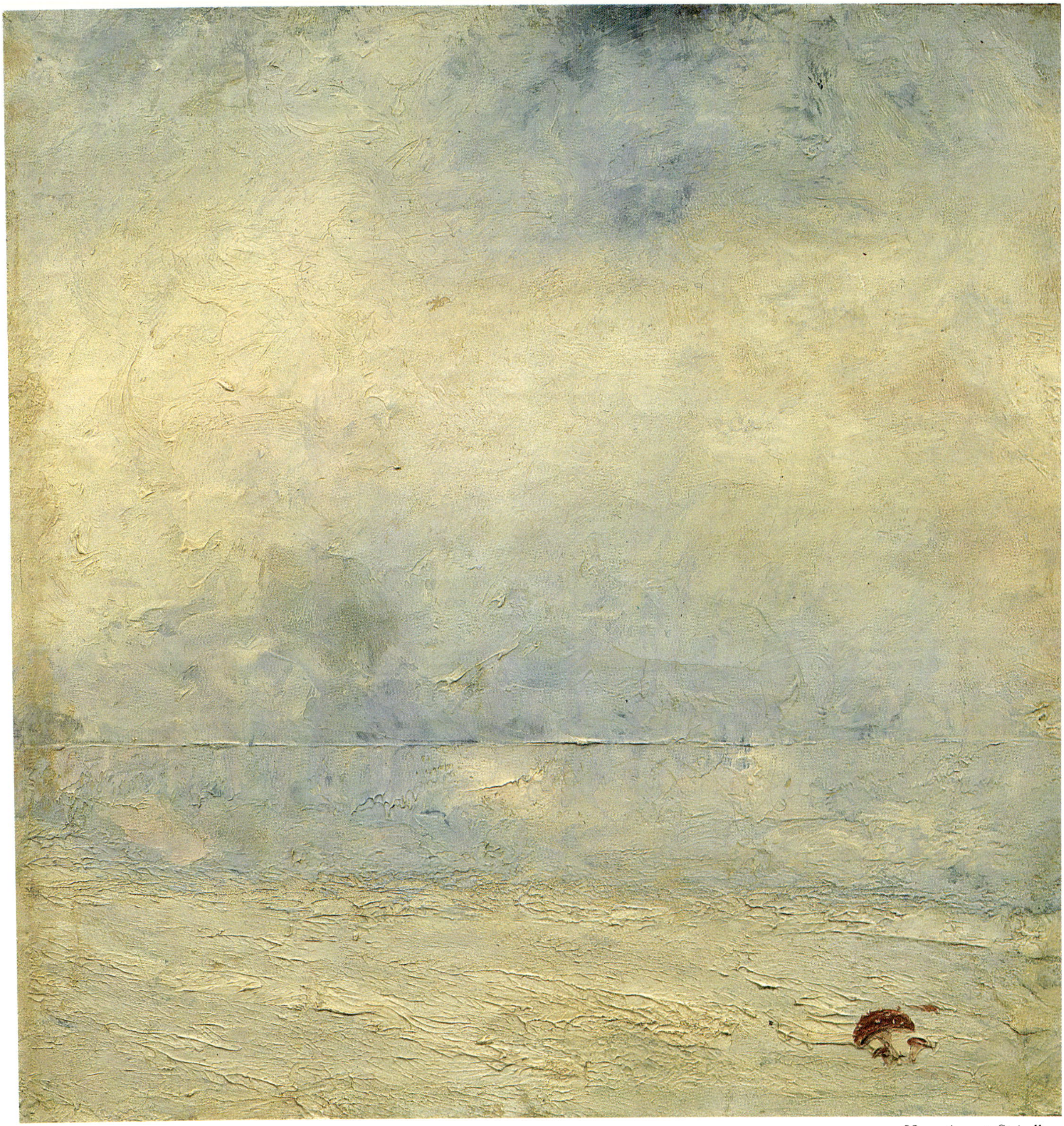

92. August Strindberg

93

Snowstorm at Sea, 1894

(Snöstorm på havet)

Oil on cardboard, 66 × 47
Not signed
Nordiska museet, Stockholm
Inv. no. 231.664

Together with Frida Uhl, the much younger Austrian journalist whom he married in 1893, Strindberg visited London, where he saw some paintings by Turner. The kindred spirit of this romantic expressionist evidently acted as a catalyst for much of Strindberg's mature painting. In 1894, while staying with his pregnant wife's maternal grandparents in Dornach on the Danube, Strindberg produced a remarkable series of large paintings and wrote the essay on chance in artistic creation. By heightening the expressiveness of colour and form to the point where principles of representation become almost meaningless, in these pictures Strindberg approached but also stopped short of abstract painting. In all his creative work the foundation in reality is so firm that even an abstract picture or a random line expresses a new naturalism.

In the autumn of 1894 Strindberg moved to Paris, intending to sell a case of paintings and make his name as a playwright and man of letters. There he met a strange Danish-Parisian painter and art dealer who commissioned him to produce paintings for a one-man exhibition. Strindberg, however, became more and more convinced that the Dane was intent on forgery; he therefore abruptly stopped painting and did not return to it for many years. But he had already completed two of his most abstract pictures, one of them *Snowstorm at Sea.*

This is an example of a recurrent motif in Strindberg's painting: waves beating against rocks, the leftward movement being part of a spiral that continues in the storm cloud racing to the right and bursting into a shower that falls on the tossing sea. Strindberg had used the motif before he saw Turner's work in 1893, but his conception clearly responded to the storm scenes for which the older painter was renowned. In *Snowstorm at Sea*, however, the palette is definitely muted, the pigment notably dry and the ground scraped to reveal patches of brown board as part of the colour scheme. The motif is entirely secondary to the handling of the materials.

The painting dates from about the time when Strindberg met Paul Gauguin and became one of his closest friends before the final departure for Tahiti. One cannot help pondering over the contrast between the colourful figure compositions in Gauguin's expressive symbolism at this time and the equally expressive paintings by Strindberg with their sombre, formless appearance.

G.S.

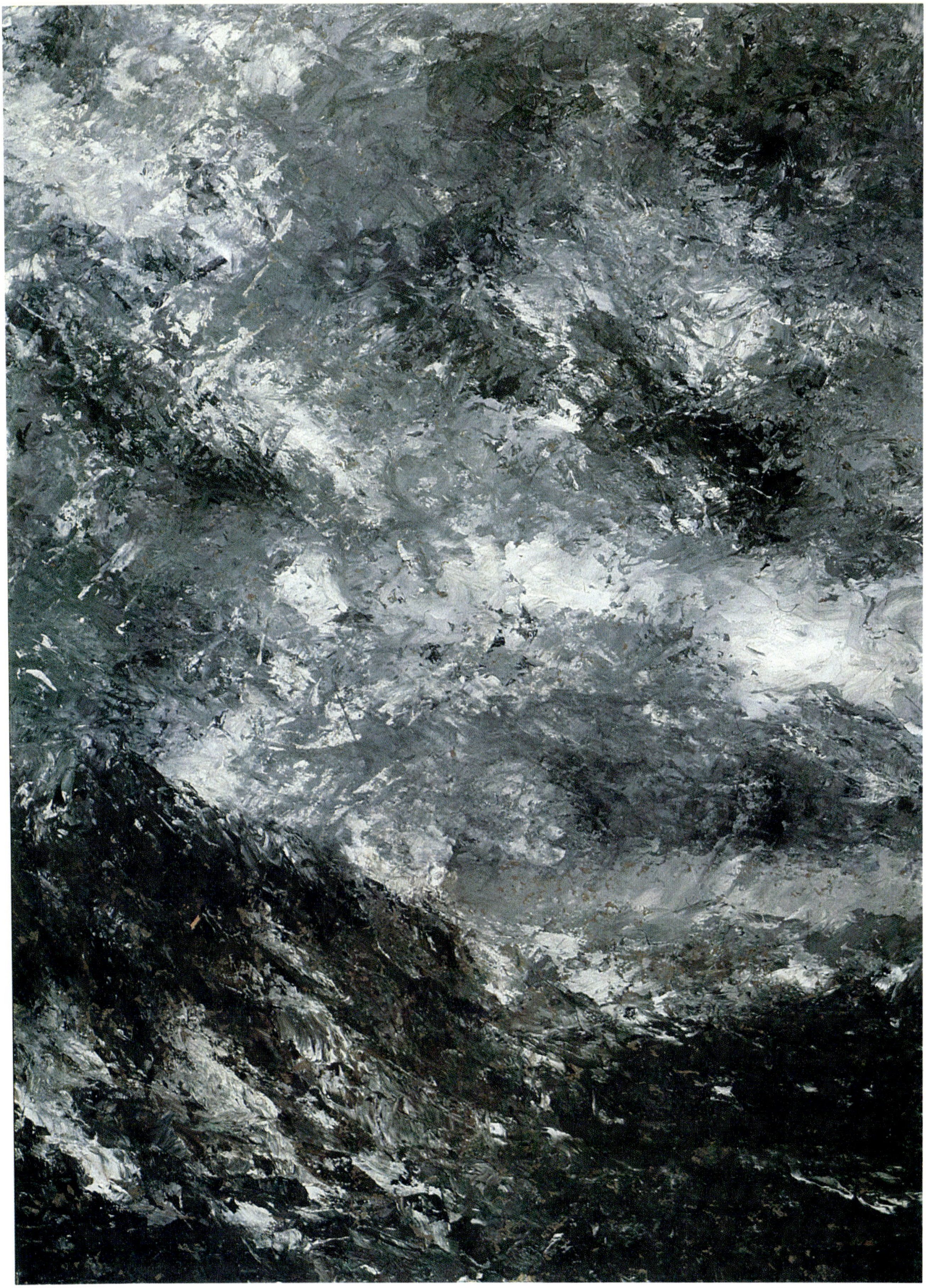

93. August Strindberg

94

Inferno-Painting, 1901

(Inferno-tavlan)

100 × 70
Not signed
Private Collection, Stockholm

Strindberg returned to painting again in 1901, at a time of bleak despair and suicidal thoughts after the first serious break with his third wife, Harriet Bosse. There is a radical change in his approach: the importance of form has given way to the preeminence of the message, while banality may even be an asset. Many paintings from this period seem to be backdrops for a drama. The cave in Plato's dialogue *Phaedo* is a recurrent theme, affording a view of this world as the imperfect reflection of the world of immutable ideas. This is a formal motif, like so many others, always present in Strindberg's painting and now acquiring a new dimension.

Inferno-Painting was named, not in allusion to the inferno which Strindberg described in the novel with that title he wrote in Paris in the 1890s, but after the 'forty-day inferno' he experienced when his young bride left him in 1901. He painted the picture after her return and during her pregnancy that year in their apartment on Karlavägen in Stockholm. Strindberg presented the painting to Richard Bergh, who had used it for the background in his famous portrait of the writer. After Strindberg's death, the painting was deposited by Bergh at the Nationalmuseum, with a view to a later donation, but when Bergh died it was returned. Since then it has been deposited for long periods at the Moderna museet, Stockholm. It has also been reproduced on a postage stamp.

G.S.

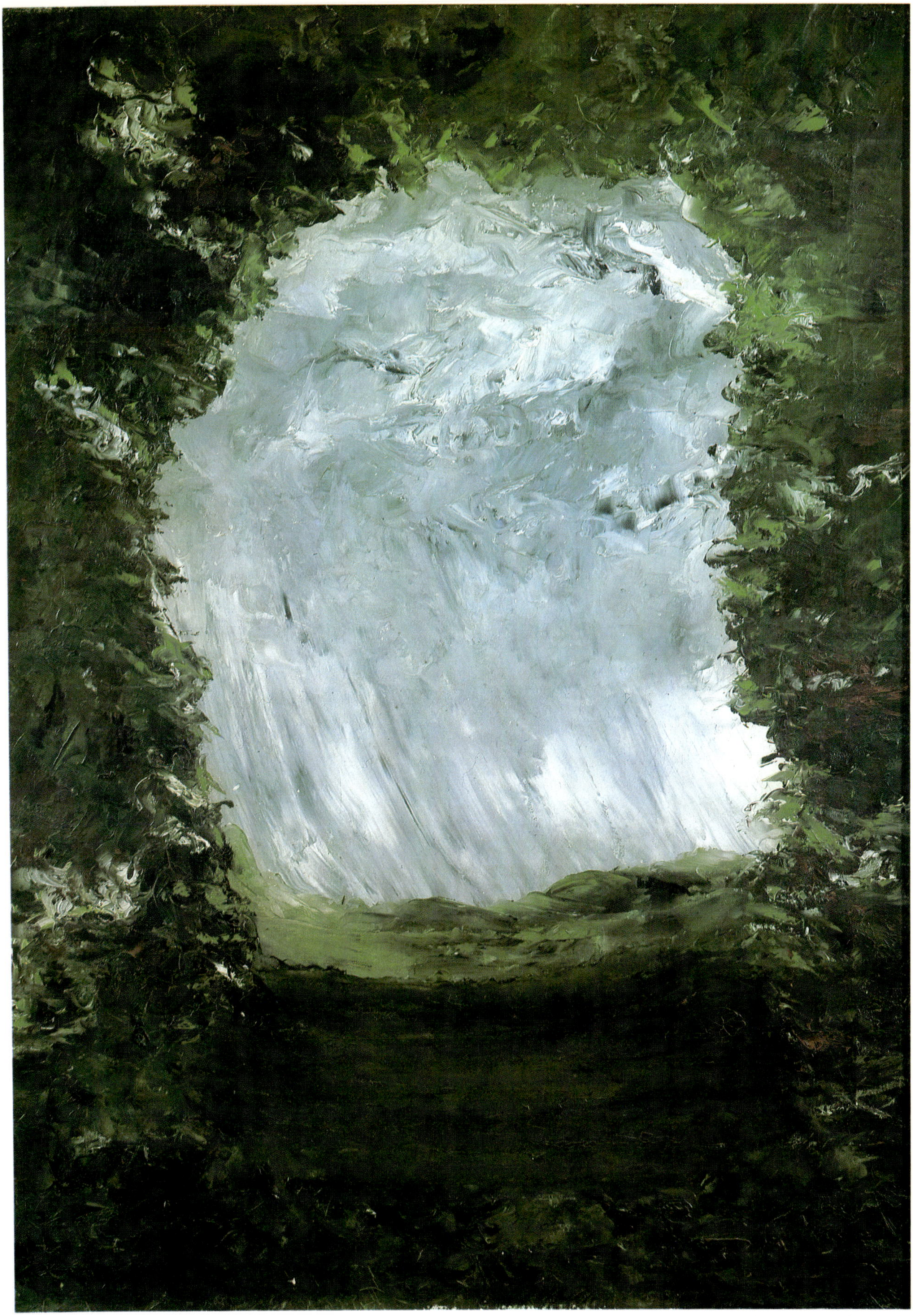

94. August Strindberg

ELLEN THESLEFF

1869–1954, Finland

Ellen Thesleff was a member of the generation of artists born in around 1870 who arrived in Paris in 1891 to study. She never adopted the realistic manner of painting, and, along with a small group of artists, had studied in Finland at Gunnar Berndtson's private academy, where training was mostly given in the style of the Impressionists.

It was natural for Ellen Thesleff to enter the spiritualist movement in Paris at the time. She was especially interested during her first year of studies in the art of Puvis de Chavannes, and in the primitive art at the Louvre. *Simplicity* became her goal. She was satisfied with following from afar others' interest in Symbolism, even though she did accept the general idea that the aim of art was spiritual beauty which lay above the visible world. 'An absolute beauty exists, but it is so exalted that reality never reaches it,' she wrote. Soon, however, she became isolated from her fellow artists by her desire to pursue an independent course. 'Only weak people are not lonely' was one of her aphorisms.

Ellen Thesleff finished her studies at the beginning of 1894 at the Académie Colarossi in Paris and travelled to Italy. The move from Paris to Italy took her to a world which she felt was truly her own. Even decades later, she emphasized the importance of the art of the Early Renaissance for her whole artistic development. She travelled to Italy again later on and spent several winters there. In 1906 she met Gordon Craig there and he taught her woodcut techniques and became a lifelong friend.

In around 1907, Ellen Thesleff adopted colourism more and more. However, the basic spiritual tone of her art remained the same. She was one of the Finnish women painters who – perhaps because they withdrew from the competitive Finnish art world – became richly creative in their later years. In its wealth and power, this work often surpassed that of their youth.

95

Thyra Elisabeth, 1892

42 × 24
Signed lower left: E Thesleff. 1892.
(Collection Bäcksbacka)
Helsingin kaupungin taidemuseo, Helsinki/
Helsingfors stads konstmuseum, Helsingfors

Even though Ellen Thesleff's attitude to Symbolism and Art Nouveau was a cautious one, her early production includes a piece which is a true work of the Symbolist period – frame and all – in its means of expression and its style. It has Puvis de Chavannes's harmony of colours, a Botticelli-like simplicity, and something of the English Pre-Raphaelites' feeling and dreaminess, as well as a softly pliant Art Nouveau line.

Stylistically, *Thyra Elisabeth* is the first example of Art Nouveau in Finland. The year that Ellen Thesleff showed this work at the annual Exhibition of Finnish Artists, her only piece there, Gallen-Kallela still believed in the lyricizing realism of his *Aino* painting (see Fig. 6).

The work received stunned and clumsy criticism. It was known to be a 'Symbolist' painting – but no one was able to explain what this meant. The poet K. A. Tavaststjerna wrote about the 'medieval-like picture of a Madonna'. He was the only critic who paid homage to the painting's poetry. 'It is certain that with this one portrait Miss Thesleff has shown herself to be one of the most interesting artists at the exhibition. Her gifts are characterized by a fine poetry, even refinement. We do not have her match when it comes to originality and the ability to choose simple means of expression.'

S.S–K.

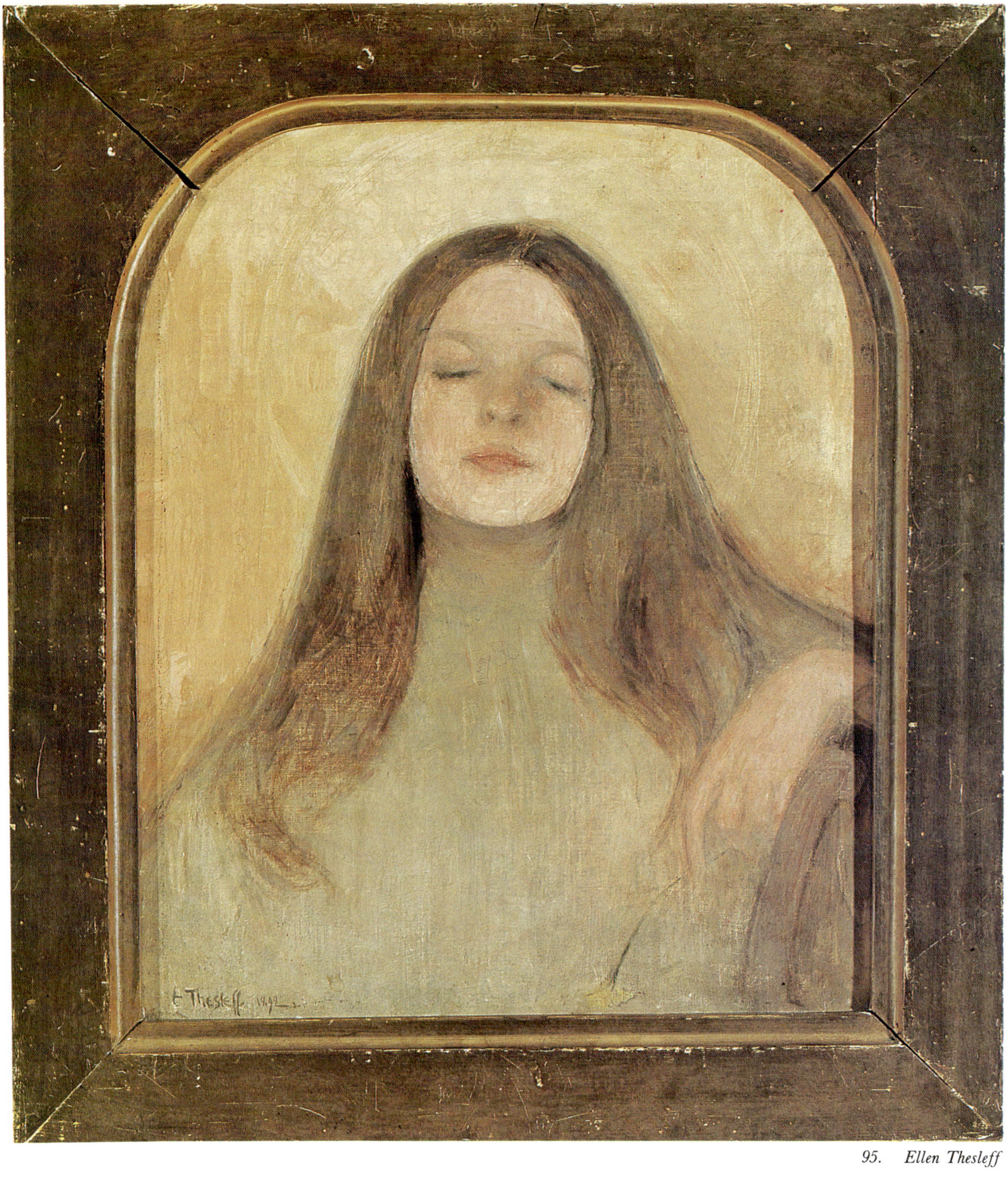

95. Ellen Thesleff

96

Spring Night, 1894

(Kevätyö, Murole)

38 × 46.5
Signed lower left: E.T. / -94
Ateneumin taidemuseo, Helsinki
Inv. no. A II 1253 (purchased in 1918)

'It is, as one can see, a synthesis of her subject-matter that Ellen Thesleff attempts to give in a way only a woman can, namely so truly that in accuracy it surpasses material reality and reaches spiritual reality.' This is how the critic and fellow artist Sigrid Schauman interpreted Ellen Thesleff's art in the 1920s.

Ellen Thesleff's *Spring Night* was on show at the exhibition which marked Finnish Symbolism's breakthrough, the Exhibition of Finnish Artists in 1894, the same one at which Gallen-Kallela showed the *Symposium (The Problem)* (No. 22).

The painting was executed in 1894, after her studies in Paris, and showed that the landscape had become something more to her than 'a piece of nature'. Amiel's words, 'un paysage quelconque est un état de l'âme', are particularly apt for this spring landscape. It is a personal paraphrase of the atmosphere of nature. The pale grey harmony of colour was originally taken from Puvis de Chavannes, but one can also see Carrière's influence. The work is also an example of the artist's spiritual merging with existence, and with nature, which is awakening along with this spring, swathed in light and the evening mist.

Critics at the time viewed Ellen Thesleff's works favourably but considered them 'minor'. They would have liked her to take on grander subjects on a larger scale: it was not great art, but it 'was beautiful to be good in small things'.

A critic from the Swedish-language newspaper *Nya Pressen* wrote: 'There is a wonderful virgin atmosphere to these paintings. Light silver-grey tones, even, flat shadows, discreet daylight, the whole bathed by a light whose source one cannot see but which is, none the less, an expression of her subjective conception of things and phenomena, full of feeling and warmth.'

S.S–K.

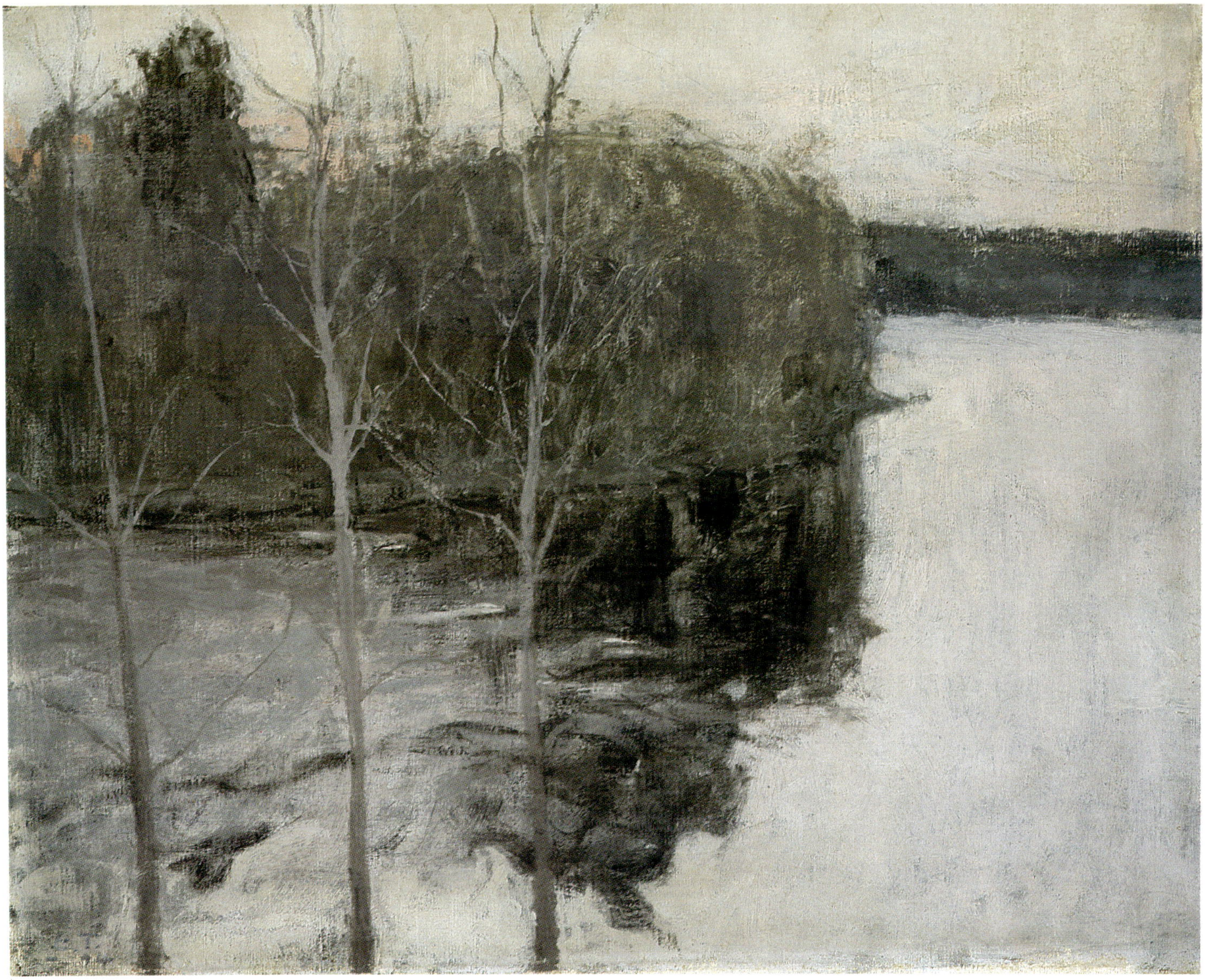

96. Ellen Thesleff

97

Self-Portrait, 1894–5

(Omakuva)

Pencil and sepia drawing, 31.5 × 23.5
Signed lower right: nov.-94/ den 4. okt.-95/ E.Th
Ateneumin taidemuseo, Helsinki
Inv. no. A III 1867 (donated in 1933)

This pencil self-portrait from 1894–5 shows the direction in which Ellen Thesleff's art developed soon after *Thyra Elisabeth.* Her palette became more limited until she achieved a Carrière-like 'black colourism'. Substance disappeared increasingly from her art. In the catalogue for the Carrière exhibition of 1891 Gustave Geffroy said that Carrière exemplified the ideals of the young generation reacting against realism. His paintings 'expressed ... in pain and noble sensitivity the vibrating and mysterious depths of life'. This same form of expression which travelled the border between reality and dreams was sought by Ellen Thesleff in her simple self-portrait. The artist probably valued this small work above many other more demanding pieces: she worked on it from the autumn of 1894 to the autumn of 1895 each time making it more profound – and submitted it both years to the Exhibition of Finnish Artists.

As she herself wrote:

'Three beings in one (I myself)
1 the original person in me, which has always been
2 the one which feels and lives a living life
3 genius, which can tear itself away from itself and see its own inner being
God is in each of us'

S.S–K.

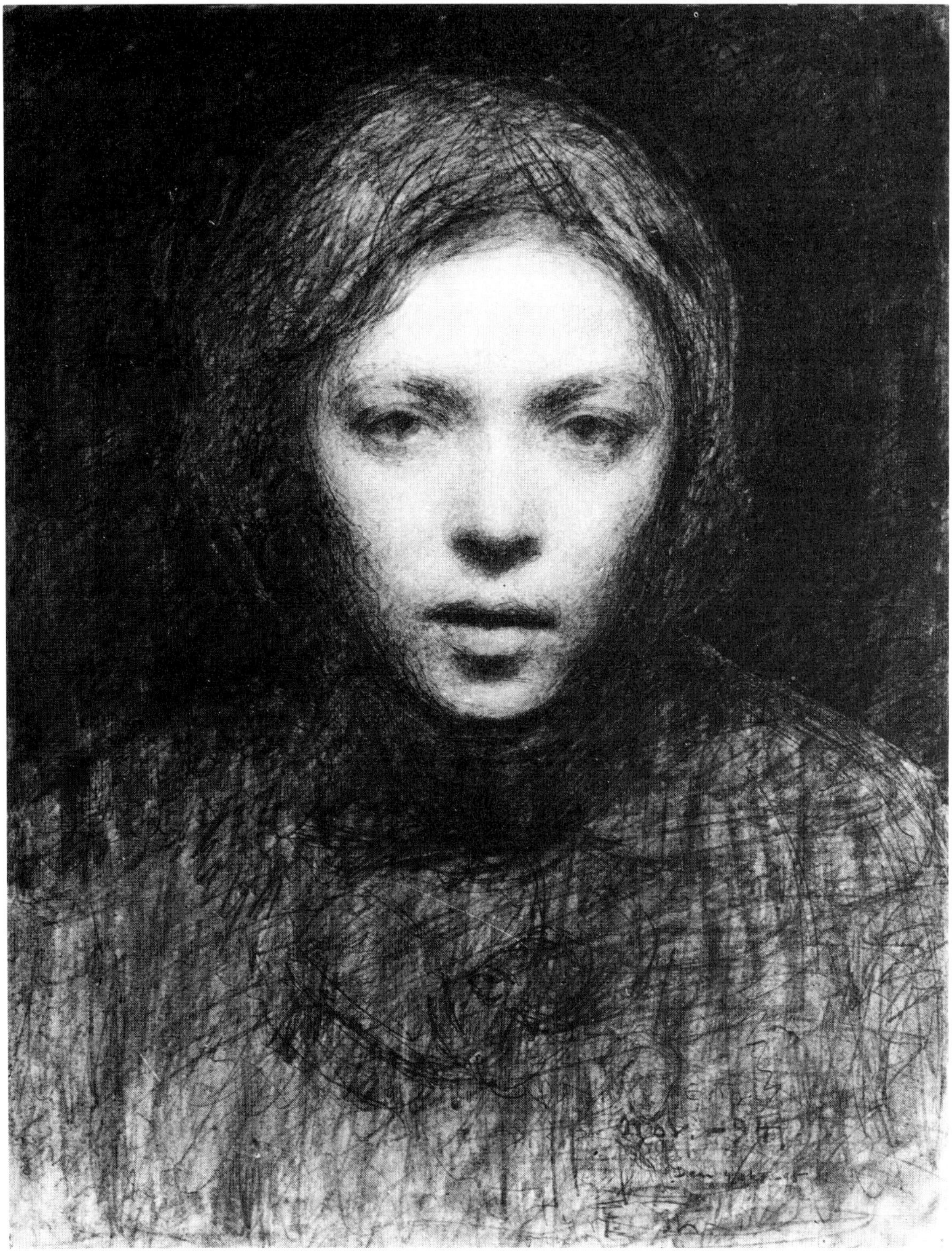

97. Ellen Thesleff

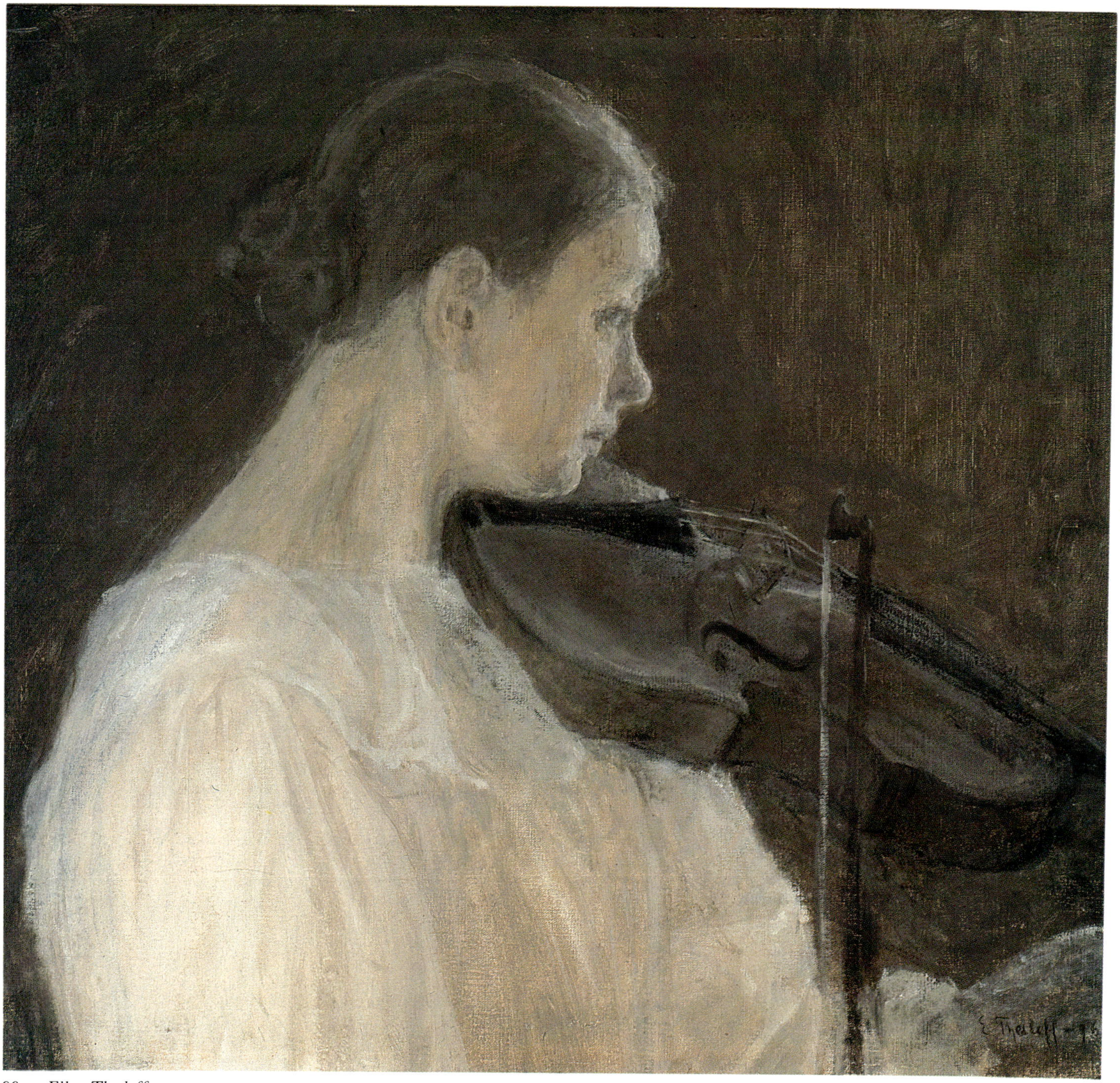

98. Ellen Thesleff

98

The Violin Player, 1896

(Viulunsoittajatar)

40 × 43
Signed lower right: E Thesleff -96
Ateneumin taidemuseo, Helsinki
Inv. no. A II 1488 (purchased in 1922)

One of Symbolism's central precepts was the mutual correspondence of the arts. The highest task of all artists was to interpret the harmony of the universe, which corresponded to the harmony of man's soul. Art had value only to the extent to which it was able to capture this harmony, which touched everything and was universal to all. Music was the highest art form, because of its purity. Therefore painting was at its purest when its form of expression approached that of music, when it was simple, separated from material things, when it had a harmony of line and colour working together in purity. In painting, too, the word *harmony*, not colour, was used.

In the last decades of the nineteenth century, women artists held an exceptionally important place in Finnish art. Their sensitivity and natural instinct suited the spiritualist expression of the 1890s. Magnus Enckell understood this. In the 1890s he observed that something quite new had come into art with women, a new view, a new sensitivity, a new way of feeling. Its inner being was closer to music than traditional art: lovely like music, simple, in a word, great art. 'You understand, it's not ladies' art, but women's art,' he wrote to his friend Yrjö Hirn, the aesthetician, in 1893. This general description suits all Ellen Thesleff's art, the opal-shimmering harmonies of the 1890s just as well as the later colourism. She used music as her subject, too, either a musician as here, or direct musical themes, such as Chopin's Waltz, Barcarolle, and Bird Fantasy among others.

S.S–K.

THÓRARINN B. THORLÁKSSON

(ÞÓRARINN B. ÞORLÁKSSON)

1867–1924, Iceland

Thórarinn B. Thorláksson was the son of a provincial Lutheran minister from a well-known clerical family. He was five years old when his father died and subsequently grew up with his elder brothers, a country pastor and a farmer. At the age of 18 he moved to the capital city of Reykjavík to study bookbinding.

From childhood Thorláksson had shown a keen interest in drawing, although he had no direct experience of art. His arrival in Reykjavík coincided with the first exhibition of works from the National Gallery of Iceland, at that time mainly comprising works by well-known contemporary Danish artists. His artistic inclination and the influence of these works led him to seek instruction in drawing. In 1889 he travelled to Copenhagen to complete his studies in bookbinding, and there was exposed to the stimulating influences of works in Danish galleries. Thereafter he began to paint in oils.

In 1895, when nearly thirty, he gave up a good job to devote himself entirely to art. He left for Copenhagen where he was to spend the next six and a half years studying art, first at the Royal Academy of Fine Arts, and later at the private school run by Harald Frederik Foss. During the summers he painted the Danish landscape. These paintings resemble those of his Danish contemporaries. He was especially taken by the works of the 'Skagen painters', in particular Peter Severin Krøyer. His teachers at the Royal Academy of Fine Arts included J. F. Vermehren and Otto Bache, but he does not seem to have been influenced by them.

In 1900 he held his first one-man exhibition, which was also the first private exhibition of an artist in Iceland. The following year one of his works, *Summer Night on Parliament Plains*, was accepted for the exhibition at Charlottenborg Palace. In addition to landscapes Thórarinn also painted portraits, interiors, still-lifes and altarpieces. However, it was in his landscapes that he attained his peak during his short but productive career as an artist. He also taught drawing at the Technical College in Reykjavík, and later became headmaster there.

During the first two decades of the twentieth century he was the moving force behind artistic life in Iceland, playing a major role in the establishment of the 'Listvinafélag' (Friends of Art Society), which built the first exhibition gallery in the country. Thórarinn's influence as an artist can also be detected in the works of painters of his generation such as Ásgrímur Jónsson, Jón Stefánsson, and Jóhannes Kjarval. Support from friends gave him a better opportunity to practise his art during his latter years, and he continued to develop as an artist to the end of his days. Three years before his death he at last had the opportunity of visiting central Europe, his only visit to the continent outside Denmark. He died at the age of 57 in 1924.

99

Thingvellir (Parliament Plains), 1900

(Þingvellir)

57.5 × 81.5
Signed lower left: Thor. B. Th. 1900.
Listasafn Íslands, Reykjavík
Inv. no. 1051 (purchased in 1956)

In 1900 Thórarinn returned to Iceland for the summer after a five-year absence in Denmark. When he began to paint the Icelandic landscape, his work was quite different from that of his Danish period. He was the first painter to perceive the landscape through the eyes of an Icelander, thereby laying the foundations for modern Icelandic art. To him the land became an image and a symbol, which he painted, not

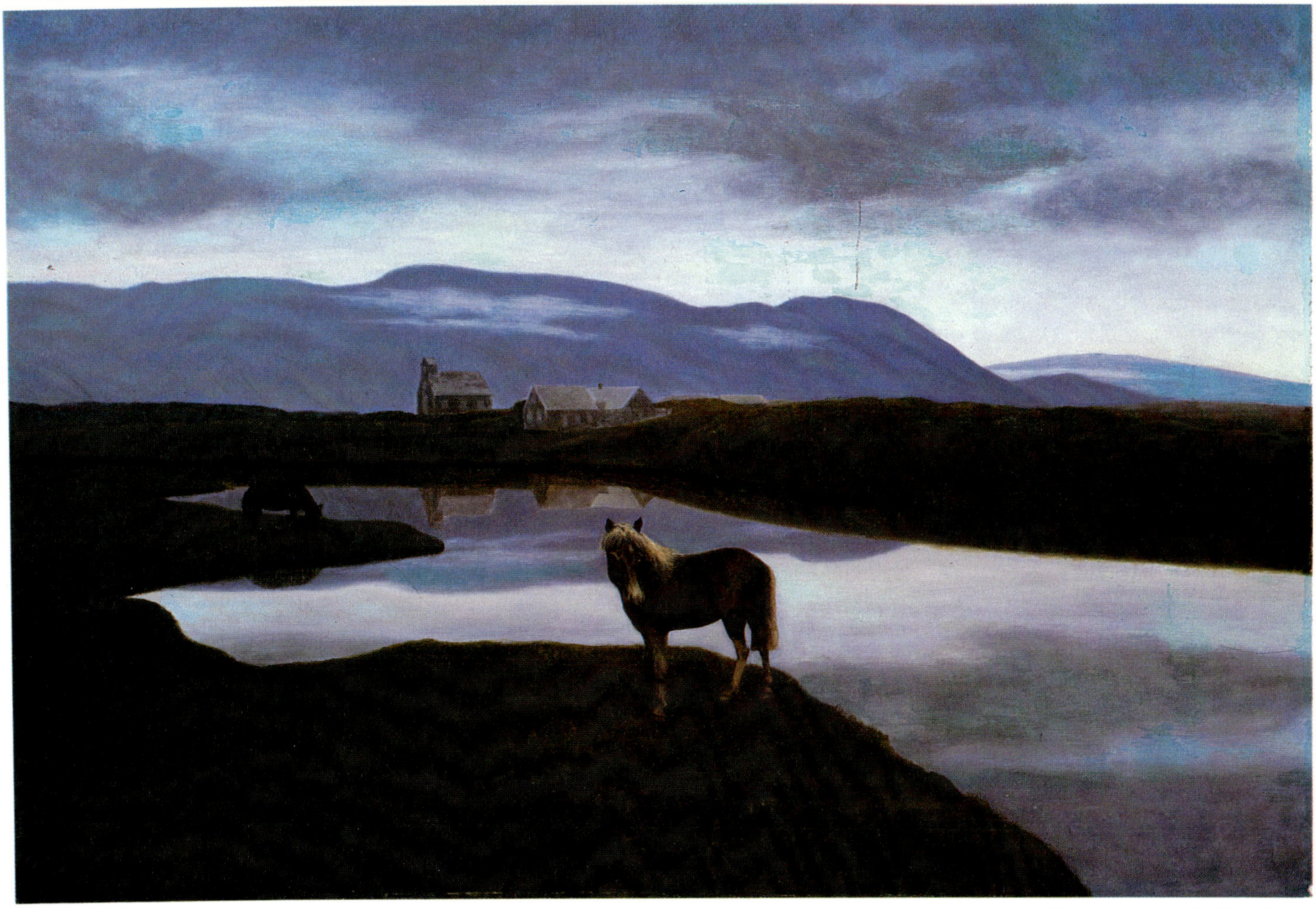

99. Thórarinn B. Thorláksson

in a naturalistic way, although it might appear so at first glance, but rather by adapting the landscape to his own ideas and feelings. In this respect, there is an obvious link between Thórarinn and some of his contemporary Icelandic poets.

For Icelanders, Thingvellir or Parliament Plains has a deep significance. It was here that Iceland's parliament, the symbol of the nation's conscience, was established in 930, and where it was subsequently held for nearly nine centuries. In addition to its rich historical background, the area is one of unique natural beauty.

This painting appears almost abstract in its simplicity. The tranquillity is absolute. Blue in its innumerable variations – from pale whitish-blue through to blackish-blue – dominates the picture and is counterbalanced by solid green interwoven with an almost unvaried brown.

Dawn tinges the eastern skies and in the distance the volcano Skjaldbreidur appears to glow. The clouds are parting for the approaching day. The mountains and the sky are reflected in the placid water. The church and houses, in greyish-blue tones, appear as lifeless objects in this enchanted landscape, but gain light and life in the reflection in the water.

In this magical atmosphere, there are only two living creatures: a black horse in the distance which faces into the picture, and in the middle ground, a reddish horse, facing the viewer. The reddish horse is a key element in the composition as its central position in the picture plane enhances the sense of space.

The relationship between the artist' and his horse gives the work an intimacy without any suggestion of sentimentality.

The painting, so personal and unaffected in its simplicity, reflects the artist's own experience of this spring night at Thingvellir.

S.J.

100

The Large Dímon, 1902

(Stóri Dímon)

24 × 42
Signed lower left: Thor. B. Th. . . . 1902.
Listasafn Íslands, Reykjavík
Inv. no. 86 (acquired in 1915)

In the spring of 1902 Thórarinn returned to settle permanently in his homeland following his years of study in Denmark. That summer he went to the south of the country to paint. The southern lowlands are the most extensive and flattest in Iceland: enormous tracts of black sands, mighty rivers (both milky glacial torrents and clear mountain rivers), sand spits, fields and meadows surrounded by mountains and glaciers to the north and the Atlantic Ocean to the south. The sense of space is enormous.

It was this vast landscape which Thórarinn chose as his subject on his return home. The painting *The Large Dímon* is from this area, deriving its title from a well-known mountain. It is a small work painted from one of the most beautiful and fertile spots in the region. But it was not the beautiful and intimate countryside which he chose to paint; instead he looked out towards the sea. The eponymous mountain appears to be nothing more than a rocky outcrop in these immeasurable expanses.

The green fields are interrupted by a dark green band which lies across the entire picture. It is thinnest and lightest to the left, but suddenly broadens and is drawn upwards at an angle and then all the way across the surface of the picture to the right. Within this green band, to the right of centre, is a brown wall which slopes down and away at an angle. It is some kind of a sod wall with a gate, which is delineated at the bottom by a pencil-fine white line, a stream which then meanders on outside the green band.

The fields continue until met by yellowish marshes where horses are grazing. The minute size of the horses helps to emphasize the sense of space and the size of the mountain. Beyond the marshes are the intertwining mountain waters of the river Thverá.

In the distance the glacial river Markarfljót runs directly across the picture, and on the far side the land rises mirage-like. In this bluish haze the river banks stand high and the farms appear as cities with towering palaces and houses. The river seems an ocean, and all the land beyond the mountain becomes a wondrous world which dances and twinkles in the haze. Over this perfectly flat, shimmering land soars a light blue sky with faint white clouds drawn with extremely fine soft brushstrokes into a long and fluffy white-blue mass. Except for the mountain, everything in these bright, light expanses is horizontal.

S.J.

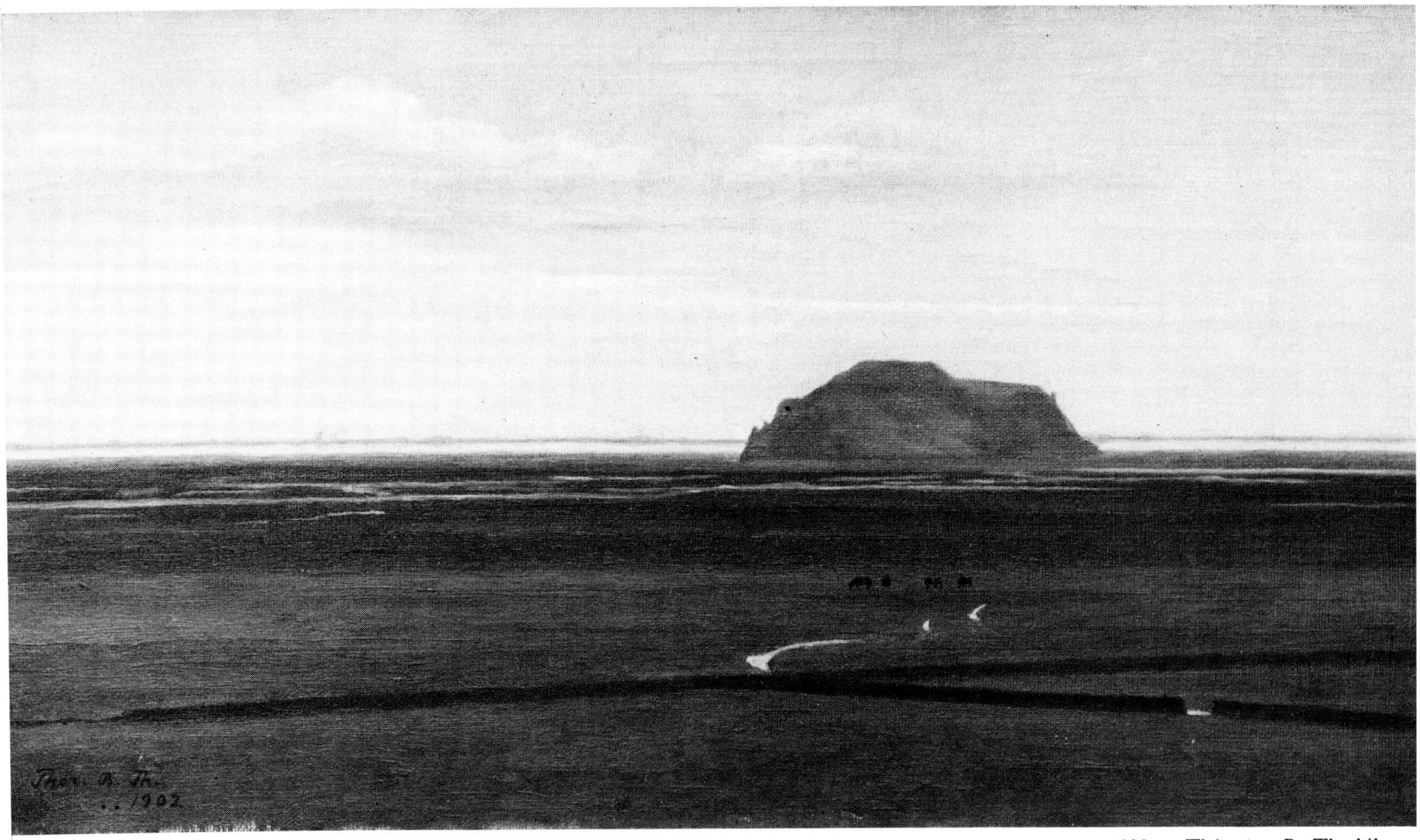

100. Thórarinn B. Thorláksson

101

Eyjafjalla Glacier, 1903

(Eyjafjallajökull)

93 × 120
Signed lower left: Thor. B. Th. 1903.
Hilmar Gardarsson, Seltjarnarnesi

Several foreign artists had visited Iceland during the nineteenth century and painted the Icelandic landscape, but they all shared a perception of the country as a peculiar natural phenomenon. Thórarinn, however, painted the country as seen by an Icelander, with reverence for its beauty, tranquillity and crystal-clear air. This was his own country, and its wealth of colours were to him unequalled in their variety; nowhere was the grass as green or the air as clear. He painted the country in the gentle embrace of spring or summer, by day and by night.

This immensely rugged, treeless land with its glaciers, mountains, waterfalls and contorted lava plains, became in his eyes one continuously beautiful and balmy summer's day of vast spaces and clear colours. In his interpretations, the mountains and glaciers became distant and enchanted, not cold, naked and rough.

Thórarinn sees Eyjafjallajökull, the towering snow-covered volcano, with gentle and colourful approach slopes in light greens, browns and purples which become bluer higher up until eventually capped by the thick white glacier itself, with its interwoven pale blues. It is difficult to discern precisely where the sky begins, for the top of the glacier merges with thick blue-white wispy clouds. This play of colours is contrasted with the expansive foreground composed of a thick green mass in tonal variations from dark green to yellowish. On the left of the picture soft, rounded grass slopes stretch far up into the bluish snow as though they were a part of the glacier. But the slopes fall away to the right and form a shallow vale through which the glacial river Markarfljót can be glimpsed where it flows through stretches of level ground in colours of brown and blue and emphasizes the vast distance between the green banks and the glacier. The green banks slope down to be met by a smaller rising bank.

Thus the artist has attempted to express both the powerful presence of the glacier and its inaccessibility; veiled by distance, it remains beyond human reach. The glacier becomes an image of dignity, intangibility and divinity for Thórarinn: it almost merges with the heavens.

In this painting there is no visible sign of any living creature; the natural state of the country is unblemished. Nothing living may disturb the peace and sanctity which the artist experienced at the time the picture was painted. This attitude of reverence is characteristic of his feelings for the land as expressed in most of his works.

Thórarinn was of a gregarious and cheerful disposition but in in the presence of nature he tended to retreat into himself and from the deep experience of this solitude he painted the glorious world of colour and form which he saw there. It was only when his work was completed that others were allowed to see the painting and share his world.

S.J.

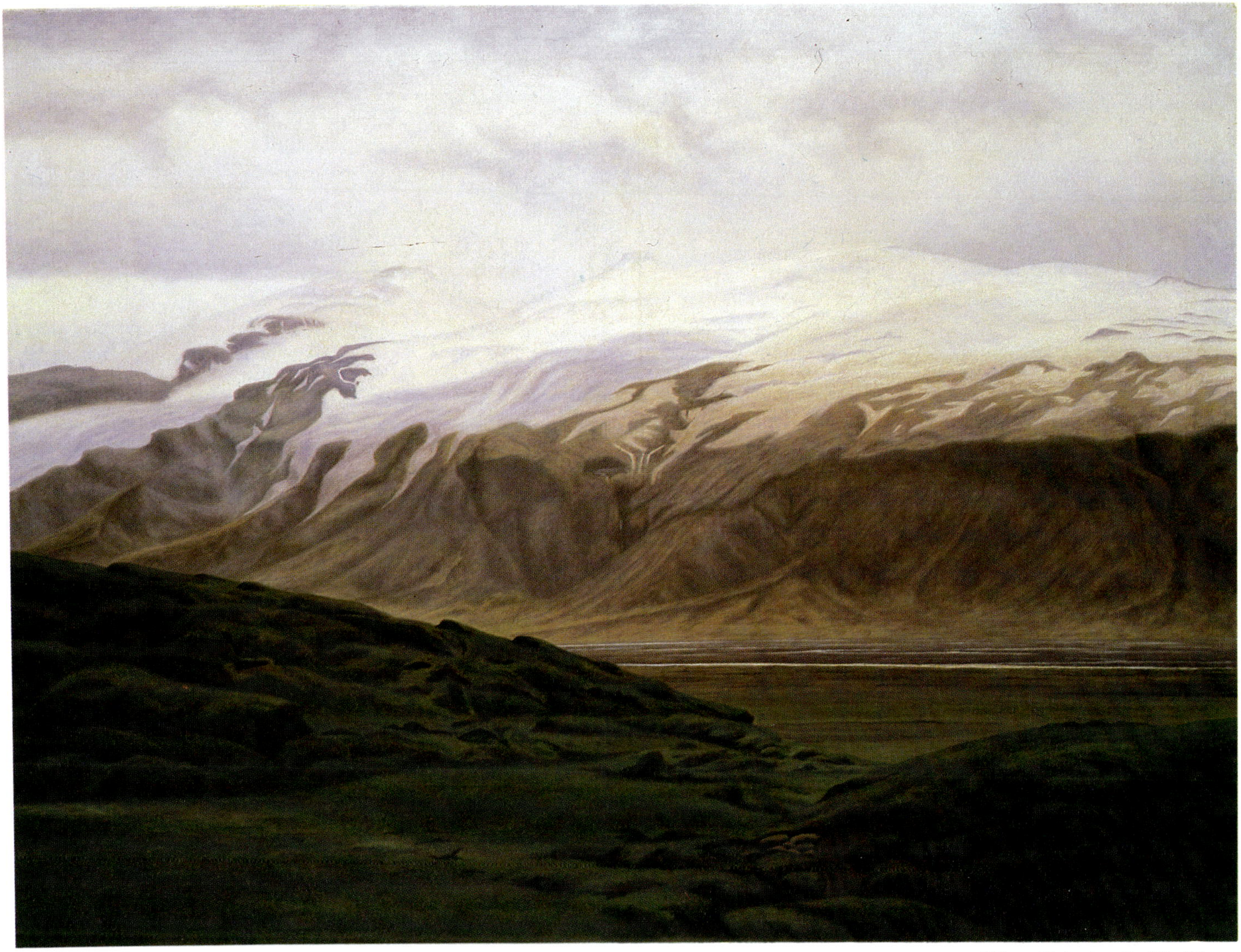

101. Thórarinn B. Thorláksson

102

Sunset by the Lake, 1905

(Sólarlag við Tjörnina)

79 × 125
Signed lower left: 19þþ05
Sverrir Thórdarson, Reykjavík

The Lake is Reykjavík's natural gem. The city also boasts a horizon of beautiful mountain ranges presided over by the mountain Esja in its continually changing cloak of colours. But the Lake lends a charm to the city centre.

This is one of Thórarinn's most singular works. An autumn evening in the city. Not a person to be seen, not a light in a window. An absolute peace reigns over this beautiful autumn evening at sunset. Here again, Thórarinn is interpreting the Icelandic landscape in his own personal way. The skies glow, mainly in yellow colours, from a pale yellow to a red which illuminates the dark red-purple banks of clouds. Dark houses of varying heights and sizes jut up into this glowing colour spectrum, and the church's spire towers heavenwards and breaks up the horizontal composition of the picture. The artist has thereby achieved a perfect balance within the picture. The houses and spire stretch clean-cut up into the sky, but the reflected outlines are softly blurred. The sky's reflection in the Lake is in a darker colour and this helps to increase the charged atmosphere of this enchanted evening.

Occasionally the reflections of the houses in the Lake stretch almost across to the other bank and the church spire disappears under the eastern bank. The houses and their reflections merge into a darkish mass so that the wide street along the Lake disappears. The eastern banks are of the same colour as the mass of houses.

The absence of living beings is particularly striking. Even in the city the landscape itself is so sacred to him that no human being may intrude. Here the beauty of the skies alone reigns supreme.

S.J.

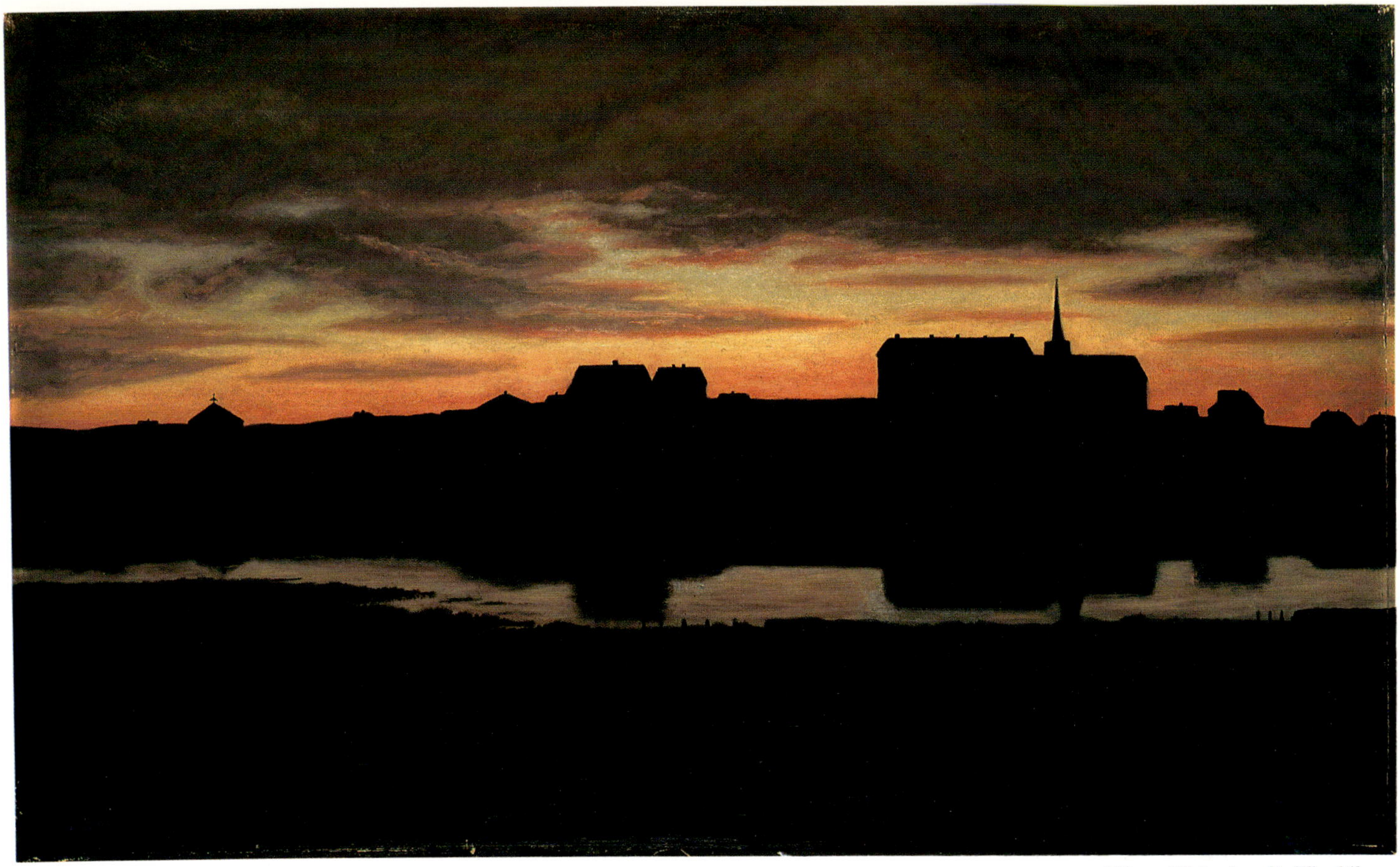

102. Thórarinn B. Thorláksson

ERIK WERENSKIOLD

1855–1938, Norway

After a brief period of study at the Royal School of Drawing in Christiania, Werenskiold set out for Munich in 1875 to join the large colony of Norwegian art students there. At the academy he studied under Løfftz and Lindenschmit, but became dissatisfied with the old-master style of painting they cultivated. He felt drawn instead towards the naturalistic trends which appeared about that time and his interest was particularly aroused by the new French art at the great international exhibition in Munich in 1878. Prevented by an illness from leaving for Paris immediately, he only arrived there in 1881 and stayed two years. Like other contemporary Scandinavian artists in Paris, he was attracted to the French naturalists and *plein-air* painters, especially Jules Bastien-Lepage, but he also had contact with the Impressionists, and wrote an article about them as early as 1882.

In Norwegian art Werenskiold represents above all the national tradition, a tradition to which he remained firmly committed throughout his long career. This attitude is most clearly expressed in his illustrations to the *Norwegian Fairy-Tales* by Asbjørnsen and Moe (1879–87) and to Snorre's *Sagas of the Norse Kings* (1899). There are marked stages in his stylistic development. In the 1880s he was one of the leading Naturalists and several of his large landscapes have become national symbols in Norwegian art. In the 1890s after renewed studies in Paris, he adapted himself to the 'mood-painting' style of the period. After the turn of the century, he was influenced by the art of Cézanne, and began to place greater emphasis on colour as a medium for light and space-creating effects; greater importance is also given to the decorative elements in the picture.

Not only as an artist but through his strong personality as well, Werenskiold made a lasting impression on the development of Norwegian culture. He was the centre of a group of outstanding artists and intellectuals whose influence was felt far into the twentieth century.

103

Autumn, 1891

(Høst)

120 × 151
Signed lower right: EWerenskiold/1891–
Göteborgs konstmuseum, Gothenburg
Inv. no. 263 (purchased in 1892)

Werenskiold was Norway's leading Naturalist landscape painter during the 1880s and the foremost representative of the national trend in the development of Norwegian art. Along with Kitty Kielland and Eilif Peterssen, he too had participated in the famous 'Fleskum summer' of 1886, but without having assimilated any traces of the new emphasis on sentiment or 'mood' which they sought to convey in their painting. At the time he was more concerned with his illustrations for the Norwegian fairy-tales. Werenskiold's stylistic change occurred later after an extended visit to Paris in 1889.

One of the first pictures in which we can see a new tendency is *Autumn*. Here he moves his viewpoint higher, and in looking down at the subject gives it a new sense of

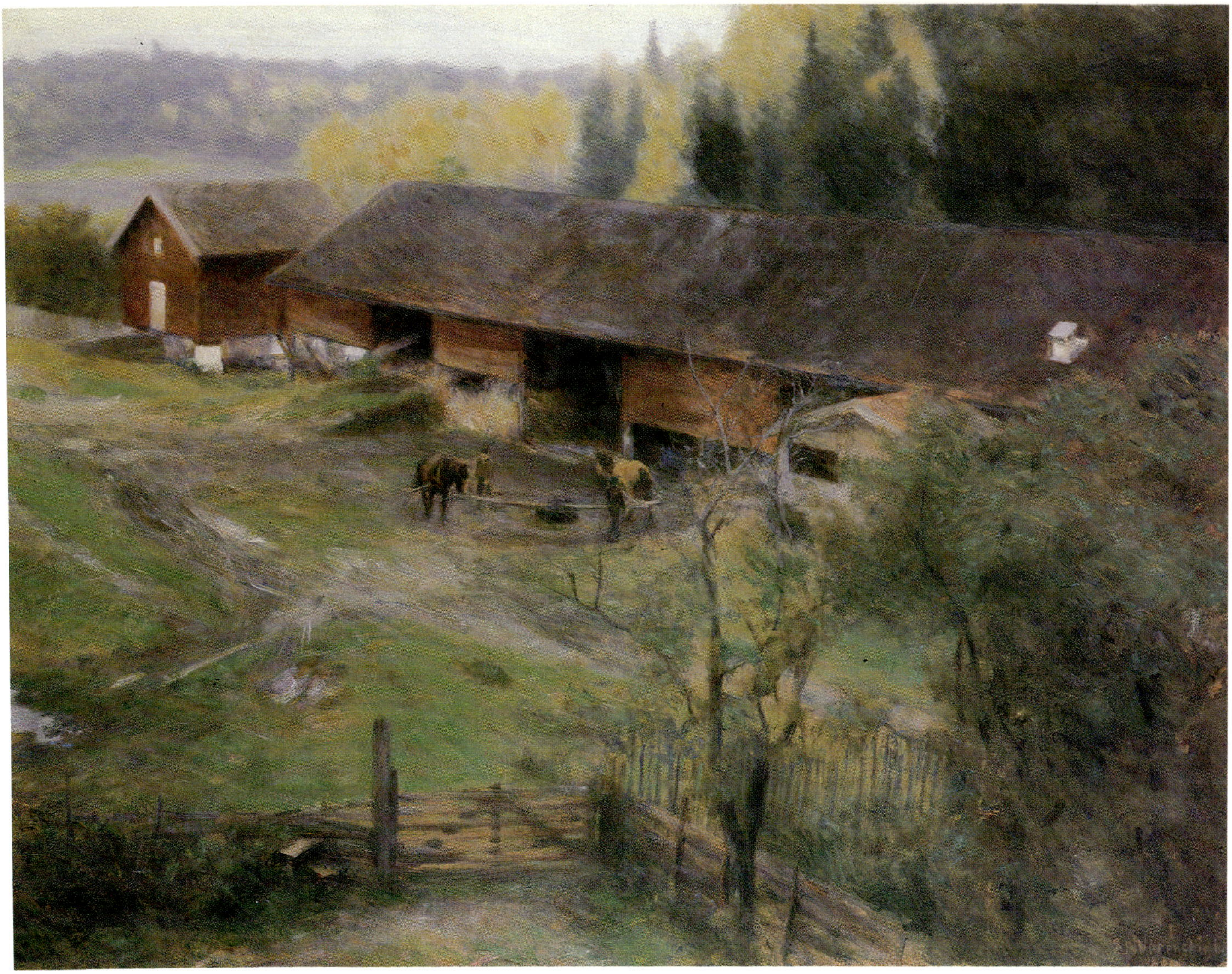

103. Erik Werenskiold

intimacy; the picture becomes an entity within itself. His previous rendering of intense bright daylight is softened, we encounter a lyrical evening mood. The last rays of sunlight envelop the scene in misty tones of colour; sharp contours are blurred, colours merge into fine and delicate nuances. Against the soft fresh green of the fields, the hazy blue of the background, and the autumn yellow of the leaves, the delicately attuned red of the barn gives life and vitality to the picture. No strong accents of colour are allowed to disturb the harmony. This picture represents a new stage in Werenskiold's stylistic development.

K.B.

104

Summer Evening at Kviteseid, 1893

(Sommeraften i Kviteseid)

79 × 100
Signed lower right: 1893. E. Werenskiold.
Nasjonalgalleriet, Oslo
Inv. no. 904 (donated in 1909)

Kviteseid is one of the innermost, isolated valleys of Telemark County, where for centuries time stood still. Telemark was a part of Norway to which Werenskiold often returned and where he found the subject-matter for many of his most outspoken 'national' pictures. It was here especially that he found inspiration for the landscapes and characters of his fairy-tale illustrations.

During his studies in Paris in 1889 Werenskiold had become acquainted with the new trends in French art. With renewed interest and better understanding, he familiarized himself with the art of the Impressionists and Neo-Impressionists; he studied Gauguin and the Pont Aven school at their exhibition that year. He was also interested in the work of Puvis de Chavannes, then popular among Norwegian artists. The first example of his reorientation can be seen in *Autumn*; with *Summer Evening at Kviteseid*, this new lyrical romantic style had found its form.

The subject is simple, a dun and a sorrel horse graze beneath leafy boughs in the twilight on the shore of a tranquil lake. An imposing mountain rises in the background. The whole picture is permeated with peace and quiet, an idyll of a Nordic summer evening.

The composition is organized in large areas and rendered with a decorative effect new in Norwegian art. The influence of Gauguin is apparent, but Werenskiold differs from the French artist in that the forms are not delineated by firm contours. They are more diffuse, and the areas of colour dissolve into a spectrum of nuances achieved by small precise brushstrokes that make the forms vibrate, a result of his studies of the Impressionists. This creates a distinctive soft atmosphere which emphasizes the lyrical and harmonious mood of the picture.

K.B.

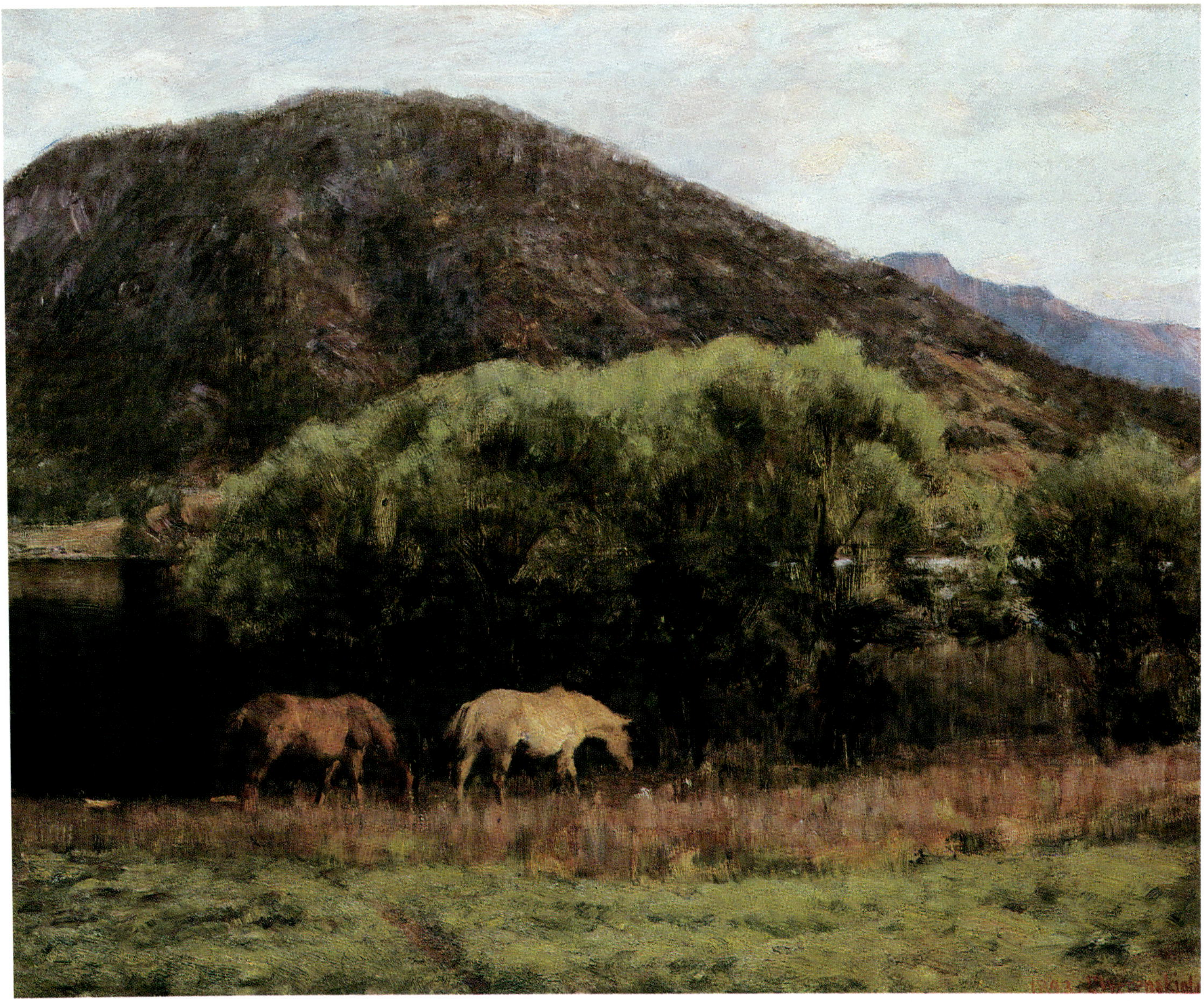

104. Erik Werenskiold

105

Portrait of Henrik Ibsen, 1895

(Portrett av Henrik Ibsen)

121.2 × 71.5
Signed lower left: E. Werenskiold. 1895.
Nasjonalgalleriet, Oslo
Inv. no. 101 (purchased in 1896)

As a portrait painter Werenskiold left a lasting impression on Norwegian art. With penetrating characterization and psychological empathy he portrayed most of the leading men and women in the Norwegian social and cultural life of the day. He had particularly close contacts with the literary world and among his many portraits of authors, the one of Ibsen is the best known.

The picture was originally intended as a study for a larger painting and is executed in what can be called a grisaille technique, where only the face is precisely defined. Werenskiold realized that in this sketch he had succeeded in interpreting the Ibsen he intended to portray, so the planned large painting was never executed.

Ibsen stands imposingly in the foreground, hands behind his back, aloof, almost unapproachable. His white hair and beard fluff halo-like about his head; behind the spectacles, one eye is slightly contracted, accentuating the sharp piercing look, a look that focuses the whole picture and which with the firm tight-lipped mouth gives a congenial portrayal of his creative willpower and penetrating vision. The background merely suggests a landscape: at the left are a few simple houses and a lake in a valley, behind Ibsen rise the contours of a mighty mountain, leading our gaze towards a snowy mountain plateau. Werenskiold said that the picture was inspired by Ibsen's poem 'On the heights'. The last verse of this poem perhaps best expresses what the artist intended to convey in this portrait of Ibsen:

> Now I am steel; for the hills I am shod;
> To the mountain-call I rally!
> The last of my lowland path is trod;
> Up here on the fells must be freedom and God,
> Men do but grope, in the valley.

(Tr. F. E. Garrett, London 1912)
K.B.

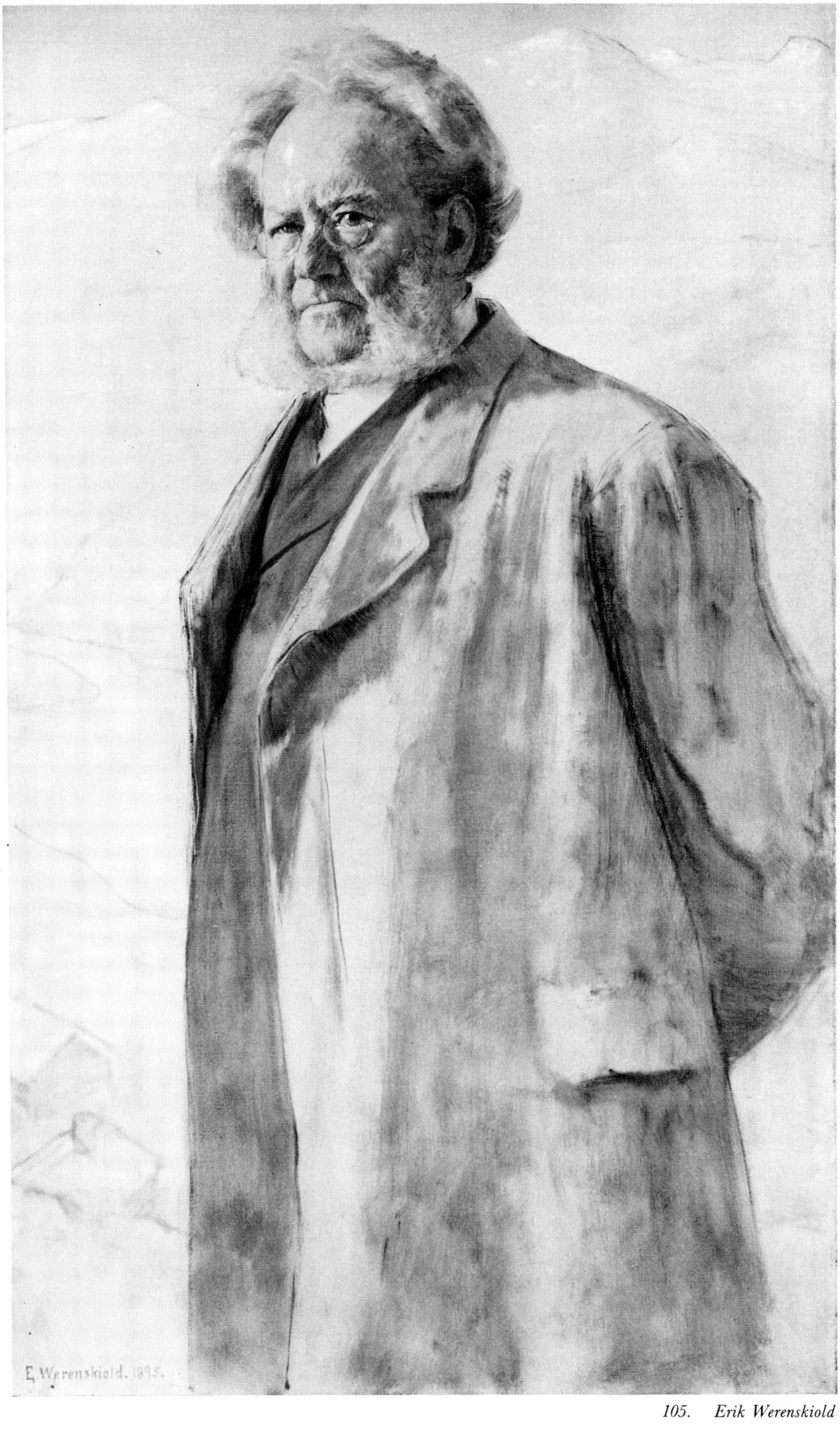

105. Erik Werenskiold

CARL WILHELMSON

1866–1928, Sweden

Carl Wilhelmson was born in the little fishing village of Fiskebäckskil in the province of Bohuslän on the west coast of Sweden. This harsh environment, with its cycle of poverty and unremitting toil, was to provide the main subject-matter for his paintings.

At the age of 15, Wilhelmson began work as a lithography apprentice at a printing works in Gothenburg. He also attended the Valand art school, under Carl Larsson. In 1890, Wilhelmson travelled to Paris, where he attended the Académie Julian. Even though he was influenced by contemporary French painting, he did not adopt features of Post-Impressionism and Synthetism in his own painting until he had returned to Sweden for good in 1896.

Wilhelmson's personal style, which marked both a clear break with Realism in its '80s form and a rejection of the National Romanticism of the '90s, made its first appearance in *Fishermen's Wives on Their Way Home From Church*, 1899. It has the terse monumentality and the clear palette which were to characterize Wilhelmson's painting in the future.

From 1897 to 1904 Wilhelmson was director of the Valand art school. In 1910, he opened his own art school in Stockholm, and in the '20s became a teacher at the Royal Academy of Fine Arts. His subjects in the 1910s and '20s were taken from Lapland, Spain, and Cornwall, as well as from Bohuslän. He also undertook a large number of portraits and monumental commissions.

106

On the Rocks at Fiskebäckskil, 1905–6

(På berget, Fiskebäckskil)

126 × 151
Signed lower right: C. Wilhelmson
Göteborgs konstmuseum, Gothenburg
Inv. no. 402 (purchased in 1908)

Like Karl Nordström, Wilhelmson depicted his own home district in the province of Bohuslän on the west coast of Sweden. Nordström was mainly concerned with the magnificent, treeless rocky landscape by the sea. For Wilhelmson, man was the main theme, though preferably in an interplay with the landscape.

Right from the beginning, Wilhelmson's pictures aimed to depict his subject clearly and truly. From the end of the 1890s, however, his style became more monumental. Under the influence of Post-Impressionist painting, Wilhelmson emphasized the surface and his pictures take on a slightly geometrical character. Colours are often strong and clear without destroying the serious overall impression. The pigment is strikingly dry and is applied to the light ground without completely covering it, so that both the canvas and the ground lend their character to the painting.

On the Rocks at Fiskebäckskil is characteristic of Wilhelmson's work. Like most of his picture, it shows the people and the landscape of Bohuslän, a landscape which is both barren and magnificent. A kind of Sunday peace and silence prevail. The people bear traces of their drudgery, but they also have a dignity. Wilhelmson might have seen this dignity in the peasants of Millet or Jules Breton, but he has given it a more stringent, less romantic form. He neither manipulates nor romanticizes the life of the people. He depicts his own milieu, people whom he knows. In *On the Rocks at Fiskebäckskil* two sea captains, a mariner and a fisherman, have gone up on the rocks to see the sun set over the sea. They sit meditatively side by side, immobile, looking for the crucial signs that bode fair weather or foul.

T.G.

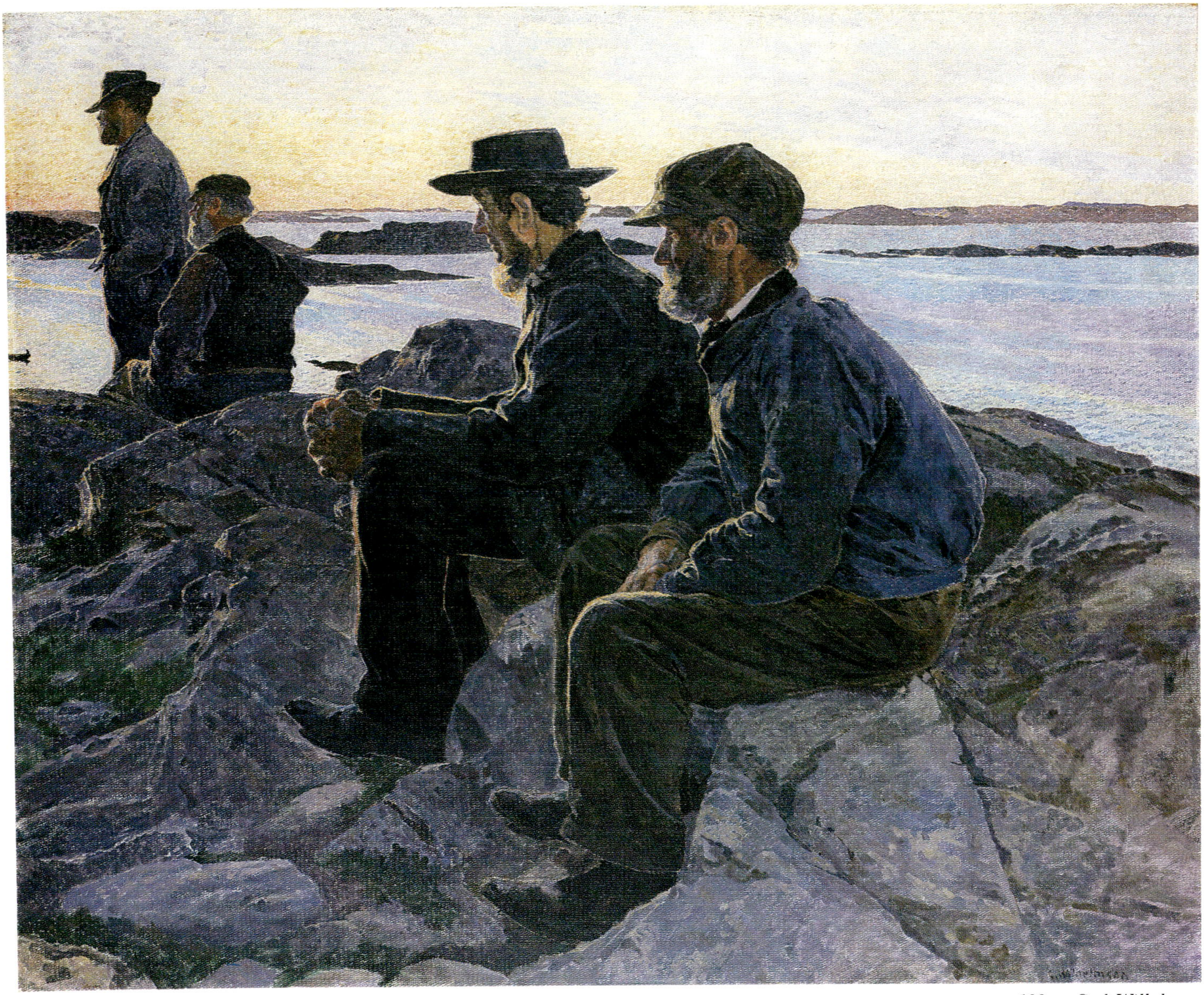

106. Carl Wilhelmson

JENS FERDINAND WILLUMSEN

1863–1958, Denmark

Willumsen was accepted at the Royal Academy of Fine Arts in Copenhagen in 1881 and at the same time took the Technical School's house construction course, which he passed in 1882. He attended the Academy's Model School from 1883 to 1885 and also visited the Artists' Study School. He worked as a painter, graphic artist, craftsman, and architect.

The success of the Bing & Grøndahl porcelain company at the Paris World Fair in 1900 was due to his contributions as artistic director. He also designed the building and lighting of the Free Exhibition, of which he was a founding member.

Like Rohde and Slott-Møller (p. 252), Willumsen began as a Naturalist with a tendency towards pessimistic Realism; the pictures from his first sojourn in Paris in 1888 still show this point of departure. He was in Paris again from 1890 to 1894 and met Gauguin in Brittany the first summer. However, he had already had an opportunity, both in Copenhagen and in Paris, to see works by Gauguin and had come into contact with other Symbolist circles, especially those around Maurice Denis and Odilon Redon (Merete Bodelsen). The question is whether what he saw actually served as a model or merely provided inspiration for his own artistic personality.

Gauguin's wood-carvings and polychrome ceramics did have a direct influence on him, but it was Gauguin's personality that was most important for Willumsen at the time. As regards his artistic independence and his work with polychrome sculpture and mixed media, it is interesting that the only Danish critic who completely understood him, Emil Hannover, reproduced and described in detail the bust of a young Greek woman in *Taarnet* (December 1893). Another Danish art historian, Francis Beckett, in June 1894, also in *Taarnet*, discussed Klinger's *Salome*, which had just been completed and had been exhibited in Berlin in the winter.

Willumsen did not seek a lyrical, decorative style. Of primary importance for him was the poetic motive, and the philosophical. Carlyle's *Sartor Resartus* was of decisive influence in this respect (Bodelsen).

Like Hammershøi (p. 122), Willumsen went his own way. Both were indebted to European art but both had a highly personal and individual contribution to make. Neither created a school, which is interesting since both were innovators.

107

After the Tempest, 1905

(Efter stormen)

Tempera and oil on canvas, 155.5 × 150
Signed lower right: J.F.W./. 1905.
Nasjonalgalleriet, Oslo
(purchased in 1913)

At the end of the 1890s, Willumsen was occupied by the applied arts. When he resumed painting after the turn of the century, he left behind the Symbolism of the preceding decade. He now developed a highly personal means of expression, an expressionism which corresponded with the often intense spiritual content of his pictures. During a stay in Pompeii, the casts of the volcano's victims, frozen in their death throes, made a deep impression on him. They showed him the terrible power of nature. They also made him aware yet again of the problem of movement. A modelled sketch for the figures in *After the Tempest* (Statens Museum for Kunst, inv. no. 5724) can be seen in this light (Poul Vad).

The tempest at sea, the shipwreck against the cliffs, is a theme well known from the Romantic painters Caspar David Friedrich and I. C. Dahl, whose paintings also have a symbolic content. Willumsen's picture is not realistic. It is a glaring yellow. A

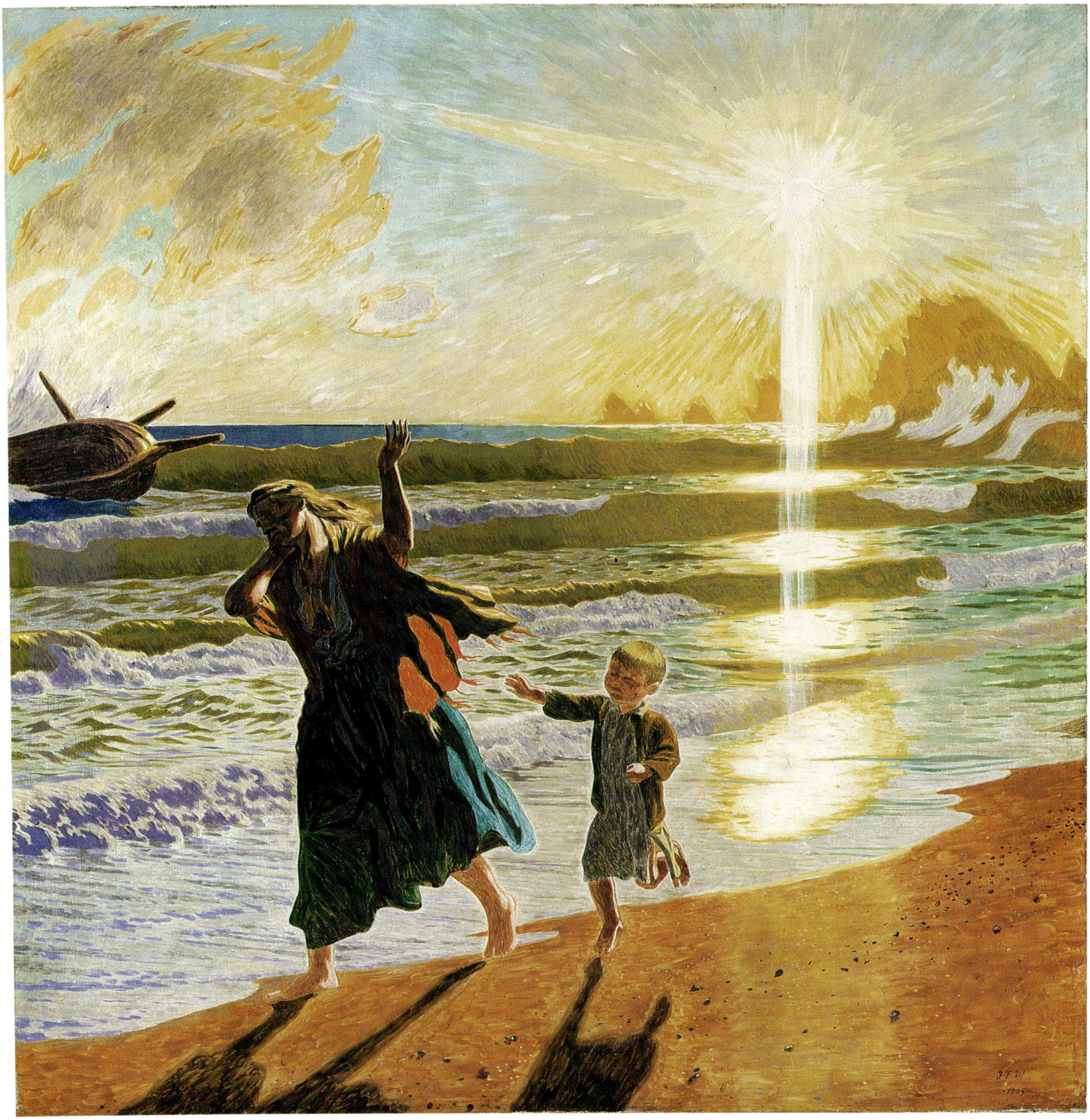

107. Jens Ferdinand Willumsen

woman is seen running along the beach crying, followed by an uncomprehending child. In the strangely frozen waves of the surf lies a capsized ship. In the background are rocks, pointed like icebergs or jagged teeth. The whole scene is bathed in a merciless light from the sun's long white rays. Nature itself is the threatening element, which crushes the woman and the child.

After the Tempest was shown in the Berlin Secession in 1906, the Free Exhibition, Copenhagen in 1908, and in Brighton in 1912.

H.W.

ANDERS ZORN

1860–1920, Sweden

Anders Zorn was the illegitimate son of a peasant woman from Dalarna and an immigrant brewer from Germany, and was brought up by his grandparents in Mora in Dalarna. He displayed a precocious talent for drawing and was admitted to the preparatory class at the Stockholm Academy of Fine Arts at the age of 15. Unhappy with the out-dated discipline demanded of him, he left the Academy in 1881 to embark upon an international career. He soon became the most cosmopolitan of all Scandinavian artists. Initially he lived mainly in London and then in Paris from 1888 to 1896, but he also travelled widely in Spain, Italy, the Balkans and North Africa. On a number of occasions he visited the United States, where his sitters included three Presidents and prominent figures from the world of business. Zorn always spent his summers in Sweden, and in 1896 he decided to settle permanently in Mora. He built his own house (now the Zornmuséet) in the 'old Scandinavian' style, completing it in 1913, and actively encouraged the revival of old local customs.

Although he had originally devoted himself almost exclusively to watercolours, he abandoned this medium in 1887–90 and began to paint in oils. From this point onwards he restricted himself to three main themes: portraits, nudes and genre scenes set in his home province. He also became famous for his etchings, many of which reproduced his paintings, and executed several sculptures.

Zorn's largest retrospective was held at Durand-Ruel in 1906.

His autobiographical notes were published by Brummer in 1982.

108

The Large Brewery, 1890

(Stora bryggeriet)

68 × 100
Signed lower right: Zorn 1890
Göteborgs konstmuseum, Gothenburg
Inv. no. 1839 (donated in 1970)

Zorn executed a series of interior views of breweries during his stay in Stockholm in 1890. The present example shows women sorting the labels that will be put on the bottles on the right; the woman in the centre is pouring beer from a barrel into bottles, and her neighbours are corking bottles. The artist had obviously made a careful study of the monotonous and unhealthy work that went on in the breweries of the time, and he portrayed it with a veracity that borders on social realism. Although Zorn did not share the socialist ideas of fellow artists like Bergh and Larsson, he made no secret of his humble origins. His *Breweries* series has led to his being compared to Strindberg, who had published his autobiographical novel *The Son of a Servant* a few years earlier (1886–7; trans. Claud Field, London, Rider 1913; Brunius and Reutersward 1979, chapter 7). Zorn himself writes:

> This time, it must have been approaching autumn, I went out to study my fellow countrywomen at their hard work in the breweries, probably mostly driven to it by my mother's example. When she was young, she had gone out to help support the family, and in Uppsala worked in the Svartbäck Brewery, where the man who was to give me life was master brewer. Something of all this, in addition to these brewery interiors, with their damp mist of warm rinsing water, wet floors and the mystical light – gaslight and daylight vying for supremacy – and the Dalecarlian girls' shining oilcloth aprons, and bare, powerful arms which put those of the brewery men to shame, and then the different headcoverings from different parishes back home.

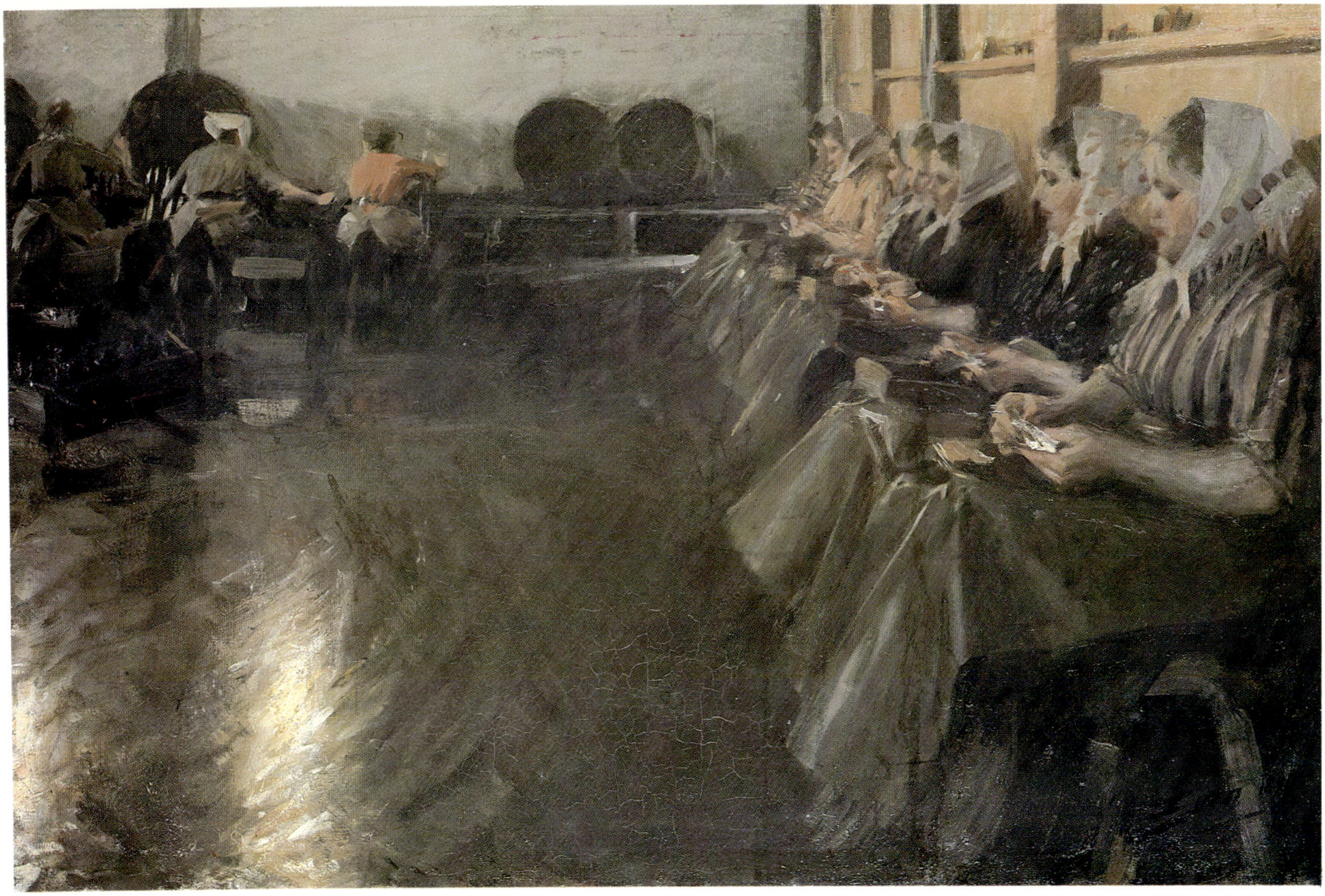

108. Anders Zorn

As with many artists, Zorn's moral and ideological preoccupations were inextricably bound up with his artistic preoccupations. It is obvious that the manual labour and the handicrafts which he often chose for his subject-matter meant a great deal to him, but it is equally obvious that it was the light and space of the breweries that caught the painter's eye. In *The Large Brewery*, he uses a technique which often reappears in his work and which has affinities with the paintings of his friend Max Liebermann. The composition is structured around a broad diagonal; the figures are pushed to the side and into the background, and the centre is occupied by a broad empty expanse of floor, with the wet bitumen reflecting the light. The subdued light filtering into the damp cellar also provides Zorn with the opportunity to play on a restricted range of soft yellow, brownish and greenish tones. The only spot of pure colour is the bright red in the left background.

P.G.

109

Mora Fair, 1892

(Mora marknad)

133 × 167.5
Signed lower left: 1892 / Zorn
Town Council, Mora

Towards the end of the nineteenth century, many artists began to feel a need to return to their roots. For Anders Zorn, that meant going back to his small home town of Mora. Throughout his cosmopolitan career he had gone there to work almost every summer, and in 1896 he settled there for good. *Mora Fair* was painted in 1892 and its church tower can be seen in the background. The painting stands out from the rest of his *oeuvre* because of the unusual dimensions chosen for a genre scene.

In *Autobiographical Notes* (Brummer 1982, p. 76), Zorn describes the subject-matter as follows:

> I had no intention of sermonizing but I did want to stick to the truth, and the man lying dead drunk in the foreground is obviously part of the truth. So is his wife, who is waiting patiently with his hat in her hand for him to be sober enough for them to go home. The groups in the background are quite typical of those one often saw at the fair in Mora. Some peasants from Orsa are paying court to the girls or getting drunk. Someone has acquired a new horse and is putting it through its paces. My grandmother is going home with a cow she has been unable to sell. This painting was admired, and I am glad to have painted the genre at least once.

While he was working on *Mora Fair*, Zorn must have been thinking of Bastien-Lepage's *Les Foins*, the painting which made such an impact on a whole generation of European painters, and not least upon the Scandinavians. Bastien-Lepage combined the 'modern' qualities of a rather Japanese compositional style and free brushwork with social and psychological preoccupations that appealed greatly to painters from the north. Zorn adopts a similar composition: the sky-line is placed high, and greenery invades the greater part of the surface. He too places a sleeping man and a woman watching over him with a vacant stare in the foreground.

The atmosphere of the two paintings is, however, very different. Bastien-Lepage's composition is dominated by the two figures, and attention is centred on the psychology of the peasant woman. In the Swedish painting, it is the mottled, bustling crowd, the lush greenery of summer, and the freshness and vivacity of the brushwork that set the tone. Bastien-Lepage's version of calm and silence gives way to one of bustling figures and rustling grass. A minor incident observed from life and illustrating the drunkenness of men and the resignation of women is integrated into the composition in a quite natural way. In several preparatory sketches Zorn had experimented where to place them in the landscape before he was satisfied with the result. This painting, which is based both on studies of contemporary life and on childhood memories, was exhibited by Zorn in Stockholm in 1892, at the Chicago World Fair in 1893, and at the Salon in Paris in 1894 before he donated it to his home town of Mora in 1905.

P.G.

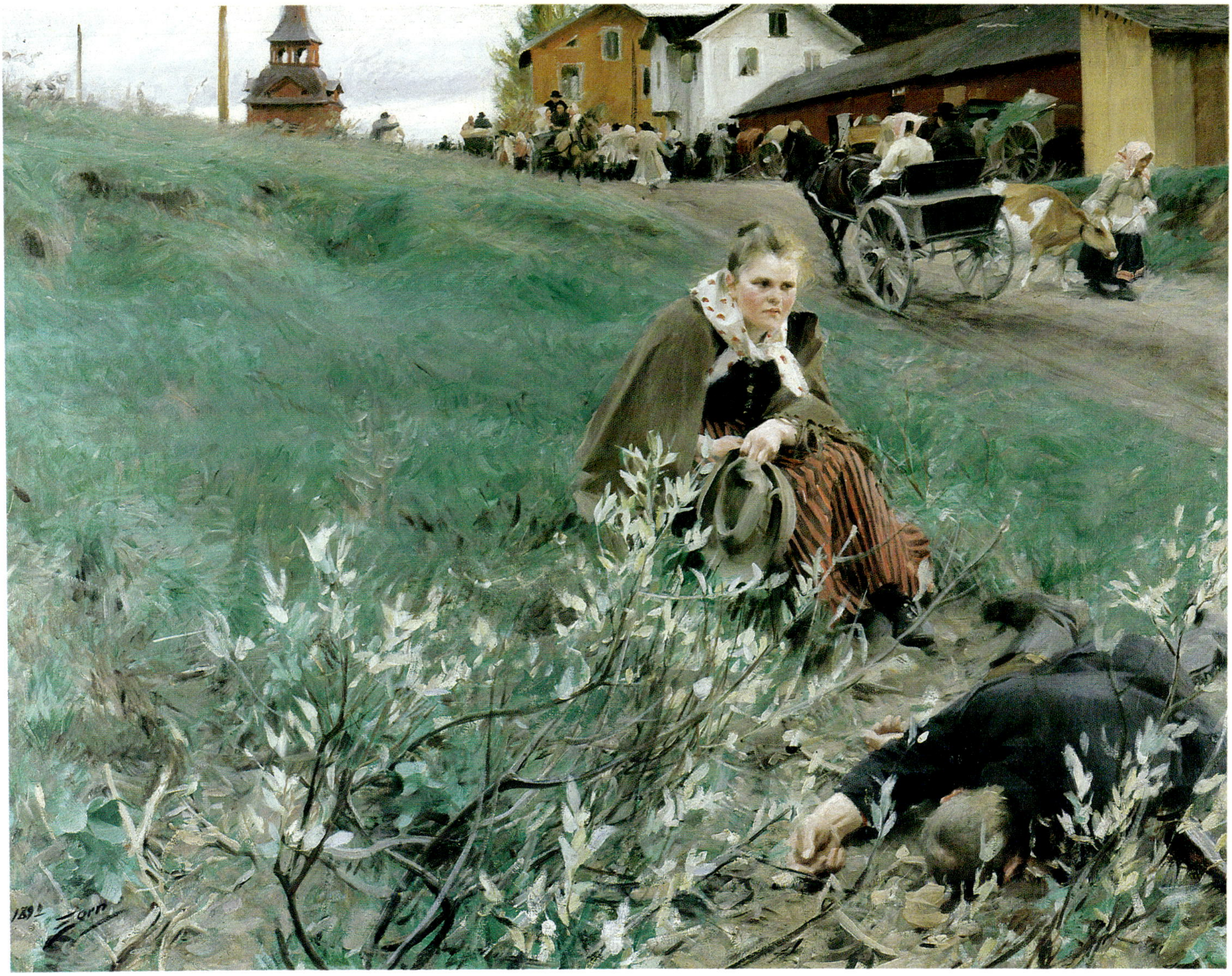

109. Anders Zorn

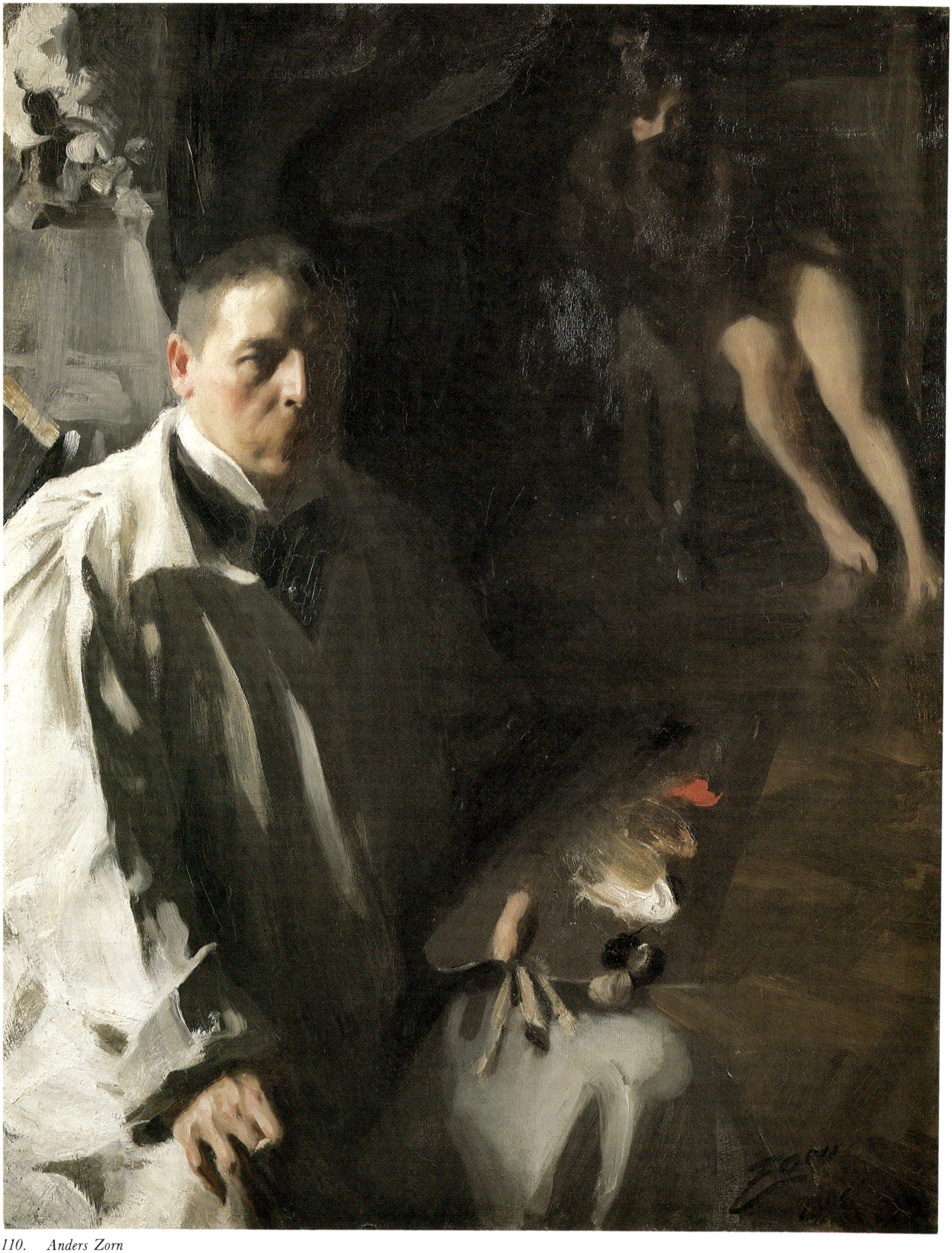

110. Anders Zorn

110

Self-Portrait, 1896

(Självporträtt)

117 × 94
Signed lower right: Zorn / 1896
Nationalmuseum, Stockholm
Inv. no. 1510 (purchased in 1897)

In 1896, Zorn returned to Sweden after having lived in Paris for eight years. Part of the last winter he spent at 71 boulevard de Clichy was devoted to this *Self-Portrait*, which was intended for the Salon du Champ de Mars. He had a great deal of difficulty with the composition, as we can see from a number of preparatory drawings and from a letter to his friend Isabella Stewart Gardner, the famous collector from Boston:

> At the time, my model was a beautiful Italian woman with a very rich head of red hair and, as I wanted to portray myself at work, I included her in the painting. But I painted her on such a large scale that we began to compete for space—I was more interested in her than in myself. For a long time I worked in desperation on my painting without realizing my mistake, and the frame was sent empty to the Salon. In order to turn it into a painting, I had to sacrifice the model. I had two days left before the *vernissage*. I relegated the model to the shadows in the far background, and the painting was then ready in time to be put into its frame at the Salon. Yet I have rarely painted anything with greater intensity than the model I had to sacrifice. It was a costly but salutary lesson to me: I learned to sacrifice incidentals for the sake of the whole.

In 1896, this 'self-made man' of 35 was already an artist with an international reputation, and a friend of the important figures from the world of culture, politics and finance who sat for him. He portrays himself here as a calm, virile and majestic figure taking a break from his work, with his palette, brushes and a cigarette in his hand. The principal models for the painting appear to have been self-portraits by Rembrandt and Titian. Zorn increasingly admired the masters of the sixteenth and seventeenth centuries, whose work he had studied at leisure in the Louvre. The example of Rembrandt, in particular, encouraged him to use chiaroscuro to suggest the depth and complexity of space and to lend his figures a certain plasticity.

The distribution of mass in pictorial space and a heightened sense of physicality had now become the hallmarks of Zorn's painting. At times, his virtuoso brushwork – the apparent 'spontaneity' is an illusion – can become superficial or overdone, but here it brings a rich, vibrant life to the canvas. This is particularly obvious in the handling of the magnificent white smock the artist is sporting.

The painting was acquired by the Nationalmuseum in 1897 at the Stockholm Exhibition of Art and Industry and was exhibited in St Petersburg in 1897 and at the Berlin Secession in 1900. Zorn produced an etching of it.

P.G.

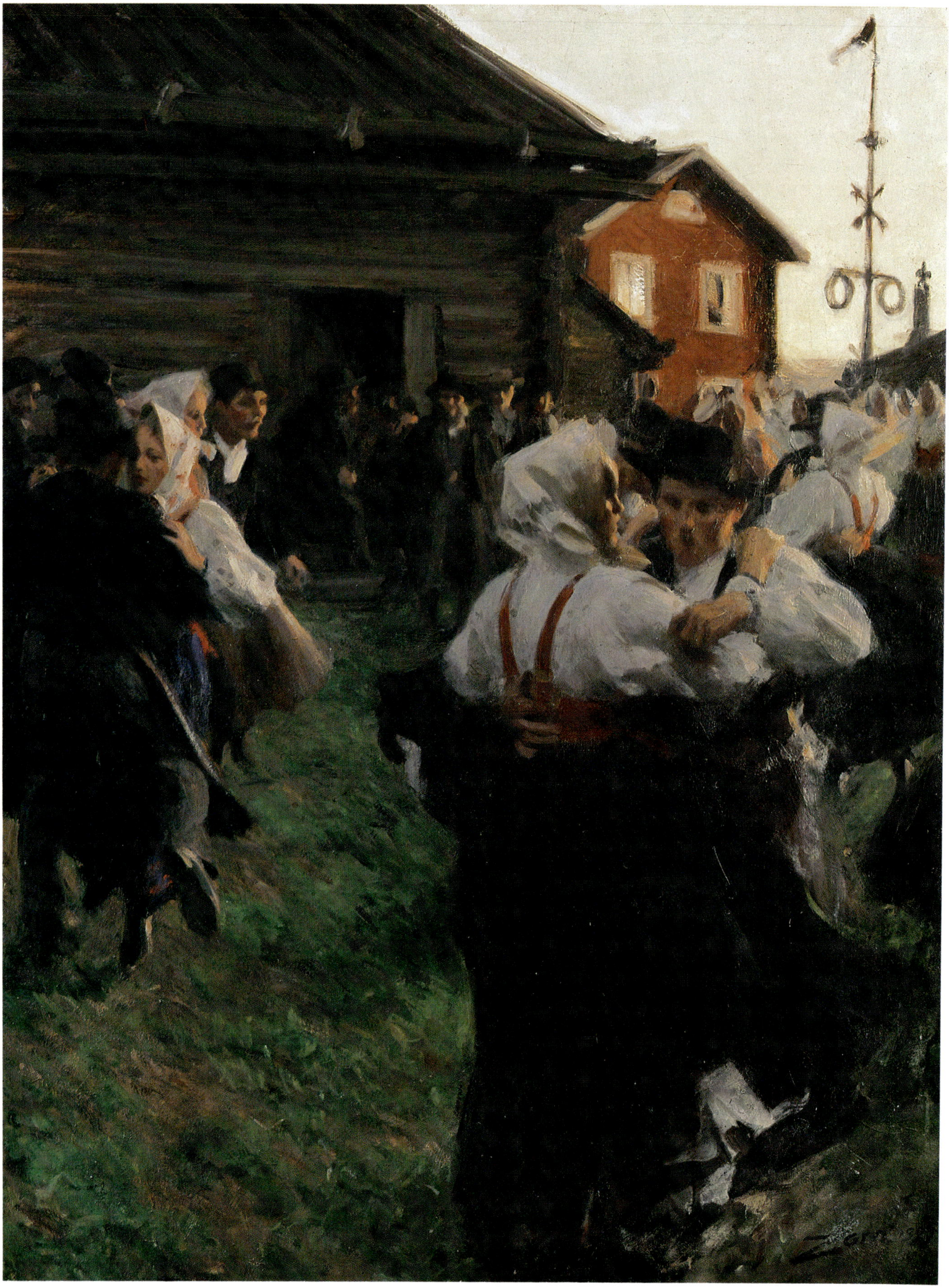

111. Anders Zorn

111

Midsummer Dance, 1897

(Midsommardans)

140 × 98
Signed lower right: Zorn 1897
Nationalmuseum, Stockholm
Inv. no. 1603 (donated in 1903)

Shortly after his definitive return to Sweden in 1896, Zorn found the theme for what is probably his most famous painting which was executed the following summer. When he visited Zorn at his home in Mora, Prince Eugen was greatly taken with the improvised peasant dances he saw, and urged his host to paint them. After some hesitation Zorn agreed to do so.

Of all the provinces of Sweden, it is perhaps Dalarna which remains most attached to its history and its ancient traditions. At the time, however, the old customs were dying out as a result of industrialization and urbanization. No one did more than Zorn to revive and encourage the old customs and handicraft traditions of his home province. His attitude was similar to that of Carl Larsson, who lived not far away in Sundborn, but in Zorn's case it took a much more obviously conservative and *passéiste* form, and the patriotic note was slightly more pronounced. Like many others at this time, he took the view that the art of the Latin countries had become artificial and decadent and that 'it is only amongst Scandinavians that one can still find a true feeling for art in all its freshness' (cited, Brummer 1982, p. 204).

When he gave the village of Morkarleby a May tree in 1896, Zorn succeeded in reviving a tradition which probably dates back to pagan times. In more recent years, the midsummer dance has become part of a somewhat touristy folklore attraction which is now found throughout Sweden.

At midnight, the peasants would erect a tall pole decorated with flowers and greenery, and then dance under the stars until the sun came up. In order to capture the opalescent light, which casts no shadows, and the atmosphere of the light summer nights of the North, Zorn decided to paint after sunset in June and July. With zest and lightness, he succeeds in capturing the enchantment of an exuberant night devoted to celebrating the return of light and *joie de vivre* after the long northern winter.

'I regard this work as containing all my deepest feelings', said Zorn on a number of occasions. It is also one of the major pictorial expressions of Sweden's National Romanticism. Zorn was one of the artists whose romanticism provided a transition from the optimistic Naturalism of the 1880s to the 'vitalist' currents that were to mark the early years of the next century. In *Midsummer Dance*, sensualism and exultation in man's vital energy – and that of *homo nordicus* in particular – are bound up with an evocation of Scandinavia's magical summer nights. In 1900, it was one of Zorn's contributions to the Paris World Fair where he was commissioner for Sweden's art section.

P.G.

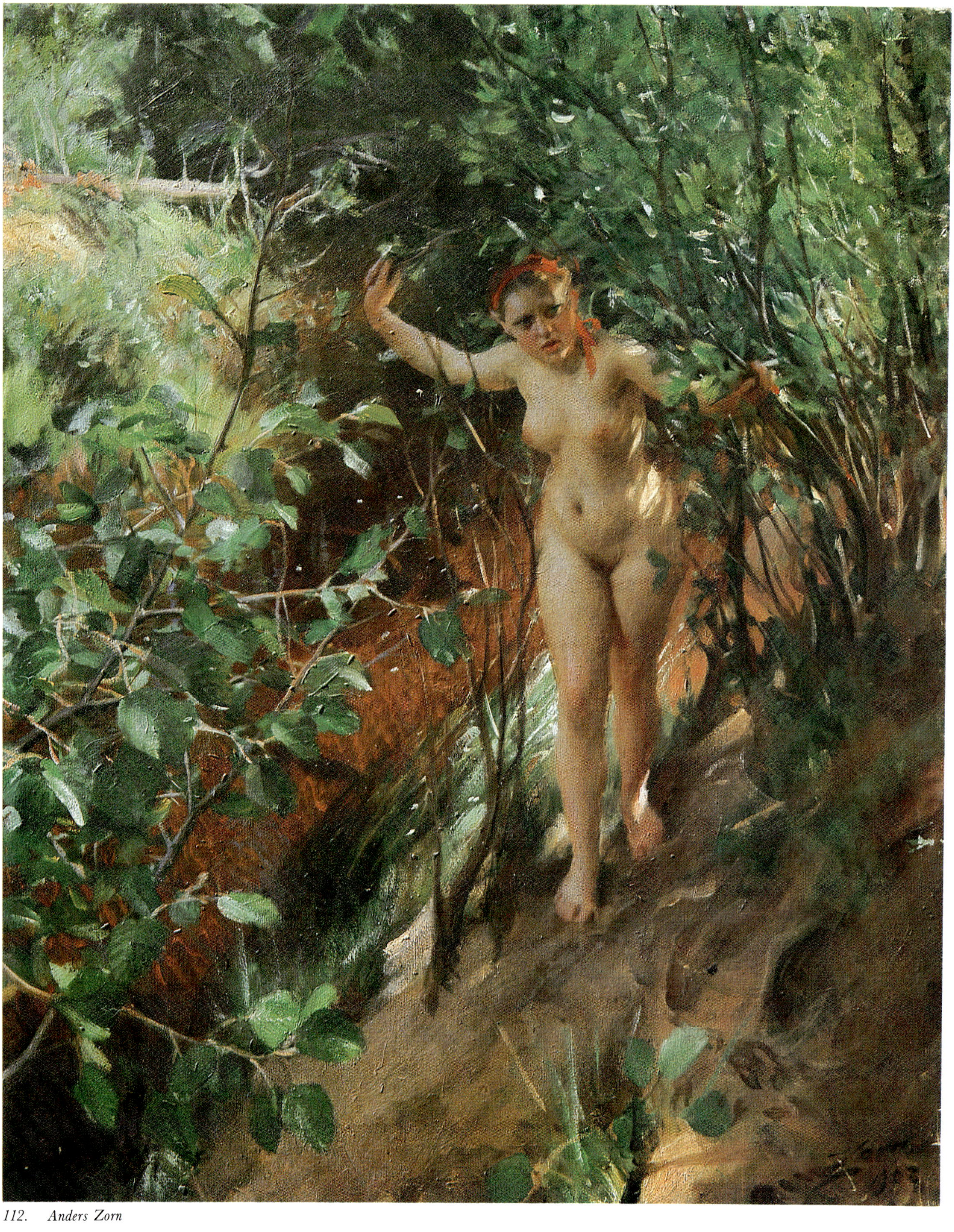

112. Anders Zorn

112

Red Sand, 1902

(Röd sand)

118.5 × 94
Signed lower right: Zorn / 1902
Zornmuséet, Mora

When he painted contemporary young women as nudes in his *Déjeuner sur l'herbe* of 1863, Edouard Manet provoked a notorious scandal. With a few rare exceptions, however, neither Manet, his Impressionist friends nor the other *plein-air* painters pursued the idea of painting nudes in landscapes. The prudery of the times was opposed to such experiments. Nudes were painted in the studio, preferably in some mythological guise. When he first tackled this theme in 1887 Anders Zorn therefore thought of himself as a pioneer. He took his models to the vast and almost deserted Stockholm archipelago and left them to wander naked among the rocks so that he could observe the effect of light on the human body.

The growing popularity of sport in Sweden and the contemporary enthusiasm for the healthy open-air life no doubt encouraged Zorn in this direction, just as they inspired his friend Liljefors to paint wild animals.

At first Zorn attempted to use colour and brushwork to dissolve his nudes into the landscape, but his very strong feeling for the solidity of forms – he was also a sculptor – led him to model his figures more firmly. In this respect, his evolution might be compared with the transition that took Renoir from Impressionism to the Classicism of the Philadelphia *Grandes Baigneuses*. It seems in fact very probable that Zorn saw and admired the *Grandes Baigneuses* when it was exhibited for the first time at the Galerie Georges Petit in the spring of 1887, and that it helped to suggest the idea of painting nudes in the open air the following summer. But it was not until some years later that he also adopted the French master's increasingly sculptural conception of the human body.

P.G.

Chronology

compiled by Jørn Otto Hansen

Year	Nordic countries	International
1792–1814		Napoleonic Wars
1808–9	Finnish War between Sweden and Russia. Russia wins. Finland becomes a Grand Duchy under Russia with its own legislation and administration. The Swedish-Finnish Constitution (1772) remained	
1810	The French Marshal Jean-Baptiste Bernadotte is chosen heir to the Swedish throne and adopts the name Carl Johan	
1812	Helsinki becomes the capital of Finland	
1814	Peace of Kiel. Denmark cedes Norway to Sweden. Union between Norway and Sweden. Norway gets a liberal constitution.	
1814–15		Congress of Vienna
1819	Thorvaldsen's statue of Christ	
1821–9		Greek War of Independence
1822		Champollion deciphers hieroglyphics
1823		Monroe Doctrine
		Schubert: *Die Winterreise*
1830	Henrik Wergeland: *Skabelsen, Mennesket og Messias*	July Revolution in France
		Revolutionary risings in Germany and Poland
		Victor Hugo: *Hernani*
1831		Berlioz: *Symphonie fantastique*
		Victor Hugo: *The Hunchback of Notre Dame*
1832	First Swedish Arts Association established in Stockholm	Goethe: *Faust II*
		Building of the National Gallery in London (until 1838)
		Parliamentary reform in England
1835	The Finnish national epic, the *Kalevala*, compiled by Elias Lönnrot	
	Fjölnir, Icelandic cultural periodical, first published	
	Hans Christian Andersen's first collection of fairy-tales published	
1837	Nasjonalgalleriet founded in Christiania	Beginning of Queen Victoria's reign (until 1901) Charles Dickens: *Oliver Twist*
1843	S. Kierkegaard: *Either/Or*	

1843–8	Scandinavism gets a foothold	
1844	J. L. Runeberg: *King Fjalar*	
	Asbjørnsen and Moe: *Folkeeventyr*	
	First Folk High School based on Grundtvig's ideas formed in Denmark	
1845	S. Kierkegaard: *Stages on Life's Way*	
1846	Fine Arts Association in Finland established in Helsinki	
1847	Thorvaldsen Museum in Copenhagen completed	
1848	Unrest in Schleswig-Holstein leads Denmark to war with Germany	February Revolution in France, followed by revolutionary risings all over Europe
	National constitutional assembly in Copenhagen	Coronation of Francis Joseph I of Austria
	J. L. Runeberg: *Tales of Ensign Stål*	German national assembly at Frankfurt Louis Napoleon elected president *The Communist Manifesto* by Marx and Engels Balzac: *La Comédie humaine* completed The Pre-Raphaelite Brotherhood formed
1849	Denmark gets a liberal constitution with expanded franchise	Courbet: *Burial at Ornans* and *The Stone Breakers*
1850	Peace between Denmark and Prussia	Richard Wagner: *Lohengrin*, first performance in Weimar
1851	Schleswig-Holstein uprising ends and the three-year war is over	Coup d'état of Louis Napoleon
1853	Icelandic national assembly held in Reykjavik	The Great Exhibition held in London
1853–6		The Crimean War
1854		Courbet: *The Artist's Studio*
		Wagner begins work on *Der Ring der Nibelungen*, completed in 1874
1855	French and English fleet bombard Sveaborg fortress outside Helsinki as part of the Crimean War	Paris World Exhibition First group show of Realist paintings in Paris
1857	Scandinavism seeks in vain to create a Scandinavian union	Gustave Flaubert: *Madame Bovary*
	B. Bjørnson publishes his first tales of rural life	Baudelaire: *Les Fleurs du mal*
1859		Charles Darwin: *On the Origin of Species by Means of Natural Selection*
1859–61		Italian War of Liberation
1860	Finland establishes its own currency, the Mark	Jacob Burckhardt: *The Civilisation of the Renaissance in Italy*
1861		Wagner's *Tannhäuser* produced in Paris
		Puvis de Chavannes: series of paintings for the Musée d'Amiens (completed 1882)

1861–5		American Civil War
1862		Victor Hugo: *Les Misérables* Millet: *Man with a hoe*
		World Exhibition in London
1863	Finnish made an official language of administration and legal proceedings	Edouard Manet: *Déjeuner sur l'herbe* Whistler: *Symphony in White*
	The king of Sweden–Norway tries to create a united Scandinavian kingdom with support from Napoleon III	
	German confederation in Frankfurt decides to declare war on Denmark	
1864	Denmark loses the war with Prussia and Austria–Hungary and loses Schleswig-Holstein and Lauenburg	Coronation of Ludwig II, king of Bavaria (until 1886)
		Arnold Böcklin: *Villa by the Seashore* (first version)
	The Finnish Artists' Association founded	
1865		Lewis Carroll: *Alice in Wonderland* S. Mallarmé: *L'après-midi d'un Faune*
1866	Nationalmuseum inaugurated in Stockholm	Austro-Prussian War Dostoyevsky: *Crime and Punishment*
1867	Alfred Nobel takes out a patent on dynamite	Second parliamentary reform in England
	Henrik Ibsen: *Peer Gynt*	Coronation of the Austrian Emperor Francis Joseph I as King of Hungary
		Japonisme becomes increasingly fashionable in France
		Manet: *The Execution of Emperor Maximilian of Mexico*
		Karl Marx: first part of *Das Kapital*
		Zola: *Thérèse Raquin*
		World Exhibition in Paris
1868		First Gladstone Cabinet Dostoyevsky: *The Idiot*
1869		Leo Tolstoy: *War and Peace*
1870	*The Seven Brothers* by Aleksis Kivi, one of the first major works written in Finnish	Schliemann begins to excavate Troy
		Courbet: *La Vague* Fantin–Latour: *The Studio in the Batignolles*
1870–1		Franco–Prussian War
1871	Georg Brandes begins his major work: *Main Currents in 19th Century Literature*	Verdi's *Aida* premiered at the opening of the Suez Canal
		Zola: *Les Rougon-Macquart* (completed 1893)
		The commune of Paris
		Wilhelm I proclaimed German Emperor at Versailles
		Germany constituted as a unified, federal state with O. von Bismarck as its first Chancellor

1872		Meeting of the emperors of Russia, Germany and Austria–Hungary in Berlin
		Monet: *Impression: Sunrise*
1873		Monet: *Gare Saint-Lazare*
		World Exhibition in Vienna
1874	Iceland celebrates its 1000th anniversary Own constitution approved	First exhibition of Impressionists in Paris
		Manet: *Boating* and *Monet Working on his Boat in Argenteuil*
	Socialdemokraten, a daily paper, is published in Copenhagen	Renoir: *La Loge*
		Mussorgsky: *Boris Godunov*
		Verdi: *Requiem*
1875	First chair in art history established in Christiania	Republican constitution in France Bizet: *Carmen*
1876	Edvard Grieg's *Peer Gynt Suite* first performed in Christiania	K. Fiedler: *Über die Beurteilung von Werken der bildenden Kunst*
		Moreau: *Hercules and the Hydra* and *Salome dancing before Herod*
		Puvis de Chavannes: panels for the Panthéon
		Renoir: *Le Moulin de la galette*
		Opening of Wagner's Bayreuth Opera House
1876–8		Balkan Crisis
		Whistler: *The Peacock Room*
1877		Bastien–Lepage: *Les Foins*
		Rodin: *The Age of Bronze*
1878		T. A. Edison makes the first incandescent lamp
		World Exhibition in Paris
1879	Henrik Ibsen: *A Doll's House* premiered at the Royal Theatre in Copenhagen	Austro-German Treaty Dostoyevsky: *Brothers Karamasov*
	Strindberg: *The Red Room*	
		Tchaikovsky: *Eugen Onegin*
1880	J. P. Jacobsen's novel *Niels Lyhne* published in Copenhagen	Maupassant: *Boule de Suif*
		Arnold Böcklin: *The Island of the Dead* (first version)
1881	Henrik Ibsen: *Ghosts*	Anton Bruckner: *Symphony No. 7*
	Nordic art exhibition and artists' meeting in Gothenburg	Renoir: *Le Déjeuner des canotiers*
	Icelandic Realists publish the cultural periodical *Verdandi*	Verlaine: *Sagesse*
1882	The Artists' Association in Finland holds its first exhibition on its own in protest against the conservative Fine Arts Association	Italy joins Austro-German alliance Prime decade of colonial acquisition for Europe

1882	The progressive artists' conflict with Denmark's Royal Academy of Fine Arts leads to its reform	Wagner: *Parsifal*
	Artists who oppose the Christiania Art Association hold their own exhibition, the first Autumn Exhibition	Manet: *A Bar at the Folies-Bergère*
1883	Nordic art exhibition in Copenhagen	Nietzsche: *Also sprach Zarathustra*
	B. Bjørnson: *Over Ævne, I (Pastor Sarg)*	World Exhibition in Amsterdam
	B. Bjørnson: *Beyond his powers*	
	L. J. Lie: *The Family in Gilje*	
	G. Brandes: *Men of the Modern Break-through*	
1884	*Politiken* newspaper in Copenhagen founded by G. Brandes' brother Edvard et al.	Three emperors' alliance renewed
	Listasafn Íslands, National Gallery of Iceland, founded	J. K. Huysmans: *À Rebours (Against the Grain)* published in Paris. The book becomes the 'bible' of the Symbolist movement
	Parliamentary rule adopted in Norway	Salon des Indépendants founded in Paris
		Seurat: *A Sunday at the Grande Jatte* (completed 1886)
	Gauguin represented at the Autumn Exhibition in Christiania	Brahms: *Symphony No. 4*
	Bruckner: *Symphony No. 7* in Christiania	
	Henrik Ibsen: *Wild Duck*	
1885	Some 80 Swedish 'opponents' submit demands to reform the Academy of Fine Arts, but the demands are rejected. They hold two of their own exhibitions	World Exhibition in Antwerp Third parliamentary reform in England
	Hans Jæger: *From Christiania's Bohemia.* The book confiscated as indecent	*Revue Wagnérienne* published in Paris
	Karl Madsen publishes the book *Japansk Maler-Kunst* (Japanese Painting) which results in a flowering of Japonism in Scandinavian crafts, especially ceramics	
	The great official 'Salon' in Helsinki	
1886	Artists' Union founded in Sweden and its first exhibition held in Stockholm	Jean Moréas: *The Symbolist manifesto* published in *Le Figaro Littéraire*, September 18
	Christian Krohg: *Albertine*. The book confiscated as indecent	Neo-Impressionists exhibit as a group at the Salon des Indépendants
	H. Ibsen: *Rosmersholm*	Pierre Loti: *Pêcheurs d'Islande*
	A. Garborg: *Menfolk*	Statue of Liberty erected in New York
	August Strindberg: *The Son of a Servant*	Leo Tolstoy: *Kreutzer Sonata*
	K. A. Tavaststjerna: *Childhood Friends*	

1886	Minna Canth: *Poor Folk*	
	Major Norwegian artists gather at Fleskum farm; 'The Fleskum Summer'	
1887	Norwegian workers' party founded	First Colonial Conference in London
	Debate on sexual morals carried on by Bjørnson's play *A Glove* in 1883	Carnot president of France
	Strindberg: *The Father* and *Miss Julie*	André Antoine founds the 'Théâtre Libre' in Paris and begins to perform modern (naturalistic) drama
	H. Ibsen: *The Lady from the Sea*	Puvis de Chavannes: murals in the Sorbonne (completed 1889)
	The Art Museum of the Ateneum (Ateneumin taidemuseo) completed in Helsinki	
		Rodin: *Burghers of Calais*
		Max Klinger: *The Judgement of Paris*
1888	G. Brandes begins his lectures on Nietzsche's philosophy	G. Mahler: *1st Symphony*, premiered the following year in Budapest
	Valdemar Vedel heralds a break with Naturalism in the periodical *Ny Jord*	Ensor: *Entry of Christ into Brussels*
		Van Gogh: Arles paintings; Gauguin visits Arles
	Nordic exhibition for industry, agriculture, and art held in Copenhagen	First Arts and Crafts exhibition in London
	Exhibition of modern French art arranged in Copenhagen by Carl Jacobsen, the owner of the Carlsberg Breweries	Debussy: *La damoiselle élue* (poem by Rossetti)
		Nicolai Rimsky-Korsakov: *Sheherazade*
		Hugo Wolf: *Mörike* and *Eichendorff Songs*
1889	Brandes publishes the article *Aristocratic Radicalism* in the periodical *Tilskueren* (German translation in *Deutsche Rundschau*, April, 1890)	Second Socialist International in Paris
		Pont-Aven group created under the leadership of Gauguin
	Munch studies in Paris and meets the circle of avant-garde painters around the art dealer Theo van Gogh; over the next few years he travels extensively in Germany and France	Monet: *Haystacks* series (1893)
		Gauguin: *The Yellow Christ*
		Van Gogh: St Remy paintings
	Impressionist exhibition at the Kunstforeninen in Copenhagen, the first real presentation of the movement in Scandinavia	Workers' celebration held for the first time in Paris on the 1st of May
	H. Branting forms the Social Democratic Party in Sweden	World Exhibition in Paris. The Eiffel Tower becomes Paris' new symbol
		'Synthetist' exhibition at the Cafe Volpini in Paris
		Gerhart Hauptmann: *Before Daybreak*
		Nietzsche becomes mentally ill after writing *Götzendämmerung* and *Ecce Homo*
		Edouard Schuré: *Les grands initiés*
		M. Klinger: *Vom Tode I* (cycle of etchings)

1890	Schism in the Swedish Artists' Union. The Swedish Artists' Association founded	Kaiser Wilhelm II dismisses Bismarck
	Akseli Gallen-Kallela and Louis Sparre explore Karelia	Maurice Denis: *Définition du Néo-Traditionnisme*
	K. Hamsun: *Hunger*	Ferdinand Hodler: *Night*
	H. Ibsen: *Hedda Gabler*	Van Gogh commits suicide
	In Copenhagen, large numbers of young Norwegian artists seek entrance to Zahrtmann's school	Cézanne: *The Card Players* (completed 1892)
		Cézanne: *Bathers* series (completed 1905)
		Seurat: *Le Cirque*
	Monet represented at the Autumn Exhibition in Christiania and the Nasjonalgalleriet purchases a painting by him	O. Wilde: *The Picture of Dorian Gray*
		Mercure de France starts publication
		Freie Volksbühne founded in Berlin
		Frank Wedekind: *Frühlings Erwachen*
		Richard Strauss: *Death and Transfiguration*
1891	Finland's special position in the Russian Empire weakened	Franco–Russian alliance
		Construction of the Trans-Siberian railroad begun
	S. Lagerlöf: *The Story of Gösta Berling*	
	A. Garborg: *Trætte Mænd*	
	H. Pontoppidan begins to publish his novel *The Promised Land*	Huysmans: *Là-Bas*
		Sudermann: the play *Sodom's End*
		T. Hardy: *Tess of the D'Urbervilles*
	Art and industrial art exhibition in Gothenburg. Scandinavian artists' meeting	First exhibition in Paris of applied art as 'art'
	A large number of Danish artists desert the official art world and create the Free Exhibition.	Paris: *La Revue Blanche* starts publication
		H. Bahr: *Überwindung des Naturalismus*
	Mogens Ballin and G. F. Clement paint in Pont-Aven in Brittany	Aurier: *Le Symbolisme en peinture*
		Gauguin travels to Tahiti
	The first independent Exhibition of Finnish Artists	First Nabis exhibition at Le Barc de Boutteville's
		Julius Langbehn: *Rembrandt als Erzieher*
		Toulouse-Lautrec produces the first modern poster
1892	The Swedish king refuses to sign the Norwegian Storting's (parliament) law on a special Norwegian consular corps, which results in a government crisis in Norway	Gladstone cabinet in England
		Hauptmann: *The Weavers*
		Monet: *Rouen Cathedral* series (completed 1894)
	Hans Larsson: *Intuition.* The Swedish philosopher's major work	Van Gogh's first one-man exhibition
	H. Ibsen: *The Master Builder*	Massenet: *Werther*

1892	A. Strindberg's 'inferno crisis'	Rose + Croix's first exhibition in Paris
	First performance of Sibelius' *Kullervo*	The Secession exhibitions founded in Berlin and Munich, partly sparked off by the scandal caused by the exhibition of E. Munch's works
	Swedish Artists' Association's first exhibition in Stockholm. Later the same year, exhibition in Copenhagen	The periodical *Blätter für Kunst* first published in Munich
	Johan Rohde visits Germany, Holland, Belgium and France viewing the newest European art, which had important consequences for Symbolist art in the Nordic countries	
1893	The political union between Norway and Sweden threatens to spark off armed conflict	The creation of the first Independent Labour party in England
	F. Nansen leaves on a Polar expedition on the ship *Fram*	Puvis de Chavannes: murals in the Hôtel de Ville, Paris
	Sigbjørn Obstfelder: *Poems*	Mallarmé: *Vers et Prose*
	Taarnet, periodical for literature and art, published in Copenhagen	Oscar Wilde: *Salomé*
	The Free Exhibition in Copenhagen shows major works by Paul Gauguin and Van Gogh	Sudermann: *Heimat* (filmed in 1938 with Zarah Leander in the main role)
	Retrospective exhibition of paintings by Ernst Josephson in Stockholm	Verdi: *Falstaff*
		Lugné-Poe founds 'Théâtre L'Oeuvre' in Paris with his staging of Maeterlinck's drama *Pelléas et Mélisande* (1892)
	Zorn in U.S.A. as Swedish commissioner for the Chicago World Fair's Columbian Exhibition	World Fair in Chicago
	R. Bergh and K. Nordström move to Varberg	Dvorak: *Symphony No. 5, From the New World*
	E. Munch exhibits in Copenhagen	The periodical *The Studio* published; A. Beardsley makes his breakthrough in it
	Willumsen begins the large relief (completed in 1928) inspired by Thomas Carlyle's *Sartor Resartus* (1836)	Hildebrand: *Das Problem der Form*
		Alois Riegl: *Stilfragen*
	The Symbolist Einar Jónsson studies sculpture in Copenhagen	Horta: Maison Tassel in Brussels
	Leading figures of the Ferkel group in Berlin: Munch, Strindberg, Przybeszewsky	
	J. Sibelius: *Karelia*	Arthur Schnitzler: *Anatol*
		Paul Verlaine: *Mes Prisons*
1894	Sven Hedin in Tibet	Sino–Japanese war (–1895)
	Herman Bang stages a number of plays by H. Ibsen in Paris for 'Théâtre L'Oeuvre'	Gladstone resigns, succeeded by Rosebery as Prime Minister
	Knut Hamsun: *Pan*	The French president Carnot murdered by an anarchist

1894	Varberg School exhibition in Stockholm	Czar Alexander III dies, succeeded by Nicholas II
	Swedish artists at the Secessionists' exhibition in Munich	The Dreyfus Case begins in Paris
	Close contacts between Finnish and Swedish artists in Paris, e.g. M. Enckell and O. Sager-Nelson	Rilke: *Erste Gedichte* R. Kipling: *The Jungle Book*
		Lumière discovers 'cinematography'
	Agnes and Harald Slott-Møller form close contacts with *The Studio*'s editor and a large number of English artists. A. Slott-Møller's decorations for Copenhagen's City Hall (M. Nyrop, 1893–1902) show traces of English arts and crafts influence	Oscar Wilde's *Salomé* performed in Paris with Sarah Bernhardt in the title role Segantini: *Angelo della Vita* Le Douanier Rousseau: *La Guerre* F. v. Stuck: *War* M. Klinger: *Brahms Phantasie* (etchings)
	Väinö Blomstedt: *Cemetery at Bourg-la-Reine* under the direct influence of Maurice Denis via Sager-Nelson	Julius Meier-Graefe: *Edvard Munch* Beardsley: Illustrations to Wilde's *Salomé*
	Thórarinn B. Thorláksson studies painting in Copenhagen	First performance of Debussy's *Prélude à l'Après-midi d'un Faune* causes a scandal
		G. Mahler: *Symphony No.2*
		Albert Langen founds his publishing house in Munich which concentrates on Nordic literature
1895		Salisbury's conservative cabinet in England
		Fauré becomes president of the French Republic
	G. Brandes: *Shakespeare*	Kiel Canal (Kaiser Wilhelm Canal) opened
	Scandinavian artists well represented at an exhibition in Berlin arranged by Münchener Freie Vereinigung	Wedekind: *Erdgeist* (dedicated to the Dane Willy Gretor whose secretary W. was for a time) Th. Fontane: *Effi Briest*
	Strindberg article about Munch in *Revue Blanche*	G. B. Shaw: *Candida* Stefan George: *Preisgedichte*
	Edvard Munch and Gallen-Kallela have a joint exhibition in Berlin	Verlaine: *Confessions* Yeats: *Poems* H. Wolf: *Corregidor* R. Strauss: *Till Eulenspiegel* Appia: *La Mise en Scène du drame Wagnerien* T. Garnier starts on his draft for La Cité Industrielle Van de Velde: Villa Bloemenwerff in Uccle Worpswede painters exhibit in Munich K. Kollwitz: *The Weavers' Revolt* Chekhov: *The Seagull* The periodical *Pan* draws attention to Scandinavian culture with contributions by Gallen-Kallela, Munch, Vigeland, Kittelsen and Zorn
	Edvard Munch: *Scream* and *The Dead Mother*	S. Freud and Breuer: *Studien über Hysterie*
1896	H. Ibsen: *Johan Gabriel Borkmann*	Theodor Herzl founds the Zionist movement
	K. Gjellerup: *The Mill* (written in German)	Jarry: *Ubu Roi* performed in Paris, causing a scandal

1896	Strindberg returns to Sweden	'Théâtre Libré' closes with the performance of Ibsen's *Peer Gynt*
	E. Munch makes decorations for Ibsen's play *Peer Gynt* in Paris	Mahler: *Symphony No.3*
	International exhibition in Dresden, attended by a number of Scandinavian artists	Strauss: *Also sprach Zarathustra*
		Puccini: *La Bohème*
		Bergson: *Matière et Mémoire*
		The periodical *Jugend* first published in Munich
		Mellerio: *Le Mouvement idéaliste en peinture*
		Kandinsky and Jawlensky in Munich
		Horta: Maison du Peuple in Brussels
		William Morris: *The Kelmscott Chaucer*
1897	Andrée tries to reach the North Pole by balloon	Spanish–American war over Cuba
	Strindberg: *The Inferno*	Turco–Greek War
	Ásgrímur Jónsson studies painting in Copenhagen	A. Chekhov: *Uncle Vanya*
	Art and industrial exhibition in Stockholm	Vienna Secession founded
	Serge Diaghilev visits Scandinavian artists with a plan to arrange an exhibition of their works in St Petersburg	Gauguin: *Where Do We Come From? What Are We? Where Are We Going?*
	Art periodical *Ateneum* founded in Finland, modelled on *The Studio* and *Pan*	
1898		Social Democratic Party founded in Russia
	Hamsun: *Victoria*	E. Zola publishes his article *J'Accuse*
		Spain loses the Philippines and Cuba to the U.S.A.
	A. Strindberg: *To Damascus*	Cézanne: last paintings in *Mont Sainte-Victoire* series
	French exhibition in Stockholm with works by Gauguin and Van Gogh	Rodin: *The Kiss* and *Balzac*
		Stanislawsky founds an artists' theatre in Moscow
	Eino Leino: *Swan of Death*	
	C. Larsson decorates the Opera House foyer in Stockholm	O. Wilde: *The Ballad of Reading Goal*
		The Berliner Sezession founded by Leistikow, Slevogt, etc.
		Leo Tolstoy: *The Resurrection*
1899	Russian oppression in Finland increased. February manifesto places all legal questions under Russian legislation. Finnish artists work to make the rest of Europe aware of Finland's struggle for freedom	First International Peace Conference, The Hague
		Darmstadt Secession
		Paul Signac: *From Delacroix to Neo-Impressionism*
	J. Sibelius: *Symphony no. 1* and *Finlandia*	Haeckel: *Die Weltratsel*
	A. Strindberg: *Advent*	A. W. Symons: *The Symbolist Movement in Literature*

1899	C. Larsson publishes *A Home*	
	The Danish sculptor Niels Hansen-Jacobsen causes a sensation in Paris at the Champ-de-Mars exhibition with his sculpture *War*	Karl Kraus founds the critical and literary periodical *Die Fackel* in Vienna Ruskin College founded at Oxford
	Special edition of Snorre's *Sagas of the Norse Kings* illustrated by leading Norwegian artists	A. Loos: Cafe Museum Monet: *Waterlilies* series (completed 1906)
1900	Finland builds its own pavilion at the World Exhibition designed by Gesellius, Lindgren, and Saarinen, with frescos by Gallen-Kallela. Europe discovers Scandinavian art at the World Exhibition	World Exhibition in Paris Von Bülow, Chancellor of Germany The Labour Representation Committee, the Labour Party's predecessor, founded in England
	Henrik Ibsen: *When we Dead Awaken*	Boxer Rebellion in China Rilke: *Geschichten vom lieben Gott*
	Thórarinn B. Thorláksson: *Thingvellir*	Arthur Evans begins the excavation of Minoan culture in Crete Puccini: *Tosca* Elgar: *The Dream of Gerontius*
	Ellen Key: *The Century of a Child*	Mahler: *Symphony No.4* Freud: *The Interpretation of Dreams* published in Vienna Bergson professor at the Collège de France Hodler: *Rückzug der Schweizer bei Marignano*, wall paintings at the Landesmuseum in Zürich P. Gauguin: *Noa Noa* P. Schultze-Naumberg: *Häuslische Kunstpflege* T. Marinetti's anti-artistic manifesto, *Burn the Muses* A. Schnitzler: *La Ronde*
1901	Nobel Prize awarded for the first time	Edward VII succeeds to the English throne
	Einar Jónsson and Thórarinn B. Thorláksson exhibit at Charlottenborg Palace in Copenhagen	Picasso's Blue Period Stuttgart Secession
	Exhibition of Danish art from 1700 to 1900 at the new City Hall in Copenhagen	
		Thomas Mann: *Buddenbrooks*
	Strindberg: *Easter* and *Dance of Death*	Anton Chekhov: *Three Sisters*
	C. Larsson settles in Sundborn	
1901–3	Gallen-Kallela paints the frescos at the Juselius Mausoleum in Pori	
1902	Munch exhibits his *Frieze of Life* in Berlin	André Gide: *L'Immoraliste*

1902	Einar Jónsson works in Rome	Debussy's *Pelléas et Mélisande*, based on Maeterlinck's play, first performed
	Jean Sibelius: *2nd Symphony*	
1903	B. Bjørnson receives the Nobel Prize for literature	Gustav Klimt: *Philosophy, Medicine, Jurisprudence*
	Jón Stefánsson studies painting in Copenhagen	Arnold Schönberg: *Gurrelieder*, based on texts by J. P. Jacobsen
	Eino Leino: *Whitsongs* I (collection based on folk-poetry)	
1904	The Russian Govenor-General murdered in Helsinki	Russo–Japanese War
	Iceland receives home rule	International Exhibition of art in Düsseldorf
		First exhibition of the Deutscher Künstlerbund in Weimar
		Leos Janácek: *Jenufa*
		Puccini: *Madame Butterfly*
		Anton Chekhov: *The Cherry Orchard*
1905	General strike in Finland	Revolution in Russia, only partly successful
		Richard Strauss: *Salomé*, after O. Wilde
	Union between Sweden and Norway dissolved	E. Heckel, Ernst Ludwig Kirchner and Karl Schmidt-Rottluff found the Expressionist artists' association *Die Brücke*; they are later joined by Nolde, Pechstein, O. Müller
	After popular referendum Prince Carl of Denmark becomes King of Norway and adopts the name Haakon VII	
1906	Unicameral parliament in Finland. Universal suffrage for males and females	Zorn retrospective exhibition at Durand-Ruel's in Paris
		Picasso: *Les demoiselles d'Avignon*
		H. Ibsen's *Ghosts* with stage setting by E. Munch, directed by Max Reinhardt, opens the Kammerspiele in Berlin
		Wedekind: *The Dance of Death*
1907	Norwegian women receive the right to vote in municipal elections	
	St John's Cathedral in Tampere, designed by Lars Sonck, decorated by Hugo Simberg and M. Enckell	
	Strindberg: *The Ghost Sonata*	H. Rousseau: *Woman with a Snake*
1908	Danish women receive the right to vote in municipal elections	Adolf Loos: *Ornament und Verbrechen* (Ornament and Crime)
	Icelandic author Jóhann Sigurjónsson's debut in Denmark with the novel *Hraun Farm*	
	Munch returns to Norway for good	
1909	Sweden approves a new democratic election reform	H. Matisse coins the term Cubism

1909	General strike in Sweden	Serge Diaghilev founds the Russian Ballet in Paris
	Selma Lagerlöf receives the Nobel Prize for literature Thórarinn B. Thorláksson and Ásgrímur Jónsson exhibit in Oslo	
	Larsson: *The House in the Sun*	
1910		G. Mahler: *Symphony No 9*
		I. Stravinsky: *The Firebird*
1914–18		First World War
1917	Finland declares its independence from Russia	The Russian Revolution
1918	Iceland becomes independent of Denmark, but remains under the Danish–Icelandic monarchy	Peace between Russia and Germany
		November revolution in Germany leading to Weimar Republic
	Civil War in Finland	Armistice signed at Compiègne
1919	Finnish independence of Russia confirmed in Dorpat	Peace Treaty of Versailles
1939–45	Finno–Soviet Winter War	World War II
	Occupation of Denmark and Norway	
	Allied forces in Iceland	
	Sweden neutral	
1944	Iceland becomes an independent republic	
1949	Denmark, Norway and Iceland join Nato	Federal Republic of Germany founded with Bonn as capital. German Democratic Republic founded with East Berlin as capital
1952	Nordic Council founded	
1957		European Economic Community founded
1973	Denmark joins Common Market	
1975		Helsinki accords on European security

Selected bibliography

General

1. Buffalo, Albright Art Gallery, *Exhibition of Contemporary Scandinavian Art*, by Christian Brinton (1913).
2. Jean Cassou, Emil Langui, Nikolaus Pevsner, *Les sources du vingtième siècle* (Paris, 1971).
3. T. K. Dersy, *History of Scandinavia* (Minneapolis: University of Minnesota Press, 1979).
4. Jean Jacques Fol, *Les pays nordiques aux XIXe et XXe siècles* (Paris: Presses universitaires de France, 1978).
5. Michael Jacobs, *The Good and Simple Life. Artist Colonies in Europe and America* (Oxford: Phaidon, 1985).
6. Carl Laurin, Emil Hannover, Jens Thiis, *Scandinavian Art* (New York: The American-Scandinavian Foundation, 1922).
7. Bo Lindwall, Nils Gösta Sandblad, *Bildkonsten i Norden*, Vol. 3: *Nordiskt Friluftsmåleri, Nordiskt Sekelskifte* (Stockholm: Prisma, 1972).
8. Borge Gedsø Madsen, *Strindberg's Naturalistic Theater. Its relation to French Naturalism* (New York: Russell and Russell, 1973).
9. Roald Nasgaard, *The Mystic North. Symbolist Landscape Painting in Northern Europe and North America 1890–1940* (Toronto: University of Toronto Press, 1984; Exhibition: Toronto, Cincinnati, 1984).
10. New York, The Brooklyn Museum, *Northern Light. Realism and Symbolism in Scandinavian Painting 1880–1910,* ed. by Kirk Varnedoe (Washington, New York, Minneapolis, Gothenburg, 1982–3).
11. Oslo, Nasjonalgalleriet, *1880-årene i nordisk maleri*, ed. by Pontus Grate and Nils-Göran Hökby (Oslo 1985; Stockholm 1985–6; Helsinki 1986; Copenhagen 1986).
12. Robert Rosenblum, *Modern Painting and the Northern Romantic Tradition: Friedrich to Rothko* (New York: Harper and Row, 1975). In German: *Die moderne Malerei und die Tradition der Romantik. Von C. D. Friedrich zu Mark Rothko*. Aus dem Amerikanischen von Reinhard Kaiser (München: Schirmer/Mosel, 1981).
13. Margareta Rossholm, *Sagan i Nordisk Sekelskifteskonst. En motivhistorisk och ideologisk undersökning* (Stockholm: K. L. Beckmans Tryckerier AB, 1974).
14. Rotterdam, Museum Boymans van Beuningen, *Het Symbolisme in Europa* (Brussels, *Le Symbolisme en Europe;* Baden-Baden, *Symbolismus in Europa;* Paris 1975–6).
15. Salme Sarajas-Korte, *Vid symbolismens källor. Den tidiga symbolismen i Finland 1890–1895* (Jakobstad, 1981). Original: *Suomen varhaissymbolismi ja sen lähteet 1890–1895* (Helsinki: Otava, 1966).
16. Ulrich Thieme and Felix Becker, *Allgemeines Lexicon der Bildenden Künstler* (Leipzig, 1907–50).
17. Gunnar Tideström, *Dikt och bild* (Lund, 1965).
18. O. G. Turville-Petre, *Myth and Religion in the North* (New York, 1964).
19. Henri Usselmann, 'Complexité et Importance des Contacts des Peintres Nordiques avec l'Impressionnisme' (PhD. Diss., The University of Gothenburg, 1979).
20. John H. Wuorinen, 'Scandinavia and the Rise of Modern National Consciousness', *Nationalism and Internationalism.* Essays inscribed to Carlton J. H. Hayes (New York, 1950).

DENMARK

General

21. Georg Brandes, 'Virkeligheden og Temperamentet hos Zola', *Tilskueren* (Copenhagen, 1887).
22. Copenhagen, Statens Museum for Kunst, *Vor Hundert Jahren. Dänemark und Deutschland 1864–1900. Gegner und Nachbarn.* Exhibition catalogue with articles by Jørn Otto Hansen et.al. (1981).
23. Copenhagen, Ordrupgaard Collection, *Gauguin and van Gogh in Copenhagen in 1893.* Exhibition catalogue ed. by Merete Bodelsen, articles by Merete Bodelsen and Kirsten Olesen (1984).
24. *Cras, Tidskrift for Kunst & Kultur* (Silkeborg, 1973–).
25. *Dansk Kunsthistorie* I–IV (Copenhagen, 1972–5).
26. Emil Hannover, *Dänische Kunst des 19. Jahrhunderts* (Leipzig, 1907).
27. Hanne Honnens de Lichtenberg, *Zahrtmanns Skole* (Copenhagen, 1979).
28. *Kunstbladet, Nordisk Tidskrift* (Copenhagen 1888–98, 1899–1903, 1909–10).
29. Julius Lange, 'Haanden paa Brystet', *Tilskueren* (Copenhagen, 1887).
30. Julius Lange, *Bastien Lepage.* 'Studiet i Marken. Skilderiet. Erindringens Kunst' (Copenhagen, 1889).
31. Karl Madsen, ed., *Kunstens Historie i Danmark* (Copenhagen, 1901–7).
32. Karl Madsen, *Skagens Maleri og Skagens Museum* (Copenhagen, 1929).
33. Vagn Poulsen, *Danish Painting and Sculpture* (Copenhagen, 1976).
34. Johan Rohde, *Journal fra en Rejse i 1892,* ed. by H. P. Rohde with introduction by N. G. Sandblad (Copenhagen, 1955).
35. Bente Scavenius, *Fremsyn-Snæversyn. Dansk Dagbladskunstkritik 1880–1901* (Copenhagen, 1983).
36. *Signum I–IV* (1960–4), ed. Poul Vad.
37. *Tilskueren. Maanedsskrift for Literatur, Samfundsspørgsmaal og almenfattelige videnskabelige Afhandlinger*, 1884–1939 (Copenhagen).
38. *Taarnet (Tårnet)* 1893–4 (Copenhagen).
39. *Weilbachs Kunstnerleksikon* 3. udg. I–III (Copenhagen, 1947–50).
40. Erik Zahle, ed., *Danmarks Malerkunst fra Middelalder til Nutid.* 4. udg. (Copenhagen, 1955).
41. *Kristian Zahrtmann, En Mindebog*, ed. by F. Hendriksen (Copenhagen, 1919).
42. Jan Zibrandtsen, *Moderne dansk Maleri*, second ed. (Copenhagen, 1967). In Danish and English.

ANNA ANCHER

S. Müller, *Nyere dansk Maleri* (Copenhagen, 1884).
K. Voss, *Breve fra Anna Ancher* (Copenhagen, 1984).
Also Bibliography refs: 32, 39, 42.

LUDVIG FIND

Merete Bodelsen, *Maleren Ludvig Find* (Copenhagen, 1943).
Ludvig Find, 'Et Par Erindringer', *Kunstmuseets Aarsskrift* XXVIII, 1941 (Copenhagen).
Also Bibliography ref: 39.

VILHELM HAMMERSHØI

Alfred Bramsen, 'Weltkunst. Der dänische Maler Vilhelm Hammershøi', *Zeitschrift für bildende Kunst.* N. F. 16 (Leipzig, 1905), pp. 176–89.
Alfred Bramsen and Sophus Michaëlis, *Vilhelm Hammershøi. Kunstneren og hans Værk* (Copenhagen and Christiania, 1918).
Copenhagen, Ordrupgaard Collection, *Vilhelm Hammershøi*, ed. by Hanne Finsen and Inge Vibeke Raaschou-Nielsen. Essays by Hanne Finsen, Thorkild Hansen, Harald Olsen (1981).
Julius Elias, 'Vilhelm Hammershøi', *Kunst und Künstler* 14 (Berlin: Cassirer, 1915–16), pp. 403–8.
H., 'Aus den Neunten Ausstellung der Berliner Secession', *Kunst und Künstler* 2 (Berlin: Cassirer, 1903–4), pp. 402–3, 405.
Ulf Linde, 'Vilhelm Hammershøi: Fem porträtt', *Thielska Galleriet Katalog* (Stockholm, 1979), pp. 50–1.
Carl V. Petersen, 'Omkring Hammershøi Udstillingen', *Tilskueren* (Copenhagen, 1916), pp. 519ff.
William Ritter, 'Vilhelm Hammershøi', *L'art et les artistes* 10 (Paris, 1909–10), pp. 264–8.
Haavard Rostrup, 'Om Vilh. Hammershøis Kunst', *Kunst og Kultur* (Oslo, 1940), pp. 177ff.
Poul Vad, *Vilhelm Hammershøi, Kunst i Danmark* (Copenhagen, 1957). Poul Vad has in preparation a book on Vilhelm Hammershøi's art to be published in 1986.
Vilhelm Wanscher, 'Vilhelm Hammershøi', *Ord och Bild* 18 (Stockholm, 1915), pp. 401–11.
Also Bibliography refs: 40, 42.

VIGGO JOHANSEN

Copenhagen, Kunstforeningen, *Viggo Johansen. Kontrafej og Komposition.* Catalogue with an article by Annette Stabell (1985).
Also Bibliography refs: 32, 39, 40, 42.

P. S. KRØYER

H. Chr. Christensen, *P. S. Krøyer,* Fortegnelse over hans oliemalerier (Copenhagen, 1923).
Ernst Mentze, *P. S. Krøyer* (Copenhagen, 1980).
Also Bibliography refs: 32, 39, 40, 42.

EJNAR NIELSEN

Copenhagen, Kunstforeningen, *Ejnar Nielsen.* Exhibition catalogue with articles by Anette Stabell and Jørn Otto Hansen (1984).
Hans Helge Madsen, *Ejnar Nielsen eller Eventyret om Gjern* (Copenhagen, 1974).
Also Bibliography refs: 39, 40, 42.

L. A. RING

H. Chr. Christensen, *Fortegnelse over Malerier og Studier af L. A. Ring i Aarene 1880–1910* (Copenhagen, 1910).
Copenhagen, Ordrupgaard Collection, *L. A. Ring 1854–1933.* Exhibition catalogue with articles by Hanne Finsen and Eske K. Mathiesen. Ed. by Inge Vibeke Raaschou-Nielsen and Jens Peter Munk (1984).
P. Hertz, *Maleren L. A. Ring* (Copenhagen, 1934).
Mogens Nykjær, 'Kærligheds natur. En tolkning af L. A. Ring: I havedøren. Kunstnerens hustru', *Cras* 1983, pp. 65ff.
Cai M. Woel, *L. A. Ring. Et Levnedsrids* (Copenhagen, 1937).
Also Bibliography refs: 39, 40, 42.

HARALD SLOTT-MØLLER

Bibliography refs: 22, 39.

J. F. WILLUMSEN

Merete Bodelsen, *Willumsen i Halvfemsernes Paris.* Summary in English (Copenhagen, 1957).
Frederikssund, J. F. Willumsens Museum, *J. F. Willumsen, og den frie Udstillings første år. 1891–98.* Exhibition catalogue with articles by Leila Krogh (1982).
Roald Nasgaard, 'Willumsen and Symbolist Art 1888–1910' (PhD. Diss., New York University, 1973).
D. L. Paul, 'Willumsen and Gauguin in the 1890s', *Apollo*, 1980, vol. CXI (London), pp. 36 ff.
Sigurd Schultz, *J. F. Willumsen. En fortolkning af hans Personlighed og Ideerne i hans Livsværk* (Copenhagen, 1948).
Poul Vad, 'Willumsen efter 1900', *Signum I*, 1961, pp. 53ff.
Vilh. Wanscher, *J. F. Willumsen* (Copenhagen, 1937).
J. F. Willumsen, *Mine Erindringer fortalt til Ernst Mentze* (Copenhagen, 1953).
Also Bibliography refs: 40, 42.

FINLAND

General

43. *Antellin kokoelmat – Antellska samlingarna*, Ateneumin taidemuseo—Konstmuseet i Ateneum (Helsinki, 1975). Catalogue.
44. 'Art in Finland', *Apollo*, May (London, 1982).
45. *Finskt sekelskifte,* ed. by Eva Nordenson, Årsbok för Svenska statens konstsamlingar, Articles by Matti Klinge, Marika Hausen, Leena Maunula etc. (Stockholm: Raben & Sjögren, 1971).
46. *Gösta Serlachiuksen taidesäätiön kokoelmat—Gösta Serlachius konststiftelses samlingar—The Collection of the Gösta Serlachius' Fine Arts Foundation* (Helsinki, 1978). Catalogue.
47. Konrad Hahm, *Die Kunst in Finnland* (Berlin, 1933).
48. *Helsingin kaupungin taidekokoelmat, Kokoelma Bäcksbacka—Helsingfors stads konstsamlingar, Samling Bäcksbacka* (Helsinki, 1976). Catalogue.
49. Helsinki, Ateneumin taidemuseo, *Två sekler finsk konst* (Exhibition series) *Realismen* (1962); *Konstmuseet i Ateneum 100 år. Jubileumsutställning (1963).*
50. Yrjö Hirn, *Lärt folk och landstrykare i det finska Finlands kulturliv* (Helsinki, 1939).
51. Eino Jutikkala and Kauko Pirinen, *A History of Finland* (Espoo: Weilin & Göös, 1984).
52. Matti Klinge, *Geschichte Finnlands im Überblick* (Helsinki: Otava, 1977). Also in French (1983) and in English (1981).
53. Alf Krohn, ed., *Les Beaux-Arts en Finlande. Bilan d'un siècle* (Helsinki, 1949). Also in English (1953).

54. W. R. Mead, 'Kalevala and the Rise of Finnish Nationality', *Folklore*, vol. 73 (Winter 1962), pp. 217–29.
55. Onni Okkonen, *L'art finlandais aux XIXe et XXe siècles* (Helsinki, 1938).
56. Onni Okkonen, *Die finnische Kunst* (Helsinki, 1943). Also in English (1946) and in French (1949).
57. Istvan Rácz, *Suomen taiteen kultakausi 1860–1930.* Introduction by Sakari Saarikivi (Helsinki, 1971).
58. Sixten Ringbom, 'Grek eller karelare? Den nationella konstens skiftande ideal', *Finsk Tidskrift* (Åbo, 1970), pp. 86–104.
59. Sixten Ringbom, ed., *Konsten i Finland* (Helsinki: Holger Schildts förlag, 1978).
60. Hans Rosenhagen, 'Finnländische Maler', *Die Kunst für Alle*, vol. 19 (Munich: Bruckmann, 1903–4), pp. 206–13.
61. Salme Sarajas-Korte, *Ateneumin taidetta* (Helsinki: Otava, 1971).
62. John Boulton Smith, *The Golden Age of Finnish Art, Art Nouveau and the National Spirit* (Helsinki: Otava, 1975, revised and enlarged edition 1986).
63. Stockholm, Nationalmuseum, *Finskt 1900* by Konstmuseet i Ateneum, Finlands Arkitekturmuseum, Konstflitföreningen i Finland. Articles by Kai Laitinen, Salme Sarajas-Korte, Asko Salokorpi, Marika Hausen (1971); Nuremberg, Vienna (1973) in German; Brussels (1974) in French and Flemish; Edinburgh (1979) list of exhibits in English.
64. Stockholm, Nationalmuseum, *Målarinnor från Finland—Seitsemän suomalaista taiteilijaa* by Finlands konstakademi, utställnings- och informationsavdelningen (1981); Helsinki, Tampere, Turku (1981–2); Copenhagen, Hamburg, *Malerinder fra Finland—Sieben finnische Malerinnen* (1983).
65. Tampere, Tampereen taidemuseo, *Tampereen Jugend.* Articles by Anneli Ilmonen, Paula Kivinen etc. (Tampere, 1973).
66. J. J. Tikkanen, *Finska konstföreningen 1846–96* (Helsinki, 1896).
67. J. J. Tikkanen, 'Die Kunst in Finnland', *Die Graphischen Künste*, XXIX (Vienna, 1906).
68. Hertta Tirranen, *Suomen taiteilijoita Juho Rissasesta Jussi Mäntyseen* (Porvoo, 1950). Interviews.
69. *Turun taidemuseo—Åbo konstmuseum* (Turku, 1984). Catalogue.
70. Ritva Tuomi, 'On the search for a national style', *Abacus, Museum of Finnish Architecture Yearbook* (Helsinki, 1979), pp. 56–96.
71. Markku and Olli Valkonen, ed., *Suomen taide*, vols 2–4 (Helsinki: WSOY, 1982–5).
Also Bibliography ref: 15.

MAGNUS ENCKELL

Nils-Gustav Hahl, *Om konst och konstindustri* (Helsingfors, 1942).
Jaakko Puokka, *Magnus Enckell, ihminen ja taiteilija* (Helsinki, 1949).
Aimo Reitala, 'On the Origins and Meaning of Magnus Enckell's Early Boy-figures', English summary. *Taidehistoriallisia tutkimuksia 3 – Konsthistoriska studier 3* (Helsinki, 1977), p. 132.
Salme Sarajas-Korte, 'Magnus Enckell and Prometheus Bound', *Ateneumin taidemuseo. Museojulkaisu* 21. 1977–8 (Helsinki, 1979), pp. 36–44.
Salme Sarajas-Korte, 'The Norwegian Influence in Finland in the early 1890s, Discussion', *Ateneumin taidemuseo. Museojulkaisu* 21. 1977–8 (Helsinki, 1979), pp. 45–8.
Salme Sarajas-Korte, 'Magnus Enckell's Melancholy', *Ateneumin Taidemuseo, Museojulkaisu* 27 (Helsinki, 1985), pp. 24–43.
Also Bibliography refs: 15, 63.

AKSELI GALLEN-KALLELA

Leena Ahtola-Moorhouse, 'Akseli Gallen-Kallela og Kalevalamotivene'. Exhibition catalogue *Kalevala-Motiver* (Oslo: Nasjonalgalleriet, 1981). Original: 'Akseli Gallen-Kallela ja Kalevala-aiheet'. *Kalevalan kankahilla, kuvarunoja Ekmanista Gallen-Kallelaan* (Helsinki, Finlands konstakademi, 1978).
Axel Gallén. Ulkomaan sanomalehdissä – I Utlandets press, in der ausländischen Presse (Helsinki, 1895).
Aivi Gallen-Kallela, ed., *Juhla-Kalevala ja Akseli Gallen-Kallelan Kalevalataide* (Helsinki: WSOY, fourth ed. 1984).
Aivi Gallen-Kallela, ed., *Juhla-Kanteletar* (Helsinki: WSOY, second ed. 1984).
Akseli Gallen-Kallela, *Boken om Gallen-Kallela* (Helsingfors, 1932). Original: *Kallela-kirja* (Porvoo, 1924).
Kirsti Gallen-Kallela, *Isäni Akseli Gallen-Kallela* I–II (Porvoo, 1964–5).
Paul Kraemer, 'Axel Gallén, Finnlands Grosser Maler', *Die Kunst für Alle*, vol. 23, December (Munich: Bruckmann, 1917), pp. 77–80.
Timo Martin and Douglas Sivén, *Akseli Gallen-Kallela: national artist of Finland.* English adaptation by Keith Bosley and Satu Salo (1985). Original: *Akseli Gallen-Kallela. Elämäkerrallinen Rapsodia* (1984). Also a Swedish edition (1985) (Helsinki: Wattikustannus).
Kerttu Niilonen, ed., *Kalela Wilderness Studio and Home* (Helsinki: Otava, 1966).
Onni Okkonen, *Akseli Gallen-Kallelan taidetta.* English summary (Porvoo: WSOY, 1948).
Onni Okkonen, *A. Gallen-Kallela. Elämä ja taide* (Monograph) (Helsinki, second ed. 1961).
Salme Sarajas-Korte, 'Om Axel Galléns Kalevalamystik', *Konsthistorisk tidskrift* (Stockholm, 1972), pp. 41–54.
Marc Treib, 'Gallen-Kallela: A Portrait of the Artist as Architect', *Architectural Association Quarterly*, vol. 7, no 3 (London, 1975), pp. 3–13.
Also Bibliography refs: 10, 15, 45, 50, 58, 59, 62, 63, 70.

PEKKA HALONEN

Outi Hämäläinen, ed., *Pekka Halonen.* English summary (Porvoo: WSOY, 1947).
Aune Lindström, *Pekka Halonen, elämä ja teokset* (Porvoo: WSOY, 1957).
Also Bibliography refs: 10, 15, 59, 62, 63, 71.

EERO JÄRNEFELT

L. Wennervirta, *Eero Järnefelt* (Helsinki, 1950).
Also Bibliography refs: 10, 15, 59, 63, 71.

HUGO SIMBERG

Pierre Gervasoni, 'Hugo Simberg, passeur vers l'Au-delà' (Paris, Sorbonne, 1985), Mèmoire de maîtrise.
Paula Kivinen, *Tampereen tuomiokirkko* (Helsinki, 1961).

Marjatta Levanto, *Tonttukuningas kuoleman puutarhassa* (Helsinki: Otava, 1985).
Pirjo Markkanen, 'Hugo Simberg's photographs', English summary. *Finnish Photographic Yearbook* (Helsinki, 1974), p. 148.
Sakari Saarikivi, ed., *Hugo Simberg. Grafiikkaa, Grafik, Graphic art* (Porvoo, 1947).
Sakari Saarikivi, *Hugo Simberg. Elämä ja tuotanto* (Porvoo, 1948). A shorter version in Swedish: *Hugo Simberg. Hans liv och verk* (Helsingfors, 1951).
Börje Sandelin, 'Döden och Fattig fan', *Ord och bild* (Stockholm, 1961), pp. 81–8.
Salme Sarajas-Korte, 'Om Hugo Simberg och Hans Christian Andersen', *Finsk Tidskrift*, no. 6 (Åbo, 1986).
Guido Simberg, *Hugo Simberg. Akvarelleja* (Porvoo, 1958).
Also Bibliography refs: 13, 15, 62, 63, 65, 68.

JUHO RISSANEN

Pietro Krohn, 'Finsk Malerkunst. Kunstforeningens udstilling 1901', *Kunst. Organ for Dansk Kunst og Kunsthaandværk*, 2. Aargang (Copenhagen, 1900).
Onni Okkonen, *Juho Rissanen. Elämäkertaa ja taidetta* (Porvoo, 1927).
Aimo Reitala, 'The Secret of Rissanen', English summary. *Ateneumin Taidemuseo, Museojulkaisu* (Helsinki, 1972), p. 41.
Sakari Saarikivi, 'Juho Rissanen', *Kuvataiteilijoiden Kuopio*, ed. by Sakari Saarikivi (Kuopio: Kustannuskiila Oy, 1982).
Olli Valkonen, 'Juho Rissasen oppivuodet 1896–1899', *Suomen taide. Vuosikirja* 1954–5 (Porvoo, 1956), pp. 41–50.
E. J. Vehmas, 'Kaksi suomalaista mestaria. Juho Rissanen & T. K. Sallinen', *Suomen taide. Vuosikirja* 1955–6 (Porvoo, 1956), pp. 19–44.
Also Bibliography refs: 59, 62, 68, 71.

HELENE SCHJERFBECK

H. Ahtela, *Helena Schjerfbeck. Kamppailu kauneudesta* (Porvoo, 1951). Swedish edition: *Helena Schjerfbeck* (Helsingfors, 1953).
Hanna and Eilif Appelberg, *Helene Schjerfbeck. En biografisk konturteckning* (Helsingfors, 1949). Finnish translation (Helsinki, 1949).
Lena Holger, 'The Convalescent Motif and the Free Replicas, Helene Schjerfbeck's Painting of a Young Girl', *Ateneumin taidemuseo. Museojulkaisu*, vol. 23, 1980 (Helsinki, 1981), pp. 40–5.
Gotthard Johansson, *Helene Schjerfbecks konst* (Stockholm, 1940).
Helene Schjerfbeck, 'Seitsemän kirjettä Maria Wiikille', *Suomen taiteen vuosikirja 1946* (Porvoo, 1946), pp. 48–69.
Soili Sinisalo, 'Helene Schjerfbeck. En ihärdig sökare – Die unermüdliche Sucherin', *Bibliography ref. 64*, pp. 32–43.
Helena Westermarck, *Mina levnadsminnen* (Åbo, 1941).
Also Bibliography refs: 5, 10, 59, 62, 71.

ELLEN THESLEFF

L. Bäcksbacka, *Ellen Thesleff* (Helsingfors, 1955).
Helsinki, Ateneumin taidemuseo, *Ellen Thesleff*. Exhibition catalogue (1969).
Salme Sarajas-Korte, 'Ellen Thesleff, Wahrheit = Schönheit', *Bibliography ref: 64*, pp. 44–55.
Ellen Thesleff, *Dikter och tankar* (Helsingfors: Konstsalongens förlag, 1954).
Also Bibliography refs: 10, 15, 59, 62, 63, 71.

ICELAND

General

72. Björn Th. Björnsson, *Íslenzk myndlist à 19. og 20.* Öld, I–II (Reykjavík: Helgafell, 1964).
73. Knut Gjerset, *History of Iceland* (New York: The Macmillan Co., 1924).
74. Georg Gretor, *Islands Kultur und seine junge Malerei* (Jena: Eugen Diederichs, 1928).
75. *Íslenzk myndlist*, ed. by Kristján Fridriksson (Reykjavík, 1943).
76. Oslo, Kunstnernes Hus, *Den offisielle islandske Kunstutstilling* (1951).
77. Richard F. Tomasson, *Iceland—The First New Society* (Minneapolis: University of Minnesota Press, 1980).
78. Waterville, Colby College Art Museum, *Icelandic Art 1900–1965*. Exhibition catalogue with article by Selma Jónsdóttir (1965).

THÓRARINN B. THORLÁKSSON

Rosemary Hoffmann and Bera Nordal, *Bibliography ref: 10*, pp. 224–7.
J. (Unknown author), 'Thórarinn B. Thorláksson', *Ódinn,* VI (1911), pp. 76–7.
Selma Jónsdóttir, 'Iceland', *Oplysningsforbundenes kunsttillæg* (Copenhagen, 1973).
Selma Jónsdóttir, 'Art in Iceland at the Turn of the Century', *Bibliography ref: 10*, pp. 57–9.
Reykjavík, Listasafn Íslands, *Thórarinn B. Thorláksson 1867–1967*. Exhibition catalogue with article by Selma Jónsdóttir (1967).
Reykjavík, Listasafn Íslands, 'Thórarinn B. Thorláksson', *Fjórir frumherjar*. Exhibition catalogue with article by Selma Jónsdóttir (1986) pp. 7–13, English translation pp. 35–41.
Hjörleifur Sigurdsson, 'Hljódláta yfirbordid', *Birtingur*, 2 (1963), pp. 36–41.
Gudrún Thórarinsdóttir, Valtýr Pétursson, *Thórarinn B. Thorláksson* (Reykjavík: Helgafell, 1982).
Kurt Zier, 'Hversu óheppilegt thad er ad hafa engan málara', *Birtingur*, 4 (1967), pp. 40–3.
Also Bibliography refs: 72, 75.

NORWAY

General

79. Henning Alsvik, Leif Østby, Reidar Revold, *Norges billedkunst i det nittende og tyvende århundre* (Oslo: Gyldendal, 1951–1953), 2 volumes.
80. Jan Askeland, *Norsk malerkunst* (Oslo: Cappelen, 1981).
81. Andreas Aubert, *Die norwegische Malerei im XIX. Jahrhundert* (Leipzig: Klinkhardt und Biermann, 1910).
82. Andreas Aubert, *Norsk kultur og norsk kunst* (Kristiania: Steen, 1917).
83. Knut Berg, Nils Messel and Marit I. Lange, 'Maleriet 1870–1914', *Norges kunsthistorie,* vol. 5 (Oslo: Gyldendal, 1981), pp. 109–307.
84. Anne M. Hasund Langballe, Gunnar Danbolt, *Bibliography of Norwegian art history* (Oslo: Universitetsforlaget, 1976).

85. Marit Ingeborg Lange, 'Fra den hellige lund til Fleskum. Kitty L. Kielland og den nordiske sommernatt', *Kunst og Kultur*, vol. 60 (Oslo, 1975), pp. 69–92.
86. Madison, Elvehjem Museum of Art, *The Art of Norway*. Exhibition catalogue (1978).
87. Magne Malmanger, 'Norsk kunstdebatt ved modernismens terskel', *Kunst og Kulturs Serie* no. 1 (Oslo, 1985).
88. Nasjonalgalleriet, *Katalog over norsk malerkunst* (Oslo: Nasjonalgalleriet, 1968).
89. Nasjonalgalleriet, *Katalog over norsk malerkunst. Tilvekst 1968–1978* (Oslo: Nasjonalgalleriet, 1979).
90. Nasjonalgalleriet, *Norske mesterverker i Nasjonalgalleriet* (Oslo: Stenersen, 1981).
91. Nasjonalgalleriet, *One hundred years of Norwegian painting*, introduction by Magne Malmanger (Oslo: Nasjonalgalleriet, 1980).
92. *Norsk biografisk leksikon* (Kristiania, Oslo: Aschehoug, 1923–83), 19 volumes.
93. *Norsk kunstnerleksikon* (Oslo: Universitetsforlaget, 1982–6), 4 volumes.
94. Jens Thiis, *Norske malere og billedhuggere,* vol. 2 (Bergen: Grieg, 1907).
95. Leif Østby, *Fra naturalisme til nyromantikk. En studie i norsk malerkunst i tiden ca. 1888–1895* (Oslo: Gyldendal, 1934).
Also Bibliography refs: 9, 10, 11.

HARRIET BACKER

Else Christie Kielland, *Harriet Backer* (Oslo: Aschehoug, 1958).
Marit I. Lange, *Harriet Backer 1845–1932. Kitty L. Kielland 1843–1914.* Exhibition catalogue (Åmot: Stiftelsen Modums Blaafarveværk, 1983).
Erling Lone, *Harriet Backer* (Kristiania: Aschehoug, 1924).
Anne Wichstrøm, 'Blant likemenn. Søkelys på Harriet Backers og Kitty L. Kiellands karrierer', *Den skjulte tradisjon*, ed. by Kari Vogt (Bergen: Sigma, 1982), pp. 172–91.
Michele Vishny, 'Harriet Backer: A Northern light', *Arts Magazine* (New York, May 1983), pp. 78–80.
Also Bibliography refs: 10, 11, 93.

HALFDAN EGEDIUS

Walther Halvorsen, *Halfdan Egedius* (Kristiania: Gyldendal, 1914).
Øistein Parmann, *Halfdan Egedius. Liv og verk* (Oslo: Dreyer, 1979).
Also Bibliography refs: 10, 13, 16, 83, 86.

KITTY LANGE KIELLAND

Gabriel Schanche Hidle, *Profiler og paletter i Rogalands kunst* (Stavanger: Stavanger Kunstforening, 1965), pp. 78–98.
Else Christie Kielland, 'Kitty L. Kielland', *Urd* (1943), pp. 376–8.
Marit I. Lange, *Harriet Backer 1845–1932. Kitty L. Kielland 1843–1914.* Exhibition catalogue (Åmot: Stiftelsen Modums Blaafarveværk, 1983).
Hild Sørby, *Jærmaleriet* (Oslo: Universitetsforlaget, 1983), pp. 15–24, 39–48.
Anne Wichstrøm, 'Blant likemenn. Søkelys på Harriet Backers og Kitty L. Kiellands karrierer', *Den skjulte tradisjon*, ed. by Kari Vogt (Bergen: Sigma, 1982), pp. 172–91.
Also Bibliography refs: 79, 85, 86, 94.

THEODOR KITTELSEN

Sidsel Helliesen, *Th. Kittelsen. De lyse årene i Sigdal.* Exhibition catalogue (Åmot: Stiftelsen Modums Blaafarveværk, 1980).
Odd Hølaas, *Th. Kittelsen. Den norske faun* (Oslo: Gyldendal, 1941).
Theodor Kittelsen i tekst, tegninger og malerier (Oslo: Gyldendal, 1945).
Theodor Kittelsen, Exhibition catalogue (Oslo: Oslo Kunstforening, 1964).
Leif Østby, *Theodor Kittelsen* (Oslo: Dreyer, 1975).

EDVARD MUNCH

Arne Eggum, *Edvard Munch. Symbols and images.* Exhibition catalogue (Washington: National Gallery of Art, 1978).
Arne Eggum, *Bibliography ref: 93.* Complete bibliography.
Arne Eggum, *Edvard Munch. Paintings, sketches and studies.* Translated by Ragnar Christophersen (London: Thames and Hudson, 1984).
Reinhold Heller, *Munch. His life and work* (London: Murray, 1984).
Ingrid Langaard, *Edvard Munch. Modningsår* (Oslo: Gyldendal, 1960).
John Boulton Smith, *Frederick Delius & Edvard Munch, their friendship and their correspondence* (England: Triad Press, 1983).
Nic. Stang, *Edvard Munch.* Translated by Carol J. Knudsen (Oslo: Tanum, 1972).
Ragna Stang, *Edvard Munch. The man and the artist* (London: Fraser, 1979).
Also Bibliography refs: 9, 10, 11, 12, 15, 94.

GERHARD MUNTHE

Hilmer Bakken, *Gerhard Munthes dekorative kunst* (Oslo: Gyldendal, 1946).
Gerhard Munthe, *Minder og meninger fra 1850-aarene til nu* (Kristiania: Cammermeyer, 1919).
Also Bibliography refs: 11, 87.

EILIF PETERSSEN

Karen Marie Ebbesen, 'Eilif Peterssens historiemalerier' (Oslo: Universitetet i Oslo, 1984) Manuscript. Thesis, 2 volumes.
Also Bibliography refs: 79, 85, 86, 94, 95.

HARALD SOHLBERG

Arne Stenseng, *Harald Sohlberg. En kunstner utenfor allfarvei* (Oslo: Gyldendal, 1963).
Leif Østby, *Harald Sohlberg* (Oslo: Gyldendal, 1936).
Also Bibliography refs: 9, 10, 79, 81.

ERIK WERENSKIOLD

Torsten Svedfelt, *Erik Werenskiolds konst* (Stockholm: Nordisk Rotogravyr, 1938).
Erik Werenskiold, published by Kunstnerforbundet (Kristiania: Aschehoug, 1913).
Erik Werenskiold, *Kunst og Kultur*, vol. 5 (1914–15), pp. 65–130.
Erik Werenskiold, *Kunst, kamp, kultur gjennem 40 aar i tekst og billeder* (Kristiania: Cammermeyer, 1917).
Leif Østby, *Erik Werenskiold* (Oslo: Dreyer, 1977).
Leif Østby, *Maleren og tegneren Erik Werenskiold 1855–1938.* Exhibition catalogue (Åmot: Stiftelsen Modums Blaafarveværk, 1985).
Also Bibliography ref: 11.

SWEDEN

General

96. Sven Alfons, Bo Lindwall and Ragnar Josephson, *Svensk konstkrönika under 100 år* (Stockholm: Natur och Kultur, 1944).
97. Ingvar Anderson, *A History of Sweden* (New York: Praeger, 1956).
98. Donald R. Floyd, 'Attitudes Toward Nature in Swedish Folklore' (PhD diss., University of California, Berkeley, 1976).
99. Alrik Gustafson, *A History of Swedish Literature* (Minneapolis: University of Minnesota Press, 1961).
100. Brita Linde, 'Ernest Thiel och hans konstgalleri' (PhD diss., University of Stockholm, 1969).
101. London, Royal Academy of Art, *Exhibition of Works by Swedish Artists 1880–1900*, by Axel Gauffin (Stockholm: P. A. Norstedt, 1924).
102. New York, The Brooklyn Museum, *The Swedish Art Exhibition*, by Christian Brinton (1916).
103. Georg Nordensvan, *Svensk konst och svenska konstnärer i nittonde århundradet*. Vol. 2: *Från Karl XV till sekelslutet* (Stockholm: Albert Bonniers Förlag, 1928).
104. Sven Sandström, *Konsten i Sverige: Det sena 1800-talets bildkonst och miljökonst* (Stockholm: Almqvist & Wiksell Förlag, 1975).
105. Franklin D. Scott, *Sweden—The Nation's History* (Minneapolis, 1977).
106. Larry Emil Scott, 'Pre-Raphaelitism and the Swedish 1890s' (PhD diss., University of Washington, 1973).
107. Stockholm, Nationalmuseum, *Konstnärsförbundet 1891–1920*, by Sixten Strömbom and Bo Wennberg (1948).
108. Stockholm, Nationalmuseum, *Opponenterna av 1885*, by Sixten Strömbom (1945).
109. Stockholm, Nationalmuseum, *Svenskt måleri från realism till expressionism* (1942).
110. Sixten Strömbom, *Nationalromantik och radikalism: Konstnärsförbundets historia 1891–1920* (Stockholm: Albert Bonniers Förlag, 1965).
111. *Svenskt konstnärslexikon*, 1–5 (Malmö: Allhems förlag, 1952–67).

RICHARD BERGH

R. Bergh, *Om konst och annat* (Stockholm, 1908, second ed., 1919).
R. Bergh, *Efterlämnade skrifter om konst och annat* (Stockholm, 1921).
B. Rapp, *Richard Bergh. Konstnär och kulturpolitiker 1890–1915*. English summary (Stockholm, 1978).
Also Bibliography refs: 11, 111.

PRINCE EUGEN

Prince Eugen, *Breven berätta (1886–1913)* (Stockholm, 1942).
Axel Gauffin, *Konstnären Prins Eugen* (Stockholm, 1915, second ed. 1947).
Axel Gauffin, 'The Landscape Paintings of Prince Eugen of Sweden', *The International Studio 45* (London, January 1912), pp. 173–85.
E. Wennerholm, *Prins Eugen. Människan och Konstnären* (Stockholm, 1982).
D. Widman, 'Prince Eugen'. *Gazette des Beaux-Arts* (Paris, juin, 1983), pp. 211–22.

GUSTAF FJAESTAD

A. Fjaestad, *Gustaf och Maja Fjaestad—ett konstnärspar* (Karlstad, 1981).
Also Bibliography ref: 9.

EUGÈNE JANSSON

Carl G. Laurin, *Stockholm through Artists' Eyes* (Stockholm, second ed. 1930).
Nils G. Wollin, *Eugène Janssons måleri* (Stockholm, 1920).
Also Bibliography ref: 10.

ERNST JOSEPHSON

E. Blomberg, *Ernst Josephson. Hans liv* (Stockholm, 1951).
E. Blomberg, *Ernst Josephsons konst* (Stockholm, 1956).
E. Blomberg, *Ernst Josephson från 'Näcken' till 'Gåslisa'* (Stockholm, 1959).
Bonn, Städtisches Kunstmuseum, *Ernst Josephson 1851–1906. Bilder und Zeichnungen*. Also Bochum Museum (1979).
Hamburg, Kunstverein, *Vor der Zeit. Carl Fredrik Hill. Ernst Josephson. Zwei Künstler des späten 19. Jahrhunderts*. Ed. by Marina Schneede, Uwe M. Schneede. Also Munich, Stuttgart (1984–5).
G. F. Hartlaub, 'Der Zeichner Josephson', *Genius* II (1920).
I. Mesterton, *Vägen till försoning. En konstpsykologisk studie i Ernst Josephsons religiösa fantasivärld* (Göteborg, 1957).
K. Wåhlin, *Ernst Josephson* I–II (Stockholm, 1911–12).

CARL LARSSON

S. and H. Alfons, *Carl Larsson, skildrad av honom själv* (Stockholm, 1952, second ed. 1977).
Carl Larsson, *Jag* (autobiography), (Stockholm, 1931).
Carl Larsson's World, Carl Larssons Welt, Le grand livre de Carl Larsson. Articles by Bo Lindwall, Görel Cavalli-Björkman, H.-C. Köster (Königstein, 1982).
New York, The Brooklyn Museum, *Carl Larsson*, by Sarah Faunce, Görel Cavalli-Björkman etc. (1983).
G. Nordensvan, *Carl Larsson* 1–2 (Stockholm, 1920–1).
Stockholm, Liljevalchs Konsthall, *Carl Larsson, Minnesutställning* (1953).

BRUNO LILJEFORS

Allan Ellenius, *Bruno Liljefors* (Uppsala, 1981).
M. Hill, 'Liljefors of Sweden: the peerless eye', *Audubon*, vol. 80, no. 5 (September 1978), pp. 70–104.
Bruno Liljefors, *Det vildas rike* (Stockholm, 1934).
Bo Lindwall and Lindorm Liljefors, *Bruno Liljefors* (Stockholm, 1960).
Läckö slott, *Bruno Liljefors—i det vildas rike* (Skövde, Västergötlands turistråd, 1982).
Jacques Tersmeden, 'Bruno Liljefors. Konst och person inför svensk och utländsk allmänhet, 1890–97.' (PhD diss., University of Umeå, 1985).

AUGUST STRINDBERG

Torsten Måtte Schmidt and G. Söderström, *Strind-*

bergs måleri (Malmö, 1972).
Göran Söderström, *August Strindberg och bildkonsten* (Uddevalla, 1972).
Also Bibliography ref: 8.

CARL WILHELMSON

A. L. Romdahl, *Carl Wilhelmson* (Stockholm, 1938).

ANDERS ZORN

Karl Asplund, *Anders Zorn. His Life and Work* (London: 'The Studio' Ltd., 1921).
Gerda Boëthius, *Zorn: Tecknaren, målaren, etsaren, skulptören* (Stockholm, 1949).
Gerda Boëthius, *Anders Zorn. An International Swedish Artist: His Life and Work* (Stockholm, 1954).
Gerda Boëthius, *Zorn. Swedish Painter and World Traveller.* Translated by Albert Read (Stockholm, 1959, reprinted, 1961).
Hans Henrik Brummer, *Zorn, svensk målare i världen* (Stockholm, 1975).
Teddy Brunius and Oscar Reutersward, *Samtal om Zorn* (Höganäs, 1979).
Loys Delteil, *Anders Zorn. Le Peintre-Graveur Illustré*, vol. 4 (Paris, 1909).
Erik Forssman, *Tecknaren Anders Zorn* (Stockholm, 1959).
Erik Forssman, *Zorn i Mora* (Stockholm: Albert Bonniers Förlag, 1960).
Freiburg, Städtische Museen, *Anders Zorn 1860–1920*, by Erik Forssman (1976).
Lawrence, Spencer Museum of Art, The University of Kansas, *The Prints of Anders Zorn*, by Elizabeth Brown (1979).
Long Beach, The University Art Museum, California State University, *Anders Zorn rediscovered* (1984).
Anders Zorn, *Självbiografiska anteckningar.* Commented and published by H.H. Brummer (Stockholm, 1982).

Photographic Credits

Kristján Pétur Gudnason, Reykjavík, Nos. 99–102
Göteborgs konstmuseum, Gothenburg, No. 53
Kari Jämsen, Kuopio, No. 75
Jacques Lathion, Oslo, Nos. 4, 7–11, 31, 46–48, 57–59, 61, 63, 67–68, 72, 86–88, 103–105, 107
Kari Lehtinen, Turku, Nos. 22–23, 35
Museokuva, Helsinki, Nos. 12–14, 25, 28, 45, 76–79, 81–84, 95–98
Nationalmuseum, Stockholm, Nos. 17, 44, 52, 111
Sven Nilsson, Stockholm, Nos. 5, 16, 19, 32, 35, 37–39, 41–43, 55, 91–94, 110
Kalervo Ojutkangas, Oulu, No. 26
Hans Petersen, Copenhagen, Nos. 1, 18, 29, 31, 33, 49, 51, 64–66, 69–71
Q-Studio, Helsinki, No. 80
Sixten Sandell, Gothenburg, Nos. 6, 15, 54, 106, 108
Douglas Sivén, Helsinki, No. 20
Ole Woldbye, Copenhagen, Nos. 40, 73
O. Væring, Oslo, Nos. 2, 3, 56, 60, 62, 89–90

THE TIME TEAM REPORTS

CHANNEL FOUR TELEVISION

CONTENTS

THE TIME TEAM

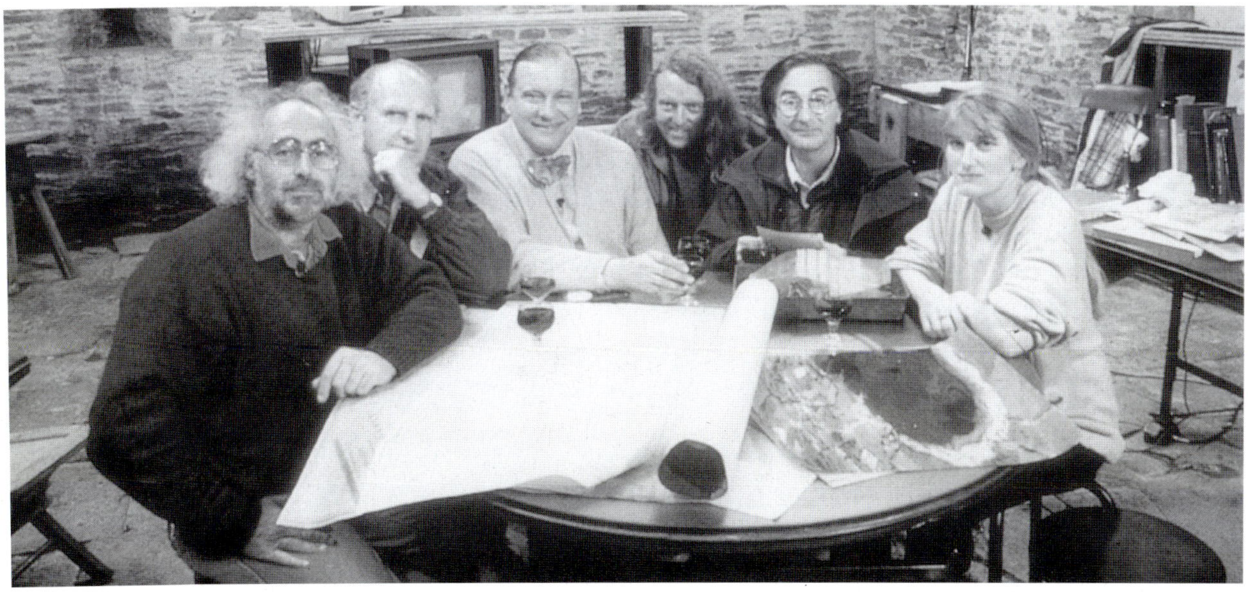

Tony Robinson, the series presenter, is probably best known as Baldrick in *Blackadder* and as the Sheriff of Nottingham in *Maid Marian and Her Merry Men*, which he also writes. He has a keen interest in history and archaeology – he is president of the Young Archaeologists Club – and is particularly fascinated by ancient Greece and the biblical lands of the Middle East.

Mick Aston, the team leader, has been involved with archaeology for more than 30 years, and is currently Reader in Archaeology at the University of Bristol. He has written numerous books and articles, including *Interpreting the Landscape*, the standard work on landscape archaeology. To date, he has appeared in three series on archaeology for Channel 4.

Victor Ambrus, a Fellow of the Royal Academy of Arts, is a freelance illustrator with over 250 books to his credit, most on historical subjects. He has twice won the Kate Greenaway Award for best illustrated children's book of the year. He is currently working on the illustrations for a new book on the Sutton Hoo excavations, written by Martin Carver

Robin Bush is a freelance lecturer, historian and broadcaster, and formerly was Deputy County Archivist for Somerset. An expert in genealogy and on the history of early emigration to the United States, he is author of numerous books on local history, including a recent definitive guide to Somerset.

Phil Harding is currently a field archaeologist with the Trust for Wessex Archaeology. Having worked in archaeology for over 25 years, he is a recognised expert in flint knapping and the Palaeolithic period.

Carenza Lewis has been a field archaeologist for the Royal Commission on Historic Monuments for England (RCHME) for nearly ten years. A specialist in the medieval period and in historic landscapes, she has worked extensively in Wessex and has recently co-edited a collection of essays on the medieval landscape of this part of England.

The *TIME TEAM (left to right)*: Mick Aston, Victor Ambrus, Robin Bush, Phil Harding, Tony Robinson and Carenza Lewis.

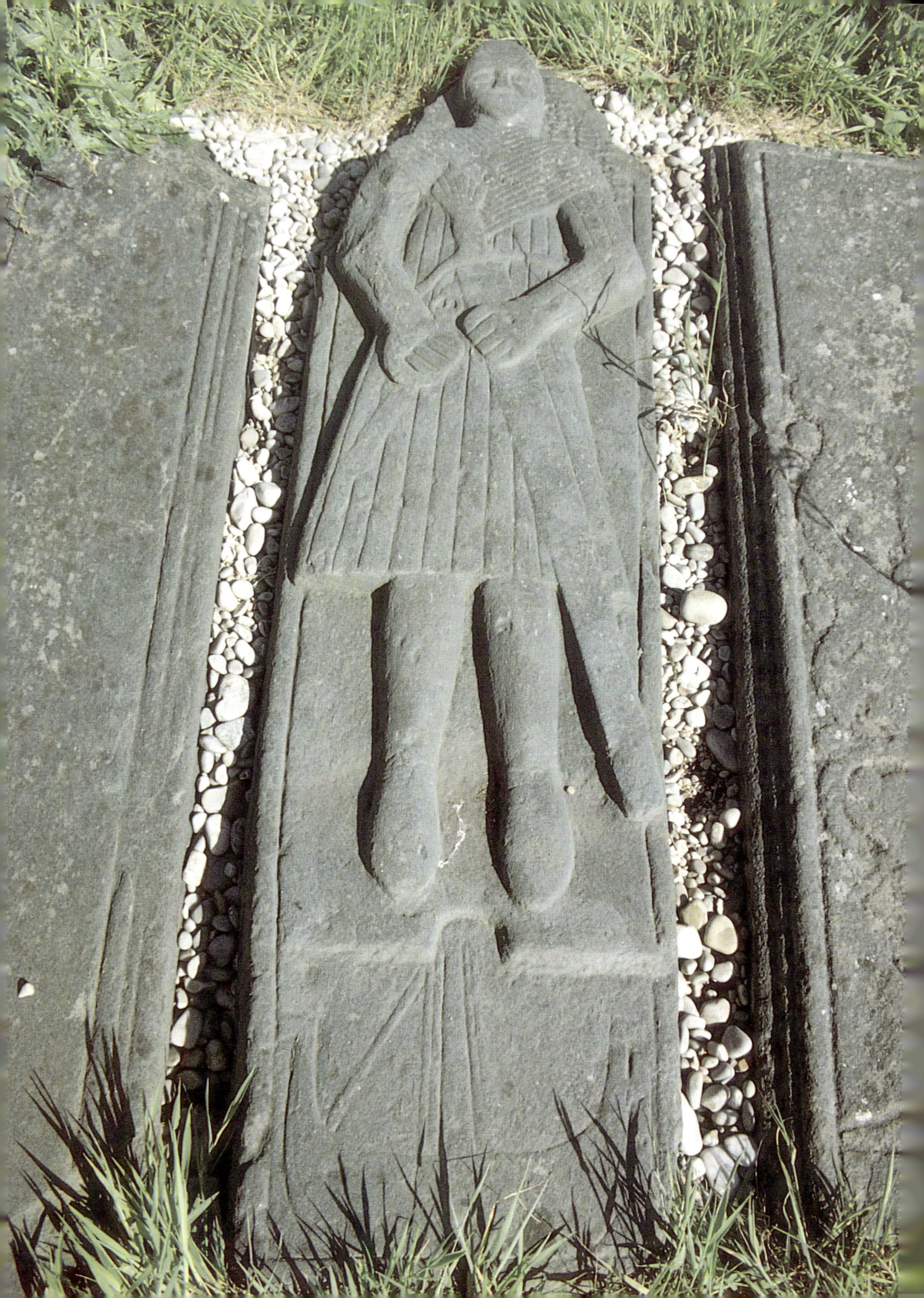

ISLAY

Western Isles, Scotland, 24–26 June 1994

TONY'S TALE, OR WHAT MIGHT HAVE HAPPENED

The islands off the west coast of Scotland exist in a world that is dominated by the sea, a world with an historical affinity with the Irish to the south and the Scottish to the east, and influenced in its early history by the Viking raiders who came from the north. Islay lies at the centre of this world. The farmers there say that, on a clear night, you can see the lights on the Irish mainland, and the prevailing winds and currents will carry a boat from the north-east coast of Ireland into Loch Indaal on the west coast of Islay, the safest bay in an area notorious for its currents and tides. Yet the island of Jura and the Scottish mainland are just short journeys across the sea. This position and the influence of these different cultures on the island's history go some way towards explaining the independence and individuality of the people who occupy Islay today.

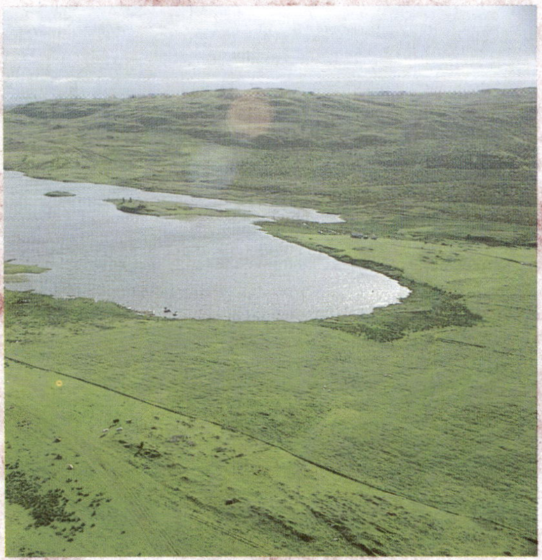

Islay – the 'flower of the islands' – has always held a special place in the history of the Scottish. Throughout it has been a focal point of the battle for control of the western sea lanes. By the 14th century, it was at the heart of a virtually independent Gaelic kingdom that controlled much of western Scotland, elected its own leaders and made its own laws, with its capital at Finlaggan in the centre of the island.

The process that would lead to this domination began around AD 1050 when the isles of western Scotland began to establish an individual identity. They were still controlled by the Norse, who, in the search for new land, had sailed their galleys there at the end of the 8th century. In 795, Iona was attacked and, in the following years, the north coast of Ireland and the Isle of Man. The Norse settled on Islay, and farms that can still be seen today have names derived from the Norse words for 'estate' (boer) and 'farm' (bolstaor), including Conisby, Bolsa and Nerabus. In the years that followed, the Norse and the local Gaelic tribes learned to live together, and the islands began to assert a certain amount of independence from their rulers in Norway.

An early ruler of Islay, Godred Crovan, who may have lived in the area of the island known as The Rhinns, can perhaps be seen as the first to establish an independent kingdom of the isles. Over the next half a century, their story was dominated by a struggle between the Norse, under kings such as Magnus Berfott, and local rulers such as Godred, who attempted to preserve their independence. Magnus was notorious for his destructive reign. Islay was repeatedly plundered, and it was only after the Irish defeated and killed the Norse king that a ruler with

(Left) Grave slab on the largest of the islets in Loch Finlaggan, showing a warrior wearing an *aketon* , with a galley at his feet. *(Mick Aston)*
(Above) Islay: the Loch of Finlaggan and its two islets. *(Mick Aston)*

his roots in the Western Isles took control: Olaf, Godred's son, who ruled from the Isle of Man. Upon his death, Olaf was succeeded by his son, another Godred, who once again threatened to destroy the peace of the isles.

At this point, a new character entered the story, one who was to be the key figure in the next stage of the islands' history. Somerled, a petty king from Argyll who had married Godred's sister Ragnhildis, became a focus for the other lords who were discontented with Godred's reign. This new leader understood the world of the seas between Ireland and Scotland. Power here depended both on a strong army and a command of the sea lanes, and Somerled strengthened the galley fleets that could defend the islands. (Some researchers believe that a new form of light, manoeuvrable galley called the nyaig *was also developed at this time.) He then attacked Godred's battle fleet in the Sound of Jura in 1156 and won control of the islands to the south of Ardnamurchan.*

Like his predecessors, Somerled was keen to preserve the isles' independence, and although he maintained contacts with the Norse and Irish, he was quick to do battle in any cause that he believed would secure his power. In the final years of his life, he attacked the Scottish mainland in a bid to expand his kingdom, but was killed in a battle in Strathclyde near Glasgow in 1164.

He was succeeded by his sons Angus, Dughall and Reginald, and it was Reginald who established his kingdom on Islay and founded the MacDonald family line. The great seal of Islay shows Somerled with his sons in a galley typical of those used to defeat Godred. With Reginald, the influence of the Norse declined and a more clearly Gaelic culture developed, still maintaining its independence from the mainland.

Finlaggan became the central point of the Lordship of the Western Isles, where the councils were held and the leaders elected. Thousands of subjects would gather for these great ceremonies, and the area round the loch would become the site for feasting. In the great hall situated on the larger of the two islets in the loch, Gaelic poetry – often attacks on the enemies of the Lords – would be read and the Gaelic harp would be played.

Four centuries of MacDonald ascendancy were to follow under such rulers as Aonghus Mor and Aonghus Og who fought with Robert Bruce at Bannockburn in 1314. The Lordship had the power to preserve its independence and expand its influence, controlling the coastal edges of the mainland and areas of Northern Ireland around Antrim. Sadly this golden era of an independent Gaelic kingdom was not to last. After 1425, under the misguided leadership of Alaisdair MacDonald, the power of the Scottish kings was overtly threatened. Relationships with the mainland were not helped when Alaisdair's successor, John, agreed, in a secret pact of 1462, to join Edward IV of England in an attack on the Scottish! In 1493, James IV of Scotland had clearly had enough and abolished the Lordship. At around this time, Islay was attacked, and the traditional enemies of the MacDonalds – the Campbells – increased their influence in the Western Highlands. The buildings around Finlaggan were destroyed, although remnants can still be seen on the islets in the loch, reminders of that lost golden age.

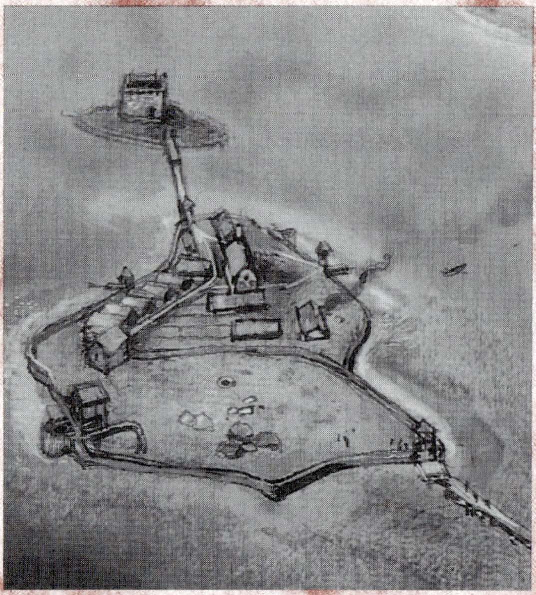

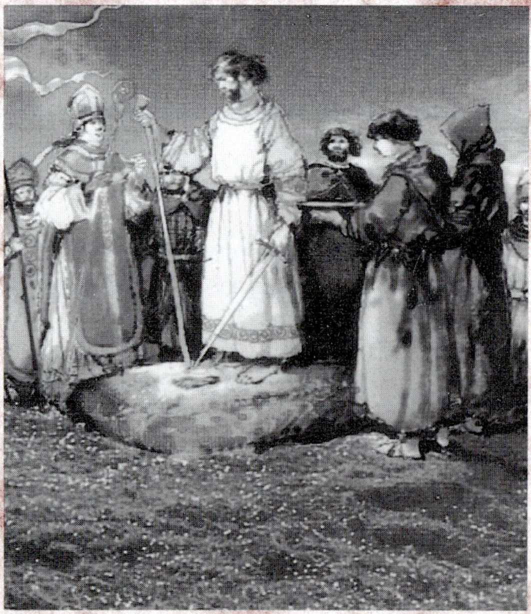

(Top) Victor's reconstruction of the Gaelic settlement on the two islets in the loch, joined by a causeway.
(Bottom) Victor's reconstruction of the inauguration ceremony at Finlaggan.

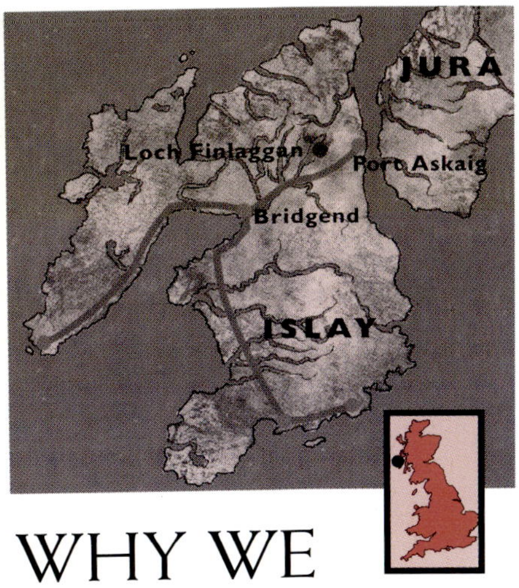

WHY WE WENT THERE

Time Team had been invited to Islay by the Finlaggan Trust, a group formed by islanders who wished to encourage interest and archaeological research in the area. Since 1989, they have been working closely with the National Museums of Scotland on the two islets in the loch. The excavations carried out there over the last five years had turned up a wealth of evidence about the Lords of the Isles, but time was running out. This was to be their last year of excavation, and there were still sites to investigate around the edge of the loch. This is where *Time Team* came in.

The Finlaggan Trust was keen to know more about the area around the main island sites. Dr David Caldwell, leader of the excavations, had become particularly interested in Cnoc Seandda, a small hill at the edge of the loch. This appeared to have a significant position, aligned as it was between the islets in the loch and the distant mountains called the Paps of Jura. When we first visited the site, there was a strong feeling that this hill could have been an alternative location for the inauguration ceremony that the Lords held to crown their new leaders. It commanded excellent views over the loch and the surrounding countryside, and its shape and the terraced area that surrounded it made it only too easy to imagine the Lords and their followers assembling there, rather than on the islets where space would have been at a premium.

David Caldwell had assisted us in gaining permission from the Trust and the estate managers to film in the area and, if necessary, undertake an evaluative excavation in the area of the mound. The farmer whose land surrounded Finlaggan, Donald Bell, was an enthusiastic supporter of the Trust, and this and the interest of the islanders themselves were a tremendous help in making us feel welcome.

So the team's brief was to look for features around the edge of the loch, investigate Cnoc Seandda and also help with a search of the waters between the islets. David Caldwell had also referred tantalisingly to a mysterious 'stone of destiny' or inauguration stone that had been lost after the destruction of the main buildings in the 15th century. This stone was described as having a footprint cut into its surface. At the high point of the ceremony, the new leader would place his foot on the stone, symbolising the continuity of his reign with those of his predecessors.

A historian of the MacDonalds, writing in the 17th century, described the rite of inauguration:

The Bishop of Argyll, the Bishop of the Isles and seven priests were sometimes present. There was a square stone 7–8 feet long and the tract of a mans foot cut thereon, upon which he stood, denoting that he should walk in the footsteps and uprightness of his predecessors – he was clothed in a white habit to show his innocence and integrity of heart, that he would be a light to his people and maintain the true religion – Then he received his forefathers sword – signifying that his duty was to protect and defend them from the incursions of their enemies in peace or war – When they were dismissed, the Lord of the Isles feasted them for a week thereafter; gave liberally to the monks, poets, bards and musicians.

From *Monro's Western Isles*

A Welsh visitor to the islands in the 18th century, Thomas Pennant, referred to the stone as still being in existence. Was it possible that it was cut into the natural rock on the top of Cnoc Seandda? *Time Team* had only a few days to find out!

Day One

The working conditions on our first day at Finlaggan were atrocious, with driving rain and the surrounding hills only just visible under a low mist. While the geophysics team began work on Cnoc Seandda, Phil and Gordon Ewart, deputy director of the National

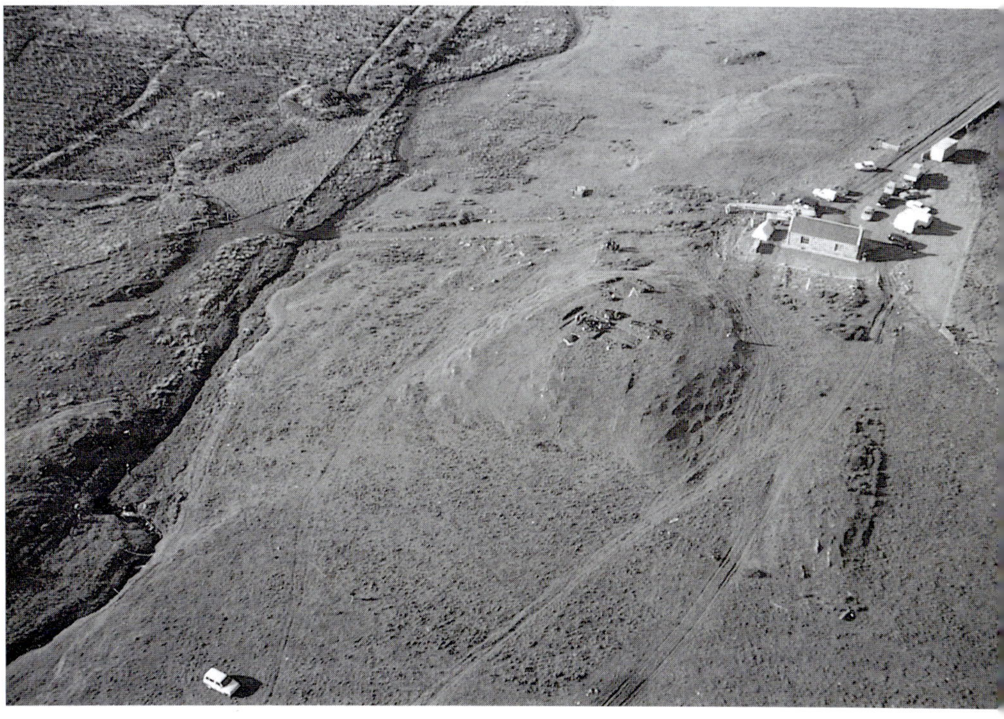

Aerial view of the excavations on top of Cnoc Seandda. *(Mick Aston)*

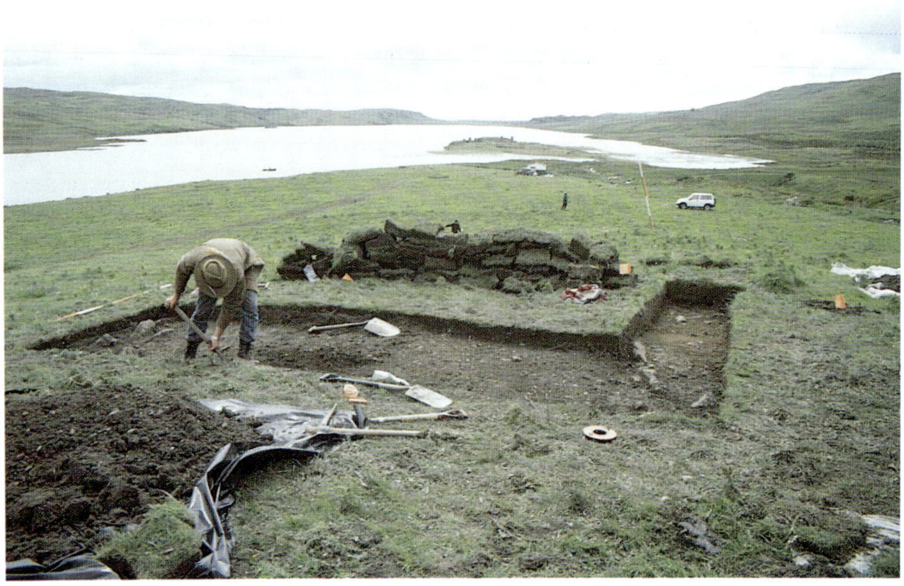

galleys, anvils and foliage in the typical West Highland style. The figure we were most interested in was wearing an *aketon*, an item of padded armour. The Trust was keen to see how this might have actually looked, and we had brought in some experts on the subject, Sue Chandler and Dave Roberts, to make a reproduction using the original materials. The *aketon* was a unique Scottish form of armour, light enough to enable the wearer to avoid his attackers and to cross the boggy landscape easily.

As our work on Cnoc Seandda continued, it became clear that evidence from a much earlier period of the loch's history was emerging. This included flint cores and blades from a period

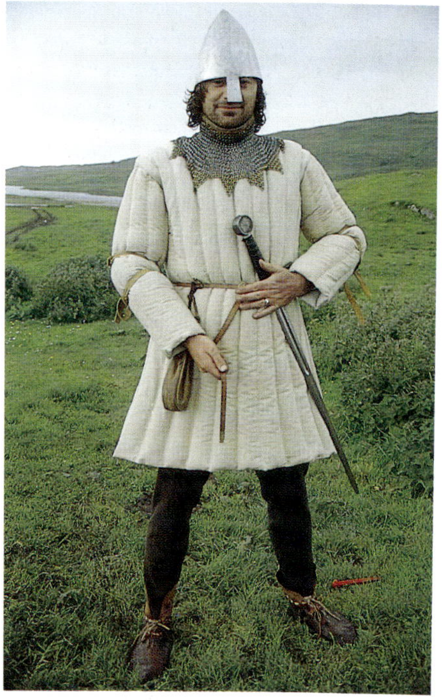

that Phil identified as *mesolithic*, around 7000 years before the Lords of the Isles. 'Cores' are the pieces of flint left after a number of blades have been chipped from the outside.

One of the critical skills for archaeologists working on sites where flints are present is the ability to identify pieces that have been deliberately worked by man. Phil's experience enabled him to do this relatively easily. Some of the key things to look for are *conchoidal rings* – that is, small rings in the surface of the flint that appear to be radiating from a bulbous point, called the 'bulb

Museums excavation, took a look at a site referred to in earlier documents as 'guard houses'. In the 17th century, Martin Martin had visited the islands and, in a book published in around 1695, described a number of features still existing around the loch. This site, called Rudh a Chrocain, appeared to be a set of turf buildings that guarded the jetty at the edge of the loch.

Working in deep mud and trenches in need of bailing out, Phil, Gordon and Alan Radley, a member of the National Museums team, managed to locate the turf walls, but little datable material came to light. Archaeologists are always hoping that a piece of pot or other evidence capable of providing a date will accompany this kind of enigmatic feature. However, in this case, the lack of pottery later than the 17th–18th centuries could point to these structures being earlier and contemporary with the Lords of the Isles.

With conditions deteriorating, it was decided to abandon the site and head for the incident room to check on the progress of the geophysics team. Luckily, the driving rain did not seem to have affected their readings, and using resistance techniques, they had begun to locate features on the top of Cnoc Seandda. The high readings found on Cnoc Seandda appeared (on the printout) to be walls cut into the natural limestone. After consulting with David, we decided to begin a limited evaluation exercise on the top of the hill, across one of the most prominent features. The first step in this process, carried out by Mick and Phil, was to deturf the area to be excavated. (The turf, if removed carefully, can eventually be replaced.) A grid was put in place so that any finds or features could be located for future reference.

While excavation got underway, assisted by members of David's team, we took the opportunity to look at some of the remains on the two islets in the loch. Perhaps the most evocative of these are the grave slabs, carved in a greenish stone, which would have been placed over the bodies of the Lord's followers, buried on one of the islets. These slabs also covered the graves of women and children, although the Lords themselves, in a continuation of tradition. were buried on the island of Iona. Some of the slabs depict the men who fought for the Lords, complete with their armour and long swords. They are also decorated with pictures of

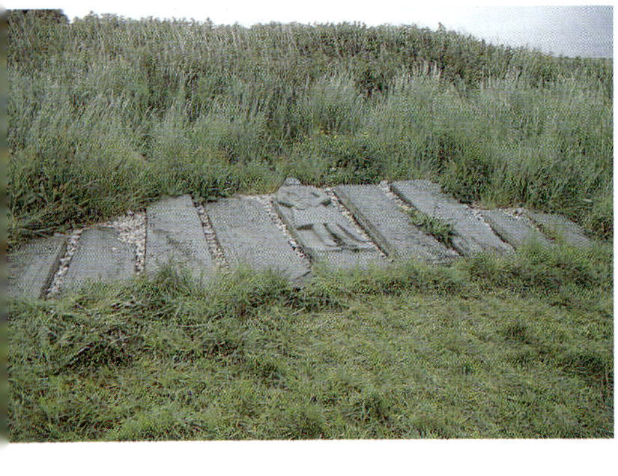

(Top left) Phil digging on Cnoc Seandda, with Loch Finlaggan beyond. *(Mick Aston)*
(Bottom left) The grave slabs on the largest islet in Loch Finlaggan. *(Mick Aston)*
(Right) 'Rat' wearing the replica *aketon*. *(Mick Aston)*

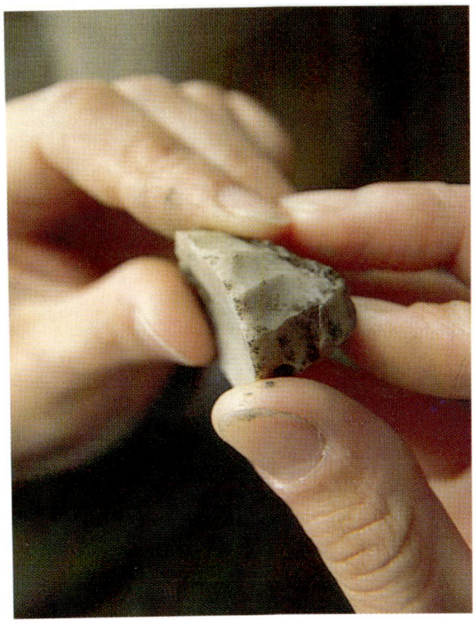

of percussion'. This is where the prehistoric flint knapper actually struck the blow, and the rings are the trace of the shock wave that passed through the flint as it was struck. In one of our pieces from the hill, a *microlith*, Phil was also able to see signs of 'retouching', where a flint had been deliberately selected in order to make a new kind of tool. Microliths were often set in wooden handles to produce what is known as a 'composite tool'.

Phil was particularly pleased to have discovered a microlith. He described it as 'diagnostic' – that is, its structure enables archaeologists to place it in a particular period. Our flint cores and blades had indicated a mesolithic date, and the microlith confirmed occupation of the site during that period.

The mesolithic material related to a time when hunters had used the hill, perhaps to watch for animals as they came to drink at the loch. The shore and hillsides would then have been covered with dense forest, and the surrounding area would have formed a rich hunting ground. Phil and the excavation team continued work on the site, gradually deepening the excavation. There was still the possibility that evidence might be found relating to the period of the Lords of the Isles.

One of the requests we had received from the National Museums of Scotland was to survey the loch and its surrounding land, as a clear picture of the ledges and mounds would be helpful in developing a wider view of the loch's history. To speed up this process, *Time Team* had brought in GPS – 'global positioning by satellite'. The system uses American military technology to track up to nine satellites in space and use these to locate positions on the ground. The system is astonishingly accurate, enabling a point anywhere on the earth's surface to be located within 5 mm in plan and 10 mm in the vertical plane. In other words, coordinates of an object as small as a coffee cup could be obtained, and these would be accurate enough to programme a missile, launched in the US, to fly straight into it!

From our point of view, the main advantage of the GPS system, apart from its accuracy, was its speed. The computations are carried out virtually at walking pace, enabling a large amount of land to be surveyed within our three-day time-scale. The coordinates obtained could be fed into our computers and used to generate a three-dimensional map on which to locate the excavations and any other features. Because of current GPS technology, many older maps are beginning to reveal mistakes, and for a number of the sites on which we work, *Time Team*'s maps are the first really accurate surveys.

Another interesting aspect of the Finlaggan excavation on the islets was the use of a metal detector. Roger McWee has been used by David Caldwell to search spoil heaps – soil and rocks produced by excavation – for any metallic objects that the excavators may have missed. A belt buckle and some medieval nails, coins and fish hooks were just some of the objects that had been located. The coins included examples from the time of Alexander III of Scotland, who reigned between 1249 and 1286, giving an early date in the history of the islets' occupation. This kind of evidence is invaluable, and shows how archaeologists and responsible members of the metal-detecting fraternity can work productively together.

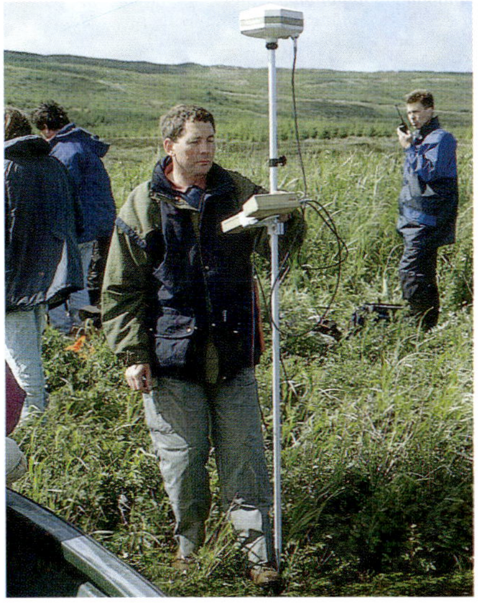

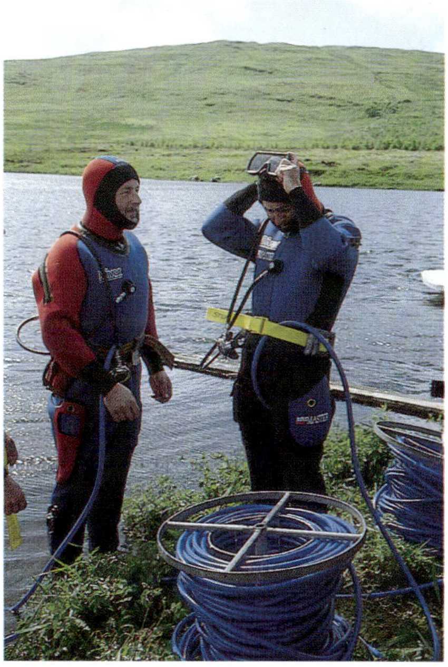

Day Two

During the first day, our diving team had been working between the islets and the causeway to the loch edge. They had been hampered by silt and had now decided to move to an area between the two islets. Dr Nick Dixon and his team from the Scottish Trust for Underwater Archaeology were equipped with breathing apparatus and a 'lift'. The latter is an underwater suction device that enables sediments to be removed from underwater objects without reducing visibility. With this equipment in place, our divers began to uncover a large area of deposits. With Tony assisting, they excavated a top

(Top left) One of the mesolithic flint cores found around Cnoc Seandda. *(Mick Aston)*
(Bottom) Simon Mears helping to carry out the GPS (global positioning by satellite) survey. *(Mick Aston)*
(Right) Dr Nick Dixon *(left)* and Tony Robinson preparing to dive in the loch between the two islets. *(Mick Aston)*

layer of what appeared to be a medieval rubbish tip, or *midden*.

This kind of feature is often the key to a medieval site. It is where all the rubbish – old pots, leftovers from meals and worn-out utensils – is thrown. Tony found a large piece of bone with butchery marks, and was able to see distinct stratified layers of material in the midden.

This stratification of finds is useful to archaeologists as it not only gives a rough chronology – the lowest level being the earliest and so on – but also enables groups of objects to be dated when found alongside others, such as coins or charcoal, which can be given accurate dates by other means. The finds that gradually emerged began to create a useful archive of evidence about life on the islets in the loch.

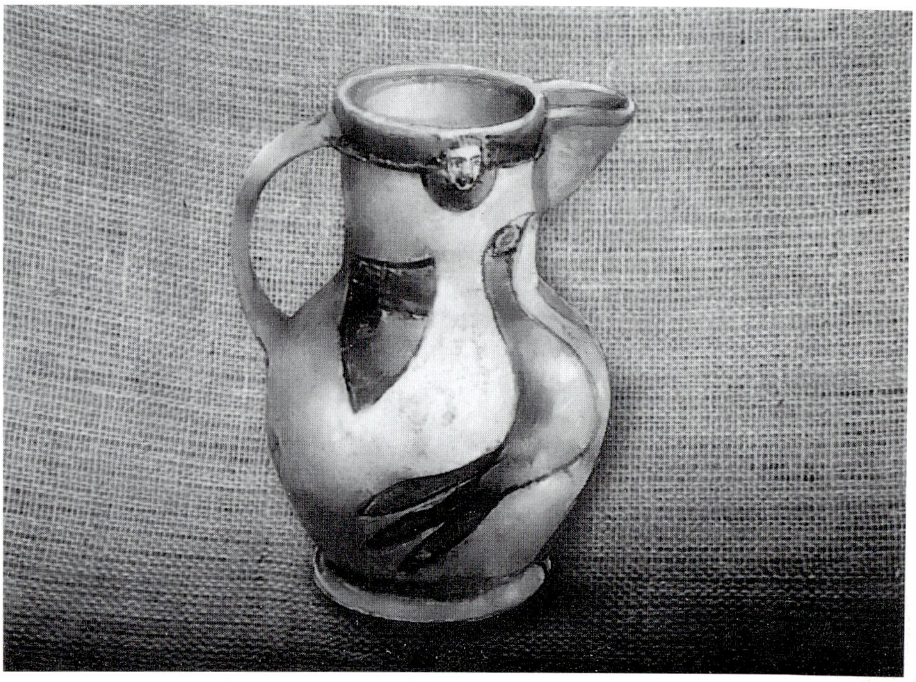

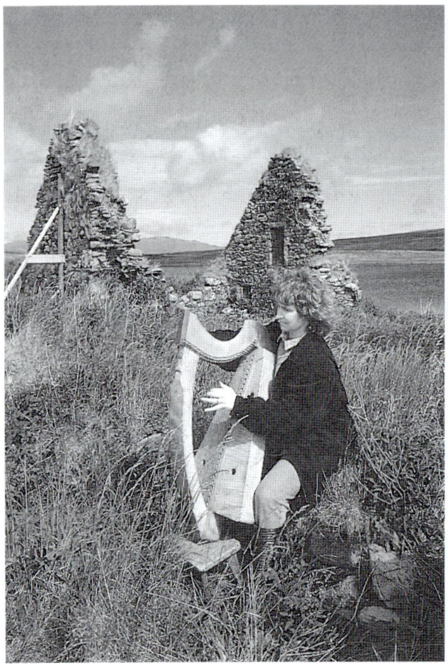

Animal bones could be analysed to show the kind of meat that had been eaten; pottery indicated the presence of expensive jugs, possibly once containing claret; and there were also scraps of organic evidence that needed further analysis.

One of the big advantages of this site being underwater is that the lack of oxygen prevents the deterioration of valuable organic materials that are lost on dry sites. Archaeologists estimate that, for some historical periods, we have lost up to 80 per cent of the evidence due to the destruction of organic materials. This made the discovery of the midden a major 'plus' for David Caldwell and his team.

The finds that had come from the midden were stored on site, along with the material that had been uncovered by previous excavations, some of which generated another request from the Finlaggan Trust. Among the previous finds were harp pins, objects which delighted Mairi MacKintyre of the Finlaggan Trust as their presence balanced the common view that the Lords were an uncultured bunch, interested only in warfare. The pins were probably from small hand-held harps called *clarsachs*. There is some evidence that these harps predated the arrival of the harp in Ireland, and in fact, the harp that traditionally appears on a bottle of Guinness is a Scottish harp! We were able to persuade harpist Alison Kinnaird to come to Finlaggan to give Mairi an idea of what a harp played on the islands would have sounded like.

We ended the second day with the excavations at Cnoc Seandda having moved into a new and critical phase. While Mick and Tony looked at the site from a helicopter, Phil and Carenza had followed their instincts and extended the area of excavation. With growing excitement, they realised that what was now beginning to emerge was a stone structure.

The feature that John had originally located on the geophysics now appeared to be a row of stones deliberately set into the top of the hill. At this stage, it was thought that this might be a prehistoric chamber or *souterrain*. We had also continued to find flints in its vicinity. Souterrains are stone chambers or underground tunnels, thought by some archaeologists to have been built for storage purposes. However, they can often have a ritual significance, and be associated with burials. Would we have enough time on our final day to find the answer?

Day Three

The bad weather had returned, but as Tony pointed out, the howling gale was now coming from a totally different direction. Phil stuck to his task of excavating the feature on the hill. How far would the stones go down?

Carenza had decided that, with space in the souterrain now becoming a little cramped, she would take the opportunity to examine Finlaggan's single standing stone. However,

(Left) Harpist Alison Kinnaird playing a *clarsach*.
(Top) Victor's reconstruction of a jug, based on a piece of ceramic found at Finlaggan.

The magnetometer used by the geophysicists is designed to detect very small, localised changes in the Earth's magnetic field. These changes are associated with geological or archaeological features near the surface. Here three strong magnetic anomalies are visible (in black). These result from either igneous (volcanic) stones or large pits filled with magnetic material. The existing standing stones can be seen at the top left.
(Geophysical Surveys of Bradford)

● Standing stone
○ Magnetic anomaly

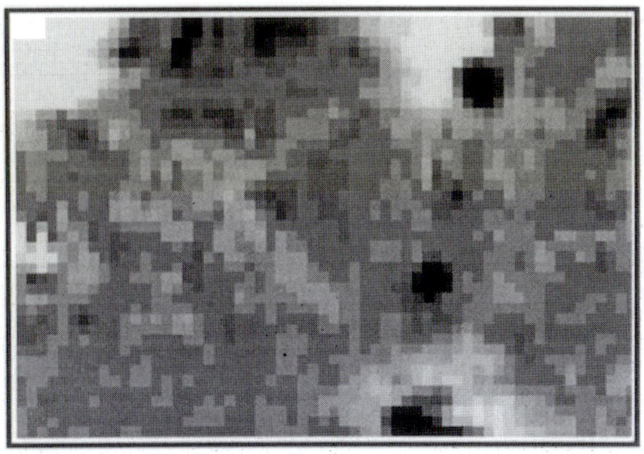

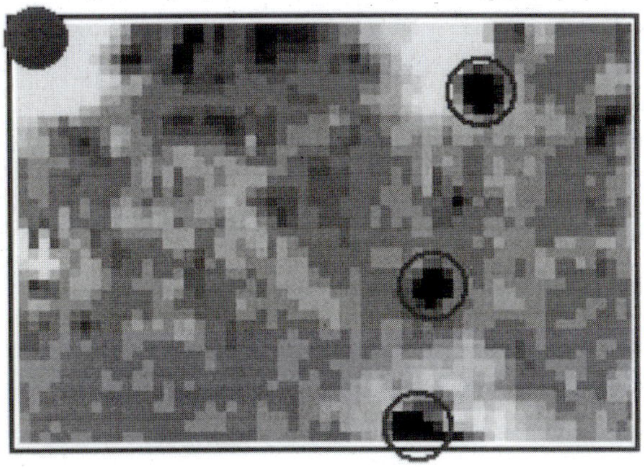

according to Robin's research, Martin Martin's 17th-century description referred to *two* stones.

On her first visit to the site, Carenza had become interested in the variations in the heights of the grasses around the stones, which may have been crop marks. These are valuable to archaeologists because they may be caused by features underneath the soil. A buried wall may restrict the root growth of crops above it, whereas, conversely, deep ditches may increase the nutrients and moisture available and therefore give patterns of increased growth or ripening. By using a sharp steel rod, Carenza confirmed that there seemed to be some kind of feature below the areas of low growth. With time running out, geophysics was called in and began a search of the field using the magnetometer.

Before we were able to get the results from the geophysics, Phil called Carenza and the rest of the team back to Cnoc Seandda with some exciting news. As he had gradually cleared out the soil from the base of the stone structure he had found there, it had become clear that this was an important feature that had been carefully built into the hill, about 5 m (16 ft) long and 1.5 m (5 ft) wide. And as he had reached what appeared to be the floor, he had uncovered bones!

A closer examination by the team and David led to the conclusion that these were animal bones that may have been deliberately buried. There were no obvious butchery marks; the bones were complete and articulated – that is, complete with joints. This was then an animal that had been buried whole for ritualistic purposes in this prehistoric chamber. By now it also had become clear that some of the stones were lintels or roofing stones that had collapsed into the chamber. With weather conditions deteriorating, the team and David Caldwell decided that more work needed to be done at a future date, as clearly this was too important archaeologically to be rushed.

However, the *Time Team* had not yet finished. With only an hour to go, the geophysics team located what looked like a series of pits or features surrounding the single standing stone. These suggested a stone row or circle. Based on this assumption, which only future excavation will prove, we were able to build up a picture of a ritualistic prehistoric landscape around Cnoc Seandda, with the chamber at its centre and a stone row aligned with the islets and the Paps of Jura.

Having come to Islay to uncover the history of the 14th century, we had, in the end, taken the history of the site back into the prehistoric period. Was this part of the reason why the Lords had been attracted to the site in the first place? Were their ritualistic activities a continuation of sacred or ceremonial activity that had been practised here over thousands of years? Hopefully more work by David Caldwell and his team will find some answers!

Final thoughts from Mick

'Finlaggan was wonderful. Even though the weather was awful on two of the three days, at least it brightened up for the helicopter flight. Flying around, we could see that the whole landscape was full of evidence of earlier people – forts, farms, field systems and mining activities. So although the prehistoric finds we made were very exciting, we perhaps should not have been surprised. Long before the Lords of the Isles, people had been living and working throughout the entire area – the Lords had simply legitimised their rule by directly relating it to the many generations that had preceded them.'

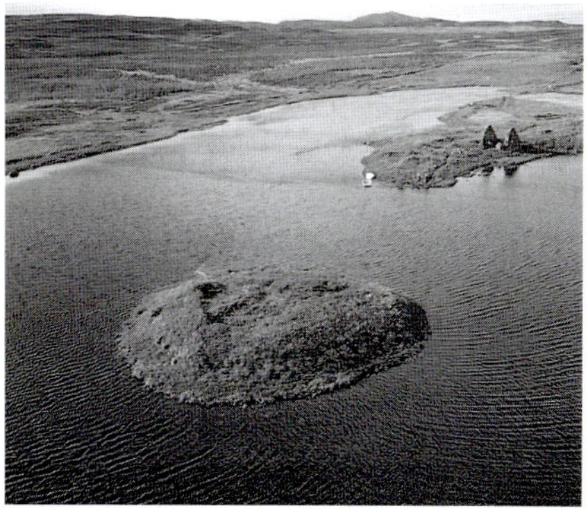

(Top) Geophysics map with caption in a box.
(Bottom right) The two islets in Loch Finlaggan. *(Mick Aston)*

TOCKENHAM

Wiltshire, 23–25 April 1994

TONY'S TALE, OR WHAT MIGHT HAVE HAPPENED

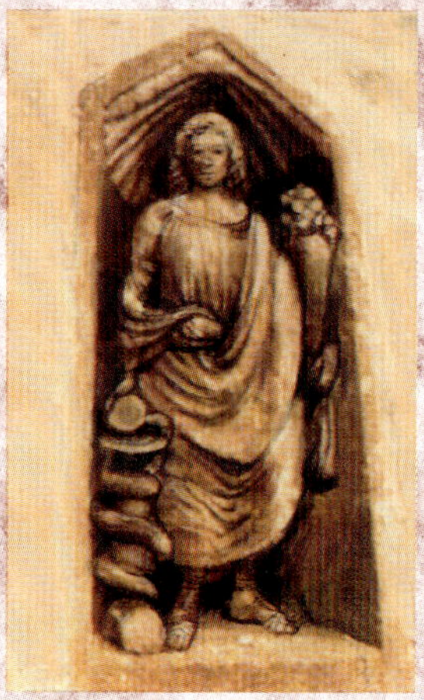

In the late 4th century AD, the Romano-British in this part of Wiltshire felt safe enough to think about the finer things in life. The battles of the past to secure the new land had been forgotten, and the local British, having adopted many Roman ways, seemed, for the time being at least, to appreciate the advantages of civilisation. Nearly 400 years separated these people from the first Roman invaders, and they were now experiencing a golden age in which the fruits of the empire could be enjoyed in peace. This was a time when villas could be sited deep in the countryside without fear of attack, rather than under the protective wings of great walled towns such as Exeter and Cirencester. The villas could be decorated by skilled teams of painters and mosaic artists. In Cirencester, about 17 miles to the north, there was a great school of mosaic art with its own distinctive styles and motifs, and for the owners of the villa near Tockenham, the prospect of a decorated floor in their main hall was an attractive one. It would give them a chance to show off their new-found wealth and display the sophistication of their tastes. They had come a long way since the time, ten generations earlier, when their ancestors had lived in an Iron Age encampment.

There was also an opportunity to show due respect to the household gods, whose worship was part of the life of most Roman homes. Although many families had begun to convert to Christianity, they continued to sustain a strong belief in the old gods. The spring and ponds at Tockenham may have been sacred to the earliest Britons, and the villa's owners perhaps felt this, too. They had learned the advantage of combining the earlier gods with the new, and as nearly all villa owners were Romano-British, born and bred in Britain, this was a natural thing to do. As well as the decorated plaster and mosaics, the richer villa owners commissioned statues and busts of the emperors. The limestone quarried near the edge of the Cotswolds was easily worked, and it was used to carve small figures representing the household deities. These were then placed in small niches in the villa walls.

The abundant springs in the area provided water for the bath house and for decorated fountains and pools. The surrounding acres were relatively fertile, and the woods were a source of fuel for the hypocaust, the Roman version of central heating that, throughout the winter months, would keep the villa at a comfortable temperature and provide hot water for baths.

After the decline of the Roman world and the invasion of the Saxons, the Tockenham villa fell into disrepair, and the great blocks of stone were robbed from the site and used for local buildings. In the early medieval period, a church was built and one of the small figures from the villa was discovered and placed in an alcove in the church wall. It was originally thought to be a representation of St Christopher and then, later, of Aesculapius, the Greek god of healing, and it still stands in the church wall today. Thus the figure that had first been worshipped as a pagan god in a Roman villa found itself in a Christian church.

Victor's reconstruction of the Roman statue set in the wall of the church.

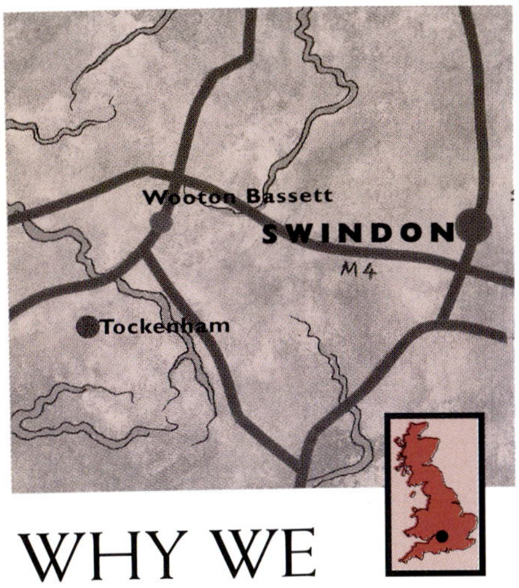

WHY WE WENT THERE

We were originally alerted to the site when a member of the local village community told us about the unusual figure in the church wall. In addition, in 1974 the local landowner had deep ploughed the area to the south of Tockenham church and discovered some pieces of pot and tile. A local archaeologist and expert on Roman villas, Bryn Walters, identified these finds as Roman. An entry was made in the Sites and Monuments Record, which would be examined in detail by Carenza in the course of *Time Team*'s work. However, the first question that needed answering was: What was the figure and how had it got there?

Day One

Assembled around the figure, Mick, Tony and Robin – after consulting the reference in Nikolaus Pevsner's *Buildings of England*, the 'bible' for exploring English buildings – decided that there was a possibility that an earlier, possibly Roman structure may have existed on the site of the church. In Pevsner's volume on Wiltshire, we found the following entry for St Giles, Tockenham:

a small nave and chancel – a bell turret with shingle spire – in the south wall, west of porch, sculpture, Roman figure of Aesculapius.

The church occupies a raised area surrounded by some springs and a small pond. The owners of the garden that lies at the edge of the church grounds had told us that a much larger pond had once existed. They had reduced its size and made it into a decorative feature. This pond may have been the location of an earlier pre-Roman shrine or an early Roman religious site, perhaps based on the worship of the gods of water or, if Pevsner's identification of the statue was correct, the god of healing. Aesculapius was the Greek god adopted by the Romans, to whom Homer, on his death bed, dedicated an offering: 'A cock to Aesculapius.' The local church had been certain enough of this identification to re-dedicate the church to St Giles, the patron saint of the crippled – the nearest Christian equivalent to Aesculapius.

Dorset, over 140 coins, unbroken pots and a spearhead were discovered in the bed of the River Horton. One of the most extensive collections came from Bath, found during the excavations by the archaeologist Barry Cunliffe.

It was decided to initiate a geophysics survey of the area around the church. We also set out to investigate the depths of the pond to see if any environmental evidence existed which might help to date the feature or, with luck, locate some object that related to an earlier Roman building. This was a bit of a long shot. The team realised that, if we were wrong, we might end up examining the mud of a late medieval garden pond!

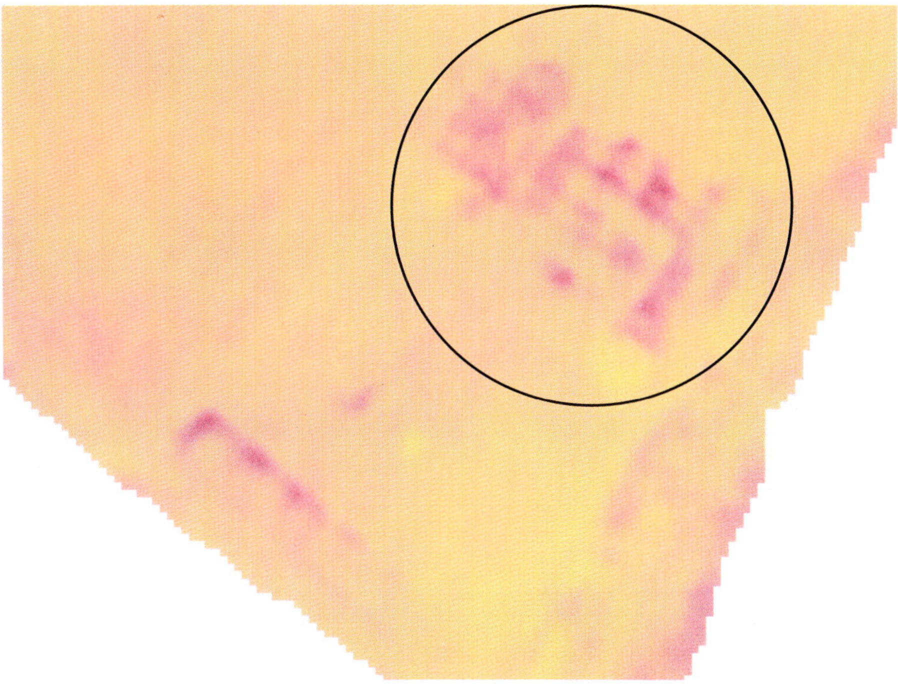

Resistance data showing the outline of the villa (circled) as revealed on Day Two. *(Geophysical Surveys of Bradford)*

If this really were an early ritualistic site dedicated to the gods of water or the god of healing, we might, if we were very lucky, find some trace of earlier buildings or evidence of the votive offerings made to the gods. It was a common practice at these kinds of sites for objects to be cast into the water: coins, weapons or small lead-cast models of weapons, tablets with curses written on them, offerings of food. The stream bed of the Walbrook in London had been found to contain a wealth of objects that had clearly not been dropped there by accident, and in

We had the advantage of two experts in environmental archaeology, Mike Allen and Julie Gardiner, who were going to work with Phil to collect and examine the pond sediments and to auger the area around it. 'Augering' involves the use of a steel tube about a metre long, which is pushed into the ground to obtain cores of soil. These can contain plant and seed remains and may also show a stratigraphy of soil levels, which reveal the build-up of deposits over time. Plant seeds and pollen can help to identify the kinds of crops that had once been grown in an

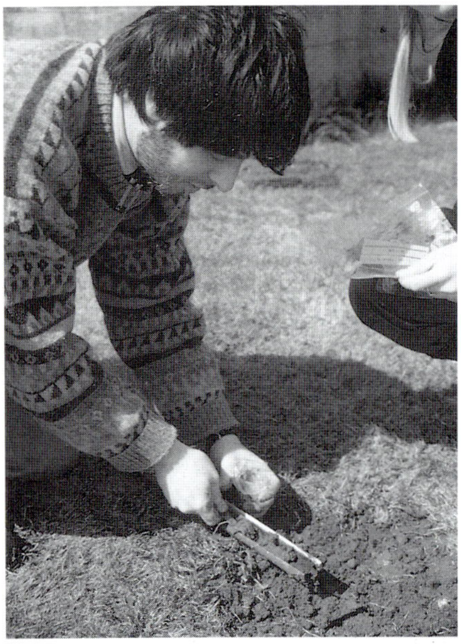

area, and can, if present in a clear stratification, show the sorts of vegetation present at a particular time.

The geophysics team were using resistivity to look for buried structures. This technique involves inserting an electric current into the ground, and then measuring the resistance changes associated with different features. The area to be searched is divided into a set of grids so that any changes can be accurately located on a map. Where the current passes through an area of dense stone such as a buried wall, there is a recording of high resistance. Where it passes through a ditch containing soil or waterlogged material, there is low resistance. These areas of high and low resistance can be plotted on a computer, and the pattern that emerges can provide the outline of a building or other such features under the ground. It is a technique which provides the team with their first non-intrusive evaluation of a site, although as John Gater and Chris Gaffney of the geophysics team are always emphasising, their findings need archaeological interpretation and are not a substitute for excavation.

In the area around the church, there seemed to be little evidence of buildings to the north-west, and with the collection of the necessary samples from the augering completed, it became clear that we would have to begin looking elsewhere. We had also by now had two other critical pieces of information. Dr Martin Henig from Oxford had examined the statue and identified it as being, not Aesculapius, but one of the lesser *genii*, or household gods. This meant that it could have come from a villa rather than a shrine. He pointed out the clear differences between our statue and Aesculapius – the toga that the figure was wearing indicated a Roman, not Greek, origin and the cornucopia in his left hand and *patera*, or Roman dish, in his right were not features associated with the god of healing. Carenza had also had a chance to examine the Sites and Monuments Record in more detail, and was convinced that the local landowner's finds indicated a possible villa site to the south of the church, from which the figure may have come.

The geophysics team were despatched to that area, while Tony and Robin examined the tithe map to see if any of the old field names gave any clues or if the map helped to show earlier boundaries. The tithe maps produced between 1836 and 1844 are the first complete record of field names we have.

It had already been noticed that, in the field where the finds had been discovered, there were a number of lumps and bumps. Stuart Ainsworth and Bernard Thomason from the RCHME began an earthwork survey and located three sets of ridge and furrow in this field. These are features left by ploughing, and they can date back to a very early period.

Prolonged ploughing leaves a distinctive set of linear mounds and ditches that are particularly visible in low sunlight. They are some of the clearest pieces of evidence for medieval farming activity and are useful because they may indicate even earlier field boundaries. Because the ploughman had to take his furrows up to the field edge, this usually left a distinctive line of furrows and ridge ends that may survive modern destruction of the hedge line. Stuart and Bernard also found and surveyed a long ridge that appeared to predate the ridge and furrow. Could this be associated with the boundary of some earlier building?

With the geophysics team working in the large field, Mick had taken the chance to invite David Barnes, the landowner. and a local metal-detector operator, Bill Giles, to come in with their finds to see if Martin Henig could throw any more light on them. Among the finds, Martin noted pieces of pottery and building tiles and a small section of stone that he believed to be a piece from a statue. The more this material was examined, the more it became apparent that an important Roman villa might be under the main field. The pieces of hypocaust tile and *tesserae* (mosaic tiles) – for this is what they turned out to be – suggested a fairly substantial building.

David Barnes indicated that he was considering ploughing the field again, and said that he would want to take as much care as possible if there was anything of importance there. Before he left, he invited Martin to have a look at a piece of old stone pipe in his garden to see if it was of interest. We would hear more about this later.

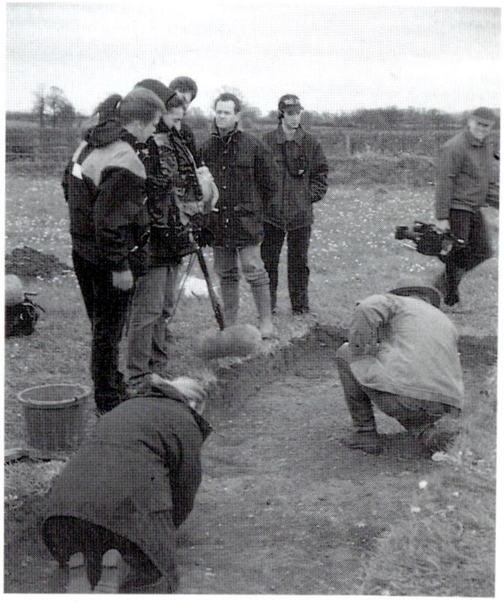

Day Two

We were all anxious to see the geophysics results, and when John printed them out in the back of his vehicle, there was a small crowd waiting to see what had been discovered. We weren't disappointed. What emerged was an almost complete plan of a Roman villa, with walls and corridors clearly visible,

(Top left) Mike Allen examining an auger sample from near the pond. *(Mick Aston)*
(Right) Working on the final trench across the villa's walls. *(Mick Aston)*

as well as a large building with what looked like an apsidal end, a feature with a half circular plan, often associated with a bath house. The geophysics team had marked out the extent of the buildings, and as Tony ran from one edge to the other, it was clear how large the structure was. However, the size and possible importance of the site raised some vital issues that had to be faced. Should we contemplate some kind of evaluative excavation to see what condition the site was in, or should it be left for further work by a team of archaeologists, who would have more time than we had? Indeed, would funds be available for work to be carried out on the site in the future?

The matter was raised with Roy Canham, the county archaeologist for Wiltshire. He was clearly concerned about the importance of the site and felt that we should proceed with care. It was decided to bring in Amanda Chadburn, an inspector with English Heritage, the next day to give us her thoughts. She would be responsible for scheduling the site and would be able to suggest the right procedure to follow. However, it was agreed that, in the meantime, some small trenches should be dug, with the landowner's permission, to see if we could get some idea of the *extent* of the site, and the *condition* and *date* of the walls or trenches outside the main body of the villa.

For the time being, with David Barnes only too keen to see what was beneath his fields, we began excavation on two sites at the edge of what appeared to have been an enclosure or garden that ran along the edge of the field. At the same time, Phil organised some groups of local villagers to conduct a fieldwalk in the fields to the west of the church to see if any other evidence might appear.

In the main field, the first trench soon began to show evidence of an earthwork and ditch that might have surrounded the edge of the villa. Pieces of Roman pottery, including roof tiles, came to light, but there appeared to be few structural remains of walls or other Roman features. However, this first trench was to come up with a surprise on the final day.

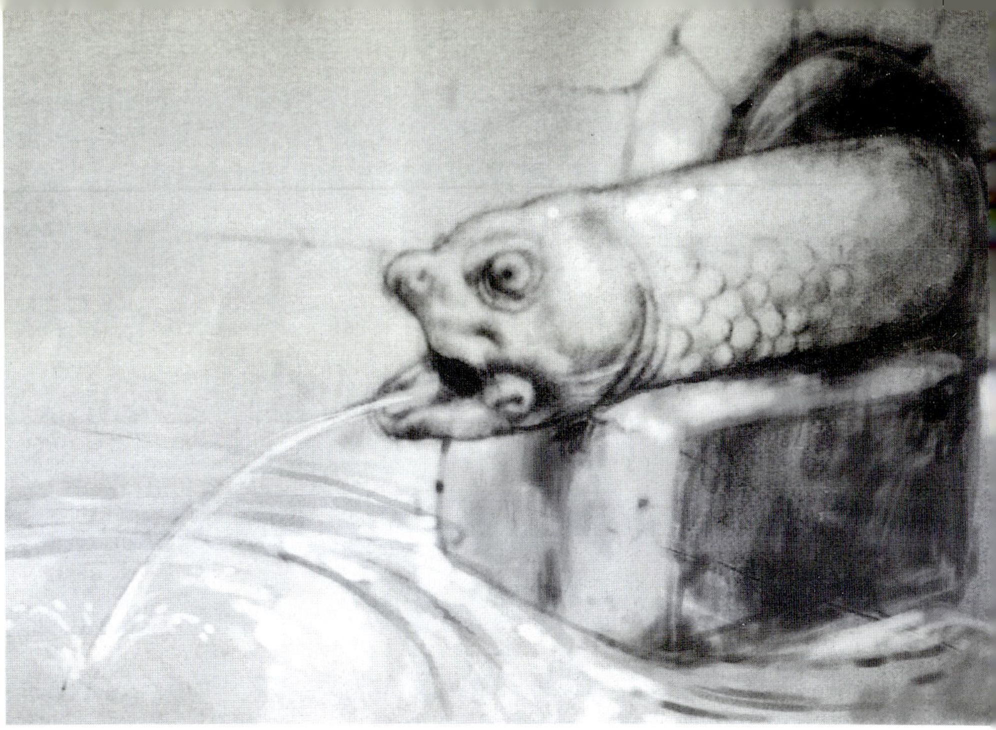

Victor's reconstruction of the decorated Romano-British water spout from David Barnes' garden. *(Mick Aston)*

At the end of Day Two we had gained little to add to our understanding of the villa complex. All manner of theories were being aired, including the idea that this was a palace of a local governor, or that it was a temple. The plan on John's computer print-out had looked so significant that it did not take much to set the archaeologists' imaginations going! The final piece of evidence to emerge that day added to the excitement. Martin revealed that the mysterious pipe object from David's garden was indeed Roman. Not only that, but it was perhaps one of the finest of its kind that he had ever seen!

It was identified as a decorated water spout in the form of a fish, complete with carved scales and gills. Martin believed that it was only at Pompeii that he had seen similar ones of such high quality. This one had lain around in David's garden for years, near an old pond. Clearly it must have come from a very fine, high-status villa.

Day Three

We had by now received a report from Mike Allen on the material dredged from the garden pond. He had discovered a large amount of burned grain from levels that might coincide with the Roman period of occupation. The important detail about the grain – which could have been an offering or, more prosaically, a bag of waste thrown into the pond – was that it had been processed. We are currently waiting for a carbon-14 date to establish the grain's exact age. What was even more surprising was that the lower levels of sediment indicated that the pond may have been formed thousands of years before the Romans arrived!

After Amanda Chadburn and Roy Canham examined the evidence from the main field, they agreed that it would be appropriate for us to excavate in the area of the main villa building. As Amanda pointed out, she did not, as yet, have clear information on the state of preservation of the villa or any evidence of its likely date. These factors would obviously play a part in the decision on whether or not the site should be scheduled and, if so, what kind of management arrangement should be made with the farmers. English Heritage see their role as working closely with landowners to ensure that sites like this are protected but in ways that farmers are also able to get the best possible use out of their land. Grants are often made to support landowners, and management schemes worked out that enable them to continue to use the area but also protect the features that have been discovered.

Excavation proceeded. We placed two small evaluation trenches across the walls of the villa, which soon revealed tesserae and fragments of building material. At quite a shallow depth, there appeared fragments of a jug and dish of Samian-ware – red gloss pottery once mistakenly believed to have originated in Samos, but which

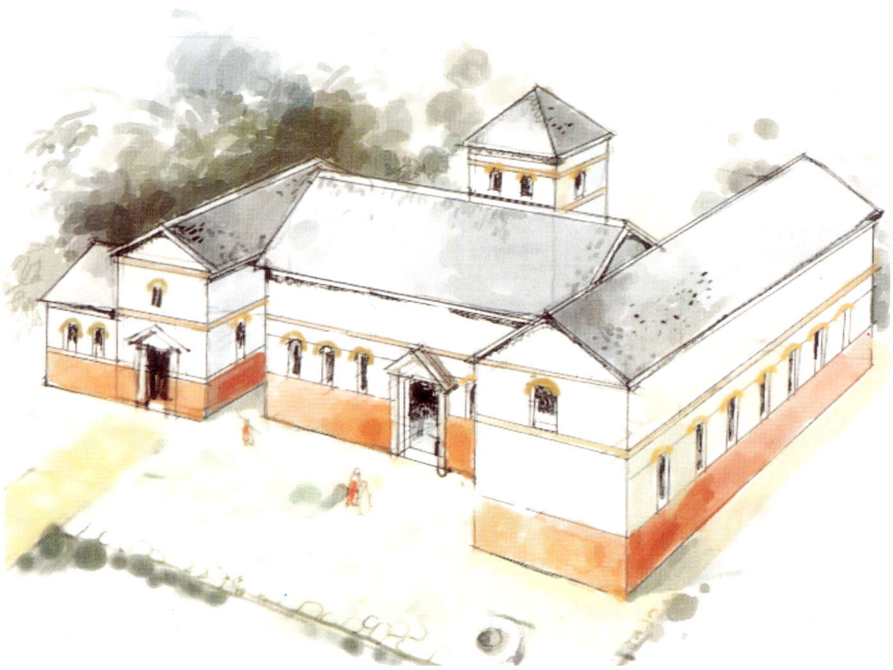

came from both southern Gaul and Britain – that had somehow survived centuries of ploughing. However, it became clear that almost all of the wall stone had been robbed. This process often leaves behind enough loosely packed soil or rubble to create what is, in effect, a ghostly imprint of the original wall on the geophysics survey. The large amounts of tesserae clearly showed the presence of mosaics, but no intact floors survived in the area we examined, and later work on the site after the team's departure confirmed this view. However, there were enough pieces of floor and ceiling tile and hypocaust segments to build up a picture of what the villa must have looked like, based on similar examples such as Chedworth, Lullingstone and Littlecote.

Phil's fieldwalkers had also come up with large amounts of prehistoric, Roman and medieval material. Although these sorts of finds are unstratified, their density is important: a large concentration may indicate a feature beneath the soil.

In the medieval period, pottery from domestic houses was thrown into rubbish heaps, which were then used for manuring the fields. This kind of material is often heavily abraded (damaged) by plough action, and it is so far from its original source that it can tell us only that there was medieval activity in the area.

However, the pottery from the fieldwalking and the excavation showed that there was occupation on this site throughout the Roman period. Some of the Samian ware could be identified as imports from Gaul, and the finest material was described as Oxfordshire red ware. Also found was a piece of *mortaria* – a dish with grit set into its surface for grinding food – and this has been identified as being similar in style to vessels in use between AD 300 and 400. None of the pottery reflected the richness of the building indicated by the geophysics plan, although the hypocaust tiles, tesserae and painted plaster and the fish sculpture clearly indicate a high-status villa, and we also found a piece of window glass.

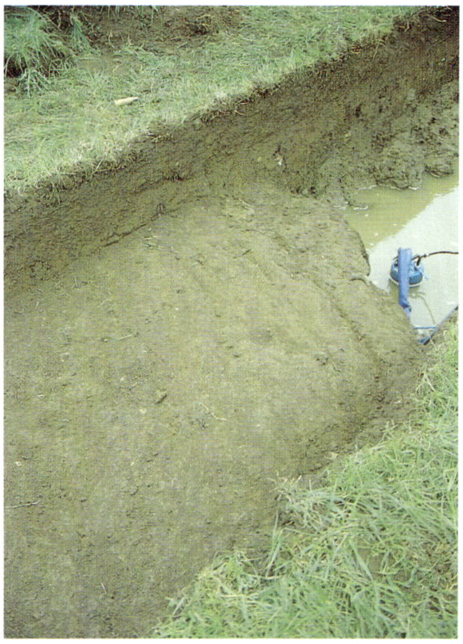

Before we left, the geophysics team began to widen their search for other features in the surrounding landscape. The process of establishing the wider context for a key building like our villa is part of the modern approach to such sites. Using a magnetometer, they were able to locate Roman field systems, ditches and pits, as well as an area of light industrial activity that may have included metalworking and pottery kilns.

The first trench now revealed its most surprising feature. At the depth of the bedrock, we found a series of long scratches in the surface. Mick identified these as 'ard marks' – caused by early ploughing. These were similar in shape to prehistoric plough marks discovered at such sites as Brean Down and Ashcombe Bottom, and were a major discovery.

Final thoughts from Mick

'Tockenham was of major interest in that it showed the process by which we can develop our understanding from a few pieces of tile to a more informed view, by adding fieldwork, geophysical surveying and environmental sampling.

'Without all this work, the likely context for the statue in the church could only have been guessed at and the fish sculpture might never have been recognised. Archaeology is all about putting things together in their context to understand the whole picture. Finds in themselves are of limited value, and it's only when we get a larger view of the context, as we have begun to get at Tockenham, that we can see the value of the original finds.'

(Top left) Victor's reconstruction of the Roman villa, based on the geophysical evidence.
(Bottom) 'Ard marks' – prehistoric plough marks found in the bedrock of the first trench. *(Mick Aston)*

WINTERBOURNE

Wiltshire, 6–8 May 1994

TONY'S TALE, OR WHAT MIGHT HAVE HAPPENED

Around AD 520 a group of invading Saxon pioneers worked their way inland from Southampton Water with the aim of establishing themselves in the area around Salisbury. We know from cemetery remains that whole families made the journey – the earliest graves include those of children. The men were well armed with weapons made from iron and carried shields with iron bosses in the centres, and the women wore beautiful gold brooches of a distinctive disc-shape and beads made from amber and glass. This was a high-status group, perhaps determined to establish their own settlement on behalf of the Saxon king, Cynric. There is also some evidence that there was pressure to emigrate because rising sea levels were flooding some of the best land in their homeland in Germany.

The Saxons as a society were warlike and predatory. Their gods were the gods of battle and war, and to die on the battlefield was a heroic death. Their system of tribal rule depended on the chief, whose aim was to expand his territory and be seen to be victorious in battle and thus able to bestow upon his followers the gifts of victory. To be a 'great giver of rings' or a 'great giver of swords' was an important element in ensuring the loyalty of the tribe.

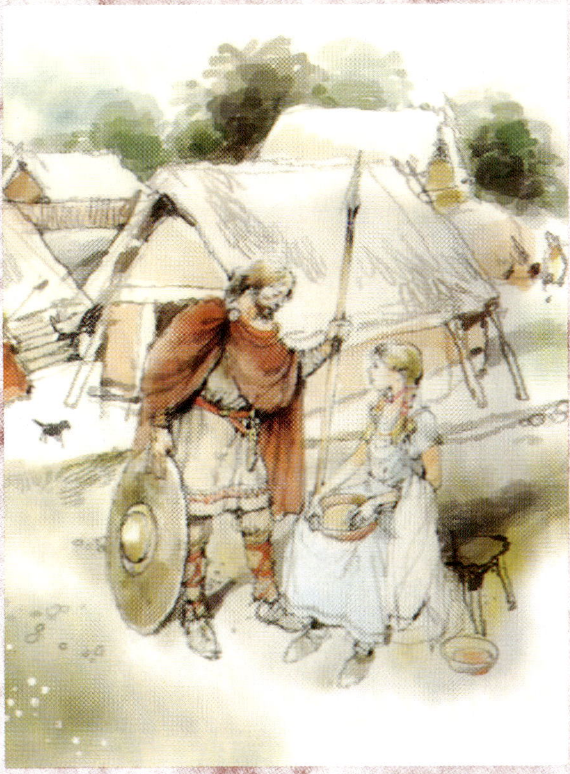

Victor's reconstruction of a Saxon village and two of the inhabitants. *(Mick Aston)*

The expansion of the Saxons, Angles and Jutes into Britain in the late 5th century was driven by this attitude. The Saxons had developed their economy and their fighting skills and organisation to the point where expansion into new and potentially rich territories had become a necessity. To make matters worse for the Christian Romano-British who awaited their arrival, the earliest invaders were pagan. Yet these were the people who would eventually create England – the land of the Anglo-Saxons.

During the next 25 years, our group established a foothold at a strategic point near Salisbury, overlooking the area where the Roman

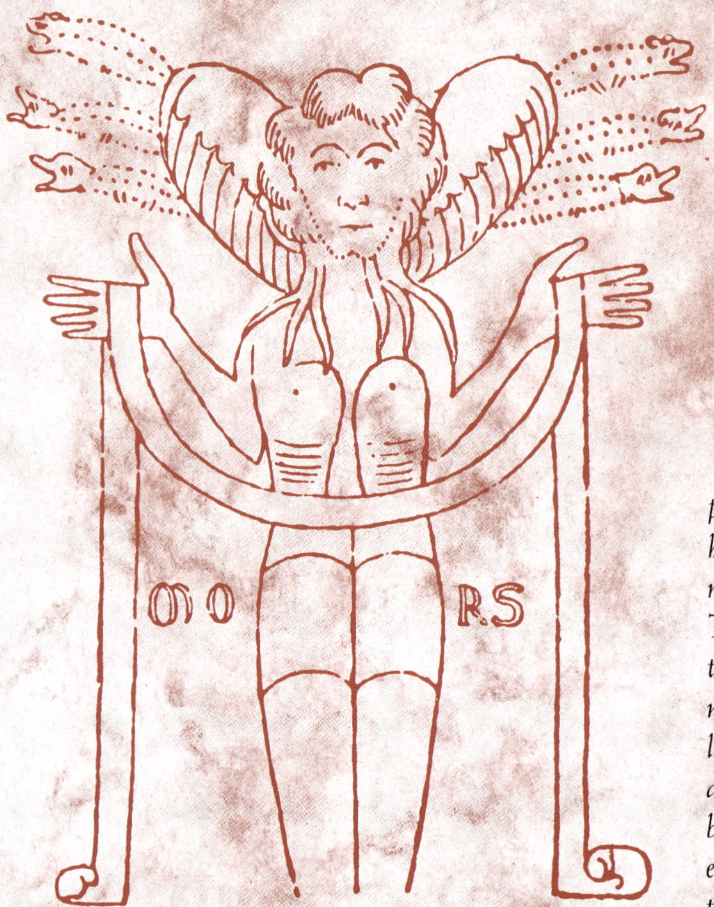

road running from Old Sarum to Silchester crosses the River Bourne. Above the valley, the chalk ridges gave them a drier area of land on which to build their wooden homes and the large wooden feasting hall that was at the centre of community life.

These early years were a dangerous time for the pioneers. Pockets of native Romano-British still occupied areas to the west – the Anglo-Saxon Chronicle records a battle taking place in AD 550 in this area – and the wet clay soils of the valley proved difficult to farm. Many of the children died early, and they along with the dead from battle were buried in the cemetery to the south of the river, near a site where earlier inhabitants, in the prehistoric Bronze Age, had built their burial mounds.

The old ceremonies and traditions of the pioneers' German homeland were adhered to, and the dead were buried with all the necessary goods to ensure their passage into the next world: swords, jewellery and rich armour to denote status; food for the journey; and coins to pay for their passage. According to their individual wishes, some members of the tribe were cremated on the site of the cemetery and the residue of their bones stored in pots marked with runic inscriptions. Those who were buried were laid facing west, as was the custom. These early graves were those of the men and women who had first created a foothold in the new land.

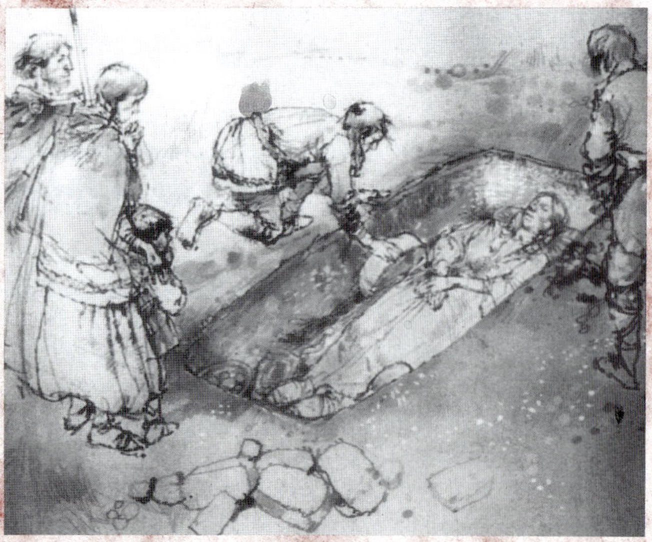

(Top) Mors, the Anglo-Saxon angel of death, from a 10th-century manuscript. From Ernst & Johanna Lehner, *Picture Book of Devils, Demons and Witchcraft*, Constable, 1971.
(Bottom) Victor's reconstruction of a Saxon burial: note the grave goods.

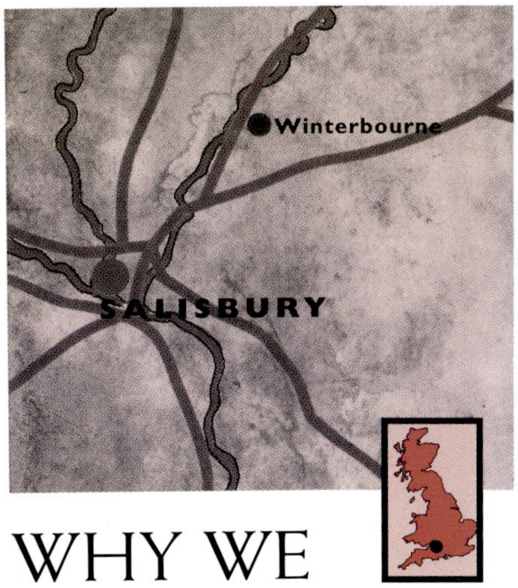

WHY WE WENT THERE

The focus for our work was a piece of building land in Winterbourne, owned by a local developer, which lay in an area of the village where other burials have been found. This land was the developer's only asset, but because of the proximity of an area of Saxon burials, he wasn't able to do anything to it until a satisfactory archaeological survey had been carried out, which may have meant the removal and the conservation of several Saxon graves. With no source of money other than the land which he couldn't sell, he was in a fix. The local county council had no funds to help out, and as they pointed out, it clearly states in their planning conditions that 'the local planning authority will require the prospective developer to arrange for an archaeological field evaluation to be carried out before the planning application is determined.' Although they are rightly governed by the principle that 'the polluter pays', often that person, if he or she does not have a large business, cannot afford the necessary archaeological work: even a small excavation may run into thousands of pounds.

Time Team, by working closely with the local county council archaeologist, were able to suggest a plan of action. Helena Cave-Penny, assistant county archaeologist for Wiltshire, drew up an evaluation proposal which proved acceptable to all those concerned. *Time Team* agreed to meet the costs of any possible conservation work, and by carrying out the necessary surveys and excavation on the site, we hoped to be able to solve both the county council's and the developer's problem. To this end, we brought in Pete Cox and AC Archaeology, an independent group of excavators, who knew the site and conditions.

Day One

When we arrived on the site, we found piles of building rubble, old sheds and broken pipes. All this would first have to be cleared before a survey could be carried out by the geophysics team. Unfortunately the mass of old metalwork and junk that would inevitably remain buried meant that magnetometry, a technique that depends on assessing variations in the earth's magnetic field, would not work. The team decided to move into an adjacent field and use resistivity.

Meanwhile, the top level of soil would be cleared. Careful use of a digger was employed here, as on these kinds of sites, a fairly clear distinction exists between the top soil and the natural layer of chalk underneath. When the surface was cleared, we began to see the outlines of shapes and marks in the chalk. Where graves have been dug, the fill that was used to cover the body, being a mixture of top soil and chalk, is a darker colour and a less regular shade than the surrounding bedrock, and this is what we were looking for.

Our local archaeologist Pete Cox had taken the necessary steps to ensure that the site would be shielded from public view. Any excavation involving human remains requires a Home Office licence and strict procedures have to be followed.

One of the key questions we had been asked to solve by Wiltshire County Council was the extent of the cemetery. It was hoped that the geophysics would reveal this, but if necessary, further trenches would have to be dug outside the main area.

Carenza and Mick were both keen to look at the aerial photos for evidence of other archaeological features in the surrounding fields. The walls and ditches of such features create different growth levels or ripening rates in crops, and these marks can often be clearly seen from the air. This might give us a clue as to the size of the cemetery.

While the key maps were being consulted and Mick and Phil were clearing the top soil from the site surface, Robin and Tony discussed the idea of grave goods and the attitude of the Anglo-Saxons towards death. As a Christian country, we have a tradition of burying our dead in relatively simple coffins with no accompanying objects. This partly stems from the Christian belief that, in the afterlife, God will provide all your requirements and that, before God, we are all equal. Grave goods would, in this context, be seen to present the opportunity for self-aggrandisement. The Saxons, being pagan, regarded the journey to their equivalent of Valhalla as requiring food, weapons, money and fine clothes to

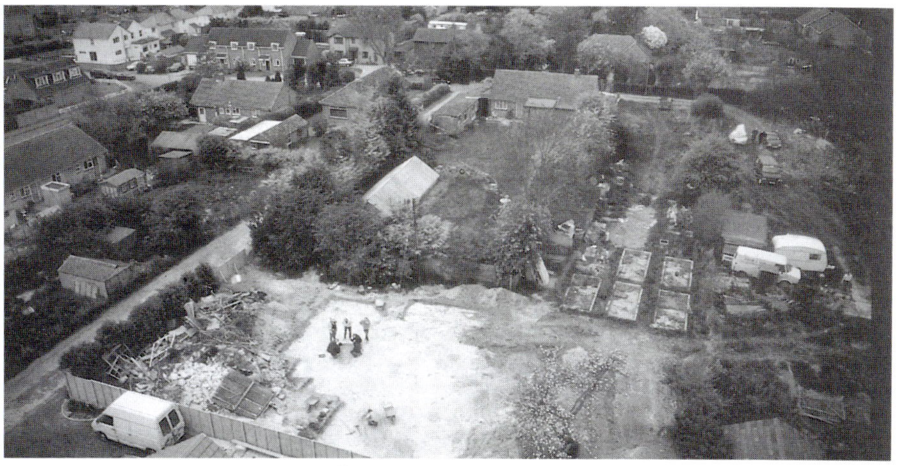

Aerial view of the excavation site at Winterbourne: note the darker patches on the chalk, indicating graves. *(Mick Aston)*

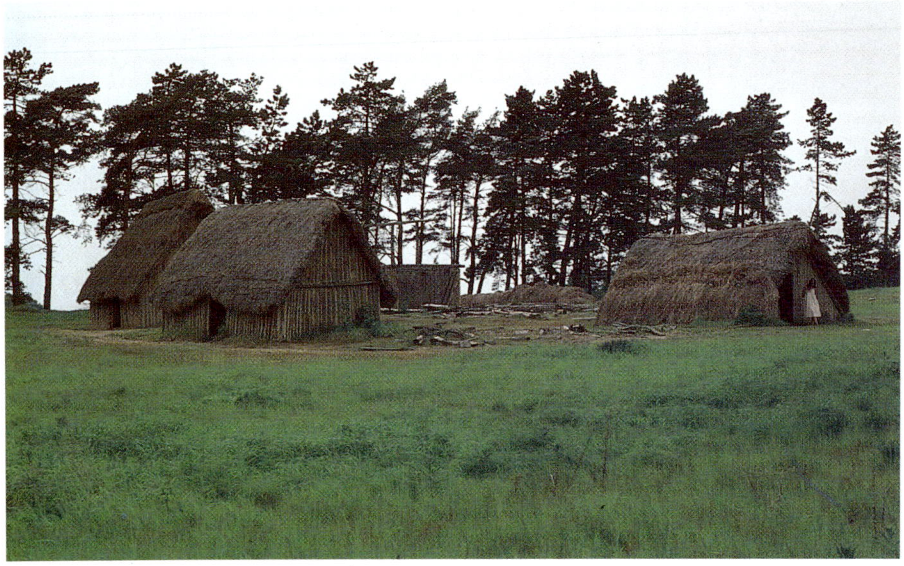

help them on their way. Also people would be buried with items that clearly showed their status on earth. The richer and higher in status you were, the more items were placed in your grave.

Grave goods might include personal pieces of jewellery as well as items of great worth such as swords and knives. This custom of placing objects with the dead has been a great boon to archaeologists – the majority of our information on the Saxons has been pieced together from finds in cemeteries. In fact, Anglo-Saxon archaeologists are often accused of having an unhealthy interest in the dead!

However, the reason they concentrate on cemetery evidence is because Saxon technology was often based on perishable organic materials such as wood, leather and bone. Their buildings were mainly of wood, particularly in the early days of their occupation, and it is often very difficult to find or interpret the evidence left by early Saxon settlements, particularly as they sometimes became sites for later medieval building in stone, which obscured or obliterated the earlier evidence.

Mick and Carenza had decided to explore the earthworks around the village church for signs of the Saxon settlement. Luckily a selection of pottery, found in the area some years before, contained pieces that were clearly of Saxon origin. It's interesting to note that the modern English word used to denote a piece of broken pot – 'sherd' – is of Anglo-Saxon origin, coming from the word that means 'a piece'. This word also forms the root for the modern word 'shire'.

Often found in Saxon graves are iron knives, the general, all-purpose implement of the period, and we wanted to see just how one was made. Our expert on early technology, Ivor Lawton, joined Phil to set up a simple furnace to create the kind of temperature needed to forge iron. The difficulty of smelting iron meant that an object like a knife would be highly prized, and an iron sword would have perhaps been the equivalent of a modern car to its Saxon owner. The key to the technology is the combination of a bellows and charcoal, which gives a higher temperature than an ordinary fire. At the end of the process, the smith had only one chance to combine the many layers of iron into a single blade. A close inspection of an iron knife or sword from this period will reveal layer upon layer of metal which produced both a strong and a sharp blade.

It is perhaps ironic that iron, although sharp, is prone to rust. A bronze blade made by people with a much earlier technology and left in the same damp environment might be in much better condition than the iron blades found in Saxon graves.

Day Two

With the top soil removed, the dark lozenge shapes of at least three graves could be seen, and excavation soon began to reveal the skeletons themselves. In many such sites, the bones are in poor condition, and very careful use of trowels and Phil's famous dental pick were needed to remove the layers of soil and sticky clay.

Because we are used to seeing cleaned and conserved objects in museums, it is easy to assume that they appear in a recognisable condition in the ground, but this is not the case. A brooch or iron pin will often appear as

Tony's journey to Valhalla

To illustrate the interpretation of grave goods, we asked Tony to assemble the sorts of things he would choose as the modern equivalent of Saxon grave goods. His choice raised some interesting questions about this kind of evidence. For instance, one interpretation of the remains of his portable telephone might be that he came from Japan – an example of the fact that objects tend to travel more widely than people. For archaeologists, a complex grave site requires careful interpretation, particularly with regard to the sources of objects. The Saxons traded widely, and great burial sites such as the one at Sutton Hoo in Suffolk have been found to contain coins and other objects from throughout Europe and beyond.

In the case of brooches, for instance, it is possible to distinguish between those from the Saxony area of Germany and the kind of brooch favoured by, say, the Jutes. However, this does not necessarily mean that their owners came from these areas.

(Above) This Anglo-Saxon settlement, reconstructed at West Stow in Suffolk, shows clearly how these immigrants from the Continent built with wood. *(Mick Aston)*
(Right) The head and shoulders of one of the adult female skeletons found at Winterbourne with *(centre left)* a disc brooch, *(centre bottom)* a crystal bead, and between the two, the brown stain of an iron pin. *(Mick Aston) (Inset)* Tony in his 'grave' with 1990s' grave goods. *(Mick Aston)*

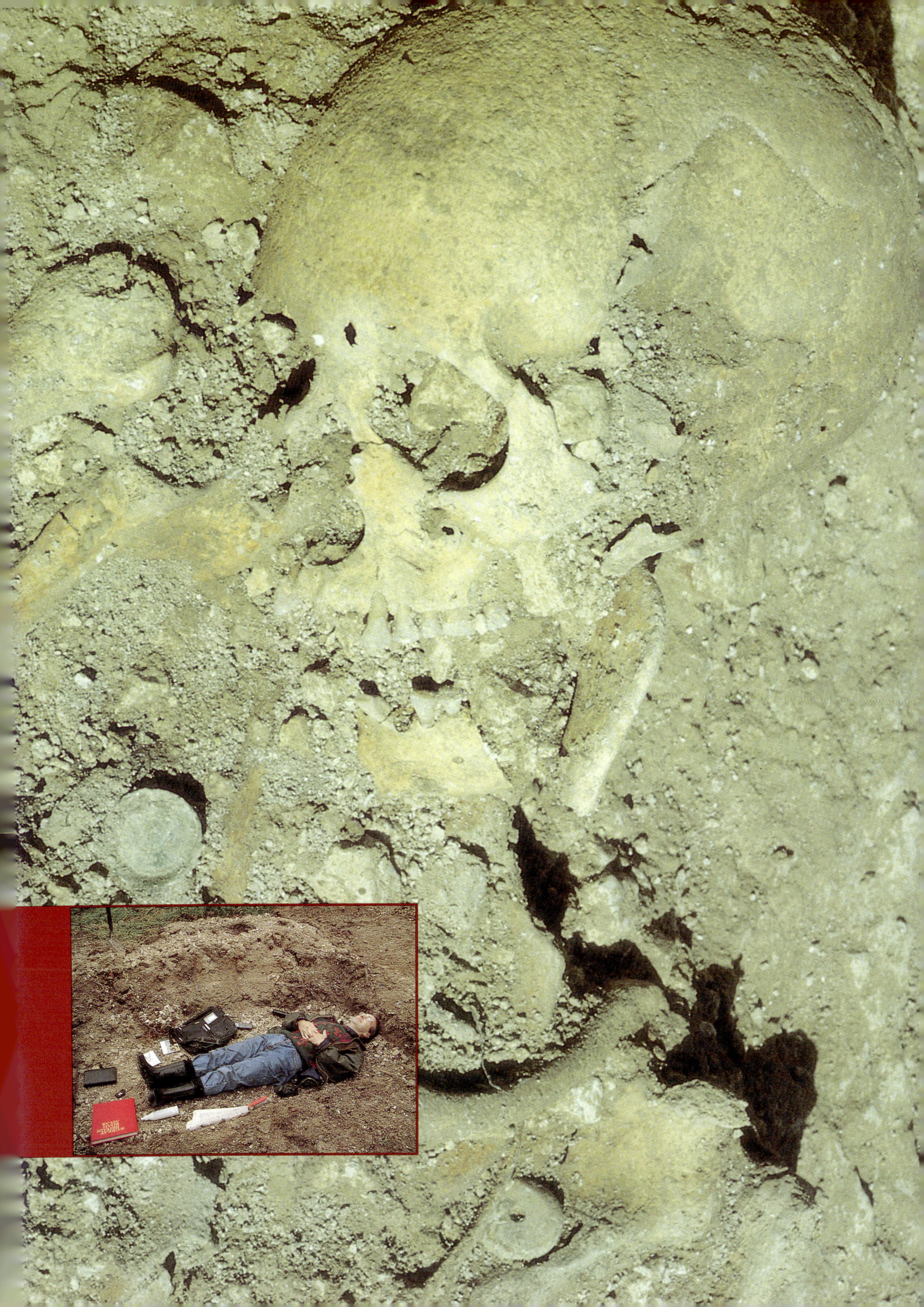

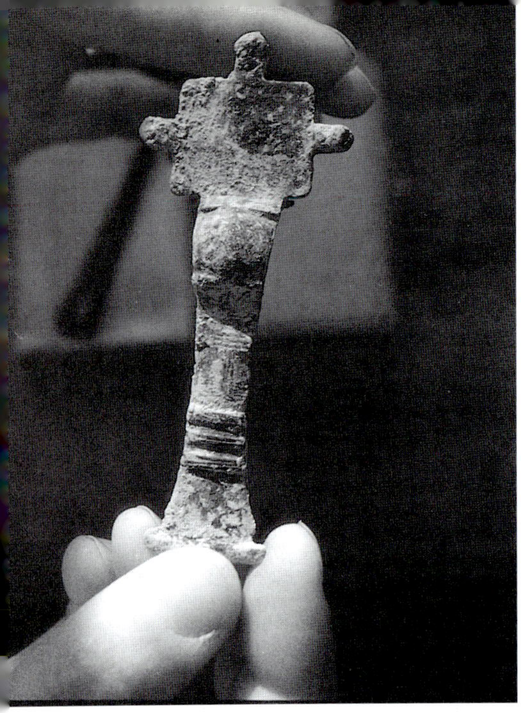

a lump of encrusted mud and decayed organic material, so it is essential for excavators to work their way carefully through the material being removed from around the bones. Subsidence in the ground and the action of tree roots and worms can often move material around within a grave. The brooch you might be hoping to find around the neck can often end up lodged behind the head or under the rib cage.

The other aspect of these kinds of grave goods is that the back of a brooch or knife may contain, in the organic encrustation, the imprint of the material or the remains of the leather belt or strap to which it was previously attached; in some cases, mineral salts from the object will have fossilised the materials underneath. Some of the most useful information we have about Saxon cloth has come from the weave patterns left on the backs of objects from graves, so archaeologists are careful to avoid cleaning any finds until they have been carefully examined. In general, the cleaning of these kinds of objects is left to the conservation lab. Ideally, excavations of this nature require the presence of a trained conservator on site to ensure that finds are handled in a way that best preserves the information they contain. In the case of iron pins, the accretions of crusted soil, rust and decayed organic matter may be all that is holding the object together.

As the skeletons became more obvious, we brought in Dr Margaret Cox, an expert in the archaeology of skeletal remains. Bones can provide useful information for the archaeologist, and it is often necessary to examine skeletons *in situ* as some of the evidence may be damaged or lost once the bones have been removed from the grave. The first piece of information that can be provided is the likely sex of the occupant. In the case of our graves, the first two skeletons were female.

The key feature for determining the sex of a skeleton is the ridge above the eyes. In males, this tends to be more pronounced; females have rounder foreheads with little sign of eyebrow ridges. In some skeletons, it is also possible to discover the pubic tubercle, which is a spur of bone that grows to support the uterus during pregnancy. Its presence shows both the sex and the fact that the woman has had a child.

It is also possible to arrive at an approximate age for skeletons. When we are born, our bones and the plates that form our skulls have areas of cartilage at their edges. As we grow older, these fuse into bone, and so a skeleton with fused bone ends and no cartilage between skull plates can be given an older age. Teeth can also be a useful indicator of age, especially in making a distinction between a child and an adolescent: differing numbers of teeth appear throughout childhood, up to the age of 16 or so when the wisdom teeth come through. The degree of wear on teeth can indicate an older person and also the kind of diet he or she ate. Saxon teeth have often been worn down by the coarse grains of their bread, but they lack the signs of dental decay that would be expected today.

The bones can also bear traces of pathology – that is, illness that occurred during the person's lifetime. The most common evidence is of osteoarthritis and damage and distortion of bone caused by excessive wear and strain. In the case of burials in a good state of preservation, it may also be possible to collect soil samples from the stomach area that might give us an idea of the kind of food eaten before death and if the person was suffering from any kind of intestinal parasite.

As we worked on the third, smaller grave, it became clear that this may have contained the body of a child. Further excavation and an examination of the bones by Margaret Cox revealed that this was the case.

It became apparent that our three graves – two adult females and one child – had been placed around the edge of another feature in the centre of the site. This was a large area of browner deposit that had been cut into the chalk, but as yet no other evidence had come to light. Mick and Pete Cox speculated that this might be some kind of earlier barrow. Whatever it was, the Saxons seemed to have respected it as relatively few burials were found in its vicinity.

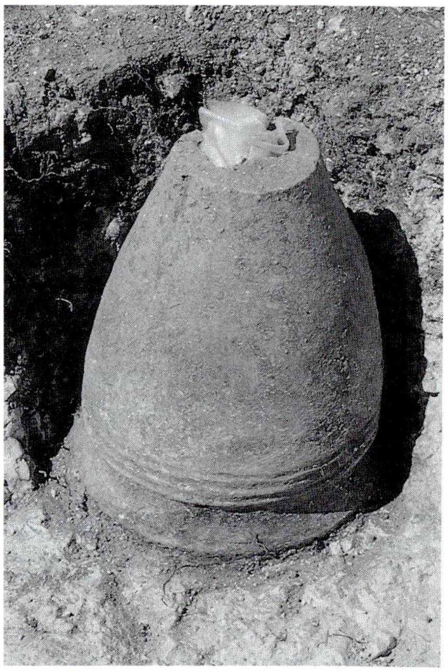

Day Three

To find out more about the site, it was decided to dig a trench away from the road towards the planted field and allotment area. Geophysics were still finding the going tough, and it might be that a small trench would locate other graves or show that they ceased to exist beyond the garden boundary.

As soon as the digger had stripped away the top soil, Pete Cox called a halt: at the edge of the central brown deposit, two holes had appeared in the ground. On examination, these turned out to be two prehistoric cremation urns taking our story back 2000 years

(Top left) A long brooch, found during earlier excavations at Winterbourne. *(Mick Aston)*
(Right) The large prehistoric cremation urn. *(Mick Aston)*

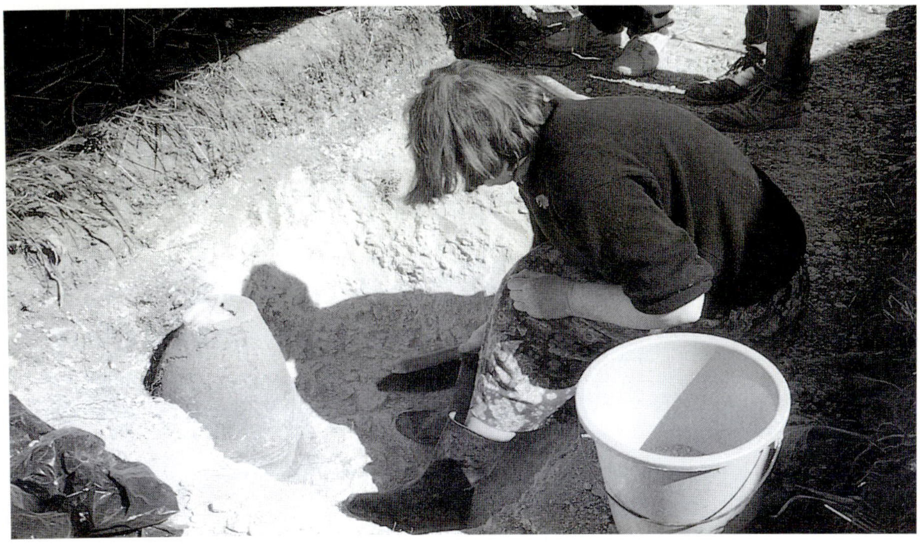

before the Saxons! This was an incredible piece of luck, especially when it became clear that inside these urns were human remains. With the aid of a torch, Mick was able to see pieces of bone – the first time anyone had seen the urns' contents since their burial in prehistoric times. The thickness and condition of the urn walls could easily be seen; conservation work had to begin immediately.

Meg Brooks from the Wiltshire Museum Conservation Service began the task of gently removing the layers of soil around the sides of the urns. Soon she was looking at a pot that was over 0.3 m (1ft) in height and, accompanying it, a smaller urn. The larger pot was decorated and beautifully shaped. However, because of cracks caused by root damage, it had to be carefully bound with bandages to hold the sides together.

As the excavators began to examine the new trench, Mick and Carenza used the helicopter to look for aerial evidence of crop marks that might indicate further burials in the adjacent fields. What became apparent was that there were a number of burial mounds with ring ditches surrounding them. These seemed to mark the edge of the Saxon cemetery and our last excavation trench appeared to cut across one of them. Burial mounds of this kind are fairly common in Wiltshire. Further excavation in this area disclosed remains which will be the subject of work by Wiltshire County Council.

As Phil revealed the last layers of the three graves, we found three examples of grave goods: an encrusted brooch, an amber bead and an iron pin. These, along with the urns, were taken to the conservation laboratories. An X-ray revealed that, underneath organic encrustation, the brooch was a bronze saucer type with a gilt coating and decorated with a circular motif.

With only a few hours to go, we made our final and perhaps most critical discovery. In the centre of the brown deposit, we uncovered pieces of cremated human bone – clearly those of the individual who had been buried in the barrow during the prehistoric period. Pete Cox and Helena Cave-Penny believed the evidence pointed to a Bronze Age pond barrow, a relatively rare feature. Unlike the more familiar barrow consisting of a mound surrounded by a ditch, a pond barrow is a circular sunken area surrounded by an outer bank. It was also apparent that the reason for the small number of graves in this area was that the Saxons had respected this prehistoric burial site. Ironically, this meant that, after the bones found during our excavation had been removed, the builder could build on the land in the area outside the pond barrow.

This barrow is considered so important that it has now been scheduled by English Heritage as an ancient monument of national archaeological importance.

Final thoughts from Mick

'This site was important for at least two reasons. First, it is relatively uncommon to find both a cemetery and evidence of a settlement together, and second, the relationship between the Saxon cemetery and the prehistoric site is of great interest. Our work, along with previous excavations and the aerial photography, clearly shows how an extensive Bronze Age cemetery of barrows – including a rare pond barrow – provided a focus for the later Saxon cemetery. These barrows, now largely ploughed level, must have been prominent mounds when the Saxon settlers arrived, and they must have either recognised their significance or respected their geographical boundaries. Being able to find the archaeological evidence for that sequence of events, with the pond barrow at its centre, makes this site unique.'

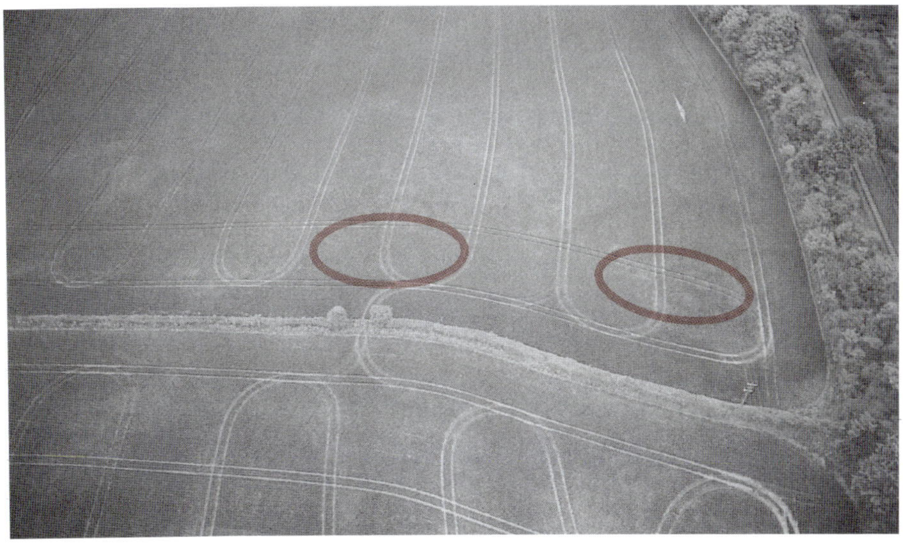

(Top left) Meg Brooks beginning the conservation of the large cremation urn. *(Mick Aston)*
(Bottom left) Aerial photograph of prehistoric ring ditches showing as cropmarks (highlighted on photograph).

LAMBETH

London, 8–10 June 1994

TONY'S TALE, OR WHAT MIGHT HAVE HAPPENED

After the invasion of AD *43, the Roman army, in their usual, efficient manner, sought to establish the quickest and easiest route north from their landing points around Chichester on the south coast. Northward lay the native British stronghold of Colchester, and the Roman emperor Claudius wanted to establish his domination over this part of the country. The Romans always wanted to advance as quickly as possible but also ensured that they developed good lines of supply – and potential routes for evacuation if this became necessary. Their way north was blocked by the Thames – not the size of today's river, but a much wider obstacle surrounded in places by low-lying swamps and tributaries that, at high tide, may have expanded up to a kilometre across.*

*Dio Cassius, the Roman historian, referred to the crossing chosen as being 'at a point where the river at high tide forms a pool'. The Roman surveyors and engineers selected the narrowest point above the area of swampy low ground. It would be a continuation of the road that came to be known as Watling Street, and eventually it would run from Dover to Canterbury, then head west through Rochester towards the Thames. North of the river it would travel to St Albans (*Verulamium*), and finally to Chester.*

The immediate problem for the soldiers who would build the road up to the Thames was – as well as being constantly on the look-out for attacks by the Britons – to bridge the areas of softer ground while taking advantage of the high areas of gravel. A foundation of wooden logs was laid and, on top of this, a layer of larger flint stones, sealed with sandy clay and finished off with gravel and pebbles rammed into the surface.

This would be the road on which the legions of Claudius would march to receive the surrender of the Britons at Colchester. It would become one of the main trade routes of the Romans in Britain, and would be the first step in creating a new town and port built by the side of the river, which would be called Londinium.

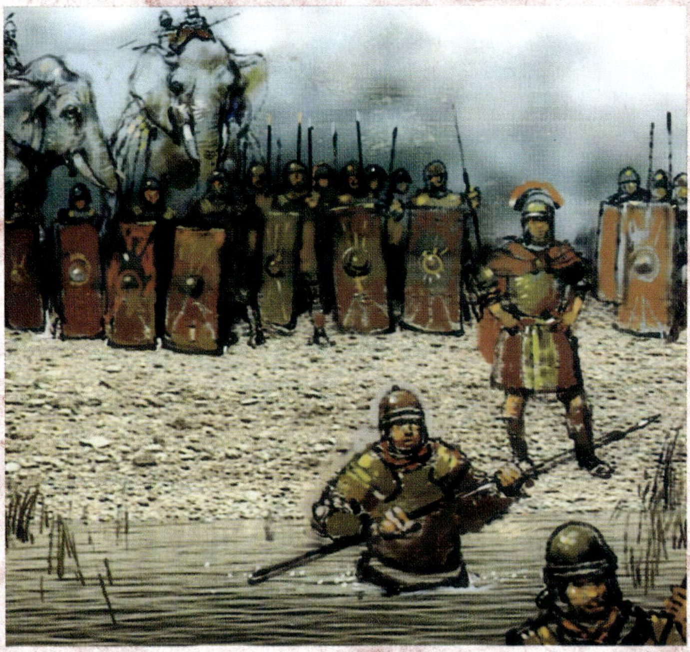

Victor's reconstruction of the Romans crossing the Thames.

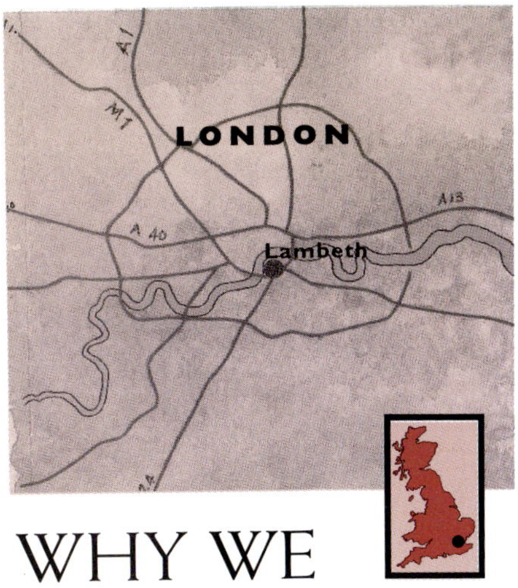

WHY WE WENT THERE

Despite London's status as one of the major cities in Europe, we know relatively little about its early origins. Roman historians such as Tacitus recorded the invasions of Britain, but their information about the capital is limited and subject to differing interpretations by archaeologists. One point of contention is the site of the earliest settlement on the Thames.

Time Team had had discussions with the Museum of London Archaeology Service (Molas), and they had raised some intriguing questions about the early history of London.

Prior to the Romans, there is little evidence of an earlier town, and it seems clear that Colchester and St Albans were more important centres to the Britons. There is also the question raised by the route of Watling Street. Just as it reaches the outskirts of present-day London, it appears to disappear at Blackheath and then to make a dog-leg towards what is now the City and the site of London Bridge. However, if a straight line is drawn from the previous course of Watling Street, it shows the road crossing the Thames at Lambeth, near where Westminster Bridge now stands. Drawing straight lines on maps and assuming that Roman roads will follow them became something of an obsession for archaeologists in the past. Yet the Romans were highly pragmatic, and if a route demanded a detour, it was taken.

However, in the case of London, two other pieces of evidence pointed to Lambeth as a possible location for an early crossing. One came in the 1930s from the archaeologist Bernard Davis, who may be regarded as coming from the 'straight-line school' of Roman archaeology, and the other came from the results of excavations in the 1960s, which revealed pieces of early pottery and possible evidence of a settlement in the Lambeth area. Davis had followed up his speculations by carrying out a number of small excavations along the supposed route, looking for evidence of man-made surfaces and worn pebbles that might be the remains of a road. In 1935, he published a report claiming to have located the road in the grounds of Lambeth Palace, and it was also here that the later finds of pottery were located. These facts were enough for the authors of at least two major histories of London to suggest that Lambeth may have been the first crossing point and therefore the area of the first Roman settlement.

After detailed negotiations with Lambeth Palace and Molas, we received permission to investigate the grounds of the Palace and the adjacent park. Would we be able to find any trace of a road and prove Davis right? Would we discover evidence of an early settlement? We had the usual three days to find out.

Day One

Entrance to the Palace grounds is via the impressive Tudor gate-tower, and it was through here that the geophysics team brought their equipment to survey the grounds where we believed Davis had dug his trenches. Stuart Ainsworth from the Royal Commission on Historic Monuments for England had already noticed some faint ridges that may have been the remains of the excavations of the 1930s, and we would be concentrating our initial work here.

Lambeth Palace is the official residence of the Archbishop of Canterbury in London. Its history began in 1190, when Archbishop Baldwin bought part of the Manor of Lambeth from the convent of St Andrew at Rochester, intending to create a college of monks. The subsequent history of the Palace was greatly influenced by the division of power in the Church of England between Canterbury, its historic base, and London. Before the latter had even developed beyond being a small hamlet, Canterbury was a powerful provincial capital and, later, a site of pilgrimage and the centre of the Church's power. London was essentially a Roman invention, and it was not until the late Middle Ages that it was able to draw away some of Canterbury's power to the capital.

The Palace's buildings have been much altered over the years and were subjected to restoration in the Gothic style in the 19th century. Still remaining, though, are the crypt of the 13th-century chapel, the Lollards tower added in 1432, the Tudor gate-tower

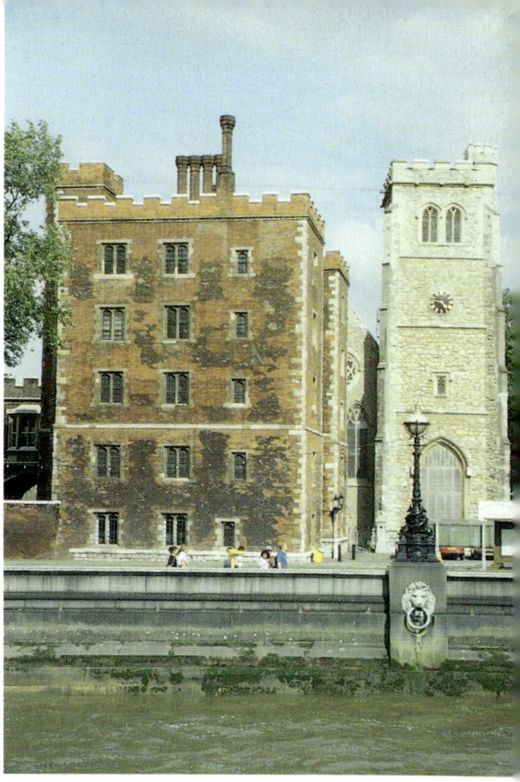

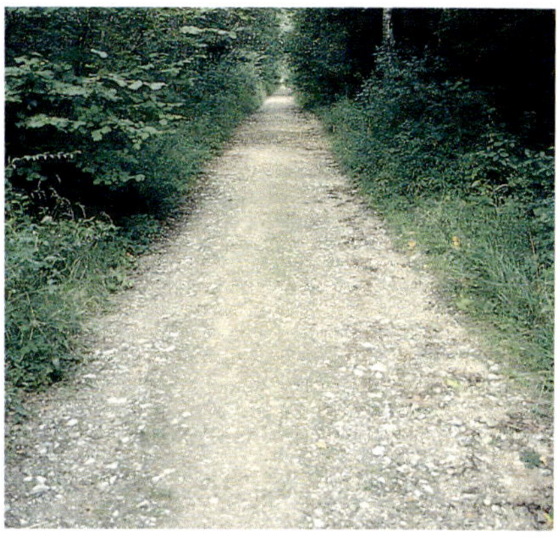

(Top right) Lambeth Palace, London. *(Mick Aston)*
(Bottom right) Watling Street. *(Ancient Art and Architecture Collection)*

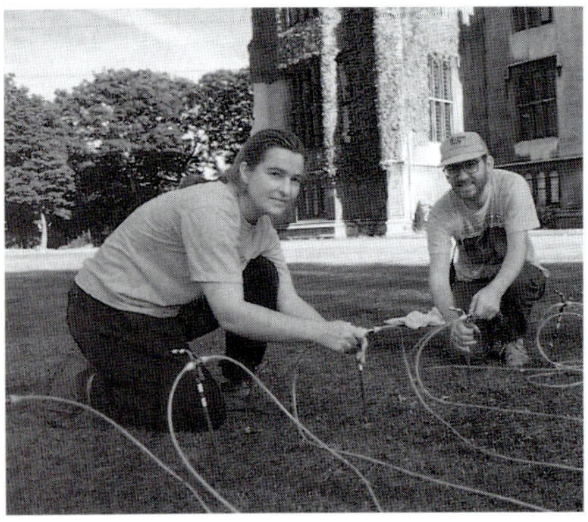

and the 17th-century Great Hall. The gardens and the park, some ten acres in all, comprise one of the few areas of central London to be left undeveloped since the Middle Ages. The staff at the Palace were keen to know if we would find any traces of the formal gardens that existed around the Palace since Tudor times.

Our plan for the search for evidence of the early settlement and Davis's road was based on locating the sites of his excavations. Geophysics soon found these, and a decision was made to excavate in two areas.

The first trench would be at the edge of the 1930s' dig; this would allow the geophysics team to carry out more concentrated work nearer the centre, using a an electrical imaging system that is designed to give a cross-section (or 'section') of the ground, which would allow us to see individual layers of soil and gravel to a depth of 1.8 m (8 ft) or more. The advantage of working like this would be that we could test Davis's findings without disturbing any other areas of archaeology that might require further work at a later date.

We had also agreed to undertake a survey of the local geology by obtaining a number of cores from within the Palace gardens and the park. These might enable us to locate underlying levels of gravel and those high points that may have been the focus for an early settlement. Molas had already surveyed an area across the river, around Westminster, and our work in Lambeth would enable them to complete this exercise.

Robin, meanwhile, had settled himself in the Palace's magnificent library, and was looking for references in early texts to crossing points on the Thames.

By the end of the first day, we located an area of gravel in the first trench, which may have been the feature that Davis had found. We also compared his drawings with the section we could see in the trench and found them to match. This showed that, as Phil remarked, 'The old boy did a pretty good job' of recording, and this made us feel optimistic about the validity of his observations about the area we were now about to excavate. In addition, the first trench had produced a piece of *mortaria*, a Roman vessel with grit set into its surface for grinding food. This was our first clear evidence of Roman activity in the area.

Day Two

At the start of the second day, we began to dig the second trench using Davis's drawings and a reference given to us by the geophysics team, who had located an area of possibly compacted gravel. This could be a natural feature or evidence of a road surface. Only excavation would give the answer.

We had also begun to look for other environmental evidence of the early crossing. A critical question was the state of the river at this point – was it tidal? One factor that would have been a likely consideration in locating a port or crossing point would have been its accessibility, and it would have been logical for the Romans to have selected a location that was tidal. This would have enabled heavily laden boats to travel as far inland as possible, assisted by the tide. Working with Jane Siddell

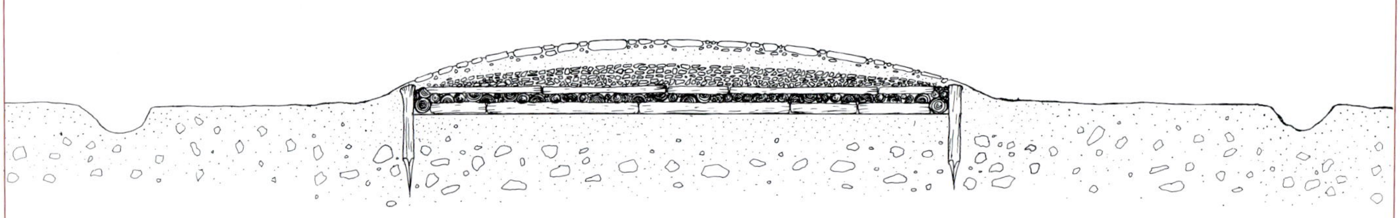

The Roman road

Time Team reproduced a section of Roman road in Lambeth Park. It was interesting to note the similarity between the gravel layers used to make this road and those that we had discovered occurring naturally in the Palace garden. Roman roads were often 6–9 m (20–30 ft) wide, and in the case of main highways such as the road between London and Colchester, they increased to 21 m (70 ft) with three lanes. It has been estimated that there were at least 3000 miles of major Roman roads in Britain, all built by the army. Building skills were obviously essential to the legionaries' training. The Royal Engineers have estimated that to build an engineered Roman road from Richborough to Westminster, a distance of some 70 miles, would have taken three years and required approximately 4000 men – 10 per cent of the Roman army in Britain in the 1st century AD. Progress would have been at a rate of two miles a month. It is perhaps not surprising that when one looks at Trajan's column in Rome – the record of that emperor's battles and victories – a large percentage of the army's activities appear to have been connected with road and fort building

(Top left) The geophysics team using the electrical imaging system. *(Mick Worthington)*

from Molas, we decided to sink some trenches down into the gravels to look for *diatoms*, microscopic single-cell algae. After death, the silica shell of the diatom's body survives, and this can be identified as belonging to a particular species. Different species are specific to different kinds of environments and reflect the nature of the soils and water in which they once lived. An analysis of the diatoms from this area might have enabled us to tell if salt water had been present and, therefore, if the river had been tidal at this point. Unfortunately, however, no diatoms were discovered in the trenches dug.

Gustav Milne from the Institute of Archaeology in London joined us to look at the way the changes in the river may have influenced the settlement pattern, and to work on a three-dimensional picture of the Thames based on bore-hole information. This would clarify which areas of the river flood plain had been higher and, therefore, candidates for settlement.

In the second, main trench where we had located layers of gravel that seemed to correspond with Davis's sections, it became apparent that these were natural. In this area of the Thames, gravel can occur in 'lenses' – thin layers – that appear to be man-made.

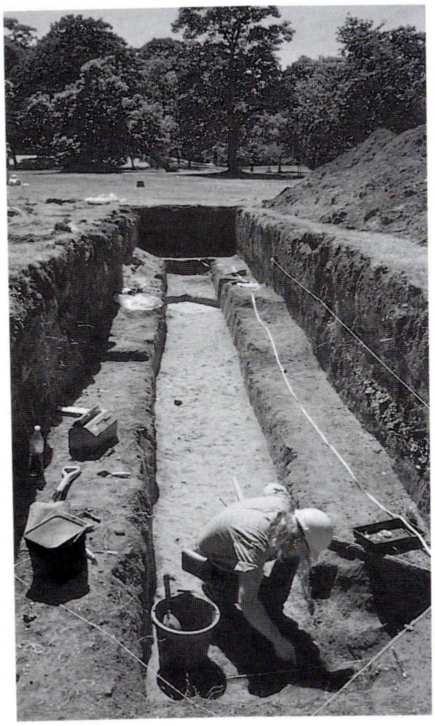

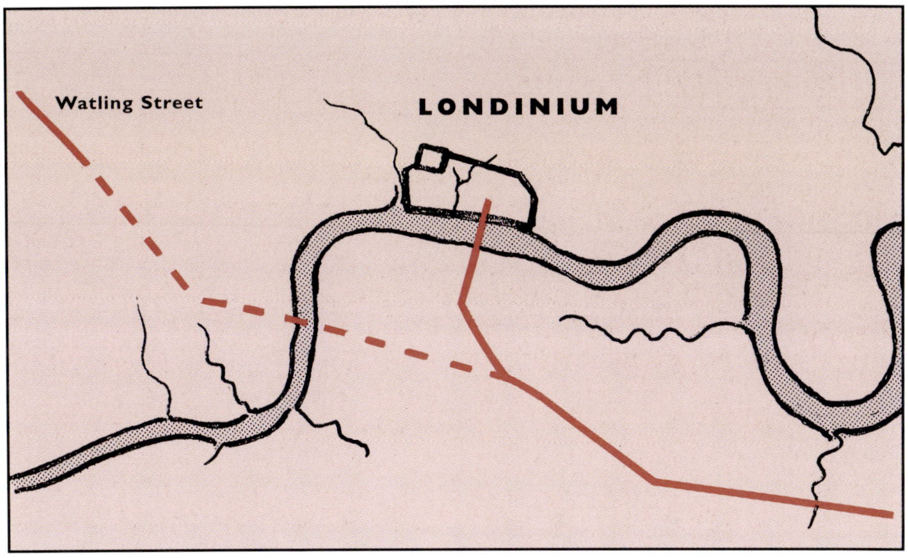

However, in trench no. 2, we were finding more Roman pottery, which had also been reported by Davis. These finds included parts of a *quern* used to grind corn, which was made out of a distinctive volcanic stone found only in Germany. This stone, identified by Mick as *Niedermendig*, was fascinating evidence of early trading connections between London and the Continent. It is also interesting to note that, of the four legions that invaded Britain with Claudius, three were German in origin. The 2nd, 9th and 20th legions were from the lower Rhine, and because of this, initial trading routes with this area may have been more easily established.

Having shown that Davis's evidence failed to prove the existence of a road, we began to look for other possibilities. Harvey Sheldon, an expert on Roman London, suggested that the road may have been further to the north, under the site of St Thomas's Hospital. Was there any other evidence? Robin was still hunting in the archives, and Mick suggested an exploration of the river on the Westminster side. Was there any sign of a ridge of higher ground that could have been used as a ford? Earlier research had thrown up the tale of a member of the House of Lords, allegedly the tallest peer in the realm, who had crossed the Thames on foot just below Westminster! Might this be a simple coincidence?

Day Three

With help from the river-based fire brigade and a piece of brick tied to the end of a tape measure (!), Mick carried out a totally unscientific analysis of water depths around Westminster. There did indeed appear to be an area of shallower water here, and the captain of the fire boat told us that this could often be felt against the hull of his boat at low water. Could this be the remnants of a natural ridge of higher land or was it just a sandbank? Only further work will provide the answer, but it did link nicely with something that Robin had found in an 18th-century history of the Palace by A. C. Ducarel. This was a reference to the 'Staingate crossing', which implied that this was an ancient route down to the river. That route is now covered by the hospital, but future building development may reveal areas of road joining Watling Street.

Harvey had also pointed out that the north bank of the Thames was less marshy and could have provided more building land for the expansion of the growing City. Excavations near London Bridge had also exposed a road that appeared to be pointing towards Lambeth. Had this been built as a connection with the former crossing point, once the City had begun to establish itself around the present site? Was the Lambeth crossing and settlement short lived?

We know that, at the time of Boudicca's attack on London in AD 60,

(Bottom left) Excavating a trench at Lambeth Palace. *(Mick Worthington)*
(Above right) The route of Watling Street. The solid line shows the known route; the dotted line indicates the possible Lambeth crossing. *(Nick Pearson)*

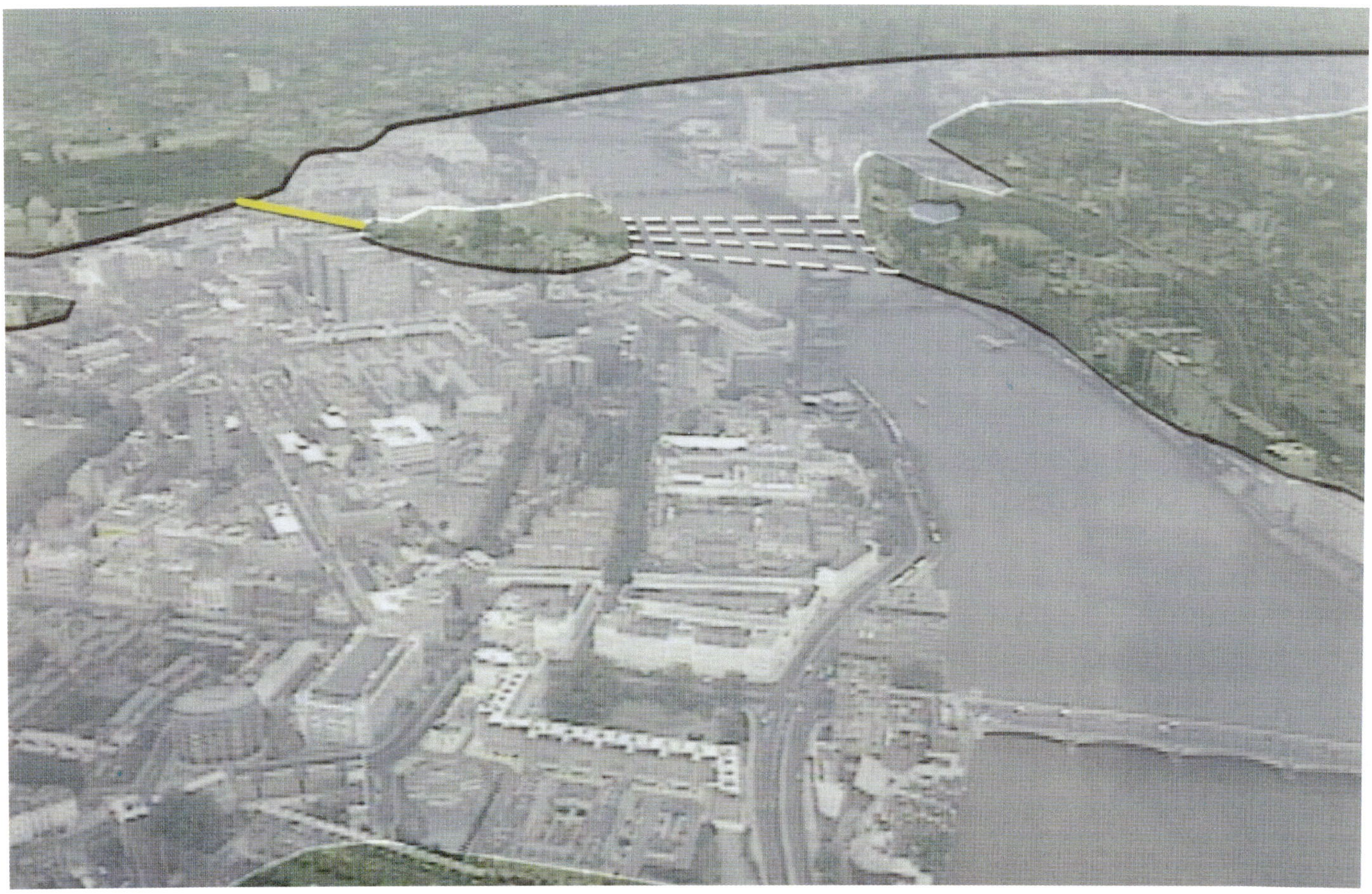

London was referred to as a thriving city. In the *Annals* by Tacitus (Book 14, para. 33) we are told that the town was 'thronged by a crowd of businessmen and merchants although not distinguished by the title of *colonia*'. '*Colonia*' was the name given to those cities occupied by Roman citizens – usually ex-legionaries and their families. Recent excavations by the Department of Urban Archaeology of the Museum of London (forerunner of Molas) at the corner of Cheapside and Queen Street in the City showed a later set of buildings built on the foundations of a destroyed site. Was this the start of the City based on its current location?

The final picture is of an initial crossing point at Lambeth or a little to the north, taking advantage of the lower water levels and the raised land on the south bank. This was later replaced by a settlement on the north bank around the current City area, taking advantage of the greater amount of dry land for the expanding conurbation and deeper water suitable for the larger merchant vessels

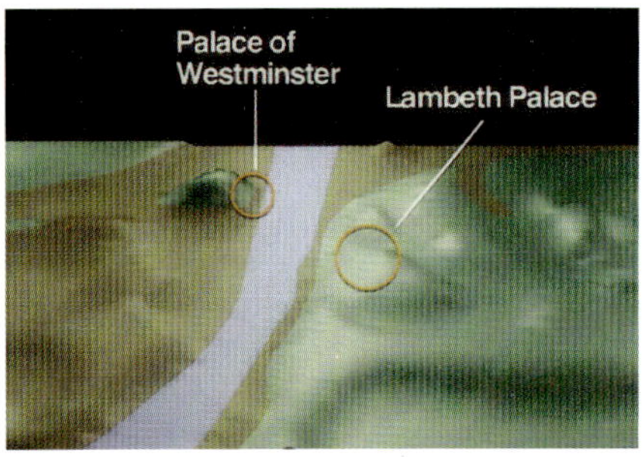

that supplied the army and traded with the Continent.

A final enigma was raised by our work on the last day. In the area of gardens in front of the Palace, the geophysics team found the remains of a substantial structure that may take us back to the earliest days of the Palace's history. It is recorded that, in 1199, the monks of Canterbury and Pope Innocent III triumphed over Hubert Walter, Archbishop of Canterbury, and King John and succeeded in having the college of monks that had been built at Lambeth razed to the ground. Was this what had appeared on the geophysics print-out? Only future excavation will answer this question.

Final thoughts from Mick

'In modern London, with its concrete and high-rise buildings, it is difficult to imagine yourself back to a time when there were fields, forests and marshes. Yet our work with Gustav Milne, Harvey Sheldon and the others enabled us to do just that. When the subsurface landscape is understood, it becomes clear why the Romans built the roads where they did, crossed the Thames and eventually established the highly successful settlement of Londinium, *under the modern City of London. Overall it is only with a full appreciation of the changing form of the river – its width, depth and shallows – that we can really comprehend what has happened since the Romans were there nearly 2000 years ago.*

(Top) Victor's reconstruction of the Thames and the Lambeth crossing as they might have been in Roman times. The photograph of modern London beneath this shows how much narrower the river is now.
(Centre) In Victor's reconstruction of the topography around the Thames during the Roman era, it is easy to see the higher ground that may have attracted the legionaries.

HYLTON CASTLE

Sunderland, 10–12 June 1994

TONY'S TALE, OR WHAT MIGHT HAVE HAPPENED

As Baron William de Hylton stood in the courtyard of his castle and stared up at the mason completing the carving of his coat of arms, he must have felt a great sense of achievement. The year was 1390 in the reign of Richard II, and the baron, who had close enough connections to the crown to display the royal coat of arms, was enjoying seeing the final touches being put on his castle – the symbol of his strength, wealth and power.

In the medieval period, the castle was one of the most significant features in the landscape. As well as having a military purpose, it also gave the owners a chance to impress the local populace. In a world dominated by the relationships of the feudal system, this was important, and Baron Hylton had not spared the decorative touches. Although not as large or commanding as those of some of his wealthier contemporaries, Hylton Castle had all the essential architectural features that were required by a man of substance. The front of the castle boasted a fine entrance – a gatehouse defended by a portcullis and decorated by the magnificent shields of those families on whom the baron could call on for support in times of trouble, including those connected by marriage to the Hyltons. The towers at each corner were complete with such structures as the 'machicolations', designed to allow boiling oil or stones to be hurled on to potential attackers, although these were more for display than having a genuine defensive purpose. The baron had also installed 'en suite' garderobes, or toilets, in the rooms, some of which commanded fine views of the estate grounds.

Now his own coat of arms was nearing completion. The helm (armoured helmet) was topped off by the head of Moses, with twin shafts of the light of knowledge streaming down upon his head. True, the castle lacked an adequate moat or a decent set of external walls, but for this part of the world, it was still a fine sight. The following years would see the building of a guest house and hall that would enable him to impress the noble guests he was hoping to invite. Like most members of the royal court, he longed for a visit from the king.

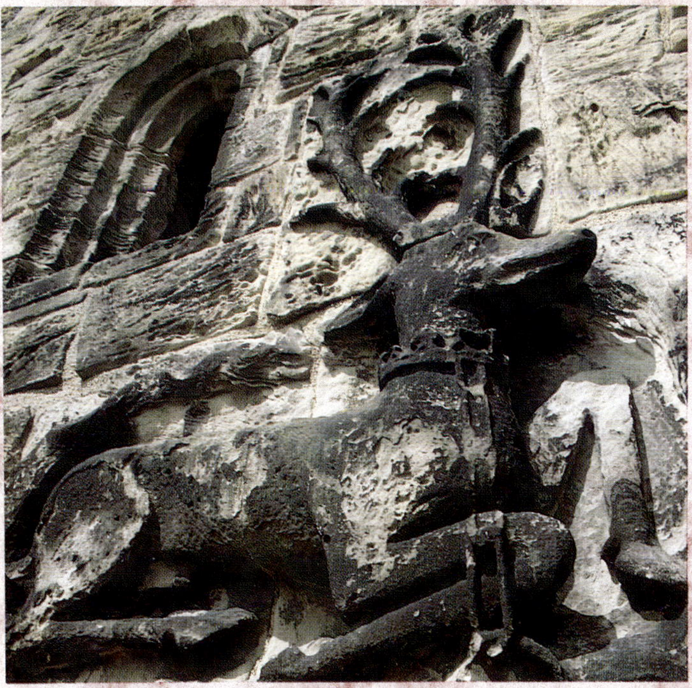

One of the coats of arms on the front of the gatehouse at Hylton Castle. *(Mick Aston)*

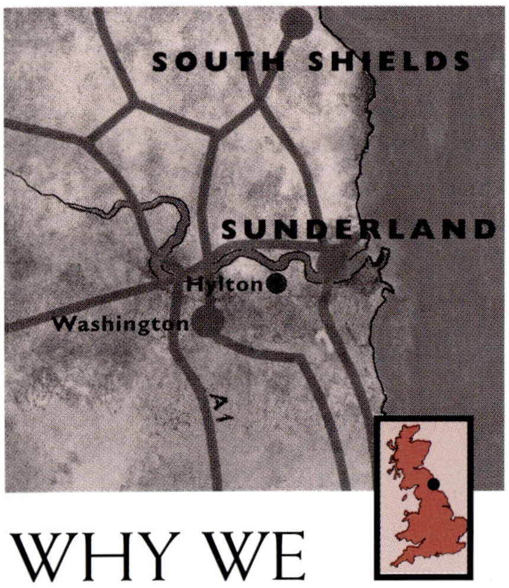

WHY WE WENT THERE

Hylton Dene is about four miles from the centre of Sunderland and close to the River Wear. It is now hemmed in by nine housing estates on land once owned, 600 years ago, by Baron William de Hylton. The castle is still surrounded by parkland, and it was the proposal to develop this land that first brought us to the area. Representatives from the community had got together with the local county council to draw up plans to redevelop the land around the castle, to be funded by the government's City Challenge scheme. It was important that any redevelopment should be done in a way that respected the historical features that still existed. *Time Team* were asked to help in assessing the condition of the castle and in uncovering any archaeological features that might still exist below ground.

This area was critically important to the community, being the only patch of clear green belt among the densely packed housing estates. The castle itself was the only feature listed as a scheduled ancient monument. English Heritage gave their support to *Time Team*'s involvement because they were keen to discover if any other areas of archaeological importance existed within the castle grounds and, if there were any, wished – as did the local community – to see this element preserved in the redevelopment.

Local legend describes the Hylton family as well established at least 140 years before the Conquest, during the reign of the Saxon king, Athelstan (AD 924–939). Lancelot Hylton assisted William the Conqueror, and on Lancelot's death in about 1070, his eldest son Henry was given 'a large tract of land on the banks of the river Were as a reward for his father's valour'. Henry went on to die in Normandy, still fighting for the Norman cause. The history of the Hylton family after this period becomes clearer and perhaps more accurate. Sir Romanus Hylton possibly built a timber hall here after 1157, of which no trace remains. Baron William de Hylton, who erected the present castle, succeeded to the title in 1347 at the age of 21, and was to die in 1435; he would be the main character in our story. The last Baron Hylton, John, died in 1746 without a male successor, and with him, the Hylton line ended.

We shouldn't let this short history of the Hylton's finish without remembering Baron Henry Hylton, described in a guide to the castle as 'slightly mad'. Rather than leave anything to his family on his demise, he bequeathed all the income of the estate to charitable causes in London!

During this period of over 600 years, from Baron William de Hylton's building of the symbol of his power to the present day, the castle was extensively renovated, modernised and altered, so that what can be seen now is an accumulation of many eras. However, considerable remains of Baron William's castle are still extant, particularly on the inside, and the essential size and proportions have remained the same. One other significant building exists in the grounds of the castle – the Chapel of St Catherine, built in the early 15th century.

Day One

After establishing our equipment in our 'medieval' incident tent, we began our work by getting the archaeological geophysicist John Gater to undertake a geophysics survey of the land to the east of the castle, along an area that we would refer to as the 'Eastern Terrace'. John, on this occasion working with Nadia Nemcek and student Louis Harvey, used resistivity detectors to survey the area. This produced three major anomalies that appeared to indicate buildings or features underground. ('Anomalies' are readings of high resistance that can be created by archaeological remains.) These readings also first raised the question of orientation, which would turn out to be the key to understanding the complex structuring of the site.

The first evidence was of a structure adjacent to the castle and *aligned with it*. This, in turn, appeared to comprise buttress-type structures and rooms with internal divisions. A second feature that was further to the east and at least 70 m (230 ft) long was also located. Again there appeared to be room divisions, but this structure was *not aligned* with the castle. A third set of buildings, still further to the east, appeared to be orientated to an area of ridge and furrow at the far end of the site.

After consultation with Steve Speak from the Tyne & Wear Museums, our main archaeological contact, it was decided to dig a series of evaluation trenches to test the anomalies and hopefully discover if some buildings existed and what condition they were in. Would they be worth preserving and would they relate to the period of the original castle? Steve and his team of excavators would be working along-

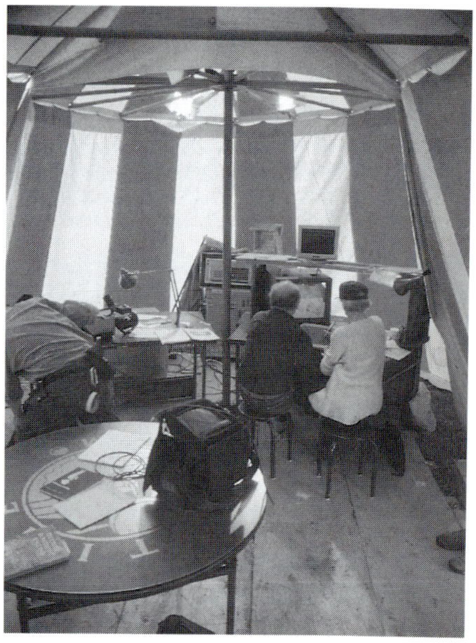

The 'medieval' incident tent. *(Mick Aston)*

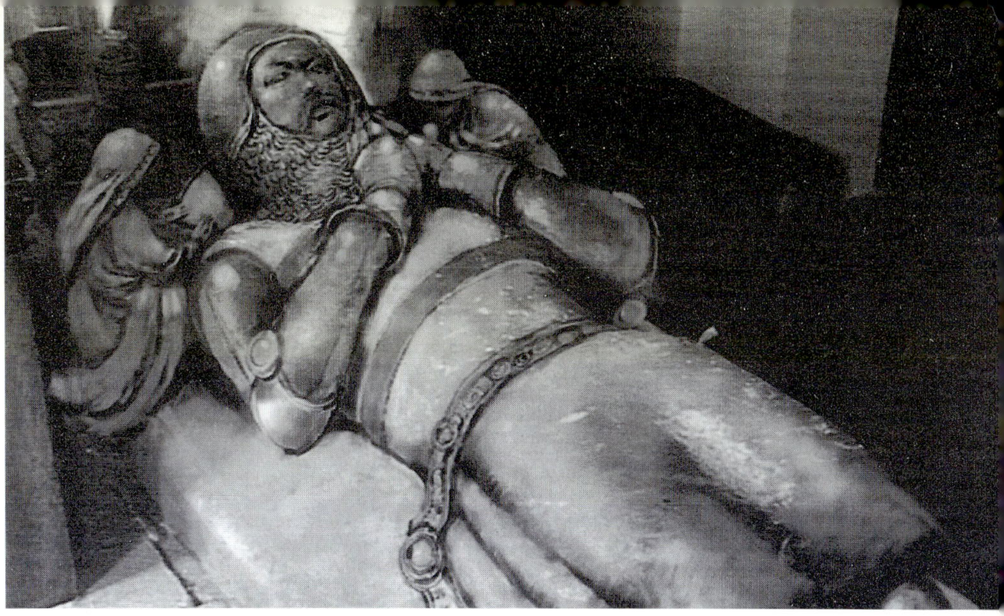

side us throughout the weekend, and their help and local knowledge proved invaluable.

Two other pieces of information came to light on this first day. To study the wider park, Stuart Ainsworth and Bernard Thomason, from the Royal Commission on Historic Monuments for England (RCHME), had begun a survey of the whole area, looking at the lumps and bumps, since it was possible that the castle had once had some parkland features or gardens. During this process, Stuart and Carenza had gone to the top of the castle to look for reference points for the survey, and from this vantage point, they noticed a series of parch marks on the terraces. Parch marks are created in dry weather by those areas of shallow soil that lie over buried features, which dry out before the surrounding ground. These marks seemed to confirm the geophysics results and increased the strength of our view that there were buildings under the surface.

The second piece of information came from Robin. He had examined an inventory written on the death of Baron William in 1435, which listed a number of buildings:

... and there are in the same manor a hall, four chambers, a chapel, two barns, a kitchen, a house constructed of stone called the gatehouse.

We were able to see the gatehouse, but what had happened to the rest of it? It was hard to tell whether the inventory refers to buildings contemporary with the baron or some left over from a previous structure. Maybe excavation would solve the puzzle.

Work began in the first two trenches in an area marked out by Stuart Ainsworth using a survey grid. Meanwhile, Victor had travelled to Monkwearmouth, one mile north of Sunderland town centre, to have a look at Baron William's tomb in St Peter's Church. Unfortunately the tomb was in a poor state of repair, and the baron had suffered the indignity of having his legs removed to make way for a church enlargement. The architectural historian Nikolaus Pevsner refers to the baron as 'legless and defaced'! However, there was enough left of the baron's tomb for Victor to begin sketching a reconstruction of the it.

We had also been asked to do some conservation work on the baron's coat of arms and, to this end, had brought in architectural conservator Graciella Ainsworth (no relation to Stuart). She would be using a high-pressure micro spray to remove the accumulation of 600 years of grime.

Day Two

At the start of Day Two, our first trench didn't seem to be producing any clear evidence of the walls or buttresses that had appeared on the geophysics survey. There was stonework there, but it looked like a mixture of a destruction deposit (created when a building has been demolished or burned down) and natural boulders used in a foundation. However, the second trench was beginning to reveal some solid stonework – a section of wall – that was aligned with the castle. Small pieces of tile were also beginning to appear. Further work in this trench would be needed.

The local community and English Heritage had also asked us to examine the interior of the castle. Beric Morley, a freelance heritage adviser and architectural historian, gave Mick a guided tour and pointed out the key features from the original building and the later alterations. He was also able to show Mick the large doorway in the eastern wall that would have led into a courtyard beyond. The division of occupation was typical of a medieval castle of this time, with the baron and his family on the upper floor in a large open hall with smaller rooms attached, and the servants and guards on the lower floor. Robin had also noted that one of the coats of arms belonged to the Washington family, one of whose descendants went on to become the first president of the United States. It has been suggested that the 'Stars and Stripes' originates from the bars and horse spur ornamentation that can be seen in the Washingtons' coat of arms.

Meanwhile, in the park, Stuart Ainsworth had discovered the first signs of a set of terraces and other features leading down to the river. Some of the latter may have been ornamental ponds, but their discovery raised a critical question: what were a set of garden features doing spread out to the south of the castle? The baron and his guests would have looked out mainly to the west and east. Rob Bell, an expert in garden archaeology, believed he had an answer. The second set of buildings located by the geophysics belonged to a

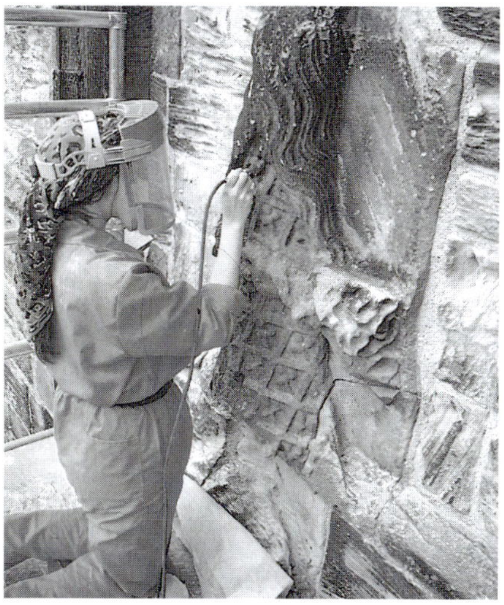

(Top) Victor's reconstruction of Baron William de Hylton's tomb at St Peter's Church, Monkwearmouth.
(Bottom right) Graciella Ainsworth cleaning Baron de Hylton's coat of arms.

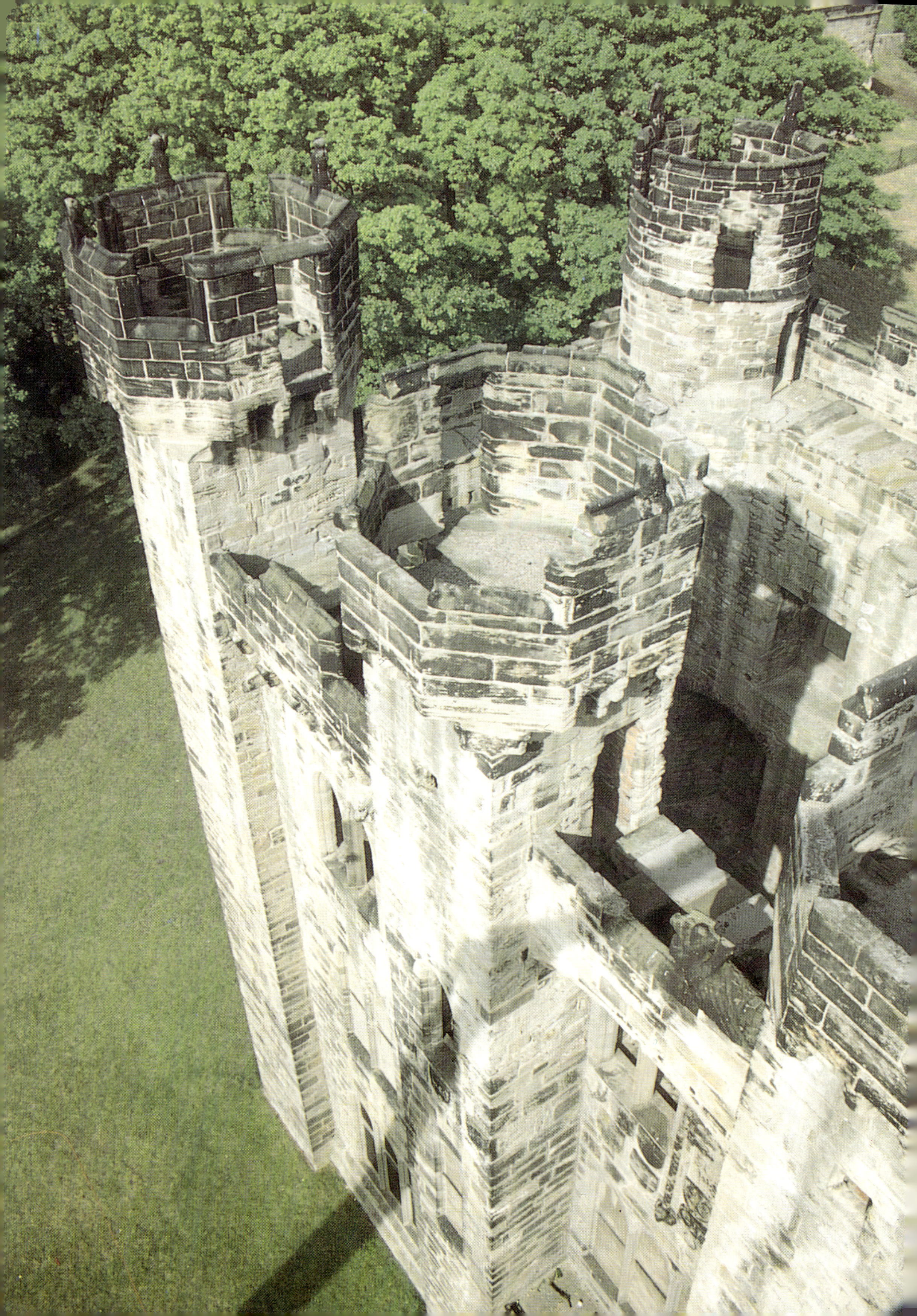

later, so far unrecorded, Elizabethan house from the 16th century, and this had faced south to enjoy the view of the terraced gardens.

From the Middle Ages onwards, gardens provided an elaborate setting for this kind of castle. They often included raised flower beds, herb gardens, an orangery, fruit garden and, occasionally, a maze. Archaeologists are becoming increasingly aware that these sorts of features can leave significant archaeological traces. If we could find clear evidence of them, the ones at Hylton could be incorporated into the design and redevelopment of the parkland.

We excavated a third trench, this one into the likely remains of the Elizabethan house. This revealed an area of badly damaged masonry that proved difficult

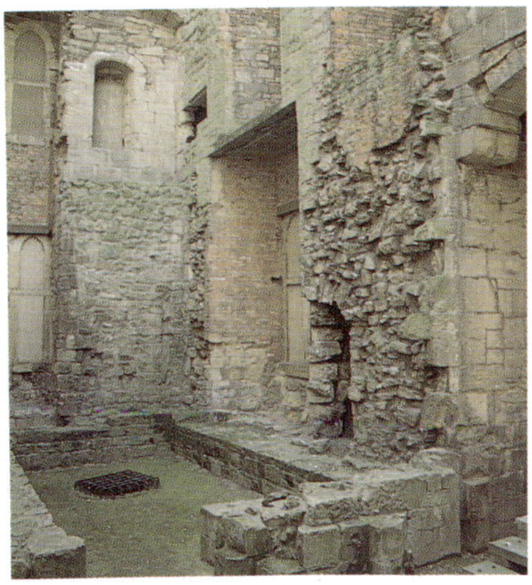

to interpret. However, we did find some pieces of fine pottery and three coins from the early Elizabethan period.

Meanwhile, from the second trench, two important pieces of information had emerged. Not only did we seem to have a clear section of wall, but we had plaster decoration on the inside, and fairly large pieces of floor tiles were beginning to emerge. Plaster of this kind indicates a high-status building, and for it to have survived intact was a remarkable piece of luck. As Steve Speak said, 'You don't find this sort of stuff in a goatshed.' He was particularly pleased to note the lack of plough damage. Ploughing in the later Middle Ages on these kinds of sites can cause tremendous damage, and the absence of the score marks and linear scrapes meant that, if other parts of the building could be located, they might be in a good state of preservation.

The tiles were identified as being contemporary with Baron William. The technology for making the tiles has changed over time, and we had enough pieces to identify these as dating from the 14th or 15th century. It was likely that they were laid in alternating light-and-dark patterns, and their size and glazed surface would have made an impressive sight for any of the baron's visitors. As is common with these kinds of floors, we were able to identify the areas of lighter-coloured mortar on which the tiles were laid. In addition, pieces of fairly substantial roof tiles were being found in trench no. 2, which gave us an idea of the kind of material that had been used to roof the hall.

The accumulation of this evidence indicated that Baron Hylton had indeed built a prestigious feasting hall or dining area to the east of the castle, reached through a central courtyard and decorated with painted plaster and glazed floor tiles.

Day Three

As with all evaluation excavation, it was important that drawings of the stonework and other remains in the trenches were made for future research. This work had to be completed before we left. Stuart Ainsworth had also mapped many of the garden features, and these and our other findings were presented to the community. They would form the basis for a redevelopment plan that would respect and use the archaeological features. It was clear that English Heritage regarded the new areas of medieval building as important enough to be scheduled as an ancient monument. Our last task of the day was to see the completion of the cleaning of the baron's own coat of arms, a little cracked at the edges but now free from grime and showing some of the detail that must have been visible in the baron's day.

With all the information that *Time Team* provided, the people of Hylton Dene and Sunderland City Council will be hoping to get further assistance from the government, the National

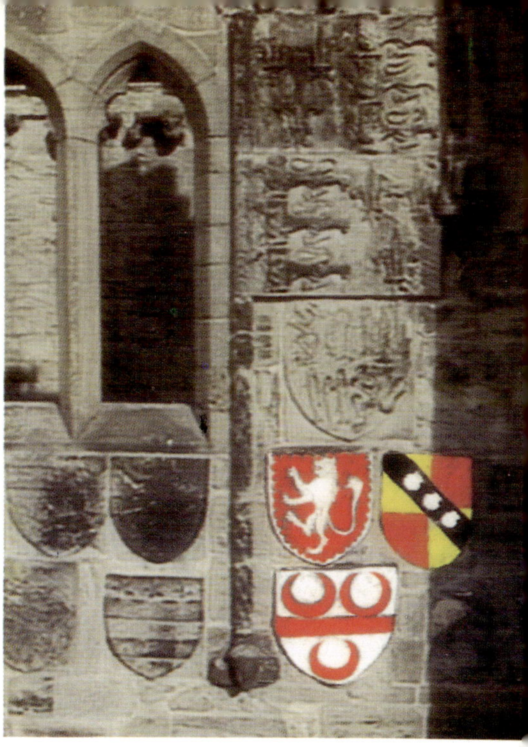

Lottery and the European Union to ensure that the baron's castle will be at the centre of a unique and valuable facility for the whole community.

Final thoughts from Mick

'For me, there were two exciting aspects of Hylton. First, it was useful to get the rest of the context of the castle from the geophysics and excavations. The isolated gatehouse was only one part – although admittedly a rather large part – of a whole complex of buildings. When and if this complex is eventually excavated, the entire site will make sense.

However, it was the earthworks of the gardens that impressed me the most. We tend to forget that these large baronial houses belonged to the wealthiest members of society, and that they wished to keep up with the latest in fashion. It was no different with garden design. Careful survey and analysis enabled us to locate the gardens at Hylton, and showed that these had undergone several phases. This, in turn, allowed us to see the medieval castle in its contemporary landscape, which could have important implications when Hylton Castle and its grounds are displayed to the public in the future.'

(Above left) The interior of the gatehouse. Baron de Hylton and his family would have been in residence on the upper floor; the servants and guards would have lived and worked on the ground floor. *(Mick Aston)*
(Above right) Victor's reconstruction of the coats of arms on the front of the gatehouse, showing how they would have been brightly painted.
(Left) The castle battlements, showing the machicolations. *(Mick Aston)*

RESOURCES

GETTING INVOLVED

If you have been fascinated by the TIME TEAM series and booklet and want to become more than an armchair archaeologist, there are dozens of organisations that can provide information and advice. Here are a few suggestions.

Council for British Archaeology

A first step is to find out what is going on near you – there are local and regional groups all over the country – and the best source of information is the Council for British Archaeology (CBA). Members include professional archaeologists, local archaeological societies and museums, and lots of interested amateurs. You, too, can become a member!

The CBA helps those who want to get involved in archaeology – in actual field work, or by participating in meetings and events – by giving information, advice and practical support. Its regional organisations provide a countrywide network.

The CBA publishes a popular news magazine called *British Archaeology*, which ranges right across the subject – from the archaeology of the Stone Age to that of the 20th century, from conservation to legislation, and from education to the latest discoveries and new ideas. The magazine also contains campaigning editorials, as well as feature articles and reviews by some of the best writers and thinkers in the field.

The CBA also caters for young people. The Young Archaeologists Club (YAC) – whose president is the *Time Team*'s Tony Robinson – is for those between 9 and 16 who take archaeology and the country's heritage seriously, but still know how to have a good time. YAC members can take part in club activities through local branches, go on field study holidays and even enter for the Young Archaeologist of the Year award. Each member receives the club's quarterly magazine *Young Archaeologist* – packed with news from Britain and from correspondents abroad, telling about things to do and places to go.

For both the *Council for British Archaeology* and the *Young Archaeologists Club*, contact:
Bowes Morrell House,
111 Walmgate, York YO1 2UA,
tel: (01904) 671417.

Current Archaeology

The six issues a year of this lively and popular colour magazine are full or news about recent finds, new books and topics of debate. There are also special offers for new subscribers. Contact:
Current Archaeology,
9 Nassington Road, London NW3 2TX,
tel: (0171) 435 7517.

English Heritage Education Service

In addition to caring for many monuments, English Heritage also has a superb Education Service to help teachers – at all levels – make full use of the historic environment. Visits to historic sites are a recommended part of the National Curriculum, and the Education Service offers guidance not only on their historical relevance but also on the part they can play in subjects as varied as English, maths, science and geography. Educational visits to English Heritage sites are free.

To obtain the free booklets *Using the Historic Environment* and *Free Educational Visits*, and the free leaflet *Resources*, which describes a host of educational publications and videos, write to:
English Heritage Education Service,
429 Oxford Street, London W1R 2HD.

The Archaeology Resource Book

This comprehensive listing of organisations, names and addresses, books, films, videos, etc. is published jointly by English Heritage and the Council for British Archaeology – 150 pages of information for only £6.00.

Records and archives

The Royal Commission on Historic Monuments for England, at its new headquarters in Swindon, houses millions of photographs of historic buildings, aerial photographs of archaeological sites, an extensive library and records of scheduled monuments. For access, contact:
National Monuments Records,
Kemble Drive, Swindon SN2 2GZ,
tel: (01793) 414618.

Historic Scotland publishes the free leaflet *Archaeological Information and Advice*, which describes public archives and other resources, the National Museums and the Council for Scottish Archaeology, as well as other regional archaeological agencies. To receive a copy, contact:
Historic Scotland,
20 Brandon Street, Edinburgh EH3 5RA,
tel: (0131) 244 3082.

Cadw, the Welsh historic monuments agency, can provide information on sites and monuments in Wales. Contact:
Cadw, Brunel House,
2 Fitzalan Road, Cardiff CF2 1UY,
tel: (01222) 500200.

FURTHER READING

Oxbow Books in Oxford specialise in archaeology and carry an enormous stock of books. They also issue free lists of new archaeology books every few months, and can supply all titles by post. Contact:
Oxbow Books,
Park End Place, Oxford OX1 1HN,
tel: (01865) 241249, fax: (01865) 794449.

Islay

Scotland's First Settlers by Caroline Wickham-Jones, Batsford in association with Historic Scotland, 1994, paperback £14.99. Featuring many reconstruction drawings, this describes how the semi-nomads of the mesolithic era lived by hunting and fishing, and by gathering shellfish, fruit and seeds. It also examines evidence from campsites, which shows the sorts of